# TODAY'S
# BEST
# NONFICTION

# TODAY'S
# BEST
# NONFICTION

THE READER'S DIGEST ASSOCIATION, INC.
PLEASANTVILLE, N.Y., MONTREAL

**TODAY'S BEST NONFICTION**

*Editor-in-Chief:* Barbara J. Morgan
*Executive Editor:* Tanis H. Erdmann
*Senior Managing Editor:* Marjorie Palmer
*Managing Editors:* Thomas Froncek, Herbert H. Lieberman, Joseph P. McGrath, James J. Menick
*Senior Staff Editors:* Anne H. Atwater, Thomas S. Clemmons, Maureen A. Mackey, Angela H. Plowden-Wardlaw, John R. Roberson, Ray Sipherd
*Senior Editors:* Dana Adkins, M. Tracy Brigden, Catherine T. Brown, Linn Carl
*Senior Associate Editors:* Christopher W. Davis, Catharine L. Edmonds, Ainslie Gilligan, Barbara M. Harrington, Paula Marchese
*Associate Editor:* Ayesha Pande
*Managing Editor, Copy Desk:* Jeane Garment
*Assistant Managing Editor, Copy Desk:* Jane F. Neighbors
*Senior Staff Copy Editors:* Maxine Bartow, Tatiana Ivanow, Marilyn J. Knowlton
*Senior Copy Editors:* Claire A. Bedolis, Jeanette Gingold, Charles Pendergast, Miriam Schneir
*Senior Associate Copy Editor:* Daphne Hougham
*Associate Copy Editors:* Fay Ahuja, Barbara Booth, Alexandra C. Koppen, Arlene Petzal
*Editorial Administrator:* Donna R. Gataletto
*Art Director:* Angelo Perrone
*Executive Art Editor:* Soren Noring
*Senior Art Editor:* George Calas, Jr.
*Senior Associate Art Editor:* Katherine Kelleher
*Associate Art Editor:* Clair Moritz
*Director, Book Rights:* Virginia Rice

**INTERNATIONAL EDITIONS**

*Executive Editor:* Gary Q. Arpin
*Senior Editors:* Eva C. Jaunzems, Antonius L. Koster
*Associate Editor:* Bonnie Grande

The condensations in this volume have been created by The Reader's Digest Association, Inc., by special arrangement with the publishers, authors, or other holders of copyrights. Letters, documents, court testimony, etc. may have been edited for space.

The original editions of the books in this volume are published and copyrighted as follows:

*The Fifties*
Published by Villard Books, a division of Random House, Inc.
distributed by Random House of Canada Limited at $35.00
© 1993 by The Amateurs Limited

*Den of Lions: Memoirs of Seven Years*
Published by Crown Publishers, Inc.
distributed by Canadian Manda Group at $29.95
© 1993 by TMS Corporation

*Above Suspicion*
Published by Simon and Schuster
distributed by Distican Inc. at $29.50
© 1993 by Joe Sharkey

*Wings of the Morning*
Published by St. Martin's Press
distributed by McClelland & Stewart Inc. at $29.99
© 1994 by Orestes Lorenzo Perez

© 1994 The Reader's Digest Association, Inc.
© 1994 The Reader's Digest Association (Canada) Ltd.

FIRST EDITION, Volume 24

*Contents*

# THE
# FIFTIES

## David Halberstam

## VOICES OF THE FIFTIES

"We conclude that in the field of public opinion the doctrine of 'separate but equal' has no place."

—*Supreme Court of the United States*

"Pat doesn't have a mink coat. But she does have a perfectly respectable Republican cloth coat. And I always tell her that she'd look good in anything."

—*Richard Nixon*

"This is Levittown! All yours for $58. You're a lucky fellow, Mr. Veteran."

—*ad in* The New York Times

"I hardly see him at night anymore since he took up sex."

—*Alfred Kinsey's wife, Clara*

"The buck stops here."

—*Harry Truman*

# PREFACE

THE fifties were captured in black and white, most often by still photographers; by contrast, the decade that followed was, more often than not, caught in living color on tape or film. Not surprisingly, in retrospect the pace of the fifties seemed slower, almost languid. Social ferment, however, was beginning just beneath this placid surface. It was during the fifties, for example, that the basic research in the development of the birth-control pill took place, but it was not until a decade later that this technological advance had a profound effect upon society. Then, apparently overnight, rather conservative—indeed cautious—sexual practices were giving way to what commentators would speak of as the sexual revolution. It was in the fifties that the nation became wired for television, a new medium experimented with by various politicians and social groups. Ten years later television had begun to alter the political and social fabric of the country, with stunning consequences.

Three decades later the fifties appear to be an orderly era, one with a minimum of social dissent. Photographs from the period tend to show people who dressed carefully: men in suits, ties, and—when outdoors—hats; women with their hair in modified pageboys, pert and upbeat. Young people seemed accepting of the given social covenants. At the beginning of the decade their music was still slow and saccharine, mirroring the generally bland popular taste. In the years following the Depression and World War II, the American dream was to exercise personal freedom not in social and political terms but rather in economic ones. Eager to be part of the burgeoning middle class, young men and women opted for material well-being, particularly if it came with some form of guaranteed employment. For the young, eager veteran just out of college (which he had attended courtesy of the GI Bill), security meant finding a good white-collar job with a large, benevolent company, getting married, having children, and buying a house in the suburbs.

In that era of general goodwill and expanding affluence, few Americans doubted the essential goodness of their society. After all, it was reflected back at them not only by contemporary books and magazines but even more powerfully in the new family sitcoms on television. These—in conjunction with their sponsors' commercial goals— sought to shape their audiences' aspirations.

However, most Americans needed little coaching in how they wanted to live. Young men who had spent three or four years fighting overseas were eager to get on with their lives; so, too, were the young women who had waited for them at home. The post–World War II rush to have children would later be described as the baby boom. (Everything else in the United States seemed to be booming, so why not the production of children as well?) It was a good time to be young. Prices and inflation remained relatively low, and nearly everyone with a decent job could afford to own a home. Even if the specter of communism lurked on the horizon—particularly as both superpowers developed nuclear weapons—Americans trusted their leaders to tell them the truth, to make sound decisions, and to keep them out of war.

For a while the traditional system of authority held. The men (and not men *and* women) who presided in politics, business, and media had generally been born in the previous century. The advent of so strong a society, in which the nation's wealth was shared by so many, represented a prosperity beyond their wildest dreams. During the course of the fifties, as younger people and segments of society who did not believe they had a fair share became empowered, pressure inevitably began to build against the entrenched political and social hierarchies.

But one did not lightly challenge a system that seemed, on the whole, to be working so well. Some social critics, irritated by the generally quiescent attitude, described a "silent" generation. Nonetheless, the era was much more interesting than it appeared on the surface. Exciting new technologies were being developed that would soon enable a vast and surprisingly broad degree of dissidence. Many people were already beginning to question the purpose of their lives and whether that purpose had become, almost involuntarily, too much about material things.

# CHAPTER ONE

N THE beginning that era was dominated by the shadow of a man no longer there—Franklin D. Roosevelt. He had died in 1945, but his impact on American politics was so profound that even the most powerful Republican leaders believed privately that their party might be permanently in the minority. Roosevelt had been cast forth in the midst of two transcending events—the Great Depression and World War II. The first was responsible for a massive reordering of the American economy and society, thereby creating a huge new base for the Democrats; the second permitted Roosevelt to emerge as an international leader in a time of great crisis and to prolong his presidency for two additional terms.

Roosevelt was the ultimate modern politician, the first great master of modern mass communications in a democracy. For millions of poor Americans and for the new immigrants and their children, his ability to exploit radio and make it seem his personal vehicle had a particular resonance. To them Roosevelt was not only President for life, he was their guide to the rites of American politics.

The effect of this on the Republican Party was devastating. In July 1949, some nine months after his own shocking defeat by Harry Truman (which seemed to promise the Roosevelt coalition would go on ad infinitum), Thomas E. Dewey met with Dwight Eisenhower, then the president of Columbia University, to begin the process of coercing Ike to run for the presidency in 1952 as a Republican. Eisenhower's notes of that meeting are unusually revealing of the Republican dilemma: "All middle-class citizens of education have a common belief that the tendencies towards centralization and paternalism must be halted and reversed. No one who voices these opinions can be elected. Consequently we must look around for someone of great popularity and who has not frittered away his political assets by taking positive stands against national planning, etc., etc. Elect such a man to Presidency, *after which* [N.B.: italics Ike's] he must lead us back to safe channels and paths." In effect Dewey was telling Eisenhower that the solid citizens who could make the right decisions for the future of the country had become a minority and that the nation had fallen into the clutches of dark and alien forces.

Not surprisingly, the Republican Party was traumatized and bitterly divided. Certainly the Democratic Party was divided as well. But for all their differences, the Democrats had a certain glue: they won, and in victory there was patronage and power, a combination that transcended ideology. For the Republicans there was only the taste of ashes. They had been out of office since 1932. The shadow of the Depression still hung over them, and the Democrats were still running against Herbert Hoover, portraying the Republicans as the party of cold, uncaring bankers. Were the Republicans forever to be trapped by those events then twenty years in the past?

Of the divisions within the Republican Party, the most obvious was a historical, regional one. On one side were the lawyers and bankers of Wall Street and their colleagues through the great eastern industrial cities. They were internationalist by tradition and by instinct: they had fought against Roosevelt's policies but had eventually come to accept certain of his premises. By contrast, the Republicans of the heartland were essentially unchanged by the great events that had overtaken them; they were resentful of World War II and suspicious of how Roosevelt had gotten them into it. They were anxious to go back to the simple, comfortable world of the twenties—before the New Deal had empowered labor unions, before air travel had shrunk the Atlantic Ocean into a pond, and before scientists had ever thought about developing intercontinental ballistic missiles to catapult atomic warheads into their midst.

They lived in God's country, a land far from oceans and far from foreigners, and they were all-powerful in their own small towns. Many had gone to college and returned home to succeed their fathers in family businesses. They had always controlled their political and economic destinies locally, and they presumed that by acting in concert with others like themselves in other small towns, they could control the national destiny. Now they looked at Washington and saw the enemy. They seemed to have lost control of their own party. That was the final insult. Confident that they represented Republicanism and true patriotism, they were at war with the eastern Republicans, who, in their eyes, were traitors, tainted by cooperation with the New Deal.

The 1948 presidential campaign proved to be a watershed for the Republicans. They were absolutely confident that Thomas E. Dewey would beat Truman, whom they saw as a small-town haberdasher, devoid of Roosevelt's charm and as uncomfortable with an open radio microphone as the average Republican. But there was the problem of Dewey's stiffness. Alice Roosevelt Longworth once described him as looking like "the little man on the wedding cake."

Dewey's strengths were his sense of purpose, his integrity, and his political cleanliness. In 1948 he refused—and this was a point of honor—to use the communist-in-government issue as a political weapon, and he refused, despite mounting pressure from the Republican right, to do any Red-baiting, even as that was becoming ever more fashionable in postwar American politics.

He was a heavy favorite to win, and he took the high road. In truth he campaigned not as the challenger but as the incumbent, as a man who had already been elected President by endless polls and surveys. The idea of a Truman victory seemed impossible to nearly everyone.

On election eve the Chicago *Tribune* had its famous headline proclaiming Dewey's victory. But even with Roosevelt gone, the Republicans blew the election. Truman won, and the Republicans now faced four more years out of office. The bitterness within the party grew. So much for the high road in American politics. The communist issue would be fair game in the near future. It was the only way the Republicans knew how to fight back.

IT WAS a mean time. The nation had come out of World War II stronger and more powerful and more affluent than ever before, but the rest of the world, alien and unsettling, seemed to press closer now than many Americans wanted it to. There would be many accusations that the Democrats had won the war but lost the peace. As David Caute wrote in *The Great Fear,* the true isolationists thought that Roosevelt had dragged us "into the wrong war: wrong allies, wrong enemies, wrong outcome." A peace that permitted Soviet hegemony over

Eastern Europe was unacceptable to many Americans. There had to be a scapegoat: these things could not merely have happened, not in a fair and just world.

In the early years of his administration Truman was hardly an ideal target for the angry conservatives; he was so solidly midwestern, small-town, and unpretentious that he was perilously close to being one of their own. If there was an enemy, someone who represented a target for all the accumulated resentment of the past and all the tensions of class, region, and education, it was Dean Acheson—he of Groton, Harvard, Wall Street, and State, the very embodiment of the eastern Establishment. His timing, as he ascended to the position of Secretary of State, was not exactly ideal. On January 21, 1949, the day on which Acheson was sworn in, Chiang Kai-shek turned over what remained of his command on the China mainland to one of his generals and left for Formosa. The civil war in China was over, and the Communists had won. It was a bad omen.

Fearless and intellectually superior, Dean Acheson possessed a highly developed sense of integrity and honor. In a world in which the old order had collapsed and a new and dangerous adversary risen up, he retained a clear view of the challenges America faced: to prop up an exhausted and shattered Europe and, at the same time, to make this policy acceptable to his own countrymen. He was far more successful at the former than the latter. In his first year as Secretary of State he was dogged by the turn of events in China and by the growing anger among the Republicans. However, it was when the Alger Hiss case broke that he became the perfect target for the right wing. The case symbolized (or seemed to symbolize) the divisions of an entire era.

A man named Whittaker Chambers charged that Hiss had been a fellow member of the Communist Party while serving in the government. At first it seemed an accusation unlikely to stick. Chambers was a confessed former underground member of the Communist Party, an admitted homosexual, and unusually sloppy in dress and personal hygiene. The man he accused of being a Communist was strikingly patrician and handsome. His aristocratic bearing seemed to confirm his political legitimacy and sum up his perfect pedigree: Johns Hopkins, Harvard Law School, and *Harvard Law Review*. At the time of the accusations, Alger Hiss was head of the Carnegie Endowment for International Peace, the chairman of whose board was none other than the respected Republican John Foster Dulles.

Even members of the House Un-American Activities Committee (HUAC), who were inclined to believe any accusations about anyone, looked down on Chambers. The House Committee was made nervous, even intimidated, by Hiss's complete denial of ever having known Chambers, and seemed on the verge of withdrawing from the case. Only a very junior member, Richard Nixon (Republican of California), persisted—among other reasons because he was being fed secret FBI documents—and kept the committee from backing off completely.

The setting was this: on August 3, 1948, the House Committee held hearings in which Whittaker Chambers not only said that he himself had been a Communist but that there was a Communist group in the government in the late thirties and that Alger Hiss was a member of it. Hiss denied the accusation. His friends rallied round. Dean Acheson, then a law partner of Hiss's brother, Donald, helped with the early legal planning; William Marbury, a prominent Baltimore attorney and a very old friend, sent a note to Donald Hiss, who had been similarly accused: "If you and Alger are party members, then you can send me an application." Hiss himself seemed to play down the seriousness of the charges, and told his wife, Priscilla, "Don't worry, little one. This will all blow over. I will handle it."

On August 5, before the committee, that is precisely what he did. Hiss seemed imposing, almost imperious, a paragon of the Establishment. "I am not and never have been a member of the Communist party," he said under oath. When asked by the chairman, Karl Mundt, if he recognized photos of Chambers, he answered, "I might mistake him for the [acting] chairman of the Committee." This line received considerable laughter. It was the high-water mark for Hiss in the case. By the end of that day, Mundt congratulated him for his forthright testimony. "Let's wash our hands of the whole mess," said F. Edward Hebert, the Louisiana Democrat. Only Richard Nixon wanted to push on. There was something about Hiss that he did not like and did not trust, and he was irritated rather than impressed by Hiss's imperiousness. Someone was clearly lying. Why not have the two men confront each other? Nixon suggested.

At the session on August 16 Hiss wavered for the first time: perhaps he had known the person testifying against him under another name. The picture of Chambers, he said, "is not completely unfamiliar." Then, rather late in the session, he said that he had written down the name of someone it might be. The name he wrote down was George Crosley.

The next day, unbeknownst to Hiss, a confrontation was arranged at room 1400 of the Commodore Hotel. With Hiss already in the room, Chambers was brought in. Hiss said that he had known this man as George Crosley. He thereupon demanded that Chambers make his accusations in a public arena, without the protection from libel offered by the committee. "I challenge you to do so, and I hope you will do it damn quickly," he said. Chambers did so on national radio.

Eight days later their public confrontation took place, and the Hiss case exploded into America's collective consciousness. At first even the general public thought that Hiss, so eminently respectable, might be wearing the white hat and Chambers, so unattractive, the black. But slowly, as evidence mounted, the tide of public opinion shifted. From the beginning Nixon was impressed by how steadfast, unflappable, and unbending Chambers was. He did not use a lawyer as Hiss did, he did not study the transcript before each session as Hiss did, and he did not qualify his statements ("to the best of my recollection") as Hiss often did.

By August 25 Karl Mundt was saying to Hiss, "You knew this man [Chambers]; you knew him very well. You knew him so well that you trusted him with your apartment . . . your automobile. You bought him lunches in the Senate Restaurant. You had him staying in your home and made him a series of small loans. There seems to be no question about that." It was a damning moment. At the end of the hearing Parnell Thomas announced that one of the two men would be tried for perjury.

For the liberals, and thoughtful people of any stripe, a dilemma arose: Could it be that this committee—so scabrous, indeed almost farcical, which had so often and so carelessly thrown around charges of communism—was actually on to something? And if so, was there a larger truth to this?

The case began to assume dimensions far greater than anyone had ever imagined, for it broke just as the lines in the cold war were becoming more sharply drawn. In March 1948 Jan Masaryk, the Czech foreign minister and an admired symbol of democratic hopes in that country, committed suicide. Then in the summer of 1948 the West used the Berlin airlift to bypass the Berlin blockade created by the Soviets. As much as anything else, those two events signaled that the wartime alliance between the Soviets and the West was over. A new, edgier political era had begun.

In response to Hiss's denials, Chambers began to escalate his charges, now accusing Hiss of espionage. This was buttressed with dramatic documentary evidence that Chambers said he had squirreled away for just such an occasion some ten years earlier, when he had left the party. The evidence—State Department documents copied in Hiss's handwriting or some documents typed on what was claimed to be Hiss's typewriter—was incriminating. Whether Hiss actually participated in espionage was never proved, and the evidence was, at best, flawed. The government briefly pondered going after him on espionage, decided its case was insufficiently strong, and went instead for a lesser, perjury, charge.

In the two ensuing trials, even those who were unbiased always had a feeling that there were missing pieces and that each of the principals was holding back something. The first trial ended in a hung jury; the vote was 8–4 for a perjury conviction against Hiss. That, according to one of Hiss's friends and lawyers, Helen Buttenweiser, was the only time she had ever seen Alger shocked—stunned by the fact that eight of his fellow citizens did not believe him. In the second trial the jury found Hiss guilty of perjury, and he was sentenced to five years in a federal prison.

When Hiss was convicted of perjury, Dean Acheson knew he would be asked about his onetime associate. He chose his words carefully. "I do not intend to turn my back on Alger Hiss," he told a reporter from the *Herald Tribune*. His words were those of a very brave man, but they were also political dynamite, and as historian Eric Goldman wrote, "a tremendous and unnecessary gift to those who were insisting that the foreign policy of the Truman Administration was being shaped by men who were soft on Communism." As Goldman noted, Richard Nixon almost immediately responded, "Traitors in the high councils of our own government have made sure that the deck is stacked on the Soviet side of the diplomatic tables."

Carving out a policy that limited Soviet expansion, and at the same time contending with but not overreacting to Soviet moves, demanded skill and resolve and vision. Americans might have dreamed of a Europe which resembled that of the pre–World War II map, but the Russians were already in place in the East. For many Americans that reality was almost impossible to accept. Acheson himself despaired of America's difficult new role of international leadership. "We have got to understand that all our lives the danger, the uncertainty, the need for alertness, for discipline, will be with us. This is new for us. It will be hard for us."

All of this profoundly affected Truman. He had come to the presidency unprepared in foreign affairs, barely briefed on major foreign-policy issues by the Roosevelt people. He had, he came to realize, arrived at a historic moment. In March 1948, after what seemed to him a series of catastrophic foreign-policy events, he wrote to his daughter, Margaret, "We are faced with exactly the same situation with which Britain and France were faced in 1938–39 with Hitler. Things look black. A decision will have to be made. I am going to make it."

# CHAPTER TWO

To the complete surprise of the nation's political Establishment and journalists, Harry Truman's fellow citizens had elected him to the presidency. It was only after he was out of office that people truly came to appreciate the full measure of the man and his virtues. In the beginning his lack of pretense and blunt manner worked against him, standing in stark contrast to Roosevelt's consummate elegance. As President, Truman was accused of demeaning the Oval Office by turning it over to Missouri roughnecks and poker-playing backroom operators who drank bourbon and told off-color jokes—his "cronies," as *Time* magazine, then the semiofficial voice of the Republican Party, called them. To some extent that charge was true, although Truman was old-fashioned enough not to permit off-color jokes.

Unlike Roosevelt, Truman had virtually no personal income, and he and his family always lived modestly. He knew the value of a dollar and would complain loudly if he thought he had been overcharged, as on the occasion of a breakfast at the famed Peabody Hotel in November 1941: "Had breakfast in the coffee shop downstairs and they charged me fifty-five centers for tomato juice, a little dab of oatmeal and milk and toast. I don't mind losing one hundred dollars on a hoss race or a poker game with friends, but I do hate to pay fifty-five centers for a quarter breakfast. . . ." The straightforward simplicity of his style would come to seem marvelously human compared with that of subsequent inhabitants of the White House, ever more image-conscious and isolated from the public by a growing number of handlers, public relations men, and pollsters.

He was the last American President who had not been to college, and yet he was quite possibly the best-read President of modern times. There was a certain jauntiness to his walk and his attitude toward life. He was not afflicted by inner doubts. He made his decisions quickly and cleanly by listening to the evidence and the best advice of those around him, and he did not look back. He was not particularly introspective. Politics was the art of the possible. At the poker table you took the hand you were dealt and you played it as best you could. Then you slept well. On his desk he kept a sign that read THE BUCK STOPS HERE.

BY THE summer of 1949 America had enjoyed a four-year monopoly of the atom bomb. That monopoly had given the country an edge in the immediate postwar era. Our defense plans, such as they were, were largely based on our exclusive control of the bomb. The initial assumption on the part of America's top scientists and intelligence analysts was that the Soviets were some five years behind us in developing nuclear weapons. As the new decade approached, we assumed that they were *still* five years behind us. There was a joke at the time, the scientist Herbert York noted, "that the Russians could not surreptitiously introduce nuclear bombs in suitcases into the United States, because they had not yet been able to perfect a suitcase." Among those who held firmly to the idea of Soviet ineptitude was Truman himself. When he first met the head of the atomic research center at Los Alamos, J. Robert Oppenheimer, in 1946, Truman asked Oppenheimer when the Russians would be able to build a bomb. Oppenheimer answered that he did not know. "*I* know," Truman said. "When?" Oppenheimer asked. "Never," the President said.

The American monopoly on nuclear weapons ended on September 3, 1949. On that day a long-range reconnaissance plane, which the United States used to sample the stratosphere, showed an unusually high level of radioactivity. A panel of nuclear specialists in Washington decided that the Russians had indeed set off an atomic bomb, and that the explosion had taken place sometime between August 26 and 29. They even figured out the general location—on the Asian part of the Soviet landmass. The American code name for the explosion, in honor of Joseph Stalin, the Soviet dictator, was Joe One.

By September 19 the five members of the Atomic Energy Commission went to tell the President that there was no doubt about what had happened. For Truman the Soviet explosion was terrible news. Already besieged for being soft on communism, he now faced the terrible decision of whether or not to pursue the development of a hydrogen bomb, a weapon far more powerful than the atomic bomb. The Soviet test left him little room in which to maneuver. Unknown to Truman at the time was the fact that he was about to inherit a major debate that had been raging in scientific circles: whether or not to go ahead with the hydrogen bomb.

On this issue the nation was at crosscurrents with itself. The fear of a German victory had quashed any doubts on the part of the scientists who had worked on the atomic bomb. There had been those who thought that a demonstration of the bomb might be as effective as actually using it. But J. Robert Oppenheimer, later pilloried for being soft during the cold war, took it upon himself to kill a petition of his fellow scientists holding that view. Right after the successful use of the atomic bomb, reporters questioned Oppenheimer about the morality of what the Los Alamos team had achieved, and he answered, in words that were to haunt him later, "A scientist cannot hold back progress because of fears of what the world will do with his discoveries." Still, there was a consensus in high-level political circles that the atomic bomb had probably saved millions of lives, given the way the Japanese had resisted American forces, island by island.

The debate over the hydrogen bomb was different in every way. It was being made in a time of peace, albeit a shaky one. Its nickname in defense and scientific circles said it all—the Superbomb or, simply, the Super. Here, with one terrible strike, was the capacity to unleash 1 million tons of TNT. Given the fact that in all World War II only 3 million tons of TNT had been used, the imagination could scarcely comprehend this new destructive power. It was far more than a more powerful alternative to the atomic bomb; it threatened the very existence of humanity. No wonder most of the scientists involved were terrified of what they had wrought.

OPPENHEIMER himself epitomized the evolution that many of the Los Alamos scientists underwent. He was the leader of the scientific community in those years, and after the successful development of the atomic bomb he was at the pinnacle of his prestige, achieving a mythic status in popular culture. His stewardship of Los Alamos was considered a sterling model for all future scientific ventures. He had worked hard to bring in the best scientists in the world and to create an esprit de corps. Visitors commented on the miraculous openness in which young physicists met with the greatest names in their profession. People spoke of Los Alamos as having a spirit of Athens, of Plato.

But after the Nagasaki bombing, to some Oppenheimer seemed the divided man—part creator of the most dangerous weapon in history, part the romantic innocent searching for some inner spiritual truth. The day after the bombing, one of his colleagues, Ernest Lawrence, found him exhausted, depressed, and wondering aloud whether the dead at Hiroshima and Nagasaki were not luckier than the living. "There was not much left in me at the moment," he later said. The job, as far as he was concerned, was done. As he withdrew from Los Alamos, so did others. He had wielded power there through sheer force of genius, and he seemed to reflect what the others would think before they had time to think it themselves. "Let the second team take over," he was later quoted as saying, a phrase that was wounding to those who stayed behind.

Even as the scientists and the administration were trying to decide what to do about the Super, some of the nation's top military men already thought war with the Soviet Union inevitable. Nor was it just military men. The members of the Atomic Energy Commission met with Senator Brien McMahon, a Democrat on the Joint Committee on Atomic Energy and a man generally considered a moderate. McMahon might have been by the standards of the day a domestic liberal, but he was a hard-liner on the subject of communism. He had become the single most important congressional figure on the issue of atomic weapons, and unlike the scientists, he had no doubts about using them. The bombing of Hiroshima, he had said on the Senate floor, was "the greatest event in world history since the birth of Jesus Christ." If the Russians got ahead of us in nuclear weaponry, that would, in his words, place "total power in the hands of total evil."

The person who would have to make the decision, of course, was Truman, and his room to maneuver was steadily shrinking. The political pressure to go ahead with the Super was relentless. In late November the Joint Chiefs of Staff, led by Omar Bradley, an officer Truman greatly admired, weighed in. It would be "intolerable" for us to let the Russians get the weapon first, the Chiefs said. By this time there were signs that the President had made up his mind to go forward with the Super and that Omar Bradley's recommendation had removed any lingering doubts.

Truman had formed a special three-man committee—of Dean Acheson; David Lilienthal, head of the Atomic Energy Commission; and Louis Johnson, Secretary of Defense—to make a final recommendation. January 31, 1950, had been set as the date for their report. Truman asked that their recommendations be unanimous, which was, in a way, a signal to Lilienthal, who had reservations about the Super, to keep his doubts within the confines of the group. Lilienthal spoke of his fears of an arms race. Acheson countered by pointing out the growing public and political pressures on Truman. Lilienthal again spoke of his own "grave reservations." Truman cut him short. He did not, the President said, believe that an H-bomb would ever be used, but because of the way the Russians were behaving, he had no other course. The meeting lasted only seven minutes. "Can the Russians do it?" Truman asked. All three men nodded yes. "In that case," Truman said, "we have no choice. We'll go ahead." It was Truman's first major decision of the decade.

As development of the hydrogen bomb proceeded, someone asked Albert Einstein, whose original equations had paved the way to the atomic age, how the Third World War would be fought. Einstein answered glumly that he had no idea what kind of weapons would be used in the Third World War, but he could assure the questioner that the war after that would be fought with stones.

# CHAPTER THREE

THE McCarthy era was about to begin. Joseph R. McCarthy, Republican Senator from Wisconsin, stepped forward on Thursday, February 9, 1950, to lend his name to a phenomenon that in fact already existed. He was the accidental demagogue. On that day he gave a speech in Wheeling, West Virginia, as part of a Lincoln Day weekend celebration. Almost casually he claimed that there were Communists in the State Department and that they controlled American foreign policy. As one of the reporters who knew him well noted later, McCarthy himself had no idea that his speech would prove so explosive. Otherwise he would have picked a bigger town than Wheeling and a more prominent group than the Ohio County Women's Republican Club. His line about Communists in the State Department was a throwaway. In the middle of the speech he said, "While I cannot take the time to name all the men in the State Department who have been named as members of the Communist Party and members of a spy ring, I have here in my hand a list of 205 that were known to the Secretary of State as being members of the Communist Party and who nevertheless are still working and shaping the policy of the State Department." That began it. Frank Desmond, a reporter for the Wheeling *Intelligencer,* put the statement in his story. Later that night Norman Yost, his managing editor, who worked as a stringer for The Associated Press, read the story and phoned in a few paragraphs to the AP office in Charleston. The story moved over the AP wire on Thursday night and made the Friday papers. The circus had begun.

On Saturday, McCarthy arrived in Reno, where he was to give a speech that night under the auspices of his colleague, Nevada Republican George "Molly" Malone. Working as a political reporter for the Reno *Gazette* at that time was a young man named Frank McCulloch. He had read the wire story from Wheeling and knew something was up. There was a certain vagueness to McCarthy's accusations, and he set out to pin him down. That afternoon he found McCarthy in Molly Malone's office. McCarthy was on the phone to his staff. "That's great, great," he was saying as he wrote down a name. "You gotta give me more names." McCulloch slid around behind the desk, the better to see what McCarthy was writing down. McCarthy made no attempt to block his view. "Howard Shipley," McCarthy wrote, and then, alongside it, the notation "HARVARD ASTR."

"I want more names," McCarthy said. "You have to give me more names." Soon he was off the phone. "What the hell does Harvard astr mean?" McCulloch asked. "A Harvard astrologer," McCarthy answered. Were these men Communists? the reporter asked. "You come to the meeting tonight and you'll find out," McCarthy said.

When he left, McCulloch went to a phone, and though it was a Saturday, he managed to find an official at Harvard. "What do you know about a Professor Howard Shipley?" he asked. "He's a scientist of some kind there." There was a long pause, and the official said that there was no Howard Shipley at Harvard. You've got to have a Howard Shipley, McCulloch insisted. Well, said the official, perhaps there was some confusion over the name because there was a Harlow Shapley on the Harvard faculty, an astronomer. Oh, thought McCulloch. I think we have a problem here.

McCarthy's carnivallike four-year spree of accusations, charges, and threats touched something deep in the American body politic, something that lasted long after his own recklessness, carelessness, and boozing ended his career in shame. McCarthyism crystallized and politicized the anxieties of a nation living in a dangerous new era. The problem with America, he was saying, was domestic subversion, as tolerated and encouraged by the Democratic Party. China had fallen, not because the forces of history were against the old feudal regime, which had collapsed of its own weight. Rather, it was because of Soviet military and political hegemony. If events in the world were not as we wanted them, then something conspiratorial had happened. Our control of events was limited because sinister forces were at work against us. With that message he changed the nature of American politics.

McCarthy was, in one writer's phrase, the political speculator who found his gusher. He was shrewd, insecure, and defensive—the poor Irish kid from the wrong side of the tracks in Appleton, Wisconsin, who fought his way out and made it to the Senate. He liked to boast of himself as a back-alley fighter. He had a wonderful sense of the resentments that existed just beneath the surface in ordinary people, for he himself burned with those same resentments. He hated the social snobbery, implied or real, in men like Acheson and Hiss. In one of his first speeches after Wheeling he hammered away at those "bright young men with silver spoons in their mouths." In fact, anti-communism was peripheral to his campaign. The names, by and large, tended to be fellow travelers from the thirties, fed to him by J. Edgar Hoover and the FBI.

But McCarthy understood the theater of it all, and he knew instinctively how to humiliate vulnerable, scared people. In the end, he produced little beyond fear and headlines. After a thousand speeches and a thousand charges, the last thing McCarthy could probably have recognized was a real Communist or a real spy ring. Perhaps the best epitaph for him came during the Eisenhower years, when he made his fateful and fatal attack on the United States Army, coming up in the end with one left-wing dentist who had been promoted by mistake. The Republican Senator Ralph Flanders said contemptuously, "He dons his war paint. He goes into his war dance. He emits war whoops. He goes forth to battle and proudly returns with the scalp of a pink dentist."

The real scandal in all this was the behavior of the members of the Washington press corps, who, more often than not, knew better. They were delighted to be a part of his traveling road show, chronicling each charge and then moving on to the next town, instead of bothering to stay behind to follow up. They had little interest in reporting how careless he was or how little it all meant to him. It was news and he was news; that was all that mattered. "McCarthy was a dream story," said Willard Edwards of the Chicago *Tribune*. "I wasn't off page one for four years."

McCarthy knew how to use the mechanics of the journalists' profession against them; he knew their deadlines,

Joseph McCarthy on the attack. The most prominent demagogue of the cold war period, he gave his name to an entire movement—McCarthyism.

when they were hungriest and needed to be fed, and when they had the least time to check out his charges. And he was nothing if not obliging: He had signals for the regulars to let them know there was a reception/press conference, with whiskey, in his room later, or that he wanted to go out with them for dinner. If they needed a story, he was always willing to give them a charge or two. If they wanted to know what the Republican leadership was thinking on other issues, he was perfectly willing to call Bob Taft, the great leader of the conservative wing of the party, and ask him a few questions while reporters listened in on an open receiver. But because of McCarthy's success with Red-baiting, the 1950 election was particularly ugly. In Florida, George Smathers beat his mentor, Senator Claude Pepper, in an unbelievably ugly primary. "Joe [Stalin] likes him and he likes Joe," said Smathers. In California, Richard Nixon, who studied Smathers' race against Pepper, defeated Congresswoman Helen Gahagan Douglas in a campaign that was virtually a case study in Red-baiting. In Illinois, Everett Dirksen defeated Senator Scott Lucas, promising to clean house on Communists and fellow travelers. The Republicans had found their issue, and the Democrats were clearly on the defensive.

"The primitives," Dean Acheson called them. Truman was blunter. "The animals," he branded them.

# CHAPTER FOUR

IT WAS a war that no one wanted, in a desolate, harsh land. "If the best minds in the world had set out to find us the worst possible location in the world to fight this damnable war, politically and militarily, the unanimous choice would have been Korea," Dean Acheson once said. South Korea became important only after the North Korean Communists struck in the night; its value was psychological rather than strategic—the enemy had crossed a border.

At the beginning of the century Korea was conquered by Japan and forced to live under a brutal occupation. At one point during World War II, Franklin Roosevelt had spoken almost carelessly of a free and independent Korea after the war. At Yalta there was talk of a trustee-ship to be administered by the Big Four. At Potsdam in July 1945

American strategists still thought the final battle against Japan would be difficult, and pressed Stalin to help. Having stayed outside the Pacific war for four years, Stalin was delighted to be a part of the dénouement. Who could have resisted a chance to gain so much for so little? But the successful use of the atomic weapon changed American thinking. Now we had no need of the Russians in the Far East. Within twenty-four hours of Hiroshima, planners in Washington were redefining America's position in Korea. Even as the Soviet troops, poised in Manchuria, were moving into the northern part of that country, word came down from the War Department to create some sort of division in Korea between the communist and noncommunist forces. On August 10, 1945, the War Office came up with a demarcation line running across the country at the relatively narrow neck near the midpoint. It was the 38th parallel. It was a rather risky gambit— that is, if the Russians rejected it as the dividing line and their troops continued to push south aggressively, there was little the Americans could do to hold the line. The offer was made to the Russians, and somewhat to our surprise they accepted. The first American units did not arrive in the South for another month.

Nothing seemed to show how unprepared America was for its new, expanded postwar role than the occupation of Korea. We had no area experts to guide us in those early, awkward days. Wary of all the Korean groups suddenly competing for our attention, we used the existing Japanese colonial administration at first, much to the dismay of the Koreans, who hoped to be liberated from the colonials. The first American commander, Major General John Hodge, took an immediate dislike to the people. They were, he said, "the same breed of cat as the Japanese."

Hodge's view seemed to reflect that of most Americans. When another American general was told that his next assignment was to head the American advisory group training the South Korean army, he retired from active service.

Eventually we created a government in the South, headed by Syngman Rhee, a volatile, manipulative figure whose main appeal to us was that he had spent most of his life in exile in America. He spoke good English, had three degrees from American universities, and since he had been out of the country for most of his life, he had not collaborated with the Japanese. He was one of the early postwar anticommunist dictators with an instinctive tendency to arrest almost anyone who did not agree with him. Only by comparison with his counterpart in the North, Kim Il Sung, did he gain: Sung not only arrested his enemies, he frequently had them summarily executed. Though Rhee, by dint of his intense anticommunism, had something of a political base in the American Congress, no one who dealt with him directly, either in Washington or Seoul, seemed to like him— certainly not the people at State or Defense. He made them particularly nervous by constantly boasting of his desire to roll back the 38th parallel and rule the entire country.

As we were desperately demobilizing our military forces after World War II, the 30,000 American troops assigned to Korea seemed a disproportionate number to many. General Hodge pushed constantly for the removal of combat troops (most significantly, including himself). By the fall of 1948 we struck a deal with the Russians: we would both withdraw our regular troops, in effect leaving behind proxy armies. At Rhee's request we left one regimental combat team until June 1949. Our role was to be solely advisory, and Rhee's troops were to become combat-ready.

America was rapidly withdrawing from South Korea, leaving behind something of an unloved and unattractive government with a new, uncertain ragtag army. The Soviets, by contrast, were leaving behind the real thing: a tough, modern dictatorship with a strong, well-trained, well-armed military force. With the aid of the Soviets, Kim Il Sung had created the North Korean People's Army, or In Min Gun. It was composed of ten divisions, some 135,000 men; its commanders were, more often than not, Koreans who had fought along with Mao and the Chinese Communists during their historic defeat of Chiang Kai-shek's army. Most important, the Russians left behind about 150 T-34 tanks, one of the most effective weapons against the Germans in World War II.

Rhee was not the only Korean leader who boasted he would conquer the entire peninsula; Kim Il Sung was every bit as audacious. In late 1949 and in the early months of 1950, there was an increasing number of border clashes, almost all of them initiated by the North.

On June 25, 1950, the North Koreans thrust across the 38th parallel. Their strike stunned America, a nation whose rhetoric and defense policies were in no way in sync. Despite all the warnings, no one

The Korean peninsula. America expected a fast victory over the invading North Koreans. But the nation soon found itself locked in a long struggle with a determined enemy.

MANCHURIA

CHINA

Yalu River

NORTH KOREA

Sea of Japan

★ Pyongyang

38th parallel

Inchon ★ Seoul

SOUTH KOREA

0   50   100
Miles

Pusan perimeter

**Pusan**

was prepared for the assault, or for the toughness of the In Min Gun. As the North Korean forces made their first overt border crossing, the panic was on. The assault consisted of ten divisions moving in four major lines. The elite troops leading the advance were highly disciplined, and they easily smashed through the relatively frail South Korean ROK (Republic of Korea) defenses. The real difference, though, was the Russian T-34 tanks. They had a broad tread and heavy armor plating, and they carried one 85-mm gun and two 7.62 machine guns. And they were at the head of a long, well-armed column moving against soldiers who had no weapons with which to stop them.

The American advisers in South Korea, in their determination to do with public relations what they could not do on the training ground, had earlier called the South Korean army the best for its size in Asia, but the truth was much less than that. Faced by the awesome force of the elite units of In Min Gun, it broke and ran. By June 28 Seoul had fallen. When Douglas MacArthur arrived in Korea on June 29, landing at a small airfield twenty miles south of Seoul, he was stunned by the sight of long lines of South Korean troops retreating. "I did not," said MacArthur angrily, "see a wounded man among them."

The news that the North Koreans had struck took the Truman administration by complete surprise. In Washington, communism was seen as a monolith, and therefore it was assumed the invasion was something that Stalin had decided on. The question therefore was what would the Communists do next, not in Korea but in the world. Truman made up his mind from the start: he would contest the Communists in Korea. "We are going to *fight*," he told his daughter, Margaret. "By God I am not going to let them have it," he told another aide. Almost all his top aides felt the same way. Omar Bradley, a man not given to hasty rhetoric, termed the invasion a "moral outrage." We had to draw the line somewhere, he said, and Korea "offered as good an occasion for drawing the line as anywhere else."

Drawing the line in Korea was to be one of the few things Truman and MacArthur would agree on. Almost immediately MacArthur, as was his wont, exceeded his authority by ordering the bombing of North Korean airfields. He was the Supreme Allied Commander in Asia, and he thought of himself as a sovereign power in the Pacific. The President and Joint Chiefs had hegemony in Europe, in his mind, but not in Asia. That was his. Essentially, he believed himself above the authority of his Commander in Chief.

But bombing would not stop the North Korean drive. On June 30, after returning from his personal inspection of the South, MacArthur reported that the South Korean army was retreating in complete chaos. The only way to hold the line against the North was to introduce American troops. He requested two divisions and one regimental combat team for immediate deployment. In Washington, Joe Collins, the army Chief of Staff, received the fateful cable from MacArthur asking permission to send American ground troops to the mainland of Asia. He did not even bother to summon the rest of the Joint Chiefs. He called MacArthur and told him his request needed presidential approval, but in the meantime he had permission to move a regimental combat team to Pusan, on the southeast tip of the Korean peninsula. MacArthur demanded a clearer mandate without delay. By then it was five a.m., June 30, in Washington. Truman was already up and the secretary of the army, Frank Pace, called to brief him. Truman immediately approved the use of the Reserve Combat Team, postponing a decision on more troops. But essentially the deed was done—and without congressional approval. Americans would fight in South Korea.

Initially Truman tried to downplay the commitment. At a meeting with reporters he said, "We are not at war." A reporter, searching for a way to describe the commitment, asked the President if it was a "police action." The President, in a moment he would later regret, noted that yes, that was an apt description.

Of the American troops ordered to Korea from Japan, only the elite 82nd Airborne was combat-ready. The rest were occupation troops, grown soft from easy duty. Many had been lured into service after the war by recruiting officers promising an ideal way to get out of small-town America and see the world. "They had enlisted," wrote one company commander, T. R. Fehrenbach, "for every reason known to man except to fight."

Yet the Americans set off for Korea astonishingly confident of an easy victory. Almost everyone, from top to bottom, seemed to share the view that the moment the North Korean soldiers saw they were fighting *Americans* rather than ROKs, they would cut and run. One colonel in the 34th Infantry, Harold Ayres, told his troops as they were arriving in Korea, "There are supposed to be North Korean soldiers north of us. These men are poorly trained. Only about half of them have weapons and we'll have no difficulty stopping them."

He and the rest of the American units were in for a rude awakening. The North Koreans were a formidable foe. Their troops were rugged peasants who showed exceptional discipline in battle. Their camouflage was excellent: they wore netting over their helmets and their uniforms so they could fix branches and leaves to them. They moved well over the hard terrain and did not necessarily stay on the roads, as the Americans did. Their battlefield tactics, borrowed from Mao's armies, were deft. What had started out as something of a game had turned into a military nightmare for the American troops.

Washington was still in shock. MacArthur began drawing up an immense list of what he needed: a marine regimental combat team, the 2nd Infantry Division, eleven artillery battalions, and an armored group of three medium tank battalions. The Pentagon recommended most of what MacArthur wanted. A fat new $11 billion supplemental appropriation bill was rushed through. Ninety-two National Guard units—or the equivalent of four National Guard divisions—and the entire Marine Corps reserve were called up. Some units, such as the two battalions of the 29th Infantry Regiment, were supposed to get six weeks of training; instead, they were, over the bitter protests of their officers, rushed immediately into battle. One day after arrival in-country they found themselves at the most forward position.

After three weeks, more than 2400 men had been lost, either dead or missing. It was one of the worst periods in American military history.

But gradually, fresh troops were pouring into the country. The quality of hardware was improving. By the same token, the North Korean army's lines of communication were now far too long and being taxed by constant bombing. Slowly the balance of force was changing. By early August the U.N. forces—for by now the United Nations had put its weight behind the conflict—actually outnumbered the In Min Gun. And while the Eighth Army had suffered terrible casualties—more than 6000 men—so had the North Koreans. American military estimates of casualties caused to the North Korean People's Army were 58,000. The North Koreans had used most of their best men and equipment in that sudden, shocking first strike. Now they were replacing elite troops with green conscripts.

If the situation was turning around, not everyone realized it. There were still top secret plans for a massive Dunkirk-like withdrawal if need be, for the summer of 1950 had proved a dark time, when America was reluctantly being drawn into a world it had never made. There was always the danger that this small war would grow larger. Averell Harriman and General Matthew Ridgway visited MacArthur in Tokyo to ask, among other things, that he make certain this did not happen. MacArthur was supremely confident; if the Chinese decided to enter the war, he would deal them such a crushing blow that it "would rock Asia and perhaps turn back Communism." Modesty was never his strong point.

DOUGLAS MacArthur had not been home in thirteen years. Truman had twice invited him to receive the appreciation of a grateful nation, but MacArthur turned him down, saying that he was too busy in Tokyo. Since a presidential request was in fact an order, Truman was furious. He suspected that MacArthur's reasons were political, that he was biding his time in order to create a Republican groundswell, with a dramatic return in time for a primary run. MacArthur's explanation was simpler but predictably vainglorious. He could not return, he told an aide. "If I returned for only a few weeks, word would spread through the Pacific that the United States is abandoning the Orient."

He was seventy years old in 1950, a towering figure who had worked long and hard to perpetuate his own legend. But not everyone thought he was the right leader for this particular war. He was older than the norm for a combat commander, and his reputation exceeded in some ways those civilians to whom he was supposed to report. Far more than most generals, he held to the idea that the commander in the field was *the* decision maker—not merely tactically but strategically as well. He was known among his peers as one who manipulated the information he passed on to his superiors in order to justify the plans he intended to carry out. There was also the danger that he had begun to see his mission in Asia in a quasi-religious light, as the leader of a holy crusade against a godless enemy.

Be that as it may, in 1950 Douglas MacArthur was at the summit of one of the most glorious careers in American history. He was the son of Arthur MacArthur, a Civil War hero who won the Congressional Medal of Honor at age eighteen and who later commanded American troops during the Philippine insurrection. His son Douglas MacArthur, at age thirty-eight, was the youngest division commander in the army. In 1930 he became the Chief of Staff of the army.

MacArthur was a complete narcissist. He was brilliant, talented, petulant, manipulative, highly political, theatrical, and given to remarkable mood swings. His favorite pronoun was the first person. In one of his most famous statements, promising his eventual return to the Philippines, he said, "*I* shall return"—not "*We* shall return." He did not share glory with subordinate commanders—he considered that a weakness—and his headquarters always made sure that he was given full credit for every victory.

He was nonetheless the most brilliant strategist in the American army, a great warrior, completely fearless—in the cool and unsympathetic eyes of George Marshall, "our most brilliant general." During World War II his leadership in the Pacific dazzled colleagues, political leaders, and military historians alike. In that campaign, starting in early 1942, he had taken a severely understrength Allied army, with little air and naval support, and charted a course of great originality. His strategy was simple: he shepherded his resources, rarely contesting the Japanese where they were strong, but instead striking at them on smaller islands, where they were weak. The day of the crude frontal attack was over, he had told Roosevelt at a meeting in Waikiki; modern weaponry had made it obsolete. Those inhuman battles of World War I, with their endless casualties, had spelled its end. Only mediocre commanders tried frontal attacks anymore. His skills, plus the growing technological might of the Allied forces and the declining resources of the enemy, came together in a masterful campaign.

After World War II was over, for some five years he served as the viceroy of Japan. His needs and those of the Japanese dovetailed perfectly—the Japanese needed to worship the man who had conquered them, and he needed to be worshipped. He prided himself on his expertise in Asia, yet his Victorian mind could not see the revolution against colonialism taking place there, most particularly in China. The China he felt he knew so well no longer existed.

Now, in the perimeter around Pusan, the tide was beginning to turn. Day by day, as August wore on, American positions grew stronger. The North Koreans were literally and figuratively running out of gas, as well as men and ammunition. This was the moment that MacArthur had been waiting for. From the first moment he had visited Korea, right after the invasion, a strategic vision had taken hold of him: In one brilliant, audacious move we would make an amphibious assault far behind their lines. They would be unprepared, since most of their army was committed to the South. We would then move quickly both north and east across the thin neck of the country to entrap them. MacArthur even had his site picked out—Inchon, on the west coast, the great national port city for Seoul. MacArthur would explain to doubters, "When we get well ashore at Inchon, the North Koreans will have no choice but to pull out or surrender."

Virtually no one agreed with him. The navy thought the plan impractical, indeed impossible, because there was no natural beach. One sunken ship could block the whole harbor. The tides could be terrible, up to thirty-two feet. Only the Bay of Fundy had higher. There were only three dates in the next two months on which the tides would be high enough to carry the big landing craft far enough in before the whole shoreline became nothing but mud—September 15, September 27, and October 11. "Make up a list of amphibious 'don'ts' and you have an exact description of the Inchon operation," one naval officer noted. Yet MacArthur remained steadfast in his vision. To him the alternative was a meat-grinder war up the Korean peninsula, with the possibility of slow progress and unacceptable casualties. "Beef cattle in the slaughterhouse," he called it.

The critical meeting on Inchon was held in Tokyo on August 23. Two members of the Joint Chiefs—Joe Collins and Admiral Forest Sherman—went to Tokyo to talk MacArthur out of it. If there must be an amphibious landing, let it be more modest, to the south of Inchon. At the August meeting, one naval officer after another got up to explain the reason why Inchon could not work, why the risks involved were too high. Finally MacArthur took the floor. The navy, he said, had never failed him before. After dismissing the doubters, he gave a great soliloquy: "I can almost hear the ticking of the second hand of destiny. We must act now or we will die. . . . We shall land at Inchon and I shall crush them." He finished, and there was a moment of silence. Then Admiral Sherman spoke: "Thank you. A great voice in a great cause." Rear Admiral James Doyle, whose job it would be to execute the landing, later said, "If MacArthur had gone on the stage you never would have heard of John Barrymore." But MacArthur had won. Inchon was his.

On the morning of September 15 the marines landed on Wolni, a small island guarding the mouth of Inchon harbor. The North Korean garrison there, composed of young, inexperienced soldiers, quickly collapsed. That afternoon 13,000 marines poured ashore against marginal resistance. Only twenty-one men were killed. North Korean forces were routed, moving back as best they could to blocking positions between Inchon and Seoul. Now, for the U.N. forces, it was a race for Seoul, and to entrap the In Min Gun before they retreated north. It was MacArthur's finest hour. If before Inchon he had been an "untouchable," now he was a god. One of the worst defeats in American military history had, overnight, been turned into a stunning success.

Seoul fell on September 26, eleven days after the landing. But even though the Allied forces moved steadily forward, the bulk of the North Korean force was slipping away. The Americans had hoped, but failed, to capture it en masse, and some 40,000 men had managed to slip through. MacArthur's forces continued to pursue to the 38th parallel. On October 1 South Korean ROK forces became the first U.N. soldiers to go north of the 38th. In the rush of events and the seeming collapse of the enemy, it was not a decision that weighed very heavily on anyone in Washington at the time. A few of the old China hands warned that North Korea was a satellite state and that neither Peking nor Moscow would tolerate it if we violated the 38th parallel. Truman, already under fire for being soft on communism, was in no position to slow down so rapid and spectacular an advance—in truth, a rout.

So it was that we blundered ahead toward the most dramatic confrontation of the cold war to that date. From the moment that the ROK forces crossed the 38th parallel, there were rumblings from

Peking. Gradually, as we pressed north toward the Yalu River and the Manchurian border, those warnings became more strident. American troops crossed the 38th parallel on October 7. The next day Mao ordered his forces to ready themselves to fight, and a massive movement of men started toward Manchuria and the Korean border.

Now Truman started to become nervous; the noise from Peking was like a distant but steady drumroll. Moreover, his own shrewdness told him that while his forces were doing well, they were doing it at a price—getting farther from their own lines of supply, ever deeper into hostile terrain, and doing this as the weather got colder. In late October he arranged a meeting with MacArthur at Wake Island. The two men were not a natural fit. Long before Korea, Truman, the good old-fashioned unvarnished populist, had written a memo on the dilemma of dealing with MacArthur: "And what to do with Mr. Prima Donna, Brass Hat, Five Star MacArthur. He's worse than the Cabots and the Lodges—they at least talked with one another before they told God what to do. Mac tells God right off." That, of course, was before they even got to know each other.

The Wake Island meeting seemed to go reasonably well, although both men remained wary of each other. Truman was concerned about Chinese intentions, but MacArthur was reassuring. The victory in Korea, he said, had already been won, and North Korean resistance would end by Thanksgiving. Truman pushed a little harder on the question of Chinese intervention. Again MacArthur belittled the possibility. At best only 50,000 or 60,000 could get across the Yalu, and if they tried to move down to Pyongyang, "there would be the greatest slaughter." This statement was a remarkable boast for so brilliant a commander. It showed, above all else, that he had spent no time studying the Chinese army or the tactics with which Mao had defeated Chiang Kai-shek.

When he made that promise, MacArthur was not thinking of the modern new Chinese army that had unleashed such a powerful force of nationalism in its victory over Chiang. Rather, he was thinking of a weak army from a feudal society. Even as he told Truman that the Chinese would not enter the war—and that if they did, he would slaughter them—the Chinese Fourth Field Army was entering the country.

The Fourth Field Army was one of the great infantry forces of the modern era, even though it consisted of peasants and remarkably little hardware. It moved on foot instead of by wheels and, lacking even the simplest of modern communication systems, coordinated its attacks with bugles—which had the additional advantage of terrifying the adversary. To say that the troops were tough and experienced was a vast understatement. They marched (or trotted) 286 miles to their assembly point at the Yalu in eighteen days, carrying only eight to ten pounds of gear and supplies: a weapon, a grenade, eighty rounds of ammunition, perhaps a week's supply of rice, and a tiny bit of meat and fish. An American soldier, by contrast, carried sixty pounds. The Chinese soldiers were not expert marksmen; rather, they were trained to attack close to their enemy and unleash bursts of automatic fire, a method that demanded that they take extremely heavy casualties.

Some people thought the Fourth Field Army was the best that the Chinese had. It was divided into six groups; each consisted of four 30,000-man armies, and each of these had three divisions of about 8000 to 10,000 men. They started crossing the Yalu, it was believed, on October 13. They used the regular bridges and built some of their own—invisible underwater fords—by means of sandbags. Their camouflage was so good, and MacArthur's intelligence was so bad, that none of their movements were detected. By the time MacArthur made his reckless pledge to Truman to slaughter them, there were probably at least 130,000 Chinese soldiers already in the country.

Though we did not know much about the Chinese, they knew a great deal about us. They received a pamphlet about the American troops just before the first battle began. The Americans, it said, were not to be underestimated. They were good soldiers, well equipped, and had the advantages of mobility and modern firepower in their attacks, enabling them to make lightning-quick strikes. But their weaknesses were noted as well: they did not fight well when forced to defend, and attacks at night would panic them, forcing them to leave behind their heavy equipment.

As both forces moved inexorably toward a confrontation at the Yalu, MacArthur was no longer merely the commander of the American forces, he was the sole policymaker as well. Washington had permitted him to cross the 38th parallel but had placed a strict ban on his going too far north. His orders were to stay away from the Yalu, but seeking to capture the North Korean army that had escaped after

Inchon, he simply disobeyed. At this point the U.N. troops, whose misfortune it was to be carrying out MacArthur's last great dream of glory, were undersupplied, underclothed, underfed, and far from their base camp. As those United Nations units moved forward, they began to feel a growing sense of isolation. Something ominous was in the air. Almost overnight the enemy seemed to have disappeared.

In Tokyo, MacArthur urged his forces on to their appointed meeting place at the Yalu. He had two major commands in operation: the Eighth Army in the west, under the command of General Walton Walker, and the X Corps, operating in the east, under the command of General Edward Almond. The optimism at MacArthur's headquarters was at its height. The war was virtually finished, he told reporters. There was talk of bringing the boys home for Christmas.

There had been an agreement between MacArthur and the Joint Chiefs of Staff ( J.C.S.) that as he moved nearer to the Yalu, he would clear all movements with them. In mid-October the J.C.S. readily approved crossing a line in the north at Chongjiu-Yongwon-Hamhung. But fearing that the Chiefs would stop his movement, MacArthur became less forthright. On October 17 he sent a directive to Washington that unilaterally set a new forward line of Sonchon-Pyongwon-Songjin, thirty miles farther north. That was still arguably within his orders. What he intended to do, though, was use this not so much as a final position but as a staging area to go even farther north.

On October 24 he ordered his troops forward. He did not clear this with the J.C.S., but the Chiefs heard of it through the army back channel and warned him that these moves were not consistent with their previous instructions. MacArthur snapped back that there were military reasons for doing this and that he had the right to go ahead based on instructions from the Wake Island meeting. That stunned Washington.

The first Republic of Korea troops reached the Yalu on October 25 and began taking the first Chinese prisoners. These men were captured all too readily and almost seemed to be offering themselves up. General Paek Sun Yup, the temporary ROK commander, spoke fluent Chinese. "Are there many of you here?" he asked. "Many," one prisoner answered.

Despite the growing evidence of a Chinese military presence, MacArthur's headquarters remained absolutely adamant that it had not encountered the Chinese. On October 30 Ned Almond went by chopper to visit an ROK unit that had taken sixteen Chinese prisoners. After looking at the prisoners and talking with their South Korean captors, he sent a message to MacArthur's headquarters that fully organized Chinese units were in the country. But his message had little impact.

Just after dusk on November 1 the Chinese forces hit an American unit with full fury for the first time. The unit was part of the 8th Cavalry Regiment, which held positions just north and west of Unsan. The Americans were facing, it was estimated later, nothing less than two, and quite possibly three, full divisions of Chinese troops.

It was a new kind of war. Just when the Americans thought they might have slowed the assault, more Chinese would come—like an endless human wave. A few men in an American defensive position would lay down a perfect field of fire and kill a hundred attacking Chinese, but then the bugles would sound; the attack would begin again. When the relief forces finally reached the site where the 3rd Battalion of the 8th Regiment had been hit, they found a ghostlike scene. There were American bodies everywhere. Not a living soul was left. One NCO thought the site resembled another Little Big Horn. It had been a devastating defeat. Some 600 men in the regiment had been lost, all told.

Yet MacArthur continued to push his units forward despite their vulnerability and the terrible cold. Sadly, he remained in Tokyo, refusing to accept the evidence that the war had changed. The front-line units were told to press on. MacArthur would not be deterred from his drive to link his forces at the Yalu.

By November 3 Truman was becoming worried by the recurring reports of Chinese intervention and the hammering of the 8th Cavalry; the J.C.S. cabled MacArthur asking the extent of Chinese involvement. The next day MacArthur replied that he now saw Chinese intervention as a "distinct possibility," to give covert assistance to the North Koreans. This would let them "salvage something from the wreckage."

MacArthur ordered his forces to bomb the Korean end of the twelve bridges across the Yalu—a violation of the old J.C.S. order to stay well clear of the Manchurian borders.

His decision alarmed Washington, which told him to desist. He sent a cable: EVERY HOUR THAT THIS IS POSTPONED WILL BE PAID FOR DEARLY IN

AMERICAN AND OTHER UNITED NATIONS BLOOD. He ended with a barely concealed threat: failure to do as he said would result in A CALAMITY OF MAJOR PROPORTIONS FOR WHICH I CANNOT ACCEPT THE RESPONSIBILITY WITHOUT HIS [Truman's] PERSONAL AND DIRECT UNDERSTANDING OF THE SITUATION.

The buck had been passed. It was Washington that had dictated policies, he seemed to be saying, for which he would no longer accept responsibility. The J.C.S. and the administration, wary of confrontation, backed down and let MacArthur bomb his bridges. It was the gravest provocation imaginable to the Chinese. It was not even tactically intelligent—in a few weeks the Yalu would freeze anyway.

In Washington the top officials—Truman, Acheson, Marshall—felt events were slipping outside their control. What were the Chinese up to? They had struck with great success, "and yet they seemed to have vanished from the face of the earth," Acheson wrote in his memoirs. "And what was MacArthur up to in the amazing military maneuver which was unfolding before our unbelieving eyes?"

When MacArthur announced on November 17 that he would make his final drive to the Yalu, Washington warned him to take only the high ground overlooking the Yalu valley and go no farther.

It was a fateful moment. By dint of his arrogance, foolishness, and vainglory MacArthur was about to take a smaller war that was already winding down and expand it to include as an adversary a communist superpower, thereby adding more than two years to its life; he was to damage profoundly America's relations with China; and he was to help start a chain of events that was poisonous in terms of domestic politics—feeding political paranoia, giving the paranoiacs what they needed most: a tangible enemy.

The drive toward the Yalu began on November 24, 1950, the day after Thanksgiving. The weather was terrible. The windchill factor made it twenty or thirty degrees below zero. Rifles froze and batteries in vehicles froze, and the jeeps and trucks could not be started. For the first day and a half the offensive went reasonably well. There was little resistance. But on the evening of November 25 the Chinese struck again. It was a terrifying moment. The Americans clung to the thin, narrow, icy roads in valleys, while above them, on the high ground, well-armed, well-led, and well-clothed Chinese troops rained down murderous fire. The Chinese came at American units in a kind of V, called Hachi-Shiki's. As they got closer, they unfolded the V and began to envelop the American position on its flanks. It was clear from the start that this was a devastating assault. Many of the American units were in desperate trouble.

Still, on November 27 the second part of the offensive was launched—the X Corps offensive, the other pincer to link up with the Eighth Army. There was a certain madness to it all. MacArthur, Joe Collins wrote years later, was marching forward "like a Greek hero of old to an unkind and inexorable fate." By November 28 it was clear that this was an epic disaster and that the great MacArthur had been outgeneraled by the Chinese.

Some 3000 men were killed, wounded, or lost that day. That it wasn't worse was a miracle. In the final few days of November alone, the 2nd Division took some 5000 casualties, or roughly one third of its men. December was just as ghastly. In the words of the British military historian Max Hastings: "Most of the Eighth Army fell apart as a fighting force in a fashion resembling the collapse of the French in 1940, the British in Singapore in 1942."

In the weeks following the Chinese attack, MacArthur seemed to be offering the President only the choice between a much larger war, in which he claimed he would ultimately triumph, or a complete rout. The meetings at the Pentagon were the bleakest that anyone could remember. The word Dunkirk hung constantly in the air. The Joint Chiefs were paralyzed by the constant bad news from the front. They no longer trusted or believed in MacArthur, but they were afraid to challenge him. Finally, as one of the meetings was breaking up, Matt Ridgway, the army vice chief of staff, grabbed General Hoyt Vandenberg and asked him why the Joint Chiefs didn't send orders to MacArthur *telling* him what to do. Vandenberg just shook his head. "What good would that do? He wouldn't obey the orders. What can we do?"

"You can relieve any commander who won't obey orders, can't you?" Ridgway asked. Vandenberg gave him a long look, both puzzled and amazed. "This was," Acheson later noted, "the first time that someone had expressed what everybody thought—that the Emperor had no clothes on." Now a collision course was set.

What probably saved the American and United Nations forces was a fluke. On December 23 General Walker, who had a reputation for driving recklessly, was killed in a jeep accident. Walker, who had commanded the Eighth Army since the American forces first arrived in Korea, was considered tough and feisty but in far over his head in terms of the larger skills needed for so demanding an assignment. Some of the top American generals had wanted to relieve him much earlier but had been afraid of the consequences as far as public relations were concerned. Now Matt Ridgway would command the Eighth Army. He got the news in Washington on December 23. The next day he left for Tokyo, where he talked with Douglas MacArthur, who told him, "The Eighth Army is yours, Matt. Do what you think best."

MATTHEW Bunker Ridgway was arguably the preeminent American soldier of this century. He was an upper-class American: his father had been a judge in Brooklyn, an uncle helped design the New York City subway system, and his mother, Julia Starbuck Ridgway, had been a concert pianist. To Matt Ridgway the military was not just a career, it was a calling. His sense of duty always had a touch of the mystical to it. "He was," noted a West Point contemporary, Russell

General Douglas MacArthur barks out his orders during the Inchon landing— his last great victory. Below: General Matt Ridgway (left) took over a demoralized army and gave it back its pride.

Reeder, "a twelfth-century knight with a twentieth-century brain."

Upon arriving in Korea, he spent the first few days visiting every frontline unit, wearing his trademark grenade pinned to one shoulder strap. Many soldiers had the impression that he wore two grenades; actually, the other object was a medical kit. From this came his nickname, Old Iron Tits. He was appalled by MacArthur's distance from the battlefield, by the paucity of division and regimental commanders at the front, and by the lack of daily intelligence on the enemy—a result of not enough patrolling.

This army had completely lost its confidence, he decided. Morale was nonexistent. The men seemed to go about in a daze, "wondering when they would hear the whistle of that homebound transport." What he wanted to create "was a toughness of soul as well as body." He chewed out the division and regimental commanders right after the start of the new year. If the ordinary soldiers had gotten soft, it was because their commanders had allowed them to do so.

He knew exactly what he wanted to do: take the high ground, employ his artillery effectively, create far stronger defensive positions, and fight better at night by using massive numbers of flares. He was going to grind the Chinese down, erode their vast numbers with his superior artillery. He was everywhere. No unit, no matter how small, was safe from his visit. "The man who came to dinner," one high official at I Corps headquarters called him sardonically. Another high officer said, "Oh God! He came to *every* briefing, *every* morning." But it was working. He was slowly breathing life back into an army that had been not merely defeated but humiliated. His goals were modest. Real estate was important to him only as a means of giving the United Nations some leverage when it came to the final negotiations for peace.

Not surprisingly, the better Matt Ridgway did, the more difficult Douglas MacArthur became. Even as Ridgway steadied his forces, MacArthur was still issuing apocalyptic cables to Washington, saying that unless we widened the war, we were going to be driven off the Korean peninsula. As Omar Bradley wrote in his autobiography, "His legendary pride had been hurt. . . . The only possible means left to MacArthur to regain his lost pride and military reputation was now to inflict an overwhelming defeat on those Red Chinese generals who had made a fool of him. In order to do this he was perfectly willing to propel us into all-out war with Red China, and possibly with the Soviet

A young corporal carries a homemade sign to the top of Heartbreak Ridge, scene of some of the fiercest fighting in Korea.

Union, igniting World War III and a nuclear holocaust."

Knowing that the Truman administration planned to announce on March 24 that it would seek a cease-fire as the first step in arranging a settlement with the Chinese, MacArthur cut the ground out from under the President by making his own announcement. He taunted the Chinese, virtually calling them a defeated army, saying that China's "exaggerated and vaunted military power" lacked the industrial base necessary for modern warfare. If only, he continued, the restrictions imposed on him were lifted, he would strike so viciously that they would be doomed to military collapse. It was not just an insult to the Chinese but a slap in the face to the President, who was seeking a means to peace.

Truman was furious. It was then that the President decided to fire his general. Truman talked the problem over with his top advisers, who warned him that firing MacArthur would initiate the biggest political battle of his administration. Truman had hoped to bring some grace to the dénouement by sending a personal emissary to break the news to the general, but word leaked out and MacArthur heard the news over the radio. That seemed to underscore the heartlessness of the decision. Still, the scandal was preferable to dealing with a provocative and disobedient commander in the field.

In Tokyo, when he heard, MacArthur turned to his wife and said, "Jeannie, we're going home at last."

The firing was as divisive an act as anyone could remember. It was not just that everyone had an opinion about what had happened but that everyone had to voice it. There were fights in bars between strangers and fights on commuter trains between men who knew each other and who had, up to that moment, been friends and had concealed their political differences.

It was to that nation, that outpouring of emotion, that MacArthur came home. At first it seemed like one vast parade that would never end. It began in Tokyo on the morning of April 16, 1951, where nearly 250,000 Japanese lined the streets to bid their postwar ruler farewell, many of them waving small Japanese and American flags. The next stop was Hawaii, and at Hickam Field the crowd was estimated by reporters at 100,000. In San Francisco some 20,000 people came out to the airport.

The last big stop on MacArthur's return was Washington. He arrived near midnight, and again the crowd at the airport was immense, though it included no member of the Truman Cabinet. In Washington, MacArthur was to address a joint session of Congress. It was the general at his most formidable—powerful, theatrical, manipulative, and wonderfully selective with the record. Among other things, he claimed in his speech that the Joint Chiefs agreed with his policies in Korea, which was a bold-faced lie.

Then came the peroration, rich in memories and pure nostalgia: "I am closing my fifty-two years of military service. When I joined the Army even before the turn of the century, it was the fulfillment of all my boyish hopes and dreams. The world has turned over many times since I took the oath on the plain at West Point, and the hopes and dreams have long since vanished. But I still remember the refrain of one of the most popular barracks ballads of that day, which proclaimed most profoundly that 'old soldiers never die; they just fade away.' And like the old soldier of that ballad, I now close my military career and just fade away—an old soldier who tried to do his duty as God gave him the light to see that duty. Good-bye."

## CHAPTER FIVE

"THERE never was a country more fabulous than America," wrote the British historian Robert Payne after visiting America in the winter of 1948–49. "She sits bestride the world like a Colossus; no other power at any time in the world's history has possessed so varied or so great an influence on other nations. Half of the wealth of the world, more than half of the productivity, are concentrated in American hands; the rest of the world lies in the shadow of American industry." Henry Luce, a leader in the internationalist wing of the

Republican Party, spoke of the coming of the American Century. He envisaged an all-powerful America spreading democracy and riches across the globe.

Driven by the revolutionary vision of Henry Ford, the United States had been the leader in mass production before World War II. Ordinary Americans could afford his creation, the Model T, while in Europe, where class lines were sharply drawn, the rather old-fashioned manufacturers preferred building expensive cars for the rich.

But after the war the Ford Motor Company hovered near bankruptcy, thanks to the madness and paranoia of its founder. If there was a symbol of America's industrial might in those years, it was General Motors, a company so powerful that to call it merely a corporation seemed woefully inadequate. It was the largest, richest corporation in the world and would, in the coming decade, become the first corporation in the history of mankind to gross a billion dollars. General Motors dominated the market so completely that when one of its top executives, Charlie "Engine" Wilson, left GM to become Eisenhower's Defense Secretary, he was widely quoted as saying that what was good for General Motors was good for the country. That is what he probably *thought,* but what he actually *said* was, "We at General Motors have always felt that what was good for the country was good for General Motors as well." In good years GM made virtually as many as or more cars than all of its competitors combined.

General Motors, in the years after the war, made ever bigger cars. It moved in that direction because it was the nature of the beast. In the late forties there had been one brief skirmish within the corporate hierarchy when Wilson wanted to do a low-price car in the Chevy division. He had in mind a car that would cost under a thousand dollars. There was even a brand name for the new car—the Cadet—and engineering on it was pursued to a relatively advanced stage.

But small cars meant smaller profits, while basic production costs stayed the same. Producing a fender for a big car, the GM analysts liked to point out, was not much more expensive than producing a fender for a little car. In December 1949 a reporter asked Wilson if there would ever be an inexpensive car priced under a thousand dollars again. No, he answered; that was in the past. "People don't want the kind of car you would have to make in order to price it under a thousand dollars. You would have to take too much out to get the price down and there are too many things you couldn't cut."

General Motors had been waiting a long time for this market of abundance; in fact, Alfred P. Sloan, the company's corporate architect, had been planning for it for some twenty-five years. But Sloan was seventy-five before the country's affluence finally caught up with his vision. It had been his belief since the mid-twenties that the American market could be broken down into a few essential niches, defined by economic and social status. The Chevy was for blue-collar people with solid jobs and for young couples just starting out who had to be careful with money; the Pontiac was for more successful people who were confident about their economic futures and wanted a sportier car—one thinks of the young man just out of law school; the Olds was, in the beginning of the decade, a bit more sedate—for the white-collar bureaucrat or old-fashioned manager; the Buick was for the town's doctor, the young lawyer who was about to be made partner, or the elite of the managerial class; the Cadillac was for the top executive or owner of the local factory. Caddies cost about $5000.

Sloan's first task was to challenge the powerful but stagnant Ford Motor Company. The era of mass car production had been inaugurated by the first Henry Ford. Before that, cars were exclusively the property of the wealthy. Ford figured out how to manufacture cars in such volume that the price dropped steadily. "For every dollar I bring the price down, I can sell a thousand more cars," he bragged. In so doing, he changed the very nature of the American economy. Under Henry Ford, that first era of auto production was, most assuredly, puritan. The Model T was simple, boxy, functional. A buyer could choose a car in any color he wanted, Ford boasted, as long as it was black. There were no frills.

Starting in the late twenties, Sloan and his colleagues at GM inaugurated the second stage of the automobile era, in which the car was not merely transportation but a reflection of status, a concept to which most Americans responded enthusiastically as they strove to move upward into the middle class, and then the upper middle class. Under Sloan, the buyer was supposed to covet an ever showier, ever more expensive car. As such, a car was not a permanent possession, it was an economic benchmark on life's journey to the top.

After World War II, Sloan pondered what Americans wanted, and he decided they wanted styling first, automatic transmissions second, and high-compression engines third. He gave carte blanche to his top designer, Harley Earl. If, in a poorer time, Henry Ford represented the Calvinist era, Harley Earl was the standard-bearer of the new age of affluence. It is possible that no one exerted as much influence on American style and taste in the fifties as he, and no one reflected more accurately what the country had become.

Earl was plucked out of Hollywood by GM in 1927. His father had been a carriage builder there, and Harley Earl had started out as one of the early customizers in the new auto business, adapting cars for the least conservative of Detroit's customers: movie stars. Even before he left Hollywood, there was a distinctive stamp to Earl cars. They were longer, lower, ever sleeker, ever more rounded, and even when they were standing still, they were to give the impression of power and motion.

His mandate came directly from Sloan, and he began a new department—the art and color department, as it was known. Now models of new cars, which had previously been tiny, were created life-size. "The trouble with small models is that your eyes don't shrink with the model," Earl liked to say. When he had arrived in Detroit, the engineering departments were all-powerful, and the advertisements for cars emphasized such features as generator capacity. But gradually, given Sloan's mandate, power shifted to the styling room.

A Harley Earl car was easy to spot. He was fascinated by jet air-

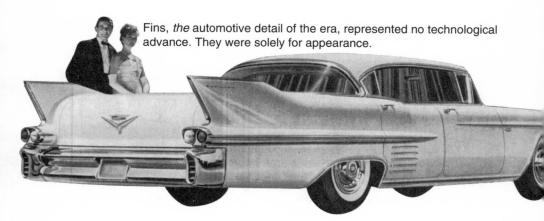

Fins, *the* automotive detail of the era, represented no technological advance. They were solely for appearance.

planes, so long and slim that they appeared to be racing into the future; he admired sharks—long, sleek, and powerful—and his futuristic cars were, in no small way, based on their shape, with a single metal dorsal fin in the rear. "My sense of proportion tells me that oblongs are more attractive than squares," he once wrote, "just as a ranch house is more attractive than a square three-story flat-roofed house or a greyhound is more attractive than a bulldog."

In a corporate culture in which the individual was *always* subordinated to the corporate good and in which a certain anonymity was increasingly valued, Harley Earl deliberately stood apart. After all, he had seen Cecil B. DeMille create his own mystique by going everywhere with a riding crop and wearing boots. "The world," Earl would say, "stands aside for the man who knows where's he's going." When he entered the room, his manner left no doubt that he expected to be catered to and, of course, listened to. Other GM executives drove Cadillacs (or the car of their division after an order came down that it was not becoming for executives of Chevy to drive Caddies), but Harley Earl drove the LeSabre, a highly futuristic car he himself had designed. Typically, it was based on a jet plane, the F-86 Sabre jet. Earl had hundreds of suits, many of them linen and in offbeat colors. Other executives allowed themselves only three colors for suits: dark blue, light gray, and dark gray. When he was meeting with the GM board, his clothes, if anything, were even more eccentric, more flamboyant than usual. His staff would watch him go before the board in a cream-colored linen suit and *blue suede shoes*. They knew he was making a statement, that he was artistic, that he knew design and taste as they did not, and, finally, that he was outside their reach and they were not to fool with him.

Not everyone admired what Earl was doing. Some critics thought his cars reflected the postwar excesses of American society. They were too large and flashy without being better, the critics believed. To the doubters he was the prince of "gorp" (the combination of fins and chrome that marked the industry's cars in those years). At Ford he was known—part respectfully, part not so respectfully—as the Cellini of Chrome. One of his foremost colleagues, the famed industrial designer Raymond Loewy, took the occasion of a 1955 speech before the Society of Automobile Engineers to criticize the entire philosophy behind Earl's cars, which he said had become like jukeboxes on

wheels. "Is it responsible to camouflage one of America's most remarkable machines as a piece of gaudy merchandise?" he asked.
Form, Loewy added, "which should be the clean-cut expression of
mechanical excellence, has become sensuous and organic." Loewy
was warning Detroit that form had overtaken function. Yet if Earl's
designs did not always please intellectuals, they were stunningly successful with car buyers.

Steadily Earl eroded the autonomy of the division heads. Design
became the critical decision, and that decision was Earl's. In fact,
because of Earl and Sloan, all the major auto companies became
caught in a vicious syndrome: a worship of the new at the expense of
the old, even if on occasion the old was better. The annual model
change forced the companies to opt for a less efficient and less attractive car, just for the sake of change. Or as George Walker, the head of
styling at Ford, said at the end of the Earl era, "The 1957 Ford was
great, but right away we had to bury it and start another. We design a
car, and the minute it's done, we hate it—we've got to do another
one. We design a car to make a man unhappy with his 1957 Ford 'long
about the end of 1958."

Earl himself became quite cynical. Young designers who went to
work for the company in the mid-fifties and who had admired his
earlier work were stunned by his attitude. Robert Cumberford remembered an early orientation meeting with a class of young
stylists. Earl stood in front of the group and looked long and hard at
them. "General Motors," he began, "is in business for only one
reason. To make money. In order to do that we make cars. But if we
could make money making garbage cans, we would make garbage
cans."

In all of this, the process was becoming increasingly sterile. It was
not merely change for change's sake, but actually a kind of pseudo
change. The industry's engineers were largely idle, as their skills were
ignored. Thus, during a time when the American car industry might
have lengthened its technological lead on foreign competitors, it
failed to do so. Instead, the industry fiddled with styling details, adding and augmenting fins, changing color combinations. Fins, the
most famous automotive detail of the era, represented no technological advance. They were solely a design element whose purpose was to
make the cars seem sleeker, bigger, and more powerful. "It gave

them [the customers] an extra receipt for their money in the form of visible prestige marking for an expensive car," Earl said, summing up the essential thrust of the industry during the decade. That failure would come back to haunt the entire industry in the seventies. Indeed, it was Earl who coined the phrase that came to symbolize that era: "dynamic obsolescence."

# CHAPTER SIX

THE American car, with its surging size and increased emphasis on style and luxury, was just one sign of the new abundance of the era. After World War II most Americans had a vision of a better life just ahead. At the core of it was owning one's own house—and as a rapidly improving network of roads and highways opened up the vast spaces of farmland surrounding American cities, the vision started to become a reality—suburbia. Indeed, people even knew what they wanted to pay for their first house: $5000, which was then roughly equal to an average family's wages for two years. Right after the war, auto workers made about $60 a week, or $3000 a year, while workers in other parts of the manufacturing sector made about $2400.

If a new car was a critical status symbol, a house was something else. More often than not, the people who intended to own one had, in the past, rented apartments, which symbolized not merely a lack of space but also a lack of independence and security. Owning a house came to be the embodiment of the new American dream. As promised by endless Hollywood films, it represented fulfillment, *contentment:* confident dads, perky moms, glowing children who attended good schools and, later, college. A house brought the American family *together* (at precisely the moment, of course, when cars and television began pulling it apart). If the first great business figure of the American Century was Henry Ford, the second, arguably, was William J. Levitt.

It was Bill Levitt who first brought Ford's techniques of mass production to housing, up to then the most neglected of American industries. Until Levitt arrived on the scene, builders were small-time operators, employing multiple subcontractors ("graduate carpenters and bricklayers," Levitt called them). The typical prewar builder put up fewer than five houses a year. Levitt revolutionized the process of home building with remarkable planning and brilliant control procedures. These techniques made it possible to provide inexpensive, attractive single-unit housing for ordinary citizens, people who had never thought of themselves as middle-class before. As much as anyone, William Levitt made the American dream possible. As Paul Goldberger of *The New York Times* noted years later, "Levittown houses were social creations more than architectural ones—they turned the detached single-family house from a distant dream to a real possibility for thousands of middle-class American families." It was, Levitt liked to boast, capitalism in the most personal sense. "No man who owns his own house and lot can be a Communist. He has too much to do."

It was the war that taught Levitt the promise of the future and how to reach for it. In 1941 he and his brother, Alfred, won a government contract to build 2350 war workers' homes in Norfolk, Virginia. At first it was a disaster; everything went wrong. Saddled with union workers who, in their view, asked for too much and produced too little, the Levitts were unable to make a profit or meet a tight schedule. They knew they had to change the essential philosophy of home building in order to meet their deadlines. They analyzed the construction process and broke it down into basic components. There were, they figured out, twenty-seven separate steps, so they would train twenty-seven separate teams—each team would specialize in one step. This solution enabled them not only to find a way around the acute shortage of skilled carpenters—for it demanded less talented workers—but also to speed up the entire process. As the war ground on, the Levitt teams became increasingly expert in mass building.

Eventually Bill Levitt served with the Seabees in the Pacific, where he was commissioned to build instant airfields for the navy. Unburdened by union restrictions and the constraints of conventional building limitations, and operating under terrible deadlines—for lives were in the balance if the airfields were not completed—Levitt took on tasks that no one thought could be done, and pulled them off. At night he sat around with other young men in the Seabees and they would brainstorm about their work—what they were doing that day, how to do it faster, and also what they would do after the war.

As for the future, Bill Levitt had no doubts. It consisted of men like himself building mass housing for the families of young veterans.

"Just beg, borrow, or steal the money and then build and build," he kept saying to his friends. When some talked about the risks involved, he would tell them to examine their own desires and needs. What did they want? A car, and then what else? A house, of course.

Even before the war, Levitt had taken out an option on a thousand acres of farmland near Hempstead, Long Island. It was relatively inexpensive—a steal, he thought—and while he was over in the Pacific, he urged his brother, Alfred, to keep up the option. Alfred Levitt, an architect, was the more artistic member of the family. He seemed not to understand his brother's grand design for the postwar years. Alfred looked at the Hempstead land and saw a lot of potato farms being cleared for a few houses; Bill Levitt looked at it and saw a gargantuan, virtually self-contained suburban community.

No industry had suffered more than housing during the Depression and World War II; housing starts fell from 1 million a year to fewer than 100,000. But during the same period the marriage rate and, not surprisingly, the birthrate increased sharply, the latter reaching the highest it had been in two decades. As everyone returned from the war, the housing situation became a crisis. Estimates placed the number of new houses needed immediately at over 5 million. A federal housing bill was rushed through that contained very little in the way of controls and a great deal in the way of federal insurance to protect builders by means of federal mortgage guarantees. The stored-up energy of two decades was unleashed.

In 1946 the Levitts pushed ahead with Bill Levitt's dream of creating his own community in Hempstead, by adding more and more acreage to what they already owned. There, some twenty miles from Manhattan, they set out to create the largest housing project in American history. At first it was called Island Trees, but inevitably the name Levittown stuck. "Well," he said years later, "the original name was something of an embarrassment. After all, here was this great new place called Island Trees, a very fancy name, and it was flat as could be as far as the eye could see, with only these two scrawny trees in the front to give it the name."

The first Levittown house could not have been simpler. It had four and a half rooms and was designed with a young family in mind. The lots were 60 by 100 feet, and Levitt was proud of the fact that the house took up only twelve percent of the lot. The living room was 12 by 16 feet. There were two bedrooms and one bathroom. A family could expand the house by converting the attic or adding on to the outside. The house was soon redesigned with the kitchen in the back so that the mothers could watch their children in the yard. The basic Levitt Cape Cod sold for $7990; later an expanded ranch-style house sold for $9500. There were no down payments, no closing costs, and no secret extras. Buyers of the first Levitt houses had to put down a deposit, which they eventually got back. It was an unusual and appealing concept: the price was the price.

At first only veterans were invited to buy. A small showcase home was erected on a plot near New York City for easy inspection. "This is Levittown!" went the ad in *The New York Times*. "All yours for $58. You're a lucky fellow, Mr. Veteran. Uncle Sam and the world's largest builder have made it possible for you to live in a charming house in a delightful community without having to pay for them with your eye teeth." The ad ran on a Monday, inviting the veterans to visit the office a week hence. On Tuesday, Bill Levitt went out to check the model home. There was a line of some thirty people. "What are you doing here?" he asked one of the men in line. "I'm out here to look at one of these Levitt houses and buy one," the man answered. "But they're not available until next Monday," Levitt protested. "Doesn't matter," the young man said. Bill Levitt was shaken. It was one thing, he realized, to sit around and brainstorm about the need for postwar housing; it was another to run smack into the full fury of it. The line grew day by day, and the ex-GIs themselves figured out how to police it, creating a system to let people take a break and eat without losing their place in line. Indeed, a kind of community began to form among those in line. These people, after all, were going to be one another's neighbors. After the office opened, 1400 contracts were drawn on a single day.

Levitt was quick to admit that he had borrowed Henry Ford's production system. But his adaptation of it was sheer genius. A car was small enough to be moved along an assembly line while the workers remained stationary. Obviously, one could not do that with houses, so why not make the teams of workers mobile, moving them from one stationary house to the next? As such, he created a new kind of assembly line—specialized groups of workers who performed their chores and moved on. The site, as Levitt liked to point out, became the

Levittown. Critics bemoaned it, but young buyers loved their new homes.

factory. The Levitts did not believe in prefabricating their houses; they had learned that it was too rigid a method. Instead, they had their own system of preassembling. Everything, William Levitt said, had to be made simple. As he saw it, America was not a country of skilled workmen—there were few of them around under the best of circumstances, and none were likely to go to work for Levitt's company, where the stress was laid not on individual, elegant workmanship, but on the maximum number of houses built in a given amount of time. Because his workers were less skilled, Levitt had many of the critical parts preassembled elsewhere. That made the on-site assembly easier, so ordinary workers, aided by power tools—just then coming into use— could take it from there. Of the tedium involved in so mechanized a process, Alfred Levitt once said, "The same man does the same thing every day, despite the psychologists. It is boring; it is bad; but the reward of the green stuff seems to alleviate the boredom of the work."

By July 1948 they were building 180 houses a week or, in effect, finishing thirty-six houses a day. Construction trucks would come in and drop off building materials at exact intervals of sixty feet. The floors were made of asphalt and the walls of composition Sheetrock. There were floormen and side men and tile men and men who did the white painting and men who did the red painting. It was, Bill Levitt noted, like clockwork: "Eighteen houses completed on the shift from eight to noon, and eighteen more houses finished on the shift from twelve twenty to four thirty." The system had to be foolproof. Anything that slowed it down—a strike by a subsidiary union, a shortage of nails or lumber—would throw off the entire schedule, and they would lose money. So they made their own nails, buying nailmaking machines and a great supply of scrap iron; they made their own cement; and they even produced their own lumber, buying thousands of acres of timberland in Oregon and building a mill there.

Some 17,000 houses were built in the first Levittown, and 82,000 people lived there. One swimming pool was built for every thousand houses. There were five schools, built by the county on public contract, which did not please pre-Levittown residents, who felt they were supporting these arrivistes. Churches were erected on land furnished by the Levitts. One man had, in effect, created a community all his own. It was a strange new world, where each day the men got in their cars or boarded trains to go off to jobs in New York City, twenty miles away; it was not unlike an old whaling port where the men periodically went off for several months to hunt their quarry, leaving their wives to tend the community. But here the men returned home at six o'clock each night.

BILL Levitt was thirty-eight when the war was over. He was the son of Abraham Levitt, a self-made success as a real estate man on Long Island. The younger Levitt was confident and intensely ambitious. His appearance was once described as like that of "a retired Marx brother turned master of ceremonies in a run-down night club." He was nothing if not tough. He went against the grain in a number of ways. In an age largely sympathetic to unions, Levitt fought them every inch of the way. The job of the union, he insisted, could be reduced to a simple idea: the protection of the slowest and least efficient worker. Because of that, Bill Levitt hired only nonunion workers. He paid them top dollar and offered all kinds of incentives that allowed them to earn extra money. Levitt workers often made twice as much a week as those who had comparable jobs elsewhere, but they did it on terms set by Bill Levitt.

The homebuyers themselves seemed pleased with Levitt homes, which over the years proved unusually sturdy. Those who bought into Levittown were, more often than not, leaping ahead of their parents in terms of their standard of living. Yet the nature of what Levitt was doing and the scope of his success made him a target for those who disliked, even feared, the new mass culture of postwar society. "*For literally nothing down,*" wrote one critic, "you too can find a box of your own in one of the fresh-air slums we're building around the edges of American cities . . . inhabited by people whose age, income, number of children, problems, habits, conversations, dress, possessions, perhaps even blood types are almost precisely like yours."

There was no small amount of snobbery to the attacks; most of it came not from dissatisfied customers, but from people who were fortunate enough, because of their backgrounds, to be able to afford more traditional middle-class housing. For those people, housing, like the choice of a profession, was a matter of preference and options.

In 1961, some ten years after the completion of the first Levittown, Lewis Mumford, one of the most distinguished architectural and social commentators of his time, described it as "a multitude of uniform, unidentifiable houses, lined up inflexibly, at uniform distances on uniform roads, in a treeless waste, inhabited by people of the same class, the same incomes, the same age group, witnessing the same television performances, eating the same tasteless prefabricated foods, from the same freezers, conforming in every outward and inward respect to a common mold."

Other critics agreed. The original version of *The Invasion of the Body Snatchers,* noted writer Ron Rosenbaum, was "about the horror of being in the 'burbs. About neighbors whose lives had so lost their individual distinctiveness they could be taken over by alien vegetable pods—*and no one would know the difference.*"

But others thought that Mumford was not quite fair. The young sociologist Herbert Gans, who decided to buy a house in the third

Levittown with his young family, was surprised by the rich and diverse quality of life there. His neighbors in Levittown had a sense of adventure and excitement. Everyone, Gans noted, "was looking forward to occupying his new home and this engendered a spirit of optimism. After all, Levittown would be a new community, and newness is often identified with perfection in American culture."

What was taking place was nothing less than the beginning of a massive migration from the cities to the farmland that surrounded them. Starting in 1950 and continuing for the next thirty years, eighteen of the nation's twenty-five top cities lost population. At the same time, the suburbs gained 60 million people. Some eighty-three percent of the nation's growth was to take place in the suburbs. Bill Levitt had helped begin a revolution. By 1955 Levitt-type subdivisions represented seventy-five percent of the new housing starts. The new auto-connected suburb would change the very nature of American society. The move to the suburbs also temporarily interrupted the progress women had been making before the war in the workplace; for the new suburbs separated women physically from the workplace, leaving them, at least for a while, isolated in a world of other mothers, children, and station wagons.

# CHAPTER SEVEN

Two brothers—who, in the beginning, failed at almost everything they did—were among the first to understand that the fundamental changes taking place in American society concerning where people lived and worked would also affect how they ate. It was then that the luck of Dick and Maurice "Mac" McDonald took a startling turn for the better.

The McDonald brothers moved to California from their native New Hampshire in 1930, driven by the grim economy of the Northeast. They tried various odd jobs on the periphery of the movie industry, with no notable success. They had never liked working for large companies and had often talked of running a place of their own. They had good reason to distrust big companies: their father, Pat McDonald, had worked in a shoe factory in Manchester, New Hampshire, for forty-two years in an age when there were no pensions or vacations. In his last year he was called in by his boss and told, "Pat, I think you've outlived your usefulness to us. I'm afraid we don't need you here anymore."

At the height of the Depression the brothers opened a small movie theater, but it quickly went bust. As far as they could tell, the only business making money at the time was a nearby hot-dog stand. So in 1937 they opened a stand near the Santa Anita racetrack; they did well from the start, but when the racing season ended, business would dry up.

Finally, Mac McDonald decided they should build a bigger place in San Bernardino, a growing blue-collar city of perhaps 100,000 people. In 1940 they opened a small drive-in restaurant there. Somewhat to their own surprise they were an immediate hit and were soon making a profit of $40,000 a year.

Their customers came in two varieties, they decided: teenage boys, with their first patched-up used cars, who liked the place as a hangout to flirt with the cute carhops; and young families, in which sometimes both parents worked, who ate there because it was relatively fast and cheap. Obviously, the brothers wanted to encourage the second group and discourage the first.

The first McDonald's, in San Bernardino, California

The McDonalds figured they needed even greater speed. On the average, customers had to wait some twenty minutes for their food. "My God, the carhops were slow," remembered Dick McDonald. "We'd say to ourselves there had to be a faster way. The cars were jamming up the lot. Customers weren't demanding it, but our intuition told us they would like speed. Everything was moving faster. The supermarkets and dime stores had already converted to self-service, and it was obvious the future of drive-ins was self-service."

The McDonalds had understood an important new trend in American life: Americans were becoming ever more mobile and living farther from their workplaces than ever before. As they commuted considerable distances, they had less time and always seemed to be in a rush. The McDonalds' customers wanted to eat quickly.

Therefore, the brothers began to look for the weaknesses in their operation that caused the delays. Clearly, the carhops would have to go, but to their surprise the McDonalds discovered another impediment to faster service: their menu was surprisingly large—including hamburgers, hot dogs, barbecue, and all manner of sandwiches—but when the McDonalds checked their receipts, they found that eighty percent of their sales consisted of hamburgers. "The more we hammered away at the barbecue business, the more hamburgers we sold," Dick McDonald said later. So they decided to get rid of the labor-intensive barbecue and sandwiches and narrow the menu to the venerable American hamburger. That would allow them to mechanize the food-preparation process as well.

Suddenly the McDonalds found themselves blossoming as brilliant innovators in the one thing they knew: fast food. In the fall of 1948 they closed down for several months, fired all their carhops, and began to reinvent the process. They replaced their small three-foot cast-iron grill with two stainless steel six-footers; the new grills were custom designed, and the stainless steel was not only easier to clean, it held the heat better. (If they had put too many hamburgers on the cast-iron grill, it lost heat.) They replaced the plates and silverware, which had a tendency to disappear anyway, with paper bags, wrappers, and paper cups. That eliminated the need for the dishwasher. They cut the menu from twenty-five items to nine, featuring hamburgers and cheeseburgers, and they made the burgers a little smaller—ten hamburgers from one pound of meat instead of eight.

The McDonalds decided they wanted a machine to make their patties. Dick pondered the question and then figured out that a candy company that made peppermint patties must have just the right device. He visited a number of candy companies until he finally found a machine where a worker, by pushing one lever, could deliver just the right amount of mix. The same machine could make hamburger patties.

The McDonalds, rather than their customers, chose the condiments: ketchup, mustard, onions, and two pickles. Under the new system, if a customer wanted something different on his hamburger, he faced a major delay. The McDonalds believed choices meant delays and chaos.

"Our whole concept was based on speed, lower prices, and volume," Dick McDonald said. In front of the drive-in, they erected a sign with a chef whose name was Speedy. MCDONALD'S FAMOUS HAMBURGERS, said the sign. BUY 'M BY THE BAG. And larger than the letters of the name was the price: 15 CENTS.

By 1950 the teenagers had departed to more tolerant hangouts and were replaced by working-class families, who, thanks to the McDonalds' low prices, could afford to feed their families restaurant meals for the first time. The kitchen was enclosed by glass, and children liked watching the burgers cooking on the stainless steel grills. The children were seen as important from the beginning, and the word was put out that the staff was to be very nice to kids because kids came equipped with parents.

What the McDonald brothers were doing with food was, as author John Love pointed out, what Henry Ford had done with automobile manufacturing (and what Bill Levitt had done with housing): they turned their kitchen into an assembly line.

Inside the kitchen everything was mechanized. There were three grill men, who did nothing but cook patties; two milk shake men; two french fries men; two dressers, who wrapped the hamburgers; and out front were three countermen, who took the orders. Much of the food was preassembled; the slack time between the rush hours was used to prepare for the next onslaught.

Here was the perfect restaurant for a new America, and it was a smashing success. There were long lines at rush hour, and by 1951 the gross annual receipts were $277,000, some forty percent higher than in the old premechanized days. By the mid-fifties the brothers were sharing profits of $100,000 a year, a dazzling figure for men selling items that cost fifteen cents apiece.

In 1952 they were on the cover of *American Restaurant* magazine. From then on, they were deluged with mail—as many as 300 letters a month—asking them how they had done it. When aspiring entrepreneurs introduced themselves to the brothers, the McDonalds were uncommonly generous in sharing expertise.

In fact, so many people were making the trek to their little hamburger stand that the McDonalds knew sooner or later they would have to franchise the operation. In 1952 they reluctantly sold their first franchise rights for a onetime fee of a thousand dollars. In truth they were already content with their lives and saw no reason to expand: they were making more money than they had dreamed of; they had lovely houses with tennis courts, new Cadillacs every year. Neither had children, and therefore there were no thoughts of leaving a financial empire to their heirs. They thought of McDonald's as a one-shot operation, and they had little interest in a great national network of hamburger stands bearing their name.

IF THE McDonald brothers knew their limits, then Ray Kroc was a man who had always seen his future as limitless. He was the classic American boomer, a self-made man, a high school dropout. He was suspicious of college graduates because he thought college tended to separate businessmen from the very people with whom they would have to deal. Kroc believed in himself and his special vision of the American dream: if he only kept trying, surely one day lightning would strike and he would become rich and successful.

As a young man, Kroc held a variety of jobs, selling, among other things, paper cups and Florida real estate, and playing piano for bands when things got really tight. His drive was incredible, and he was always spurred by the fact that his father, a successful Western Union operator, had become rich speculating in land in the twenties and then had lost everything in the Depression. On the day of the senior Kroc's death, his desk contained his last paycheck from the telegraph company and a garnishment notice for the amount of his wages.

Ray Kroc was *always* looking for the idea or invention that would make his fortune. On his route as a paper-cup salesman he made the acquaintanceship of a man named Earl Prince, an engineer who also ran a chain of dairy parlors. In the late thirties Prince, in no small part pushed by Kroc, developed a machine that used a single motor to drive five separate spindles, thus greatly accelerating the milk shake–making process. He called it the Multimixer, and it was a powerful machine, or, as Ray Kroc liked to boast, "You could mix concrete with the damn thing." When Kroc's employer, the Lily-Tulip paper-cup company, turned down the idea of selling it across the country, Kroc decided to handle it himself. In 1939 he started his own business— Malt-A-Mixer.

The war put his dream on hold because the materials for the Multi-mixer were no longer available, but when the war was over, his business exploded. He and two associates sold 9000 Multimixers a year, and Kroc was making $25,000 a year. It was not the big strike he had hoped for, but by the standards of the time, he was wealthy.

By the early fifties the tide was running out on Multimixers and sales were dramatically down. Kroc had the foresight to realize that it was not so much the product that was the problem as its prize customer—the neighborhood drugstore. The great move to the suburbs was the death knell for that small-town institution.

By 1954 Kroc was looking for an alternative source of income. He was still selling Multimixers at the time, and the one thing that puzzled him was the success of a small hamburger spot in San Bernardino, which seemed to buck the national trend: the rest of the nation wanted fewer Multimixers; this place called McDonald's needed ever more. In early 1954 the McDonald brothers ordered their ninth and tenth machines—that meant they were making something on the order of fifty milk shakes at a time. In addition, Kroc was getting calls from other fast-food operators, who told him they wanted the same kind of mixers that McDonald's was using.

Soon afterward Kroc went to San Bernardino to take a look. He was stunned. He arrived an hour before lunch, but there were already long lines. He immediately liked what he saw: attendants in spiffy white shirts and trousers and white paper hats. Kroc got in line and began to talk with the customers. He innocently pointed out that he had never waited on line for a hamburger before. The regulars, as he had hoped, gave him unsolicited testimonials: the place was clean, it was fast, it was cheap, and the hamburgers were good. Orders, he was amazed to discover, were being filled in about fifteen seconds apiece. The hamburgers cost fifteen cents each, a slice of cheese cost four cents more, a shake was twenty cents, and a coffee was a nickel. One out of three customers wanted a shake, and even here the McDonalds had improved upon Kroc's beloved Multimixer. Ed Toman, an inventor friend, had taken the machine and cut four inches off the spindles. That meant that the shakes could be made right in the twelve-inch paper cups—there was no need to transfer from the mixer to the cup. Kroc sat all afternoon and watched.

The McDonalds were glad to see him—he was, after all, something of a celebrity in the business. Mr. Multimixer, they called him. They assured him that this was a typical day. Kroc asked the McDonalds when the rush stopped. "Sometime late tonight when we close," Dick McDonald said. At first Ray Kroc began to think how good it would be to expand McDonald's because of what it could mean to his Multimixer business. And the more he thought about it, the more he was convinced he had seen the future and it was hamburgers.

At the moment Ray Kroc entered their world, the McDonald brothers had issued all of nine franchises and were looking for a new manager to handle franchising. Soon after his visit Kroc called Dick McDonald. "Have you found a franchising agent yet?" he asked. "No, Ray, not yet," McDonald answered. "Well then, what about me?" Kroc said.

Ray Kroc took over the franchise end at the age of fifty-two, a diabetic who had already lost his gallbladder. Starting out all over in a new field when most men were starting to think about retirement, he was unbelievably hardworking and ambitious, and his ability to outwork everyone in his office was soon a legend. He made $12,000 at the start, half of what he had made as a Multimixer man. But he was sure this was the big break he had always been looking for. "It was," he once said, "practically life or death for me."

Years later he was asked why he went with the McDonald brothers when he could so easily have stolen their system. Part of it was the name itself. McDonald's simply sounded right to him. He did not think that a chain named Kroc's would have the same appeal. In addition, he had been in and out of a thousand kitchens in his years as a paper-cup and mixer salesman, and this was by far the best operation he'd ever seen. He knew that the McDonalds had learned to do things right only after making many mistakes, and it was well worth whatever it cost him to avoid repeating those mistakes.

He saw immediately that the prime customers were families— young couples, a little unsure of themselves, often with children in tow. They were comfortable at McDonald's, as they might not have been at a more traditional restaurant; they came, ordered, and ate in the car, and if their children were misbehaving, it wouldn't annoy the other clients. It was an inexpensive, easy night out for the family. At first the various franchises did their best business on Saturday night and next best on Friday night—the customers obviously regarded it as a treat. Then they began to do well on Sunday afternoon, and then, at last, on the weeknights. Soon there were advertising slogans reflecting the thrust of the business: "Give Mom a night out," and then "Give Mom a night off." As Fred Turner, Kroc's heir to the company, later noted, these were the forerunners of the famous McDonald's slogan "You deserve a break today."

At the center of all of the hoopla was a very small piece of meat, soon to be standardized in the McDonald's handbook at 1.6 ounces. It was made of "commercial-grade" ground chuck and formed into a patty $3\frac{5}{8}$ inches in diameter. The fat content was between seventeen and twenty percent. It was served with a quarter ounce of onion, a teaspoon of mustard, a tablespoon of ketchup, and a pickle one inch in diameter. There was, in Kroc's mind, something beautiful about a hamburger—as opposed to, say, a hot dog.

Kroc opened his own first hamburger stand in Des Plaines, suburban Chicago, in April 1955; at the time, he was so desperately short of cash that he had to borrow the money necessary to put up his showplace McDonald's. He even offered the banks half the stock in his company for a mere $25,000. Fortunately for his own financial future, and probably also for the future of McDonald's, he found no takers.

He was a hands-on owner, the first person there every morning, setting up, checking things out, then going into downtown Chicago, working all day at his headquarters, trying to expand the network, and then stopping back at night to close and clean up. "Every night you'd see him coming down the street, walking close to the gutter, picking up every McDonald's wrapper and cup along the way," said Fred Turner, who started as one of Kroc's first grill men and later became chairman of the company. "He'd come into the store with both hands full of cups and wrappers. He was the store's outside pickup man." Actually, cleanliness and order were fetishes with him. He gave his top people little packets with nail files, combs, and brushes, and for one executive, whose nose hair he judged as too long, he included a tiny pair of scissors. He demanded that all his employees be clean, down to their fingernails, and sometimes he even asked them to brush their teeth more carefully. He wanted no beards or mustaches, no wrinkled clothes, and no gum chewing. Every day the windows at all McDonald's had to be cleaned, the parking lot had to be hosed down, and the garbage cans scrubbed. Mopping of the floors inside was a continuous process.

From the start, his restaurant was successful; by the second full year it did a total volume of $200,000, which meant that his pretax profits were around twenty percent, or $40,000. His hard work became legend within the company. He remained wary of talent and education. "Nothing in the world can take the place of persistence," he liked to say. "Genius will not. Talent will not. The world is filled with unsuccessful men of talent. Education alone will not. The world is filled with educated derelicts."

The most important component of Kroc's ethic was hard work, and the second most important was thrift. The ketchup came in large cans, and employees were told to open any supposedly empty cans and scrape out every last bit of remaining ketchup. Even if it was only a spoonful, spoonfuls from thousands of cans added up. Even after he had become a millionaire, Kroc would visit various McDonald's to patrol for unused packets of sugar, salt, and pepper that had been left on the tables, in order to keep them from being thrown out.

Ray Kroc was this way not just about his business but about his personal life. There were frequent letters to the wives of McDonald's employees imploring them to be thrifty: cigarettes should be bought by the carton; socks, toilet paper, and toothpaste should be bought in quantity and on sale. "When beef, steaks, and chops are extremely high," he added in one letter, "it certainly seems logical to use more fish, fowl, casserole dishes, and things of that sort that really have more flavor and save a lot of money. The same is true of baked goods. I had some pumpkin bread that Virginia Lea baked that was made with canned pumpkin, orange juice, flour, dates, and nuts that was out of this world."

In the beginning Kroc stumbled on his way to figuring out who were the perfect franchisees. He went first to his pals at his suburban Chicago country club, sure that these were the paradigms of America's business success. Later he realized they lacked the true grit and absolute commitment that Kroc demanded for his new empire. They were, it turned out, men who had already made it, and they either looked down on the hamburger business or thought it something of a lark. Few were willing to work the backbreaking hours that owning one of these restaurants demanded or surrender as much independence as Kroc demanded. One old pal decided to charge eighteen cents instead of fifteen cents for a hamburger, and even worse, he wore a beard—which Kroc hated. Many of his old friendships turned so sour through business involvements that Kroc found it difficult to mention their names.

The best owners, he learned, were people who had not yet made it, but who were ready to bet their entire lives on one break—people like him. They had worked hard all their lives, saved a surprising amount of money, and always dreamed of owning their own business. Often both husband and wife would be involved, and they did not so much work there as live there. He gave Sandy and Betty Agate an early franchise in Waukegan, Illinois, because he was encouraged by the simplicity of their background and remarkable determination: Sandy was a pressman who went to night school to get a degree in optometry, and Betty, who was Jewish, sold Catholic Bibles door to door. Their franchise became one of the early showplaces. When potential franchisees showed up, Kroc often sent them to see the Agates, who would tell their entire success story and even show their tax returns. Kroc gloried in the success of such families, and it did not bother him at all if they were making a great deal more money than he was in those early years. His ego was always invested in the success of the chain, not his own financial gain.

He had started franchising in 1955, when his own McDonald's was one of only two he had awarded. At first he moved very slowly. In 1956 he awarded twelve more. In 1957 there were forty; by 1958, seventy-nine; by 1959, 145; and by 1960, 228. As the new decade began, they were planning to open a hundred new restaurants a year. The word was out and the rush was on. Soon the company was becoming more identified with Ray Kroc than with the McDonald brothers. "I put the hamburger on the assembly line," Ray Kroc said in 1959, and in the larger sense, at least, he was right.

His success mounted as the highway became ever more a part of the social fabric of American life. Powerful new competitors entered the field, but by and large Kroc treated them with scorn; they were out to make money, he said, not perform a service. They had no quality-control systems, no love of the product, no desire to make every small part of the chain as good as its whole.

His entire life became McDonald's. He would talk about little else, and had no interest in those who did not share his obsession. It was said that an earlier marriage foundered because his wife did not love McDonald's enough; a third marriage succeeded because it was to a woman already steeped in the culture of the company. Finally he had someone to talk to. Everything about the company, he thought, was pure artistry. "Consider, for example, the hamburger bun," he once said. "It requires a certain kind of mind to see the beauty in a hamburger bun. Yet is it any more unusual to find grace in the texture and softly curved silhouette of a bun than to reflect lovingly on the hackles of a favorite fishing fly? Not if you're a McDonald's man. Not if you view the bun as an essential material in the art of serving a great many meals fast. Then this plump yeasty mass becomes an object worthy of sober study."

By 1961 Kroc had started preliminary talks with the McDonalds about buying them out. The brothers were doing well. They made an annual profit of $100,000 on their own stand, and in 1960 they took in an additional $189,000 from the franchises—they got one half of one percent on sales, which by then had reached $37.8 million. The relationship between Kroc and the brothers was becoming ever more strained. Their heart had always been in their own stand. He had come to think of them as careless and lazy, people who thought small, willing to sit on the sidelines and make an easy profit while he did all the heavy lifting.

The brothers themselves wanted out, but they wanted out on their terms. They wanted $2.7 million to sell the name and the company to Kroc, which meant $1 million after taxes for each brother. It was a great deal of money. Nevertheless, Kroc sensed it was a bargain: the chain was growing at roughly 100 stands a year, and would hit his magic goal of 1000 by the end of the decade.

With the help of his financial aides, Kroc put together a loan and bought out the brothers. The real glory years for the chain were just beginning. Kroc's old estimate of 1000 outlets had been far too modest; some thirty-seven years after he took over the franchising, there were 8600 McDonald's in America and 12,000 in the rest of the world. He achieved wealth beyond his wildest dreams—$600 million by some estimates—but was completely uninterested in what wealth could bring him (other than buying a baseball team, something he had always wanted). He told one reporter, "I have never worshipped money and I never worked for money. I worked for pride and accomplishment. Money can become a nuisance. It's a hell of a lot more fun chasin' it than gettin' it. The fun is in the race."

## CHAPTER EIGHT

As the booming postwar economy changed the face of American business, a technological breakthrough transformed the communications industry, sending powerful shock waves through all levels of the society. It was called television.

As the decade started, the television map of America was a spotty affair. In 1953 there were 108 stations, but only twenty-four cities had two or more. In those days the networks were patched together for a particular big event—a heavyweight fight or the World Series. But Americans had already begun to adapt their habits to accommodate their favorite programs. Studies showed that when a popular program was on, toilets flushed all over certain cities, as if on cue, during commercials or the moment the program was over. Radio listenership was significantly down.

The first example of the unprecedented power of television was the meteoric rise of Milton Berle. Berle was the quintessential vaudeville slapstick comic. His humor was manic and often vulgar, depending heavily on sight gags. He arrived on television in 1948, almost by chance. He had heard that the Texaco people were looking for a master of ceremonies for a television version of *Texaco Star Theatre*. Berle knew instinctively that television was right for him. Texaco tried out several hosts, but it was obvious that Berle was the most successful.

Almost from the start, his Tuesday night show on NBC was an *event*. The early history of television and the story of Berle's show were close to being one and the same thing. Those who didn't have television sets visited those who did. The very success of Berle's show accelerated the sale of television sets; those Americans who did not yet own sets would return home after watching him at their neighbors' houses and decide that, yes, it was finally time to take the plunge. A year into the show, his fame was so great that his face was on the cover of both *Time* and *Newsweek* in the same week. He was television's first superstar.

Milton Berle was forty-two in 1950, but his entire life had been spent in the theater. At the age of six he won a Charlie Chaplin look-alike contest wearing his father's clothes and shoes and a mustache cut from his mother's furs. Before he was ten, he was on the vaudeville circuit, and while still in his teens he was opening the Palace. He would do anything for a laugh—don a wig, a dress, or false teeth; fall on his face or take a pie in it. There was never a pause for the audience to catch its breath.

In the late fall of 1948, his television show enjoyed a 94.7 rating, which meant that of all the sets in the country being used, 94.7 percent were tuned to him. In the beginning NBC had lost money on its television shows, but by 1950 the tide turned: sales for broadcast time tripled. In 1952 the industry made a profit of $41 million.

At this earliest stage of its history, television was primarily an urban phenomenon. According to *Variety*, of the 1,082,100 television sets operating in American homes in 1949, some 450,000 were in New York City and most of the remaining ones were in Philadelphia, Washington, Boston, Chicago, Detroit, and Los Angeles. Berle was a classic Borscht Belt comedian. His live audience was primarily Jewish and urban; therefore, he was playing to what might be considered a home crowd. Five million people watched his show and thirty-five percent of them lived in New York.

It was a marvelous time for him. He was being paid $5000 a week to do what he knew best and what he probably would have done for nothing. People who called him at home would have to listen to five or six jokes before they could get a word in. In 1951, fearing that he would go to a rival network, NBC signed him to a thirty-year contract for $200,000 a year. It was at precisely that moment that he started to slip. In part he was done in by the coaxial cable. Its coming meant television was reaching into smaller towns and rural areas. People there were not native Berle fans, and his flip references to New York neighborhoods and stores fell on alien ears. As his ratings began to decline, he became more manic than ever, rushing across the stage, feverishly interrupting other acts. For his fifth season, 1952–53, the format of the show was changed. There was to be more form, less freewheeling by Berle himself—the very thing that in the beginning had seemed to make the show so popular. It ended up fifth in the ratings for that year. By 1954–55 he had fallen to thirteenth, and the next year he was dropped from the show. Berle became the first figure to experience both the power and the volatility of television. The highs were higher than anything in the past, and it generated an astonishing intimacy between performer and audience. But because of that intimacy, the audience could be fickle, and a star could descend just as quickly as he rose. It was a lesson that various entertainers, actors, and even politicians were going to learn the hard way.

By 1952 TELEVISION was seeping ever more deeply into the nation's bloodstream. People now expected to *see* events, not merely read about or hear them. At the same time, the line between what happened in real life and what people saw on television began to merge: many Americans were now living far from their families, in brand-new suburbs where they barely knew their neighbors; sometimes they felt closer to the people they watched on television than they did to their neighbors and distant families.

Nothing showed the power of this new medium to soften the edge between real life and fantasy better than the coming of Lucille Ball. In 1951 she was forty years old, in the middle of a less-than-dazzling show-business career. In films she was seen more as a comedienne than as an actress, and she tended to draw what one executive termed second-banana roles—generally in low-budget films—that did not go to the top stars. "The queen of the B movies," she was sometimes called. She had enjoyed some measure of success in radio, and in 1948, hoping to save her shaky eight-year marriage to Cuban bandleader Desi Arnaz, she opted to do a radio comedy show called *My Favorite Husband* so that she would not have to travel away from home so much. Her radio husband was a pleasant midwestern banker from Minneapolis, as Lucy herself later said, "certainly not—great heavens—Desi Arnaz from Cuba."

In 1950, when CBS executives asked her to do a weekly situation comedy on television, no one was unduly excited. That was their mistake, for Lucille Ball was destined for television, where her slapstick talents could be properly appreciated. Lucy had a marvelous comic voice, but like Berle, she was primarily a visual comedienne. She had a perfect sense of timing, a wonderfully expressive face, and was just wacky and naïve enough to generate sympathy rather than irritation.

Lucy and Desi Arnaz were an unlikely couple, not merely on television but in real life as well. If Lucy was to be a dizzy housewife, she deserved, at least in the minds of the CBS executives, a straight-arrow husband to put up patiently with her foibles, but no, she insisted that Arnaz be cast as her husband. The people at CBS were appalled. No one, a CBS executive told her, would believe a show in which she was married to a Cuban bandleader. "What do you mean nobody'll believe it?" she answered. "We *are* married." She remained adamant, and finally CBS gave in.

But Lucy understood something that the producers initially did not: viewers certainly knew that Desi was her real husband, and that made the show itself all the more believable. Since Desi played a Cuban bandleader on the show—his profession in real life—who could tell where reality ended and the show began?

*I Love Lucy* premiered on Monday, October 15, 1951. The first episode was called "The Girls Want to Go to a Nightclub." An announcer introduced the show by speaking from the Ricardos' living room. "Good evening

Lucy and Desi. No one, TV executives said, would believe a sitcom featuring a daffy redhead married to a Cuban bandleader.

and welcome. In a moment we'll look in on Lucille Ball and Desi Arnaz. But before we do, may I ask you a very personal question? Do you inhale? Well, I do. And chances are you do too. And because you inhale you're better off—much better off—smoking Philip Morris and for good reason. You see, Philip Morris is the one cigarette proved definitely less irritating, definitely milder than any other leading brand. That's why when you inhale you're better off smoking Philip Morris. . . . And now Lucille Ball and Desi Arnaz in *I Love Lucy*."

The first episode was characteristic of what was to come. Ricky and his sidekick, Fred, want to go to the fights even though it is Fred and Ethel's wedding anniversary; Lucy and Ethel want to go to a nightclub. The men arrange for blind dates. Lucy and Ethel find out, dress up in outrageous costumes, and pose as the dates. The reviews were generally good, although *The New York Times* critic was dubious—he thought it was all a bit lowbrow.

In fact, the show had perfect pitch. Broad in its humor yet able to appeal to a wide variety of tastes, it was number one in New York within four months. Soon as many as two out of three television sets were tuned to Lucy. Marshall Field, the prominent Chicago department

Above: Milton Berle in full regalia. Right: In the fifties, for better or worse, television changed the way America lived.

store, which had used Monday as its clearance-sale night, surrendered and switched to Thursday by putting a sign in its window: WE LOVE LUCY TOO SO WE'RE CLOSING ON MONDAY NIGHTS.

The great strength of the Lucy show—a television writer named Jack Sher and his wife, Marilyn, pointed out—was the mirror it held up to every married couple in America: "Not a regular mirror that reflects the truth, nor a magic mirror that portrays fantasy. But a Coney Island kind of mirror that distorts, exaggerates, and makes vastly amusing every little incident, foible, and idiosyncrasy of married life."

Lucy cut across all age-groups. Children loved her, could readily understand her routines, and seemed to like the idea of an adult who seemed so childlike. In later years her shows would probably have been deemed sexist, and actually they were. In one way or another they were all a takeoff on women-driver jokes. Lucy could not really do anything right; she had a God-given instinct to get into trouble. There was Lucy trying to make wine by crushing grapes with her feet, Lucy shoving too many marshmallows in her mouth, Lucy trying on the wrong size slippers, Lucy being crunched in the face with a pie. No one was ever better at such stunts, and no one sacrificed her body and her face more readily to them. Onstage she became the dippy person she was playing, and yet it was a show starring not just one wacko but *two*.

To everybody's surprise, Desi was just as good, the straight man who was anything but straight. He knew exactly when to be appalled, and irritated or amazed, by her, by the fact that *she had done it again*. Traditionally, straight men did not get laughs—they were there to be the foil—but with Desi, there was always some word or phrase he could mispronounce. That seemed also to soften the humor of the show. It was not just Lucy who was screwy; it was the two of them—and their neighbors too. At the end, though, there was Desi embracing her. All was forgiven, and everything came out all right.

Their real lives were not quite so idyllic. It was always a difficult relationship: Desi was a drinker and a womanizer. "If I stayed mad at every woman that Desi had an affair with, I'd have been angry with half of the nicest girls in Hollywood," Lucy once said. As their son, Desi Arnaz, Jr., once noted, "I learned pretty early to relate to *I Love Lucy* as a television show and to my parents as actors on it. There wasn't much relationship between what I saw on TV and what was really going on at home. Those were difficult years—all those funny things happening on television each week to people who looked like my parents, then the same people agonizing through some terrible times at home, and each of them trying to convince my sister and me separately that the other was in the wrong."

By April 7, 1952, there were 10.6 million households tuning in— the first time in history that a television show had reached so many people. By 1954 as many as 50 million people watched certain segments. The show was so popular that it lifted not just its advertisers but CBS and the entire industry; in 1953 CBS-TV showed a net profit for the first time—in no small part because of Lucille Ball—and a year later television became the largest advertising medium in the world.

# CHAPTER NINE

AFTER his return General MacArthur waited for political lightning to strike. It never did. The polls reflected both his personal triumph and the wariness of the American people toward his policies: fifty-four percent of those polled by Gallup favored MacArthur's more aggressive tactics against China, but only thirty percent favored them if they meant escalating the war. For a short time, as MacArthur spoke all over the country, the crowds remained big. But since he did it still wearing his uniform, there was something unsettling about his attacks on the President of the United States. Gradually his crowds grew smaller and less enthusiastic; his supporters diminished to a coterie of powerful, wealthy, conservative isolationists. To his own surprise, MacArthur did just what he had promised—he faded away. As the excitement he'd bottled the year before died, he was left with a job as chairman of the board of Remington Rand. A cartoon in *The New Yorker* captured the banality of his fall. It pictured the general's office, and hanging on the doorknob was a sign that said OUT TO LUNCH. I SHALL RETURN.

But Truman's firing of MacArthur did have a profound effect on the 1952 presidential race, wounding the President even more than it had the general. It also advanced the political chances of another

general, Dwight Eisenhower. The country was not in the mood to
return to isolationism. It wanted to be reassured, not threatened. Who
better to do that than a man who was a hero and an internationalist.

Yet by all rights the 1952 Republican nomination belonged to
Robert Taft. He was the choice of the grassroots conservatives. And if
Eisenhower was the only man who could stop him, no one, in late
1951, knew whether he was even a Republican, let alone a politician.
Taft had waited twelve years and had been exceptionally loyal to his
party. But his strengths were also his weaknesses. He appealed to a
narrow slice of the electorate, and it was said that he could not win a
national election. Before Taft announced his candidacy, he wrote
down the pros and cons. Perhaps, he noted, he was a little old and his
health was not quite as good as it should be. But on the pro side he
wrote down, "Opportunity to save liberty in U.S."

Taft was the last major isolationist of American politics, and his
political base was rooted in an America of the past—prewar, pre-
superpower. He was the scion of a great political family—the Tafts of
Ohio—that included a solicitor general, and a Chief Justice and a
President of the United States.

In 1948 he was at the height of his political powers, so dominating
a figure in the Senate that *The New Republic* wrote that "Congress now
consists of the House, the Senate, and Bob Taft." His career was also
on a collision course with political realities. Despite others' attempts
to make him better at public relations, he retained a basic wariness of
any attempts to shape his public image. Photo opportunities were
arranged to show him with a dead turkey, which readers were apparently to believe he had shot. He posed in a business suit with the dead
bird; he and the turkey seemed to have no connection with each
other. On another occasion he was photographed landing a very
dead sailfish from a boat still obviously tied to a wharf.

He tried for the nomination in 1948, but Thomas Dewey crushed
him at the convention. It seemed his best chance was in 1952. The
others who had taken the nomination away before were gone. Willkie
had been a comet, fueled by the approach of World War II; Dewey
had had his chance twice.

The only cloud on the political horizon was General Dwight David
Eisenhower. Who was Ike? Was he a Republican? Did he want the
presidency?

On these questions the general himself was coy. Right after the war, MacArthur had given a large dinner for him in Tokyo, and after the guests had all left, MacArthur predicted that one or the other of them was bound to be President. But the Pacific commander speculated it would not be himself. He had been away too long and was too out of touch with the Republican leadership. Eisenhower was irritated by MacArthur's words and by the suggestion that he had a covert political agenda. He launched into a long lecture about the separation of the military from civilian politics, as well as his own lack of desire to run for office. When he was finished, MacArthur patted him on the knee and said, "That's all right, Ike. You go on like that and you'll get it for sure."

By late 1951 the eastern wing of the Republican Party was working harder than ever to bring Ike home from Paris, where he was serving as the first commander of NATO. His supplicants explained that it was not going to be that easy, that he could win the Republican nomination, particularly if he got in early enough, but in fact the nominating process would most likely be harder than the general election—an all-out battle against passionate, well-entrenched Republican conservatives. Slowly Eisenhower began to inch toward running.

In early January, 1952, Eisenhower allowed his name to be entered in the New Hampshire primary, and on January 27 he finally announced that he was a Republican. On March 11, the night of the primary, he got together as usual with his pals in Paris for a game of bridge. Dr. Howard Snyder, the general's personal physician, left early so that he could go home and listen to the returns. Snyder promised to call if there was any important news. "Don't call me," Eisenhower said. "I'm not interested. Call Al [Gruenther, a man who bet on almost everything] if you want to speak to anyone. He's got some money on it." In New Hampshire, without even showing up, Ike beat Taft 46,661–35,838. The race was on, like it or not.

On April 12 Dwight Eisenhower asked to be relieved of his military command so he could come home to fight for the Republican nomination. He came back to his hometown, Abilene, Kansas, in early June, knowing that he would not get the nomination by acclamation and that he was getting a late start. The homecoming did not go well; it was virtually obliterated by a downpour. CBS covered it live, and the camera caught Ike buttoned up in his slicker, with his rain hat on. Perhaps it was not only the weather but the strain of the arduous new role of politician that seemed to dim Ike's ever present grin and immense aura of personal vitality. Instead, he looked like a tired, somewhat dispirited old man doing something he did not want to do. When he took his rain hat off, what little remained of his hair blew in the wind, making him seem even more forlorn and lost. Instead of the heroic conqueror of Nazi Germany, he seemed a rather shaky elderly Midwesterner.

What followed was one of the most bitterly contested struggles for a nomination in American history: Taft against Eisenhower, with liberals Earl Warren and Harold Stassen hoping for a deadlocked convention. Politics seemed uglier than usual; the Korean War dragged on; McCarthy was in full bloom.

In the end, the Taft people were crushed by a combination of Eisenhower's popularity and the political muscle of his allies. During the convention Eisenhower's supporters were better organized and better on the floor, and their communications gear was more modern than that of their opponents. They knew how to play to the media, including television. But the mood was nasty. At one point John Wayne, who was a Taft man, jumped out of his cab to shout at an old mess sergeant running an Ike sound truck, "Why don't you get a red flag?"

Taft himself seemed immobilized by the events. Just before the first ballot started, he turned to an aide and suggested he talk to Senator Bill Knowland, a conservative in the California delegation. Perhaps, said Taft, he and Knowland could meet after the first ballot and strike some kind of deal. Back came the message: "Knowland says there isn't going to be any second ballot." The nomination was Ike's.

It was a bitter moment for Taft. He would never be President. Embody the Republican Party's heart and soul he might, but his own colleagues believed he could not win.

Richard Nixon was nominated as Vice President on Eisenhower's ticket. Eisenhower himself had no clear preference for a running mate. The night he was nominated, Herbert Brownell, one of his top people, asked whom he would pick as his Vice President. "I thought the convention had to do that," Ike answered. At the first meeting the Eisenhower staff held after the nomination, they discussed the vice-

The 1952 Republican Convention was a bitter one. But you'd never know it from the smiling faces of the victorious candidates and their wives—Mamie and Ike on the left, Nixon and Pat on the right.

presidency. "What about Nixon?" he was asked. Nixon held the exact center of a bitterly divided party and was acceptable to virtually everyone, including McCarthy. Henry Cabot Lodge, Ike's official campaign manager, had to herd Nixon past reporters to avert a premature press conference, but he put his arm around Nixon and told the reporters, "He has done as much to rid this country of Communists as any man I know." So it was that Richard Nixon was introduced to the country for the first time as a national candidate.

In 1952 the Democrats were nothing less than desperate. They had been in power for too long—twenty years—and while the record of the sitting President, Harry Truman, might one day provide fertile territory for revisionist historians to take a second look at a courageous man operating in an extremely difficult time, there was no escaping the fact that at the time, he was an unpopular President in an unpopular party burdened by an unpopular war. That year the Democrats turned to a short, slightly overweight, rather aristocratic figure named Adlai Stevenson, just completing his first term as the reform-minded governor of Illinois.

He was bright, funny, and literate, and he seemed incapable of uttering a sentence that did not sound polished. His style was unaffected by the clichés of professional politics; if canned, warmed-over thoughts did not offend his audience, they most certainly offended *him*. He was a snob about many things—particularly in his choice of friends and in his social attitudes. He was quick to give credit to others, except in the area of speech writing; there he became highly irate when other Democrats even so much as suggested that their words had come from Adlai Stevenson's mouth.

Stevenson's ancestors were part of Illinois's landed gentry and no strangers to politics. His great-grandfather Jesse Fell had been Abraham Lincoln's campaign manager, and the first Adlai Stevenson had served as Vice President of the United States under Grover Cleveland. The current Adlai was the adored son of parents who were somewhat disappointed in themselves. Lewis Stevenson, his father, had never quite lived up to his own ambitions or those of his rather wealthy wife, and there was considerable tension in the marriage. In one fight Lewis had said to Helen Stevenson, "Well, you took me for better or worse," and she had answered, "Well, you are worse than I took you for!"

For all his self-effacing qualities, Adlai Stevenson had a certain sense of political entitlement, thanks to his privileged background. He was the most reluctant of candidates; he liked being governor of Illinois. Early on, he suspected that the Republican candidate would be Eisenhower, and he did not think he could beat him. He wanted to run for the presidency one day, but he wanted to wait.

When the President offered the governor the nomination, the governor told him he did not want it. At first the President tried to persuade him. "Adlai," Truman said. "If a knuckle-head like me can be President and not do too badly, think what a really educated, smart guy could do in the job." But when it became clear that Stevenson truly did not want the job, Truman became enraged. Here he was, not merely the President but a devoted man of the party offering the highest position in the country to a mere one-term governor, and he was being rebuffed. But the pressure did not abate. If anything, Stevenson's reluctance made him even more attractive. Suddenly he was the candidate everyone wanted.

Curiously, Stevenson was now able to have it both ways: to campaign without campaigning, to be the candidate produced by the party professionals who nonetheless excited the independents and reformers. If he ended up with the nomination, it would be not as the candidate of the Truman administration, but as the candidate in his own right. He was not unaware of the process he had set in motion. His strategy was simple: he would not enter the primaries, but if the party so decided, he would accept its nomination at the Democratic Convention. In fact, that was pretty much how it turned out. By this time Truman had switched his allegiance to Alben Barkley, but in the end, to the annoyance of the sitting President, the convention nominated Stevenson on the third ballot.

THE people at Batten, Barton, Durstine & Osborn were appalled by Eisenhower's initial failure to come across well on television. BBD&O, then the third-largest advertising agency in the country, was more or less the Republican house firm. Ben Duffy, the head of the agency, decided that they had to recast Ike. He was stiff and awkward in his formal presentations; therefore, it was important to show him in commercials and in quasi-spontaneous appearances—reacting to other people, becoming more like the attractive, magnetic Ike everyone knew and loved.

As BBD&O was developing the overall theme for Ike's campaign, Rosser Reeves, head of the Ted Bates Agency, was working on Ike's television spots. Reeves became, in the process, one of the two or three most influential men to emerge in politics in 1952—yet his name rarely appeared in the millions of words written about the campaign.

Rosser Reeves was not a politician, and he had little use for politicians in general; he was an advertising man, and in 1952 he helped change the nature of American politics by introducing the television spot. He was a dominating presence, perhaps the most successful advertising man of his time in terms of reaching a mass audience. If others were making a name in advertising with the elegance and sophistication of their work in the exciting new medium of television, then Reeves was a throwback to the more primitive days of advertising, when the main idea was to hit people over the head with the product as bluntly as possible. It was not to be beautiful; it was not to be artistic. It was not to amuse viewers, who might not even buy the product. It was to sell.

Rosser Reeves had decided early in his career that the most effective advertising campaigns were not the ones with the biggest budgets but the ones that held relentlessly to a single theme. Advertising, he believed, particularly in the age of television, was primal. Reeves liked to tell the story of the mule trainer called in to deal with a recalcitrant mule, who had begun the treatment by first hitting the mule in the head with a two-by-four, explaining to the astonished owner, "Well, first I've got to get his attention."

One of his campaigns for Anacin was a classic example of this. It portrayed the inside of the head of a headache sufferer. Inside were a pounding hammer, a coiled spring, and a jagged electric bolt, but they were relieved by little bubbles making their way up the body from the stomach. The Anacin ads, he later admitted, "were the most hated commercials in the history of advertising." But they increased Anacin sales from $18 million to $54 million a year in an eighteen-month period. "Not bad," Reeves once said, "for something written between cocktails at lunch."

Reeves had admired Ted Bates, whose agency he eventually took over, because Bates had, in his words, "the most unconfused mind" he had ever seen. What he had learned from Bates more than anything else, he would say, was that a commercial should be cut to the essentials. Most commercials were too long and too repetitious, wasting viewer time (and goodwill) and advertiser money. Far more effective, he eventually decided, was the spot: in quick, out quick, and done. This new medium of television was so powerful that less could easily be more. He gradually evolved the principle of USP, or the unique selling proposition. Reeves had an uncanny ability to determine the essence of a product and then make it seem dramatically different from its competitors (when in fact the difference was often negligible). At the heart of USP was finding one feature about the product that was allegedly unique and pummeling the public with it. "The prince of hard sell," he was called.

In an age in which advertising in general prospered from the growing affluence of the society, Reeves prospered more; he took Ted Bates from $16 million in billings in 1945, and no place among the top ten firms, to number five, with $130 million in billings in 1960.

For the 1948 presidential campaign, Reeves had proposed a series of radio spots to Tom Dewey, who had turned them down, saying he felt they would not be dignified. His decision not to use them had left Reeves convinced that if Dewey had been a bit more modern, he might have been elected President that year. So in 1952, when a group of Texas oilmen ("I had some oil interests at the time," Reeves once noted) who supported Eisenhower asked him to come up with a retaliatory slogan to the Democrats' "You never had it so good," he told them that what they needed was not a slogan but a campaign of quick television spots featuring the general speaking to the American people on a vast range of issues—in short, punchy, unanswerable takes. Some of Reeves' people got together and came up with a plan called How to Insure an Eisenhower Victory in November. It recommended that $2 million be spent in the last three weeks on spots— "the quickest, most effective and cheapest means of getting across a message in the shortest possible time." With that, American politics and American television advertising were about to be married by a man who did not believe in overestimating the intelligence and attention span of his audience.

Reeves, who was relatively new to politics, went out and did his homework. He read a popular book by Samuel Lubell, one of the early analysts on ethnic voting in America, and came away with the belief that the Dewey people had been incalculably stupid in their campaign. A shift of very few votes in just a few critical states would have won the election for him. Reeves was so impressed by the Lubell study that he hired a brilliant young man named Michael Levin, a disciple of Lubell's and a firm believer in the value of polling. The Lubell study and Levin's research convinced Reeves even more that spots were the answer for the Republicans. The election was going to be close, so they had to concentrate their best efforts on key areas in the swing states. The spots had many advantages, he argued: they were a relatively low-cost way to exploit an expensive new medium; they could be fine-tuned to reach undecided voters; there was a vital element of control to them—the candidate never ended up saying things that surprised his backers or himself; and finally, they allowed the campaign manager to concentrate money and effort in critical areas. If they did the spots in the last few weeks of the campaign, the Democrats would be hard-pressed to answer them. The oilmen liked the idea, and shortly thereafter the forty-two-year-old Reeves, under the aegis of Citizens for Eisenhower, took a six-week unpaid leave from Ted Bates to work for the Eisenhower campaign.

Earlier in the year, Reeves had sat with some friends when Douglas MacArthur delivered the keynote speech to the Republican Convention. One of his friends had thought MacArthur's speech powerful, but Reeves thought the prose too purple and that MacArthur had wandered all over the map, failing to dramatize the very issues he stood for. To make his point, Reeves sent out a research team to interview 250 people about the speech. Only two percent of the people had any idea of what the general had said. That, as far as Reeves was concerned, proved his point. In September, as he sat in the St. Regis Hotel reading Ike's clips from newspapers across the country, he concluded that Ike was as bad as MacArthur, talking in all kinds of directions about too many different things. This was a disaster. "You don't do that in advertising," he said. "You lose penetration." Reeves zeroed in on three essential themes: Ike cleaning up corruption; Ike the soldier who was, in truth, a man of peace; or Ike who would clean out the Communists in government. He found the American people were worried about Korea above all, as the war there dragged on. With that, Reeves thought he had his USP, so to speak: Eisenhower, the man who will bring us peace. That slogan was brought to the general for his approval, and much to the surprise of Reeves and his group, the general demurred. He, no more than anyone else in the world, could guarantee peace. So the slogan was made even simpler and better: Eisenhower, man of peace.

Soon Reeves had worked out an entire strategy for the spots. He wanted them to air at critical times, between two highly popular regular shows. ("You get the audience built up at huge costs by other people," he wrote in a memo.) The announcer would say, "Eisenhower answers the nation!" Then an ordinary citizen would ask a question, and Ike would answer it in words crafted by Reeves from Eisenhower's speeches. The candidate approved of the idea, but was not entirely comfortable with it; it was something, he made clear, that the people who knew more about this game of politics were insisting he do. Most assuredly, he did not like the fact that these same people were running around telling him that his forehead shone too much.

The subject of the relationship between his bald dome and the television camera had already considerably irritated the candidate. It had first arisen back in Paris, when David Schoenbrun, a CBS correspondent, had pointed out that he had something of a problem. Ike had told him he knew he was bald, but what could he do about it? When Schoenbrun suggested the use of makeup to take some of the shine off his head, Ike said, "Why don't you just get an actor. That's what you really want." But gradually Reeves and his people persuaded Ike to overcome his reservations.

In order to film the spots, Ike and his closest aides decided to give Reeves only one day, in early September, which was a reflection of how seriously the candidate took it all. Reeves knew he was working with a reluctant candidate and that he would have to accept the limitations imposed on him. He wrote all the spots himself. When Ike arrived at the studio, it was obvious he was uncomfortable in this alien place. He had brought along his trusted brother Milton to act as censor. It was Milton's job to look through proposed spots and announce which ones the candidate would and would not do. "No," Milton would say, to Reeves' annoyance, about words taken verbatim from one of Ike's speeches. "Ike will never say this." But he had already said it in a speech, Reeves would protest. "He's not going to say it again," Milton would answer with finality.

Technically, everything was quite primitive. This was before the TelePrompTer, and Reeves had wanted to shoot Ike without his glasses, but Ike could not see the prompter board. So Reeves improvised a giant handwritten board that Eisenhower could see without glasses. Now, at least, Ike would look like he did in his photos—hale and hearty, not like some aging, tired banker. If the candidate initially had some misgivings, once he started doing the spots, he relaxed. Seeing that things were going better than expected, Reeves wrote additional spots, and the general did them.

Now that he had Ike's answers in the can, Reeves needed to get the questions. He sent film crews to Radio City Music Hall to search out the most typical-looking and typical-sounding Americans they could find—"real people in their own clothes, with wonderful native accents." Typically, a woman would be directed to say, "You know what things cost today. High prices are driving me crazy." Then Ike answers, "Yes, my Mamie gets after me about the high cost of living. It's another reason why I say it's time for a change. Time to get back to an honest dollar and an honest dollar's work." Or a man asks, "Mr. Eisenhower, are we going to have to fight another war?" Then Ike answers, "No, not if we have a sound program for peace. And I'll add this: We won't spend hundreds of billions and still not have enough tanks and planes for Korea."

It was pioneer work, Rosser Reeves liked to say, in the art of penetrating a specific market with a high-density campaign and yet using a minimal amount of time and money. The campaign spent $1.5 million on the spots in those states where the campaign was perceived as being close. Marya Mannes, writing in the liberal *Reporter,* had mocked this new marriage of Madison Avenue with the American political system: "Feeling sluggish, feeling sick?/Take a dose of Ike and Dick./Philip Morris, Lucky Strike,/Alka Seltzer, I like Ike." By chance the executive editor of the *Reporter,* Harlan Cleveland, lived next door to Reeves. One day Reeves asked Cleveland what his magazine's objection was. "It was selling the President like toothpaste," Cleveland answered. Reeves answered that the essence of democracy was an informed public. "Is there anything wrong with a twenty-minute speech? Or a ten-minute speech?"

"No."

"Then what's wrong with a one-minute speech or a fifteen-second speech?" Reeves replied. " 'You can't say anything in a fifteen-second speech,' " Reeves quoted Cleveland as saying. Then Reeves dissented: "As a man who has been responsible for five hundred million dollars' worth of advertising, I know more about this than you do." There was a pause in their conversation; Reeves was sure he had his man now. "Harlan," he said. "Do you remember the speech that Churchill gave at Westminster College in Fulton, Missouri? What did he say there?"

"That an Iron Curtain had descended on Europe," Cleveland said. What else did he say? Reeves pushed. Cleveland could not remember. "That was a fifteen-second spot from Churchill," Reeves said, "just like the one during the war about 'never have so many owed so much to so few.' That was a Churchill spot, too. He was very good at spots."

If Ike adapted, albeit somewhat uneasily, to the new communications technology, Stevenson did not. He hated the idea of using advertising with the political process. "This is the worst thing I've ever heard of," he told Lou Cowan (a CBS executive on loan to the campaign) when he heard of the Eisenhower spots—"selling the presidency like cereal. How can you talk seriously about issues with one-minute spots!" Though there were already 17 million television sets in the country, Stevenson essentially refused to recognize the medium. Ironically, he was quite good at it: television caught him as he was—his lack of false airs, his natural grace, and, above all, his charm. Because he did not seek exposure and did not take it seriously, he was not stilted when he went on. Still, he did not like speaking to an invisible audience of millions. No amount of pressure and cajoling from his staff could convince him of the new medium's importance. He did not watch television himself—he bore it with the snobbery of the elite class.

In no small way, there were certain new class lines forming during the campaign. Stevenson was immensely popular with the new, emerging postwar intellectual elite—what writer Michael Arlen years later termed "the new G.I. Bill intellectuals." The Republicans were hardly bothered by this. That September columnist Stewart Alsop called his younger brother John, a powerful figure in the Connecticut Republican Party, to suggest that Stevenson was doing well among the people he ran into. "Sure," answered John Alsop. "All the eggheads are for Stevenson, but how many eggheads are there?" Thus Stevenson became the candidate of the eggheads.

It was nonetheless a handsome campaign in a bad time. Stevenson, believing he had not even the smallest chance of winning, was therefore not tempted to compromise. Right after he gained the nomination, he was told by his advisers to make some kind of accommodation with Texas conservatives on the issue of offshore oil rights; otherwise, he was warned, he would probably lose Texas and the election. "But I don't *have* to win," he answered. Instead, he went before the American Legion, a citadel of jingoism and political reaction, and told the audience that McCarthy's kind of patriotism was a disgrace. Besides his own inevitable defeat, the result was that at a moment when the Democratic Party should have been in complete disrepute—after having been in power for more than twenty years—it was reinvigorated. Stevenson made it seem an open and exciting place for a generation of younger Americans who might otherwise never have thought of working for a political candidate.

"When an American says he loves his country," he said in one memorable speech, "he means not only that he loves the New England hills, the prairies glistening in the sun, or the wide, rising plains, the mountains or the seas. He means that he loves an inner air, an inner light in which freedom lives and in which a man can draw the breath of self-respect." In a speech he gave to the Liberal Party, he spoke of the right-wingers who hoped to ride into power with Eisenhower—"the men who hunt Communists in the Bureau of Wild

Life and Fisheries while hesitating to aid the gallant men and women who are resisting the real thing in the front lines of Europe and Asia. . . . They are finally the men who seemingly believe that we can confound the Kremlin by frightening ourselves to death." Stevenson's gift to the nation was his language, elegant and well crafted, thoughtful and calming.

The most dramatic moment in the campaign came early, and it was also connected with television. In mid-September it was discovered that a group of wealthy California businessmen had created a fund designed to alleviate the financial pressures on Richard Nixon, a politician without financial resources of his own. The idea was that the money be used for the young Senator's travel, for his Christmas cards and other small expenses. "They are so poor that they haven't a maid and we must see to it that they have a maid," said Dana Smith, one of the chief organizers. The Nixon fund was not unique. Similar funds had been used by other politicians, including Adlai Stevenson, it would turn out. Many Congressmen enhanced their salaries by placing their wives on the payroll in various administrative or secretarial positions, something that Nixon, to his credit, had not done. Neither Nixon nor the organizers were particularly secretive about the fund. In mid-September, when reporters first asked Nixon about it, he was quite open and relaxed, and suggested that they go see Dana Smith. Smith, in turn, spoke enthusiastically about what they were doing and suggested that it might be a model for others. The fund apparently had a total of over $16,000. The contributions ranged from $100 to $500. The early stories did not seem to cause much of a stir. Most newspapers played the story inside, if at all. Then on September 18 the New York *Post*, a liberal newspaper decidedly unsympathetic to Nixon, played the story big: SECRET NIXON FUND screamed the banner headline. SECRET RICH MEN'S TRUST FUND KEEPS NIXON IN STYLE FAR BEYOND HIS SALARY said the head.

"We never comment on a New York *Post* story," Jim Hagerty, Ike's press secretary, said immediately. But the Eisenhower people froze. The whole campaign was premised on his cleanliness. He was the man who was going to, as the saying went, clean up the mess in Washington. A decision was taken aboard the Eisenhower train that the general must be protected and not tainted by this, even if it meant letting Nixon take the heat.

With that, the burden was on Nixon to clear himself in Ike's eyes. How he was going to do this was unclear. Nor were the candidates' logistics much given to coming up with a coherent mutual strategy. Ike was on his train, traveling in the Midwest, surrounded largely by people from the liberal eastern wing of the party, men who had never wanted Nixon on the ticket in the first place.

Each candidate was now behaving exactly in character. Ike, the commanding general, was aloof—so carefully sheltered by his own staff that he did not sense that his very inaction was giving the story momentum and validity. On the Nixon train, whistle-stopping in California, the vice-presidential candidate, always given to black moods and periods of despair, fell to brooding and self-pity. His staff cursed the general, who could have put the entire thing behind them in a minute and had chosen not to do so. Nixon later said that Ike had made him feel like "the little boy caught with jam on his face."

Gradually the idea was born among those sympathetic to Nixon that he should make a special television appearance to clear himself.

On Tuesday, September 23, Nixon bared his soul to the entire nation—at least his financial soul. He had everything to gain and nothing to lose, with his political career hanging in the balance. Ike's people wanted copies of the speech before Nixon went on, but the vice-presidential candidate, angry over what he considered Eisenhower's waffling, was not about to give them anything. For Nixon it was all rather exhilarating—it was the kind of challenge he could understand and rise to. The speech was thereafter known as the Checkers speech—after a reference to his dog, Checkers—although Nixon himself, who loved the speech and thought of it as one of the high-water marks of his career, much preferred to refer to it as the Fund speech. Still, Nixon was proud of the reference to his girls' dog because it was a version of a famous Roosevelt speech that featured Roosevelt's little dog, Fala.

He knew exactly how he wanted to portray himself—as the ordinary American, like so many other veterans back from World War II, just starting out in life, more than a little modest about his service to his country. ("Let me say that my service record was not a particularly unusual one. I went to the South Pacific. I guess I'm entitled to a couple of battle stars. I got a couple of letters of commendation, but I was just there when the bombs started falling.") He wanted his audience to know he had never been rich and that he was being smeared in the process of fighting Communists for ordinary Americans (which he would continue to do, no matter how this all came out). There was no advance copy of the speech; he spoke from notes.

Ted Rogers, who was in charge of television for Nixon, told the people at the broadcast studio to make the setting as natural as possible—no flags, no gimmicks. Nixon was the one who insisted that Pat go on with him. She was his only prop, a reminder that they were a typical young American couple. Rogers was dubious about putting her on—he thought it might be in bad taste—but Nixon was firm. It was not just politics for him, Rogers realized; it was as if he were fighting some kind of war—Nixon against the world.

Nixon spoke to the nation for thirty minutes. He outlined his family's finances in exceptional detail. Pat Nixon came to hate the speech because in her eyes it unveiled the poverty of their past. "Why do we have to tell people how little we have and how much we owe?" she had asked. The speech itself was extremely maudlin: "Pat doesn't have a mink coat. But she does have a perfectly respectable Republican cloth coat. And I always tell her that she'd look good in anything." Then there was the dog: "And you know the kids love that dog, and I just want to say this right now—that regardless of what they say about it, we're going to keep it." But above all, there was the respect and obedience to Eisenhower ("And remember, folks, Eisenhower is a great man, believe me. He is a great man . . ."), while telling his listeners to send telegrams to the Republican National Committee, a conservative group hostile to Ike and sympathetic to Nixon. He cast the issue not in political terms but in personal ones. He had come to the American people and told them he was drowning and asked them to save him. Most surely they would now reach out.

He was in tears as he finished, sure that he had blown it and that he had not even gotten in the Republican National Committee's address in time. Rogers, though, was dazzled by how well it had worked, how Nixon had ended just on the right note without even knowing it, "walking off the set into the Warner Brothers sunset," as Rogers later said. The phone response showed that Rogers was right. Ike, watching in Cleveland, was not amused by the way in which Nixon had taken the play away from him.

So Nixon saved his spot on the ticket. There was a price, of course. Ike never entirely trusted him again, and Nixon became increasingly contemptuous of Eisenhower's political judgment. There was also the belief on the part of the nation's tastemakers that there was something a little unsavory about the entire episode: the self-pity, the willingness to use wife, children, and dog. "He may aspire to the grace and nobility of Quakerism but if so he has yet to comprehend the core of the faith," Richard Rovere wrote. "It would be hard to think of anything more wildly at variance with the spirit of the Society of Friends than his appeal for the pity and sympathy of his countrymen on the ground that his wife did not own a mink coat."

The big winner in the whole episode was not Nixon but television. Nixon had given a powerful demonstration of what it could do. In effect, Richard Nixon had summoned his own instant convention, deputizing millions of Americans sitting in their homes as the delegates to it. With a shrewd, emotional speech, he had gone over Eisenhower's head and rehabilitated himself. The old political bosses could provide an audience of several thousand; television could provide one of millions, without the risk of hostile questioning.

The person who learned this lesson best was Nixon himself. The entire tone of his campaign began to change. If his bus was ready to roll, and the print reporters—to his mind his principal enemies in the fund scandal—were not ready, his attitude now, thought Ted Rogers, was, "We don't need them." He had become convinced that television could carry him above any obstacles the print reporters might put in his way. He was the new electronic man in the new electronic age.

# CHAPTER TEN

IN THE summer of 1951 Marlon Brando opened in his first big film, the screen version of Tennessee Williams' *A Streetcar Named Desire*. There was never any doubt he would get the part after his Broadway performance in the play; he exuded a raw sexual power onstage that could only translate into box-office power. Brando was paid $75,000, reasonably good money at that time for a first starring role.

*A Streetcar Named Desire* was not just a play—it was an event. Its frank treatment of sophisticated sexual themes marked it as part of a powerful new current in American society and cultural life. Even the plot seemed emblematic—the brutal assault on Blanche's prim Victorian pretensions by Stanley Kowalski's primal sexuality. Every night on Broadway the audience would leave the theater visibly shaken—not only in response to Blanche's tragic breakdown but also in some small way, perhaps, because they had gotten a glimpse of the violent changes just beginning to transform their own culture and lives.

That *Streetcar,* first on Broadway and then on film, seemed to transcend a mere theatrical triumph to become a cultural benchmark was due to three remarkable talents, all then at that zenith of their powers: Tennessee Williams, perhaps the greatest American playwright; Marlon Brando, the most original American actor of his time; and Elia Kazan, the great director. The cumulative force of these three men caused an explosion that shattered the pleasant conventions of American life. Different though they were in many ways, all three were outsiders, liberated by the changing times and eager to assault existing conventions.

Williams was gay, his private life an open secret. Kazan was a Greek American, driven by the feverish energy of the outsider looking in. Brando was a self-invented outsider, a middle-class American who scorned the conventions of middle-class life.

*Streetcar* derived its vitality from the talents of all three, and the person who realized that from the start was Williams. For *Streetcar* he passionately pursued Kazan, although at that point hardly the best-known or preeminent director on Broadway. Still, Williams was certain Kazan could put over the poetic vision of the play. Williams recognized his own limitations, and in a letter to Kazan he wrote, "The cloudy dream type, which I admit to being, needs the complementary eye of the more objective and dynamic worker. I believe you are also a dreamer. There are dreamy touches in your direction which are vastly provocative, but you have the dynamism my works need."

When Kazan started on *Streetcar,* he had thought of conventional casting and offered the part to John Garfield, the quintessential tough but good guy. But Garfield set down terms that were impossible: he would play Kowalski for only four months, and he demanded a guarantee of the movie role. Kazan thought it was Garfield's polite Hollywood way of saying he did not want the part. That brought him

Not everyone was conservative in the fifties—certainly not the rebellious Marlon Brando, shown here with Vivien Leigh in *A Streetcar Named Desire*.

to Brando. Kazan had used him for a bit part in a play called *Truckline* and had witnessed the energy he projected onstage. Kazan began thinking of him as Stanley. But a traditional audition was out of the question. Brando had a bad reputation for auditions, where he mumbled and strayed emotionally.

Since Brando disdained telephone ownership, Kazan had to send out word through the Greenwich Village underground that he was searching for the actor. Then he passed him the script. At first Brando was uneasy with it; he hated the Kowalski character—it was just the kind of male brutality that offended him. But there was a power to the play that was irresistible. Finally they got in touch. "Well, what is it, yes or no?" Kazan asked. Yes, said Brando. Kazan lent him twenty dollars and sent him to do an informal reading for Williams, then in Provincetown.

A day after Brando arrived, Williams called Kazan, so enthusiastic as to be "near hysteria." Brando was in. Back in New York City, he tried to insult the producer, Irene Selznick, daughter of fabled motion-picture producer Louis B. Mayer, by putting down the world of Hollywood. But she remained immune to his provocation, and she signed him to the part at $550 a week.

Brando was, of course, always a great original. He was the new American rebel, rebelling not against physical hardship or harsh economic conditions, but rather against conventionality and the boredom engendered by his boyhood in the Midwest and a strict father. Marlon Brando, Sr., a limestone salesman in Omaha, was a man much given to setting strict rules at home. Yet when he himself was off on sales trips in Chicago or elsewhere, he strayed from his puritan ethic to drink and chase women. Brando's mother, Dodie, was talented, charming, and almost fey—a would-be actress who was a leader in local amateur theater. Caught in this unsuccessful marriage, she found her own manner of freedom in alcohol. Later, when Dodie visited her children in New York, they would try to hide her liquor. But she always foiled them by sneaking the bottles under the bath towels they had dropped on the bathroom floor. This, she said, was the perfect hiding place: "One thing I know, none of my children ever picks up the towels from the bathroom floor." The respective influence of the parents on their three children can be judged by the fact that Marlon became an actor, Jocelyn became an actress, and Frances became a painter. No one went into conventional careers in business.

Brando's resentment of his father's authoritarianism would stay with him throughout his life. "I hate ultimatums," Marlon would say later. That would be obvious in his work and his career from the start. In 1943, at the age of nineteen, he came to New York City intending to be an actor. If a counterculture existed anywhere in America in the forties and early fifties, it was in Greenwich Village. Here were Italian restaurants with candles stuck in old Chianti bottles, coffeehouses with poets and artists, small theaters and clubs that featured modern jazz. The battle cry was the rejection of commercialism and materialism. In one of his first important films, *The Wild One,* Brando plays a member of a motorcycle club. "What are you rebelling against?" asks a girl in the small town. "Waddya got?" asks Brando.

He loved the Village from the start. It was everything that Omaha was not. Here he could get by in T-shirts, blue jeans, and, if necessary, a leather jacket. Even for the Village, he lived like a gypsy, moving around constantly, rarely having an apartment of his own. If by chance he had money, he spent it or gave it away. If he didn't have money, he borrowed it. Material possessions seemed to mean little to him. He seemed to covet something different: personal freedom. His was not so much a political rebellion as a restlessness with the conventions of the American middle class.

But at this point in his career there was already a sense that he was going to make it. From the very start he got work—more, it sometimes seemed, than he needed or wanted. "This puppy thing will be the best actor on the American stage," Stella Adler, the actress and teacher, said.

Yet he was oddly ambivalent about his talent and the search for success. He hated auditions, for they meant pleasing a person in authority. He was at once ambitious and not ambitious.

The ambivalence came from both fear of failure and fear of success, which might force him toward a place in a world he was rejecting and present him with too many choices. Success led inevitably to materialism, he was sure, and that was not something he sought. Thus he was the first in a tradition of new American rebels that would include James Dean and Jack Kerouac.

"Marlon," said Truman Capote, who wrote knowingly about him, "always turns against whatever he's working on. Some element of it. Either the script or the director or somebody in the cast. Not because of something very rational—just because it seems to comfort him to be dissatisfied, let steam off about something. It's part of his pattern."

Brando brought a new dimension to narcissism as well. The rules did not please him, so he reinvented a society in which he set the rules. Inevitably, it all led to becoming only more self-obsessed. In his mind he owed nothing to anyone and accepted no larger obligations. At one point Robert Mitchum was asked on a talk show if he had ever made a movie with Brando. He answered mordantly, "Brando's never made a movie with anyone."

On some level, though, he knew it all worked for him, and his provocative behavior made his looks and sexuality seem even more remarkable and powerful. For the New York theater world he was a breath of fresh air, the man who broke the rules and thereby achieved a more natural kind of acting.

*Streetcar* opened in December 1947. The confluence of these three outsiders—Brando, Williams, and Kazan—reflected a changing America and changing sensibilities. It represented a new and more tolerant social order, where words and images once banned were now

permitted. Ten years earlier America might not have been ready for
Williams' plays, an immigrant like Kazan might not have been able to
find his way to Broadway, and Brando might have been rejected by
those running the theater. But now they had all arrived at the same
place at the same time.

The synergy of talents was extraordinary. Each strengthened and
amplified the others' talents: Williams without Kazan might have
been too poetic and not sufficiently dramatic; Kazan without Williams
might have been too political and raw; and both without Brando
might have lacked the star who brought their work to the very center
of American cultural life, first in the theater, and even more remarkably in Hollywood, which reached far beyond a narrow cultural elite.
Each of the three was in his own way rebelling against the puritanism
of American life and the conventional quality of the American dream.
Thanks to Hollywood, they could now bring their views to an audience of millions.

AMONG those deeply moved by *A Streetcar Named Desire* was a college
professor from Bloomington, Indiana. His name was Alfred Kinsey,
and in 1950, when he saw the play on Broadway, he had already
published the first of his two pioneering works, *Sexual Behavior in the
Human Male,* popularly known as the Kinsey Report. Kinsey knew
immediately that he and Williams were, in different ways, doing something very similar—they were tearing away the façade that Americans
used to hide their sexual selves. As a result of his work, Kinsey was
both fascinated and troubled by the vast difference between American sexual behavior the society wanted to believe existed and American sexual practices as they actually existed; in other words, it was one
thing to do it, but it was quite another thing to admit doing it. For
example, at least eighty percent of successful businessmen, his interviews had shown, had had extramarital affairs. "What a gap between
social front and reality!" he noted.

Alfred Kinsey was no bohemian. He lived in the Midwest, had
married the first woman he ever dated, and stayed married to her for
his entire life. Almost surely, his close friends thought, he had had no
extramarital affairs. Because he was an entomologist and loved to
collect bugs, he and his bride went camping on their honeymoon. In
his classes at the University of Indiana he always sported a bow tie and

a crew cut. Kinsey did not smoke, and he rarely drank. On Sundays he and his wife, Clara, would invite faculty and graduate-student friends to their home to listen to records of classical music. There the Kinseys served such homey desserts as persimmon pudding. They took these evenings very seriously—Kinsey was immensely proud of his record collection. When the wife of one faculty member suggested that they play some boogie-woogie, the couple was never invited back.

His greatest passion was his work. He approached it with an intensity that was rooted in the Calvinist zeal of his forefathers. As a young man, he had gone on vacation with friends but complained later that the time might have been better spent working, and in fact he generally worked every day of the year except Christmas Day. He seemed to be the least likely candidate to become one of the most controversial figures of his generation. During the early forties he published *Edible Wild Plants of North America,* which was voted the most important book of the year by the trustees of the Massachusetts Horticultural Society. He was a highly respected professor of zoology in a good department at Indiana University. Esteemed by his colleagues for his world-class collection of gall wasps, he was also popular with his students, a kind and humane teacher who was always generous with his time.

Then in 1938 a group of his students came to him and asked questions about marriage. He was touched by their innocence. At first he refrained from answering, fearing he knew too little. He went out and read everything he could on the subject and was appalled by the inadequate available material—both in quantity and quality. Some of the students petitioned the university to start a course on sexuality and marriage. From the start, it was Kinsey's course, and it was a huge success. It soon became his obsession. Clara Kinsey was known on occasion to tell friends, "I hardly see him at night anymore since he took up sex." What was probably true, some of his colleagues thought, was that he was already a little restless with the study of insects and was looking for a larger challenge.

When he began his studies of human sexuality, one of his oldest friends, Edgar Anderson, by then the director of the Missouri Botanical Garden in St. Louis, wrote him: "It was heartwarming to see you settling down into what I suppose will be your real life work. One would never have believed that all sides of you could have found a project big enough to need them all. I was amused to see how the

Scotch Presbyterian reformer in you had finally got together with the scientific fanatic with his zeal for masses of neat data in orderly boxes and drawers. The monographer Kinsey, the naturalist Kinsey, and the camp counsellor Kinsey all rolling into one at last and going full steam ahead."

He began by taking sexual histories of his students. He conducted the interviews in his tiny office, locking the door and sending his assistant elsewhere. The enrollment for the class grew every year. Soon 400 students were signing up for it. But more and more his heart was in the research. By 1939 he wrote to a friend that the interviews were "a scientific gold mine." Soon he was not only taking the sexual histories of his students but traveling out of town on weekends, at first to Chicago and then to other communities in the Midwest, to find additional subjects. The project took an increasing amount of his time, and there was an inevitable conservative reaction against him in Indiana. Complaints began to come in from parents and local ministers. One of his early critics, Professor Thurman Rice of the University of Indiana Medical School, was enraged because Kinsey had not, in the course of teaching, denounced premarital sex.

At first Kinsey had limited resources: he used part of his own small salary to finance his research. Then in 1941 he got his first grant from a foundation, for $1600; in 1943 he received his first grant from the Medical Sciences Division of the Rockefeller Foundation, a gift of $23,000; by 1947 that figure was $40,000. The foundation thereby became the principal financial backer of his studies. By 1947 he was preparing to publish the first book of his results—a simple report on the human animal studied in one of its highest-priority biological acts. His conclusions do not seem startling today: that healthy sex led to a healthy marriage; that there was more extramarital sex on the part of both men and women than they wanted to admit; that masturbation did not cause mental problems, as superstition held; that there was more homosexuality than people wanted to admit.

To publish his findings, Kinsey chose W. B. Saunders, an old-line medical-book firm in Philadelphia. The original printing was slated for 10,000, but as prepublication interest grew, Saunders increased it to 25,000. The book cost $6.50, which made it expensive for those days; had 804 pages; and weighed three pounds. Kinsey had received no advance against royalties from the publisher, and whatever money

*"Is there a <u>Mrs.</u> Kinsey?"*

he made, he turned back to his own think tank, which by then was known as the Institute for Sex Research of Indiana University.

Though he continued to sign himself on letters "Alfred Kinsey, professor of zoology," his days as a mere professor were behind him. His name was suddenly a household word; everyone knew of him as the sex doctor. There was a famous Peter Arno cartoon in *The New Yorker* showing a woman reading the report and asking her husband with a horrified expression, "Is there a *Mrs.* Kinsey?" Within ten days of the book's release, the publisher had to order a sixth printing, making a phenomenal 185,000 copies in print. To the astonishment of everyone, particularly Kinsey, the book roared up the best-seller lists, a fact somewhat embarrassing to *The New York Times,* which at first neither accepted advertising for Kinsey's book nor reviewed it. The early critical response was good. The first reviews saw his samples adequate, his scientific judgments modest, his tone serious. Polls taken of ordinary Americans showed that not only did they agree with his evidence but they believed such studies were helpful.

Then his critics weighed in. They furiously disagreed with almost everything: his figures on premarital sex; his figures on extramarital sex; his figures on homosexuality; above all, his failure to condemn what he had found. Not only had he angered the traditional conservative bastions of social mores—the Protestant churches on the right and the Catholic Church—but, to his surprise, he had enraged the most powerful voices in the liberal Protestant clergy as well. By trying to study our sexual patterns, he was accused instead of trying to lower our moral standards.

Kinsey was at first stunned, then angered by the response, but he was never embittered. He was appalled by the failure of other scientists and doctors to come to his defense. He sensed in certain cases that the lack of support stemmed from professional jealousy. In time, as the attacks grew more strident, he did not hesitate, when talking with friends, to compare himself with such scientists as Galileo, who had been pilloried in the past for challenging the myths and the ignorance of his age. What surprised him most was the absence of scientific standards in most of the assaults. His critics were, he noted, merely "exposing their emotional (not their scientific) selves in their attacks."

But Kinsey held back from displaying his dismay in public. Besides, there was a second book to finish. His biggest fear was that he might lose his key source of support, the Rockefeller Foundation. Alan Gregg, who was in effect Kinsey's man at the foundation, warned that it might be harder than he had expected to sustain the funding. Perhaps the royalties from the book could pay for the research, Gregg suggested. Kinsey wrote Gregg that there was only a limited amount the royalties could do in terms of support. If anything, Kinsey wanted to expand the budget—there was always so much more to do.

The trouble, Kinsey learned, was the new head of the Rockefeller Foundation, Dean Rusk. Rusk had come over after serving as assistant secretary of state for Far Eastern affairs. Cautious, wary of the power of conservatives in Congress, he was not eager to take serious political risks on behalf of something that must have seemed as peripheral to him as Kinsey's sex research.

The second book, *Sexual Behavior in the Human Female,* was published in the fall of 1953. Kinsey was well aware that it was even more explosive than the first—he was, after all, discussing wives, mothers, and daughters. Like the first book, it was a sensation. The first printing was 25,000 copies. Within ten days the publishers were in their sixth printing, for a total of 185,000. It would eventually sell some 250,000 copies.

Again the initial reception was essentially positive; some of the magazine reporting was thoughtful. Then the firestorm began anew.

"It is impossible to estimate the damage this book will do to the already deteriorating morals of America," Billy Graham pronounced. Again Kinsey was disheartened: "I am still uncertain what the basic reason for the bitter attack on us may be. Their arguments become absurd when they attempt to find specific flaws in the book and basically I think they are attacking on general principles."

The new book was the final straw for the Rockefeller Foundation. In November 1953 Kinsey's supporters there made passionate presentations on his behalf. His work, they argued, was among the most important the foundation was sponsoring. They put in a request for $80,000. An unsympathetic Rusk rejected it. It was a shattering moment. Kinsey was devastated. "Damn that Rusk!" he would say from time to time.

Kinsey merely redoubled his efforts. If he had been a workaholic before, now there was a manic quality to his activities. His friends began to worry about his health. He suffered from insomnia, began to take sleeping pills, and started showing up groggy at work in the morning. Long-standing problems with his heart grew more serious. On several occasions he was hospitalized, and by the middle of 1956 he was forced to stay home and rest. That summer he conducted interviews number 7984 and 7985. "It is a shame," he noted, "that there comes a time that you have to work up data and publish it instead of continuing gathering. Frankly, I very much enjoy the gathering." He was ever the scientist, delighted by discovery. On August 25, 1956, he died, at the age of sixty-two.


# CHAPTER ELEVEN

B Y THE fall of 1953 Eisenhower was settled in the White House. A truce, albeit an uneasy one, had finally been signed in Korea. Now Eisenhower's administration was formulating what it would later call the New Look, a reformulation of American foreign policy and military posture. It reflected the President's belief that the true strength of America came from a healthy economy and that a heavy defense budget would diminish that strength. Cutting defense spending inevitably meant a greater dependence on atomic weapons.

Ike had arrived in office with the Korean War inflating the military budget to $42 billion. One of the first things George Humphrey, the Secretary of the Treasury, did was to help pare the defense budget down to $34.5 billion.

An adjunct to the New Look, first identified by Secretary of State John Foster Dulles in January 1954, was the doctrine of massive retaliation. (What Dulles actually said was that local defense measures would now be replaced throughout the world "by the further deterrence of massive retaliatory power.") That meant we would react instantaneously, to even the smallest provocation, with nuclear weapons; therefore, an enemy would most assuredly not dare provoke us. The policy seemed to guarantee that all future wars would be short and inexpensive. But such military critics as Matt Ridgway were hardly impressed. He saw the world as far more disorderly, with all kinds of threats, requiring flexibility in the ways we might respond. Nor did he see nuclear weapons as a practical option in the many messy situations that were already developing around the world. What about insurgencies and brushfire wars that did not necessarily fit into the superpower nuclear equation? Was the New Look a viable strategy there, or was it primarily a bluff?

In early May, 1953, Ike appointed new Chiefs of Staff. Arthur Radford, the embodiment of what the Republican right wanted, replaced Omar Bradley as Chairman of the Joint Chiefs. There was, it would turn out, a world of difference between the old-fashioned Bradley and the modern, eager young Arthur Radford.

Radford was a product of the modern navy, a man of both Annapolis and of aircraft carriers, whose career had raced ahead, propelled by the force of modern technology. He was unusually interested in Southeast Asia and had decided it was the coming battleground between the West and communism; he considered himself something of an expert on the region.

If the critics of the Truman-Acheson years had seemed to envision a simpler world—in which nothing limited American power, and the atomic weapon offered an easy answer to every military dilemma— they now had in Admiral Radford a Chairman of the J.C.S. who shared their views. Both assumed that the communist world was a monolith, and easily bluffed by nuclear threats.

The problem with military policies that are built to domestic specifications and do not take into account the complexity of the real world is that eventually the real world intrudes. So it happened to Eisenhower, Dulles, and Admiral Radford in the spring of 1954, in the most unlikely of places: Indochina, where the French were still fighting an exhausting colonial war. That spring it seemed they were about to suffer a decisive defeat at Dien Bien Phu, a cluster of small villages in the Thai mountains along the Laotian border.

The French Expeditionary Force of some 500,000 men—some French, some Vietnamese, some North Africans, and some Europeans in the French Foreign Legion—was being swallowed up in the rice paddies and jungles. Their opponents, the Vietminh—the communist-nationalist insurgents—were gaining confidence and fighting with greater audacity. That inevitably posed something of a problem for the new Republican administration. The conflict in French Indochina—later to be known as Vietnam—was not yet an American war, but it was in many ways an American-sponsored war. Even before the outbreak of hostilities in Korea, Truman, eager to take a stronger stand against Asian communism, had started helping finance the French war. By the end of 1953 we had spent over $1 billion in aid and escalated our rhetoric to classify the struggle between the Vietminh and the French, not as a colonial war, but as part of the larger struggle of the Western democracies against communism.

By 1953 we had more interest in continuing the Indochina war than the French did. The reality was that they had systematically underestimated the capacity of the Vietminh to wage a guerrilla war. Every year in Vietnam, France lost a third of the graduating class from St. Cyr, its military college. *La guerre sale* (the dirty war), it was called by this time back in France. And increasingly the French wanted out.

By mid-1953 it was clear to most military observers that the French were on the defensive, as the hemorrhaging of their forces continued and as domestic support for the war continued to shrink. Even worse, there were signs that with the Korean War over, the Chinese Communists—despite historical tension between them and the Vietnamese nationalists—were supplying heavy weaponry.

In late May, 1953, the French had sent General Henri Navarre, one of their top staff advisers, to take command there. Navarre wasted no time in developing a plan that minimized contact with the Vietminh for more than a year while he rebuilt his forces, with significant reinforcements from France. Starting in the fall of 1954, he intended to strike against the Vietminh with these beefed-up units. Significantly, he did not aim for victory; rather, he hoped to demonstrate a French presence so strong that the Vietminh would finally come to the negotiating table.

By all rights the Navarre plan should have excluded a battle for a small and not particularly valuable outpost along the Laotian border. Yet a plan for Dien Bien Phu had existed for some time before Navarre arrived. Slowly, almost inevitably, Navarre and his command incorporated it into his larger plan, deciding to send several French battalions into Dien Bien Phu and hoping that the Viets would attack them there. It would be the set-piece battle the French had wanted for some time; instead of fighting an army of ghosts who disappeared into the night time and again, the Vietminh would be tricked into standing and fighting, and the French would finally be able to use their superior weaponry. The French believed they were setting the trap and the Vietminh would rise to the bait. It proved to be a trap all right, but for which side was the question.

On November 20, 1953, two battalions of French forces parachuted into Dien Bien Phu. For weeks before the battle, various visitors to the post noted that the French unit there seemed to be encircled and that the surrounding high ground belonged to the Vietminh. When they pointed this out to the garrison's artillery commander, Colonel Charles Piroth, he treated the idea with ridicule. He claimed the Vietminh could never get their artillery through to this distant outpost, and even if they did somehow manage, they would never be able to supply the troops with enough ammunition. The French would smash them, he added. Asked a few weeks before the battle began whether he wanted additional artillery pieces, Piroth scorned the idea; he had all the weapons he needed, he answered.

Once again the French had made a fatal mistake. The Viets had a secret new, if rather primitive, weapon: the bicycle. They had reinforced 2000 of them with extra supports so that peasants could load and push them through the primitive trails to Dien Bien Phu. The bikes could carry up to 500 pounds, more than five times the weight of most of the peasants themselves and more than twice what an elephant could carry. Resupply was less of a problem for them than the French imagined. Slowly, steadily, usually by moving at night, some 50,000 Vietminh soldiers gathered on the high ground around the French post—four times as many men as the French had assembled and four times as many as Navarre thought the Vietminh were capable of gathering. An additional 100,000 peasants were there to help supply the combat soldiers. In addition, they were well supplied with heavy weapons, including 105 20-mm howitzers.

On March 13, 1954, the siege of Dien Bien Phu began. "Hell in a very small place," the historian Bernard Fall called it. Within two days Colonel Piroth was desperate; he could not believe that he was so badly outgunned. When one of his superiors asked him where the Vietminh guns were, he pointed to a spot on the headquarters map and said, "They may be there." Then he quickly pointed to another spot. "Or there." Can you silence them? he was asked. He shrugged his shoulders and refused to eat. "I am completely dishonored," he told one friend. "I have guaranteed deCastries [the camp commander] that the enemy artillery couldn't touch us, but now we are going to lose the battle. I'm leaving." Soon thereafter Piroth pulled a pin on a grenade and committed suicide.

On the first night, a major stronghold on the northeast sector, Beatrice, fell, and on the second night, so did another, Gabrielle. That gave the Vietminh two of three key points on the northern rim of the valley; on the third night, they gained the third when the Thai tribesmen deserted at Anne Marie. Suddenly this war with its thousand little skirmishes was focused on one dramatic and poignant battle. Dien Bien Phu became a household word, and the question of whether the embattled French garrison would survive was taken up as an international issue. The French lacked the resources to rescue the surrounded troops. The only hope was some form of American intervention, but even conservative congressional leaders were wary of getting involved. Here then was the first test of the New Look and of the new Eisenhower-Dulles doctrine, the keystone of which was that no additional Asian country should fall to the Communists.

For the next two months Secretary of State John Foster Dulles was a man constantly in motion—cajoling, pushing, and stroking allies. Ostensibly, he wanted some kind of joint Allied intervention in Indochina to rescue the French garrison, most likely by pounding the general area with the American air force, perhaps even using, if need be, atomic weapons. What he actually wanted to happen has always intrigued historians of the period. Certainly those who opposed intervention—General Matt Ridgway, for instance—thought he did want to intervene. What was clear is that he did not want the administration to be blamed for being soft on communism or for losing Indochina. Therefore, the most important thing was to make sure that if the worst happened, the blame was assigned elsewhere, either to the Allies or to Congress.

But the problems of putting together some sort of joint action were immense. The French, stunned by the tragedy facing them at Dien Bien Phu, seemed to have lost all taste for battle. The British were just finishing up their own hard war in Malaya, and having given up India without firing a shot, they had little interest in shedding British blood for what was to them very clearly a colonial war for a French cause. Nor was Eisenhower eager for another Asian war. He had just finished in Korea, for which there had been little public support from the start. Indochina promised, if anything, to be even worse.

As the idea of intervention began to die, Dulles continued to speak publicly of the importance of the garrison. However, in a private cable to Eisenhower from Paris on April 23, he noted that the situation there was hopeless but that there was "no military or logical reason why loss of Dien Bien Phu should lead to collapse of the French." Then Dulles finally went on national television and blamed the British; we would have gone in, he seemed to be saying, but for the Allies. That took care of the domestic politics. We had not lost the war; our allies had.

The post fell on May 7. The news reached Paris in the late morning of that day, and the French prime minister, Joseph Laniel, dressed entirely in black, barely able to control his voice, broke the news to the National Assembly. It was a terrible moment, filled with the deep, bitter shame of a nation betraying fighting men halfway around the world. That night all French television and radio networks canceled their regularly scheduled programs and instead played the Berlioz *Requiem.* It was over.

At a conference in Geneva, Vietnam was divided up, with the North becoming a communist state under the Vietminh leader Ho Chi Minh and the South an anticommunist society under Ngo Dinh Diem, a Catholic mandarin who had sat out the war in America and was now being installed by the Americans. Both sides, ironically, resented the Geneva settlement. The North, with good reason, felt it had been on the verge of a total victory but had been pressured by the Soviets to settle for half the pie. By contrast, in America there was a feeling that somehow the French had sold out and given the Communists a victory at the conference table. Dulles came to believe that Dien Bien Phu was a boon to us. "We have a clean base there now without the taint of colonialism," he said later with stunning innocence. "Dien Bien Phu was a blessing in disguise." Some blessing, some disguise.

How wrong Dulles was to claim that we had escaped the taint of colonialism, the next generation of American policymakers would find out. We thought the war in Indochina was over; the other side knew it had just begun.

# CHAPTER TWELVE

B Y THE early 1950s the Supreme Court was in chaos—racked, ironically, by long-simmering divisions among the four Justices appointed by Roosevelt. If nothing else, the conflict reflected something of the political contradictions and deviousness of the man who had appointed them. The personal squabbles among the four intellectually towering figures—Felix Frankfurter, Robert Jackson, Hugo Black, and William O. Douglas—sometimes seemed more serious than the political ones. When Harlan Fiske Stone, the Chief Justice, died in 1946, Truman chose his old friend former Congressman Fred Vinson to replace Stone, because he believed Vinson to be likable and extremely skilled as a conciliator.

But Vinson's skill of bringing people together, which had served him so well in the Congress, deserted him on the Court, where he faced questions too complicated and subtle for the old-fashioned compromise solutions he was accustomed to. Moreover, the men he was now dealing with were different by temperament from the kind of men Vinson had dealt with in the past. Frankfurter, Black, Jackson, and Douglas were men of formidable intellect, matched only by their overwhelming egos. They did not welcome Vinson as a kindred spirit;

instead, they looked down on him as second-rate. "This man," Philip Elman, an influential Frankfurter clerk, wrote his boss, "is a pygmy, morally and mentally. And so uncouth."

The most unfortunate aspect in all this was that a number of transcending questions were wending their way toward the Court docket. The most important of these dealt with the question of separate-but-equal school facilities in the South. By this time a number of cases challenging the right of states to segregate their schools—including one filed in (of all unlikely but highly segregated places) Topeka, Kansas—had worked their way through the judicial process and had reached the Supreme Court. The Kansas case had been filed in 1951 by a black welder named Oliver Brown, who objected to the fact that his eight-year-old daughter, Linda, had to go twenty-one blocks by bus to a black school when there was a white school only seven blocks from her house. Brown, a mild, religious man, was hardly a local radical. He had tried hard to register his daughter at the all-white Sumner School but finally decided to sue the local school board. The case was filed under the title *Brown* v. *Board of Education* of Topeka.

In the South the concept of separate but equal had always been a sham. It might have been separate, but it never was equal. The southern states were spending twice as much to educate white children as they were black children and four times as much for school facilities. White teacher salaries were thirty percent higher, and there was virtually no transportation for black children to and from school.

If the pace with which the challenge to segregation moved through the courts was, in the words of one writer, a "glacially slow process," then there was finally a sense of steady progress in the postwar years. Thurgood Marshall, the shrewd, folksy black lawyer, had started working for the NAACP in 1936 for the grand sum of $2400 a year, plus expenses, and he carried the burden of much of the litigation. Marshall argued most of the early civil rights cases in small southern courtrooms and suffered the worst indignities of segregation himself, not to mention the threat of physical danger. On occasion he liked to reminisce about the small town in Mississippi where a local resident had told him, "Nigguh, I thought you oughta know the sun ain't nevah set on a live nigguh in this town." So, he noted, he had "wrapped my constitutional rights in cellophane, tucked 'em in my hip pocket," and caught the next train out of there. Marshall and a handful of colleagues attacked the segregationists where they were most vulnerable—in the border and southwestern states, where racism was less virulent.

By 1950 the Supreme Court had begun to tilt away from segregation and had outlawed it in graduate schools. Marshall and his handful of colleagues had carefully and indeed cautiously escalated what had begun as piecemeal raids on the periphery of segregation into a full-scale assault upon its very core. That meant taking on the precedent of *Plessy* v. *Ferguson,* the critical decision made some sixty years earlier. In the aftermath of the Civil War, there had been considerable impetus to give blacks full citizenship. The Thirteenth Amendment had outlawed slavery, and the Fourteenth Amendment ruled that state governments could not deny black citizens due process or equal protection. But by the latter part of the nineteenth century a series of separate-but-equal laws authorized segregation throughout the South. Most of these laws seemed in direct conflict, legally and spiritually, with the Fourteenth Amendment. Among these was a Louisiana law that said all railroad trains should have separate-but-equal accommodations. In June 1892 a black man named Homer Adolph Plessy deliberately tested the law on a trip from New Orleans to Covington, Louisiana. He was asked to leave by the conductor, then arrested and tried before Judge John Ferguson in New Orleans. Plessy argued that the arrest had violated his rights under the Fourteenth Amendment, but Judge Ferguson ruled against him.

Eventually the case found its way to the Supreme Court, where Justice Henry Billings Brown (a rather bland Massachusetts judge who had paid someone to take his place in the Union army) handed down the decision against Plessy. Brown argued that it was not clear which rights were actually covered by the Fourteenth Amendment, and he noted that the government could not force citizens to commingle. Somewhat disingenuously Brown argued that segregation laws did not necessarily imply the inferiority of either race. It was a remarkably insensitive decision, reversing the tide of legal equality begun after the Civil War. The vote against Plessy was 7–1, the one dissenting cast by John Marshall Harlan, the leading intellect of the Court and himself a very conservative man. In a passionate dissent, he noted that if the state could do this to blacks on the railroad, could it not do it elsewhere to other groups, "of native and naturalized citizens of the United States, or of Protestants and Roman Catholics?"

For the next fifty years a legal, political, and social crisis built. In the vacuum of presidential and congressional inaction on the subject, the issue was finally passed on again to the Supreme Court in the form of *Brown* v. *Board of Education*. Whether Chief Justice Vinson himself would be willing to help reverse the *Plessy* decision was a serious question among those who knew him well. When the Court met in conference in December 1952, Vinson observed, "However we construe it, Congress did not pass a statute deterring or ordering no segregation." He was clearly very nervous about the course ahead. Since Tom Clark tended to vote with Vinson on such issues, Frankfurter, a conservative who nevertheless was convinced that segregation had to end, foresaw a decision that would end segregation but by a close vote. A narrow margin would make implementation difficult, if not impossible. As a delaying tactic, Frankfurter suggested rehearing *Brown*. The new hearings were scheduled for December 1953, but in September, Vinson died suddenly of a heart attack. "This is the first indication I have ever had that there is a God," said Frankfurter.

The question now was who Dwight Eisenhower would pick as the new Chief Justice. The President announced that his choice would be a political moderate like himself. Speculation began to center on Earl Warren, the liberal governor of California, who was coming to the end of his third term. ("He's a Democrat and doesn't know it," Harry Truman once said of him.)

It was easy to underestimate Earl Warren. He was not particularly articulate, and he prided himself on being homespun. He seemed so relaxed and agreeable that it was easy for new acquaintances to underestimate his ferocious sense of purpose. He had been a distinguished governor of California, tough-minded and pragmatic about government, its limits, and how best it could benefit ordinary people. He was both an optimist and an activist. If he did not exactly bring an ideology to the Court, then he brought the faith of someone who had seen personally what government could and should do to ameliorate the lives of ordinary people.

That the great figures on the bench had so much more judicial experience—Black with sixteen years of service on the Court, Frankfurter and Douglas with fourteen each, and Jackson with twelve—did not daunt him. As he saw it, they knew more about the law, but he knew more about the consequences of the law and its effect on ordinary citizens. His law clerk, Earl Pollock, said years later that there were three things that mattered to Earl Warren: the first was the concept of equality; the second was education; and the third was the right of young people to a decent life. He had spent a lifetime refining his view of the role of government, and he came to the Court ready to implement it.

Warren's greatest skill, perhaps, was his ability to cut to the core of an issue. He immediately came to the conclusion that the Court had to confront *Plessy* directly. *Plessy*, he believed, could only exist based on the idea of Negro inferiority. He was not eager to overturn so important a law from the past, but he did not want to continue punishing black children by sending them to inferior schools. That had to end. The law, he said in one meeting and in words noted by Frankfurter, "cannot in 'this day and age' set them apart."

At this point it was all a matter of tactics and strategy. Warren wanted "a minimum of emotion and strife." He did not want to inflame the South or to divide the country unnecessarily, but he did want, if at all possible, to make this a unanimous decision. He wanted the Court to speak with one voice.

The process of bringing this particular Court together for a unanimous decision was not an easy one. After the first conference of the Justices, on December 13, 1953, Warren moved with great political skill. The stakes were so high that the Justices were unusually secretive about their discussions, in many cases holding back information even from their clerks, lest word leak out of the divisions that existed within. When Frankfurter circulated a memo on the case, he wrote on it, "I need hardly add that the typewriting was done under the condition of strictest security."

By April only one man on the Court still favored legal segregation— Stanley Reed, a member of the southern gentry from Kentucky. At this point Warren was lunching regularly with him. Finally the Chief Justice made his move. "Stan, you're all by yourself in this now," he said. "You've got to decide whether it's really the best thing for the country." In the end, Reed caved in; all he asked was for a decision that made the dismantling gradual rather than violent and quick.

The Court's 9–0 decision was a personal triumph for Warren. Frankfurter, not often given to praise, wrote, "Dear Chief: This is a day that will live in glory. It's also a great day in the history of the court, and not the least for the course of deliberation which brought about the result. I congratulate you." So it was that on May 17, 1954, Earl Warren read the unanimous opinion of the Supreme Court on an issue that had haunted America for almost a century: "We conclude that in the field of public opinion the doctrine of 'separate but equal' has no place. Separate educational facilities are inherently unequal."

The *Brown* v. *Board of Education* decision not only legally ended segregation, it deprived segregationist practices of their moral legitimacy as well. It was therefore perhaps the single most important moment in the decade, the moment that separated the old order from the new and helped create the tumultuous era just arriving. It instantaneously broadened the concept of freedom, and by and large it placed the Court on a path that tilted it to establish rights to outsiders. *Brown* v. *Board of Education* was just the beginning of a startling new period of change, not just in the area of civil rights but in all aspects of social behavior. One era was ending and another beginning.

ON THE evening of December 1, 1955, Mrs. Rosa Parks' entire body ached; her feet, neck, and shoulders were especially sore. Parks was a tailor's assistant in a Montgomery, Alabama, department store. Hers was an exhausting job that paid a minimal salary; she made alterations and had to handle a large commercial steam press as well. On this particular day, she finished work and walked a few blocks as usual to the bus stop. The first bus on her route was so crowded that she realized there would be no place left to sit, and she desperately needed to get off her feet. She decided to wait for a less crowded bus. Eventually a bus arrived that had a fair number of seats available. She paid her ten cents, boarded the bus, and took a seat in the rear, or black, section of the bus, near the dividing line between the white and black sections. On Montgomery's public buses, the first ten rows were for white people, the last twenty-six for blacks. In many cities in the South, the line dividing sections on buses was fixed. This was not true in Montgomery; by custom, the driver had the power, if need be, to expand the white section and shrink the black section by ordering blacks to give up their seats to whites.

Three other blacks boarded the bus and sat next to Mrs. Parks in the same row. Gradually, as the bus continued on its rounds, more whites got on. Finally, with the white section filled, a white man boarded. The driver, J. F. Blake, turned to look behind him at the first row of blacks and said, "You let him have those front seats." That was not a suggestion; it was an order. It meant that not only did one seat have to be freed but the other three blacks would have to move as well, lest the white man have to sit next to a black. All four blacks knew what Blake meant, but no one moved. Blake looked behind him again and added, "You all better make it light on yourselves and let me have those seats." The three other blacks reluctantly got up and moved toward the back. Rosa Parks did not. She was frightened, but she was tired. She did not want to give up her seat, and she most certainly did not want to stand up the rest of the way. She had just spent her entire day working in a department store, tailoring and pressing clothes for white people, and now she was being told that she had no rights.

"Look, woman, I told you I wanted the seat. Are you going to stand up?" Blake said. Finally Rosa Parks spoke. "No," she said. Then Blake warned her, "If you don't stand up, I'm going to have you arrested." She told him to go right ahead, but she was not going to move.

Blake got off the bus and went to phone the police, thereby involuntarily entering the nation's history books.

Parks continued to sit. In so doing, she became the first prominent figure of what became the movement. Perhaps the most interesting thing about her was how ordinary she was, almost the prototype of the black women who toiled so hard and had so little to show for it. She had not, she later explained, thought about getting arrested that day. Later the stunned white leaders of Montgomery repeatedly charged that Parks' refusal was part of a carefully orchestrated plan on the part of the local NAACP, of which she was an officer. But that was not true. What she did represented one person's exhaustion with a system that dehumanized all black people. Something inside her finally snapped.

Soon two Montgomery policemen arrived. Was it true that the driver had asked her to get up? they asked. Yes, she said. Why hadn't she obeyed? She felt she shouldn't have to. "Why do you push us around?" she asked. One of the policemen answered, "I don't know, but the law is the law, and you're under arrest." Only then did she get up. The police took Parks to jail, where she was charged with violating the city's segregation laws. She was allowed one phone call, and she called her home. She was the first person ever so charged—the first of many tactical mistakes on the part of city officials, for it gave the local black community the case on which to hang a lawsuit.

After her phone call home, the news of her arrest spread quickly through the black community. E. D. Nixon, the head of the local NAACP and Parks' friend, called the police station to find out what had happened. He was told it was none of his business. So he telephoned a local activist who said he would post bond.

E. D. Nixon was a Pullman car porter, a union man, and a powerful presence in the black community. He was not displeased by what had happened. This was the case he had been looking for. Mrs. Parks was the perfect defendant: She had worked with him in the NAACP for twelve years, and he knew she was a strong, confident person. If she said she was going to do something, she did it.

That night Nixon talked to Rosa Parks and her family. He badly wanted to use her case to test the constitutionality of the bus law. Would she agree, he asked, to be a test case? The idea frightened Raymond Parks, her husband, a local barber who knew the violence that traditionally awaited those blacks foolhardy enough to challenge the system. He warned her, "Oh, the white folks will kill you, Rosa. Don't do anything to make trouble." She was torn. She did not want to put her family at risk, but neither did she want the younger black people who came after her to face such indignities. Nor did she want to face them anymore herself.

"If you think we can get anywhere with it, I'll go along with it," she told Nixon.

Nixon went home and sketched a map of Montgomery—where blacks lived and where they worked. The distances between them were not, he decided, insurmountable. "You know what?" he told his wife.

"What?" she asked.

"We're going to boycott the buses," he said.

In Montgomery the majority of bus riders were black, particularly black women who went across town, from a world of black poverty to white affluence, to work as domestics. Nevertheless, a black challenge to the bus company was a formidable undertaking. Despite the earlier ruling of the Supreme Court, the Deep South remained totally segregated. Whites held complete political, judicial, and psychological power. In a city like Montgomery it was as if the Court had not ruled on *Brown.*

Before the whites would take the blacks seriously, the blacks had to take themselves seriously—that was the task facing the black leadership of Montgomery in December 1955. One of their great problems was the terrible divisions within the black leadership itself—by religion, by generation, by age, by class. There was no doubt that Ed Nixon was a forceful figure, willing on many occasions to take risks that few others would; but some felt that he was too abrasive, too eager for glory, and not sensitive enough to others.

At the first organizational meeting, held the day after Parks was arrested, there was quick agreement on the need for a one-day boycott, starting on Monday morning. There was also a decision to hold a meeting of the black leadership, which included many ministers, on Monday afternoon, and a large public protest meeting was set for Monday night.

At the Monday afternoon meeting one of the ministers suggested that future meetings be secret, closed to the press, so that the whites would know as little as possible about what they were doing and who their leaders were. Meetings closed to the press! Ed Nixon got up and began to taunt them. "How in hell are you going to have protest meetings without letting the white folks know?" he began. Then he reminded them that those being hurt were the black women of the city, the most powerless of the powerless, the domestics who went off every day to work for whites. These were the people who suffered the greatest pain from segregation and made up the core of every black church in town. "Let me tell you gentlemen one thing. You ministers have lived off the sweat of these washwomen all these years and you have never done anything for them," he said. "I am just ashamed of you. You said that God has called you to lead the people and now you are gone to pieces because the man tells you that the newspapers will be here and your picture might come out in the newspaper. If you the preachers are not the leaders then we will have to pray that God will send us more leaders."

That ringing assault contained all too much truth. It was a young minister named Martin Luther King, Jr., who answered Nixon and said that he was not a coward, that they should act in the open. With that, the Reverend Dr. King had at once taken a strong position for the boycott, but he had also shown he was not completely Nixon's man. Before the meeting was over, Martin Luther King, Jr., was named president of the new group, to be called the Montgomery Improvement Association. It was not a role he sought—he was new in town, had a young family, and wanted first and foremost to do a good job at his first church.

But with a certain inevitability the movement sought him. He was a brilliant speaker. He had the ability to make complex ideas simple. He could expand an idea, blending the rational with the emotional. That gave him the great ability to move others—blacks at first and soon, remarkably enough, whites as well. He could reach people of all classes and backgrounds; he could inspire men and women with nothing but his words.

On the first day of the boycott, the Holt Street Baptist Church was filled by late afternoon, and a crowd estimated at between 6000 and 10,000 gathered in the street to hear the meeting broadcast over loudspeakers. That night the black people of Montgomery got their first taste of Martin King's oratory. He started out by making one point clear: their action was different from those of the White Citizens' Councils, which were using the threat of violence to stop black political and legal progress in the Deep South. "Now, let us say that we are not here advocating violence. We have overcome that. I want it to be known throughout Montgomery and throughout the nation that we are a Christian people. The only weapon that we have in our hands this evening is the weapon of protest." They were nothing less than ordinary Americans, he was saying, seeking the most ordinary of American rights in a democracy they loved as much as white people loved it. They were, in effect, setting out to make America whole. "If we are wrong, the Constitution of the United States is wrong. If we are wrong, God Almighty is wrong. If we are wrong, Jesus of Nazareth was merely a utopian dreamer and never came down to earth! If we are wrong, justice is a lie." By then the crowd was with him, cheering each incantation. "And we are determined here in Montgomery to work and fight until justice runs down like water and righteousness like a mighty stream." When it was over, it was clear that the right man had arrived in the right city at the right time; this would be no one-day boycott, but one that would continue until the white community addressed black grievances.

That the black ministry at this moment was to produce an exceptional generation of leaders—of whom King was merely the most visible—was not surprising. It was the obvious repository for black talent at that time. There were not a lot of black lawyers around in those days, and the usual political avenues were blocked in the Deep South. Therefore, the new black ministry was where talented young black men went to learn how to lead their people. It was outside the reach of the white community, a rare place where a young, well-educated black man could rise by merit alone.

When the bus boycott began, Martin Luther King, Jr., was twenty-six years old. He was a black Brahmin, working toward a doctorate in theology, a symbol of the new, more confident, better-educated black leaders now just beginning to appear in the postwar South. His father, Martin Luther King, Sr., known as Daddy King, was pastor of the Ebenezer Baptist Church, a prosperous black church in Atlanta. Martin Luther King, Jr., the second of three children, grew up in a gentle environment, a member of the black elite of Atlanta, loved and secure. Years later James Baldwin wrote that King lacked the self-doubts that burdened most blacks of their generation. "Martin," Baldwin wrote, "never went around fighting himself the way the rest of us did."

To the white leadership in Montgomery, Martin King was just another faceless preacher, surely ignorant. Indeed, in the early days of the boycott the whites kept calling him Preacher King, as if by denying him his proper title, they could diminish him. They had no idea how to deal with him.

When the boycott proved to be remarkably successful on the first day, the mayor of Montgomery, W. A. Gayle, did not sense that something historic was taking place, nor did he move to accommodate the blacks, who were in fact not asking for integrated buses, but merely a minimal level of courtesy and a fixed line between the sections. Gayle turned to a friend and said, "Comes the first rainy day and the Negroes will be back on the buses." Soon it did rain, but the boycott continued. A month after the boycott began, it was so successful that the bus-line operators were asking for permission to double the price from ten to twenty cents a ride. They were granted a five-cent raise.

The mayor was petulant. "No other city in the South of our size has treated the Negroes more fairly," he said. Now he wanted his fellow whites to be made of sterner stuff and to stop helping their maids and workers to get to work by giving them transportation money and, worse, giving them rides.

The Montgomery authorities stopped the local black cabdrivers from ferrying people to and from work in groups of five and six for ten cents a ride (there was an old city ordinance that said the minimum fare for a ride had to be forty-five cents), but money poured in from the outside to buy some fifteen new station wagons. Eventually the Montgomery Improvement Association had some thirty cars of its own.

Inevitably, the city leaders resorted to what had always worked in the past: the use of police power. The city fathers decided that they had to break the back of the carpool, and soon the police started arresting carpool drivers. On January 26, 1956, some eight weeks into the boycott, Martin Luther King, Jr., was arrested for driving thirty miles an hour in a twenty-five-mile-an-hour zone. He was taken to the police station and fingerprinted. At first it appeared that he would be kept overnight, but because the crowd of blacks outside the station kept growing larger and noisier, the police let King go on his own recognizance. Two days later King's house was bombed by a white extremist, the first in a series of such incidents at the homes of black leaders and at black churches.

In unity and nonviolence the blacks found new strength, particularly as the nation began to take notice. Things that had for so long terrified them—the idea of being arrested and spending the night in prison, for example—became a badge of honor. Their purpose now was greater than their terror.

King was, in effect, taking a crash course in the uses of modern media and proving a fast learner. Montgomery was becoming a big story, and the longer it went on, the bigger it became. In the past it had been within the power of such papers as the *Advertiser* and its afternoon twin, the far more racist Alabama *Journal*, either to grant or not grant coverage to black protests and to slant the coverage in terms most satisfying to the whites. But that power deserted the local newspapers now because they no longer had a monopoly on news. Just a year earlier, on Christmas Day, 1954, WSFA-TV had gone on the air. The news director—and star reporter as well—was a young man from

Oklahoma named Frank McGee, then in his early thirties. He was in fact a very good reporter, and he immediately decided that the bus boycott was a very big story. Unlike his local print counterparts, he did not take the protest as a social affront. Rather, he realized it was the kind of high drama that lent itself exceptionally well to television. That was particularly true as the whites blindly continued to resist and the story continued to escalate.

The NBC network news show, also still in its infancy, started to use McGee with increasing regularity on the network, with a direct feed from Montgomery. It was not only a good story, in which ordinary Americans were asserting their demands for the most basic civil rights, but it was also helping Frank McGee's career. (Within a year of the bus settlement, he became one of NBC's first national network correspondents.)

Soon Montgomery was flooded with members of the national press. The more coverage there was, the more witnesses there were and the harder it was for the white leadership to inflict

Right: Martin Luther King, Jr., was a young minister when the Montgomery bus boycott began. Below: Rosa Parks' refusal to give up her seat touched off the boycott. Here, a year after the boycott began, she at last sits in the front of a bus.

physical violence upon the blacks. In addition, the more coverage there was, the more it gave courage to the leadership and its followers. Everyone sensed that the country and the world were now taking notice.

The sympathies of the national press corps were not with the mayor of Montgomery, or with police commissioner Clyde Sellers, who said, "I wouldn't trade my Southern birthright for 100 Negro votes." Rather, the national reporters were impressed with the dignity of Rosa Parks and the seriousness of the young Martin King.

Ironically, it was the white leaders of Montgomery who first helped to create the singular importance of Martin King. They needed a villain, and if they could weaken, discredit, or scare him, then their problems would be solved, they thought. Gradually he became the focal point of the boycott. "I have the feeling," Bayard Rustin, the nation's most experienced civil rights organizer, told him at the time, "that the Lord has laid his hands on you, and that is a dangerous, dangerous thing."

For a time, the role was almost too much for King. The amount of hate mail was staggering, and it was filled with threats that he had to take seriously. His father pleaded with him to leave Montgomery and return to Atlanta. "It's better to be a live dog than a dead lion," Daddy King said. His son realized for the first time how sheltered his existence had been, how ill prepared he was to deal with the racial violence that was waiting just beneath the surface in the South.

The boycott continued. In late February the white leadership cited an obscure state law prohibiting boycotts and indicted eighty-nine leaders, including twenty-four ministers and all the drivers of the carpools. The real target, however, was King. He happened to be in Nashville lecturing when the indictments were announced. Back in Montgomery, many of the other leaders were giving themselves up in groups to show their defiance. King flew back to Montgomery by way of Atlanta. In Atlanta, his father pleaded with him not to go back. "They gon' to kill my boy," he told the Atlanta police chief. But Martin Luther King, Jr., was firm. Not to return, to desert his friends at this point, would be the height of cowardice, he told them. "I have begun the struggle," he said, "and I can't turn back. I have reached the point of no return." At that point his father broke down and began to sob.

On November 13, 1956, almost a year after the boycott had begun, King went to court to defend himself and the carpools against the local authorities, who had declared the boycott "a public nuisance." King was hardly optimistic about the outcome in a Montgomery court, but suddenly, during a recess, an AP reporter handed him a note that included an AP bulletin reporting that the Supreme Court had judged the Montgomery bus-segregation law to be unconstitutional. The blacks had won. King, always aware of the need to be magnanimous in victory, spoke at a mass rally to point out this should not be viewed as a victory of blacks over whites but as a victory for American justice and democracy.

On December 21 the city prepared to desegregate its buses. An empty bus pulled up to a corner near Dr. King's home. Martin Luther King, Jr., boarded it. The white driver smiled at him and said, "I believe you are Reverend King." "Yes, I am," Martin Luther King, Jr., said. "We are glad to have you with us this morning," the driver said.

So the battle was won. But the war was hardly over.

# CHAPTER THIRTEEN

THE Supreme Court ruling on *Brown* v. *Board of Education,* which occurred in the middle of the decade, was the first important break between the older, more staid America that existed at the start of the era and the new, fast-paced, tumultuous America that saw the decade's end. The second was Elvis Presley. In cultural terms his coming was nothing less than the start of a revolution. "Elvis Presley," said Leonard Bernstein, the distinguished American composer and conductor, "is the greatest cultural force in the twentieth century. He changed everything—music, language, clothes, it's a whole new social revolution. Because of him a man like me barely knows his musical grammar anymore." Or as John Lennon, one of Elvis' admirers, once said, "Before Elvis there was nothing."

If he was a revolutionary, then he was an accidental one, an innately talented young man who arrived at the right place at the right time. He had no political interests at all, and though his music symbolized the coming together of black and white cultures in the mainstream in a way that had never happened before, that seemed to hold little interest for him. What he really wanted from the start was to go to Hollywood and be a movie star like James Dean or Marlon Brando, a rebel up on the screen. If he would never rival Brando and Dean as a movie actor, he learned from them one critical lesson: never to smile. That was the key to their success, he was sure. He was also sure he could manage the same kind of sultry good looks they had. As a teenager, he spent hours in front of a mirror working on that look, and he used it to maximum effect later, in his own appearances.

Sam Phillips, Memphis recording man, enthusiast of black music, had been looking for years for someone like Elvis—a white boy who could sing like a black boy. Elvis Presley walked into Phillips' studio in the summer of 1953. He had been sent there by another talent scout, who had not wanted anything to do with him—or with those awful pegged pants, the pink and black clothes. He was an odd mixture of a hood—the haircut, the clothes, the sullen, alienated look—and a sweet little boy—curiously gentle and respectful, indeed willing and anxious to try whatever anyone wanted. Everyone was sir or ma'am. Few young Americans, before or after, have looked so rebellious and been so polite.

Sam Phillips immediately liked Presley's early greaser style. "And the sideburns, I liked that too. Everyone in town thought *I* was weird, and here was this kid and he was as weird as I was," Phillips recalled. He listened to Presley a few times and was sure that Elvis had some kind of special talent, but he just wasn't sure what it was. Elvis was not a particularly good guitar picker, but there was a sound almost buried in there that was distinctive. He sang everything: white, black, gospel, country, crooners.

Phillips called Scotty Moore, an electric-guitar player, and Bill Black, a bassist, to work with Elvis. They were to try to bring forth whatever it was that was there. After a few weeks of working together, the three of them went to Phillips' studio to record. Phillips by chance entered the date in his log: July 5, 1954. For a time, the session did not go particularly well. Elvis' voice was good, but it was too sweet, thought Phillips. Then Elvis started picking on a piece by a famed black bluesman named Arthur Crudup—"That's All Right, Mama." Suddenly Elvis Presley let go: he was playing and jumping around in the studio like all the gospel singers, black and white, he had watched onstage. Soon his two sidemen joined him. "What the hell are you doing?" Phillips asked. Scotty Moore said he didn't know. "Well, find out real quick and don't lose it," Phillips said. They turned it into a record. Having covered a black blues singer for one side, it seemed only fitting to use Presley's version of bluegrass singer Bill Monroe's "Blue Moon of Kentucky" on the other.

Phillips was sure the record was a winner, and he sent it to a local disc jockey named Dewey Phillips (no relation), who had a show called *Red, Hot and Blue*, on WHBQ. He was very big with the young white kids—Elvis himself had listened faithfully to him almost every night since he was fourteen years old. Dewey Phillips played traditional white artists all the time, but just as regularly he played the great black singers, blues and gospel.

Dewey agreed to play Elvis' first disc. The night he did, Elvis was so nervous that he went to a movie by himself. The two songs were such a success that all Dewey Phillips did that night was flip the record back and forth. The switchboard started lighting up immediately. Finally the disc jockey decided he wanted to interview Elvis on the air, and he called Sam Phillips and told him to bring the boy in. The Presleys did not have a phone, but Sam called over to their neighbors and they got Elvis' mother. Gladys and Vernon Presley had to go looking for their elusive son in the movie theater. "Mama, what's happening?" he asked. "Plenty, son," she answered, "but it's all good."

Off they went to the station. There he was introduced to Dewey Phillips, who was going to interview him. "Mr. Phillips," he said. "I don't know nothin' about being interviewed." "Just don't say nothing dirty," Phillips said.

AFTER Elvis Presley's sensational debut on Dewey Phillips' show, his career skyrocketed. He was what first the region and then the nation wanted: a white boy to explode into the beat, to capture it for the whites. The success spread steadily. Deejays in Texas picked up on it, and soon after that, Elvis was making regular appearances on the *Louisiana Hayride,* which was second only to the *Grand Ole Opry* as a showcase of country white talent. He began traveling the South with a company of country musicians headlined by Hank Snow. But almost overnight he became the star of the touring group, something that did not escape the attention of Colonel Tom Parker, Snow's manager. Parker, it appeared, though he did not own Presley's contract, was encouraging the large companies to move in and buy the contract from Sam Phillips, who lacked the resources to promote and sustain a major success. The colonel had friends at RCA, the traditional recording powerhouse. When the negotiations were over, Sam Phillips had $35,000 and Elvis was the property of RCA.

Presley's timing was nearly perfect. In 1954 a white musician named Bill Haley did a version of "Shake, Rattle, and Roll." By the summer of 1955 it was number one on the white chart and number four on the rhythm-and-blues (or black) chart. In that same year Chuck Berry brought out "Maybellene," which was the first successful assault on the main chart by a black musician; "Maybellene" went to the top of the rhythm-and-blues chart and went to number five on the white chart. The crossover was in full force. Parents might disapprove of the beat and of their children listening to what they *knew* was black music, but it did not matter. Elvis Presley and rock music were *happening*.

A new young generation of Americans was breaking away from the habits of its parents and defining itself by its music. There was nothing the parents could do. This new generation was armed with both money and the new inexpensive appliances with which to listen to the music. In the early fifties a series of technological breakthroughs brought small transistorized radios that sold for twenty-five to fifty dollars. Soon an Elvis Presley–model record player was selling for $47.95.

This was the new, wealthier America. Elvis Presley began to make it in 1955, after ten years of rare broad-based middle-class prosperity. Among the principal beneficiaries of that prosperity were the teenagers. They had almost no memory of the Depression and the world war that followed it. There was no instinct on their part to save. In the past when American teenagers had made money, their earnings, more often than not, had gone to help support their parents or had been saved for one treasured and long-desired purchase, like a baseball glove or a bike.

But now, as the new middle class emerged in the country, it was creating as a by-product a brand-new consuming class. *Scholastic* magazine's Institute of Student Opinion showed that by early 1956 there were 13 million teenagers in the country. The average teenager, the magazine said, had an income of $10.55 a week. That figure seemed remarkable at the time; it was close to what the average American family had had in disposable income, after all essential bills were paid, fifteen years earlier.

For the first time in American life the young were becoming a separate, defined part of the culture. Because they had money, they were a market, and because they were a market, they were listened to and catered to. Elvis was the first beneficiary. In effect, he was entering millions of American homes on the sly; if the parents had had their way, he would most assuredly have been barred.

Certainly Ed Sullivan would have liked to keep him out. Ed Sullivan hosted *The Toast of the Town,* the most successful variety show in America on this strange new piece of turf called network television. Broadcast at eight p.m. on Sundays—an hour when families were likely to gather together—Sullivan's show provided a pleasant, safe blend of acts, including some performers of exceptional talent. In addition, there seemed to be a guarantee that nothing would happen that was at all threatening. Sullivan was, after all, involved in the most delicate business imaginable—selecting acts to perform live in millions of American living rooms, a place where no one had ever performed before. There was something for everyone, and Sullivan made sure that there was always one act for the children.

Sullivan himself was shrewd enough to minimize his own appearances, since his style was widely perceived as being exceptionally wooden. He would introduce a number, get off the stage, and reappear in time to lead the applause. "Let's hear it for . . ." he would say, and then give the name of the act. Once, after Sergio Franchi had sung the Lord's Prayer, Sullivan turned to his audience and said, "Let's hear it for the Lord's Prayer."

In 1956 his show was at the exact center of American mass culture, and he wanted no part of Elvis Presley, who was now enraging ministers and parent groups by dint of his onstage gyrations and the overt sexuality of his music.

Earlier, as Elvis conquered the South with regional appearances, he had begun to perfect his act. Some of it was natural instinct—he had to carry a beat, and it was hard to carry a beat while standing still. So he began to gyrate as he had seen endless gospel singers gyrate. The first time he had done it, he had been driven by pure instinct, and the

Elvis stepped up to a microphone, strummed his guitar, swiveled his hips— and America's music was never the same.

crowd began to shout. From then on, it became part of his act; if you were going to do a live show, he explained, you had to have an act. That's what people came to see. Otherwise they could just as well stay at home and play records.

A country singer named Bob Luman once said of an early Elvis concert, "This cat came out in a coat and a pink shirt and socks and he had this sneer on his face and he stood behind the mike for five minutes, I'll bet, before he made a move. Then he hit his guitar a lick and he broke two strings. I'd been playing for ten years and I hadn't broken a total of two strings. So there he was, these two strings dangling, and he hadn't done anything yet, and these high school girls were screaming and fainting and running up to the stage and then he started to move his hips real slow like he had a thing for his guitar."

The teenyboppers started to maul him. They did not mean him any harm, Luman explained. What they wanted "was pieces of you for souvenirs." By the end of 1955 RCA was ready to push his records nationally, and he had signed to do four Saturday night shows on a Jackie Gleason production called *Stage Show.* He got $1250 a show for the Gleason appearances, plus, of course, national exposure. Gleason knew exactly what was happening. "He's a guitar-playing Marlon Brando," he said. Only part of what worked for Elvis was the music, Gleason knew. It was also the movement and the style. And a great deal of it was the look—sultry, alienated, a little misunderstood, the rebel who wanted to rebel without ever leaving home. He was perfect because he was the safe rebel. He never intended to cause trouble— he was a classic mama's boy. Gladys Presley had barely let him out of her sight until he was in high school. Now finally on the threshold of great success, he used his royalties in that first year to buy three new homes, each larger than the last, for his parents. He also gave each of his parents a new Cadillac, though the one he gave his mother never got license plates, since she did not drive.

By 1956 he had become both a national celebrity and a national issue. His success, amplified as it was by the newfound wealth of the nation and the new technology of radio, record players, and, finally, television, defied the imagination. His record of "Hound Dog" sold 2 million copies, and "Don't Be Cruel" sold 3 million. His singles were not merely taking off, they were defying traditional musical categories: "Heartbreak Hotel" was number one on the white chart, number one on the country chart, and number five on the rhythm-and-blues chart; "Don't Be Cruel" and "Hound Dog" became number one on all three charts. In April 1956 he was selling $75,000 worth of records a day.

That month he made a rather sedate appearance on *The Milton Berle Show,* and in June, Berle had him back. This time Elvis cut loose, causing an immense number of protests about the vulgarity of his act. Ed Sullivan announced that Presley's act was so suggestive that it would never go on his show. Within three weeks Sullivan had to change his mind. His competition, *The Steve Allen Show,* booked Presley for July 1. It was the first time Steve Allen had beaten Ed Sullivan in the ratings. Sullivan signed Elvis for $50,000 to do three shows. It was a figure then unheard of.

The battle was over. Ed Sullivan had conceded, and the new music had entered the mainstream of American culture. Sullivan was pleased; Elvis' ratings were extraordinary. Sullivan also wanted to make clear that he had not lowered America's morals. "I want to say to Elvis Presley and the country that this is a real decent, fine boy," he told his audience after the third show. "We've never had a pleasanter experience on our show with a big name than we've had with you. You're thoroughly all right." It was the deftest of surrenders; it appeared to be the generous speech of a man receiving a surrender, while in fact it was the speech of a man who had just surrendered himself. Market economics had won. The old order had been challenged and had not held. New forces were at work, driven by technology. The young did not have to listen to their parents anymore.

# CHAPTER FOURTEEN

I N THE home, it was to be a new, even easier age—the good life without sweat. "Never before so much for so few," wrote *Life* magazine in 1954. It was in fact an astonishing age of abundance, an age of wondrous kitchen and household aids, ever bigger, but not ever more expensive, as in the auto industry. The very success of the item meant that the price kept coming down: consumers were buying more for less.

If there was one figure who came to symbolize the dazzling new American kitchen and all its astonishing appliances, as well as the revolution in selling and advertising that was taking place, it was Betty Furness—the Lady from Westinghouse.

Her chief asset was that she was attractive, but not in a way that made women jealous. Men liked her looks, but even more important, women, the prime targets of these commercials, liked her too. She came across like the women portrayed in photos and ads in women's magazines—bright, upbeat and confident, and modern without looking too glamorous. She was the all-American wife in the all-American kitchen. She could handle anything in this sparkling new workplace that promised to make household chores, if not downright obsolete, at least easy.

The sale of Westinghouse appliances boomed, and there was no doubt that there was a connection with this pleasant, attractive woman's appearances as the Westinghouse hostess. "You can be sure if it's Westinghouse," she said at the end of each commercial, and it became her trademark.

The power that Betty Furness had as a commercial symbol for Westinghouse was a reflection of the growing power of television as a vehicle for advertising and also of the growing power of advertising in American life. For the fifties was a decade that revolutionized Madison Avenue. At the turn of the century, the home had been a reasonably safe haven from the purveyors of goods (partly because there was so little disposable income). Radio advertising had been clever and deft, and had greatly expanded the possibilities for reaching the consumer, but television opened up the field even more dramatically and offered a vast array of new techniques, from the subtle and sophisticated to hammering away with a brief, repetitive message. "We discovered," said BBD&O's Rosser Reeves, "that this was no tame kitten; we had a ferocious man-eating tiger. We could take the same advertising campaign from print or radio and put it on TV, and even when there were very few sets, sales would go through the roof." The speed with which television's power ascended awed even those who prophesied it: in 1949 Madison Avenue's total television billings were $12.3 million; the next year they jumped to $40.8 million; and the year after that they jumped to $128 million.

Television, of course, could do what radio never could, for it was visual. "Show the product," said Ben Duffy, one of the men who was writing the rules even as he learned them, "and show it in use." Many advertisers did that and more: a Remington razor shaved the fuzz off a peach, as Stephen Fox noted in *The Mirror Makers,* and a Band-Aid was used to show it was strong enough to lift an egg.

It was a salesman's dream. The nation had not only been wired to sell but it had been wired to sell through pictures, going right into the home. It was, Rosser Reeves said, like "shooting fish in a barrel."

IN ALL of this, no one was paying very close attention to what the new home-oriented, seemingly drudgery-free life was doing to the psyche of American women. The pictures of them on television and in magazines showed them as relentlessly happy—liberated from endless household tasks by wondrous new machines they had just bought. Since the photos showed them happy, and since there was no doubt that there were more and better household appliances every year, it was presumed that they were in fact happy. That was one of the more interesting questions of the era. The great migration to the well-applianced home of the suburbs reflected a number of profound trends taking place in the society, not the least important of which was the changing role of women, particularly middle-class women. Up until then during this century women had made fairly constant progress in the spheres of politics, education, and employment opportunities. That trend came to a stunning halt in the years after the war. In the postwar years the sheer affluence of the country meant that many families could now live a middle-class existence on only one income. In addition, the migration to the suburbs physically separated women from the workplace. The new culture of consumerism told women they should be homemakers and saw them merely as potential buyers for all the new washers and dryers, freezers, floor waxers, pressure cookers, and blenders.

At this particular moment it was impossible to underestimate the importance and influence of the women's magazines—*Ladies' Home Journal, Redbook, McCall's,* and *Mademoiselle*—on middle-class young women. Isolated in the suburbs, they felt uneasy and lonely and largely without guidance. In an age before the coming of midday television talk shows largely designed for housewives, women's magazines made up the core reading material for suburban wives. If the magazines' staffs at the lower rungs consisted mostly of women, the magazines were almost always edited by men. In addition, editorial content, much more than in most general-circulation magazines, echoed the thrust of the advertising. If the advertising was designed to let women know what the newest appliances were and how to use them, then the accompanying articles were designed to show that

"You can be sure if it's Westinghouse," Betty Furness promised us.

Betty Friedan and daughter, Emily. Later Friedan would write *The Feminine Mystique*—and launch the feminist movement.

women could not live up to their destinies without them.

The ideal that fifties women were to strive for was articulated by *McCall's* in 1954: togetherness. A family was as one; its ambitions were twined. The husband was designated leader and hero, out there every day braving the treacherous corporate world to win a better life for his family; the wife was his mainstay on the domestic side, duly appreciative of the immense sacrifices being made for her and her children. There was no divergence within. A family was a single perfect universe—instead of a complicated, fragile mechanism of conflicting political and emotional pulls. Families portrayed in women's magazines exhibited no conflicts or contradictions or unfulfilled ambitions. Thanks, probably, to the drive for togetherness, the new homes all seemed to have what was called a family room. Here the family came together, ate, watched television, and possibly even talked.

And who was responsible ultimately for togetherness if not the wife? "The two big steps that women must take are to help their husbands decide where they are going and use their pretty heads to help them get there," wrote Mrs. Dale Carnegie, wife of one of the nation's leading experts on how to be likable, in the April 1955 *Better Homes and Gardens*. Those women who were not happy and did not feel fulfilled were encouraged to think that the fault was theirs and that they were the exception to blissful normality.

ONE of the first women to challenge the fallacy of universal contentment among young suburban wives was a young woman from the heartland of the country. Born and reared in Peoria, Illinois, she entered the elite Smith College in 1939, finding there everything she had longed for, a world where women were rewarded for being smart and different instead of being punished for it. She graduated in 1942, summa cum laude, full of optimism about the future even though the war was still going on. Several scholarships for graduate work were offered her. Ambitious, admired by her classmates, Betty Goldstein was certain that she would lead a life dramatically different from her mother's. But at graduation time Betty Goldstein turned down the scholarships because she was interested in a young man; since he had not been offered a comparable scholarship, she was afraid it would tear their relationship apart if she accepted hers. That decision, she later wrote, turned her instantly into a cliché. Looking back on her life, Betty Goldstein Friedan, one of the first voices of the feminist movement, noted that the young man's face was more quickly forgotten than the terms of the scholarships themselves.

Instead of getting married, she moved to the exciting intellectual world of Greenwich Village and became part of a group of liberal young people involved in labor issues and civil rights—before it was fashionable. When the war was over, she met a young veteran named Carl Friedan, who seemed funny and charming, and in 1947 they were married. In 1949 they had their first child.

Ms. Friedan soon found herself part of the great suburban migration as she and her family moved to larger and larger houses in the suburbs. As that happened, she was cut off from what she had been, first physically and then increasingly intellectually and socially as well. Betty Friedan now poured her energy into being a housewife and mother, into furnishing the houses and shopping, cooking, and cleaning for her family.

In some ways her life was full, she would later decide, and in some ways it was quite empty. She liked being a mother, and she liked her friends, but she worried that she had not lived up to her potential. She began to write freelance for women's magazines. It was a sign that while the domestic side of her life was rich, it was not rich enough.

Her early articles—"Millionaire's Wife" (*Cosmopolitan,* September 1956), "Two Are an Island" (*Mademoiselle,* July 1955), and "Day Camp in the Driveways" (*Parents',* May 1957)—were not the achievements she had had in mind when she left Smith.

Then something happened that changed her life. As she and two friends were planning to return to Smith for their fifteenth reunion, in 1957, they were asked to do a report on what had happened to the members of their class of '42. She made up a questionnaire and got an assignment from *McCall's* to pay for her time. The piece was to be called "The Togetherness Woman." The questions were: What difficulties have you found in working out your role as a woman? What are the chief satisfactions and frustrations of your life today? How have you changed inside? What do you wish you had done differently? The answers stunned her. She had tapped into a great reservoir of doubt, frustration, anxiety, and resentment. The women felt unfulfilled and isolated with their children; they often viewed their husbands as visitors from a far more exciting world.

The project also emphasized Friedan's own frustrations. All those years trying to be a good wife and mother suddenly seemed wasted; it had been wrong to suppress her feelings rather than to deal with them. The surprise was that there were thousands of women like her out there.

As she wrote later in her book *The Feminine Mystique,* "It was a strange stirring, a yearning that women suffered in the middle of the twentieth century in the United States. Each suburban wife struggled with it alone. As she made the beds, shopped for groceries, matched slip cover materials, ate peanut butter sandwiches with her children, lay beside her husband at night, she was afraid to ask of herself the silent question—'Is this all?' "

As she walked around the Smith campus during her reunion, she had been struck by the passivity of the young women of the class of 1957. When Ms. Friedan asked these young women about their futures, they regarded her with blank looks. They were going to get married and have children, of course. She thought, This is happening at Smith, a place where I found nothing but intellectual excitement when I was their age. Something had gotten deep into the bloodstream of this generation, she decided.

She left and started to write the piece for *McCall's,* but it turned out very different from the one she had intended to write. It reflected the despair and depression she had found among her contemporaries, and it was critical of women who lived through their husbands and children. *McCall's,* the inventor of "togetherness," not surprisingly turned it down. She sent it to *Ladies' Home Journal,* where it was so rewritten that it seemed to make the opposite points, and she pulled it. That left *Redbook,* where Bob Stein, an old friend, worked. He turned it down and called her agent. "Look," he said over the phone. "Only the most neurotic housewife would identify with this."

She was, she realized later, challenging the magazines themselves.

She was saying that it was wrong to mislead women to think they should feel one way when in fact they often felt quite differently. She had discovered a crisis of considerable proportions, and these magazines would only deny it.

Suddenly she envisioned "The Togetherness Woman" as a book. She called George Brockway, an editor at Norton publishing, and he seemed delighted with the idea.

The economics of publishing were significantly different from those of magazines. Books were not dependent upon ads; they were dependent upon ideas, and the more provocative the idea, the more attention and, often, the better the sales. Brockway knew there had already been a number of attacks on conformity in American society, particularly as it affected men. Here was an attack that would talk about its effect on women. He was impressed by Ms. Friedan. She was focused and, to his mind, wildly ambitious.

She told Brockway she would finish it in a year; instead, it took five years. Later she wrote that no one—not her husband, her editor, or anyone who knew her—thought she would ever finish it. She did so while taking care of three children. She later described herself as being like all the other mothers in suburbia, where she "hid, like secret drinking in the morning, the book I was writing when my suburban neighbors came for coffee."

Her research was prodigious. Three days a week she went to the New York Public Library for research. The chief villains, she decided, were the women's magazines. What stunned her was the fact that this had not always been true. In the same magazines in the late thirties and forties, there had been a sense of women moving steadily into the male professional world; then women's magazines had created a very different kind of role model—of a career woman who knew how to take care of herself and who could make it on her own.

But starting around 1949, these magazines changed dramatically. It was as if someone had thrown a giant switch. The new woman did not exist on her own. She was seen only in the light of supporting her husband and his career and caring for the children.

The more Ms. Friedan investigated, the more she found that the world created in the magazines and the television sitcoms was, for many women at least, a fantasy world. Despite all the confidence and happiness among women portrayed in the magazines, there was underneath it all a crisis in the suburbs. It was the crisis of a generation of women who had left college with high idealism and who had come to feel increasingly frustrated.

Nor, she found, did all the marvelous new appliances truly lighten the load of the housewife. If anything, they seemed to extend it—there was some kind of Parkinson's Law at work here: The more timesaving machines there were, the more things there were to do with them. She had stumbled across something that a number of others, primarily psychiatrists, had noticed: a certain emotional malaise, bordering on depression, among many women of the era. One psychiatrist called it the housewife's blight. No one wrote about it in popular magazines, certainly not in the monthly women's magazines.

So, gathering material over several years, she began to write a book that would come out in 1963, not as *The Togetherness Woman,* but as *The Feminine Mystique.* She was approaching forty as she began, but she was regenerated by the importance of the project; it seemed to give her her own life back. The result was a seminal book on what had happened to women in America. It started selling slowly, but word of it grew and grew, and eventually, with 3 million copies in print, it became a handbook for the new feminist movement that was gradually beginning to come together.

# CHAPTER FIFTEEN

Iᴺ 1956 ᴛʜᴇ most surprising book on the best-seller list was *Peyton Place* by Grace Metalious, a young woman who had never published a word before. It was brought out in hardcover by Julian Messner, a small publisher, and went on to become the third best-selling hardcover novel of the year. *Peyton Place* was such a phenomenon that the title entered the language as a generic term for all the small towns that appeared placid on the surface but underneath were filled with dark secrets, most of them sexual. In her book Metalious tore away the staid façade of Peyton Place/Gilmanton, New Hampshire, to reveal a hotbed of lust and sexual intrigue. "To a tourist these towns look as peaceful as a postcard," Ms. Metalious told Hal Boyle of The Associated Press in an early interview. "But if you go beneath that picture, it's like turning over a rock with your foot—all kinds of strange things crawl out. Everybody who lives in town knows what's going on—there are no secrets—but they don't want outsiders to know."

Indeed, the principal occupation of *Peyton Place* seemed not so much farming or working in the town's textile factory but gossiping; people there not only led secret lives, they devoted most of their waking hours to sitting around and talking about them—at least about everyone else's.

Constance MacKenzie, the prim, attractive young widow who ran the town's dress shop, dreaded the idea that people might learn that in her brief time in New York she had an affair with a married man, who was the father of her daughter. Another local girl was sexually assaulted and impregnated by her sinister stepfather, and the kindly local doctor decided to save the young girl's reputation by disguising an abortion as an emergency appendectomy.

If there ever was a book that reflected the changing nature of the American book business as it changed to the new high-powered world of paperbacks from the more genteel old-fashioned world of hardcover publishing, it was *Peyton Place*. Published as a paperback in the fall of 1957, it quickly sold 3 million copies, and it kept right on selling. By the middle of 1958 its sales were over 6 million. By 1966 there were some 10 million copies in print.

At the time of publication Ms. Metalious' novel was perceived as being successful for the most basic of reasons: it told the blunt truth about a small town at a time when that was still sensational. Gradually, however, as the society evolved into the sixties and seventies, there was a revisionist view of that success, a sense that at least some of it had been due to Ms. Metalious' powerful and visceral comprehension of the problems faced by women in the modern world. Cultural detectives tracking the evolution of the feminist movement could find in her pages the emergence of independent women who dissented from the proscribed lives and limited opportunities reserved for women. Metalious, they suspected—for there was little evidence of this in the initial reviews of the book—had touched a nerve without anyone's realizing it.

Kenneth Davis noted in his book on the paperback revolution, *Two-Bit Culture*, that the women in *Peyton Place* "were on the cutting edge of a movement that had not yet arrived and still had no voice. They wanted more than to simply find the right man, settle down and begin breeding and keeping house."

Rather, Davis pointed out, Metalious' characters might have come right out of the Kinsey Report on women. They had sexual feelings that contrasted starkly with the attitudes women were then supposed to have, as set down in endless books written by men. Nor were Metalious' women nearly as admiring of men as they were supposed to be. In fact, they often considered men unreliable and childish. They did not want to be controlled by men; they wanted to be independent and to have careers in places like New York or, if they remained in towns like Peyton Place, to have some control over their lives.

Metalious was, at first glance, an unlikely feminist hero. She never fully articulated her own vision and probably would have been surprised to find some thirty years later that women at colleges read her book not so much as literature, but as part of the change in the politics of gender. With a few rare exceptions she was not close to other women, and as her literary career progressed and her own life began to unravel, she wrote of the frustrations of women with less skill and perception than she had in her first book.

Metalious had written as she did—roughly, simply, but powerfully— because it could have been her own story. She was a lower-middle-class French-Canadian girl who grew up in small towns in New Hampshire, living always involuntarily in a matriarchy. In high school she was bright and different, and teachers noticed her. Nonetheless, a literary future seemed out of reach. It seemed dimmer still when in February 1943, at the age of eighteen, she married George Metalious, a high school friend, because she was pregnant.

Grace and George were not unlike many couples trying to make their way after the war. George had served in the army, then come back to a child and a wife he barely knew. They struggled for a time, had a second child, and George went to the University of New Hampshire on the GI Bill. His wife took a job to support them, a common arrangement in those days. But Grace was different in one way— above all, she wanted to write. It was the only way she could escape the dreary world that seemed to be closing in around her. And although her housekeeping was terrible, her work habits were excellent. She wrote faithfully every day.

By 1953 she began to send manuscripts to publishers. By early 1955 she had finished her first novel, a rather routine semiautobiographical story about a young couple struggling through GI Bill life at a New England college. Entitled *The Quiet Place,* it was rejected everywhere it was sent.

Around the same time, she sent off her second novel, entitled *The Tree and the Blossom.* She had read *King's Row,* an extremely popular novel of the forties that dealt with the incestuous relationship of an adolescent girl and her father. By chance, a similar incident had occurred in the small town where Metalious lived: a young girl had shot her father to protect herself and the rest of her family. In that, Metalious seized on a sensational incident that would give her novel a special darkness. The novel, which was renamed *Peyton Place,* was mailed to publishers in May 1955.

It was turned down at several houses but was finally published by Julian Messner. The head of the firm, Kitty Messner, thought the book might sell 3000 copies—standard for a first novel—but the editor Howard Goodkind, who handled the publicity, thought it could be promoted into a best seller; he suggested spending an additional $5000 to create a special promotion campaign for the book emphasizing its controversial nature. That sum was a considerable risk in those days, but Messner agreed.

By the time the novel was published, in late September, the publicity machine had done its job, and the book shot up some best-seller lists. It sold 60,000 copies in the first ten days. The reviews were generally respectful. Carlos Baker, the distinguished Hemingway scholar, placed Metalious in the tradition of American writers who had helped expose the underside of small-town American life. Interestingly enough, a critic named Sterling North, writing in the New York *World Telegram,* who had earlier praised blunt language when used by male writers, was appalled by Metalious' use of the same words: "Never before in my memory has a young mother published a book in language approximately that of a longshoreman on a bellicose binge."

Fame and success were sweet at first. The people in New York were touched by the contrast between Grace's sweetness—and indeed vulnerability—and the harsh quality of her life as depicted in the book. All her dreams seemed to be coming true. She sold the book to the movies for $250,000, and the first check was for $75,000.

But if she had been well prepared to overcome the adversities of her life, she proved significantly less able to deal with the pressures of her success. The writer of *Peyton Place* was supposed to be both sexy and glamorous, after all, and Grace Metalious was a rather plain young woman. She was uneasy about the press and television appearances that were a part of the book's promotion, and she particularly disliked it when someone asked whether or not the book was autobiographical. She made an appearance on an early television talk show called *Night Beat,* hosted by a young man named Mike Wallace, then gaining a reputation for himself as a tough interviewer. She thought she had been assured he would not ask the autobiography question. Almost as soon as the interview began, Wallace asked her, "Grace, tell me, is *Peyton Place* your autobiography?" She struck back by calling him Myron, his real name, which she had been told beforehand he did not like to be called, and by asking him how many times he had been married, another sensitive point.

Even before the book's publication, her own marriage had started falling apart. Liberated by her success and her changed financial position, she ended her marriage, took up with a disc jockey, and married him. She began to spend money freely; at the same time, she stopped writing. Driven mostly by Hollywood producer Jerry Wald, she eventually wrote a listless sequel she was not proud of, called *Return to Peyton Place*. At the last minute a writer named Warren Miller was brought in to doctor it into a readable book. Nonetheless, *Return* also sold well, though not as well as its predecessor.

By 1960 George Metalious had come back into her life, and she published *The Tight White Collar,* which became her favorite book. It sold well, but, again, not nearly as well as *Peyton Place.* To shrewd editors it was obvious that her audience was beginning to slip away. Soon she had serious financial problems. When *Peyton Place* had been a success, she had worked out an agreement with her lawyer to place her and her family on a budget of $18,000 a year, a good deal of money then. But she never lived by the agreement.

The remaining years of her life were sad. Always a heavy drinker, she began to drink more. Metalious left her in the fall of 1963, and a few months later, in February 1964, Grace Metalious died of chronic liver disease.

# CHAPTER SIXTEEN

I N 1955, IN a quiet ceremony in Huntsville, Alabama, Wernher von Braun, at forty-three, became an American citizen. This was not a particularly good time for von Braun and his German colleagues in the American space program at Huntsville. To a nation trying on the uncomfortable new role of international power, space seemed a futuristic fantasy—and an expensive one at that. This was particularly true for the President and most of his chief advisers, men born in the previous century. But for von Braun, who believed the space age was already here (thanks in no small part to his own V-2 rockets, used by the Germans in World War II), this was unusually frustrating.

Von Braun was probably at the moment the leading rocket scientist in the world. His V-2 was the first successful ballistic missile, and in the last year of the war, 1300 of them had been fired at London with mounting success. At the end of World War II, von Braun and his team of German rocket scientists chose America as their future home as the Red Army pushed toward Peenemünde, where the Germans were headquartered. The choice was relatively easy. "We despise the French; we are mortally afraid of the Soviets; we do not believe the British can afford us; so that leaves the Americans," one team member said later, recalling how the scientists viewed their choices at the time.

The group slipped out of Peenemünde, burying most of their important papers in a deserted mine, and with the aid of faked papers reached Bavaria and the American forces. Wernher's brother, Magnus von Braun, who spoke relatively good English, went out to hunt for an American soldier to whom they could surrender. In time, one was found, and Magnus announced to a rather startled private, "My name is Magnus von Braun. My brother invented the V-2. We want to surrender." When Wernher himself appeared soon after, there was considerable doubt that he could actually be the father of the V-2. He was, said one American, "too young, too fat, too jovial." Then he began to talk. The American scientists were dazzled; his knowledge was so complete, and he easily blended the practical with the visionary. When von Braun spoke, listeners paid attention.

The Russians were furious when they learned that the Germans had slipped away. Stalin was a major promoter of the uses of science and technology, and he was well aware of the importance of Peenemünde. "This is absolutely intolerable," he said, according to reliable defectors, when he learned the rocket camp was empty. "We defeated Nazi armies; we occupied Berlin and Peenemünde, but the Americans got the rocket engineers. How and why was this allowed to happen?" In a way the Red Army's race toward Peenemünde was symbolic: it was, without anyone knowing it, the beginning of the race for outer space, or what Winston Churchill called the wizard war.

The Americans, by getting the German scientists, had pulled off one of the coups of the war. In 1945 the Germans were far ahead of other nations in rocket developments; the Soviets were second; and the Americans, having diverted much of their scientific resources to developing nuclear weapons, were third. But getting von Braun and his colleagues instantly made the Americans competitive.

After surrendering, von Braun and his people first ended up at the White Sands Proving Ground in New Mexico. Von Braun was, he liked to say, not a prisoner of war but a prisoner of peace. The early days at White Sands were hardly easy ones. They were men between countries in terms of loyalty; Germany was gone, but they were not yet Americans. Actually, their real loyalty was not to any nation but to science, and their special vision was little understood by others. They were paid six dollars a day. They were not even allowed to send packages back to Germany. By 1947 the Germans were beginning to be accepted. Many of their families had arrived, and that year von Braun was allowed to go back to Germany to marry his eighteen-year-old first cousin. Nonetheless, some of the doubts were still there, and when eventually a movie was made about von Braun's life, *I Aim at the Stars,* Mort Sahl, the comedian, added the line "But sometimes I hit London."

Von Braun quickly found that Germany had been far ahead of the Americans in rocket development. The first American rocket his team worked with was a WAC Corporal. It was much smaller than the V-2 and much slower. By 1950 the German team was transferred to the army rocket center at Huntsville, Alabama. Von Braun dreamed of placing a satellite in space, but that demanded multiple-stage rockets—that is, rockets that launched other rockets to gain even higher altitude and greater speed.

Von Braun was not merely a brilliant rocket scientist but a kind of space poet who envisioned manned space flights to the moon and Mars. His most practical thoughts always seemed to others like dreams and fantasies. Years later, in July 1969, on the eve of the Apollo 11 launch of a manned trip to the moon, a news conference was held at which several NASA officials answered questions. Reporters repeatedly asked the officials what the true significance of the moon landing was. None of the officials had an answer except von Braun. For him the moon shot was one more major step in human evolution. It was comparable, he said, to the moment when life emerged from the sea and established itself on land.

However, from 1945 through 1951 von Braun had no ballistic missile program to speak of. Only as the Russians started working on a missile did our program begin to move ahead. It was no small irony that a team of scientists who had chosen America because of its limitless financial resources was almost from the start saddled with limitations that were primarily financial.

By the summer of 1956 von Braun was absolutely certain that the Soviets were planning to launch a satellite. He was completely confident that he and his colleagues could do it too if they could only get the go-ahead from Washington. But if von Braun dreamed of men in space, the people in charge of his budget dreamed of orderly figures and of tidy weapons systems that they already understood. In America rocket scientists still operated on what was effectively the back burner.

On the morning of October 4, 1957, the Soviets launched the world's first space satellite. It was a relatively small aluminum alloy sphere that weighed 184 pounds and was 22.8 inches in diameter. It had two radio transmitters. The Russians called it Sputnik, which means "fellow traveler" in Russian.

No one in the Eisenhower administration, despite all the warnings, was prepared. Even worse, and this was almost surely generational, none of the senior men even saw at first what a psychological victory it was for the Soviets. But the younger men in the administration—Richard Nixon, Henry Cabot Lodge, Nelson Rockefeller—understood immediately the propaganda value of Sputnik. They knew that in the age of atomic weapons, any kind of scientific breakthrough on the part of the Soviets was seen as a threat.

Soon there was Sputnik II. Launched on November 3, 1957, it

weighed 1120.29 pounds—some six times more than its predecessor—its orbit was even higher, and it carried a small dog, Laika. Clearly, the Soviets intended to put a man in space soon. It was another psychological triumph. But the worst was still to come. Jim Hagerty, Ike's press secretary, had announced right after Sputnik that the navy, which had also been working on a satellite, planned to put one in orbit very soon.

Hagerty's announcement stunned the navy, but the navy team speeded up its schedule. Smarting from the Soviet success, the White House not only announced the launch but in effect showcased it as a major media event. At the launch, in the words of Kurt Stehling, a German engineer, "it seemed as if the gates of hell had opened up. Brilliant stiletto flames shot out from the side of the rocket near the engine. The vehicle agonizingly hesitated for a moment, quivered

A model of the first Russian satellite, Sputnik, which won the opening round of the space race

again, and in front of our unbelieving, shocked eyes, began to topple. It sank like a flaming sword into a scabbard down into the blast tube. For a moment or two there was complete disbelief. I could see it in the faces. I could feel it myself. This just couldn't be. The fire died down and we saw America's supposed response to the Soviet satellite lying amid the scattered glowing debris, still beeping away, unharmed."

U.S. CALLS IT KAPUTNIK, chuckled the London *Daily Express*. OH, WHAT A FLOPNIK! headlined the London *Daily Herald*. It was a "Stayput-nik," said another paper. The Soviets gloated.

So von Braun's team was left to recoup American prestige. Hopes were pinned on his Missile #29. The launch date was set, with no premature publicity. Finally everything seemed to come together. With some 100 reporters in the grandstand, the launch took place at 10:47:56 p.m. on January 31, 1958. They knew immediately it was a good one. Everything seemed to work perfectly. At six minutes and fifty seconds into the flight, the final rocket—or kick stage—ignited and burned for six seconds and hurled the satellite into space. America, after some significant and quite unnecessary humiliations, was finally in the space race.

# CHAPTER SEVENTEEN

LOU Cowan, one of the most inventive figures in the early days of television, needed a gimmick for a game show, one so compelling that millions of Americans would faithfully tune in. The radio quiz shows had been, in retrospect, small potatoes, with prizes to match. On *Take It Or Leave It*, the ultimate challenge was the "$64 question"—a phrase that even worked itself into the American vernacular by 1945. In the new age of television, though, everything had to be bigger and better. Americans were not going to sit home, glued to their television sets, wondering whether some electronic stranger who had briefly entered their living rooms was going to be able to double his winnings from thirty-two dollars to sixty-four dollars. In the postwar era that was pocket money.

Such was the dilemma facing Lou Cowan in early 1955. He needed high drama, and what better way to achieve that than a *very* large prize? Six hundred and forty dollars? Not so terribly exciting. But $64,000 gets into the realm of the almost impossible, he thought.

The name of the program was *The $64,000 Question*. It aired for the first time from ten to ten thirty p.m. in June 1955 on CBS. It was an immediate hit. Five weeks after its première, *The $64,000 Question* was the top-rated show on television. Approximately 47.5 million people were watching. The sales of its sponsor, Revlon ("the greatest name in cosmetics"), skyrocketed. The head of Hazel Bishop, a rival cosmetics company, subsequently blamed his company's disappointing year on the fact that "a new television program sponsored by your company's principal competitor captured the imagination of the public." It was the most primal lesson yet on the commercial power of television.

Not surprisingly, *The $64,000 Question* produced a Pavlovian response to its success. Suddenly the networks were flooded with imitations, all of them for big prize money. One organization came up with *The $64,000 Challenge*. Others produced *Tic Tac Dough, Twenty-One*, and *The Big Moment*.

By 1956 the appeal of these shows appeared to be limitless. Then subtly, and soon not so subtly, there was the inevitable pressure that television seemed to inspire: to improve the show by manipulation, to *cast* it—that is, to ensure each contestant would find some special resonance with the millions of people watching at home. The process began naturally enough at first with the preference to choose a contestant possessed of considerable charm over a contestant without it. Soon the producers, by pretesting, were able to tell where a candidate's strengths lay and what his weaknesses were. As the pressure built for ratings, the manipulations grew more serious. Some guests would be put through dry runs, only to find that when they appeared on the live shows, the questions were remarkably similar to the ones they had answered correctly in the rehearsal.

More and more, with so many different shows vying for public approval, the producers found it was the quality of the contestants—and the degree to which the nation identified with them—that made the difference. When the Barry and Enright company, one of the big hitters in the world of game shows, introduced its new game in March 1956, called *Twenty-One*, loosely based on the card game of the same name, its producer, Dan Enright, was confident it would be an immediate success. The première was, he said later, a dismal failure—"just plain dull." The day after, Marty Rosenhouse, the sponsor, made an irate call to say he did not intend to own a turkey. "Do whatever you have to do," he told Enright. Those were the marching orders for Enright and his staff.

Fixing the show did not particularly bother Enright. The quiz shows had never been about intelligence or integrity as far as he was concerned; they were about drama and entertainment. It was a predatory world, Enright believed, and he excelled in it. He was not, Dan Enright reflected years later, a very nice man in those days. He was totally compelled by work, wildly ambitious, and utterly self-involved. "I was determined to be successful no matter what it cost," he said, "and I was greedy, greedy, not for money, but for authority, power, prestige and respect."

Soon—with considerable fixing—*Twenty-One* became a huge success. Enright cast it as he might a musical comedy. He wanted not just winners and losers but heroes and villains. His first break came early, when a young man named Herb Stempel wrote asking for a chance to be a candidate. Stempel had seen the debut of *Twenty-One* and had thought the questions rather simple. He had, he had always been told, a photographic memory. "The walking encyclopedia," one uncle called him. At the time, Stempel was an impoverished graduate student at City University. He was invited to the offices of Barry and Enright, given an exam consisting of 363 questions, of which he got 251 correct—the highest score anyone had gotten so far on the entrance exam. He was perfect for the show, except for one thing—he was short, stocky, and not particularly appealing on television.

He was, Enright decided, unlikable. And so Enright decided to exploit that and emphasize his unattractive side. Stempel had grown up in a poor section of the Bronx. His father, who had been a postal clerk, died when he was seven, and his mother suffered from high blood pressure and was on welfare from the time of her husband's death to when she died. There had seemed to Stempel an unfairness about his childhood from the start: Other kids had fathers; he did not. Other kids had some money; he did not. But his photographic memory was remarkable. Yet for all the knowledge stored in Stempel's head, Enright thought, he was socially limited and almost unable to sustain a conversation.

A few days after their first meeting Enright came by to see Stempel at the latter's home in Queens. Enright opened an attaché case and pulled out a bunch of cards similar to the ones used on *Twenty-One*. He began going over the questions in a dry run with Herb Stempel. It was, Stempel began to realize, a rehearsal for *Twenty-One*.

"How would you like to win twenty-five thousand dollars?" Enright asked. "Who wouldn't," Stempel answered. With that, Enright had made him a co-conspirator, demolishing any leverage Stempel might have if qualms arose in the future.

Enright checked out his new contestant's wardrobe. Since he was to be portrayed as a penniless ex-GI working his way through school, he was to wear his worst clothes: an ill-fitting double-breasted blue suit that had belonged to Stempel's father-in-law. He also selected a blue shirt with a frayed collar to go with it. Enright made Stempel get a marine-style haircut, which made him look somewhat like a Nazi soldier. Stempel realized the role he was to play was the nerd, the square, the human computer. It was a cruel thing to do, Enright reflected years later—to make a man who obviously had considerable emotional problems go before the American people in as unattractive an incarnation as possible.

Good soldier that he was, Stempel was not a satisfactory winner for *Twenty-One*. His only real value was as a loser. The show needed a hero in a white hat—a handsome young gladiator to defeat him. In October the producers found him in the person of a young English instructor at Columbia University named Charles Van Doren.

Of all the people associated with the quiz-show scandals, Van Doren remains the one most indelibly burned on most people's memory. He was the bearer of one of the most illustrious names in American intellectual life, and he captivated the audience as no one else ever did. His manner—shy, gentle, somewhat self-deprecating, like a young, more intellectual Jimmy Stewart—was immensely attractive. He was smart enough to win, yet modest enough to seem just a little uneasy with his success. His father was the celebrated Columbia professor Mark Van Doren, winner of a Pulitzer Prize for his poetry. His uncle Carl was just as famous a man of letters.

It was a masterful stroke of casting—Van Doren turned out to be a superb performer. In contrast to the unattractive Stempel, he was, in Enright's phrase, the kind of young man "you'd love to have your daughter marry." He never seemed to lose his boyish innocence, which in fact he had lost from the start.

Coached by Enright's staff on how to answer, Charles Van Doren became very good at the theatrics of the show. He learned to stutter, to seem to grope toward answers he had already been given. He was good at the game, but not too good; the questions were answerable, his struggling implied, but they were not easy.

To Herb Stempel, Van Doren was the enemy, and the epitome of all the injustices he had suffered in terms of privilege and looks. "I felt here was a guy, Van Doren, that had a fancy name, Ivy League education, and I had just the opposite, the hard way up," he once told Enright. That Stempel, because of the deal he had made with the devil, would now have to give up his television celebrity—and lose to someone he was sure he could beat—was the unkindest cut of all.

The dénouement for Herb Stempel came on the night of December 5, 1956. According to Enright's script, he was to lose by answering incorrectly a question the answer to which he knew perfectly well: which movie had won the Academy Award for best picture in 1955. The answer was *Marty,* and Stempel had seen the movie three times. He loved it because he could identify with its principal character, an unattractive but sensitive man who has as many feelings as someone who is handsome. That it was a movie he cared about made it all the harder. On the day of the program, NBC hyped the confrontation all day long: "Is Herb Stempel going to win over one hundred and eleven thousand dollars on *Twenty-One* tonight?" an announcer would say over and over again as the day wore on. Stempel would talk back to the television set in his room: "No, he's not going to win over one hundred and eleven thousand dollars, he's going to take a dive."

Once the program began, he came perilously close to answering the *Marty* question correctly, breaking Enright's rules and just going for it. But he played by the rules, and Van Doren ended up riding a tiger. In time he became a national hero, with a record fifteen appearances on the show. Hundreds of letters came in each day telling him how he represented America's hope for a more serious, cerebral future. NBC signed him to a three-year contract that included regular stints on the *Today* show. In the end, his total winnings came to

The nation was shocked to learn that the graceful and charming Charles Van Doren (left) had cheated to beat Herb Stempel on the quiz show *Twenty-One*.

$129,000, but given the draconian taxes of the period, he actually took home only about $28,000.

Stempel had quickly squandered his own prize money in a series of bad investments. His bitterness festered. He began to bug Enright, demanding a chance to play Van Doren in a clean, unfixed game. Enright became increasingly aware that Stempel was a live hand grenade, a wronged man who wanted revenge. No one had really understood the impact of all this on his psyche.

Stempel began to look for reporters who might write about the scandal. At first the press was wary of picking up the story, because there was no way of corroborating it. The fixing had been done one-on-one, with no witnesses. Deniability was critical. If a contestant changed his mind and wanted to talk, it was to be his word against that of a program executive; thus, charges of fraud against the program could be neutralized.

Then, inevitably, the whole scam unraveled. A woman who had been coached left her notebook in the outer office of one show. Another contestant saw the notebook—which contained many of the answers the woman was asked to give as a contestant—and complained. Others came forward. Finally the district attorney's office launched a broad investigation of quiz shows. The evidence of rigging was overwhelming, but for reasons never quite clear, the judge in the case impounded all the evidence. With that, the quiz-show scandal was passed to a congressional committee.

Gradually the congressional investigation kept coming back to focus on Charles Van Doren, the young man who had charmed the entire nation. Van Doren steadfastly maintained his innocence and claimed that he had received no help. That meant he continued to lie—to the prosecutors, to the New York grand jury investigating the quiz shows, to the media, to his employers, to his family, and to his own lawyer. Nevertheless, the committee managed to gather more than enough information to show that the programs were rigged.

On November 2, 1959, a crush of journalists and photographers recorded Van Doren on the committee's witness stand, beginning, "I would give almost anything I have to reverse the course of my life in the last three years. . . . I was involved, deeply involved, in a deception. The fact that I, too, was very much deceived cannot keep me from being the principal victim of that deception, because I was its principal symbol. There may be a kind of justice in that." Aware of Van Doren's great popularity, the committee members handled him gently and repeatedly praised him for his candor. Only one Congressman announced that he saw no particular point in praising someone of Van Doren's exceptional talents and intelligence for simply telling the truth. With that, the room suddenly exploded with applause, leaving no doubt that ordinary people would not so easily forgive Van Doren.

Herb Stempel had taken a train to Washington, paying for the trip with his own money, to see Van Doren's appearance. In the crowded congressional hearing room, he wanted some kind of vindication, but he was bitterly disappointed by what happened. "I felt terribly hurt by the way they praised him," he said years later. Afterward Stempel grabbed one of the New York assistant D.A.s who had worked on the case and started to complain about the professors at City University who had turned down his proposal for a Ph.D. thesis. Even at what might have been a moment of triumph, it still seemed that he regarded himself as a victim.

The scandal illuminated some things about television in addition to its growing addictive power. The first was the capacity of a virtual stranger, with the right manner, to project a kind of pseudo-intimacy and to become an old and trusted friend in a stunningly short time. That would have profound ramifications as television increasingly became the prime instrument of politics. The other thing the scandal showed, and this was to be perhaps its most powerful lesson, was that television *cast* everything it touched—politics, news shows, and sit-coms. The demands of entertainment and theater were at least as powerful as substance. Among the first to benefit from that new casting requirement was a young junior Senator from Massachusetts, who, like Charles Van Doren, was young, attractive, upper-class. If Charles Van Doren was the major new star of television in the late fifties, he was to be replaced by John Kennedy as the new decade started.

As for Charles Van Doren, he quickly dropped out of the public arena. He moved to Chicago with his young family, and drawing on a family connection with Mortimer Adler, the editor of the Great Books series, he worked for the *Encyclopædia Britannica* as an editor. His life in Chicago was largely private, and he was not often seen in that city's journalistic and literary circles. He and his wife, Geraldine Bernstein Van Doren, whom he had first met when she had a job answering the mail prompted by his early success on *Twenty-One*, reared two children there. He never wrote or spoke about the quiz-show events. When, on different occasions, journalists telephoned, suggesting that they were working on an article about that period and asked to speak with him, they were told that Mr. Van Doren was living a very happy life and did not need or want to get involved in their project.

## CHAPTER EIGHTEEN

LATE in his presidency Dwight Eisenhower came under increasing scrutiny personally. Sputnik had been only the first of several psychological setbacks for America. Soon after, in November 1957, a confidential document called the Gaither report leaked out. It was prepared by a blue-chip panel appointed by Eisenhower himself, and it was a chilling piece of work. Based on information available to most laymen, it implied that we were slipping in our nuclear capacity while the Soviets were becoming stronger all the time. The evidence, it reported, "clearly indicates an increasing threat which may become critical in 1959 or early 1960." The report recommended $25 billion be spent for the building of bomb shelters all over the country and another $19 billion on increased budgeting for weaponry.

Eisenhower was now in a difficult position. He and other senior members of his administration were well aware of a CIA project that kept them well informed on what the Russians were up to. The project involved a lightweight airplane that could fly at an altitude of 70,000 feet, above the range of the Soviets' air defense, and from that height take pictures of the ground below. The plane was called a U-2. The photographic technology it carried was developed by the great American photographic genius, Ed Land, who had invented the Polaroid camera.

Eisenhower had been stunned by the photos from the first U-2 flights. Not only could the plane take a clear photograph of a parking lot fourteen miles down but you could even see, he said, "the lines marking the parking areas for individual cars."

In a sense, the U-2 helped stabilize the relationship between the two superpowers, but because the information it provided was super-secret and could not be introduced into the democratic system, Eisenhower was oddly paralyzed. He knew the Soviet threat was overrated. But what he knew, ordinary citizens could not know. He had nothing to offer but himself and his word in defense of his policies. The proof lay locked in the CIA's vaults.

It is our contradictions that make us interesting. Eisenhower, the famed general, wanted more to be a man of peace than a man of war. He had hoped, after the war, for a rapprochement with the Russians, but his anticommunism seemed to harden during much of his administration. He could barely restrain his contempt toward Adlai Stevenson when Stevenson raised the issue of limiting nuclear testing in 1956, and yet in the final years of his administration Eisenhower hungered, more than anything, for some form of accord with the Russians on limiting nuclear testing and perhaps even on limiting the production of nuclear weapons.

By 1958 he had begun to reduce the number of U-2 flights. He had always been uneasy with them. He knew they were provocative, and he himself would point out that nothing would move the United States more quickly to war than the knowledge that the Soviets were overflying us and taking pictures. He was beginning to build new links to Khrushchev. In 1959 the Soviet leader had visited the United States. He'd spent time with Eisenhower in his hometown, and on the whole the trip had gone well. Ike did not want the budding trust between them jeopardized by the U-2 flights.

What the President did not know was that the U-2 pilots themselves were becoming more nervous. There was evidence by the fall of 1958 that the Soviets were not only tracking them with radar but firing SAMs (surface-to-air missiles) that were coming—as one U-2 pilot, Francis Gary Powers, put it—uncomfortably close. At the same time, the planes themselves were becoming heavier as more equipment was being added.

On the last day of April, 1960, at the U-2 base in Turkey, Powers climbed into his plane at five twenty a.m. For the first time, a U-2 was to fly all the way across the Soviet Union. At six twenty-six Powers was allowed to take off. He soon picked up the trail of a Russian jet. It was traveling at supersonic speed toward him. But he remained confident; Soviet planes still flew far below him. He was flying toward Sverdlovsk for what would be the first U-2 trip over that city, when he heard a dull thump. A tremendous orange flash hit the cockpit. *My God,* he thought to himself. *I've had it now.* Later Powers decided that what had happened to him was a near miss, which tore the fragile craft apart but spared his life.

The plane was completely out of control, hurtling toward the ground. He managed to get out, then got his parachute open. When he landed, he was quickly picked up by a local farmer and turned over to the KGB.

The Americans took a terrible beating in the propaganda game that followed. A planned summit in Paris, which Eisenhower had hoped would lead to a limited test-ban treaty, was a disaster. Khrushchev chose to thunder his way through it. He shouted so loudly that French President Charles de Gaulle, the host, tried to quiet him by saying, "The acoustics in this room are excellent. We can all hear the chairman."

Years later Chip Bohlen, one of the top American kremlinologists, said that Khrushchev took the U-2 as a personal insult; it was a per-

When Francis Gary Powers' spy plane crashed in Russia, it took with it all hope for a greater American-Soviet détente.

sonal embarrassment because he had promised his colleagues in the Politburo that Eisenhower could be trusted. (Khrushchev himself later said that the U-2 affair was the beginning of the end for him in terms of his ability to hold power.)

For Eisenhower there would be no test-ban treaty. That which he had wanted most—a genuine beginning of peace—had been shot down along with Powers. His administration would end, he said bitterly, much as it had begun—without any real progress. "I had longed," he said just before he died, "to give the United States and the world a lasting peace. I was able only to contribute to a stalemate."

Yet Eisenhower may have underestimated the most important achievement of his administration—the fact that the worst did not happen. In the years of his presidency both superpowers developed the hydrogen bomb. Yet his own essential decency and the respect his own nation held for him allowed him to soften the most terrible furies of that time and permit a relatively safe passage through those years.

As the decade came to a close, Eisenhower's Vice President, Richard Nixon, was approaching a critical moment in his career: his run for the presidency in 1960. The Democrats, he suspected, were about to nominate John Kennedy, who would make a formidable opponent.

Kennedy was young, attractive, contemporary, skilled as few politicians of his generation were at using the media. He had been a natural on television—from the start the camera had liked him. He was attractive, he did not posture, and he was cool by instinct. Television was a cool medium—the more overheated a candidate, the less well he did on it. Kennedy's gestures and his speaking voice seemed natural. His speeches were full of humor, irony, and self-deprecation, and that helped him in what was to be the defining moment of the 1960 campaign—the first presidential debate.

By contrast, television was a problem for Nixon. Not only were his physical gestures awkward, but his speaking tone was self-conscious and artificial. What often came through was a sense of insincerity. To Eisenhower's secretary, Anne Whitman, "the Vice President sometimes seems like a man who is acting like a nice man rather than being one." That was a critical distinction, particularly for a man entering the television age, because if there was one thing the piercing eye of the television camera was able to convey to people, it was what was authentic and what was artificial.

The first debate changed the nature of politics in America, and it also crowned the importance of television politically and culturally. Until that night in Chicago, Kennedy had been the upstart, a little-known junior Senator who had hardly bothered to take the Senate seriously. Nixon, on the other hand, had been Vice President for eight years; he was experienced, had visited endless foreign countries and met with all the leaders of the world. He also fancied himself a not inconsiderable debater, and he was confident he would do well against Kennedy.

John Kennedy, who viewed Nixon with an upper-class snobbishness, arrived in Chicago early. He had spent much of the previous week in California, and he was tanned and glowing with good health. Knowing that this was the most important moment in the campaign, he had minimized his schedule and spent much of his time in his hotel resting. He also practiced with his staff members, who posed likely questions and likely Nixon answers.

Nixon, by contrast, arrived in terrible shape. He had been ill earlier in the campaign with an infected knee, and he had never entirely recovered. His staff tried to tell him to rest and prepare himself, but no one could tell him anything. Old and once trusted advisers had been cut off. Frustrated by Eisenhower's offhand treatment of him for the last seven and a half years, Nixon had become megalomaniacal in 1960 as far as his veteran staff was concerned, determined to be his own campaign manager as well as the candidate.

The first debate was set for Monday, September 26. Nixon, ill and exhausted, flew out late on Sunday night and went on a motorcade through Chicago, stopping for rallies in five wards and then getting to bed very late. On Monday his face was gray and ashen, and his shirt hung loosely around his neck, like that of a dying man.

At the studio, both candidates turned down the makeup offered by the station. It was gamesmanship: each man feared that if he used makeup, then the next day there would be newspaper stories about it or, even worse, a photo. But Kennedy had a good tan, and an aide did a slight touch-up with commercial makeup. Because of his dark beard, Nixon used something called Shavestick. The CBS professionals were shocked by Nixon's appearance.

Nixon was extremely sensitive to heat, and he sweated profusely when the television lights were on. He had started out in the debates by looking ghastly, gray, and exhausted. Then while some 80 million of his fellow Americans watched, it got worse. He began to sweat. Soon there were rivers of sweat on his gray face, and as the Shavestick washed down it, Nixon went into a kind of cosmetic meltdown. "That night," columnist Russell Baker wrote thirty years later, "image replaced the printed word as the natural language of politics."

When it was all over, Nixon thought he had won; Kennedy knew otherwise. The next day Kennedy drew huge crowds wherever he went, and the people seemed to feel a personal relationship with the candidate. For Nixon the news was a great deal worse. The parents of Rose Woods, his longtime secretary, called from Ohio to ask if there was anything wrong with him. Even Hannah Nixon called Rose to inquire about her son's health.

Later Ted Rogers, one of his advisers, mused that eight years of Nixon's experience as Vice President had been wiped out in one evening. Rogers wondered how Nixon could have been so careless about so vital a moment in the campaign, and later he decided that it was the sum of everything that had gone before: anger over Eisenhower's treatment of him as Vice President; his subsequent determination to make all the important decisions in this campaign himself and to listen to none of his old advisers; and, finally, his belief that because of the Checkers speech, he was an expert on television. Unfortunately, anyone who understood the medium could have warned him that Kennedy would be a formidable foe in front of a television camera.

THE debate between these two young men, each born in this century, each young enough to be Dwight Eisenhower's son, seemed to underscore how quickly the society had changed in so short a time. It showed not only how powerful the electronic medium had become but also how much it was already speeding the pace of life in America. Not everyone was pleased by the change wrought in American politics by television. Dean Acheson was not moved by either candidate as he watched the debate, and it had made him feel older. To him both candidates appeared to be cold, mechanistic figures who had, with the aid of pollsters and advertising executives, figured out, down to the last decimal point, what stand to take on every issue. "Do you get a funny sort of sense that, so far at least, there are no human candidates in this campaign?" he wrote Harry Truman. "They seem improbable, skillful technicians. Both are surrounded by clever people who dash off smart memoranda, but it is not all pulled together on either side, by or into a man. The ideas are too contrived. . . . These two . . . bore the hell out of me."

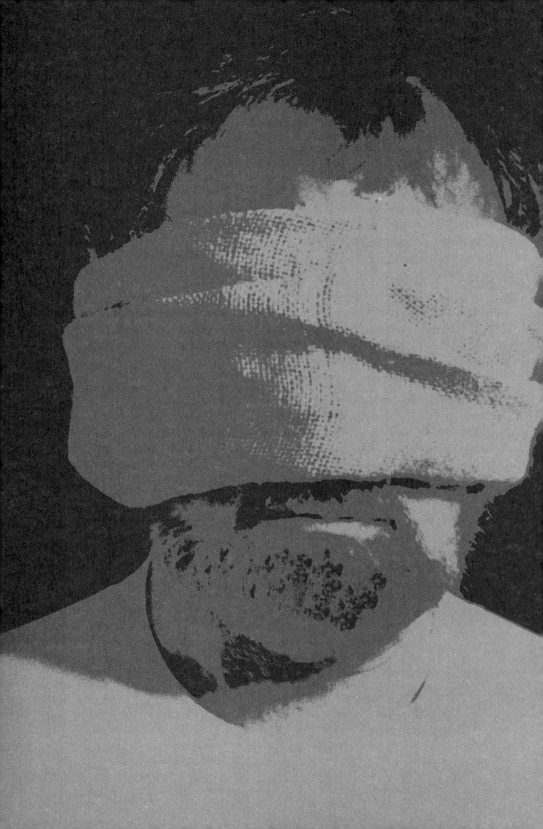

# TERRY ANDERSON

# DEN OF LIONS

## MEMOIRS OF SEVEN YEARS

. . . Three very Arab looking young men threw open the doors of the Mercedes and jumped out, each holding a 9-mm pistol in his hand. By the time I realized what was happening, one of the men was beside my car, pushing his pistol at my head. "Get out," he said fiercely. "I will shoot. I will shoot."

"Okay," I answered quickly. "Okay. No problem."

He reached in and pulled the glasses from my face, [then] pulled me along beside him, toward the Mercedes.

"Get in. I will shoot," he hissed at me, pushing me into the back seat.

Another young man jumped in, then shoved my body down. I could feel a gun barrel pushing at my neck.

—*Den of Lions*

*Come away with me from Lebanon, my bride,*
*Come away with me from Lebanon;*
*Away from the peak of Amana,*
*Of Senir and of Hermon,*
*Away from the den of lions*
*And the mountains of leopards.*
                              —Song of Solomon 4:8


# Prologue

DAMASCUS, *Syria. December 4, 1991.*   Madeleine walked hesitantly into the large room. She was looking in the wrong direction and didn't see me standing near the couch watching her.

It was after midnight of an incredibly long day. I hadn't slept the night before, waiting in that other, much smaller room—the last of so many prisons—for the end of our seven-year nightmare. It already seemed a thousand miles away, faded and dreamlike in my mind, drowned by the wave of emotion that had been building ever since Tom Sutherland and Terry Waite had been taken out of our cell fifteen days ago, leaving me alone, the last of the American hostages.

I had been taken out of the cell, still blindfolded, just after dark. A short car ride, a last tirade from Ali about evil America, then the handover to Syrian intelligence—a colonel, who put his hand on my shoulder and told me, "You're free." I took off my blindfold and dropped it beside me, onto the road. Into the small sedan. No rush of joy, no real feeling at all for the first few minutes, just the strangeness of being able to look around freely. The night was clear. I recognized the road—Baalbek, as we had thought. Past the ancient Roman ruins. Everything seemed new, especially the highway. Lots of new apartments, small office buildings. Last time I was there, seven years ago, the road was still narrow, potholed, and the years of war had left their mark everywhere. No sign of it now.

The beauty of the stars, unseen for so long, suddenly hit me. I leaned forward, peered up through the windshield awkwardly. After a minute or two I heard the driver exchange a few words with the three agents in the back seat. Everyone laughed. I looked over, and he pointed up. There was a clear sunroof above me. I spent much of the forty-five-minute ride leaning back. The Big Dipper. Orion's Belt? Where is Cassiopeia? Then the lights of Damascus dimmed the stars.

A long, boring session at Syrian intelligence headquarters as some general talked on and on. I shifted restlessly. Patience. You should have learned that by now.

Then the short ride to the Foreign Ministry. I knew the drill, had listened so many times as my fellow hostages went through the dance. Into a small room, where the American ambassador, Syrian deputy foreign minister, others are waiting. I'm introduced to the slim, handsome man standing quietly against the wall—Giandomenico Picco, the assistant U.N. secretary-general who had negotiated the series of releases over the last year, whom we had followed in his travels so intensely, hunching over the radio to catch each hint of progress.

"I've been wanting to meet you for a long time," I joked.

He smiled, shaking my hand. "Me, too."

Short briefing, then down the hall into a small room jammed with reporters, cameras, glaring lights. I was almost frightened, until I saw the enormous shaggy gray beard of Alex Efty, the AP's Cyprus correspondent. He grabbed me in a bear hug. There was Bill Foley, grinning at me over his camera. He looked as if he was crying! Others, old friends, colleagues, jammed shoulder to shoulder.

Speeches from the ambassador, the foreign minister, Giandomenico, mercifully brief. I made the obligatory gesture of thanks to the United Nations, Syria, Iran, answered a few questions, then begged to be excused. "I have an appointment with a couple of very beautiful ladies, and I'm late already." Laughter, a graceful exit.

The Syrians gone, I was in the hands of the Americans now, in the ambassador's car. My stomach felt hollow. The tension seemed to vibrate through my chest, almost audible. Not unpleasant, but building. A few minutes. Lord, thank You. Let it be all right.

Into the ambassador's residence. A pleasant young lady whose name I missed guided me into a room.

"Do you want to see Madeleine now?"

"Yes. Of course I do."

Everyone left immediately. I stood in front of the couch, glanced around. Typical embassy—comfortable, expensively furnished.

Dear God, there she is. She looked so scared, even smaller than her five-one frame. Her hair was still long, heavy, and deep black. She glanced my way, spotted me, her eyes huge and dark. We walked slowly toward each other, and she was in my arms, her body slim and taut against mine. "It's all right. It's over. It's okay," I murmured. She was crying, holding tight. I could feel the tears pressing against the back of my eyes. "It's over."

The feel of her, the smell of her, recalled so many times over the years until it was more imagination than memory, instantly seemed to erase the 2454 days we had been apart, as if it had been only hours since I left her in bed, sleepy, six months pregnant, content. Almost seven years. March 16, 1985.

# CHAPTER ONE

## Terry

*BEIRUT, Lebanon. 8:00 a.m. March 16, 1985.* The green Mercedes, sparkling clean in the morning sunlight, drifted to a halt in the narrow road. Don Mell, the young AP photographer I was dropping off at his apartment after our tennis game, had noticed it earlier, but hadn't mentioned it—it didn't seem important. Now, though, it struck him as odd, especially the curtains drawn over the rear window.

"A hamster-mobile," he remarked, using the nickname given by journalists to the armed young men swarming around Beirut.

The joke, already worn, seemed even less amusing when three very Arab looking young men threw open the doors of the Mercedes and jumped out, each holding a 9-mm pistol in his right hand. My mind seemed to stall for a few seconds. By the time I realized what was happening, one of the men was beside the driver's door of my car, yanking it open and pushing his pistol at my head. "Get out," he said fiercely. "I will shoot. I will shoot."

"Okay," I answered quickly. "Okay. No problem."

He reached in and pulled the glasses from my face. As I slid out of the seat, half crouched, he put his hand around my shoulders, forcing me to remain bent over. "Come, come quickly."

I glanced at Don, a vague blur on the other side of the car, willing him to run, not daring to shout the words. He stood frozen.

The young man pulled me along beside him, toward the Mercedes, just four or five yards away, still forcing me to remain half bent.

"Get in. I will shoot," he hissed at me, pushing me into the back seat. "Get down. Get down."

I tried to crouch in the narrow space between the front and back seats. Another young man jumped in the other door, threw an old blanket over me, then shoved my head and body down with both his feet. I could feel a gun barrel pushing at my neck.

The car lurched into gear and accelerated madly, almost slid around a corner. The front-seat passenger leaned over the back of his seat. "Don't worry. It's political," he said in a normal tone as the car lurched back and forth, the driver cutting in and out of traffic.

The strange comment, apparently meant to be reassuring, wasn't. As my mind began to function again, it made me think of the other Americans kidnapped in Beirut for political reasons. William Buckley, missing twelve months. The Reverend Benjamin Weir, missing ten months. Father Lawrence Martin Jenco, missing two months.

There wasn't any real fear yet—it was drowned by adrenaline. Just a repeating mental refrain: Anderson, you're in deep, deep trouble.

The car rocked as it careened around corner after corner. The left side of my face was pressed hard against the carpeted floor. I could follow the route—I'd been through these streets so many times: through Basta, the slum area filled with Shiite refugees, then up the hill into Hamra, down Bliss Street in front of the American University campus, tires screeching down the twisting, steep descent to the Corniche along the Mediterranean. Then a long, straight stretch down the coast to another slum—Ouzai, on the edge of the airport.

After fifteen or twenty minutes the car turned off the main highway, straight into what seemed to be a garage. A metal door clanged down, cutting off the street noise. The doors were yanked open, and hands grabbed at me, pulling me upright. There were mutterings in Arabic—short, guttural, incomprehensible.

Someone slipped the blanket away, slipping a dirty cloth around my head, then wrapping plastic tape around and around. Other hands grabbed my tennis shoes, yanking them off. Someone pulled off the gold chain around my neck. Then the gold bracelet on my right wrist, the watch on my left, also went. "Don't," I said involuntarily. "They're gifts. Don't take them."

"We are not thieves," one of the men said. He stuck my watch into my sock. Not the chain or bracelet. I never saw either again.

More tape, around my wrists and arms. I was pulled out of the car and guided clumsily to the side of the garage, pushed down onto a filthy blanket smelling of oil and gasoline.

My legs were taped tightly. I could no longer sit upright, and slid sideways. One of the men propped me against the wall.

The men talked among themselves for a few minutes; then several left. Only one seemed to be still with me, pacing back and forth.

After a while—twenty minutes? an hour?—they came back. I was pulled upright, guided across the floor, and seated again.

"What is your name?" a voice asked, heavily accented.

"Terry Anderson. I am a journalist."

"Your company?"

"The Associated Press. A wire service."

The man seemed uninterested in my answers. "You are a spy."

"No. I am a journalist. What do you want from me?"

The interrogation went on, almost aimlessly, without heat. Accusations. Denials.

"Why do you have this?" A hand shoved something at me. Peering along my nose, through the gap it made in the tape around my head, I saw the gold charm from my chain—an inscription from the Koran.

"It was a gift. My wife gave it to me."

"She is Muslim?"

"No. Maronite. Catholic."

"You are not Muslim. Why do you wear words from the Koran?"

"They are beautiful. They are the words of God."

He was obviously unsatisfied and muttered to his companions. Then more serious questions.

"What other Americans do you know? Who works at your office?"

"I can't tell you that."

"You must say. Give us the names of all the Americans you know."

"No. I can't do that."

"We can make you."

"I know you can try. You can hurt me. But I can't give you the names of my friends."

"We have electricity. You know?"

"Yes, I know. But I still won't give you names. They are my friends. I can't help you kidnap them."

More demands. Refusals. Strangely, the procedure was still without heat. It didn't seem as if they really meant the threats.

It ended after perhaps forty minutes. The men left, except for one. He shoved me back against the wall, resumed pacing.

I could think of nothing except Madeleine, still in bed, sleepily kissing me good-bye at seven a.m. Six months pregnant, her belly making a mound of the blanket. She would know soon, probably knew already. Don would have gone straight to the office, alerted the AP people there. They would have gone to our apartment, just a few hundred yards from where I was kidnapped.

I began crying silently, rocking forward and back against the wall. Who would tell her? How? I twisted my wrists against the tape, struggling against it. The guard came, bent over, and surprisingly gently put his hand on my arm. "No. No. No good."

I stopped struggling and tried to compose my mind. Breathe evenly, smoothly. Calm. Don't think. Calm.

After several hours had passed, I realized I needed to urinate. I groped mentally for the scraps of Arabic I had picked up in the past two years. "Hello. Excuse me. *Chebab.*" Mister.

*"Shu?"* What?

"I need toilet. Toilet."

He pulled me upright, back against the wall. Then he picked up a tin can and held it near the front of my tennis shorts. I pulled them down in front with my thumbs and tried to urinate, but couldn't, through embarrassment and awkwardness. "Sorry." Without replying, he put down the can, then lowered me to the floor. A few minutes later he brought me half a hamburger and a Coke. *"Jowan?"* Hungry?

"Thank you." Taking a bite, I realized I hadn't eaten since the night before. I finished the Coke, which he held, then again told him, "Toilet." He helped me up, picked up the can, and held it. This time, success. Relief. Back to the floor.

It was probably around midnight before the others returned. They checked and renewed the tape, adding more around my mouth. Two of them picked me up by my legs and shoulders and carried me back to the car, dumping me in the trunk. The lid closed.

PRIORITY:—URGENT—
THE ASSOCIATED PRESS
DATE: Saturday, March 16, 1985
SLUG: Reporter Kidnapped
DATELINE: BEIRUT, Lebanon

Terry A. Anderson, Chief Middle East Correspondent of The Associated Press, was kidnapped by armed men off a street in mostly Moslem west Beirut on Saturday morning.

Donald Mell, a photographer for the AP, witnessed the abduction and said three bearded men, two armed with pistols, forced Anderson into a green Mercedes and sped off.

Nate Polowetzky, foreign editor of The Associated Press, said in New York: "We are deeply concerned about the events in Beirut, and are seeking all possible information regarding the welfare of Associated Press correspondent Terry Anderson. We will, of course, pursue all avenues for his release and safe return."

*BEIRUT. March 17, 1985.*    The apartment building we ended up in was only half finished. Peering through gaps in the tape around my eyes as I was hauled and bumped up flight after flight of stairs, I could see shoes and slippers in front of the apartment doors on the first few floors, then bare concrete, roughly finished, and empty door frames.

Finally we arrived. I was dumped on a steel cot. A chain with two-inch links was attached to both my feet and fastened with a large padlock on each ankle. Another chain was wrapped around my left wrist and padlocked, and another on my right.

The chains, apparently fastened to the walls, were not long enough for me to sit up, even if I had been allowed. It was quickly made apparent to me that I was not.

I have in my mind a mélange of images of those first few weeks: sharp, crystal-clear moments from which I can call up every detail— the creaking of the metal cot, the sounds of my guards arguing among themselves, the noises of the street outside. These are surrounded by blurred hours and days, colors and emotions, rage and tears, frustration and remorse.

Slowly I was taught the rules of this new existence, with a combination of slaps and punches when I did something wrong. No noise, no speaking. Even rolling from side to side on the bed to relieve the painful muscle cramps brought on by lying still for hours would earn a slap or a poke with a gun. "Hssst. No move."

Occasionally, three or four young militiamen would burst into the room, fresh from the fighting outside. They'd curse or spit: "Death to America"—they were a cliché come alive. I'd felt their hatred before, in brief encounters with the bearded fanatics increasingly common in Lebanon. Now, though, I was helpless, a toy these young men were using to play out their power fantasies.

TWENTY-FOUR days. It must be about the eighth of April. I'd kept track by scratching a line in the wall next to my head each gray dawn. My body was locked for hours each day in cramps from the effort of not moving. I was exhausted by the ceaselessly churning thoughts in my head. Around and around, over and over. Replaying endless scenarios in which I escaped, gunned the car, jumped out, and dropped my kidnapper with a karate blow—useless, childish plays. Humiliation of trying to pee in a bottle while lying down. Humiliation of being poked and prodded and cursed at. I knew I was on the edge of madness, of losing control completely, breaking down.

Finally, as one of the guards walked past my cot, I called out softly, *"Chebab."* Hey.

*"Shu?"*

*"Tehki Inglisi?"* Speak English?

*"Lahsa."* One moment. He left, came back with another guard.

"What?"

"I can't do this anymore. I am not an animal. I am a human being. You can't treat me like this."

"What do you want?"

"A book. A Bible. And to move. You must loosen these chains. I will go crazy."

A grunt. "I speak chef."

"Thank you."

The next day, late in the afternoon, the English-speaking guard came in and threw a heavy object on the bed. I reached for it, felt the smooth covers of a book.

The guard came around to the head of the bed. "Good?"

"Yes, very good, thank you."

He began fiddling with the chain on my right hand. He got the lock open, then replaced it, but allowing a foot or so more chain. Moving around the bed, he did the same on the other side.

"Sit up. But no look."

I sat up slowly, stiffly. He pulled the blanket off me and draped it over my head, leaving it hanging in front of my face. "Now look."

I cautiously pulled my blindfold up a bit, until I could see the book. Red, new. A Bible, the Revised Standard Version. I caressed it gently, then leaned forward so the blanket would hang down over my face but allow light from the bulb above me to fall on the book in my lap. My back started aching almost immediately, but I ignored it.

I read the title page, the publishing and copyright information, the notes of the editors, slowly, carefully. Then: Genesis.

"In the beginning . . ."

## Madeleine

*BEIRUT. March 16, 1985.* When I opened my eyes, I was looking straight at the clock on the wall: eight thirty a.m. Terry's not back from his tennis game yet. When he woke me with a kiss at seven, he said he'd be back by this time. We'd promised each other that no matter what happened, we would always be on time for our meetings. When someone you love is late in Beirut, you worry.

He'll be home any minute now, I thought. It's Saturday, my day off, and I can use another hour of sleep. I dozed off. It was about ten o'clock when our cleaning lady, Umm Mahmoud, opened the bedroom door, waking me. I was shocked at her coming into our bedroom. "What are you doing, Umm Mahmoud?"

"Oh, we thought you were at your mother's," she answered.

That's crazy. Why should she think I'm at my mother's? This is my home. Why is she looking at me so strangely? And who are "we"?

"Where is Terry?" I asked.

She mumbled something I couldn't understand, but I realized something was wrong. "Mustapha wants to talk to you," she said.

---

It should be apparent to all that the conversations in this book cannot be exact, despite the use of quotation marks. Neither Madeleine nor I had notes to refer to in writing it—only our memories. We are both satisfied that those memories are clear and that what we have quoted ourselves and others as saying is substantially accurate. Any errors are due to mistakes of memory.     —TERRY ANDERSON

Why would our landlord want to see me now?

I dressed hurriedly and ran out of the apartment and down to Mustapha's place on the ground floor. He was standing outside his door with his sister and her two daughters. They all looked upset, even angry. As they saw me, they fell silent.

"What's going on, Mustapha?"

He said that Bill Foley, a friend and former AP photographer who lived on the first floor, wanted to talk to me.

I knew something was badly wrong. I ran up the stairs to Bill's flat. The door was open, and as he heard me coming, he came out. He looked sadly into my eyes and opened his arms to me. His girlfriend, Cary, was standing behind him. My mind was racing. I couldn't believe what I was beginning to think. It couldn't be true.

"Did they take him, Bill? Did they take Terry?"

He held me tightly, nodded his head. I could feel him crying.

The first thing I thought of was, I want to be with him, I want to be there, too, wherever he is. I felt terribly lost and confused.

Cary, who was crying also, took me into the apartment, tried to calm me down. I could hear her repeating, "It will be all right. I'm sure he'll be freed soon."

I can't believe she's talking about Terry. I can't think anymore. Oh, my God, Terry kidnapped. It's not true. There must be a mistake.

Bill told me what Don Mell had told him: A car followed them from the sports club, and as Terry stopped to let Don out at his apartment building, three men with pistols grabbed Terry, put him in their car, and drove off. Don tried to follow them with Terry's car but lost them after a few blocks. He came to our place to tell me, knocked on the door, but, when I didn't respond, went on to the office.

"I want to see Don," I told Bill. My mind was numb. Everything seemed like a dream. I couldn't feel my body.

As we left the building, a CBS-TV crew was waiting to talk to me. The cameraman asked if I would say something. I was crying. "What can I tell you? I have nothing to tell you."

I had worked on the story when the Reverend Ben Weir was kidnapped. I had seen his wife in our office, at NBC. I had watched her cry and felt her pain. My mind rejected the thought of being one of those women whose man had been taken.

When we arrived at the AP office, all our friends were working on the story. As I came in, they all stopped for a few seconds. One by one they came to me, reassured me. They seemed as lost as I was. The phones were ringing; some of our friends were calling government officials, militia offices, party leaders. It was complete chaos.

I knew I had to do something, but I didn't know what. One thing kept running through my mind. Terry. Terry will come back tonight. He'll convince those people of the mistake they are making. Surely it's the same people who took another hostage a few weeks ago. They let him go after a day. It must be the same people. It can't be Islamic Jihad. It can't be. As long as we don't hear from them, we're okay.

I stayed in the office most of the day, watching, waiting for something to happen, but nothing did. There was no news, no result for all the effort everyone was making.

Finally Scheherazade Faramarzi, one of our friends at the AP bureau, asked me if I wanted her to come and stay with me that night. I was very grateful, and said yes. The next morning she came with me to the AP office. There had been no calls, no claims of responsibility.

We were as afraid of knowing Terry's whereabouts as we were of not knowing. As long as we didn't hear from the Jihad, Terry had a better chance to come home sooner rather than later. Scheherazade and I went home to the apartment.

It was around seven p.m. when a neighbor who lived below us came to tell me there was a call for me in her house. The AP had been trying to reach me, but couldn't get through on our phone. Telephone service in Beirut was often erratic at best.

My heart was beating very fast. I was afraid to pick up the phone. The voice on the line sounded deep and apologetic. Whoever it was said he was very sorry, but he had just had a call from Reuters News Agency saying a man claiming to be from the Islamic Jihad had called them to claim Terry's kidnapping. He continued talking, but I couldn't hear him. I could only hear my voice screaming, "Oh, please God, why? Not the Jihad." Suddenly there were more people in the room, crying with me.

I have never been as scared in my life as I was that moment. Terry, in the hands of those people. What will they do to him? I thought about the baby I was carrying, of Terry and me.

O, God, have mercy on us.

I went to the office every day that first week, hoping for news, something. Pictures of Terry were distributed in Beirut by the AP, as well as in the Bekáa Valley, eastern Lebanon, southern Lebanon. The silence was killing me. I knew that the longer they kept silent, the longer it was likely he would stay there. They had already been holding three hostages for many months: William Buckley, the Reverend Benjamin Weir, and Father Martin Jenco. Another hostage, Jeremy Levin, managed to get away in February—whether he'd escaped or been released was still a mystery. Now Terry had joined the list. The Shiite fundamentalists' hatred of America had made them blind to any human rights. And their power had been growing rapidly in the last year.

Lebanon was being ruled by the weakest government since the war began, divided among parties from all sects. The Christians who had dominated the country since its birth in 1943 were split, with even the powerful Maronite Catholic sect divided among feudal families. The Maronites were locked in deadly enmity with the Druse, a fierce sect dominating a large section of Lebanon's central mountains.

The Muslims were split between Sunnis—careful businessmen and old families, in large part—and Shiites, mostly poor laborers from southern Lebanon and the Bekáa Valley. But the once quiescent Shiites, oppressed and exploited by the other sects, had become angry and radicalized. They were inspired by the Islamic Revolution of their fellow Shiites in Iran and by the unofficial but undoubted fact that they outnumbered all the other sects, and probably made up more than half of Lebanon's population of three or four million. The fundamentalists in Iran were sending money and mullahs to preach revolution and hatred of the West to the Shiites. Israel, now ruling their home territory in the south with a heavy hand, only fueled the fire.

All of these factions were locked in a struggle over the rigid and now outdated unwritten agreement, called the National Covenant, dictated by the French before they left Lebanon: the Maronites would provide a president, the Sunnis a prime minister, the Shia a speaker of parliament, and the Druse some senior military men.

That already terribly complicated situation was further inflamed by an influx of Palestinians who had been kicked out of Jordan in 1970 and insisted on waging their war against Israel from Lebanese soil, and the meddling of Syria, the next-door giant from which all that was now Lebanon had been taken just fifty years before, and which refused to really acknowledge that independence.

The mixture had erupted into civil war in 1975—a war that had still not ended and would continue for sixteen years.

Among the most fearsome of the many radical groups that plagued Lebanon was the one that called itself Islamic Jihad—Islamic Holy War. It was believed to be a cell of Hezbollah, the Iranian-founded Party of God, and was creating an atmosphere of terror that enveloped Westerners and Lebanese.

Tens of thousands of Shiites had been driven out of their homes in southern Lebanon during the first Israeli invasion, in 1978, then by the 1982 Israeli invasion and continuing occupation. They took refuge in Beirut's suburbs—a matter both inconvenient and unpleasant for the Lebanese who originally lived there.

I am a Maronite Catholic, but was still living in the old West Beirut neighborhood where I was brought up. It had changed greatly over the years. Once a pleasant area near the harbor, Minet El-Hosn was now filled with refugees, mostly Shiites. All of my family's longtime neighbors and friends had left during the first few years of the war. There were still many non-Shiites there—both Christians and Sunni Muslims—but the fundamentalists had managed to take control.

My family consisted almost entirely of women—my mother, two sisters, two nieces. We also had a brother, but he had left the country. As the power of the fundamentalists became established, it became harder and harder to lead our own lives. We were obliged to take account of Shiite sensibilities in dress, behavior, even in practicing our religion. We could not be seen with any man not known to be a fiancé or husband. We did not even dare to make the sign of the cross, or go to midnight Mass at Christmas.

Whether it was the new sense of power the fundamentalists were gaining after years of oppression or the ambition they had for themselves and for their cause, some kind of a monster was being born. The fundamentalists seemed to hate everything and everyone who was not of their religion. They believed the West and Satan America were behind every evil that occurred in Lebanon, and Israel was America's instrument for bringing that evil about.

By no means did all Shiites think that way. Most were just ordinary Lebanese trying to live their lives. But those who disagreed could not express their opinion. It was not practical to oppose the power that protected them and fed their children when they could not do it themselves.

When the civil war had started in 1975, I had gone ahead with plans I had to travel to England. Like many Lebanese, I thought the war would last only a few months. I was wrong. This war was fiercer than anything the Lebanese had ever witnessed. The hatred that had accumulated between the Christians on one side and the Palestinians and their Lebanese Muslim allies on the other was beyond comprehension. I spent about a year in England visiting my sister and her family, then four years in Sweden after I married a Swedish man. The marriage didn't work, and after our divorce I finally returned to my country. My family had told me of the changes, but still I was shocked to see what had happened in those five years. The destruction caused by the civil war was truly shameful.

I went to work for an American television network, ABC, covering the Israeli invasion in 1982 and the war. It was during that time that I met Terry at a party given by a CNN cameraman. Terry offered me a drink and sat next to me. I had never seen him before. He was very fat, with a beard that made his face look big and round. After talking to me for a few minutes, he moved on. I thought, I wonder if I will ever go out with this man. He wasn't my type at all.

At the beginning of 1984 I started working with NBC News. The war had taken a different shape. Lebanon was exporting terrorism, and the Lebanese had learned a new trade—kidnapping Westerners.

NBC and AP worked together a lot. We used AP's wire reports, and I had seen Terry's copy frequently. I admired his accuracy and writing style. Bonnie Anderson (no relation), the NBC correspondent, gave a party at her flat, and Terry came.

It was the first time we had said more than a few casual words to each other. A few weeks later Terry called to ask me out for dinner. I declined, but left the possibility open for another time. I wasn't sure I wanted to go out with him. He called again, and again my answer was, "Maybe another time." I knew I should tell him I wasn't interested, and I still don't know what made me hesitant to do that.

Finally, after several invitations, I accepted. During the evening he told me he was married. He told me his wife had returned to Japan and would not be rejoining him. He was to be reposted to Mexico at the end of the year, but she didn't want to go. The marriage had not been going well. But his respect for Mickey and love for their daughter, Gabrielle, showed me something I had not seen in other men.

Terry liked to surprise me and often did as we continued to see each other. But his biggest surprise came after a few months, when he said he had told AP headquarters in New York he wanted to stay in Lebanon, and they had agreed. Two days later he told me he had asked his wife for a divorce.

I knew what he was trying to tell me. I was overwhelmed. This man was changing his life for me. He was proposing. When I said yes, I decided I would give him nothing but love and happiness.

It wasn't long before I became pregnant. We didn't expect it; I thought I couldn't. Though I had been married before, I had never gotten pregnant.

Destiny is not something you choose. It is chosen for you. Meeting Terry, falling in love with him, and carrying his baby were things that God had chosen for us. We felt we were made for each other. Planning our lives and our family was the most normal thing to do, as though we had been together for years. We traveled to the States in January 1985 to visit Terry's father, who was critically ill. I met his sisters and brothers and felt immediately as one of the family.

Then March 16, 1985, came and ended our wonderful dream. The traders knocked at our door, but they weren't buying or selling. They just robbed us of our happiness and planted hate instead of love in my heart. Hate that only Terry's return could eliminate.

THOSE first days were very painful, and endless. Hoping that Terry would show up any minute, I stayed home constantly. I could not let myself think of how he was feeling, how scared he must be. I felt ashamed. These are my people who are doing this to us. I often wondered if he was thinking the same thing. More people were kidnapped. On March 22 two Frenchmen were abducted. Other abductions followed. It was obvious nothing was going to stop the kidnappers unless their demands were met. But no one seemed to know what the demands were.

It was at this point that I realized I had to leave Lebanon. It had been three weeks since Terry's abduction, and I was entering my eighth month of pregnancy. AP had arranged with Terry's sister

Peggy Say for me to fly to Batavia, New York, his hometown, and stay with her. I had refused earlier when they suggested it, but as the time grew nearer when I would be unable to fly because of my pregnancy, I was afraid that Terry might get released and sent back to the States and I would be stuck, not able to join him. The thought of being in Lebanon while Terry was somewhere in the States was unbearable. So I left.

# CHAPTER TWO
## Terry

*BEIRUT, 1982.*  When Israel invaded southern Lebanon on June 6, 1982, southern Africa was quiet, and I was restless. I'd been covering the region out of Johannesburg for nearly a year, and while the country was beautiful and the people interesting, it had failed to take hold of me. The stench of apartheid overwhelmed everything. As soon as the news of the Israeli invasion broke on the AP wire, I was on the phone to my foreign editor, Nate Polowetzky: "Do you need help? Can I go?"

Nate urged caution, told me to wait a few days. Finally, though, he called back. Yes, go to Israel.

Twenty-four hours later I landed in Tel Aviv and went down to the AP office. Bureau Chief Larry Thorson gave me a short briefing, then handed me the keys to a rental car.

I had little knowledge of the Middle East. I'd spent most of my time overseas in Asia, and my only foreign language was Japanese—hardly likely to be useful in Lebanon. Still, I was excited. It was a war, it was the world's biggest story, and I was a journalist.

Buoyed by the high that was still drowning out the effects of a twenty-four-hour airplane flight, I drove to the very northern tip of Israel, met up with an AP photographer, and crossed into Lebanon escorted, as all foreign journalists had to be, by an Israeli press officer.

Those first few days were a disaster. I battled constantly with the Israeli press handlers and censors. After a week I decided to part company and arranged transportation to East Beirut, where the AP was setting up a separate office, as the situation in its old location—the western, Muslim half of the capital—grew daily more chaotic.

East Beirut was held by the Christians, who had encouraged the Israelis to invade their country to drive out the hated Palestinians and shore up Christian domination of the Muslims. It was fairly safe. The Israeli forces ringing the western half of the city were concentrating their fury on the Muslims and Palestinians trapped there.

It was a peculiar war, where we could sit in lawn chairs on top of our hotel, the Alexandre, just a few dozen yards from the Green Line— the no-man's-land of destruction dividing the city—and watch Israeli tanks and planes destroying the western half. During the day AP Middle East news editor Tom Baldwin and I would range up and down the front line, gathering material for our stories. At night we would go out to one of the several fine French or Lebanese restaurants that remained open just blocks away from the hotel.

Lebanon fascinated me with its endless complications, its cross-currents, and subwars within larger wars. The more I learned, the more I saw parallels with Asia. This Middle Eastern country was more eastern than middle. Somehow it had already captured me. I was hooked both as a newsman and as an individual.

Then there was the incredible violence. I'd seen violence before— many times in my six years as a foreign correspondent, as a reporter in the States, and before that as a marine in Vietnam. But the intensity and sheer ferocity of these people appalled me.

Lebanese factions murdered each other, and each others' families, with sickening regularity. Christians would drag live Palestinians at high speed behind their cars. The Syrians wiped out the entire town of Hama—one of their own—to quash a small rebellion. Israel smashed Beirut without regard for the half million Lebanese caught there, without even a small attempt to distinguish among combatants and noncombatants, men, women, or children.

After a few days in East Beirut, I crossed over the front line, moving into the AP office in besieged West Beirut with AP Middle East correspondent Nick Tatro. Through the fiercely hot Mediterranean summer days I wandered through the city and talked to refugees. I climbed office and apartment buildings, stair after weary stair, to watch Israeli F-14s and Kfirs swoop down and lay their terrible cargoes almost gently on the homes and businesses below them, untouched by the Korean War–vintage antiaircraft guns of the Palestinian and Muslim militias defending the city. Then I would take to the streets again, trying to get to the bombed areas, check on the destruction, watch the bodies and pieces of bodies being loaded into whatever emergency vehicles could get to the scene.

Despite the horrors, the blood, and despair that surrounded us, the fascination never faded. And mixed with it was the awful, heady rush of danger. We covered that war almost as if it were a horror movie, feeling ourselves exempt from death, careening from sporadic encounters with wild-eyed gunmen to terrifying, stretched-out minutes huddling under shells and bombs or cowering from snipers, only to return to the Commodore Hotel bar and blandly trade the day's war stories with our colleagues over a giant gin and tonic.

The pose of observer, the veteran immune to the pain of others, was just that, though—a pose. No one, not the most cynical correspondent, got through that summer in Beirut without pain.

For me, it was the dark, deep eyes of Palestinian and Lebanese children, the sight of doctors operating on grievously wounded people, hunched over the table to keep the plaster dust, shaken from the ceiling by shells, from drifting into the gaping, bloody holes. Beirut in the summer of 1982 was summed up for me by the pitted body of three-year-old Ahmed Baitam lying on an intensive care bed in Barbir Hospital, on the Green Line, while doctors tried to bring him out of shock. The pits covering his skinny frame were from phosphorus. The doctors failed, and he died while I watched. The bodies of his five-day-old twin sisters were in a morgue drawer down the hall. Fourteen members of that single family died when two shells hit the basement they were hiding in.

But Beirut was also an incredibly stubborn, brave, independent people: Elias, my Christian driver, whose baby cried constantly because of the shelling and sniping he'd heard since birth; Elias' cousin, Tony, dubbed by the AP staff the Wonder Driver because of his willingness to go anywhere, anytime; and day after day the thousands of Lebanese who just kept trying to live their lives, go to work, raise their kids, while their country went mad.

In August, as the tortured negotiations among the United States, the Lebanese government, the Palestinians, and the Israelis approached an end, Nick Tatro called me into his office. Middle East news editor Tom Baldwin would have to leave. His wife, Toni, was seven months pregnant. Would I exchange jobs with Tom?

I barely hesitated. Of course, given the expectation that the war would be ending soon and my wife and daughter, Gabrielle, could join me, I'd love to have the post. We agreed that I would return to Johannesburg and close up my house, take a short vacation, and return to Beirut.

I ARRIVED back in early October of 1982, Japanese wife and daughter in tow. Mickey was understandably nervous, and the first view of the southern suburbs of Beirut from the airplane did little to reinforce my assurances that "it will be all right." But after nearly fourteen years of marriage I was accustomed to dismissing Mickey's concerns.

A sweet, quiet, and very traditional lady from Hiroshima, she had been trailing along behind me ever since I talked her into ignoring her parents' fierce objections and marrying me while I was serving with the Marine Corps in Japan. I had just turned twenty-one, and she was a young twenty-two.

The marriage had not gone well. We "married in a fever," as the song goes, and that carried us for a while. But I was too young and bullish to use any sensitivity in our relationship, and the gaps in temperament and culture were too great to allow real communication. I had often left her to cope alone while I was off covering something I thought more important. She never complained—a Japanese woman from a conservative family has limited expectations of marriage.

As we lived our parallel lives, though, my expectations had changed, and I had often fulfilled them with a series of other women. I even used that pathetic cliché: If she doesn't know, it can't hurt her. Of course, she knew, and was hurt, but never spoke of it.

So far, the level of unhappiness had not reached the critical point. I knew the break would never come from her, and I hadn't had the nerve to face the pain it would inflict on our daughter, Gabrielle, a beautiful and cheerful sprite of seven—let alone on Mickey herself.

This tour in Beirut was exciting to me. For Mickey, it was just another strange place, and a frightening one at that. It would prove, finally, too much for our marriage to survive.

Much had changed in the city. The fighting was over. During my vacation the PLO had left, and the Israelis, flagrantly ignoring the agreement they'd just signed, had used the assassination of Lebanon's President-elect Bashir Gemayel in September 1982 as an excuse to move into West Beirut. Lebanese Christian Phalangist militiamen, with at least the tacit permission of the Israeli army, had massacred hundreds of men, women, and children in the Sabra and Chatilla refugee camps, prompting the immediate return of the multinational force—the units of American, French, and Italian troops sent into Beirut to oversee the evacuation of the PLO. At the airport, a 2000-man unit of U.S. marines was settling in, sending out patrols in jeeps and on foot. Forceful, confident, they reflected the spirit and plea-sure they felt in this job: peacekeeping.

As I settled into my new job during the late fall of 1982, a feeling of optimism was flooding Beirut. The Lebanese, with their incredible spirit, were busily rebuilding. I tried to get a handle on the larger responsibilities of being Middle East news editor, traveling to Syria and Iraq and Jordan and Bahrain and Cyprus, getting acquainted with the different problems and power structures of each.

But it was still Lebanon that gripped me. Despite the ravages of the war, it retained an atmosphere—a mélange of the Orient and Eu-rope, sophistication and wealth, and simplicity and poverty. And it seemed to be in a renaissance. Even the Lebanese, so long deceived, believed that the good days were returning.

The pessimism of veterans like Farouk Nassar, who had watched thirty years of Middle East crises for the AP, or Robert Fisk, the London *Times* correspondent who was rapidly becoming my best friend, seemed excessive, cynical.

I had quickly grown to like and admire Robert after I met him in the first weeks of the war. With his brilliant analytical mind and cold, critical look at everything that passed before him, he saw things at a different angle, fifteen or twenty degrees at variation from the rest of the world. That and his penetrating intelligence threw a light on events that couldn't be found anywhere else but on the pages of the *Times* of London.

We spent many days in the field together, and many evenings on the balcony of my apartment arguing about Lebanon and the world. Above all, he tried to keep me alive. He drilled the fundamentals into me each time we ventured into the dangerous world that was Lebanon, among the militias and armies and snipers: "There are no good guys. The gunmen are all little furry creatures with yellow teeth and small brains and guns. All of them—even the British and

French and Americans. Sooner or later they all behave like hamsters."

I often wondered where Fisky put the pain. I know he felt it, had seen him wince, seen the anger in his eyes as we watched the bodies pile up. That's where his profound neutrality came from. He had seen them all do it, counted the bodies on every side, until there could be no sides for him. What was left was rage at everybody who misused power, low or high.

I respected him greatly, but everything I saw and heard during that late fall of 1982 and early 1983 belied his caution and pessimism. The Lebanese, the Americans at the embassy, everyone saw an end to the war, an end finally to the bad times. The divided city suddenly was, at least nominally, open. Traffic moved from east to west and back again. Schools opened; the nightlife, which never totally disappeared even during the siege, grew brighter, more frantic.

Through the spring and summer I worked frantically. I paid little attention to what I saw as an increasingly fruitless marriage, neglected my growing daughter, drank and smoked heavily. My boss, Nick Tatro, was expecting a transfer any week, and I wanted his job badly. It was one of the top foreign service positions in the AP and would represent a major jump in my career. Chief Middle East correspondent for The Associated Press. To become an expert on this horribly complicated, violent region in a year? I *would* do it.

I became even more determined as the optimism faded to unease, and the unease to fear, in Beirut. The new Christian-dominated government, under Amin Gemayel, was heavy-handed in its dealings with the other sects. Fighting broke out in Beirut when the government evicted Shia refugees from a school they had occupied, with no provision made to house them elsewhere. Bulldozers began plowing under the shacks of thousands of other refugees along the coast so rich Christians could reclaim the land for new apartment buildings.

In south Lebanon, resistance to the Israelis grew, despite severe reprisals and random sweeps of the villages by Israeli-led militiamen. In the beautiful mountains above Beirut, Christian Phalangists, who had encouraged the Israeli invasion, began "arresting" Druse men at random checkpoints. Those arrested usually just disappeared. Fighting broke out in villages where the two sects had lived in relative peace. Innocent villagers and travelers were murdered out of hand because they carried the wrong identity card.

In Washington, the goal of the multinational force seemed to become blurred. Over strong protests from both the U.S. embassy and the marine command, the Reagan administration shifted from peacekeeping to "support of the legitimate government." The problem with that was the Gemayel government had little claim to legitimacy and less to governing.

Western reporters had become accustomed to wandering freely around Lebanon, accepted by even the most radical of factions as journalists, separate from and independent of the U.S. and British governments. The PLO knew the value of treating the press well. Now, though, the atmosphere was changing. With the victory of Ayatollah Khomeini in Iran, Iranian money poured into Lebanon to influence the Shia. Conflicts between Christians, Muslims, Druse, and Palestinians sharpened. The shift of position in Washington was noted quickly by all the other players in the Lebanese war, and sharply changed the view they held of the multinational force and even of Western reporters. The radicals got more radical, the contempt and hatred for America and the West a little more personal.

Ten Italians and five U.S. marines were wounded on March 16, 1983, in separate attacks. Later in the day the Agence France-Presse office in Beirut received a call from a Lebanese man. He said he was from an organization called Islamic Jihad, which no one had heard of, and wanted to claim responsibility for the attacks. Such claims were common. With no basis on which to judge, we usually ignored them.

On a sunny April day, as I lingered in my apartment on the Corniche Manara, facing the Mediterranean, the building shuddered from a massive explosion. I ran down to the street. Nothing—except a few stunned people looking east. The U.S. embassy was that way, just seven hundred meters down the road. I began to run toward it, and as I rounded the small bend, I saw that the embassy was blanketed in black smoke. Two men were carrying a body down the small driveway to the street. The smoke lifted momentarily. The building's entire center section had collapsed on itself.

More mutilated bodies, unrecognizable as Lebanese or American, were being pulled out as Beirut's emergency crews arrived. One body, in a white shirt, was hanging head down from the fifth or sixth floor, its lower part trapped in the wreckage, blood staining the concrete.

Gradually swarms of journalists and investigators pieced together the story. A man in a black pickup truck had driven through the light wooden gate at the embassy, slamming into the building, just beside the front door, and detonating his cargo of explosives. Sixty-three people died, including a line of Lebanese waiting for visas and seventeen Americans in the embassy itself. The American victims included a half dozen men meeting in a conference room on one of the upper floors—virtually the entire Middle East section of the Central Intelligence Agency.

The explosion eliminated the embassy for all practical purposes. It also destroyed the confidence of both Lebanese and Americans in what we were doing there, and wiped out American intelligence-gathering capability in the country during a crucial period.

As BEIRUT and Lebanon were disintegrating, so was my life. I did get the job I wanted. I was now the chief Middle East correspondent and wholly wrapped up in keeping track of the increasingly weird events in Lebanon, handling a spirited, feuding staff of journalists, administering a million-dollar budget, and coordinating coverage for a dozen other countries. Overwork, too much alcohol, and the emotional and psychological toll of unending violence left me with little room for anyone else and little interest in my marriage. My wife and I had almost nothing to say to each other. There was no hostility; there was simply nothing in the relationship. Yet guilt kept me from doing anything about my feelings.

Events continued to pile up around us. In August the Lebanese army and Syrian-backed Druse militiamen began a fierce battle over positions in the mountains overlooking Beirut. The army took a major drubbing and broke up. Half its men took their weapons over to the various Shia and Druse militia in West Beirut and the southern suburbs. The other half fell under the sway of rightist Christian Phalange leaders in the eastern half of the capital.

The marines at the airport were now in a militarily untenable position, lined on one side by a warren of concrete buildings inhabited by Shia—many of them radical fundamentalists—and directly under the guns of the Druse in the mountains. Politically, they were in worse trouble, as U.S. support for the Gemayel government increased, alienating all the other factions. The marines and the other members of the multinational force would pay a terrible price for that policy.

On October 23, 1983, two explosions came within seconds of each other, at six twenty a.m. The closest was heavy enough to make the walls of my apartment house shudder. As I headed downstairs, AP photographer Bill Foley was emerging from his apartment, two floors down. Scrambling for the car, we tuned in the radio for the first flashes.

"Where was it?"

"Rauche. French headquarters, they said."

Traffic was light. In three or four minutes we came up the hill and turned left into the narrow street where the French paratroopers had their headquarters. *Had* was the operative word. The building had almost disappeared, collapsing into a pile of broken concrete. French soldiers and officers were stumbling around in shock. One man was gently holding a hand that stuck up out of the mess, the man who owned it completely buried but still alive.

Shouting questions, interrogating men who could barely speak, we quickly learned that dozens of soldiers were buried in the rubble. Foley was scurrying about, snapping picture after picture. Then someone shouted at me, "They've hit the marines, too."

I grabbed Foley, practically dragged him to the car. Another frantic five miles to the airport. Another pall of smoke, screaming sirens. Something was terribly wrong.

Two stunned marines, smoke-smudged faces streaked with tears, manned a large gap in the chain-link fence of the airport. They said nothing as we climbed through. The bodies were already being laid in rows a few yards from the pile of smoking concrete that had been the main barracks for the 1200-man marine-and-navy unit.

Five minutes trying to count the torn bodies, talk to crying marines, get some kind of account of what happened. A truck bomber—a suicidal man who smiled as he ran his truck directly into the building's entrance.

The horror was overcoming me. There were bound to be men I knew in that smoking rubble. I'd been a marine for six years. These were *my* people.

U.S. intelligence was quick to assign a name to the man behind the attack—Hussein Mussawi, an almost unknown Shia Muslim who had split from Amal, the main Shia political and militia group, to form something called Islamic Amal. He also seemed to be providing the muscle for a new, ultrafundamentalist coalition of mullahs that called itself Hezbollah—the Party of God.*

After the marine bombing, Lebanon seemed to fall apart. Any faint optimism, any discussion of a future for the country seemed fatuous. The marines hunkered down in bunkers at the airport and behind a massive concrete-and-earth wall at the British embassy, now shared with U.S. diplomats. A marine amphibious armored vehicle and machine-gun post were both just below the window of my apartment, next to the embassy. Shells fell sporadically on the city and suburbs, and the battles in the mountains continued throughout the year.

In December 1983 a group of Iranian-inspired Shia launched an attempt to destabilize Kuwait with attacks on the U.S. and French embassies, power stations, and other installations. Though people were killed, the attempt failed miserably. Seventeen Shia were convicted and jailed. The event, far off in the Persian Gulf, got wide coverage but was soon forgotten, at least in the West. There was no hint that the repercussions would involve half a dozen countries and leave dozens of Westerners, including me, in chains for months or years.

The climax came on February 5, 1984, when Druse and Shia militias took over West Beirut, driving the Lebanese army out of the city in a complete rout. The next morning, along with dozens of other Americans and Westerners, my wife and daughter boarded a marine helicopter in front of our apartment building and left for Cyprus. That "temporary" separation from them became permanent. It was the end of hope for Lebanon for the next eight years, and the effective end of my sixteen-year marriage.

In Beirut the warnings had been there as early as the beginning of 1984. But they went nearly unnoticed in the general chaos. In January 1984 Malcolm Kerr, president of the American University of

---

*As sources within Lebanon and Iran would show, Hezbollah had without question carried out the attack on the embassy. More importantly, it had set up as early as 1982 a special operations center, known as Ali's Center, to gather information on Westerners in Beirut. Operatives, including many women, were assigned to follow Westerners.

William Buckley was a top target. At some point my name was linked with his in the data bank at Ali's Center—probably because I had developed a friendship with another embassy official. Another bit was added to my file after Buckley's kidnapping when I refused to buy pictures of him and another hostage, the Reverend Ben Weir, from a couple whom I believed to be linked closely to the kidnappers, then reported the attempted sale to the embassy. Eventually Ali's Center would list me as the "second man" in the CIA in Beirut. Needless to say, I was never a witting or unwitting "asset" of the CIA or any other intelligence agency.

Beirut, was murdered in his office in what turned out to be a carefully planned operation by Hezbollah after Kerr was labeled a dangerous spy.

In March, Jeremy Levin, bureau chief for CNN, went missing. A week later William Buckley, station chief for the CIA in Lebanon, was taken almost from his front door, despite a professional's security precautions. Each kidnapping was dutifully reported, then virtually forgotten by the Beirut press corps, struggling to keep up with the never-ending permutations in Lebanon's rat's nest of a war.

Foreigners were becoming more and more nervous about going out at night. We found our amusements in parties at each others' flats, drinking and dancing almost frenetically. At one party I chatted up a slim, stunning Lebanese woman with long black hair and beautiful eyes. Her name was Madeleine Bassil, and she worked as a researcher and production assistant at NBC. A couple of weeks later I asked her if she'd like to have dinner, but got turned down. I tried again after a few days. No luck. Again. Finally she agreed.

On May 8 the Reverend Benjamin Weir, a Presbyterian missionary who had lived in Lebanon thirty years, mostly among the Shia in the south, was snatched from the sidewalk near his Beirut apartment.

At the end of July the last U.S. marines, still guarding the combined British-U.S. embassy, were pulled out. A relief—the armored vehicle and machine guns were gone from under my window, the concrete-and-earth barrier blocking the Corniche taken away. The seaside promenade was again filled with evening strollers and the tiny trucks that sold the bitterly strong Lebanese coffee.

As always, the summer was bright, hot, the Mediterranean sun never letting up as I drove from one end of the country to the other. Southern Lebanon: hundred-year-old olive orchards, scores of bright green orange trees, bulldozed by the Israeli army after a sniper attack; the bare, gray-green mountains, thousand-foot drops off winding one-lane roads; massacres in this Druse or that Christian village; the Bekáa, with its ever larger number of tiny fanatical groups.

Despite the frantic pace—or perhaps because of it, because of the things I'd seen over the past two years—I began to do some heavy thinking. I'd never been introspective, never stopped pushing long enough to think about where I was going, what I was becoming. I was a mess physically, morally. It couldn't go on. I began cutting down on my drinking, trying to get some exercise, running on the Corniche along the sea in the early mornings.

I asked my wife for a divorce—painful, so painful, especially trying to explain why to an eight-year-old daughter who loved both her parents blindly. Madeleine and I had by now begun dating steadily, quietly. I proposed, and asked her to move into my apartment. She agreed. Both of us were working twelve-, fourteen-hour days. The peace of that small third-floor flat, with its lovely expanse of sea just across the road, was the antidote to each day's craziness.

I also began once again to read the Bible. I was raised a Roman Catholic but had left the church as a teenager. I'd remained interested in religion, almost as an intellectual exercise, I thought, and had read widely—Buddhism, Islam, Judaism, Christianity. This time, though, I knew I was looking for something more than intellectual stimulation. I just didn't know what.

Madeleine was getting increasingly nervous about my safety. She wouldn't let me speak English as we wandered through the streets; she speculated about the unshaven young men sitting idly in cars near the apartment. I paid little attention. I'd wandered freely through the country for two years. Sure, it was dangerous. I could handle it.

Madeleine became pregnant. She wasn't supposed to be able to, had never conceived in her first marriage. There was never any question of what to do. It was inconvenient, but to give up a child she'd always longed to have, and one I welcomed, was unthinkable.

In December 1984 we took a couple of weeks off. We stayed with Madeleine's sister and brother-in-law in Sunderland, England. I ran in the bitter cold dawn along the sea and wandered through the streets of the small industrial town, just trying to come down from the tension and excitement of the Middle East.

As we walked around Sunderland and Newcastle, I kept catching sight of the tall, sharply pointed traditional steeple of the local Catholic church. Every time I turned around, it was there. Finally, during lunch at a nearby restaurant with Madeleine and her sister, I excused myself, walked around the corner, and entered the church. I sat down in a pew and just looked at the altar. I didn't pray—not really. But I felt a perfect sense of being at home where I belonged. After so many years of avoiding it, I recognized myself: I'm a Catholic, a Christian. The sense of relief was powerful and immediate. I didn't know what

I was going to do with my new knowledge, whether I could live up to the obligations and duties it would impose. I would have to work that out later. For now, just knowing was enough.

Madeleine and I returned to Beirut in time for Christmas, 1984, and resumed the frantic pace of our jobs. By the end of 1984 the city had settled into permanent chaos. Armed men wandered the streets, and car thefts were common. A German man was shot to death, apparently when he refused to give up his car to some thug.

On January 8, 1985, Father Lawrence Martin Jenco was forced from his car in Beirut. The priest was head of Catholic Charities in Lebanon, charged with distributing millions of dollars to the needy—Christian or Muslim. The usual anonymous caller to a Western news agency said he and the other missing Americans would go free "if all Americans leave Lebanon."

On February 14 Jerry Levin, the CNN bureau chief who had been taken in 1984, escaped from his kidnappers. He told Syrian officials his guards had forgotten to fix his chains properly and he had climbed out a third-story window, using sheets and blankets to lower himself to the ground. He seemed shaken and distraught, but in reasonable health. I joked to a couple of friends: "They had a priest, a minister, an embassy official, and a journalist. They've lost the journalist. I suppose they'll be looking for a replacement."

At the beginning of March, I went to Cairo for a regional bureau chiefs' meeting. Lou Boccardi, the newly appointed president of the AP, was there for an International Press Institute meeting. He asked me several times about Beirut, expressing concern for my safety, but did not press the question when I assured him I didn't want to leave.

Just two days after I returned to Beirut, a car bomb went off outside the office of Sheik Mohammed Hussein Fadlallah, a fundamentalist mullah considered the most radical Shiite leader and identified by Western intelligence as the spiritual adviser to Hezbollah—the Party of God. Hezbollah's leaders were closely tied to Iran and virulently anti-American. More a loose coalition than a unified group, Hezbollah was engaged in a power struggle with the more moderate Amal, for long the primary political and military force of the Shiites. At first a great deal weaker than its rival, Hezbollah was using its Iranian-supplied money well and had grown into a powerful force.

Don Mell, Scheherazade Faramarzi, and I went to talk to Fadlallah the morning after the explosion. The scene was all too familiar—buildings torn, piles of rubble in the street, gunmen everywhere. The blast had killed nearly eighty people but missed Fadlallah. Most of the victims were civilians—many women and children.

The hostility we encountered was incredible, hatred blasting from the eyes of the militiamen and civilians all around us. On top of one pile of rubble was a makeshift sign: MADE IN AMERICA. Fadlallah was not available, and we left quickly.

The U.S. embassy had been quietly warning Americans to leave Beirut—a warning that most of the newspeople ignored. After the United States vetoed a U.N. resolution condemning the Israeli occupation of southern Lebanon on March 12, the U.N. ordered out all Americans working for its international agencies. Many diplomats were also leaving. I talked with Nate Polowetzky, the AP foreign editor, by Telex. He pressed me about the danger. I reassured him. "Frankly, I think the danger is greater from thugs just after money or a car."

On March 15, I went home for lunch, as had become my habit. As I drove along the Corniche on my way back, a new Mercedes pulled up beside me, then cut in sharply. I stepped on the gas, swerving to the right and then back into my lane ahead of the Mercedes. A minute later, as I turned up the hill toward Hamra, they tried again, on the smaller side road. This time I glanced into the car. Four bearded young men, but no guns in sight. I swerved sharply down an even smaller road, catching the driver of the Mercedes by surprise. By the time he stopped and backed up to make the turn, I was fifty yards ahead. The other car chased me for a few hundred yards but dropped off when we approached a Lebanese army checkpoint.

In the office, I told my news editor, Gerry Labelle, and Fisk what had happened. "Were they trying to kidnap you?" Labelle asked.

"I'm not sure. I think so."

Fisk offered the use of his car for a few days. I declined, and asked them both not to say anything. "Madeleine would get upset."

That evening Fisk dropped in, and we talked about the danger of kidnapping, carefully avoiding mention of the day's incident. Fisk was adamant—he'd never let them take him. He'd fight. "Don't be a fool, Fisky. If you fight, you'll get killed. Go along. At least you'll be alive."

He left, and Maddy and I went to bed early, since I had to be up at six a.m. for my tennis date with Don Mell.

# CHAPTER THREE

## Terry

*BEIRUT. April 1985.* I've had the Bible two days now. It's what—April 9? 10? Hard to keep track. The guards haul in several large sheets of plywood and some two-by-fours and begin hammering. Late in the afternoon they unfasten my chains. "Get up." One guard pushes me forward and into a narrow closetlike space they had made with the plywood, just wide enough to hold a cot, with a plastic shower curtain hanging at one end.

I lie down on the cot, and they refasten my chains. I can sit up and even lean back against the wall. "When closed, you can lift *couvrez-yeux*," one of the guards says in bastard English-French, rattling the curtain. "We come, you close eyes. You see me, you dead. Okay?"

"Yes, okay."

The curtain closes. I cautiously lift the blindfold—the first time in nearly four weeks. Cot, blanket, water bottle, pee bottle. Bible. Curtain. Nothing else. I lie back. The plywood partition ends a foot or so from the high ceiling. The chains run underneath, perhaps to a bolt in the wall or floor. The guards' movements, just on the other side of the plywood, are plain.

The curtain is suddenly yanked aside. I grab at the blindfold, lying on the bed. Too late.

*"Couvrez-yeux,"* he shouts. "No look. No look."

"Okay. Okay." Fumbling the cloth back in place.

"No good. You no good." A slap on the head. "Keep here. No put down. Keep here."

"Yes, I understand. Sorry."

"You see, you dead."

Silly. I'd already seen, and he knew it. Typical militiaman—small, thin, scruffy beard, sharp Arab nose, black hair. Completely inseparable from a thousand—ten thousand—others.

IT'S surprising what you can remember when you have nothing to do but remember. At first the mind is a blank. Where are all the things I learned, the books I read, the poems I memorized? There's nothing there—just a formless, gray-black misery. God, help me.

Start with the memories. Forget the stupidity of walking out into the street after one kidnap attempt, the very next morning, to give them your open, stupid self. That's done. You're paying. Think about Madeleine—so beautiful, all dark and flashing and loving. You're so lucky to win this woman now, after all these years. What is she doing? What is she feeling? Stop. It hurts too much.

What about Mickey and Gabrielle? I've hurt them both greatly. Especially Gabrielle. She sounded so sad, had so much pain in her voice the last time I talked to her on the phone. She's eight. How can she understand? Thou shalt not commit adultery. So many times, in so many places. No excuses. You did it. Accept it. Be sorry.

But I'm not sorry about Madeleine. No matter what. We didn't plan this child. But so much joy when it happened. So short a time together—what, ten, eleven months? Worth all this, if I die today, worth it.

All the other memories. The people. The mistakes, offenses. How arrogant I was! It must have been hard to like me. Did they all? Or was I just tolerated? I don't like me much. How can anyone else?

Hours, days, nights, weeks. Gray dawn after gray dawn.

An English-speaking man came in today and dictated a letter to me. At least I know why I've been kidnapped, or at least the "official" reason. He gave me a pen and paper, then told me to write:

> I am fine. I received your message. You should know that I am a victim of the American policy that favors Israel and which forced the detained persons in Kuwait to do what they did. My freedom is tied to the freedom of the detained over there. The American government still does not care about us. I ask you to do your best to pressure the American government to release the detained people over there because we are very close to being hanged in the case that this term is not met. Please move very swiftly to end my detention because I cannot take it anymore.

No discussion allowed. I asked about the message I was supposed to have received, but got no answer. After he left, I thought about those people who had been arrested in Kuwait in 1984. A straight swap, it looks like. Unfortunately, I can't believe the United States will allow itself to be pressured by terrorists. It's going to be a long time.

THE DAYS BEGIN TO SETTLE INTO A kind of routine: Sleepless nights, shifting and turning, trying to ease the stiffness of lying on a bed twenty-four hours a day. Listen to the roaches, occasionally watch one or two or three crawl slowly up the wall. Hear the muttering in Arabic as the guards awaken. Food—usually a sandwich of Arabic bread and dry yellow cheese. Brief trip down the hall to the filthy bathroom. Back to the cot. Read the Bible for a while. Lunch—perhaps a bowl of soup, or cold rice with canned vegetables dumped on top. The evenings are sometimes enlivened by short visits from one or two of the young men, sometimes to ask questions in broken English, sometimes just to amuse themselves. Occasionally one or two will kneel on my chest, poke their guns in my ear or neck, and hiss threats: "You dead. I kill you."

"Sure. *Tfaddal.* Go ahead. You kill me, my problems are over."

Late afternoon. The guards begin hammering again, on the other side of the room. A few hours later, well after dark, there's a subdued stir and bustle. Clank of chains, the snap of padlocks. A few words in English: "Sit. No speak." Another hostage? Who?

The next morning my trip to the bathroom is delayed. Someone else is being taken, perhaps two people. As the second returns past the door of my room, a guard stops him. *"Riyada. Sportif. Yallah."*

I hear the sound of someone jogging in place, doing jumping jacks, for five or ten minutes; then he's taken into another room.

My turn. Before getting onto the cot afterward, I speak to a guard. *"Riyada?* Exercise? Sport?"

He slaps my face hard. Again and again. "Sport? You want sport?" Slap, slap. "No sport here. *Yallah.*"

Brief shock, then an explosion of burning, blinding rage. Almost physically I clamp down on it. Don't move. Don't show *anything.*

Back on the cot. Chains pulled tight, painfully tight, and padlocks snapped. My feet begin to swell almost instantly. Four, five hours. Another guard brings lunch. "My feet, the chains. No good."

He pulls on the chain, then hisses, "Sssst. Who do?"

"The other guard."

"He *majnoon.*" Crazy. He opens the locks, eases the chains.

My undershorts, tennis shorts, and T-shirt are filthy—unchanged since my kidnapping. My hair feels stiff. I smell of sweat and urine. My teeth are starting to hurt. No chance to wash during the brief trips to the toilet each day. The dirt offends me. I'd been taught thoroughly in the Marine Corps, in Vietnam—no matter what, stay clean. Stay healthy, and you might stay alive. The next morning, in the bathroom, I strip and begin to wash with the hose connected to a tap on the wall. The door slams open.

"What you do?"

Crouching naked on the floor, back to the guard, blindfold lying on the bathtub. "I'm washing. Very dirty."

"Come. *Yallah*. Finish."

I wipe myself off with my T-shirt, get dressed, put the blindfold back. In the hall the guards push close. "Why you wash?" Fist hitting my chest. "I no say wash. Why you wash?"

"I'm dirty. Not good."

"No wash. I say when." Another blow, not hard, on the breast.

Two or three days later the guards bring in white cotton shorts and T-shirt, and a pair of cheap briefs. This time I'm allowed to use the tub, take a real shower, not just a quick hose-down.

The weather has shifted fully now. May in the Mediterranean, and even the nights are hot. From time to time I can hear a guard speaking to others in broken English—the same kinds of things he says to me: "Stand up." "Sit." *"Couvrez-yeux."* Once, he uses a name— William. Buckley? Probably. There are now, I think, three other hostages in the apartment, all in chains. Who are the other two?

Despite the severe, repeated warning—"If you see us, you are dead"—I sometimes take peeks through the curtains, or under my blindfold as I'm going to and from the bathroom. No matter how tight the strip of cloth is, it's always possible to see along my nose, and the guards know it. The images are blurry—I'm very nearsighted, and they took my glasses—but I can't resist the urge once in a while.

I'm beginning to sort out the guards, mainly by voice. One, who gives his name as Sayeed, speaks reasonably good English and seems friendlier than the others. Sometimes he comes for a talk, usually about "evil America." I try to explain to him that yes, Americans have done bad things, but we're not evil. The discussions are fruitless, but they help pass the time. And every time we talk, it might help them to see me as an individual, a human being.

Sayeed seems the most religious of the guards, praying five times a day. He never sits directly on my cot, always bringing a small board to put on top of the blanket. He won't touch me after I've been to the toilet, explaining once that he must remain clean to pray.

I ask Sayeed, "How can you do this? Doesn't the Koran say you may not punish someone for another's sins?"

The question bothers him. He goes to the chief, an older man held in great respect by all the guards. Later he comes back. "The chef says I must not talk with you about this. He says you think like a snake."

One of the guards is simply evil. Calling himself Michel, he claims to be a Christian from East Beirut—an obvious lie. He prays the same as all of them. He delights in sneaking up to the curtain at the end of my cot and snatching it suddenly open, then screaming, "No look. You look. I kill." Sometimes he creeps up and just sticks the barrel of the pistol through the curtain. "Bam. Bam," he says quietly.

Michel throws the little fruit we get—a banana, an orange—over the top of the partition. Often it falls on the floor, where my chains prevent me from reaching it. The two or three bananas there already smell, bringing dozens of huge cockroaches. Once Michel sets a bowl of soup at the top of the bed, just out of my reach. Stretching painfully for it, chained arm stretched out straight behind me, I knock it over onto the bed. He laughs and walks away, leaving the mess. It stays overnight, until another guard helps me clean up.

It's difficult to talk to these men, to bring myself to be polite, to act as if I care what they think. Their minds are alien to me. Only the loneliness, the hours and days without speaking a word, bring me to talk to them. That, and the devouring desire to find out what the hell is going on, what the chances are of getting out of here. But on that subject they have little to say. "Soon, and very soon. *Inshallah*"—God willing—is the unvarying response.

One day Sayeed and another guard come in and release my chains. "You go home now," Sayeed says. I don't believe him, but my stomach tightens, and my heart begins racing. Amid much bustle I'm taken into the hallway and pushed down on a mattress on the floor. A chain is again fastened to my leg, and Sayeed laughs.

My new position is uncomfortable—every time a guard goes by or a hostage is taken to the toilet, he has to walk across the bottom of my mattress. Already I'm becoming possessive, almost neurotic, about my space. The constant procession of feet tromping on my bed drives me to distraction. I try pulling up the end of the mattress every time I hear someone coming, but quickly tire of it. Several times I snap at the guards: "Don't walk on the bed. It's dirty." They pay no attention.

There had been no explanation for the move into the hall, and there is none a few days later when they again unchain me and move me back into the large room I had come from, though this time in a cubicle on the other side. I lie on the cot, listening to the sound of airplanes taking off, loud, close. We must be right at the end of the runway, in Hay El-sellum, or Bourj Al-Barajneh. I can remember the slum neighborhoods well, the one- and two-story concrete homes, the narrow, shell-pitted roads.

I'm allowed to wash more often—perhaps twice a week—but still am filthy most of the time. The room is a mess, with bits of rotting food and dirt underfoot. The rough army blanket I've been given has obviously never been washed.

I can hear the guards talking to Buckley. He's put in my former place, perhaps six feet away from me. He's ill. All of us have had colds for the past week or so, filling the small apartment with coughing and sneezing. Buckley is the only one not recovering. Instead, he develops a fever, mutters to himself. One phrase is clear: "Oh, God. I've lasted a year, and now my body is going." He goes delirious, moaning in the night. I ask about him, but am rebuffed.

A new hostage is brought in late in the evening. He speaks loudly. When asked, he gives his name to one of the guards—David Jacobsen, administrator at the teaching hospital of the American University of Beirut. He is placed on a mattress just outside the plastic curtain of my cubicle, and chained to the wall. I peek cautiously during a quiet moment. Tall. Long, thin pale legs. Blindfold like mine. I don't dare whisper to him—the guards are lying on their mattresses just two or three feet away.

One or two days later, in the evening, the chief comes in. He's always referred to as the Hajj, a title of honor given to those who have made the pilgrimage to Mecca, and the guards show much deference to him. He walks over to Buckley's cot. In Arabic he mutters, *"Mareed. Ktir, ktir mareed."* Sick, very sick. Then he goes out.

The guards won't give Buckley water or juice. They believe that anyone with a fever should not be given liquids—exactly the opposite of proper treatment. He pleads for an orange. Finally, in the night, there is the sound of him gasping, floundering about. The guards come in. A thump, as if Buckley kicked the wall. Then silence. After a few minutes the guards carry him out of the room. The conviction leaps to my mind—he has died. I begin praying for him.

The next day I ask Sayeed, "Where's Buckley? Is he okay?"

"Oh, yes. He is in a very good place," Sayeed replies lightly.

There is a patch on the wall just above my bed—a hole in the cement, filled with soft plaster. Someone has scratched in it JESUS LIVES. Not one of the guards, for sure. It must have been whichever hostage was here before me. I begin again to keep track of the days as best I can, casting my mind back to try to figure out how long I've been here—seventy, seventy-five days? It's hard to remember. They're all the same, and I've been moved from bed to bed several times, losing my scratch marks in the wall. I try to count the days in my head, but when I wake up each morning, I can't seem to recall what the previous day's number was.

Since Sayeed seems the friendliest of the guards, I ask for books every time he comes. "I'm not a dog. I can't just sit here day after day. I have to have something for my mind. Please get me books."

One morning Sayeed drops several hardbound books on the bed: a collection of essays about Iran, one on the origins of Shiism, a book about the Druse I'd heard about but never read, and a 1950s political science textbook, *The State,* by a British Communist.

I devour them all in two days, reading all night. Then I read them again and ask for more. "You finish already?"

"Yes. I read very fast. Can you get me more?"

He laughs. No more books arrive.

The nights are still horrible. Filled with half dreams. No real sleep—just dozing, jerking awake. I pray often. Bargains, pleas. God, I'll do better. I'll go to church. I'll give to the poor, spend my life on good causes. How far do I have to go? Renounce Madeleine, our child? Not possible. Even if I die here. Besides, how does it help to cause more pain and heartache? How could God ask that?

What about the anger, the hatred that fills me toward these people? How can I pray for them? Love thy enemy. I can't. That's too much. How do you love evil? Hate the sin, love the sinner. What does that mean? How can you separate a person from his actions?

I reach so hard to touch God, concentrating, waiting for some acknowledgment from Him that I exist, that He's listening. I get back only blankness. I know I'm not evil—these people are evil. But I *feel* sinful, unworthy. If I were God, I wouldn't talk to me, either.

Long nights, squirrel-in-a-cage nights. Mind spinning; thoughts, emotions whirling. Anger. Frustration. Pain. Guilt. My mind so tired, my spirit so sore. And more to come, more and more. I just can't do it.

But at the bottom, in surrender so complete there is no coherent thought, no real pain, no feeling, just exhaustion, just waiting, there is something else: Warmth/light/softness. Acceptance, by me, of me. Rest. After a while, some strength. Enough for now.

It happens once, twice. A few hours later it fades, and the anger and frustration and longing are back. But the memory is there, the sense of presence. And sometimes the place is reached again briefly. Meanwhile, the hours are endured, the days gotten through. And the nights are spent in prayer and the effort to get back to that place.

A FEW days after Buckley's disappearance, late at night, the guards bring in the Hajj and a man who says he is a doctor. He takes my pulse and blood pressure, asks me about my health. "I'm okay," I tell him, "but I need exercise, and I need to be able to wash more."

The next day the guards begin bustling about early in the morning. They sweep and scrub the floor, give me clean shorts and T-shirt. For the next few days I'm allowed to shower, and I get maybe ten minutes to do stretches and push-ups before I'm chained up again.

The new routines don't last long. A week later, around midnight, several guards and the Hajj come into the room. I can hear them unchaining the others; then they come to unlock my padlocks. "Quiet. No speak," one says to me. I'm led out of the apartment and down the stairs, out the door and down a dirt road for a hundred or a hundred and fifty yards, then into another building. This time we stay on the first floor. Into a room—clean, tiled floor. Mattress. A chain is wrapped around my left ankle and padlocked. Another hostage is chained across the room. The guards go out, and the door closes.

Cautiously I raise my blindfold slightly. I can see the blurred image of a man leaning against the wall, peeking back at me from under the rag wrapped around his eyes. Jacobsen? I think so, but it doesn't matter at all. After all these weeks, at least I have a companion. The relief is immediate, immense. Can we talk? Don't know—no instructions. He grins through a thick brown beard. I wave, smile at him.

## Madeleine

*NEW YORK. April 1985.* It was Easter Sunday when I arrived at John F. Kennedy Airport, in New York City. Terry's cousin Tom, a policeman, was waiting for me and helped me through immigration. His wife, Sue, and Terry's sister Peggy Say, who had just moved to New York from Florida, were waiting outside. Peg and I hugged each other and started crying. We caught another plane for Rochester, New York. Peg, her husband, David, and I stayed with David's mother in nearby Batavia for a week before we found a house.

It's difficult to explain how I felt in those times. Far away from home and family, waiting for Terry to come back, expecting a child without a father around—this was not the way we had planned it. I don't remember going to bed one night without crying. Terry was so far away now.

Terry's father, his brothers, and his sister Judy were also in Batavia for a while. It felt good to be with his family. They were all trying to find out what they could do for him. His younger sister Judy, Peggy, and I went to Washington, D.C., ten days after I arrived in the States. With the help of the AP people there, we managed to meet with some State Department officials. They promised nothing, saying only they were doing their best to get the hostages released.

I was very disappointed to discover the Americans really had no idea where the hostages were or how to end the problem. Like all Lebanese, I believed the American government had the power to do anything. I learned quickly that we were dealing not only with Lebanese terrorists who were ignorant of the Western world but with Americans who were equally ignorant of Lebanon.

On May 15 pictures of several hostages were released by Islamic Jihad, with a warning and a demand for the release of their friends being held in Kuwait. One of the pictures was Terry's. It's absurd to say I was happy, but I was. A picture of Terry meant he was alive. He looked angry in the picture, which meant he was feeling something, he was not giving up. I used to imagine how he must be fighting to keep his dignity intact. He also did not have his glasses on in the picture. I knew he was unable to see much without them. Just the thought of him practically blind in the hands of those people was unbearable. I would have given my life to prevent what was happening to him.

Two more Frenchmen were kidnapped three days after the statement, then an Englishman and another American, David Jacobsen.

On June 6, I went into labor. David junior, Peggy's stepson, and Peg drove me to the hospital, but it wasn't until noon the next day that I started getting contractions. I was nervous and trying to breathe as I had been taught in the prepartum classes. The doctors put me on a monitor to check how the baby was doing; then Peg came into the room. She told me I had to decide whether to give them permission for a cesarean delivery. Apparently the baby was under stress every time I contracted.

I couldn't believe it. All through my pregnancy I felt well. I had exercised with Terry every day. Now I felt as if I had failed him and my motherhood. Nothing had gone right since he was kidnapped.

Ten minutes later I was in the operating room, numb from anesthesia, except for my head. I could feel the tears in my eyes. As I looked at the ceiling, my thoughts wandered to when I had met Terry, and then how he was the first to decide I was pregnant. I had laughed at him. At the age of thirty-four I had given up on the idea of ever getting pregnant. How happy he was, how proud he made me feel to be a woman when it was confirmed. How he held me and kissed me in the elevator at the hospital when we got the test results. For six and a half months I saw nothing but admiration and love in his eyes whenever he looked at me, at my growing belly.

It was all a miracle—a miracle that came to life at 12:51 p.m., Friday, June 7, 1985. The pediatrician held the baby to my face and said, "Here is your daughter, Madeleine." I looked at her tiny face, her black hair and fair skin. "She is beautiful," I said. They took her away. I cried and cried. This was not what we planned for. I wanted so much to see her and Terry together.

Two days after our daughter, Sulome Theresa, was born, I heard about the abduction of another American, Tom Sutherland. It was obvious that whatever effort the Americans were making to free the hostages was not working. The kidnappers needed more hostages. I held Sulome tight and wondered when she would see her father. How long, and what is it going to take, before we become a family?

# CHAPTER FOUR

*JULY 3, 1985.*   David Kimche, director general of the Israeli Foreign Ministry, visited Robert "Bud" McFarlane, President Reagan's national security adviser, at the White House.

Kimche informed McFarlane that top Israelis had been meeting for some time with an Iranian who claimed to represent certain "elements" in the government of Iran who were interested in changing that country's policies. They were clearly hinting at a coup. Kimche said only a few people in the Israeli government knew of the meetings, and asked specifically that the American CIA not be informed.

In fact, the United States already knew of the talks and even knew that Israel had been shipping arms to the Iranians as early as 1981. In all their testimony in the later hearings and trials concerning Iran-contra, U.S. officials insisted that they had never approved of such weapons transfers. Again in fact, Secretary of State Alexander Haig had given the go-ahead to Prime Minister Yitzhak Shamir.

The weapons shipments stopped, apparently because Haig withdrew his approval. But in early 1985 the CIA produced a new analysis of U.S. policies on Iran. Based wholly on speculation, the new analysis suggested there was likely to be opposition to the Khomeini regime in Iran because of the economic failure of the new government. To encourage such opposition, "evidence" of "bona fides" would have to be produced. In the Middle East that meant one thing—weapons.

A "study memorandum" was circulated to all Cabinet officers and drew sharp reaction. McFarlane said in a 1993 interview, "Cap Weinberger [the Secretary of Defense] was quite sharp in saying that this was out of the question. We cannot do this. George Shultz [the Secretary of State] agreed."

McFarlane was primarily interested in overall U.S. policy on Iran. His boss, Ronald Reagan, was interested almost to the point of obsession in gaining the release of American hostages in Lebanon. Everything the United States had tried so far had failed.

"It was clear that Reagan's concern was the release of the hostages, come what may," McFarlane said. "Come what may being the Iran-contra affair. He believed that at the end of the day his commitment to releasing the hostages was not only right but . . . politically sound. That Americans would find it defensible to do damn near anything in the world if you could release those hostages. It broke the law, it went against policy, it offended allies, it [angered] the Congress. And he really did think about those things. That was not a high price to pay."

At that first meeting with McFarlane in July of 1985, Kimche made no suggestion of any weapons-for-hostages deal. He was simply informing his country's ally and sponsor that he was in touch with an Iranian named Ghorbanifar, who claimed to represent Iranian officials interested in a rapprochement. He also did not mention that Ghorbanifar, a well-known arms merchant, had a reputation for lying and exaggeration. Was the United States open to such a dialogue? McFarlane briefed the President. "He [Reagan] said, 'Well, if there's a basis for believing that these people are genuine, then of course we're open to a dialogue. Tell them that.' And I did."

It was not, of course, that simple. This was the Middle East.

Ten days later came another message from Kimche, via an Israeli arms dealer named Al Shwimmer. The Iranian "dissidents" had decided they were too vulnerable. They would arrange the release of the hostages, but just as the CIA study had predicted, they needed some evidence of their clout—specifically, weapons. More specifically, one hundred antitank missiles (TOWs).

Once again, McFarlane says, he briefed the President. "Reagan's response was, 'Well, no, we can't do that. We cannot ship American weapons to Iran until we know just who it is we're dealing with.' "

He wasn't shocked at the idea, McFarlane recalled. He just wanted to make sure the United States gave missiles to the right people.

A few days later Kimche was back with another, slightly altered proposal. Would the United States approve of Israel's giving its own (U.S.-supplied) weapons to the Iranians and, by the way, promise immediate replacement of whatever the Israelis gave away?

"So we had another meeting with the President and the same cast, and I went through this all with them," McFarlane related. As in all the previous discussions of the subject, Weinberger and Shultz objected. William Casey (CIA director) and Don Regan (White House chief of staff) were generally in favor. "Bush said, 'Yeah, it's worth a try,' " according to McFarlane. Reagan, of course, was all for it.

Thus, in July of 1985, arms-for-hostages was born.

# Terry

*BEIRUT. July 1985.* Jacobsen is a tall man, with a quick smile and a penchant for monologues. The administrator for American University Hospital, he'd been in Beirut only about six months when he was taken.

The morning after our arrival in the new quarters, we're given permission from the guards to talk quietly, and we quickly exchange stories. David had been snatched as he walked the short distance from the university to the hospital, without a guard. One of the kidnappers walloped him over the head with a gun, stunning him long enough to get him in the car. He'd been brought directly to the apartment where I was being kept. He'd also heard Buckley in delirium and was as convinced as I was that he died. The only difference was David thought that last loud thump was the guards knocking Buckley on the head. I don't agree, but there's no way, of course, to know.

Jacobsen seems fairly cheerful. His biggest immediate problem is his eyes—he's very farsighted, and his glasses were lost in the kidnapping. When the guards bring my Bible, David says he is a committed Christian. I begin reading to him, a few minutes in the morning and afternoon—mostly psalms or Paul's letters.

At first the guards don't bother us much, and the room is a great deal cleaner than our previous one. The building is obviously someone's house, not a prison. There are no windows in the room. The inside doorknob has been removed, and a steel plate covers the hole.

We're also able to get a little more exercise, with only one three-foot-long chain on an ankle. I learn to pace one step in each direction without tripping on the chain. I do sit-ups and push-ups throughout the day, using the physical exertion as a tranquilizer, whenever my spirits drop too low or my mind spins too fast.

One evening the Hajj stops by. Already I have learned to recognize his voice, a light tenor, soft but authoritative. He sits down on the floor and starts a conversation, with Sayeed next to him translating. First he apologizes for the chains. It's necessary, he says, for security. Besides, the seventeen Shia jailed in Kuwait are suffering much worse conditions.

"When are we going home?"—the first and obvious question for both David and me.

"Soon, *Inshallah*," the Hajj replies, but it's quickly apparent that he's just making reassuring noises. In fact, according to him, the U.S. government is refusing to negotiate. "They say we are terrorists." The word angers him. "We are not terrorists. We do this because it's the only way."

"Hajj, look in the dictionary. That's what terrorist means—someone who uses violence for political purposes."

The reply is quick, almost practiced. "What can we do? Your government will not pay attention to us."

"Talk to the Kuwaitis. If you want your people out of Kuwait, you should be talking to them."

"They won't do anything." He is scornful. "They are just puppets of the Americans. If your government tells them to let our brothers go, they will do it."

"It's not that simple, Hajj. The American government can't interfere in these cases. The Shia were sentenced for trying to kill many people. The American government isn't going to ask Kuwait to let them go."

"They must. Or you will not go home. How can we make the government talk to us?"

"Convince them that you're reasonable. Let one of us go."

He doesn't sound convinced, of course. It's very strange to be talking like this with my kidnapper, pretending that it's all perfectly normal, rational. Pretending that I'm not enraged, frustrated, and terribly terribly lonely.

I'm blindfolded—I can't see his face, can't look into his eyes. Does he really believe I'm a human being, like himself? Does he feel any of my pain? If he does, how can he do this?

He asks if we need anything. Books, a radio, newspapers, we reply. To fill the hours. To stay in touch with the world and not feel so alone. He promises to get us something, then leaves.

After the door is closed, David and I raise our blindfolds and look at each other. "Do you really think he'll do anything?"

"Probably not. But it can't hurt to argue with him. Maybe something will happen. Maybe we'll get a few books, anyway."

Two small fans keep the room reasonably cool—when they operate. But, as always in Beirut, electricity is erratic. When it goes out, the room quickly becomes stifling. It is full summer now—the beginning of July. Three and a half months.

After some argument the guards agree to open the door when the power is out. They do so early one morning. We've been aware of prisoners in the next room, listened to them going back and forth to the toilet in the morning. We've had several long discussions, trying to figure out who they are. Today, eagerly but carefully, we sit back against the wall and slowly tilt our heads to peek through the gaps in the blindfolds as our neighbors are escorted past our door one by one.

David recognizes a colleague at the university, Dr. Tom Sutherland. "He looks like a ghost," he says. "He's so pale, and walks like a zombie."

Later in the day I ask Sayeed about them. Surprisingly, he tells me. "They are Americans. A priest—Jenco. Ben Weir. And a professor at the American University—Sutherland."

David tells Sayeed he knows Tom Sutherland, had worked with him at the university, and would like to talk to him.

"Tell the Hajj I am a Catholic," I add. "I want to talk to the priest, Father Jenco. I want to say confession."

"Confession? What do you mean?"

"It is part of my religion. To talk with a priest about my sins."

"You can tell me your sins." He laughs.

"No. I have to do this if I can. It's part of my religion."

"Okay. I will ask."

A day later Sayeed and two other guards bring Father Jenco into our room, seating him on David's bed. Sayeed takes David into their room, where Ben Weir and Tom Sutherland remained.

We all, of course, remain blindfolded, and two guards stay in the room. Half lying on the floor, chained leg stretched out behind me, I grope toward the priest with my right hand, saying softly, "How are you, Father?" I find his hand and squeeze it gently.

Sayeed returns. Turning toward him, I say, "I want to say confession now. Can you close the door? We have to be alone."

The guards exchange a few words in Arabic; then Sayeed says, "You have ten minutes." They go out the door and close it behind them.

Cautiously I raise my blindfold. Father Jenco, a white-haired man with a gentle smile, is sitting cross-legged. We clasp hands. "Hi, Father," I say. "I'm Terry Anderson. I don't know where to start. It's been a very long time since I said confession."

"It doesn't matter. Just go ahead." He nods in encouragement.

The discussion goes on for twenty minutes or more, twice the time the guards had agreed to. Father Jenco's responses are always quiet, gentle. Mostly, he just listens. For a Catholic, ritual confession is an emotional ceremony, no matter how informal the setting. This was my first confession in twenty-five years. This smiling, soft-spoken priest, also a hostage, dressed like me in white cotton shorts and T-shirt, frightened, in his own pain and anger, received the full flood of my emotions, guilts, and concerns, returning warmth, love, and understanding.

By the end of our session both he and I are crying. Finally I kneel beside him. "Father, forgive me, for I have sinned in word and in thought, in what I have done and what I have not done."

He rests his right hand lightly on my head. "In the name of a gentle, loving God, you are forgiven." He pulls my head gently to his shoulder and hugs me. We sit back and look at each other. In a few moments we hear a guard turning the lock on the door, and we pull our blindfolds down over our eyes.

DAVID Jacobsen and I broke into amazed laughter the other night. We were sitting in the room, with the guard Michel just outside the open door, when we heard a bell outside in the street. David asked, "What is that? It sounds like an ice-cream truck."

"Yes, *bouza*," Michel said.

"Well, why don't you go get some? It's hot."

"Okay." And he did. The only guard there (that we knew of), and we sent him out for ice cream! Weird, but delicious.

The Hajj delivered a stack of old *Herald Tribunes* and a few magazines—*Time* and *Newsweek*. Mostly a couple of weeks old, but better than nothing. In one, there was a short piece on Buckley— Islamic Jihad announcing they had killed him. No surprise. We both were sure he died that night. And Islamic Jihad would certainly try to turn his death to its advantage. Means nothing much, though it's an indication the negotiations are not going well. Also no surprise.

David and I are now allowed to get together once a week for services with Father Martin Jenco, Pastor Ben Weir, and Tom Sutherland. David worries about Tom—says he seems listless, pale, and without spirit. There's no news of progress toward a release for anyone.

Tonight something is going on. All the guards are here, and I heard the Hajj's voice. Sayeed releases my chain and David's. We're guided out of the room, down some stairs, and into another room. Rough concrete floor. Dirty. Someone in the room, on a mattress. The door closes, and we raise our blindfolds. It's Tom Sutherland. We shake hands. He is really in bad shape. Says they've been giving him a hard time over some paper in his briefcase, calling him a spy, threatening him. No sign of Father Martin or Pastor Weir.

Within a few minutes Sayeed comes back in and tells Tom to pick up his mattress, then takes him out. Almost immediately Sayeed's back and tells me the same thing. I'm taken down more stairs, into a huge, echoing subbasement. There is a line of cells on the right side of the room, about chest high. Steel doors. I'm shoved into a cell. It's not quite big enough for the mattress on the floor—I have to pull the end up for the guard to close the door. The ceiling is too low for me to stand up. Michel quickly comes back, carrying a length of chain. He chains my feet, a padlock on each foot, passes the chain out through a low, barred opening, and padlocks the chain outside.

After he's left, I can hear Tom moving around in the next cell. I call out to him softly. "Tom. Are you okay? What's this about?"

"I don't know. They say I'm a spy. This is some kind of punishment."

But why me? No one has accused me of being a spy recently.

Tom and I spend one night in the horse stalls, as he refers to them. The mosquitoes are bad, and some kind of machinery roars all night. The next evening I'm taken out and back upstairs. David is still in the new cell. I tell him what it's like in the subbasement. "I don't think Tom can last long down there. It's pretty awful."

When Sayeed comes back, I ask him why he put us down in the stalls, then brought me back and left Tom there.

"He's a bad man."

"No, he isn't. He's a professor, not a spy. A good man."

Sayeed explains that they had found a paper in Tom's briefcase— some kind of discussion of Islam. The problem apparently is not so much what was in the paper as that Tom denied having it, said he'd never seen it. That has awakened the hamsters' paranoia. If he's worried enough to deny it, it must be bad, is their kind of logic.

He even showed the paper to David and me. It is simply an address to some conference that explains basic concepts of Islam. Very academic, totally harmless. We try to tell Sayeed that it means nothing. But he's stuck on the idea that Tom's denial means it must be important. I go back to arguing the main point.

"You have to get him out of there. He won't be able to stand it long."

"I can't. It's an order. He must stay."

"Do you want him alive? He's not a bad man. Look. If he has to stay, take me back as well. He can't stay there alone."

The discussion goes on. Finally Sayeed leaves. Half an hour later he's back with Tom. Rejoicing. Embraces among the three of us.

Sayeed explains. "I took a *fatwa* from the Koran." This kind of *fatwa* is a religious ruling made by randomly choosing a verse from the Koran and interpreting it as being a yes-or-no answer to a question. This time it was yes. I can hardly believe the explanation. Sayeed is reasonably intelligent, somewhat educated. Yet he believes in this procedure, to the point that he will violate his orders. At any rate, Tom is back, shaken and scared, but with us.

Sayeed asks if we would like to have Father Martin and Pastor Ben with us as well. Five in a room this size? No hesitation. We all answer, "Yes, of course." The next day they are both brought into our cell, and five mattresses are jammed in. It's going to be hard to live like this, but we need each other badly. At least I need them. Anything to keep my mind going, to keep away those whirling, useless thoughts.

WE WORK out a routine that allows the five of us to exist in this ten- by twelve-foot room. The companionship is wonderful—Father Martin and Ben Weir seem to be gentle, quiet men. They've already formed a deep bond, sharing their faith without paying any attention to the dogmas that separate them. Father Martin conducts Mass one day; Pastor Ben leads the service the next.

Tom seems a little uncomfortable but goes along. From what he's said, he was once a regularly churchgoing Presbyterian but drifted away. He seems to be worried sick about the pressure he's under from our hosts. He talks about nothing else. We can't persuade him that they're not serious about his being a spy, and in fact we can't be sure. He takes little part in our discussions, spending most of his time just lying on his mattress. A couple of times he's talked about suicide—about putting his head in one of the plastic sacks we get for garbage. I've not been too patient with him—I don't think he's serious about it, and anyway it's a damned difficult way to kill yourself.

David is enthusiastic about the services. He's a regular at the Crystal Cathedral in California, which I gather is some sort of conservative, evangelistic Protestant group. He seems to be conservative about almost everything—a solid Orange County Republican. We couldn't disagree more on just about every issue, and it's beginning to show.

Every morning after breakfast we pick up our mattresses and lean them against the wall. Then we pace around in a circle, one behind the other, gradually beginning to run faster and faster. Father Martin, Ben, and Tom each end up dropping out of the circle and stepping into the center of the room. David and I circle them, picking up speed, racing madly into exhaustion. Finally we both give up, sweating and heaving for breath. The exercise is too much for this small room, but it's a purge.

Several times Sayeed and I have wrestled—me blindfolded, trying to use the little aikido I learned in Japan against his karate. Not very successfully, obviously. I dumped Sayeed on the floor once, fell on top of him, and ended up with a disarranged blindfold, staring into his face from about four inches away. He didn't even blink. Nonetheless, we've all become pretty careful about keeping the blindfold in place. Ben is the twitchiest about it. He's got a set of swimming goggles with the lenses covered by tape, and every time there's a noise at the door, he jumps for the corner, faces inward, and snatches his goggles down. He must have had a bad time earlier. He's been a captive well over a year. He and Father Martin were kept together in the mountains for a time, along with Levin and Buckley.

We've gotten some new guards—Fadl and Mahmoud. Of course, like all the names we know, they're just made up. These two men are friendly. Mahmoud speaks some English, Fadl very little.

We're all desperate for news. Ben speaks fluent Arabic—he spent thirty years in Lebanon. He frequently lies on the floor (at our urging), next to the door, to see what he can pick up from the guards' talk. Not much—apparently it's mostly what you would expect uneducated young men to say during a stint of boring duty. At least we can keep track of the date. Today is August 30, 1985: 168 days.

WE'VE been moved again, back to the same room David and I were in a few weeks ago, but this time, all five of us. The Hajj has also given us a radio, a little seven-band Sony. We can even get Armed Forces Radio on it and listen to all the American news reports—the networks, AP, and UPI. Heard Peg's voice the other night—the first time any of our families have been on. I choked up completely and started crying.

David and I seem to be bickering a lot. The longer we're together, the harder it is for the two of us to get along. Tom is still very quiet and very depressed.

We've just had a startling announcement from the Hajj. They've decided to let one of us go home, "as a humanitarian gesture"! It's also an effort to persuade the Reagan administration that these people are serious about wanting to negotiate. The most startling part, though, is that he says we're to choose which one. We're all stunned.

Then the Hajj adds that it cannot be Tom. He will be the last to go home, he says. He also says it should not be me. We protest. Ben argues in Arabic with him fruitlessly. He leaves.

How are we going to handle this? We all deserve to go home, and we all want it badly. I can see it on everyone's face, and I know it's on mine. What a terrible, terrible thing to do to us. Perhaps we should refuse to choose. But then maybe no one will go. No, we will try.

We quickly decide that whatever choice is made, it must be unanimous, and it should be by secret ballot. We also agree that we will ignore the Hajj's stricture about Tom and me. We walk around in our circle for half an hour. Very little talking. Finally I speak.

"We all want to go. I think if it can't be me, it should be David. He's articulate and forceful. If someone is to speak for us, to persuade Reagan to begin talks, he'd do it well."

David's grateful but says little. Pastor Ben says he does not want to go, that he will stay. Father Martin says the same.

We sit down, tear up some paper, and begin the ballot. First time, one vote for everyone except Ben, two for me. Another ballot, same result. We take a break, get up, and begin walking in a circle again. After a few minutes I ask, "Anybody want to say anything else?"

"Why? You want to campaign?" David snaps. I don't reply.

Another ballot. This time it's two for David, three for me. I'm in a quandary. Should I vote for myself? Or David? How long will this go on? Again. Same. Again. Now it's four for me, one for David.

"Well, that's that," Father Martin says, obviously assuming the single vote for David is mine. "No, Father. It has to be unanimous," I tell him. It takes him a few seconds to realize that both David and I are voting for ourselves. I'm ashamed at the silence.

Last ballot. Five for me. We sit back. I can feel the tears building. Father Martin hugs me, then Ben, Tom. Finally David.

"Thank you," I manage. "I'm very grateful. I also feel guilty. You all deserve to go as much as I do."

I'm also scared. The Hajj said he didn't want it to be me. Will he veto the choice? I can't believe it will happen; I feel somehow it's not right. I'm ashamed of wanting it so bad.

We call Sayeed, tell him of our choice. He laughs. "We have already chosen." We ask him why. The Hajj told us to choose. "I will tell the Hajj. He will talk to you."

A night of misery, joy, confused prayer. I try as hard as I can not to believe it. But it's no use. I can't help thinking about being free, seeing Maddy, the baby I know she's had, Gabrielle. The shame and guilt won't go away. I can't even look at Ben. And the others, they must be terribly disappointed.

Finally the Hajj appears. No discussion, no greeting. He speaks in Arabic to Ben at length, angrily. Ben gasps. "Oh, no. Oh, no."

What is it? I know already.

"He says I'm the one. I'm going tonight. I tried to argue, but he won't listen. I'm sorry."

The disappointment overwhelms me. I expected it. I was prepared for it. But it hurts. Oh, God, how it hurts.

Ben is quickly given a haircut, clothes. We get a brief chance to embrace him, wish him luck. "I'm sorry," he says to me again. "Don't worry," I reply. "You should have been the one we chose anyway." He's hustled out, and the four of us sit quietly for a while. Then the lights are turned out. I pray, reaching for calm, for acceptance. Slowly, slowly it comes. Lord, I don't know what You want of me. Help me.

# CHAPTER FIVE

*WASHINGTON. September 19, 1985.*   Peggy Say and her brother Glenn Richard Anderson, Jr., were jammed against each other in the middle pew of the huge Presbyterian church, sweating and nervous. No one had had a chance to speak privately with Ben Weir before this press conference. Neither knew whether he had seen their little brother Terry in prison, whether Terry was ill or desperate.

There was an explosion of applause, bursts of blinding light from flashbulbs. Weir walked onto the stage, looking healthy and fit. The expected questions, until finally The One: "Pastor Weir, did you see the other hostages?"

"Yes, just a few days ago. And they were well."

Peg began crying. Rich clapped and shouted with the others. Weir went on gravely: "If something isn't done soon, the captors are going to execute the hostages. They have released me to urge the administration to act immediately, or the consequences will be fatal."

The gravity of the message was nearly buried in the rush of knowing that their brother was alive and well. Later Peg, Rich, and members of other hostage families met with the Presbyterian pastor. He related personal anecdotes and conversations about the other hostages, passed on messages—all the details the families were longing to hear.

Peg had come out swinging in the last few months. The Associated Press agreed to pay her expenses and phone bills; the hostage families had become a vocal lobby, harassing the government, appearing on talk shows and newscasts. None of them were quite sure what should be done, but they were demanding that *someone* do *something*.

The families demanded a meeting with President Reagan. They got Vice President Bush first, to his dismay.

The meeting was heated and angry. The relatives held Bush personally responsible for the lack of action and demanded an accounting. They accused, berated, argued, and pointed fingers. The Vice President just slid lower in his chair, as if he really felt somehow guilty.

Finally, when Peggy accused Bush of being unchristian, he sat bolt upright, shaking his finger at them all and shouting in Ben Weir's face: "I don't care what you think. I'm telling you that we are responsible for you sitting in that chair today. It was your government that got you free!"

The response was not quite accurate. The U.S. government was not responsible, but it knew about the deal that brought Weir home.

Those 100 antitank missiles—TOWs—that Kimche and McFarlane had talked about and President Reagan had approved, magically become 508 TOWs, had in fact been the key. The original Iranian promise to free all the hostages in exchange for the weapons had melted down to their freeing one. McFarlane had tried to make that one William Buckley, not knowing that Buckley was dead. Naturally, the kidnappers could not produce Buckley, so they had freed Weir.

McFarlane said in a 1993 interview that "Reagan was disappointed" that only one hostage was released. "But not at all moved to turn it off. To the contrary. He said, 'Well, it is bearing fruit.' "

The Iranians thought so, too. Shortly after Weir's release, Shwimmer and Ghorbanifar, the arms dealers, were back at the table with Israeli and American officials. Now they wanted Hawks, Sidewinders, Phoenix, and even Harpoon missiles. Real weapons. And real money.

It was very clear that these things were not intended for any dissident faction in the Iranian army or government. They would be used directly in the war against Iraq.

McFarlane told them they had gone too far. The Israelis and their Iranian intermediaries backed off, but only to work out new terms. No Harpoons, no Phoenix or Sidewinders. But okay on the Hawks. The Americans gave the green light if the weapons came out of the Israeli inventory. Of course, being the Middle East, it again was not that easy.

*NOVEMBER 18, 1985.* "Colonel North? This is Yitzhak Rabin." The Israeli defense minister. "We have a problem, and Mr. McFarlane says you can solve it."

On an open (insecure) line the Israeli official explained, using only a few euphemisms and code words. Israel wanted to send the shipment of seventy-five Hawk missiles to Iran via a discreet route, but didn't have a plane available that could handle it. "And, obviously, they wanted us more actively engaged in [the swap]. I say that without any proof, but in hindsight it appears that's what they wanted," Lieutenant Colonel Oliver North asserted in a 1993 interview.

If that's what they wanted, it worked. As the shipment became more complicated, North worked his phones to keep it on track. The United States was now "operationally" involved.

Everybody involved—and that meant nearly everybody at the top level of the U.S. government—can now remember warning everybody else about what they were doing. McFarlane warned the Israelis, the President, the Cabinet members. Weinberger and Shultz protested directly, writing memos detailing their objections. Just for the record, apparently, because none of those warnings or objections was strong enough to derail the project.

North arranged the logistics through retired air force major general Richard Secord, now a freelance businessman with close ties to the CIA; Colin Powell, then a major general and military assistant to Weinberger; and the CIA's Duane (Dewey) Clarridge. Nearly all of the top officials brought in had to be told what it was about.

The weapons made it to Iran. But again, this was the Middle East.

"The Israelis [had] put together the oldest and most beat-up Hawks they could find," McFarlane said. "As you might expect, the Iranians were livid about it, because not only were they getting bad stuff but the Israelis had the effrontery to ship it in boxes with a lot of Hebrew on the outside into Tehran airport."

McFarlane blames the screwup mainly on the arms dealers involved—Shwimmer on the Israeli side and Ghorbanifar for the Iranians. After all, there were millions of dollars involved. Regardless of who was to blame, no hostages were freed.


## Terry

*BEIRUT. September 1985.*   Since Ben left, relations between David and me have deteriorated. We seem to fight all the time. David keeps referring to the necessary "pecking order," as if we were all a flock of chickens. Tom says almost nothing, and Father Martin is straining to keep things on an even keel. It's as if with Ben gone, the equilibrium in the room has been lost.

This morning, while David was in the bathroom, I asked Tom and Father Martin what was wrong. Their answer was a solid blast at me.

"You challenge David all the time. You seem to want to top him, to prove something to him. It's like a pair of bulls trying to dominate the same herd."

I was shocked. Naturally, I'd assumed the others would agree with me that David was causing the trouble.

I thought about it for a bit, and when David came back, I apologized. "If I've done things to offend you, I'm sorry. I'd like to start over." I assumed he would make the same sort of remarks, we'd shake hands and try to get along. What he said was, "Yes, you have. You've been a bastard." That just enraged me again, but I kept my temper.

I've been sitting here thinking about all that. It's not a view of myself I like—argumentative, bullheaded, trampling on other people. It's hard to accept, but I have to, since both Father Martin and Tom agree. Once again I'm faced directly with the contradiction between what I believe I am and what others see me as. This place is like a hall of mirrors. There's no hiding from the others, and there's no ignoring the reflections they give me of myself.

WE'VE been moved again. We were all taken out blindfolded sometime after midnight and shoved into the back of a small van with several guards. If we were near the airport, then I think I followed the route well enough to know where we are now, in an apartment somewhere near the old Kuwaiti embassy. We are in a large room, perhaps fifteen by eighteen, with four mattresses laid out for David, Tom, Father Martin, and me. Steel plates on the windows.

Within a day or two we discover that there are other prisoners in the apartment. Counting steps and the flushing of the toilet, we figure there are four of them in the next room. Even with at least eight hostages, though, the guards seem remarkably casual. They leave the door of our cell open because of the stifling heat, and even allow us to go back and forth to the bathroom without escort. Of course, we quickly find there is no likelihood of escape. Too many guards, too high up, several locks on the front door of the apartment.

One day, as I leave the bathroom, I hear a hiss from the slightly opened door of the room next to ours. Dropping my toothbrush, I squat down and grope for it, peering under my blindfold. "We are French. Who are you?" the voice says in English. "I am an American. Anderson." Then I quickly stand up and continue to our room.

We have heard on the radio, which we are given from time to time, that there are four French hostages, along with several Brits, an Italian, a Korean, and some others. These must be the French. Tom, who speaks fluent French, knocks on the wall to the rhythm of the "Marseillaise," and we hear the rhythm repeated back to us.

Our days quickly settle back into a deadly routine. David and I still argue, but much more cautiously. Tom still seems apathetic, tiring quickly of any discussion. Father Martin and I talk about religion and the Catholic Church. He's a kind, gentle man, but he's not always easy to get along with. The strain of captivity, the petty humiliations we're all subjected to are as hard for him as for any of us, despite his strong faith and personal dedication.

I have to laugh sometimes. I'm the only other Catholic here, and he treats me sometimes like a particularly annoying altar boy. He snaps at me and orders me around in a way quite different from the way he talks to David and Tom. I don't mind, though I can't quite say why. I wouldn't accept that kind of treatment from anyone else.

Every day we walk in a circle, sometimes for hours, one behind the other. Father Martin can't stand to have David behind him, complaining that he creeps up too close. Tom doesn't want me behind him for some reason. So we always fall in in the same order—David, me, Father Martin, Tom. When someone steps out of the circle, then steps back in the wrong place, there's a quick shuffle to get everyone back where he belongs. We've all become terribly possessive about the small space we have to ourselves. When a guard, or even one of the other hostages, steps on my mattress, I feel a quick burst of rage.

There has been a running fight with the guards over the bathroom. For some reason they're limiting our daily trips to seven minutes, in which we have to move our bowels, wash, brush our teeth, wash our underwear and plastic dishes, and fill our water bottles. That's all we get—the one trip to the toilet each morning. If we miss that chance, we have to hold it until the next day. Often by the time the morning trip comes around, we're in physical pain. The humiliation of not being able to go to the bathroom when we need to is great. There doesn't seem to be any reason for it, except the guards don't want to waste more than an hour taking all eight of us to the toilet. Don't know why—they do nothing the rest of the day. Incredibly lazy.

I think I'm finally learning to control my thoughts of Madeleine, my pain and guilt, and to think only of her grace and beauty and the wonderful sense of knowing each other we had so quickly. Still, I often have to push her into the back of my mind. I don't find the sexual frustration surprising or too hard to deal with. But I'm still surprised at the intensity of the pain sometimes when I think of her and what this is putting her through.

I've just been given another sharp and unpleasant look at myself. I finally got Tom Sutherland talking, and he told me that I was crushing him, that I'd been aggressively argumentative in all our discussions, and that he felt I thought he was stupid. His ego has been crushed by these hamsters' constantly hassling him about being a spy, and he's telling me I make him feel worse.

I feel like a total s____. I haven't been paying attention to the effect my "intellectual" exercises have been having on this man, already deeply depressed and suffering. I've got to be much much more careful. He's not in any shape to take criticism, or smart remarks and put-downs. These things have no place in here, anyway. I wonder if any of my friends really liked me at all. I seem to come across as an arrogant loudmouth. I'm not a bad man. I'm not. Or at least I don't mean to be. Do intentions count? Not for much, I guess.

I flew into a rage at the guards. Two of them took me into the living room to show me some pictures. They were of dead children being held aloft by a screaming, chanting crowd apparently after a major explosion of some sort.

"America do. Reagan do," one guard said in his pidgin English.

The pictures appalled me—so explicit, so bloody, such small bodies. I threw them down on the floor. "No. Not America. Lebanese. Lebanese did this to each other."

I refused to look when they picked them up and shoved them at me again. I pulled the blindfold down firmly over my nose and started praying out loud, ignoring their shouting. After a minute or two they took me back into the room. "I'm sorry," the guard said.

I was trembling with rage. The others asked me what was wrong. I couldn't describe the pictures or explain. I just sat against the wall and put my head on my knees until I could calm down.

I thought of the boy I had seen die at Barbir Hospital in 1982, of the small bodies in a refrigerated truck outside a Tripoli hospital in 1983. So many children. I never learned to control the awful wrench at the sight of them.

It's October 29, 1985 two days after my birthday: 227 days. The guards told me today that I have a child and that there would be something about it on television. I knew the baby must have been born in June—four months ago. They brought in a small television for the evening newscast, which had a short montage: Gabrielle standing with a couple of her cousins—I couldn't tell where; then short pieces of Peg, Dad, and Rich speaking; and, finally, a few seconds showing a baby girl—just video of a photo. Couldn't see much—a baby face, big eyes. There was no sound in English, just an Arabic commentary.

By the end of the two minutes or so, I was crying, crouched close in front of the television, peering under my blindfold, trying not to let the guards standing behind me or the others know how much it hurt.

When the guards left, I got up and walked rapidly around and around the room. The others were quiet. The thoughts were roiling around in my head: Madeleine, the baby, where are they? The brief shot of Gabrielle—she looked so sad. Suddenly I stopped and faced into a corner and started sobbing. What have I done to this so bright and happy child? The sadness on that always cheerful face was like a fist in my chest. Father Martin came over and put his arm around my shoulders. I flinched. I wasn't ready to be consoled.

After a while I went and sat next to him. He'd been hurt when I rejected his comfort. "I'm sorry, Father. I just needed a few minutes."

We talked a bit about Gabrielle and how I felt about that picture. That hurt, that guilt won't go away for a long time, if ever.

In the morning the guards brought in a newspaper with a picture of the baby and a short story, obviously about the messages that were sent in the television story. With some difficulty I spelled out the Arabic under the picture: her name is Sulome Theresa. So now I know—another beautiful child. Sulome Theresa.


## Madeleine

*Sunderland, England. October 1985.* Relations between Peg and me had gotten very bad, and I felt I had to get out of the house we had shared in Batavia. I felt she was changing from the pressure and attention of being on television. The worst part for me was knowing she was not telling me everything she was learning from officials she talked to. I couldn't understand it and felt humiliated. I rented a room in the house of a friend in Batavia, Marsha Barton.

Terry's father and brothers went back to Florida. Terry's sister Judy stayed in Batavia, although relations between her and Peg were also strained. A single mother with three children, Judy had a full-time job, so I didn't see much of her. It was unbearable living in this situation. I became very depressed all the time. It was lonely with my first child, in Terry's hometown without him. It was time I left.

I arrived in England, where my sister Nahla lived, in October 1985. A mother of two, she helped me a great deal in my new role as a mother. She was, as always, very concerned about my mental and physical condition. I had ached for such care and concern ever since Terry's abduction.

Psychologically, I was deteriorating slowly, and when the captors in one statement claimed they had killed William Buckley in retaliation for Israeli air raids on PLO headquarters in Tunis, I began to imagine the worst. Knowing how important Buckley must have been to them, I feared for Terry's fate. Holding my baby in my arms and crying, I spoke out loud, with no one else in the room, wishing him a happy birthday, fearing for his condition. Two days after his birthday a videotaped birthday message from his family and friends in Batavia was broadcast on Beirut TV stations.

Those few days were the most terrible since he was taken. On November 7 a caller claiming to be a member of the Islamic Jihad said the group would execute all American hostages it held because "indirect negotiations with the United States have reached a dead end." Another caller claimed that all American hostages had been killed and their bodies dumped in a bombed-out factory in Beirut.

It was terrifying to imagine Terry dead. How could he die now? We haven't started our life together yet. He hasn't seen his daughter or felt the warmth of her body. Why is this happening? Why did he have to ignore their first attempt to kidnap him? I was angry with him; I wished I was dead, too, so I could face him with my anger.

The next day letters from the four American hostages were delivered to the AP bureau in Beirut. They denied the claim of their death. Terry's message to me also said that he had seen the videotaped birthday message from his family made in Batavia and finally knew he had a daughter and that her name was Sulome.

# CHAPTER SIX
## Terry

*BEIRUT. November 1985.* The fighting outside has been getting worse—a lot of shelling, automatic weapons fire. The guards are nervous. I have fantasies about this apartment house being blown open, the guards being killed, the blast freeing us. Sometimes the fantasy turns into a nightmare of me hanging head down from the wreckage, six stories above the ground, like the man at the U.S. embassy.

The night is filled with the sound of guns and with the same thoughts all of us who believe in God must confront sooner or later. If God is omnipotent and loving, where does evil fit in? Where does justice come in? Okay, perhaps I deserve what I'm getting. But what about the children?

I find it hard to believe in a God who cares endlessly about every one of us, who monitors our every deed, and guides all things. So many things are obviously unguided, and so many others just cruel. I also cannot believe in an accountant God, who weighs my sins and metes out appropriate punishment. These men are not, in any way I can understand, God's instruments. This is not my punishment for adultery or indifference or all the petty dishonesties I've been guilty of in my life.

This is man's work, the product of political and economic forces, mixed with the needs and greeds of petty, evil men and the indifference of others. God is there to help me, to give me guidance and solace, and to keep me in the knowledge that no matter how much I may be humiliated, no matter how much I may come to dislike myself as my knowledge of myself grows, his love is unquestioning. He did not place me here, but He will help me get through it, even unto death, with grace and dignity.

OUR radio, which had been taken away from us, has reappeared without explanation. Within days we hear Ben Weir in New York, in some kind of press conference with a special representative of the Archbishop of Canterbury, a man named Terry Waite. Waite offered to act as an intermediary, to travel to Lebanon to talk with our captors. It's the first promising news we've ever heard. Perhaps the Hajj's gambit in freeing Ben is working?

After excitedly discussing it among ourselves, we call the guards. I explain to them what we heard, and suggest they answer Waite's proposal. "He obviously wants to talk to you. The Hajj said you couldn't get anyone to negotiate. Why not answer him?"

Mahmoud and the others listen, then say they'll tell "the chefs."

A couple of days later a new man appears. He says his name is Ali, and he's very friendly. He talks with a peculiar accent, very American and quite fluent, but with a strange, lisping *s*.

We will be allowed to write letters to our families, to the Archbishop of Canterbury, and to the President and members of Congress. We are to say that if the archbishop wants to help, he should send his intermediary to Kuwait, not Beirut, and try to get their friends released. We are to urge the President to do something to end this situation.

It's not entirely satisfactory, but it's something. The four of us compose joint letters. Then we begin working on our private letters.

I include a will, and a power of attorney for both Maddy and Peg. It will alarm them, but with my divorce likely still pending and a new child, I can't take a chance. As long as I'm alive, I can rely on the AP to take care of Maddy and the child, as well as Mickey and Gabrielle. I dread the idea of leaving them all without any resources if I die.

Ali says our letters will be delivered later, and proves to be telling the truth. The news is on the radio within hours—the letters were all dropped off at the AP. We're all totally hyped up. Is this the beginning of the end? We don't dare hope too much. The letters are not magic bullets. No one is going to say, "Gee, they're suffering. Let's begin negotiating." But it does help increase the pressure on those who might be able to do something to win our freedom.


## Madeleine

*SUNDERLAND, England. November 11, 1985.* "Madeleine, my love, my heart, I saw our daughter on TV the other night and I cried for joy. . . . I never cease thinking about you—I talk to you (in my head) every night and in the early mornings. Maddy, love, I'm sorry to have brought you pain, mostly through my arrogance in not being careful enough. It is little return for the happiness you brought me. I hope I can bring you as much happiness in the many years we will have together."

THE letters, the first direct contact from Terry since March 16, renewed my mind and soul and gave me new energy. Robert Fisk, who was in the Beirut AP bureau, made copies of a long letter addressed to me and Terry's family and sent them express mail to London. When he called, he said he was encouraged. One of the letters that Terry wrote was for President Reagan, urging him to try to secure their release. Another was addressed to the Archbishop of Canterbury, appealing for his assistant, Terry Waite, to mediate. At that point, I was sure my Terry would soon come home.

I don't remember how many times I read Terry's letter—twenty, thirty times. In his letter, I saw a man in terrible pain and yet making sure that his pain was not inflicted on us. I saw a father who could cry with joy only looking at a photograph of his child's face. The letter gave me strength that held me together for a long time.

All my hopes were high, and I started getting ready to receive Terry by Christmas. The days that followed were extremely tense. Waiting for a phone call or a message that would send me and my daughter to the first plane to meet Terry both gave me a ticket to heaven and brought me to the edge of a nervous breakdown.

## Terry

*BEIRUT. November 1985.*   The comments from our families are coming thick and fast. There's even a picture in the local paper of Tom's wife, Jean, reading his letter in the AP office. The reported comments from Washington are a little slower and considerably briefer. "No negotiations with terrorists. No pressure on Kuwait."

It's incredibly strange to sit here in our underwear, blindfolds on our foreheads, absorbing the abuse and petty humiliations of these young men, then listen to our letters being read and reacted to in Washington and New York by the world's mighty. We all drink in the attention, huddle over the radio constantly, debate every word endlessly. It's impossible not to believe now that something is happening, that perhaps one of us, two of us, all of us, might be going home soon.

In all the news reports, though, there's no mention of Madeleine. I believe I know why. She's Lebanese, a Christian who lives in West Beirut, whose family is also in the Muslim half of the city. And she's incredibly vulnerable—an unmarried woman with a child by an American. There are those here, Christian and Muslim, who would kill her just for that. She does not dare to speak out. I understand completely. Yet I long for her voice, for some word, for some indication of what has happened to her. There can be no doubt of our love. But how long can a beautiful young woman, alone with a new child, rest her hopes and her life on the few short months we had?

The days go on, one after the other, mounting up with frightening speed. We talk, or argue, about almost anything—politics or how the rear end of a car works. Tom and I tried to figure that out for hours one day. I keep making decks of cards out of the endpapers from the few magazines and books we have. When the guards find them in their periodic minor searches, they take them away, so we all huddle around one of the mattresses, with a blanket handy to throw over the cards when anyone comes in the door. We play almost entirely hearts, and play intensely. Father Martin and Tom have the least card sense, David is pretty good, and, fortunately or unfortunately, I'm better than all three. They're always trying to talk each other into ganging up on me—we play cutthroat, not partners—but can't hold their coalition together.

Father Martin accused me of dumping Dirty Gerty (the queen of spades—thirteen negative points) on him deliberately on every occasion. I quietly kept track for a couple of days and astounded him when I proved it was just the opposite—I was *his* favorite victim by far, not he mine. I am a pretty vicious player, though. I've always been very competitive; games are totally unenjoyable to me unless I play to win, whether it's points or money. The vehemence of our play is the only safe outlet for our emotions—and I'm not sure it's all that safe.

The cards, though, can take up only an hour or two. The rest of the time, it's back into our heads mostly. It's not a good idea to nap, because we already have great difficulty sleeping at night. Best to stay awake—but how? Prayers can't take up too much time, though we have services twice a day. Mostly we're just supremely bored. When is something going to happen? Anything? What in hell is going on?

It's close to Christmas, and we've heard on the radio that Terry Waite is in town. He seems to hold a press conference at least twice a day and sounds very optimistic. The roller coaster is climbing again. But the downhill part isn't far behind. On Christmas Eve we hear him telling the newspeople that he's leaving Beirut without having gotten anywhere. Our church services are understandably somber, and there is no conversation afterward. We all just sit or lie quietly on our mattresses.

The depression is enormous, a thick, black blanket smothering me. Despite all our caution, all our effort not to believe anything good would happen immediately, we really did believe it. At least I find out now that I did. To face again the knowledge that it will be weeks, months before there's even a chance of freedom is just too much. I can't do it. Please, God, I have to keep going. It will end. But when?

*Beirut. March 1986.* Ali is back with his smarm and lies. Brought us several big bags of fruit—bananas and tangerines and apples, more than we can possibly eat before they go bad. He insists he's not part of this group, just "helping my friends." He asks us if we need anything—books, of course—and implies that there is movement in the negotiations and something might happen "soon, and very soon." Back on the roller coaster again. It's just impossible for us not to allow ourselves to hope, no matter how many disappointments there have been, no matter how much we distrust this man. He makes my skin crawl, but I pretend to accept his friendliness.

During the next couple of visits the promises of release become more explicit, more direct. A deal is being made, Ali says. We are measured for clothes, and he brings in new shirts, trousers, even shoes for the four of us! "A few days," he says. Are we going home? Can we believe this man? Tom bangs out the "Marseillaise" on the wall to the Frenchmen next door and gets a triumphant-sounding repeat back. We're full of speculation, yet all of us are afraid to believe. Ali is so explicit, though. He couldn't tell that direct a lie, could he? What would be the point?

Then, suddenly, the roller coaster plunges down. Ali brings in a *Time* and *Newsweek* telling of the bombing of Libya. On April 14, 1986, American warplanes attacked Libya. At first Ali insists it won't make any difference. He's certainly contemptuous of Muammar al-Qaddafi, whom all these people dismiss as a madman. But as the days pass and the promises grow vaguer, it's clear whatever was going on has been blasted to bits with Qaddafi's headquarters.

Once again we go into depression, fighting the slide as hard as we had fought the climb. The days gradually drift back into the fog of breakfast, walking, bathroom, lunch, and so on. The conversation by now lags often. We've talked ourselves out, just about.

Then Ali's back. We are going home, he says. The clothes are brought out. The excitement builds. Ali gives slow, clear instructions. "You will all be taken out to a bus waiting outside. Your blindfolds will be removed, but keep your eyes on the ground. Don't look at anyone. You will be driven a short distance."

We wait several hours—endless. Finally, in the evening, the door opens, and several guards come in. The Hajj is there. Much bustle. David is taken out. A few minutes later Tom. The guards come in again. I stand up, and am guided out the door, down the hall, and straight into the bedroom at the end.

The guards guide me to a straight-backed plastic chair, and I sit down, enveloped in depression. It was all obviously a cruel hoax. Within a few minutes Tom says something to the guards, making me aware he also is in the room. But I hear nothing from David. We sit for an hour, a second hour. The two guards, Sayeed and someone else, grow bored. The two begin chanting in Arabic. Louder, louder. Then Sayeed leans close to my ear and switches to English. "Death to America. Death to America." The normally friendly young man has gone off on some Shia mind trip, hypnotized by the chant, by hatred. I lean forward and begin to pray, trying to ignore the noise, trying to lift the blackness that envelops my mind. "Dear Lord, You who take away the sins of the world, grant me peace. Lord, help me. Our Father . . ."

After several hours David is brought in and pushed into another chair. Sayeed and the others grow quiet. The Hajj appears, gives orders. The three of us are taken back to our room, and the others leave.

Lifting our blindfolds, we look at each other. Father Martin has obviously gone—home, it seems. But the joy we should feel for him doesn't come.

David tells Tom and me that he was asked to make a videotape for Father Martin to carry. He said he wrote a plea for the U.S. government to do something. Then he was brought in to us without seeing Father Martin.

We sort through the few things left beside his mattress. He has apparently been allowed to take nothing. His Bible, stuffed with markers, is still there, a tiny book of prayers. We prop his mattress up against the wall, rearrange ours to give us all a little more room. The conversation is brief. Finally we compose ourselves for sleep.

## CHAPTER SEVEN

*DAMASCUS. July 26, 1986.* The Syrian military car pulled up to the crowd of reporters and officials in front of the Syrian Foreign Ministry. Father Martin Jenco stepped out, blinking in the sunshine.

"Where's the sister of Terry Anderson?" he asked the crowd. Those around him moved back slightly, making a path to where Peggy Say stood. The two rushed into each other's arms. Both were crying and laughing as the secret policemen pulled them toward the building.

"How is Terry?" Peg asked quickly.

"He's okay. He's holding up."

There wasn't time for much more. Jenco was most concerned with the videotape he'd been given by his captors and the threat they'd made: if it isn't broadcast on television by midnight, the hostages will be executed. The threat was absurd. But no one could ever be sure.

The priest was swept away by Syrian officials to be handed over to the American ambassador, the tape still in his hand.

Peg rushed back to her hotel, where she called the AP to tell them about the tape. After some tussle with officials at the embassy, the AP got the tape and passed it to all the networks, barely making the deadline imposed by the captors for its broadcast.

When Jenco paused briefly for a news conference at the airport in Damascus, Terry Waite appeared at his side. "It's no coincidence I am here," the Church of England envoy told the reporters. Waite had not actually been involved in any way in the negotiations that led up to the priest's release. He didn't even know about them. He was on a visit to Jordan when Oliver North called him up and told him to go to Damascus immediately. The American figured that Waite's high public profile would provide decent cover for secret arms-for-hostages deals. Waite didn't question the orders.

Jenco's release ended Peg's trip to Damascus. She had arrived two weeks earlier as part of her crusade for her brother's freedom. But it was clear that only one hostage was coming out this time.

Peg was a long way from the scared housewife she had started out as sixteen months before. Though still often confused by the whirl-wind of media and politicians, she was by now totally focused on the goal that had become an obsession. Find some way to get Terry out.

The death in April of Peter Kilbourne, an American University librarian who was kidnapped in December 1984, had outraged and bewildered Peggy. She knew and liked Peter's family. She also knew that North and all the others involved were virtually certain that if the United States attacked Libya, hostages would be killed. They went ahead, and three hostages died—bought from their captors by the Iraqi chargé d'affaires in Beirut and personally executed by him.

Peg had by now lost a good deal of her awe of people in power. She had sat and argued in dozens of meetings with U.S. officials. One of her most frequent targets was a marine officer she had met in her search through Washington—Lieutenant Colonel Oliver North. He was an aide to National Security Adviser Bud McFarlane; surprisingly, he was sympathetic and willing to talk to her.

"She was very angry, very upset at the lack of progress," North said later. "You [could] not listen to her long, anguished ordeal and not be moved by it. You'd have to have a heart of steel."

North was in fact one of the few men who could have told Peg all about the efforts to free the hostages, if the subject hadn't been top top secret. "I would say, 'Peg, the State [Department] has told you all they can. We are trying everything possible to get Terry home.' "

"Everything possible" had expanded over the ten months since Ben Weir's release into a tortuously complicated edifice involving the extreme stretching, if not outright violation, of a number of U.S. laws; barefaced and repeated lying to the public and one another by top government officials, including the President; and even actions that could arguably be said to violate the U.S. Constitution.

There was little pretense anymore to a broad diplomatic purpose behind the effort. It was now obviously a straight swap—arms for hostages. There was also no attempt to reconcile these dealings with the frequently repeated public policy on terrorism: no deals with terrorists. Or to square them with the administration's strong efforts to prevent its allies from selling weapons to Iran.

How could Ronald Reagan sign a secret presidential finding, authorizing the negotiations in the face of these contradictions, backed up by the strongest objections from his senior Cabinet members?

Emotion, according to those close to Reagan. Sheer emotion that deepened with each encounter with relatives of the hostages.

"He'd listen to the families, and the dimensions of their pain that he absorbed more than [anything] I ever saw him absorb. This was something that *really* moved him," McFarlane recalled.

"It made Ronald Reagan decide to take whatever political risk was necessary," North agreed. "I'd said to Bud, Regan, [James] Baker— 'Don't meet with the families. I don't think that's a good idea.' "

With the President emotionally involved, no amount of protest was going to kill the initiative begun by Israel so long before.

Ollie North had by now negotiated a detailed package of weapons and missiles and an exact timetable with the Iranians, through the arms dealers Ghorbanifar and Shwimmer. The proposal was to receive final approval at a meeting in London, in December 1985, among the Iranians and the Americans.

Shultz and Weinberger made one last effort to stop the process. At a meeting with the President they again forcefully put forward their objections, and this time were joined by McFarlane, who was in the process of resigning. Reagan apparently gave in, authorizing McFarlane to go to the London meeting with one message for the Iranians: no more weapons.

McFarlane did so in a blunt presentation to Ghorbanifar, Shwimmer, and Kimche. North sat in on the meeting. McFarlane reminded them all that what had begun as an attempt to open a dialogue with Iran had become a haggle over human lives. It had to stop. The United States wanted to continue talking to Tehran, but first the hostages had to come home, and not in exchange for missiles.

The reaction was an outburst of contempt from Ghorbanifar, who curtly dismissed the Americans' second thoughts and concern with principle. He was a weapons dealer, he said. That was his business. That was what this was all about from the beginning.

"You're a fool," he concluded. "You're going to get every one of us killed. And I don't want to have anything else to do with you."

Hussein Mussawi (seated), believed to be associated with the secret terrorist group Islamic Jihad, which claimed responsibility for Terry's abduction. Photo taken during a 1983 interview with Anderson.

Left: Terry in 1984. And above: Embracing Madeleine at a party in West Beirut shortly before his abduction.

Right: Photo released by Terry's captors in October 1988, three days before his forty-first birthday—and three years after his abduction.

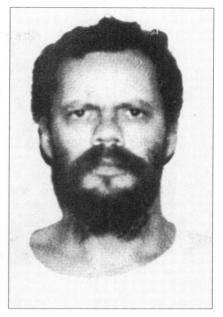

Left: Peggy Say and Don Mell, who was with Terry when he was abducted, discuss his plight with the Reverend Jesse Jackson. Below: Sulome visits her father's office, Christmas Eve, 1990.

Left: Terry's first wife, Mickey, and their daughter, Gabrielle, in Venice, 1977.

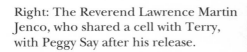

Right: The Reverend Lawrence Martin Jenco, who shared a cell with Terry, with Peggy Say after his release.

Brian Keenan, one of the most rebellious of the hostages, with his sisters in Damascus just after his release

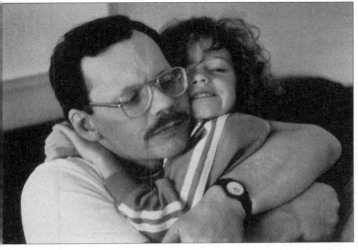

Left: Christmas morning, 1991. Terry with Sulome shortly after his release.

Right: Celebrating freedom. Terry, Madeleine, and Sulome, with fellow hostage John McCarthy and his fiancée, Jill Morrell, in Antigua.
Below: Giandomenico Picco (center) engineered the final release of the hostages. His efforts won him the United Nations Association Award, presented to him here as Anderson looks on.

An obvious, if unpleasant, end, McFarlane thought as he left.

Not quite. North stayed after his boss left. The two differ on what his instructions were, but the results are not in doubt. The dialogue continued.

McFarlane was replaced within days by Admiral John Poindexter as Reagan's national security adviser. The deal was alive again, but the Americans no longer trusted Ghorbanifar. They wanted to deal directly with someone in the Iranian government.

On February 17 a shipment of five hundred TOWs was flown from Israel to Bandar Abbas, in southwest Iran.

On February 24 North sat down in a Frankfurt, Germany, hotel room with not just one, but half a dozen Iranian officials. The meeting consisted mostly of North's speech about Washington wanting a better dialogue with Iran, and the ritual tirade about the inequities of the West from the Iranians. At the end of the meeting a ten-page list of weapons and parts was pushed across the table to North.

On February 27 a second shipment of five hundred TOWs was flown from Israel to Bandar Abbas. No hostages were released. However, North got something else out of the deal. The Americans had heavily overcharged Iran for the missiles. But in the complicated bookkeeping involved in the top secret deal, only the lower, correct amount was credited to the Department of Defense. Even after Ghorbanifar and everyone else took their cuts of the $10 million deal, millions were left over—with no need to account for it. That money, it occurred to North very quickly, could be used for another project dear to both his and Reagan's hearts: the Nicaraguan contras.

Congress, enraged by the unofficial war the Reagan administration was waging against the leftist government of Nicaragua, had cut off all official funds for the contras, the antigovernment guerrillas. North had been deeply involved in the U.S. support effort for the contras. It was both a priority of President Reagan, his boss, and a matter of strong personal and ideological conviction for North.

This windfall from the missiles sold to Iran would buy a lot of weapons and supplies for the contras. It was more than enough to offset the disappointment caused by Iran's reneging on the promised release of the American hostages. And the arms-for-hostages process would go on.

In April, Reagan called once again on the now retired McFarlane.

The Iranians were ready to receive a top U.S. official in Tehran—secretly, of course. Would McFarlane go?

"Well, I was pleased. I was surprised, but I told him sure," McFarlane said. "The only thing I asked was, 'Are Shultz and Weinberger involved?' And he said they were on board."

The trip, as explained by North, would involve meeting top Iranian officials, primarily President Rafsanjani himself, for substantive discussions. Hostages would come up only as the prerequisite for any further rapprochement.

And, by the way, North added, the last shipment of weapons would be made concurrently. Three loads of spare parts for missiles.

The May 25 trip was yet another disaster. The Iranians who met them were low-level functionaries. There was no meeting scheduled with Rafsanjani. "Ghorbanifar and North had lied," McFarlane said. The official that McFarlane finally talked to clearly believed McFarlane was there to deliver weapons. He had nothing to say about hostages.

McFarlane blew a gasket. He ordered planes that were waiting in Israel, loaded with spare parts, to unload. Then he headed for the Tehran airport, ignoring pleas from North, Ghorbanifar, and even the Iranians for more time to work out something. Once again the whole deal had been blown out of the water. Apparently. Only apparently.

Over the next few weeks the Iranians were told there could be no further discussions until at least one or two hostages were released. If that was done, according to North, the Hawk spare parts could be brought into the deal again and maybe even a couple of radars.

Father Jenco was released on July 26.

On July 30 President Reagan authorized the release of some of the spare parts the Iranians wanted. Three pallets of electronic spares for Hawk missiles arrived in Iran on August 3, 1986.

## Terry

*BEIRUT. July 28, 1986.*   It has been two days since Father Martin left. The guards say he has been taken to Damascus, where my sister Peg met him. That afternoon they bring in a small black-and-white television. David, Tom, and I cautiously lift our blindfolds to watch the news reports of Father Martin's arrival. We hear snatches of reports, but Sayeed quickly turns the sound down if it gets too detailed.

Then a commentator appears. American. There's a wide yellow banner across the top left side of the screen saying, SECRET MESSAGE? The commentator speculates on whether a reference to William Buckley's family in the tape David made contains a code. Buckley was single and had no family, he notes.

I can feel my back grow cold. There is no comment from the guards. When the report is over, they disconnect the television and leave, still saying little.

As soon as they are gone, we grill David. What was that about? He said he sent his condolences to Buckley's wife and children. Where did you learn about this alleged family? "You told me," he says. "No, I knew nothing about Buckley, knew nothing about a family." We're unable to trace the source of the bad information. If our hosts believe it, I can't help feeling, we're in for trouble.

The next day the guards storm in, accompanied by Ali and the Hajj. "You are spies. You are evil," Ali shouts. We're subjected to a ten-minute harangue, our protests of innocence ignored. David and Tom are taken out of the room.

"Stand up," Ali says to me, apparently translating for the Hajj. "Face the wall. Put your arms up." Then they leave.

After a few seconds, feeling silly standing with my arms up in an empty room, I sit down and try to compose my mind. I can hear shouting outside the door, but can't guess what's going on. I don't want to think about it.

The door opens a half hour later.

"Why are you sitting down?" Ali says fiercely.

"You left. I thought you were finished with me. You want me to stand up? Okay." I face the wall and put my arms up. Tom and David are brought back in, and the harangue begins again, Ali translating for the Hajj. "You are spies. We trusted you, and you betrayed us."

"No, we didn't," I try to interject.

"Shut up. Don't speak." He continues. We will be punished. Maybe killed. And so on. Finally it runs down. The two of them leave.

After the door closes, we begin the discussion. Tom and David say they were put against a wall, threatened. There was a lot of shouting, but no physical punishment. What happens now? No way to know.

It doesn't take long. The next evening the guards are back. We are abruptly ordered up, then taken down the stairs into a waiting van. A short ride, then we are unloaded. From glimpses under the edge of the blindfold, the building seems to be deserted, half finished. One by one we are lowered through a hole in the floor, into a dirty basement, then taken into a six- by six-foot cell with a steel door. No light, nothing but filth on the floor. Bustling of the guards, then we're pushed out and into the cell next door. Two of the same size knocked together, the remains of the wall between still there. The door slams.

Mattresses for each of us, two in one half, one in the other. Water bottles. Nothing else. I'm frightened. This place is grim, the worst place we've been. How long are we going to be here? They must have been planning to move us after Father Martin was released, just as they did after Ben went home. But these conditions? How are we going to make it? What now?

## Madeleine

LARNACA, *Cyprus. August 1986.* Father Jenco called me a couple of weeks after his release. We talked for an hour. I loved hearing him talk about Terry. Everything the priest said about him made my heart jump. I felt so proud of Terry, and so sorry for him.

Father Jenco told me only the gentle things about Terry. He told me how much Terry loved me, and his plans for our future. I knew these things, but it still made me very happy hearing them.

Sulome was six months old at the start of the year and already filling my life with joy that I never dreamed of. Her movements were very steady, and her bright green eyes would look at me with love. My sorrow for her grew as she did. I'd grown up without my father. My parents separated when I was a few months old. I always hated the fact that my father never lived with us. Here my child was going through the same thing.

On the first anniversary of Terry's kidnapping, March 16, 1986, there was still no news, no progress. On the contrary, more foreigners were being kidnapped. I felt I was living in the dark. I began to feel the distance between us. I had to leave England, to get closer to Terry.

I decided to go back to Lebanon, but my family in Beirut wouldn't hear of it. The situation there was getting worse. Scheherazade Faramarzi, who had been transferred by the AP to Nicosia, asked me if I would consider coming to Cyprus. I welcomed the suggestion and on April 6 flew with Sulome to the island. It turned out to be a very good move. For the first few months we stayed with Scheherazade, who became the best friend anyone could wish for.

Just a few days after we arrived, U.S. Navy jets attacked two military bases in Libya. Within days, there were news reports that Peter Kilbourne, and two other Britons kidnapped two weeks earlier, had been murdered in Beirut. Kilbourne had been missing two years, and no group had ever claimed responsibility for his kidnapping.

Sulome and I adjusted to Cyprus quickly. She was ten months old when we arrived, almost walking. I wasn't ready to be sociable, but enjoyed the warm weather and the closeness to Lebanon and my family. But mostly I was close to Terry. I could breathe the same air he was breathing, and if I wanted, I could take a short plane ride and be in the same neighborhood where we always suspected he was.

Sulome and I moved to Larnaca, on the south coast of the island. Summer began, and everything I did felt strange. To be free to enjoy the sea and sun and sand felt like cheating. I limited my movements to taking Sulome to the beach and straight home.

Sulome's birthday was on June 7, and that day Terry's brother Glenn Richard junior died in the States. His father had died three months earlier of cancer. During his father's funeral Rich had had a stroke. While he was recovering from surgery, doctors discovered he also had inoperable, fatal cancer.

I had liked Rich very much. Although I had met him only a few times, he always made me feel we had known each other a long time. That he died on Sulome's birthday made me feel even closer to this wonderful man.

Peggy came to Cyprus in the middle of July. She had been refused a visa to Syria previously, but with the help of Margaret Papandreou, the American-born wife of the Greek prime minister, she had gotten one this time. We spoke by phone a few times, but did not meet. Finally we had another argument on the phone, ending with her calling me names and slamming down the receiver. I decided never to have contact with her again.

On July 26 Father Jenco was released. Terry Waite appeared with him in Damascus, and it looked as if things were really happening.

But the optimism lasted only a short time. Frank Reed and Joseph Cicippio were kidnapped in Beirut just three days apart, on September 9 and 12. Their captors announced themselves as the Arab Revolutionary Cells. The strange name only meant Islamic Jihad had increased its membership. It was also a sign that whatever reasons they had to release Father Jenco, they didn't have them anymore.

It was hard to accept that it might be a very long time before we saw Terry again. I was again going into deep depressions. I felt like a yo-yo.

## Terry

*BEIRUT. August 1986.* It's a week, maybe ten days, since we were brought here. August what—3, 5? The guards will say nothing. We simply sit through the day in the dark cell. Now that David and I have almost entirely ceased arguing, it seems that Tom has decided to join the fray. He's emerging from his quiet depression, but usually to fight with David. He seems to have taken a deep dislike to him. I try to mediate, but I'm in no shape myself to play mother hen.

This place is truly horrible, and the guards seem to have taken in the atmosphere of the prison. We're jammed in tight against each other, with no room to move except one by one. We've lost everything—books, paper, pen, any access to news.

The cell is filthy with cockroaches, spiders, and various other vermin, and mice and rats can be heard scurrying about at night. Two of the new guards seem really vicious. So far they haven't taken any overt action, but often stand in the doorway after delivering the garbage they call food, and curse in Arabic. I can feel the hatred boiling off them like steam.

We can hear others in the cells on either side and across the way. Once in a while we peek through a small fan in the bottom of the steel door of our cell—the electricity is often cut, so it doesn't work—as the others are taken to the toilet. I believe I heard someone ask in a strong English accent for a cigarette. But so far no contact, not even a face or a wave. We haven't been able to figure out if the Frenchmen are here.

Tom asks regularly about my faith. He is still groping, not really believing, but unwilling to give up that faint hope that if our government can't get us out, something or someone called God might do so.

There isn't much I can do to help him. I don't believe in that kind of miracle anymore. My faith has to do with a knowledge, a deep assurance that there is a God and that He requires something of me.

DAVID is gone from the cell. First he was asked to write a letter. He was taken out for some time and, when he came back, said they had dictated exactly what he was to write—a demand for negotiations. He said he made some spelling errors to make sure those who read it would know it wasn't voluntary. A day or two later the guards were back, and this time very angry. Apparently news stories had noted the errors, making exactly the conclusion David had wanted, but broadcasting it all over the world. We could hear the angry discussion down the hall. David was put in another cell on the other side. We can hear him say a few words now and then to the guards.

I have long depressions that sometimes reduce me to tears at night. I try to hide them from Tom, but I know he feels them and has his own. We spend long periods not talking, just lying on the mattresses day and night.

I was sitting with my back to the wall a week or so ago, thinking about various incidents in my life. For some reason, an incident at Kennedy Airport in New York came to mind: A deaf man gave me a card with the signing alphabet sketched on it. He was raising money. I gave him some, looked at the card, remembered I already knew the alphabet from high school, and put it in my pocket.

Sitting in the dark, I tried to recall the signs, learned from two deaf friends when I was fifteen or sixteen and never used since. Surprisingly, I could remember perhaps two thirds of them. I tried out some alternatives for the ones I couldn't recall clearly, then showed them to Tom, suggesting he learn them, too, in case we were forbidden to speak, for instance. Over the next few days we practiced a bit, becoming fairly fluent in the simple spelling out of words. No particular reason—just a way to pass the time, of which we have an abundance.

HALLELUJAH! We've established contact with two other prisoners—John McCarthy and Brian Keenan. Tom spotted them looking out the little window of their cell across the way some days ago, and waved. They waved back. Then Brian held a piece of paper out the window—dangerous—that said, "I am Irish, my friend is English."

Standing on tiptoe to see out the window of our cell, which is just a little too high for my five seven, I tried to say, "We are American," and spell out our names in the air. Didn't seem to work too well. I'd managed to squirrel away a pen and some paper. I dug them out of the mattress and wrote a long note. I tried to be witty about our lodgings, told them who we are, and signed it "Up the Union."

Then I held the note up and told them with gestures it would be in the bathroom we all use, at the end of the corridor.

The next morning I stuck it in the pipe under the sink. I didn't want to think about what the guards would do if they found it, but they didn't. Brian and John got it, then put a reply in the pipe the next morning. In it, Brian made it very clear: yes, he's Irish, and a Protestant from Belfast, but he's a fervent supporter of the armed struggle and not in any way in favor of the union of England and Ireland.

Not an auspicious beginning. The old Anderson two-step: one foot forward, the other in my mouth. Anyway, in the next exchange, I suggested they learn the signing alphabet, and we spent two days, with the help of a couple of notes, showing them through the bars. Now we can talk! And we are doing so at length. I've quizzed John, who's a producer for ITN, about Maddy, but he knows nothing. Brian was an English teacher at the American University—strangely enough, hired by Tom's wife. He was able to tell Tom quite a bit about Jean, which has cheered Tom up considerably.

It's fantastic to be able to talk to someone else, someone who at least was outside more recently than we were. John was taken April 17, and Brian, April 11—just four months for both of them. They were dismayed to learn we were all being held by Islamic Jihad and that they have been tossed in with two people who have been held more than a year. But they both seem amazingly upbeat, full of jokes and cheerful chat.

Another new hostage—an American by his voice—has also joined us. He's in the cell to the left of ours. We hear his voice all the time. He seems to be a Muslim and prays often. But the prayers are very strange, full of demands of God that he be released.

The guards have spent the last several days installing a new tile floor in the cells, sealing up many of the holes that the bugs lived in. At least the place is a little cleaner now, if not more hospitable.

One thing hasn't improved, our food. Real garbage—hunks of mutton bones, cold rice, dry cheese sandwiches. McCarthy says they give the meat to their dogs and the bones to us.

David has made a videotape. The guards turned off the fans, even though there was electricity, and in the dead underground silence we could hear him reading a script in the guards' room—a demand for negotiations, an emotional appeal to the U.S. government. Tom and I speculate on whether that means negotiations are under way, or if it's another effort to get them going. It's September now, and we've been more than two months with no news at all. Nothing.

I'M ALONE now. "Trust Me" Ali, as we refer to him, showed up and told me I had to make a videotape. He dictated a bunch of stuff to me in a very arrogant way, all of it propaganda: rationalizations of their actions, attacks on Reagan, vague but ominous threats. I thought long and hard about whether or not I would do it. I wasn't really afraid of what they would do if I refused—there isn't much more they can do to me without killing me. There were lots of things in my mind about aiding and comforting the enemy, the old stuff from the Marine Corps. But in the end I decided nobody would really think these were my opinions, and it was likely to be the only way I could reassure Maddy that I'm alive and well. So I did it.

Ali promised me flatly that I would continue to stay with Tom. They took me into the guards' area, where they set up a camera and I read the script. Then they brought me back to a different cell, facing a wall so I can't communicate with anyone. I've been here a couple of weeks now. I'm so filled with rage and loneliness I can barely think.

I've got to keep my mind disciplined. I've got to hold on. But it's hard. I slip frequently into depressions, lie for hours on the mattress, just wallowing in misery. This isolation is almost more than I can bear. I can occasionally hear Tom's or John's voice, but there's no way to contact them except with notes in the bathroom. We've exchanged a couple, but they are getting nervous about it and obviously don't want to continue unless there's something important to say. Of course, there isn't anything to say.

I've been asking for the Bible since I was put in here, and finally they brought it to me. But it's very hard to read it. There's no light in the cell, just a flickering fluorescent lamp in the corridor. I have to hold the book up by the window to see anything and even then can barely make out the words. I don't think I could ever have imagined being this miserable.

WHEN they brought lunch today, I refused it. The food revolts me. The guard insisted. "You must eat."

"I don't want it. I'm not hungry."

"You must. Take."

It was another bowl of revolting, fat chunks of mutton over cold rice. I picked it up and threw it at the wastebasket. Of course, I had pulled my blindfold down when the guard came to the cell door. The dish hit the wall, and the food splattered on the floor. The guard cursed in Arabic and left. A few minutes later Sayeed came in. He sat down and said, "Why did you do that?"

"I don't want to eat. I'm not hungry. And it's bad food."

"You must not throw it away." The Shiites, like many groups in the Middle East, consider food sacred. To waste it is a sin.

"They want to beat you," he added. "I have told them they cannot. But you must not throw the food." He left before I could ask him why he won't let them thump on me. He never seemed to consider it very important before.

I'm afraid I'm beginning to lose my mind. This solitary confinement is killing me. There is nothing to hold on to, no way to anchor my mind. I try praying every day. But there's nothing there, just a blankness. I'm talking to myself, not God. I never realized how much I needed to be around others, to feed off them mentally. Do I have anything of my own inside me? Is there any core there? Is everything I thought I was just based on a reflection of others?

THINGS sure get weird around here. The guards brought in a birthday cake on my birthday, October 27! A huge two-layer thing. They took me up to their room, sat me down, and told me they were going to tape me eating the cake. I sat and watched under the edge of my blindfold as they stuck thirty-nine candles on top of the cake, then tried to light them. Of course, being hamsters, they lit them from the outside in, burning themselves half a dozen times trying to light the last candles on the inner ring. Finally they brought out the camera, but the light wouldn't work. Keystone Kops! Anyway, I got a piece of cake, asked them to divide up the rest among the other prisoners, and went back to my little cell.

My second birthday in captivity: 592 days. I hope Maddy sees the tape.

I'VE seen Sulome! Two days after my birthday the guards brought in a small television and showed me a tape of my daughter. She was so beautiful that it was painful to watch. Maddy spoke over the tape—a birthday message full of such love and such sadness. Then Sulome came on, holding my picture and saying, "I love you, I love you, I love you." A magnificent birthday present. I could barely see it the first time because of my tears. I asked them to play it again, and they did. Then I was allowed to write a short note to my family. I don't know if any of these letters—they've allowed us to write three or four over the past year and a half—have gotten through.

Each time I see something like this, it's a blend of great joy and great pain. It shatters the little world I live in, sends me careening between euphoria and love and enormous depression and regret. I would not give up these messages from the outside for anything, and yet sometimes they hurt too much. But at least the pain makes me know I'm alive.

My prayers are terribly mixed up now. God must be confused. Sometimes I'm so grateful for what I've had—an exciting life, so many wonderful people, even, finally, a great passionate love that was and is returned with equal intensity. Then I feel, Okay, if it ends now, I've had my share and more. I've returned little for all that, and I have many, many things to regret. I can't ask Him for more, having used so poorly what He's given me.

I'm beyond the promises and pleas: "Just get me out of here, I'll be good, I'll do this or that." It's acceptance I'm working on now. I find it easier to say to God, "Whatever You want will inevitably be. I have no choice but to accept." That's where some peace lies.

The guards are mostly leaving me alone these days. Not much harassment. Just the daily trip to the bathroom, food deliveries three times a day, and that's it. Be grateful for small favors, I guess.

FRANK Reed, the guy we've heard praying all the time, is even worse than I thought. He seems to have gone completely off the wall. Sayeed came in the other day and told me Frank's name, said he was sick and they wanted me to talk to him. Sayeed and a couple of other guards took me across to Frank's cell. I sat down and peeked under my blindfold. I could see him backed into a corner and all hunched up. Sayeed stood just behind me. "Hi. I'm Terry Anderson," I said first. He didn't reply. "They have said we can talk." He still wouldn't speak.

"I think it would be better if you left," I told Sayeed. He went out and closed the door but stayed just outside. I lifted my blindfold. "You can raise your blindfold," I said to Frank. "They're gone."

He still did not move. Finally he muttered, "I don't want to talk."

"Do you want me to leave?"

"Yes."

I knocked on the door, and Sayeed came to take me back to my cell. "He's very sick," I told him. "I don't know what you've done to him, but he's not well. He wouldn't talk to me."

That was it. I can't imagine a hostage in these circumstances refusing to talk to another American. He's almost catatonic. Must have had a very bad time. God help him.

I'm back in contact with the others. I've been moved to another cell down the line—no reason given. I can see John and Brian across the way, and they can see Tom, who is just next door to me. We've been talking again with the hand language, with the two of them taking turns relaying messages between Tom and me.

John says Tom is in pretty bad shape, very depressed and talking about suicide again. They're worried about him. John and Brian seem okay, still sounding fairly cheerful.

I told them about my brief contact with Frank. They also think he's gone nuts. No word on David. Nobody can see his cell, which is around the wall that blocks off half the cells. It's an incredible relief for me to be able to talk to someone again.

DAVID has gone home, I think. That's what one of the guards said to me, though of course there's no way to know if he's lying. But there was a lot of bustling around the other night. As I was being escorted through the guards' room to the bathroom, I peeked under the blindfold and saw David sitting on the floor against the wall, fully dressed.

Good luck for him, but I wonder why David? They had seemed to be going by order of kidnapping—Ben Weir, then Father Martin. I should have been next. If they skipped me this time, does that mean they'll keep me to the last? Three or four releases in two years. Not a rapid schedule. But maybe things have broken; maybe we'll all get out of here soon. Please, God.

## CHAPTER EIGHT

*BEIRUT. November 2, 1986.*    David Jacobsen was pushed out of the car on the Corniche Manara, in front of the Riviera Hotel. The area was a Druse neighborhood, and Druse militiamen quickly organized a motorcade to whisk him across the Green Line to the embassy, in the eastern hills overlooking the city.

Jacobsen's release was the perfect example of the flat, unadorned purchase of a hostage by the American government. It was exactly what everyone involved had indicated was unthinkable. The price: a mere five hundred TOW antitank missiles, f.o.b. Tehran.

The details of the deal were worked out in two meetings between Oliver North and Ali Bahramani, a nephew of Iranian President Rafsanjani. The process had nearly broken down when Islamic Jihad snatched two more Americans off the streets of Beirut—Frank Reed, the head of a private international school, and Joe Cicippio, comptroller of the American University. There was no way the Americans were going to accept an unending process—pay for one hostage, see another kidnapped. They said so, loudly, to their new contact.

But Bahramani vehemently denied that the Lebanese radicals had broken any understanding. They didn't have Reed or Cicippio, he insisted. North, reluctant to see his carefully built initiative go up in smoke, accepted the assurances. They were, as you might expect, total lies. Reed and Cicippio were already in the hands of the same people holding Jacobsen and the others.

In their eagerness to develop this new contact, North and several other U.S. officials had already agreed not only to the five hundred TOWs for each hostage. They had thrown in considerable U.S. intelligence information about alleged Soviet designs on Iran and the Gulf, as well as intimating other military equipment might be forthcoming if the Iranians could pay for it.

That, it seems, was important. Though the congressional ban on funding the Nicaraguan contras was expiring and North no longer needed the secrecy of transferring Iranian payments to that project, the idea of more free, unbudgeted money for that particular cause was a powerful incentive to keep things moving.

With a couple of minor hitches and delays, the whole thing went smoothly. The TOWs were shipped to Israel on October 27, after Iran made a $4 million payment into a secret account. On the next day, they were moved on by the Israelis to Iran.

Six days later Jacobsen was unceremoniously dumped in front of the Riviera. However, within days of his release, pamphlets were being distributed in Tehran's bazaar detailing the arms-for-hostages negotiations, including McFarlane's trip to Tehran. The pamphlets were the result of a power struggle going on in Iran and revealed that high officials had been buying weapons from the United States. This was a major shock to the Iranians—their revolutionary government had been dealing with both the Little Satan (Israel) and the Great Satan (America). The revelations were an even bigger shock in the West— to the American people, who had heard Ronald Reagan trumpet "no deals with terrorists" so often; and to America's allies, who had been subject to frequent lectures about the evil of selling arms to Iran.

The shaky, terribly complicated structure North and the others had erected came crashing down. There would be no more American hostages released for nearly four years.

## Madeleine

*LARNACA, Cyprus. November 1986.* Even after Jacobsen's release we held on to the hope that Terry would also be coming out. The rumors had said for two weeks that two Americans would be released.

The tension had begun to build again on October 3, when a videotape of Terry and David was released by Islamic Jihad. Terry looked fine: strong, with his will unbroken. His gaze was straight, and he was wearing glasses. That made me happy, because I knew he couldn't see beyond his nose without them.

After the videotape the rumors multiplied. The AP called to advise me to get ready. For three days I packed, unpacked, and packed again, trying to make sure I missed nothing. It was a torment to wait for days with no real assurance he was coming out. I struggled to believe, and to pretend not to believe so I wouldn't be disappointed.

Then David came out. Everyone was excited, hoping Terry would be next—soon. The atmosphere was overwhelming; I felt I could fly without wings. Even Sulome knew something was happening. She clung to me, and I had to take her everywhere I went.

The next day I was still waiting for something to happen. Then I heard the report about the arms-for-hostages dealings. If there had been a chance for Terry's release, the publication of the pamphlets in a pro-Syrian magazine, *Al-Shiraa,* killed it. Even if the captors knew of such a deal, they would never want it known that they were not really in control of the hostages, that Iran was the boss. Their demand for the release of their friends in Kuwaiti jails would be jeopardized. They wouldn't have a way to save face anymore.

I fell into another deep depression. I felt as though I had been battling with a very strong power for days, and I was exhausted. I hated living in furnished apartments where nothing was familiar. My responsibility to my daughter was weighing heavily on me. Here I have the most precious gift God had ever given me, a daughter, and yet I can't enjoy her. I was raising Sulome as a duty, not a pleasure. I was waking up in the morning because I had not died at night. I felt trapped. Everything around me was beautiful and within hand's reach, but I was not allowed to touch. I could not touch. I blamed Terry for everything. I would cry alone, and angrily call him names. But nothing eased the deep pain of my loneliness.

## Terry

*BEIRUT. November 1986.* Things have gotten very bad. Frank Reed managed to get out of his cell and wander up and down the hall for a while, talking to everyone. But he couldn't get through the steel doors at the end of the hall and eventually went back in and shut his cell door. The guards must have been watching. Nothing happened immediately, but after a couple of hours a chief showed up, and they dragged Frank out of his cell and into the guards' room, where they beat him badly. "You want to escape?" someone asked him loudly.

Then I heard a heavy blow, as if he'd been hit in the chest with a stick, followed by the sound of a body falling to the floor. The beating seemed to go on for hours but probably lasted thirty or forty minutes.

Eventually they took him to a cell on the end of the row and left him. A few minutes later he started shouting. "I want my clothes. I'm going home. Bring me my clothes!"

Two of the guards rushed in and beat him some more. He was yelling, "Sayeed. Help me. Help me!" He must be under the delusion that Sayeed is his friend. Finally it stopped.

It is impossible to describe how it feels to hear someone being beaten like that. To hear the ugly, dull thumps and slaps, and be able to do nothing. I felt physically ill and so utterly helpless.

Now Tom's gotten it. He got caught looking out his cell window. They took him into the guards' room and beat him for what seemed like half an hour. Then they put him in his cell and closed the steel flap that covers the small window in the door. One of the guards, Michel, apparently was away during the first beating. When he returned, he decided he wanted his share of the fun and opened up Tom's cell door to begin beating him again, until another guard stopped him. Tom is completely in the dark now, and we have no contact.

The guards have gotten really ugly. They seem to enjoy this atmosphere of anger and hatred. The physical surroundings—dark, wet, and dirty—seem to contribute. The guards are ready to use the smallest excuse to start the beatings again. So far, though, they haven't touched me. I don't know if I'm grateful or not. I don't want to be beaten, but to be exempt while others are is not a good thing.

Brian's joined the list of victims. They decided to give us all haircuts, as they have from time to time, and Brian objected to getting his beard cut. He's had it since he was sixteen. They beat him up, then shaved it off. This is getting out of hand. At least Tom's out of purdah. They opened the flap covering his window again, after more than a week, and we can talk. He's really shaken but seems to be recovering.

A grim Christmas Day. They asked if I wanted to send a message to my family for Christmas, and gave me a pen and one piece of paper. I just couldn't think of anything to say. Finally I wrote a two-line note: "I miss you all very much. I'm still well, but very tired."

Then as I was talking with the hand signals to Tom, I took off my glasses briefly. They slipped out of my hand, and the lenses got smashed. Now I can't read Tom's hand signals. Not much to celebrate this year, except I'm still alive and healthy.

## CHAPTER NINE

*WASHINGTON—London—New York. January—February 1987.*   Terry Waite left again for Lebanon in January. His decision to meet again with the kidnappers came as a surprise. The stink over Iran-contra arms-for-hostages was so strong it could almost be seen trailing after the various top-level American officials as they marched in and out of congressional hearings and the offices of various investigators. As usual when scandal hits, each official told a different story. Even President Reagan had to come up with several versions when his own Cabinet members pointed out to him that he was lying to the public.

Waite had clearly been used as a front man by North, set up to take credit for the releases and detract attention from the secret dealings between Washington and Tehran. The fact was pointed out in both English and American newspapers. The mere linking of his name with North's was dangerous. The Church of England envoy had been told flatly by his Islamic Jihad contacts during his last trip to get out of town and not to come back without something to offer. He had been able to get nothing from anyone. The Americans no longer wanted to talk to anyone about possible deals. The Iranians and Kuwaitis both refused him visas.

Waite knew it was dangerous, but he was determined. His reputation had been stained. He had not accomplished what he had set out to do more than a year before—get all the hostages out. He would try again.

In hindsight, Waite would admit to being reckless. Not for making another attempt, but because he had dismissed the guards he had been provided with by the Druse. He had to argue with them to get them to allow him to go to a meeting with the kidnappers' representative alone. But they eventually gave in to his stubbornness.

As day stretched into day with no word from him, rumors flew madly. He was in serious negotiations in the Bekáa Valley. He was close to success. Finally the truth came out. He had been taken.

On January 17 a West German businessman was kidnapped in Beirut. Three days later another West German was taken.

A third German and a Saudi were snatched off the streets in Beirut. The U.S. Department of State banned all travel to Lebanon and ordered the 1500 American citizens in the country to leave at once.


## Terry

SOUTHERN *Lebanon. March 1987.*   We have been moved again, twice. First, to an ordinary apartment on the edge of the southern suburbs of Beirut; then again, deep into southern Lebanon, seemingly into the middle of what used to be called the Iron Triangle. The name referred to a group of fervently Hezbollah villages bordering the strip of Lebanon still occupied by Israel. This had always been the center of Shiite resistance to the Israeli occupation, the source of many of the attacks on Israeli troops.

We certainly didn't come from Beirut first class. Frank, Tom, and I were loaded into trucks. But first we were all wrapped from head to foot with plastic shipping tape, with only a small space for the nose to allow us to breathe. I was literally packed into a tiny compartment under the floor of a van, with two guards shoving on me to get the lid of the little coffinlike enclosure sealed.

Then we drove for several hours—obviously south, because that's the only way you can go that long on a relatively flat, good road in Lebanon. I even noted when we passed through Sidon, going around the little traffic circle in the center of the city.

The trip was hell. It was raining, and I got thoroughly soaked from the puddles we splashed through. Also, the fumes from the van's engine made me feel desperately ill. Every time we hit a pothole or a bump, my nose banged into the metal floor above me. When we finally arrived and were taken into what seemed to be a mosque, my nose was bleeding and I was shivering constantly.

Tom and Frank arrived at the same time. Don't know what happened to John and Brian. We stayed in that place just overnight, then were put into car trunks and driven a short distance to another, similar, large building. The guards have fixed up a secret basement room here, with a door in the floor of a closet. Our cell is about twenty feet long and perhaps eight or nine feet wide. We each have a cot, and we're each chained to a U bolt in the wall.

We're constrained to near total silence and allowed little movement. On some nights of the week meetings are held upstairs. When that happens, a guard is put in with us with an AK-47. We are forbidden to move, or even cough, for several hours.

This place is metaphorically, as well as literally, a hole. It's dirty and full of mosquitoes. The light, a bare bulb hanging from the ceiling, is never turned off. The guards are suspicious and unfriendly.

Once again the depression is enormously deep. Only our physical misery distracts us from our black, endless thoughts. Neither Frank nor Tom is in terribly good psychological shape, though Frank is much the worse of the two. He just lies there for hours without moving or raising his blindfold, even when the guards are not around. Seems to still be semicatatonic. Tom is just deeply depressed and pessimistic. With very good reason. I keep saying that something must be happening. But it doesn't convince him, or even me. We all know that Terry Waite has been kidnapped, too. We heard it on the guards' radio in Beirut. Clearly, something terrible has gone wrong.

Sometimes I wake abruptly from the light dozing that passes for sleep these days, after dreaming of Madeleine. I can feel her so clearly, the curve of her hip, the smell of her hair. I wake up to an awful emptiness in my arms. I still can't think of her for more than a few moments at a time without the pain threatening to engulf me.

I can often feel the panic sneaking up, the weight of the months and years that have gone by while we lie on these mattresses, the incredible waste. I push it away and busy my mind with mental games or frantic efforts at conversation. Tom keeps careful track of the time—"This is my six-hundredth, seven-hundredth day. It's twenty-three days till my birthday, till Christmas, till Easter." I snarl at him, "Don't tell me, Tom. I don't want to know." I can't stand to think about all those weeks, months piling one on top of the other.

ANOTHER move, to some kind of small villa maybe five miles or so from the place we were just in. It's slightly better than the last place. We're each chained to ringbolts in the floor and to each other.

They've put up very heavy steel doors to cover a pair of French doors in the bedroom, with no fewer than five padlocks and a chain on them. There's no door to the room, just a blanket hung up to screen us from the guards in the next room. No exercise again and just one trip to the toilet a day. Damn few showers as well.

But John and Brian have rejoined us. We can hear them occasionally. They seem to be in a disused toilet area.

A few things are better. We can talk quietly, and they even gave me some cardboard and a pen. I made a Monopoly game, and a Scrabble board, with little bits of paper for the letters. We play every day. The games seem to be helping Frank emerge from his shell. He's interested in them, and I've even been able to persuade him to talk about his work. (He ran a couple of small private schools in Beirut with a Lebanese partner.) But he remains very frail, narrowly balanced on the edge of sanity.

We're allowed to watch a small black-and-white television sometimes, but only the entertainment programs. The guards turn it off ten minutes before the news comes on, and back on ten minutes afterward. That means, of course, even the entertainment programs we are allowed to see are truncated, and we rarely learn how any of the stories end. Nonetheless, I watch it whenever we have it.

The TV has confirmed our location, anyway. The main channel we see is Middle East Broadcasting, a Christian Broadcasting Network station that we all knew was located in the Israeli-occupied border zone: The 700 Club with Pat Robertson, and the like. None of the channels could be seen in Lebanon outside the far south, near the Israeli border.

They even gave us back our watches, taken from us so long ago. Tom's is electric, and the battery has run down, so it's useless. But mine, an old self-winding gold watch Madeleine gave me, is still going. At least we know what time it is, and that pleases Tom, who seems to need to know. I don't much care—we've got no appointments.

Tom got terribly ill for about a week recently. He suffered from recurrent high fever and could not eat at all. I badgered the guards for several days before they finally got some medicine for him. Then he wouldn't take it. He said it made him sicker. I spent every day and night pushing and persuading him to take the medicine when he was supposed to, and to eat something at every meal. Most everything he threw up. All this frightened me badly, but he's come out of it now.

Taking care of Tom and trying to work on Frank, get him interested in things and talking, is at least keeping me occupied. Prevents me from spending too much time in my now familiar black depression. I spend most of my prayer time on them, though there's plenty of time left over for mea culpas and pleading for some kind of inner peace on my own behalf. There's absolutely no news—nothing.

## CHAPTER TEN

*WASHINGTON, D.C. March 1987.* The doors that had opened so readily over the past two years for Peg Say were now all firmly shut. No one in the Reagan administration wanted to even hear the word hostage. Even when she did succeed in getting into someone's office, the faces were all new. The men she had come to know were all gone.

In one such meeting, a new liaison man named Michael Mahoney told Peg bluntly, the hostages were being "devalued." The kidnappers were to be persuaded that their victims had no value to the United States. And by the way, the family members of hostages would never again have access to high government officials.

Peg was dismayed and angry. Sure, the families had demanded that something be done. They had not demanded it be illegal, foolish, and ineffective. Three hostages had come home through North's efforts. Six other Americans were now hostage. The net result was not exactly a win. But it was not the families' fault. Nor that of the hostages.

But as the administration was trying to push the whole issue off its collective desk, interest in and sympathy for the hostages were growing in the small towns and cities across America. Cards and letters from schoolchildren and adults were piling up in the offices of No Greater Love, an organization set up to help the families of victims of war and terrorism. Friends and relatives of the hostages were on this or that talk show or news show every day.

In Beirut, Lebanese television carried a videotape of two-year-old Sulome Anderson blowing out the candles on a birthday cake. "Our hearts are broken. Where is Daddy?" she asked, waving a picture of her father. The Lebanese announcer came back on the screen wiping tears from his eyes.

## Terry

*BEIRUT. November 1987.* I'm finally out of that mess in southern Lebanon and back in Beirut, though I was alone for a while. No explanation. They just came in and told me to stand up. They taped me up completely. Then it was into the secret compartment again, and north for several hours. It was not a pleasant trip.

I did have a couple of seconds to hand my watch to Tom. I'd like to have kept it, since it was a present from Maddy. But he needs it worse than I do.

I was chained to the wall again in one of the apartments we lived in a year or so ago. No news, no TV. I had some books and read them mostly by candlelight. I even have the red Bible again.

Then I got a surprising new companion. I was moved from the bedroom I was in to another just down the hall in the same apartment, where one of the Frenchmen, Marcel Fontaine, has been kept for some time. We're now chained to the same wall, our mattresses lying head to head on one side of the room. He's a small man, thin, and very quiet. Of course, we told each other our stories immediately. Fontaine was kidnapped just a week after I was—March 22, 1985. So we've both been held for thirty-three months. There were four Frenchmen held together for some time, and they were the ones who were in the next room in the apartment Tom dubbed the "Marseillaise." But one, Michel Seurat, died of some kind of cancer while we were all there.

It seems Fontaine was separated from his two companions, Jean-Paul Kauffmann and Marcel Carton, some weeks ago. He doesn't think they've been freed, but has little information.

It's pleasant to have someone else here after three or four weeks in solitary, especially a man as undemanding as Marcel. He talks little. His English is limited, and he has a very thick accent. He was a consul at the French embassy in Beirut. He seems very conservative and likes books about conspiracies: *The Hundred Families That Rule France* is one of his favorites. We have a number of French books, and he's helping me with my vocabulary, though he says my accent is atrocious and he can hardly understand when I speak French.

We get half an hour or so off the chain each day for exercise. I jog back and forth across the room and do sit-ups. All the large muscles in my arms and legs and chest have shrunk or turned to flab. Got to stay in shape. But it's difficult. I exercise hard for a week or two, then do almost nothing for days. I just can't seem to keep it up.

These days we seem suspended, just floating through the weeks, trying not to notice the time going by. Nearly three years.

I ALMOST cracked. For no particular reason, except frustration. I was trying to persuade the guards to get the chiefs to let me send a message home for Christmas. Nothing. No response. "We will tell the chef." "We have told the chef." "We have no orders." Just nothing.

Suddenly, during the exercise period, thinking about home, about Madeleine and Sulome and everyone, my mind started spinning out of control. I walked over to the wall and began beating my forehead against it, hard, trying to make it all stop. After a couple dozen thumps, Fontaine knocked on the closed door for the guards. Mahmoud came in, ran across the room, and pushed me down on the mattress. "What are you doing?" It wasn't until then I noticed my head was bleeding.

He chained me up again, got a cloth and wiped off the blood, then asked me, "Why are you doing this?"

I didn't know why. "Don't ignore me," I said. "When I talk to you, give me an answer."

"You must not do this." That was all. The next day one of the chiefs came in and examined my head, but did not speak to me.

I thought I was doing so well. I thought I had myself under control and could deal with all this with some dignity. Now I don't know how long I'll be able to make it. I'm scared, not of them, but of myself.

Fontaine had a bad time New Year's Eve just because of the guards' stupidity and laziness. Apparently, every year the French families put a message on Radio France International at midnight, and the French hostages have always been allowed to listen. This time he told Mahmoud about the upcoming message several days in advance and asked him to get permission to give us a radio for it. Mahmoud said the guards will tape the message, but we can't have a radio.

That was frustrating. What was worse, though, was that on New Year's Day, Mahmoud brought in a tape machine, saying he had done the taping. But when he pushed the PLAY button, we discovered the batteries had been too weak. Total loss, until next year—God forbid.

It is so enraging to be at the mercy of these young men and to find them not vicious, just stupid, lazy, and indifferent. They cannot imagine what those messages mean to us. There's no reason for them not to give them to us. I know there have been dozens for me over the years, and I've received only four or five. It's just so uselessly stupid.

Weeks of nothing but boredom. It's spring now, not that it means anything to us. The steel on the windows is too tightly sealed for us to see anything but a small line of daylight around the sides. I've seen the sun once now in three years. Back in 1985 the guards took David and me into a room with an open window and let us look at the sky for about five minutes. That's it.

FONTAINE'S gone. They told us one day that one of the two of us was going home. He was convinced it would be me. I once again tried, not very successfully, not to believe it. That night several of them came in, including the Hajj. I recognized his voice immediately. They told me to stand up, released my chain, and took me out of the room, but only to the other bedroom. I stayed there for a couple of hours; then they took me back, and Fontaine was gone.

The Hajj came over to talk to me. He took my hand and held it gently while we talked. "*Keefak,* Terry?" How are you?

"*Salaam aleikum,* Hajj. What is happening? Has Fontaine been set free?" Mahmoud translated. The Hajj said that all the French had gone home. "Everything is very good. There are good negotiations."

I asked him when I would go home, and he said, "Maybe one month." Then he left.

So once again the roller coaster starts up. There have been so many "good negotiations." So many near releases.

## Madeleine

*NICOSIA, Cyprus. April 1988.*    On April 8, 1988, a Kuwaiti airliner was hijacked by Islamic Jihad. The plane was taken from one airport to another around the Middle East, and two Kuwaiti passengers were killed before it finally landed at Larnaca. The hijackers were demanding the release of the seventeen Shia jailed in Kuwait and threatening to kill their American hostages if any attempt was made to attack the plane. They displayed a photo of Terry to prove they were the ones who held the Americans. Eventually the passengers were released and the hijackers allowed to go free.

I was again, of course, worried and depressed. But this time the bad feelings lasted less time.

In a deep depression a few months ago, I had called an old friend for help, Cassandra Ludington, wife of the AP bureau chief. Cassandra had come over to my apartment in minutes, then brought me back to her own home. While her two sons took Sulome out to the garden, I sat with her in her living room, crying for more than three hours.

Cassandra had tried before to get me out of my solitude. From then on I began to go out more often, and after the first few times Cass asked, I agreed to go to church with her. In the beginning it felt as if I were intruding. I didn't feel godly at all. When others were praying or singing hymns, I was crying. It didn't feel right, and yet I knew I needed to reach some sort of peace with God.

The more I cried in church, the more I felt at peace. I don't know what happens when we are in the house of God. All I knew was that I didn't seem to be alone anymore. I had my friends and the church and the refound belief that God was helping me and my family.

That assurance was confirmed on May 4, when three French hostages were released. I went to Paris to meet Marcel Fontaine. He looked pale and seemed withdrawn, but he reassured me Terry was in good shape and in good spirits. Like all the freed hostages before him, Fontaine also told me of Terry's love for me, how all these years he has never ceased thinking of me. The joy that these words can give a woman is extraordinary: to know that you and the one you love are on the same level of feeling for each other without the look of the eyes and the touch of the flesh. My love for him grew deeper every day.

According to Fontaine, Terry, with his stubbornness, always managed to get the guards to give them what they needed, and their conditions had improved during the months they were together. Again, as always, I was very proud of Terry. But also very angry and sad that he was now left alone in his cell to deal with those animals.

For Sulome, at the age of three, the absence of her father was natural and not yet a major element in her life. But now I saw her begin to feel the meaning of it around her friends and their fathers.

She would watch them play, or see them go off together, knowing she had no part in it. Her eyes would drop sadly, and she would look around for me, seeking protection from her own discovery. Every time I saw that look in her eyes, I wished I could enter her heart to soothe it with my love. I had no way to stop her from hurting.

I realized now was the time to explain about her father and the reasons for his absence. I didn't know if it would make sense to her. But I could bring her closer to him by telling her about him whenever we got a photo or a videotape. I never told her he was in danger.

On his birthday that year, October 27, the Jihad's statement included a picture of Terry with a birthday cake, bending to blow out the candles. I couldn't tell if it was a smile on his face or a look of sarcasm. He appeared thin and feeble, different from all his other photos. I cried until there were no more tears in my eyes.

By this time we had moved from the furnished apartment I hated to a new house. Now I drove Sulome up into the mountains of Cyprus, far away from everything and everybody, and told her about her daddy's birthday. By a tree next to a small river, she and I found a strange kind of peace. Sulome asked to write her name on the tree. With a knife I carved her name, and the date: October 27, 1988. We would do the same thing each of the next three years on that day.

A few days later, on October 31, a videotape came. He looked stronger than in the photo, but resigned. He appealed to the next President, Bush or Dukakis, to end his captivity, saying he found it difficult to keep his spirit and courage high any longer.

## Terry

*BAALBEK, Lebanon. May–December 1988.*  It didn't take them long to move me again after Fontaine left, and it was another memorable move. They woke me before dawn on May 6, just two days after he was set free. No nonsense about my going home this time. They taped my hands lightly, then placed small round Band-Aids over my eyes. The Hajj picked up my prescription sunglasses—virtually the only one of my possessions they've hung on to—and put them on my face. Then they dressed me in a chador—with the black hood covering my head completely. There was a piece of gauze set into the front of the hood, over the eyes, where a woman would ordinarily look out. After the usual interminable wait, I was taken outside and put in the back seat of a car, a Mercedes that seemed identical to the one they used for my kidnapping thirty-eight months ago.

The Hajj drove the car himself, with me and a guard sitting in the back. They never noticed, through the veil, that the Band-Aids came off my eyes almost immediately. With the prescription glasses I could see everything around me. We drove through the narrow streets of southern Beirut for about twenty minutes, dodging rubble in the roadway, edging past burned-out cars, bumping through shell holes. The devastation was incredible. Obviously this area had been hit hard and repeatedly over the months.

Finally we backed into a driveway and up to a large truck. Dear God, I thought. It's the coffin again. They pulled me out, pulled off the chador, and wrapped me up in the shipping tape, head to foot. Then they slid me back into the secret compartment, and this time one of the guards got in with me.

The ride was a long one—five or six hours—and extremely hot. Up out of Beirut over the mountains and into what was obviously the Bekáa Valley. For the last two hours, I was ill from the heat and exhaust fumes, and frightened of throwing up. I had to concentrate totally to keep my stomach under control—with all the tape over my mouth, I would have choked to death on my own vomit.

The truck stopped eventually, and I was taken out, unwrapped, and left lying on the ground, outside what seemed to be an isolated villa. One of the guards poured a bottle of water on my head, then gave me some to drink. Then they took me inside and down into a secret cellar. A chain was placed on my wrist, and they left.

There was a moment of silence after the door closed. I cautiously lifted my blindfold and saw Tom Sutherland and Frank Reed sitting against the wall. Tom spoke first. "I thought you'd gone home, but the Frenchmen said they were sure you hadn't."

Reed had been kept in isolation for the last year or so, since we saw him last. But Tom had been put in with Jean-Paul Kauffmann and Marcel Carton for about six months. We couldn't figure out why they'd shifted everybody around that way.

It was both good to have company again, especially Tom, and terribly depressing to know that there was no likelihood of release.

They wouldn't have carted us all out here to the Bekáa if they planned to let us go soon.

The basement cell we are in is long and narrow, perhaps twenty or twenty-five feet by twelve. There is a walled-off toilet in one corner, but of course we can't reach it because of the chains. We have a light in the ceiling that is on all the time. In one corner is a long pipe leading up to the surface, with a small fan that brings in air. No chink of daylight, except at the end of the pipe.

Tom and Frank are at daggers drawn. They bicker constantly. Tom seems to have developed a deep dislike for Frank, and Frank is, as usual, oblivious to everything. He sits for hours at a time slouched against the wall, his blindfold down over his eyes. Occasionally, he rouses to join a discussion for a few minutes, usually to disagree over some "fact" or other. Of course, we have no way to check anything, so it's just one man's "fact" against another's. Pointless to argue.

Tom and I argue as well. But usually it's an academic argument, a debate. Since we've been separated, he's gotten a good deal more self-confident, even aggressive at times. Apparently, he got on very well with Kauffmann and Carton. It's good to see him get back some confidence. His self-esteem was badly shattered over the first few months by the guards' violence and suspicion. I didn't help, with my steamroller style of discussion. He began to think he was stupid, and I couldn't really convince him that I like and admire him, that his knowledge of so many things and kindness and liking for people make me a bit jealous. He is a good and gentle man who just was not prepared for this kind of hell. Who could be?

I've lost a good deal of my aggressiveness, I think, after so much time alone. But I'm still hungry to use my mind. Tom and I talk for hours about anything that comes to mind—how to wire a house for electricity, how a three-way switch works. Anything.

Suddenly our long-repeated pleas for a radio have again borne fruit. The guards brought in a small Sony, and now we can listen to all the newscasts we want. No reason given once again for its return. There isn't much about the hostages these days. Seems everything is still stalled by the Iran-contra aftermath. But we're able to follow the presidential campaign in the States. Of course, Tom is a good Republican and supports Bush. I remain a liberal Democrat, and for

Dukakis. Though I have to confess I don't know much about him. He seems very dry and cold.

We speculate off and on whether the election will mean anything for us. Bush's getting elected means no change likely. Dukakis, being unschooled in foreign policy, is probably too pro-Israeli to accomplish much. It's clear, though, that our case has been ruled out of bounds for the election. Neither the Republicans nor the Democrats will stray from the mantra: No negotiations with terrorists. Correct policy, but discouraging.

JOHN and Brian are with us! Just a week after we arrived here, the guards came in and dumped two more mattresses against the wall. The next day they brought them in. We had to pretend to introduce ourselves, still blindfolded while the guards were in the room. Couldn't, of course, acknowledge that we'd already been talking for months in the Beirut prison with the sign language.

The first couple of days with them were great—lots of talk, exchanging stories of the past year. John is an incredible mimic, a fan of the Goon Squad and *Saturday Night Live*. Strangely enough, he took American studies at his university, but has never visited the States.

Brian is still the tough Belfast boy. He's an English major with a thorough knowledge of literature. Very funny at times. The two of them have developed an incredibly close relationship, despite their vast differences. Makes the rest of us a bit jealous.

They're fresh meat for Tom and me. All those months of probing each other's minds, of discussing so many things. John is diffident in the talks, rarely holding the floor for long. Brian needs to be coaxed a bit but, once started, has a great deal to say. I'm afraid my eagerness puts him off. He looked at me late one night, after one discussion of books, and said, "You just suck my mind dry."

Even Frank joins in now and then, emerging from his shell and talking about Boston, usually when we're quiet for a while. He's got a lot of very funny stories to tell. It's too bad he's so fragile. Don't know how he can sit there, sometimes for days, never lifting his blindfold.

I've got a picture of Sulome tucked inside the Bible. Sometimes I take it out and just look at it for ten or fifteen minutes. She's almost three now. I wonder where they are. What is Madeleine doing? Haven't had a message from them in so long now. The guards have brought in a couple of newspaper clips telling of various rallies and events. John said he saw, accidentally, part of a television program on him—a rock concert hosted by the Friends of John McCarthy. I know there are a couple of similar committees for me—Journalists' Committee to Free Terry Anderson, and so on. Frank has never had a message, except his name included in the list of American hostages now and then. He never says anything about it. Doesn't even talk much about his Lebanese wife anymore, just occasionally his son, Tarek. What's going on inside that head? How badly has he been damaged?

Late at night, after some of us start to doze off, there is generally a quiet talk going on between whichever two of us can't sleep. Frequently it's John and I whispering to each other at three or four o'clock in the morning as we share one of our four daily cigarettes. John is an enormously civil man. He rarely complains, and I've never seen him angry. I know he's as lonely and discouraged as any of us, but he just keeps his cool and his sense of humor. Doesn't talk much about his feelings, unlike the rest of us.

Brian is finding it very very difficult, I think, to make the daily compromises we all have to make in our relationships with the guards. He hates them, as we all do. But he sees it as absolutely necessary to his own integrity to let them know he hates them. He can react to this situation only in the terms he learned growing up in Northern Ireland. There, open defiance and openly expressed hatred are the rule. Here, he sees us talking with these young men, even making jokes with them. He understands the polite fiction we all engage in, but he can't bring himself to take part in it.

I think John, with his urbanity and wit and ability to get along, has been Brian's buffer. In return, Brian's steely integrity has helped John in those times we all have when we question ourselves. Have we been tamed? Shouldn't we make it hard for them, not easy? We're so well trained now. We yank our blindfolds down when they come in; we stick out our legs for the chains. Sometimes, when they forget to lock us up, we even remind them. We've all done the same thing, feeling sick and helpless and weak: locked the chain around our own leg. And hated ourselves for it.

We accept so many assaults on our dignity: shoves and pokes, yanks on the chain, a piece of fruit tossed at us as if we could see and catch it while blindfolded. I still get angry. Each new guard has to be taught:

I will be treated with a decent minimum of respect. I am a hostage, not a criminal. And, first of all, I am a man, not an animal.

Most of the guards who have been with us for some time accept these things. I think they know it wouldn't take much to drive us to despair, to not caring about consequences. And in fact the guards don't usually want to make things more difficult. They just don't understand how much their every move affects us.

John and I nearly got ourselves in deep trouble. One of the surlier guards suddenly decided he wanted to learn English. He sat down in our cell and, after explaining in Arabic what he wanted, picked up John's plastic cup and held it under McCarthy's nose, where he could see it under the blindfold. *"Shu Inglisi?"* he asked. What English?

"Cup," John replied soberly.

Then the guard picked up a plastic spoon. *"Shu?"*

"Cup," John said. I sat up straighter, surprised. I couldn't see what he was holding, but guessed he hadn't picked up the same object twice.

"Cup?" the hamster asked.

"No, cup," John said, giving it a slightly different pronunciation.

The guard reached over to my mattress and picked up my Bible. *"Shu?"*

Trying to appear serious, I leaned forward and peered under my blindfold. "Cup," I said.

"Cup?"

"No, cu-u-u-p," I replied.

After one or two more tries, he suddenly twigged to what we were doing, said something rapid and low in Arabic, got up, and left. We started giggling and couldn't stop for ten minutes. It may not have been smart, but it was fun.

It's amazing sometimes how much laughing we do. John's imitations, Brian's terrible shaggy-dog stories, Tom's awful puns and drinking songs, Frank's tales of Boston. Even the idiotic and frustrating things the guards do set us off in giggles. There's often a bitter touch to it. But not always.

SOME optimistic news for John, and maybe Brian, on the radio. Britain and Iran have agreed to reopen relations. Britain could hardly do that without some kind of understanding about British hostages.

No further mention of the Americans, no speculation about more releases. Nothing. The days go so slowly, yet pile up so quickly. It's October 6, 1988. Three and a half years. I can't even remember all the places I've been kept. And I can't allow myself to think of that time wasted, that huge chunk of my life gone.

FRANK has been taken away—allegedly to go home, though none of us believe it. They have played this cruel hoax before on all of us, but to do it to Frank is especially vicious. A couple of guards came in, and one of them said, "You go home now, Abu Tarek," using Frank's nickname. They unchained Frank and took him out, without giving him a chance to say more than good-bye to the rest of us.

Why were we all so sure he wasn't going home? It was just wrong. There was something in the way the guard spoke that said it was a lie. It has now been two days, and there's still nothing on the radio. Frank is certainly in another prison, perhaps alone. Why do they have to do it like this? He has never fully recovered from his last stint in isolation. There is something in him that seems to invite abuse from the guards. I fear for his sanity. But then, I fear for my own sanity if it goes on too much longer.

CHRISTMAS, and things have suddenly turned horrible again. One of the surlier guards went berserk last night. It seems the guard yanked on Brian's chain when he was locking him up after the toilet trip. Brian yanked back and made some sort of move as if he were going to take a swing at the hamster. We heard the guard curse and run out the door. He was back in a few seconds with tape and another guard. They taped Brian up completely, then beat him severely with a stick and a rifle. In the end, when the one guard was repeatedly cocking the AK-47 and threatening to kill Brian, the other guard stopped him. They left Brian taped and went out.

All through it, as I lay there in my blindfold, I said nothing. Tom and John did the same. Brian is maybe six feet away from me. I could hear the blows as if they were hitting me, could hear Brian's involuntary cries of pain. I feel weak and violated. I know I couldn't have done anything. If I had tried to interfere, it would simply have made it worse. As always, the only thing to do is curl up and wait for them to calm down. But to lie here and know it's the proper thing does not take away the disgust at myself, the feeling that I've behaved weakly.

Brian was badly bruised, but not seriously injured. At least nothing was broken.

When they brought in food perhaps an hour or so later, I pushed it aside. "No. I do not eat," I said. One of the guards started shouting in Arabic. Then Tom and John refused their food as well. Brian was offered none. The guards were extremely angry, but left.

Today, Christmas Day, we refused breakfast and lunch. In the afternoon Mahmoud came in. We told him about the beating (of course, he already knew), and we said that they had to take the guard who did it away. He had no reason to do such a thing, and we couldn't accept it.

Mahmoud argued with us and told us we had to eat or there would be big trouble. A short time after he left, a new guard came into the cell. They taped me up and carried me upstairs, propped me in a kneeling position in the kitchen, and asked me about the hunger strike. I repeated what we had said earlier—the bad guard would have to go. We couldn't live with him.

They made some mild threats, then launched a ridiculous charade. Taking an air gun, they fired it next to my head, then gave out theatrical groans, apparently for the benefit of the other three hostages downstairs. After a few minutes of that silliness they told me that I was to persuade the others to eat or we would be separated and put in isolation again. Then they carried me back to the basement cell, carefully placed plates of cookies in the center of the room, and left.

I explained to John, Tom, and Brian. After some giggles about the mock execution, we sobered. The threat about isolation was a serious one. None of us thought we could take that again easily. At the same time, we had gotten no concession on the guard. If we gave in this time, the usefulness of hunger strikes was at an end forever.

We agreed that each of us had to decide for himself without pressure. I told the others I thought we had better not push it this time, that things would get rough. I would eat. Tom and John decided the same. Brian indicated he probably would, but not right now.

I picked up a cookie and ate it, facing the camera they had installed some weeks earlier in a corner of the room, near the ceiling. That was it. The Great Protest was over. Happy Christmas, 1988.

## Madeleine

*NICOSIA, Cyprus. December 1988.*   As 1988 ended, my life had become
a routine of ups and downs. But with my family, friends, and the God
I had come to know again helping me, I felt stronger after each
disappointment. I was trying my best to prepare for whatever the
future had in store for us.

In a resurgence of my womanhood, I was many times tempted to
find a boyfriend. It scared me to feel this way. I knew that it would
hurt Terry, but I still wanted to know I could feel like a woman. That
all the sorrow and pain, and the guilt, had not destroyed my ability to
appeal to a man.

Every time I was depressed, I attributed it to loneliness and need.
And I found quickly, to my surprise, that there were many men willing
to approach me. But I didn't want just any man. I wanted the man I
had said yes to when he asked me to spend the rest of my life with
him. I wanted Sulome's father. Terry.

I felt shame and guilt, knowing that Terry was chained in Lebanon,
while I was here in freedom, fantasizing about my needs.

The year 1989 was one of silence. Silence from both the captors
and the United States. It also began as a year of sickness for us. In
early February, Sulome had a severe case of pneumonia. She was hot
and sweating, and her heartbeat was so fast I thought she was having
a heart attack. My friends helped me rush her to the emergency ward
of the local hospital. At the X-ray station I broke down and cried,
sobbing so loudly everybody was staring at me. The fear of losing
Sulome frightened me so badly. But my tears were for Terry's absence
as well. I needed him very much now, and so did Sulome.

Sulome was in the hospital a week, and I almost lived there with
her. She was home for two weeks after that before she could go back
to school. Within days I was in bed with a throat infection and high
fever. I had overexhausted myself. The AP sent two doctors to see me
at my home, and Cassandra was always there.

After I was on my feet again, I decided to go see a psychiatrist. I was
out of patience with myself, and unable to take more depressions and
frustration. My desires and beliefs were all confusing. I wasn't even

sure I loved Terry. I felt something that had gone beyond love, to a place that I could not understand and yet never wanted to let go of.

I had been to see a psychiatrist in 1986. He had told me: "You should leave your daughter with a nanny and go out to work. Find yourself something to do, or you will end up finding a man."

I thought he was crazy. How could I leave my daughter with someone else? Was she supposed to miss both her father and her mother? And I couldn't understand his linking working and finding a man. Terry had been gone only a year at that point. The last thing I wanted was another man. I never went back.

This second psychiatrist was more diplomatic. "You are a woman. Why are you denying it?" He wanted to explore my childhood and why I was fighting my natural needs.

But after a few sessions I realized I did not want to be faced with what he thought was right for me. He could not convince me that Terry would not mind if I had relations with another man. I was thinking of my daughter as well. I could not be with anyone other than her father, unless I knew our relationship was over completely.

Again I decided not to see the psychiatrist anymore, and put that part of my life back in limbo.


## Terry

*BEIRUT. January 1989.*    Back to the big city again. On January 27 Mahmoud and another guard came into the cell. They took me upstairs and wrapped me in the familiar plastic shipping tape. Then it was into the secret compartment in the truck and off to Beirut. I spent a week in the same apartment we had been in before, but alone this time. The brown stain where I had bashed my head a year or so ago was still there. It was almost a relief being by myself after so long with several other people. I had a few books and the Bible. Then I was taken out again and dumped into the trunk of a car. I felt a second body being dumped on top of me, and was immediately sure it was Tom. Don't know why. We didn't exchange a word or a signal. But I was certain, and correct, as I found out after a short ride.

The two of us were escorted blindfolded up to an apartment, where we were chained side by side to a filing cabinet. The chains were very short—there were only about six inches between our ankles—and one chain ran from my wrist to his ankle and my ankle to his wrist. Seemed a bit excessive, but no point in arguing.

We spent eight days like that, barely able to move, until finally we were moved into a bedroom at the other end of the apartment. The room had been fixed up with steel plates over the windows and iron straps bolted into the walls for our chains.

At least now they've given us some books—a box of paperbacks ranging from political textbooks to trashy thrillers. Even a couple of pornographic novels. Worse, several are Barbara Cartland romances.

This place is reasonably clean. It's a large room, maybe fifteen feet by twenty. Tom and I are chained to opposite sides, just close enough to be able to hand things to each other. Still no radio and no news. There seems to be a lot of shelling going on between East and West Beirut. We're apparently only a few blocks west of the Green Line, so we get shells quite near fairly frequently. Sometimes bits of shrapnel rattle off the steel plates covering the windows.

Tom and I occasionally discuss the books we're reading but otherwise stay mostly quiet. After several years together we don't really have much to say anymore, I guess.

WE'VE been here three months now. It's about the middle of April—fourteenth or fifteenth, we think. I'm now well into my fifth year. We're mostly just floating along, trying not to notice the days passing. I have to fight not to think about the months and years lost, about Madeleine and Sulome and Gabrielle. I've become more practiced at pushing such things away, but the 1500 days are just a massive, horrible weight sitting in my chest.

In the night, when the blackness in my head grows, the only thing that will push it away is prayer. Sometimes I feel a real joy in it, a real understanding of what it means to be loved by God as I know myself to be—faulted, proud, self-indulgent. Those times ease the pain of this existence so much, give me hope that I can not only stick this out but perhaps emerge whole, and live a better life when it's over.

Had a couple of long sessions with "Trust Me" Ali, who has been showing up occasionally lately. He's giving us the usual crap about "good negotiations" and "something will happen soon." Right. Anyway, I've been trying to persuade him to let us have a radio. Wonder of wonders, finally won! We now have a Sony transistor radio and have been catching up on the world's disasters.

First obvious news is that Beirut is falling apart again. President Amin Gemayel appointed his army commander, General Michel Aoun (a Christian), acting prime minister when his term ended in 1988. The Muslims in West Beirut refused to accept it, because the prime minister is supposed to be a Sunni Muslim. The country has had two governments ever since, neither of them effective. Aoun has announced he's going to drive Syria out of Lebanon. He's instituted a blockade of West Beirut, and there is all kinds of fighting between the two sides. That's what all the shelling we've been hearing is about.

Nothing on about the hostages. We seem to be in limbo again as far as the world is concerned.

At least we know the date. April 1, 1989: 1477 days.

## CHAPTER ELEVEN

*NEW YORK. March 1989.*   Associated Press top executive Larry Heinzerling had been summoned without explanation. From the large office of Lou Boccardi, president of the AP, you could see ice-skaters bobbing and weaving. The winter scene in Rockefeller Center made Heinzerling smile.

Boccardi waved Heinzerling to a chair. As always, he was direct. "I want you to take over the Terry Anderson case, starting today. Go to Washington next week for the anniversary ceremonies, and then let's see where we go from there."

The AP had come under considerable criticism for its efforts on Anderson's behalf. Since those efforts had been made without fanfare or publicity, many thought the AP had not done enough.

Boccardi and other AP executives had over the past four years met with countless American and foreign officials, including Lieutenant Colonel Oliver North and Anglican Church envoy Terry Waite, now a hostage himself. It had fully financed the varied activities of Peggy Say. It had supported and watched over both Anderson families—in Japan and Cyprus.

It was now more than two years after North's 1986 arms-for-hostages debacle, and all government attempts at finding a solution remained frozen. In Washington, you could not even discuss hostages or Iran and use the word negotiation in the same breath. The subject had been banned by the incoming Bush administration.

Heinzerling's new assignment was a tough one, even for the former foreign correspondent. It was full time and open-ended: he was to try every avenue in pursuit of Anderson's freedom. He had carte blanche, though Boccardi was adamant that the AP avoid any action that could endanger Anderson or prolong his captivity. There were only three rules: First, he could not discuss his work with anyone but Boccardi. Second, the AP would offer no ransom. Third, he could meet anyone, anywhere, at any time, but would keep forever every confidence he agreed to. The AP also had to keep its most precious asset—its reputation for covering the news fully and objectively. The agency could not take a position, pro or con, on any government policy. The AP had never in a hundred and forty years taken an editorial position on anything.

As Heinzerling went about his part of the crusade, clocking tens of thousands of miles on airplanes, meeting in bizarre places with mysterious and sometimes scary people, he would cross paths often with another man on a very similar mission.

GIANDOMENICO Picco, the six-foot-six suave and handsome Italian deputy to U.N. Secretary-General Javier Pérez de Cuéllar, was personally responsible for saving more lives than could be counted. He had managed to negotiate a lasting cease-fire in the seemingly endless war in Afghanistan, then immediately moved on to one even more intractable: Iran-Iraq. There also he was finally successful, almost single-handedly working out the terms of the cease-fire that ended the eight-year-old conflict. A million Iranians and Iraqis had died already. How many more would have if the fighting had continued?

Picco had watched from afar the mess that was Iran-contra. He had raised the subject of the Western hostages several times during his trips to Tehran in connection with the Iran-Iraq War. Always he had been rebuffed. It was not yet time.

Finally the break came. In Washington, President Bush had publicly indicated his willingness to come to some accommodation with Tehran. "Goodwill begets goodwill," he said in his inauguration speech. It was a clear call for the Iranians to offer something.

In yet another meeting in Tehran, Picco found a high official who was willing to discuss the question of the hostages. Officially the position was unchanged: "This is not our responsibility. We have nothing to do with it." But the very fact that someone so high was even willing to dedicate an official meeting to the subject was enough for the veteran diplomat. The Iranians were ready to play.

Picco began his odyssey. He had nothing to offer other than his reputation, skill, and patience. He knew there would be no deal as such, because the Americans would in no way make any kind of payoff. He also knew the process would be difficult, painstaking, and dangerous. But he was absolutely determined that it would succeed.

Others were already having sporadic success. The Swiss government and the International Red Cross in Geneva were deeply involved in a highly secret initiative that apparently had been the key to the release of Frank Reed. It was believed Reed was chosen because he was so sick. His mental condition had worsened, until he believed he was having conversations with U.S. embassy officials in Beirut via a radio in his head. His release involved a more or less straight swap of hostages for Lebanese held by the Israelis.

At the same time, the process of negotiations over Iranian money held by the United States continued at The Hague. Neither party would admit any connection between those talks and the hostages. Certainly the release of large sums by the Americans to the Iranians helped the atmosphere a great deal.

At the United Nations, Picco was trying to put together a package that would provide release of *all* the hostages. The Swiss process was not good enough. "That was not a solution," Picco insisted later. "At that pace, it could have gone on for ten years." He wanted everyone out in months.

The aim was ambitious to the point of ridiculousness. He still had nothing much to give anyone. The Americans were now interested, but completely unwilling to consider any deal and still scared to death of the word negotiation. The Iranian government apparently wanted to end the whole episode, but did not have complete control over its own radicals, let alone the fundamentalists in Lebanon.

What Picco did have that no one else had was his reputation for total honesty; complete stubbornness; a negotiating ability honed in Cyprus, Afghanistan, and the Middle East; and a boss who was willing to take his lead on this subject. Secretary-General Pérez de Cuéllar allowed Picco to go where and when he needed to, and questioned him little. He made the phone calls or initiated the conversations Picco suggested, and kept the sprawling U.N. bureaucracy off his assistant's back.

It would be more than a year after that first, faint indication of interest in Tehran before this most discreet of U.N. officials was ready to take his plan where it would finally have to be presented—an anonymous apartment in the southern suburbs of Beirut.

## Terry

*BEIRUT. June 1989.*   Whatever progress is being made in the negotiations, as Ali insists there is, it hasn't stopped these people from adding to their stock. Another Briton, an old man named Jackie Mann, has been kidnapped on the street in Beirut. Not a good sign for us—and, of course, not good for Mr. Mann either.

Ayatollah Khomeini has died in Iran. Saw incredible scenes on the television—which the guards let us watch now—of huge mobs weeping and wailing and beating their heads. We've already spent several hours speculating on whether his death will mean any major changes in Iran and any hope for us. Probably not. But we can hope.

We're getting lots of books these days—boxfuls. It's still a pretty mixed bag, trash and good stuff. But at least we have plenty to read. And plenty of time to do it.

Hard to keep cheerful as the weeks pile up.

THREE months with little news, then an avalanche of messages. It's my birthday, October 27, and I've watched tapes of messages from my family on five channels, at least twice each. Saw Sulome, but not Madeleine, though her voice was there with a beautiful message of love. Heard Peg, and people in New York and Washington, telling me of their support. An incredible day!

THERE's been a flurry of hostage stuff on the radio and television over the past two months, all hopeful again. For the first time the Tehran *Times,* an English-language newspaper said to be a mouthpiece for Iranian President Rafsanjani, called for the unconditional release of all hostages in Beirut. Even Sheik Fadlallah, the one identified commonly as spiritual leader of Hezbollah, is calling for our release. The news said he just got back from a visit to Tehran. Maybe he got his marching orders?

At least we know where we are now. Woke up to a hail of AK-47 fire outside the building this morning. We heard just an hour later on the radio that Syrian soldiers had gotten into a gunfight with the bodyguards of Sheik Subhi Tewfali, secretary-general of Hezbollah, just outside Tewfali's headquarters in the southern suburbs of Beirut. Since that was the only gunfight reported today, we are quite obviously being held by Tewfali. So much for Hezbollah's denial that they have anything to do with Islamic Jihad. Of course, we never believed the denials, and I don't think anyone else did either.

MORE insanity among the Lebanese. General Michel Aoun, in the midst of his "war of liberation" against the Syrians and the rival Muslim government of Lebanon, has suddenly launched into a vicious war against his erstwhile allies, the Lebanese Forces Christian militia. Aoun's regular army forces and the militiamen have been bashing each other all over East Beirut and destroying much of the city along the way. I think Aoun has gone completely off his rocker.

Still a lot of hints and rumors on the hostages. It's all very confusing, but it seems obvious something is stirring, and Tom and I can't help feeling hopeful. I don't know what to think. I'm just trying to chug along, keep things even, and not get on the roller coaster again.

It's April 1, 1990. I just finished my fifth year: 1841 days.


## Madeleine

*NICOSIA, Cyprus. June 1989–June 1990.*    Sulome turned four years old on June 7, 1989. She seems to change from day to day—so small, always bringing happiness to my heart. Now that she could talk and understand so much more than when she was smaller, our relations were more interesting. Her questions about her daddy were more penetrating, and I could only answer with the truth. She often cried after I talked about him, but the tears were always followed by smiles and hugs, as if she was thanking me for making her understand. She gave me strength, and the assurance that at least with her, I had not failed.

October 27, 1989. Terry's forty-second birthday, and another year gone from his life. As we had done the year before, Sulome and I went to the mountains for a picnic alone, to celebrate Terry's birthday under the same tree and carve the date in its trunk. Again we taped a birthday message for him and sent it to the Lebanese TV stations.

In February 1990 the first positive news in a long time began coming out of Iran. Clergymen there and in Lebanon were saying that the hostage problem would be solved before the end of the year. Radical fundamentalist leaders, who before had opposed releasing the hostages, began saying the same thing. For me the rumors had ceased to raise my hopes or cause me to change my daily routine.

Larry Heinzerling was also encouraged by the information he was receiving. Larry helped me keep my sanity with his persistent kindness. By now, I learned later, he had full knowledge of the negotiations and arrangements for release of all the hostages. But he called me only when he was absolutely sure of what he was telling me.

The support the American people were giving the hostages was sowing seeds of change. The hostage saga was beginning to turn against those who caused it. The radical fundamentalists in Iran who sponsored the kidnappers were in trouble with the new regime of President Rafsanjani. The President's brother, Mahmoud Rafsanjani, was shuttling from Iran to Lebanon to Syria almost every week in an effort to get the hostages released. The Lebanese civil war was ending, and the government was regaining some small measure of sovereignty.

In March of 1990, as Terry entered his sixth year in captivity, I was for the first time holding high hopes that the year would be the last. The dream was finally coming true. I started speculating on possible dates for his release. I knew, as everyone did, that the kidnappers would have to find some way to save face.

I also began taking care of myself a little. Although I knew Terry liked my hair long, I decided to cut it, to look fresh and new and young when he came home. I bought some new clothes and started going to an aerobics class. Although the fear of disappointment haunted me, I had to do these things for my own sanity.

# CHAPTER TWELVE

*Nicosia, Cyprus. June 1990.*   Heinzerling had become obsessed with the campaign to free Anderson ever since he had been assigned to it by the AP. His travels never seemed to cease, and when he did make it home, he took the obsession with him. Anderson's plight intruded on everything, touching children, spouse, and acquaintances.

Heinzerling had become an expert, devouring books on Shiites, terrorism, Lebanon, and Syria during the hour-long train rides from his home in Princeton, New Jersey, to work in New York. He would leave for Washington or Bonn, Geneva or Jerusalem, Tehran or Damascus on almost no notice.

On a sticky July night in 1990 he found himself in Nicosia, Cyprus, en route from Jerusalem to Damascus. He was making a brief stop to update Anderson's fiancée, Madeleine, on his so-far fruitless efforts. The AP bureau chief, Nick Ludington, and his wife, Cass, the closest of Madeleine's friends, invited him to an office party for another staffer. Madeleine was routinely invited to such affairs, but almost never came. This time she did, a visibly lonely and depressed woman.

An hour into the party, Heinzerling looked around for her. Cass pointed to the front door. There, alone on the steps, sat Madeleine playing with a cat. He sat beside her.

"What are you doing out here by yourself?"

"Oh, I just wanted some time alone," she said gently.

The scene somehow summed up the entire tragedy for Heinzerling. The lovely young woman could not enjoy a party, because it would be a betrayal of Terry. But sitting at home with the demons of despair would bring on deeper depression. So she had come, but remained alone in a tortured compromise. Madeleine, like Terry, was caught up in suspended time. He had no choices; she had many, and they were all difficult. Whose experience was worse?

Madeleine was obviously deeply in love but inwardly terrified. What would follow so many years of rage, separation, and pain? What would emerge from Lebanon when the hostages were finally released? How could she survive, wondering each day, Does Terry still love me? How would she cope with a possibly broken man, a stranger?

Heinzerling could only admire the balance and devotion she exhibited. "I guess it's impossible to enjoy yourself with so many people here to remind you of Terry," he said to her. He touched her arm gently. "It's going to be okay."

"Do you really believe it?" she asked.

"Yes," he said firmly, though he knew the solution was still not in sight. Then he rose and left her with the cat, the sound of crickets in the July night, and the pain etched on her face.


## Terry

*BEIRUT. August 1990.*   We seem to have been swallowed up by greater events. The Middle East has gone into another convulsion with the invasion of Kuwait by Iraq, and the U.S. leading a jihad against Saddam Hussein. As usual, our analysis focuses almost wholly on what this will mean for us.

One bit of good news has leaked out in the general avalanche: the seventeen Shia radicals held in Kuwaiti jails have disappeared, apparently freed during the invasion. Their whereabouts are unknown.

Unfortunately, I have to conclude that whatever was going on toward our release before this war is very likely to be put on hold. None of the parties that would have to be involved—the U.S. government, the Iranian government, maybe the U.N.—will have any time for such a minor issue for the next few months.


BRIAN's gone home! And Tom and I are back with John. The guards just came in, ordered us to stand up, taped our arms and around our eyes, then dumped us in a car trunk for a ten-minute ride.

When we were unwrapped in our new abode—another apartment in the southern suburbs of Beirut—John was sitting against the wall, bearded and grinning with relief.

It seems Brian and he had been together, along with Frank Reed, for more than a year. Suddenly Reed was taken out nearly four months ago; then two days ago they came for Brian. John said that when Brian realized he was being freed, he actually fought with the guards, shouting he would not go without John. John said he was frightened at being left alone again, afraid he couldn't take it.

They've had absolutely no news. No radio, no TV, nothing. He was amazed when we asked the guards for our radio and they brought it in immediately! We spent the first couple of days together listening to the news about Brian, and bringing John up to date on the Iraqi invasion and dozens of other things we've heard over the past year. Once again the roller coaster is on the rise. We're all almost euphoric, convinced that something is really happening.

The apartment is the same one I was kept in with Fontaine, and again later. The blood mark from beating my head on the wall is still there, a little faded but obvious.

John says Reed was in very bad shape when he and Brian were put together with him. He had been abused badly and was being treated with contempt by the guards until John and Brian protested.

John also said there was another prisoner in the apartment, in the next room, and both he and Brian believed it was Terry Waite. They had communicated sporadically and vaguely with knocks on the wall, but couldn't really exchange any information.

There isn't any explanation for why we have been allowed a radio and TV and books. Frank Reed, John, and Brian, held by the same people only a few blocks away, have had nothing. Only thing we can figure out is that we kept asking, whereas after a while they gave up.

The routine has improved here again. The food is better, with more fruit and fresh vegetables and meat, and the guards are more accommodating. We even get half an hour off the chain to exercise. Tom and I are amazingly fat after nearly eighteen months without even standing up more than ten minutes a day. Have to work it all off.

It's great to have John with us again, and incredible how he's kept his sense of humor and cheerful nature. Like suddenly walking outside and into a fresh breeze.


## Madeleine

*Nicosia, Cyprus. August 1990.*   Brian Keenan was released on August 24. It was very encouraging when he reported that he had been with Terry less than a year ago. It was the first news of Terry for two years.

I flew with Sulome to England, met with Larry Heinzerling there, and we all went on to Dublin. We telephoned Brian, and in a whispering voice he said he would very much like to meet me and that he had a message from Terry. He sounded affectionate and warm.

He met me at the small airport at Galway, on the west coast of Ireland, where he was staying in a friend's cottage. The first thing that struck me was that his eyes were red and he had difficulty looking straight at anything. He told me he had not seen strong light since the day he was kidnapped. His voice was still a whisper, and his hands were shaking. We sat and talked for hours. I was shocked at his condition, a result of so many years in the hands of merciless thugs.

Brian had a lot of stories about Terry to tell me. How he was maintaining himself, what kept him going. "Terry loves you so much you will never know," he said.

He told me about the places they had been held in, sometimes in conditions not fit for animals. I could have stayed forever listening to him talk, feeling close to Terry. When the day ended, I felt as if I were leaving my heart with Brian.

I didn't realize what the meeting was doing to Sulome until much later, when she started asking me about Brian.

"Is Mr. Keenan sick, Mummy?"

"No, he isn't," I said. "Why are you asking that?"

"He is shaking all the time, and he has no voice." Before I could say anything, she continued. "Is Daddy very sick, Mummy?" Her eyes were wide, and there were tears in them. I didn't know what to say. I didn't think Terry was in such bad shape, but I had no real idea. I held her tight, and we both started crying.

"If Daddy comes home sick and shaking like Mr. Keenan, we will have to help him get better, and give him lots of love, because Mr. Keenan said Daddy misses us a lot and is always thinking of us," I said.

I think the magic words were "help him." Sulome began telling me how she would read for him and make him tea every day and take him out for walks and hold his hand. Her ideas went on for a long time. Still, we were depressed for many weeks.

Terry was forty-three years old on October 27, 1990—his sixth birthday in captivity. Again Sulome and I went into the mountains, to the same tree, and carved another date on it, wondering if we would be back next year. The Iraqi invasion had taken up the interest of the world, especially the United States. The issue of the Lebanon hostages was dead again.

I decided to take Sulome to Lebanon to spend Christmas with my family. It was my first time back since Terry was kidnapped in 1985.

Peace seemed to be blooming in Lebanon, especially Beirut. We drove immediately into the mountains above the city, where I had planned to stay. On the way, we passed through the southern slums, where the hostages were believed to be held. Signs carried slogans: DEATH TO AMERICA and THE STRUGGLE AGAINST SATAN AMERICA STARTS HERE.

That Christmas, I wrote a letter to Terry trying to tell him how close we were to him and yet so far from him.


## Terry

*BEIRUT. September 1990.* September 5, 1990. My two-thousandth day.

I've established contact with Terry Waite. He is next door, as John and Brian thought. I began by tapping on the wall and, when he tapped back, painstakingly tapped out the series 1-2-3-4 . . . to 26. Then, using numbers for the alphabet (1 = *a*, 2 = *b*, and so on) I tapped out our names. It took a while, but he caught on. I spent all one night tapping out a summary of all the news: Brian's release, Frank's release, the comments and promises of Iran, Syria, and others. Then the world news: the Berlin Wall's falling, communism's demise in eastern Europe, free elections in the Soviet Union—all the incredible things that have happened since he was taken three years ago. He thought I was crazy.

He's been in isolation all that time without even a scrap of news. I knew he was brave, risking his life for us. But he must also be incredibly tough. Sounds sane and rational. When I apologized for dragging him into this with the letters we sent so long ago to the Archbishop of Canterbury, there was no bitterness in his gracious reply.

It takes an agonizingly long time to exchange any message, what with stops and starts, misspellings and miscountings. My knuckles are already scraped raw from the concrete wall. But he obviously needs this contact so badly, I can't stop.

ASKED the guards about Terry Waite—or at least about "the other hostage in the apartment." Got short shrift and lies. "He is a bad man, a Lebanese," one guard, Abu Ali, told me. It was the second time, and he ended by saying, "Do not ask about this again." Guess that's that.

My knees have swollen like footballs. Apparently pushing the exercise too much. I run back and forth across the room almost constantly during my half hour off the chain. Then I do some sit-ups and use volumes of the *Encyclopedia Americana* we have as weights. It's awkward, but it serves the purpose. At least I'm losing some of the gut.

Tom spends all night every night with the radio to his ear, listening to the news. He told me while John was in the bathroom that he had heard John's mother had died some time ago. Didn't know whether to tell him or not. I advised him to do so. "It's his right to know. I would want to know something like that." When John returned, Tom tried to tell him, but stumbled and hesitated so much that I finally broke in to say it gently as I could, but directly.

Of course, John took it well, but it was obviously a great blow. He was very quiet all day, trying to absorb it.

John has never talked much about himself or those close to him. But we've begun talking a bit more, especially late at night, when Tom is dozing or listening to the radio. I was surprised to discover John's diffidence is not just politeness but a reflection of fairly low self-esteem. Thinks he wasted his university career and doesn't have a deep mind. I've always found him intelligent and knowledgeable. Are all the jokes, the ready wit, partially defensive?

He doesn't say much about his fiancée, Jill, though we've all heard several times of the incredible campaign she's waging on his behalf. Perhaps too painful. I know I have difficulty talking about Madeleine, or even thinking about her too much.

AT LEAST part of Lebanon's seemingly unending civil war is over. The Syrians have stormed the presidential palace, killing seven hundred and fifty of General Aoun's followers. Aoun's days as acting prime minister of a rump government are over, and he's hiding in the French embassy. All the bombast, and he fled at the first push. The now totally legitimized President Elias Hrawi says nearly all the various militia groups in the country have agreed to withdraw from the capital and eventually be disarmed. Once again it all sounds good. But so many past failures make it hard for anyone to believe in anything.

HAD A CHANCE TO LEARN PERSONALLY whether my advice to Tom about breaking bad news quickly was right. When I woke up this morning, he told me quietly but straight—both my dad and Rich are dead. At least, I'm sure it's Rich. The radio report said only that my father and brother had died during my captivity. It has to be Rich.

I had tried not to think about Dad too much. I knew that with his emphysema and other problems, he was unlikely to have lasted this long. But Rich. He has had cancer since he was sixteen. I feared for him, but couldn't think about it. It seems wrong, incomplete. He was always my big brother, always there when I had to get out of the house. Argumentative, stubborn. Interested in everything, passionate about all sorts of injustice and stupidity.

Once again I have to retreat into prayer. Find acceptance, comfort. It will be there, I know. It always is.

FINALLY met Terry Waite. We have all been packed up and hauled back to the Bekáa Valley. We're now in an unfinished half basement of what seems to be a villa. John, Tom, and I are chained to the wall in a kind of hallway, three in a row. Terry Waite is in the next room. He was allowed to talk with us for about fifteen minutes today.

Very emotional. The man has been held in total isolation for nearly four years! We've whispered to him in the next room several times since we moved here—even got caught twice, but the guards didn't seem outraged. Just told us to stop.

I heard the Hajj's voice in the hallway this morning and told Mahmoud to ask him to come speak with us. He did, and assured us things were going very well. "Our friends are home," he said, confirming that the Shiite prisoners in Kuwait were set free.

*"Mabrouk,"* I said. Congratulations. "Now can we go home?"

"Soon," he said. But he was vague about what remained to be done. New demands? Anyway, that's one obstacle out of the way.

"Look, Hajj," I said at the end. "We know that's Terry Waite next door. He knows we're here. You know that we know. The whole world knows. Why don't you let the poor man come in here with us?"

He laughed and patted my hand. Then he gave some orders in Arabic, and a few minutes later they brought Waite in.

They sat him down on Tom's bed, then allowed us to talk quietly. We hugged each other; then Tom and John did the same. He's so big!

Six feet seven inches. But skinny. He's not well. We've heard him coughing and gasping for breath for hours in the next room. Asthma, apparently. He says it was brought on by the insect spray they used in the last place. Also emotional strain, I think.

They've given him some medicine, but it doesn't seem to help much. The best thing they can do is let him go. But that doesn't seem likely in the near future. There've been some reports linking Sheik Obeid, the Shiite cleric the Israelis kidnapped, to us. That would be a tough one, because the Israelis aren't going to let him go unless they get their own missing soldiers back.

Lord, don't let it get complicated again. Eight more weeks until Christmas—my sixth in here.

THEY'VE moved us all upstairs, into a bedroom of this villa. It's fixed up just like all the other prisons we've been in: steel plates over the windows, door handle removed. Terry Waite is with us. The four of us are chained up along one wall of the room, on mattresses.

We've got a small black-and-white TV and now two radios. T.W.— his new nickname, to distinguish the two Terrys—brought the small one they finally gave him in the last place.

The conditions aren't bad—they've given us two plastic chess sets and a couple of decks of cards, so we play chess and bridge all the time. I've taught John how to play chess, and he's picked it up amazingly quickly. Tom and T.W. have also learned, but both are still beginners. Tom taught us three bridge, although T.W. is nearly hopeless—no card sense at all.

Our biggest problem is his health. He's very sick. Spends hours, usually late at night, gasping and wheezing until it seems he'll collapse. The medicine doesn't do much good. I usually end up sitting up with him, talking to him until three or four o'clock, trying to keep him calm—almost hypnotizing him. "Breathe slowly, T.W. Don't hyperventilate. Slowly and deeply." For hours, until the attack passes. He's becoming enormously dependent on me, and it scares me because I have no idea if I'm doing anything right. He's desperate.

The sad thing is the attacks and the strain are affecting the relationships among us. Tom and John, and to some extent I, find it extremely wearing to listen to the loud gasps and whistling wheezes for hours. We're sympathetic. We know he's sick. Nonetheless, it is a strain. We're not all that stable psychologically ourselves, after all these years. Tom especially tends to take it as a personal, almost deliberate, affront, to turn it into a grievance. He doesn't like T.W., anyway—which is surprising, since for the first few days he took to him enormously. Don't know what made him turn. We're all peculiar, anyway, I think. Surprise, surprise.

A QUIET Christmas. We're all fighting hard to maintain an even keel through the incredible mix of optimistic and pessimistic signs we hear on the radio. Our hosts' promises that we would all be home by the end of the year are obviously not going to be kept. At the same time, it's equally obvious that a great deal of activity is going on.

## CHAPTER THIRTEEN

*New York. January 1991.*   Giandomenico Picco thought he had it all set up. After more than a year of meticulous work involving repeated trips to Tehran, Geneva, Washington, and elsewhere, all the parties had agreed it was time to end the hostage problem.

The U.N. diplomat had not been involved in the last couple of hostage releases: Brian Keenan and Frank Reed. Those had been negotiated one by one—Keenan by the Irish, Reed by the Swiss government. Each apparently involved winning some concession from Israel, such as the release of some Shiites from Khiam prison in southern Lebanon, run by Israel's proxy militia, the South Lebanese army. But these one-offs got more and more difficult each time.

Having other people working on the same problem made it more complicated. But Picco was interested only in a complete solution, one that would lead to all the hostages' being released. It was a complicated deal. To put it plainly, Picco was winging it. He was telling the Iranians, and through them the kidnappers, that he had agreement from Israel and the United States on things he hadn't even asked them about just yet.

"When you do these things, you are like in a vicious circle," Picco said in an interview in 1993. "One side says, 'I agree if they agree,' and the other says, 'I agree if they agree.' So what do you do?"

Apparently, act as if you've got an agreement that you haven't. So far Picco had been able to offer the Iranians and their protégés a considerable amount in the field of public relations—or, more pertinently, "face." Still the discreet diplomat, he would not say even in the 1993 interview what exactly he had promised. But it certainly involved a U.N. finding that Iraq was primarily to blame for the incredibly bloody Iran-Iraq War. That was important to Tehran both for reasons of principle and because it held out the hope, however faint, of eventual reparations. A report by Pérez de Cuéllar was issued on December 10, 1991, formally blaming Iraq for starting the war.

Pérez de Cuéllar, ever ready to help his assistant, also agreed to travel to Tehran to discuss the fulfillment of U.N. resolutions concerning war damage. While the question of the billions of dollars of Iranian money Washington had impounded was not directly involved, it didn't hurt that several large payments were made to Iran during the period of Picco's negotiations.

That left mainly the problem of satisfying the Lebanese kidnappers themselves. Although subject to Iranian influence and funded by Iranian money, they were by no means Iranian puppets. In fact, there had been a breach growing between Hezbollah and Tehran for some time. The seventeen fundamentalists who had been jailed in Kuwait had been freed. Nonetheless, other factions demanded some sort of satisfaction before an overall agreement to release all the hostages could be concluded.

Picco was confident the Israelis would go along with the idea of releasing Lebanese prisoners from the prison at Khiam and would probably even agree to let go some prisoners in Israel itself. They would, of course, have to receive something concerning their own soldiers who were missing or being held in Lebanon. That also could be arranged.

Then came the first major hitch.

Picco was in Beirut, meeting with an intermediary to discuss details of what had already been agreed to in principle. But his interlocutor suddenly told him, "There are problems. We need some time."

"When you start hearing that in Beirut, it's bad news. I didn't like it," Picco said later. "I made the decision that I have to play everything I've got. And the only thing I've got is me."

The diplomat demanded an immediate meeting directly with the kidnappers. The intermediary agreed to do his best.

As Picco waited at the apartment he was using in Beirut, the folly of his proposal struck him. "I really began to think, My God, what have you said?" Picco didn't even tell his boss, Pérez de Cuéllar, what he was going to do, because he knew the Secretary-General would forbid him. Within hours he had his answer—the meeting was on. Following instructions, Picco left his apartment and walked down a Beirut street. A car pulled up beside him, the door opened, and he got in. He was immediately blindfolded.

The trip took some time. Picco thought of his teenage son, and of Terry Waite, who had also counted on the immunity of a negotiator. When they arrived at their destination, Picco was gently helped out and into an apartment. He was searched, but politely. When he was finally allowed to sit down, he guessed there were perhaps a dozen people there with him.

"Mr. Picco, why should we trust you?" one of the unseen men asked him abruptly.

"There is a very good reason," Picco answered quietly. "I have made a great act of faith coming to see you, totally alone. I have put my life in your hands. If you have half the guts I have shown, the least you can do is trust me."

With the challenge out of the way, the discussion continued. It quickly became apparent that the "problems" were simply a lack of resolve on the part of the kidnappers to end the hostage problem. There seemed to be a disagreement among the factions involved.

"I tried to explain to them that by not going ahead, there would be more difficulties, not less," Picco recalled. He knew he had to get the problem settled immediately—or, at the very least, get them to agree to another meeting within hours to continue the discussion. He could not allow the process he had set up so carefully to bog down.

The first meeting lasted several hours. A second was set for the next night. Picco was scared but determined. And his pushing worked. "At the second meeting I met a hostage," he said. He would not say which one, and none of the hostages has revealed such a meeting. "I think what I told him helped him" was Picco's only comment. More important, he won agreement from the kidnappers to go ahead with the plan. All the hostages would be out by the end of 1991. Then it was time to begin settling the details. How many prisoners from Khiam for how many hostages and exactly what information about the missing Israelis? Who would move first? What was the schedule?

First, Picco went to the Americans. He asked the Bush administration to provide an "introduction" to the Israelis—really, an endorsement of what he was doing. He got it. Then he added Tel Aviv to his shuttle schedule. There would be more meetings with the kidnappers, always frightening. By now Picco was not afraid of being harmed by the men he was talking to. But he knew others in Hezbollah did not want him succeeding, and would try to stop him.

Picco was growing ever more confident that it could be pulled off. But as always, the devil would be in the details.

## Terry

*BEIRUT. February 1991.* I've finally managed to get the guards to understand that Terry Waite needs something more for his asthma. One night they took him to a doctor in Baalbek. T.W. said the doctor gave the guards some prescriptions for pills. Unfortunately, the new pills haven't helped that much. He still has attacks, and the other night he passed out briefly. I think he's near collapse.

It's frightening to guess, when I have so little knowledge, but finally I suggested they get more of the same medicine he's taking, except in an inhaler rather than as pills. Dad used one for his severe emphysema, and it worked very well. They got one, and it was almost like magic. The asthma attacks immediately became less frequent and less severe.

Now, though, with T.W. more active and alert, tension in the room has increased. Tom's dislike for Terry has deepened into outright antagonism. We've tried to talk quietly and calmly about the problem, but it hasn't worked very well. T.W. is not very observant or very good at reading moods. Often each of us just wants to be alone and undisturbed with our thoughts. Tom and John and I have learned to read those signs in each other and heed them. T.W. wants to talk all the time, no matter what we want.

When he does engage in conversation, he has the large man's habit of moving in close, until he looms over you. I tried the other day to ask him not to do that; it is disconcerting and disturbing. In here we've grown jealous of our personal space. He just couldn't understand.

Thankfully, we have more to do now. For some reason the guards bring in a stack of magazines every two weeks: *Time, Newsweek, Business Week,* even *Fortune.* We've also got the radios to listen to, and we do so constantly with no objections from the guards.

In fact, the attitude of our guards has changed dramatically. They make an effort to be friendly and try to bring us the food we ask for. We still have occasional clashes, but they are very restrained when they get upset. The violent outbursts are gone. One of them said to me the other day, "I have been told I cannot get angry at you." Obviously, the chiefs have warned them against giving us a hard time.

*MARCH 16, 1991.* My sixth anniversary. A deal seems to be falling into place. Hezbollah is saying it's willing to swap Israel's missing soldiers for the Lebanese held in Khiam prison and Sheik Obeid. The Israelis have made it plain they will go along eagerly. There have even been stories saying there's a new leader of Hezbollah, Abbas Mussawi, replacing our former host, Subhi Tewfali. The stories all say Mussawi is more pro-Iranian than Tewfali was, and more willing to go along with what Iran wants. And Iran seems to want an end to the hostage problem, which is keeping it from improving economic relations with other countries.

We spend a good deal more of our time talking about our futures now. What we'd like to do when we get out, where we'll go for a vacation. It still feels dangerous to give full rein to optimism. Something can still go wrong. It has so many times before.

JOHN's gone home. There was no ceremony and no notice. The guards just came in and told him to stand up, then unlocked his chains and took him out. I had time only for a quick "Good luck."

Within hours we were watching him on television. Even the local Shiite stations in the Bekáa Valley carried the live CNN coverage. He looked so incredibly cheerful and young, stepping out the door of the military airplane in Britain, smiling and waving. The news that he's carrying a message for U.N. Secretary-General Pérez de Cuéllar has been greeted with enthusiasm. I told Tom, "This has to be part of the ritual dance. They've already made a deal. This has all been agreed to beforehand." I sounded a great deal more confident than I felt.

# Madeleine

*NICOSIA, Cyprus. August 1991.* Larry Heinzerling told me that his contacts were giving him hope that things were moving. I had been skeptical when I first heard in 1990 that a U.N. official was taking up the negotiations for the hostages as a humanitarian matter. I thought how little humanity my people had shown themselves to have. But Larry gave me encouraging reports of U.N. assistant secretary-general Giandomenico Picco's work.

By the middle of 1991 there were so many stories about possible deals and releases that it was impossible to keep track of them. Some involved the Shiites held in southern Lebanon by the Israelis; other rumors brought in Israeli soldiers captured in Lebanon. Despite the flood of reports, Sulome's sixth birthday came and went on June 7, 1991, with our most important wish still ungranted.

But on August 6 Islamic Jihad issued a statement, accompanied by Terry's picture. They said they were sending a special envoy to U.N. Secretary-General de Cuéllar in a bid to end the hostage affair.

Two days later John McCarthy was released after five years as a hostage. I watched his arrival in England, when he stepped out of the airplane looking healthy, full of life. It was the first real indication that maybe the hostage affair was finally coming to an end.

John called from the hospital where he stayed for the first few days of his freedom. "If you think I look well, you should see Terry," he told me. "He looks ten times better. He has even put on some weight." He laughed. "He is trying to lose it before he comes home."

As he spoke, tears were running down my face. Sulome was sitting next to me and, without understanding, began crying as well. I gave her the phone, and John told her, "Do you know your daddy has your picture hanging over his bed, and it is his best companion when he is away from you and your mummy?"

Her face went red, and she didn't know what to say. She looked at me happily and told me what John had said. When I took the phone back, John's voice was choked up. "This is the first child I have spoken with for over five years," he said. After talking for what seemed forever, we arranged to meet in England a week later.

We flew to London, then met Larry Heinzerling and took a car to a secret location to meet John. The limousine driver turned out to be a member of a private security team hired by the World Television News, John's employers, to protect his privacy.

The peaceful green countryside we were passing through seemed to encourage memories of the past six and a half years. I thought of the many, many lonely nights—dreaming of Terry beside me, listening to my complaints about the day with a smile, then making love with me. It is actually coming to an end. Loneliness will no longer be part of my daily routine. I won't have to be both father and mother.

The country home we were approaching appeared so peaceful, even in the pouring rain. As the car stopped, John came walking out, a big, bright smile on his face. His father and brother followed him.

"I can't believe how well you look," John said when we embraced. We were crying, while at the same time I had a huge grin on my face.

Inside the friendly, warm home, we talked for nearly two hours. After lunch John and I went for a walk. John told me how Terry loved me and what Sulome and I meant to him. When I asked if Terry knew I was still waiting for him, John had no answer. "We both really understood if you and Jill could not wait for us that long," he said, referring to his fiancée. Then he added with a great smile, "But you did wait, and it is wonderful."

John said one of his captors had told him all the hostages would be released within two months. We went home with our hopes high. I believed strongly Terry would be home by Christmas.

The weeks passed as in a dream. Sulome was trying to decide which of her friends should get her birds, her cats, and tortoises, while I was giving away our plants and other things we would not need when we left Cyprus. Although the fear of something's going wrong was always there, this time preparation was like food for my soul. I needed the time to get ready.

John had also said he and Terry and the others always listened to the radio, especially the BBC. A friend of mine, BBC correspondent Keith Graves, told me some of the other families were using the network to send messages to their hostage relatives. I knew now if I did the same, Terry would certainly hear it. For the first time, I spoke on the radio myself, along with my daughter, in an interview Keith did for the BBC's *Outlook* program.

On November 16, 1991, Larry Heinzerling called to tell me that Tom Sutherland and Terry Waite were about to be released. "Your Terry will be last, but it won't be very long before he's home," he said.

Two days later both men were released, carrying a message that Terry would be freed in five days. The joy that engulfed our house cannot be described. My mother, who was staying with me, was dancing like a teenage girl. For Sulome the dream was finally becoming a reality. "Am I really going to see my daddy?" she asked. "What will he do when he sees me?"

On November 20 Tom Sutherland called from Wiesbaden, the U.S. military base in Germany, where the hostages were taken after their release. He sounded so happy, and I felt very close to him, knowing he was the one who had spent the most time with Terry. Tom carried a letter from Terry. "You cannot imagine how happy that [BBC] message made Terry feel," he said. "You have a special man in Terry, and he loves you now as much as he loved you before." Tom again reassured me that "although Terry would have always liked to hear your voice or see your face on TV with Sulome, he understands and respects the fact that you chose not to." When Tom repeated almost the same words as John McCarthy had told me, I knew that somewhere in the long silence I had put doubts in Terry's mind that I was waiting for him. But Tom insisted that Terry was not hurt, especially not now, after the message.

Tom sent Terry's letter by mail, and I received it three days later. It was short but said everything. I saw in it a confident man, one who had crossed from heaven to hell and come back with knowledge and control. I also saw a man who was taken for years from every humane thing and yet kept love in his heart.

## CHAPTER FOURTEEN

*Beirut. August 8–9, 1991.* McCarthy's release had finally come off, just as Picco had planned it. It was the beginning of the end, the launching of the carefully worked out dance that involved the release of all the hostages and the release of hundreds of Israeli prisoners. Picco hadn't worked out all the details, but he remained confident that the agreement would go through—until a French medical worker was kidnapped in Beirut a day after McCarthy's release. The anonymous kidnappers threatened to kill him if any more American hostages were freed. The unexpected move threw those Picco was negotiating with, and him, into a panic.

"They were absolutely unprepared to continue," Picco said. He demanded another meeting immediately. The drill was the same— the anonymous men in a car, the blindfold, the complicated route.

By now the fundamentalists are more comfortable with the Italian and remove the blindfold when he arrives. He can see just the man sitting in front of him, not the dozen or so standing behind him.

The meeting is stormy and very long. "I feel in my bones the danger of things falling apart. I know at this moment, while I sit with them, it may just evaporate in thin air."

The Islamic Jihad official told Picco that they had not kidnapped the Frenchman. "You want us to give you another hostage?" he asked. "You want the Frenchman killed?"

Picco was not going to let it happen. He ignored his interlocutors' flat refusal to continue the releases. He demanded. He shouted.

"This is where the big boys come in," Picco recalled telling them. "You are the big boys. You have to do both things. You have to make sure that nothing happens to the French guy, and you've got to release another hostage."

"What if something goes wrong?" Picco was asked.

"I can't foresee that," he replied immediately. "Because if something goes wrong, then you and I are out of business. It's finished.

"If you stop it [the release process], it means you can't deliver. If you can't deliver . . . whatever happens to me, you will have no others [to negotiate with] in the future. It's finished for you. You've lost your credibility."

The discussions and arguments went on for five hours. "It was tense, very tense. There was utter confusion" among the Lebanese fundamentalists in the room.

Picco finally clinched it when he said, "Whoever has taken the Frenchman is challenging you. Not only is he challenging but he's winning if you don't release the next hostage. So you want to lose, or you want to win? Who is in charge here?"

Another hostage was released on Saturday, August 11. The Frenchman was released by his unknown kidnappers at the same time.

## Terry

MADELEINE has finally broken her long silence and gone on the BBC's *Outlook* program with the most beautiful message I could imagine. All those doubts and fears evaporated as I listened to her husky, warm voice tell me how much she loved me, how she and Sulome were waiting for my release so we could all begin again.

"Terry, I'm amazed. You have given us great hope about your health, the way you look, and the way you are. You have maintained the Terry that I know, the image of you in Sulome's head and heart. You have been always in our hearts.

"I love you, Terry. I'll always love you. And I'm looking forward to a brighter future, where we can pick up where we left behind. I miss you, and we are out here waiting."

Seven years, and she has never wavered, has never given up. A weight, a fear that I had always refused to think about, is gone.

I'M ALONE, as I began. It's very much a relief, instead of the incredible shock and strain it was nearly seven years ago.

Two new chiefs came in late in the afternoon to announce that Tom and T.W. were to be released. They added that I would be going home within five days. The hostage problem is over.

They were in a fair hurry and told Tom and T.W. that they had only twenty minutes or so to get ready. I asked them for some favors: that they take off my chains, since if I was going home in days, they weren't necessary; and that they allow me to write a letter for Tom and T.W. to carry to Madeleine and my family.

The first request was granted as soon as I asked. They also agreed to let me write a letter, and gave me a pen and some paper. I quickly wrote a two-page note to Maddy and my family, embraced both Tom and T.W., and they were gone.

The place is quiet now. I have the two small radios and heard the two of them in Damascus. Giandomenico Picco is getting the credit for negotiating their release. There's a great deal of speculation about when I might come out.

My guards are quite friendly now and disturb me very little. I spend the day listening to the radio and exercising. I jog around the room for thirty or forty-five minutes at a time and do a lot of push-ups and sit-ups. And I think about what it will be like when I go free.

I told Tom I want Madeleine to be there, with Sulome, when I go to Damascus. I'd like my older daughter, Gabrielle, to come as well. I also asked if Robert Fisk, my best friend, would be able to come. He will be the best one to tell me all that's happened over the years, to bring me up to date.

It is very strange planning all this, after so long. I still have a strong reluctance to allow myself to be caught up in the expectation of a quick release. What happens if something goes wrong? How would I withstand the disappointment? But everything seems to be so certain.

I spent long hours in the night looking back, trying to crystallize what I thought about all the things I'd seen, the places I'd been, and what I really felt. My newfound faith, for instance, what had brought me back to being a Christian. And about journalism. I could see now what it had done to me and so many of my friends and colleagues. So much violence to take in as daily fare, so much of other people's pain, and nowhere to put it except in a few pages of copy or a couple of minutes of film.

I know now I could never really go back to that. I couldn't stand any more violence, and I had never been interested in becoming an editor or an administrator. It was only pride and ambition and the taste for power that brought me as far as becoming an AP bureau chief.

The days passed quickly. Five days, maybe a week, the two new chiefs had said. I never expected them to keep to that schedule— timing was never a major virtue of the hamsters. After the first week I occasionally had the terrible thought that something had gone wrong, but Mahmoud and the other guards always assured me that everything was "good, and very good." And there was so much on the radio about the end of the hostage problem and my release.

JOE Cicippio is out. It took a little longer than the five days they had promised, but at least it's moving again. Israel is also back in the game, releasing twenty-five of the prisoners from Khiam. Maybe it really will be "soon, and very soon."

# Madeleine

*NICOSIA, Cyprus. December 1, 1991.* Early on Sunday morning the phone rang. It was Nick Ludington, AP bureau chief in Cyprus. "Do you have your little bag ready to go, Madeleine?" he asked. The words I had waited for so long. "Is Terry coming home?" were the only words I found to say.

"I don't know if it is today," he said. "But we must leave for Damascus today, and Larry [Heinzerling] will meet us there. He called me at three this morning on his way to a plane to Damascus."

An enormous feeling of unreality came over me, and I just stood there for what felt like forever after Nick hung up, holding the telephone, afraid I might wake up from the dream if I put it down.

In Damascus, we all moved into a small hotel, trying to avoid the places journalists usually stayed. It was difficult to sleep that night. Sulome prayed that her daddy would quickly be released, and asked to make sure he knew he must take her to the circus as soon as possible.

In the morning Larry Heinzerling arrived to explain what was happening. He didn't know how long we would have to wait, but was taking all the necessary steps, such as getting the papers needed at the U.S. embassy for Sulome and me and himself to get on the military plane that would take Terry from here to Wiesbaden.

On Monday we stayed at the hotel. The press had received the word that Terry was coming out, and newspeople were converging on Damascus. They were looking everywhere for us. I was still not ready to meet or talk to anybody, so we remained at the hotel all day.

Sulome, with little to play with, kept asking the same questions: "How long are we going to stay in the hotel, Mummy? When is Daddy coming home?" I was running out of patience, explaining it all to her for the tenth time. The wait was exhausting my spirit and my nerves.

There was still no word by Tuesday evening. As I put Sulome to bed, crying and nervous, her uncertainty made me feel lost and doubtful as well. What if they decided not to let him go? What shall we do after coming so far—physically and emotionally?

At ten a.m. Wednesday, Nick came in to say that the Iranian news agency had just announced that Terry had been freed and was on his way to Damascus. A bomb of emotions burst in me. Nick took me in his arms, saying, *"Mabrouk."* Congratulations. "It's finally over."

I asked if the AP wanted some pictures, and he sent for a photographer. Then the U.S. embassy sent a car to take us to the house of the deputy chief of mission, the ambassador's deputy. We would wait there for word of Terry's whereabouts.

That was definitely the longest day I ever experienced—something that's easy to say but very difficult to live through. The waiting and the strange surroundings were also a great strain for Sulome, who was on the verge of a tantrum.

The ambassador, Christopher Ross, arrived about four p.m. He said he had no news so far. He waited with us until midnight, when the phone rang for him. He told us before leaving, "When I call you to get ready, a car will come and take you to my house."

Sulome had long since gone to sleep. I got her out of bed, and the call came half an hour later.

Those moments in the car on the way to the ambassador's house— the ending of almost seven years of broken hearts, misery, and deprivation—were the most meaningful and happiest moments of my entire life. My body was in the car, but my soul was floating out in the night, trying to push time forward. I was numb, clinging to Sulome, who remained asleep. I felt God's blessing on us.


### Terry

*BAALBEK, Lebanon. December 4, 1991.* The 2454th day, and the last. The two new subchiefs came in this morning to say that I would be going home tonight. They talked with me awhile about various things. Strangely, they seemed most concerned with justifying themselves and the last seven years. They said that their group now realized that this had all been a mistake, and they had gotten little out of it. They knew that the release last year of their brothers in Kuwait—the main goal they'd had for all those years—had nothing to do with the hostages they had held so long. "This tactic [kidnapping] is not useful. We will not do it again," one of them said. "We are not giving up. But we will use other means."

He did not explain what that meant, and I was not interested enough to pursue the subject.

They gave me a new shirt, a pair of trousers, and some shoes, then left. I've been sitting here playing solitaire and listening to the radio. It's very strange—all the news reports say I've been turned over to the Syrians already and am on my way to Damascus. They say there's a delay because of snow in the mountains between Beirut and Damascus. Of course, I'm in the Bekáa, and there's no snow.

My mind is so full, spinning so fast. Maddy—she's in Damascus, according to the radio, with Sulome. How is she feeling? What will we say to each other after so much pain? It is so good knowing she is waiting and we can start again. What has it been like for her? How could she wait so long? I know the depth of my love. Hers must be so much greater, her strength so incredible.

I know the drill at Damascus. I've seen it so many times. The first ceremony at the Syrian Foreign Ministry. Thank everybody, even the Iranians—ironic that, but necessary, I suppose.

What do I say about my kidnappers? I have no love for them. The small kindnesses of a few guards over the years mean nothing compared to nearly seven years chained to a wall. But I don't hate them. I could, easily, but I cannot let myself. My life will begin again in a few hours. What am I going to make of it? Can I keep the faith and the determination of this time? Will I be able to keep from slipping back to the self-indulgence, the arrogance that I know I was full of then?

I am forty-four years old. I don't feel it. I still felt young when I was taken seven years ago. I feel young today. But I'm not.

All my thoughts are fleeting. I can't concentrate on anything except the cards. Lunch comes, then dinner. Mahmoud asks me as he brings the food, "Are you happy?"

"I'll be happy when I'm free, Mahmoud."

It's dark outside now. They always prefer darkness to fall before making any move. The door opens. Several guards come in. Mahmoud says, as he has so many times, "Stand up."

No tape this time. Just the blindfold. The new subchiefs are there. One of them hands me a small bouquet. Half a dozen carnations. "Give this to your wife and tell her we're sorry."

Someone takes my arm, guides me through the door, outside, and into a car. "Trust Me" Ali is in the back seat with me. He's ranting about Bush's ingratitude, his failure to mention the Khiam prisoners in his first statement about my release. I'm impatient. Shut up, man. I don't need any more of this.

The car stops. I'm pulled out. Someone puts his hand on my shoulder. "I'm a Syrian colonel. You're free."

## Madeleine

*DAMASCUS. December 4, 1991.*   There were more than a dozen people in the hallway of the ambassador's house as we entered. Larry took Sulome from me and put her down on a couch, still asleep and looking like an angel. My legs couldn't hold me up anymore, and I abruptly sat down on the nearest couch.

It was only a minute, but felt like forever, before the ambassador came in and said, "You can go in now, Madeleine. Terry wants to see you." I looked at him blankly and sat glued to the seat. I realized I was afraid to leave the room. I was afraid to see him. After all these years of imagining what it would be like, I was now afraid of it.

I stood up and walked in the direction the ambassador was pointing. I was looking for another room with a door, but as I turned the corner from the living room, I saw Terry standing right in front of me, his hands behind his back, waiting. He looked just as well as when I last saw him, on that Saturday morning, March 16, 1985. His eyes were full of love. We walked into each other's arms, and in the warmth of his body I found myself at last. His arms, as always, could wrap around my whole body. "Don't ever leave me again," I whispered, crying.

"It's over, it's over," his soft voice reassured me. Yes, it was over.

## Afterword

*BRONXVILLE, New York. April 1993.*   Madeleine and I were married on April 18, 1993, before a few friends and family in the living room of the old home we bought late last year.

We cannot say we have come full circle, because we are a long way from where we were when we first planned to marry, nine years ago. Much of that distance we traveled separately, enduring our own private trials and pain. We had many close and dear friends to help us, and we had the knowledge of each other's love to sustain us. But we also had the terrible uncertainty of what those years were doing to us, fearing that the changes we saw in ourselves would somehow overwhelm that love. We were forced to look inside ourselves, alone, to find the strength and faith we both needed so desperately.

In the past seventeen months we have traveled even further on our personal journey, but this time together. Again we had the aid of many dear friends, as well as the full support of our "family" at The Associated Press.

The AP arranged for us to fly straight from our incredibly warm homecomings in New York and Washington to the Caribbean island of Antigua. AP president Lou Boccardi borrowed two Royal Air Force psychiatrists, Dr. Keron Fletcher and Dr. Ken Craig. They charted for us the difficulties we faced in renewing our life together, in knitting ourselves into a close family with our beautiful six-year-old daughter, Sulome, and in handling the pressures of being public people and the many demands of living in this so busy world.

It has been at times difficult, but always fascinating. There has been far more joy than tears, and enormous happiness. The warmth and concern shown for us everywhere we go has helped greatly.

While no one chooses the kind of terrible events that engulfed us, we have much to be thankful for out of those years of testing. We know ourselves, and each other, much better than we might have. We know the depth and strength of our love. And we have a deeper, stronger faith in God.

"That which does not destroy me makes me stronger," Nietzsche wrote. We are stronger, and our life is full of joy.

DEPARTMENT OF JUSTICE
FEDERAL BUREAU OF INVESTIGATION
FIDELITY
BRAVERY
INTEGRITY

# ABOVE SUSPICION

## by Joe Sharkey

When Mark Putnam was
a kid, he would have killed
to be an FBI agent.
He never dreamed he'd
kill to stay one.

. . . The situation was unprecedented in the eighty-three-year history of the FBI: an agent appeared to be facing a charge of criminal homicide. Worse, the offender wasn't some rogue cowboy on some drug-addled flameout. Of all of the eight thousand agents in the bureau, it had to be *this* guy—this earnest, likable, gifted young man who seemed to project every virtue that the bureau imagined itself as representing. The guy they would have put on a recruiting poster now qualified for a wanted poster.

—*Above Suspicion*

# 1

THE baby threw up just as the eighteen-wheel coal truck with the word Jesus across its front plate barreled out of a blind switchback and bore down on them in the rainy February afternoon like a forty-ton avalanche of soot.

Skidding on the slick mountain road, Mark Putnam managed to pull the 1980 Oldsmobile off to the side, where he slowed to a crawl, the passenger door nearly scraping the granite wall that went a hundred feet up. The coal truck rumbled by with its horn shrieking.

"Oh, my God," Kathy Putnam said in a low voice from the back seat, where two-year-old Danielle lay across her lap, miserable with car sickness and fatigue.

Kathy cleaned up with a diaper. Her gaze met her husband's dark eyes in the rearview mirror. "Listen, Kat, we don't have to do this," he said with a grimace, and added, only partly in jest, "Do you want to turn around and go back to Connecticut?"

Kathy was nothing if not a good sport. Three years before, when she and Mark had dashed off to get married in New York City, she had known what she was getting into. Mark was a young man with one overriding goal: he intended to be an FBI man. Theirs was a marriage remarkable for its synergy—her hard-nosed realism applied to his unchecked zeal; his fortitude to her diffidence, creating a force that augmented their individual strengths. Together, they'd gotten him into the FBI. If Mark's first assignment was in Pikeville, a forlorn outpost in the isolated mountainous coalfields of eastern Kentucky, then they would make a go of it and wait for a better one. Kathy smiled and tickled the baby's chin. "It's going to be okay. You'll see."

Mark guided the car, its engine straining, up the steep mountain road. "The road has to end somewhere," he said disconsolately.

In a while they were relieved to see a sign, CONGESTED AREA, but it only marked the truck pull-off for a coal-mine operation below the blasted rocks and stepped contours of a strip-mined mountain; heaps of coal chunks clattered noisily on conveyor tracks that crisscrossed down from outcrops high up the ridge. Broken trees and shattered boulders lay scattered on the site in huge mounds. Staring in wonder, they drove past and started another steep climb.

Soon they saw evidence of a settlement: unpainted little frame houses set on shelves of land hacked into the hills; tumbledown bungalows and rust-streaked trailers pushed up close against the two-lane highway. On a sagging front porch a woman in a faded print housedress and muddy field boots studied them from a rocker.

A mile farther the highway abruptly swept down, opening into four lanes at the base of a deep gorge blasted through the rock, with walls one hundred feet high, veined with glistening narrow seams of coal. They sped past another road sign, PIKEVILLE—POP. 4500, and past an exit that wound around into a small community shadowed by mountains and skirted by a meandering river. A jumble of neat buildings dominated by a brick courthouse with a weather vane on top, Pikeville looked like a village in a model railroad display.

A mile beyond the exit the road narrowed and began to climb once more. Mark made a U-turn and drove back into town.

KATHY Putnam was twenty-seven years old in 1987, six months younger than her husband. She and Mark had both grown up in Connecticut, where they had met five years earlier. With their daughter, they made a handsome family—Mark, dark and sensitive, a muscular young man who stayed in shape by running and lifting weights; Kathy, with her delicate features and untamed light brown hair, hopelessly unathletic; and amiable Danielle, with her mother's quick smile and her father's flashing eyes. If the FBI had commissioned a recruitment commercial, the Putnams would have been in it.

But the commercial would probably have shown the family arriving somewhere other than isolated Pikeville, the seat of Pike County,

Kentucky, a corrugated chunk of land shaped like a lump of coal. It sprawls over 785 square miles, most of them between two rivers, the Levisa Fork and the Tug Fork, which tumble out of the high watershed of the western Appalachian range down to the Cumberland Plateau.

It is a land extravagantly endowed with mineral and other natural resources and thus cursed with plunder. Timber barons cleared the mountains of their magnificent hardwood forests after the Civil War, and when they were gone, coal barons slashed their way in for the wealth underneath.

Dogpatch is what some new arrivals call the place, a term that conveys the disdain outsiders often bring to their first encounters with "hillbillies." Dogpatch is, after all, the world of "Li'l Abner," the comic strip whose characters embodied popular conceptions of hillbillies as befuddled lummoxes, sexually amenable Daisy Maes, bumptious elders, and shotgun-toting wild men, all coexisting in dim-witted bliss in a junkyard Eden where tranquillity is occasionally shattered by a thumping mountain feud. As with most enduring stereotypes, there is always authentication available to those who look for it. Pikeville and the neighboring Tug Valley, along the border with West Virginia, were in fact the locale for the Hatfield-McCoy Feud of the late nineteenth century. In the hilly rural areas out of town grown men still go barefoot in the summer, the dole is a way of life, the teenage pregnancy rate is among the highest in the country, and feuds simmer over generations like stewpots.

It is a place whose young people have long plotted to leave. By the end of the 1950s three quarters of the annual crop of high school graduates were migrating out of the plateau. What they left behind was a society as stratified as its landscape—the rich clustered in small towns like Pikeville, among the banks and courthouses; the poor clinging stubbornly to life in smoky hollows and along ridges, with walls of granite at their backs and thick veins of rich bituminous coal underfoot. Long accustomed to the appraisal of outsiders, inured to flash floods, mud slides, mine explosions, and rockfalls, the population includes some of the most cantankerous and individualistic humans alive on the continent. These are the people Mark Putnam, special agent of the Federal Bureau of Investigation, twenty-seven years old and all of one week out of the academy, was sent to serve.

Shortly after the Putnams arrived, the senior agent from the Louisville office, a man seldom seen in Pikeville, drove down to offer a welcome. He told Mark frankly that he would have been better off in a central office like Lexington, where there were dozens of more experienced agents to teach him the ropes. But the supervisor pointed out the bright side to Mark's situation.

"I'll be right up-front with you, Mark. This is an office that needs new blood. It has a lot of potential that hasn't been worked at for years. You're obviously gung ho, and there's a lot to keep you busy if you want to work it. Look at it as a potential career maker."

"I'm going to bust my ass for you," Mark told him.

"Just do your caseload. I won't kid you—nobody else wants to come here, which is why you got it. Luck of the draw, I guess."

There was another unspoken reason for the assignment. The FBI likes to insist that its files be as neat as its agents' attire, but over years of indifference the Pikeville bureau had become an administrative disaster. The office needed more than new blood; it needed a clerk to straighten out the mess. Whatever his nascent abilities as a crime-fighter, Mark Putnam had a skill that put him at the top of the list for Pikeville: for four years after college, while he and Kathy worked toward getting him accepted as a special agent, Mark had been a clerk in the busy FBI office in New Haven, Connecticut.

It was characteristic of the Putnams' marriage that Kathy had been the one to motivate him for the assignment—after initially intervening and trying to have it changed. Before they packed up the car in Connecticut, Mark had told her, "I'm afraid I'm going to screw this up and ruin my career before it gets going. I'm a rookie and a Yankee, with no law-enforcement experience." His wife had called the special agent in charge in Louisville to point that out. She was told that the assignment was firm and that the Pikeville office could be a career maker if he handled himself well.

Determined to do just that, Mark reported to work on a Monday morning in late February, 1987. The Pikeville FBI office was a tiny room on the ground-floor front of the federal building, with a window that looked out on sleepy Main Street. It was staffed by Dan Brennan and Sam Smith, who were awaiting transfer to more appealing locales. The new man had to squeeze past their desks to get to his makeshift work area, which consisted of a chair, a telephone, and a cleared space on the table that held the paper shredder, mail bin, and answering machine. There was no secretary.

The office fleet consisted of a beat-up Dodge Diplomat with nearly a hundred thousand hard miles on it and a four-wheel-drive Bronco, both of them already claimed by the two veteran agents. Kathy needed the Olds to get them settled in their new home. With a territory of several thousand square miles to cover in eastern Kentucky and West Virginia, Mark resented having to arrange for a bureau car like a teenager asking his father for the keys.

After his first few weeks on the job Mark talked Dan Brennan into a compromise arrangement to fit the twelve-hour days he'd already begun to work. Late in the afternoon Mark would drive Dan home, then use the Dodge well into the evenings to get into the hill towns to investigate cases that had piled up. Because Mark reported to work at seven in the morning, two hours earlier than his colleagues, he would leave the car in Brennan's driveway at night and jog home, then jog the mile to work the next day.

Mark's long workdays left Kathy largely on her own to establish their home. Thanks to her skill at managing money, they had enough saved up to make the down payment on an $89,000 two-story colonial in Cedar Creek, a small subdivision at the northern edge of town, accessible across a sway bridge over the Levisa Fork.

Kathy loved the house. "It had seven rooms, hand-embroidered curtains, a nice kitchen, two full baths, lots of room, nice landscaping. It seemed perfect for a small family like ours."

Mark's only objection was the mountain that pushed into the backyard. The muddy hulk left the house in a cold, damp shadow for much of the day.

In any case, he had little time to brood about it. Desperate to assimilate and learn, Mark soon found a way to get into the hills during the day without a car. He surprised local law-enforcement officers, who tended to resent the FBI for its haughtiness and its preoccupation with its image, by asking to tag along on their patrols. It amused Mark that the cops who befriended him were named Hatfield and McCoy. Paul Hatfield, Fred McCoy, and Bertie Hatfield, all of the Pike County sheriff's office, let him ride with them and introduced him to the old coal towns and hill settlements. Bertie, a laconic sheriff's deputy who also sold used cars from a small lot in Freeburn, an old coal company town on the banks of the Tug Fork, became a particularly good ally.

MONEY talks, as cops know, but its voice carried particular resonance in eastern Kentucky, where information has long been a commodity. All law-enforcement agencies paid for information, but the FBI had especially deep pockets. All an agent had to do was fill out a voucher with the amount and a few sentences describing the information likely to be yielded. Within a week a check for $500 or $1000 would come from Louisville.

Later Mark would recall his amazement at discovering how the system worked. "I'd go to an informant, 'I've got something for you.' The guy would be just awestruck that I was actually giving him the whole five hundred dollars or thousand dollars and not holding out like two hundred dollars for myself. After a while I didn't have to go out and drum up business—it just came to me."

# 2

To A bank robber, eastern Kentucky offers unusual challenges and opportunities. In some ways it is not an ideal place to rob a bank. For one thing, the region has an FBI office, and bank robbery is a federal crime. For another, robbing a bank is usually a daylight pursuit requiring the capacity to get away in a car—not an easy task in a place where the nearest interstate is two hours of bad road away.

On the other hand, banks in isolated mountain settlements tend to be guarded with about as much fortification as a hot dog stand. During the late spring and summer of 1987 in the Tug Valley, small banks were being knocked off not only efficiently but in a similar manner. Carl Edward "Cat Eyes" Lockhart, recently released from prison on probation, apparently had gone back to work.

As bank robbers go, Cat Eyes had much of the audacity of John Dillinger, only a little of the skill, and none of the discretion.

He was a soft-spoken, dark-haired local boy with luminous green eyes that provided him with his nickname. From childhood, his stated goal in life had been to be a bank robber. Having achieved that, he had just been released from a Virginia penitentiary after serving seven years of an eighteen-year sentence for a brazen robbery in 1980. He had gotten away with $300,000 from a small-town bank in Virginia.

Cat Eyes was a legend in the Tug Valley, mostly for having spent the $300,000 in a wild three-month spree, driving through several southern states with a friend. The desperadoes' odyssey had culminated in a truly spectacular week of debauchery and gambling in Nashville, where the boys dropped their last $50,000 before turning up frazzled and broke back home. There they were promptly arrested.

In June, Bertie Hatfield called up his new friend Mark Putnam and told him he thought Cat Eyes Lockhart was behind the latest spurt of bank robberies.

"How do you know it's him?"

"Well, all of a sudden he's rich. One thing about the guy, he spends it." Bertie also explained that all the reports mentioned the robber's bulky coveralls and ski mask—Cat Eyes' favorite disguise.

"Any ideas on how we catch him?"

Bertie had a good one. He offered to introduce Mark to Kenneth Smith, Cat Eyes' boyhood friend, unabashed admirer, and host.

After Cat was paroled, Kenneth Smith—himself on probation for drug possession—invited Cat and his girlfriend, Sherri Justice, to come and stay awhile. Kenneth had been married to a Freeburn girl, Susie Daniels, for five years. They'd divorced a few years earlier, but still lived together off and on. Susie claimed it was for the sake of their two children, although people close to her knew that the drugs Kenneth usually managed to get were part of the allure. Kenneth liked cocaine and booze; Susan preferred pills. Their four-room wood-frame bungalow on the Tug Fork in Vulcan, West Virginia, had long been a social center for the disaffiliated—a place to drop by, drink beer, snort cocaine, and, to those so inclined, crash for the night.

Bertie suggested to Mark that Kenneth Smith, chronically broke but with expensive tastes, might be open to the kind of persuasion that the FBI's deep pockets could provide. In August, Bertie had Kenneth come to Pikeville to see Mark.

The meeting wasn't promising. Kenneth would cooperate only in exchange for being removed from probation. He also wanted a weekly salary, with bonuses for specific information. Afterward Mark contacted Kenneth's parole officer, who said, "Forget it. The guy is totally unreliable." Besides, for a drug dealer, Kenneth had a notoriously bad memory. His ex-wife kept track of the details.

Bertie, who had known twenty-five-year-old Susie all her life, suggested to Mark that they approach her instead. He warned Mark that Susie "ran her mouth" frequently. Still, with the suspected bank robber living in her house, she had the right connections, and she had secretly provided Bertie with useful information in the past.

By this time Susie had begun to weary of her houseguests. Cat, who was broke again, ate like a wolf and ran up the phone bill, calling his former prison buddies long-distance. And even though Susie was working a common Tug Valley welfare scam, collecting monthly checks from both West Virginia and Kentucky, money didn't go far with six people in the house—more, if you counted Susie's troublesome younger brother Tennis and the others who drifted in and out. She also worried about the effect on her two children, Miranda Lynn, five years old, and Brady, who had just turned two. By the summer she and Kenneth were fighting openly over the situation.

To get to Susie, Bertie decided to introduce Mark to Tennis, whom Bertie had also used as an occasional informant. On the night before they were to get together, however, Bertie called Mark at home.

"We got big problems. Tennis shot somebody."

They went directly to Susan's house. It had been a family dispute. Tennis had fled after the shooting, but while they were there, he walked in. Mark persuaded him to give himself up. They called the West Virginia State Police barracks just up the river past Matewan.

As they waited for the troopers to arrive, Susie, her eyes blazing resentment, took the occasion to unload on Mark. A relative of hers had once helped the FBI in a case, she said angrily, and never got the money that was promised. Fair, she insisted, was fair.

As they drove back to Kentucky, Mark said, "Bertie, that girl is trouble."

"You're right about that," his companion replied.

Mark said, "Keep working on her, will you?"

Not long afterward, when another mountain-town bank was robbed, Bertie called Mark and said, "Okay, she wants to meet."

They drove to Williamson, a gritty river town on the West Virginia side of the Tug. Susie arrived accompanied by Kenneth and Tennis, now out on bail on a manslaughter charge. They sat at a table in a small restaurant, Kenneth dominating the conversation while Mark made eye contact with Susie, who at least gave him a smile. After a while he asked her, "Listen, could I talk to you alone for a minute?"

Kenneth glowered when his ex-wife, tossing back her brown hair, followed the FBI man outside. Through the window he watched them get into Bertie's car and sit there talking.

Mark tried to size her up. She was street-smart, that much was obvious. There was an edge to her, which was something he liked in women. She wasn't about to be pushed around. He didn't think she was particularly attractive, although she was generally considered to be fairly pretty, with small features and an engaging smile.

"So what do you want to talk about?" she asked.

"I want to know if you're interested in helping me."

"Now, why would I want to do something like that?"

He explained that money was available. She shook her head disdainfully. He kept at her, thinking, I am going to break this girl.

She changed the subject.

"I see you're married. Tell me what your wife looks like. Pretty?"

"Yes, she's pretty."

"She have a good body?"

"She keeps herself in very good shape, Susie," he said, glancing at her legs, exposed in high-cut shorts. Momentarily flustered, she placed her palms unconsciously across her thighs. At five feet five and a hundred and twenty-five pounds she was self-conscious about the ten pounds she had put on during the summer.

"Don't call me Susie. I hate it. It's Susan."

"Okay, Susan." He smiled at her. "Will you help?"

She said she'd think about it, and they went back to the restaurant.

Over the next week Mark and Susan met twice more, privately, and as an understanding evolved, he explained the payment process: "First you have to give me something to take back." Taking out a notebook, Mark got her talking about Cat Eyes.

She doled out information in expert increments, and he let her talk. Mark, like many naturally quiet men, was an exceptionally good listener, and it was apparent to him that this was a woman more accustomed to giving attention than to getting it. From time to time he would ask a pertinent question, and she would add a pertinent piece of information. Yes, she finally said, she thought that Cat Eyes was planning on robbing another bank.

"How do you know?"

"He's living with me and Kenneth. Him and his girlfriend."

Mark was aware of that, but he played the game. "How come?"

"He's broke. Kenneth likes him."

"Do you?"

"I suppose. I just don't want to adopt him."

"Doesn't he pay you?"

"No."

"Sounds to me like he's taking advantage of you."

That got her attention. She agreed to meet Mark in Pikeville. Before long, they were meeting two and three times a week.

IN SIXTEEN weeks of training, new agents received a few lectures on what motivates informants: money, revenge, or, occasionally, a sense of duty. The delicate business of actually developing and maintaining relationships with informants, which is the backbone of the FBI's investigative process, is passed over with a few precepts, the most important of which is, "Don't get personally involved." But even the dullest rookie recognized that the only way to develop a worthwhile informant was through personal trust and loyalty.

Money paved the way, however. To "open" a new informant, an agent was allotted $5000, to be distributed at the agent's discretion, and more down the road, depending on the usefulness of the information. From the beginning Susan understood that she stood to earn thousands of dollars if she delivered. Mark had determined that Susan could provide specific information in a criminal case and could probably open doors to him in future investigations. But he was nervous about spending the government's money. He wrote out a requisition and sent it to his supervisor, Terry Hulse, in the Covington branch office, near Cincinnati. When Hulse phoned to talk about it, Mark wondered uneasily if he had done something naïve. Hulse asked, "Mark, are you sure about this money for this informant?"

"What do you mean?"

"You're only going to give this girl five hundred dollars? I mean, she's giving you information on this guy—you know this guy's doing this robbery, don't you?"

"Yeah, I'm about ninety-five percent sure he's doing it."

"So keep her on board. Give her more money."

Mark said, "This girl's holding back—we're playing a kind of cat-and-mouse game right now. I just want to get her in the habit."

"Okay, I'll buy it. I like it. But let me tell you something. The money is there. Use it."

At their next meeting, when he gave Susan the $500, she seemed a little upset.

"Hey, there's more, but the information has got to back it up," Mark said. He didn't realize that, to Susan, taking the money was a major step, a break with her past. He wouldn't understand until it was too late that once she made that break, for her there would be no going back.

By the summer of 1987 Susan had already lived a hard fifteen years since she announced at the end of seventh grade that she had "better things to do" and dropped out of school in Freeburn. She had already been in a couple of fights with girls in elementary school, and she fought easily and ferociously enough to be ostracized among her better-mannered classmates. In a household where a smack across the face was a routine occurrence, in a social world where a young girl with a fast mouth sometimes had to defend herself with her fists, Susan arrived at adolescence with physical threats already firmly established in her life. She was poor—her family was on welfare nearly all of her life—and she resented it. Susan had grown up the fifth of nine children of a chronically unemployed coal miner, Sid Daniels, and his long-suffering wife, Tracy Eldridge Daniels. The children shared clothes—and even shoes—in a drafty house high up a mountain gulch in Freeburn known as Barrenshea Hollow.

It was a place where trouble never was far away. Susan started school in 1966, at a time when cheap oil was flooding the country and the Appalachian coal industry, already battered by unemployment caused by the growth of efficient strip mining, sank into one of its cyclical severe depressions. At the time, the majority of Pike County students dropped out by ninth grade.

Natural peril intensified the fatalism of a child's life in a mountain hollow where mine disasters were a routine part of life, and spring rains often unleashed great mudbanks of strip-mine debris and boulders from eroded mountaintops onto populated areas below. Catastrophic floods devastated the Tug Valley twice during Susan's youth—in 1963, and again in 1977. In the latter year the river, swollen by fifteen inches of rain that fell on still frozen ground, crested at fifty feet and swept away hundreds of homes in the valley.

Few of the four hundred or so people in Freeburn had telephones in Susan's childhood years, but many acquired television sets. When she was a little girl, Susan decided that she wanted to be a secretary, like the ones she saw on television shows. Secretaries had respect from men. Secretaries dressed beautifully and lived in cities. Secretaries were helpers, and Susan, at her best, was a helper.

Like most out-of-work miners, her father drank hard. Like most women in the hollow, her mother remained in the background. Susan had few friends. Instead, she had what were referred to as notions.

The highlight of Susan's grade school years was belonging to the Patriotettes, the all-girl drill team. The little girl from Barrenshea Hollow loved her red-and-white Patriotettes uniform and wore it proudly in ragtag holiday parades. In her seventh-grade yearbook Susan's picture stands out among those of her classmates with pigtails and scrubbed faces. She is the only one wearing a beret.

IN 1977 SUSAN saw her first opportunity to get out. She met twenty-two-year-old Kenneth Smith, a good-looking local boy who could be charming when he wanted something. When Kenneth spotted her and whistled, Susan simply got on the back of his motorcycle and rode off with him to a trailer he rented on the far side of the mountain, in another old coal-company town called Majestic.

Kenneth earned his money by selling drugs. Like most dealers, he visited cities from time to time. Susan resolved to go with him, and he was smart enough to realize that she was an asset, since she had a good memory and an affinity for numbers. She helped him with small-time deals in cocaine, marijuana, acid, and bootleg depressants and stimulants. In time she began referring to herself as his "executive assistant," a phrase she had picked up from television.

For the first time, Susan was able to buy the clothes she liked—not only for herself but for friends and relatives. But the prosperity didn't continue. When Susan was seventeen, Kenneth was arrested for drug possession, jumped bail, and fled, sending her to Louisiana to stay with one of his brothers and his wife. While there, broke and miserable without Kenneth, she worked in a fast-food restaurant. When that didn't pay, she turned to occasional prostitution.

In time Kenneth joined her. They later moved to Indiana, where they married and had a daughter, Miranda. Thrilled at being parents, they tried to settle into respectability. Kenneth took a job as a carpenter's assistant, and Susan worked hard to decorate their trailer with frilly curtains, throw rugs, and pillows.

As the novelty of parenthood passed into drudgery, they again turned to drugs for recreation and then, after Kenneth lost his job, for financial support as well. They began fighting. Kenneth would beat her and in the morning vow to reform. It was a pattern that Susan never managed to break.

From Indiana they moved to a cheap apartment in Cicero, Illinois, a run-down suburb outside of Chicago. There they established drug contacts that would later keep them supplied in the Tug Valley.

By the time Susan was in her early twenties, she and Kenneth were back in the Tug. Facing trial on the old drug charge, Kenneth pleaded guilty and got off with probation. At home the fighting got so bad that Susan ran away. She wandered for months, staying with friends and relatives, who would sometimes find her curled up on their couch in the morning.

During this time she began showing up regularly at a country-and-western bar on Route 23, the main highway through Pikeville, across from a road called Harmons Branch. The bar's owner, also the featured singer, was a burly man named Marlow Tackett, who had hopes of making it in Nashville. Susan sat at a table night after night and pined for him. She told people she was planning to become his manager and to help take him to the big time. Years later, when asked about her, Marlow would barely remember the girl from Freeburn.

Miserable and destitute, Susan finally returned to Kenneth. A second child, Brady, was born in 1985. She and Kenneth divorced soon afterward, which enabled her to get better welfare benefits. In 1987 they were still living unhappily together in the rented house beside the river, when Mark Putnam came into her life. In Susan's world Mark was a novelty—a handsome, motivated, polished man who was *interested* in her as someone who had something to offer. With no special effort he treated her like a lady, and she responded.

THE PAYOFF FOR MARK CAME IN September. Susan told him that Cat Eyes had brought home a duffel bag containing two sawed-off shotguns and some ski masks. Cat was clearly making big plans, Susan reported. "Watch the papers," Cat had told her with a wink.

The FBI quietly warned local banks to be on the alert.

Cat had chosen a branch of the First National Bank in Ferrells Creek, in the hills fifteen miles from Pikeville and five miles from the Virginia border. In Virginia the roads were good. Cat had arranged for a getaway van and an accomplice to drive it.

On the morning of September 10, 1987, Cat entered the bank and approached the teller's window. The teller, Rosemary Childers, looked up with some alarm. Cat was wearing a huge pair of lumberjack's coveralls that swathed him from neck to foot, and a black knit ski mask turned around backward, with two eyeholes clumsily cut out in front so he would not expose too much of his face, especially his distinctive green eyes. He was holding a sawed-off shotgun.

Cat plopped a pillowcase down on the counter and said to the teller, "Fill it up with money."

While the teller took stacks of bills from her cash drawer, Cat Eyes raised the gun and swung around, ordering the six or seven other people in the bank: "Freeze, and put your hands up!" Some were confused at the sequence of the command; tentatively, hands went up.

Childers took this opportunity to drop a dye pack into the pillowcase along with the money. A dye pack is a security device that looks like a standard stack of bank money, a hundred bills thick, with a real $10 bill on the top. Once it passes through the electronic beam at a bank's door, a timing switch is triggered. The next time it is jostled, the device explodes, splattering red dye on the culprit and his loot.

"Into the vault," Cat Eyes shouted to the bewildered group of employees and customers. There was some commotion while Rosemary Childers went to look for the key. When she found it and opened the vault, Cat ordered her to take the stacks of bills from a shelf and drop them into his pillowcase, which he held open like a trick-or-treater. She made a show of dropping in a second dye pack. Cat Eyes spotted this one. "And no dye bombs," he said. Sheepishly the woman removed it. The pillowcase now contained $12,807.

Cat Eyes closed the vault door—thoughtfully not all the way—and ran to the exit with a shout of glee. Just outside, he paused to perform a small victory jig. At once the dye pack exploded, initially causing Cat to think he had been shot. When he realized what had happened, he dashed for the van, screaming at his accomplice to get going.

The van was found ditched on a side road at Ferrells Creek, along with a couple of hundred dollars soaked with red dye.

CAT didn't return to Susan's house, which the authorities were watching. But a week later, in the Tug Valley branch of the Pikeville National Bank in South Williamson, an alert bank teller, Debby White, became suspicious when a polite but nervous dark-haired man with amazing green eyes came in to exchange a wad of $2 bills—182 of them in all—all stained at the edges with red dye.

As Cat left the bank, she called the state police, who promptly notified the FBI. Mark was out of town to serve a fugitive warrant, and Dan Brennan finally got through to him on the phone and explained the situation. "Talk to Susan," Mark said. "She'll fill you in."

Susan refused. "I only talk to Mark," she told Brennan.

When Mark found her the next day, he was baffled by her loyalty. "It's your case," she said. "I don't want you to give away the credit."

She told him where Cat was—at his mother's house in West Virginia. When Mark and Dan Brennan arrived with state police to handcuff the suspect, Cat insisted that he walk beside Mark, for the benefit of the newspaper photographer who showed up.

Susan was furious that Mark had to share credit for the arrest. She stopped by the office the next day and found him there alone. He counted out fifteen $100 bills and gave them to her, but she tried to give one back. "I want you to have this."

He shrank from it. "I can't take that, Susan!"

She insisted. "You did all the work, and you're getting screwed out of any credit."

"You don't understand how this organization works. You're making me a hero. Maybe I didn't get the big write-up in the paper, but my bosses know who did the work, and I get the credit for you."

"I want you to have this. I won't take it back."

She dropped the money on his desk and walked out.

In a panic he thought, Is she trying to set me up?

He phoned his supervisor in Covington, who told him to write a covering memo and put the money in the safe toward the next payment, which would come if and when Susan testified against Cat Eyes.

Later, when Mark broached that subject, Susan said she would consider testifying but that she was afraid for her life. If she testified, she wanted enough money to move out of the area with her children.

Mark asked, "How much money do you think you'll need?"

"Four thousand dollars."

"No problem," he said.

## 3

Mark knew enough about what he was up against in eastern Kentucky to regard Susan as more than a source of information. To an outsider anxious to assimilate, she offered the invaluable cachet of acceptance: being seen with a local girl made him look more like one of the boys. For her the opposite was true. To the extent that he found camouflage with her, she was flushed out into the open. Susan had known instinctively that once she made her pact with Mark there would be no turning back. As if to ensure that, she had made it a point to tell everyone in Freeburn that she was working for the FBI.

Far more than her husband, Kathy implicitly understood Susan's dilemma. From the beginning she approached Susan with a mixture of empathy and wariness that enabled Susan, a woman acutely alert to opportunity, to find the rapidly blurring line between Mark's professional and personal lives and quickly step over it.

The unlikely alliance between the two women developed on the telephone during the summer and fall of 1987. Susan had taken her role as an informant quite seriously, regarding it as a full-time job that required her to report in frequently. Since Mark was out on the road so much and the office had no secretary, Kathy fielded many of his phone calls from their home. Susan called the house for the first time about a week after her initial meeting with Mark.

"Kathy? This is Susan Smith," she had begun. "I don't know if your husband told you about me or not. I'm working as his informer on an important case. Is he there? He was supposed to meet up with me at the office, but I don't know where he is."

Kathy told her she'd relay the message when Mark got in. Mark had told her about Susan, including the meeting outside the restaurant. He'd also told her something that they both found amusing and somewhat curious. According to Bertie, after the meeting Kenneth had stormed around Freeburn maintaining that the FBI man had actually "screwed" his ex-wife in the back seat of the car in broad daylight.

This whetted Kathy's curiosity about what sort of person would be living with a wild man like Kenneth Smith. She was pleasantly surprised to find that she liked Susan. She decided that Susan was friendly, sincere, engagingly ditsy at times, and more than a little bit vulnerable when it came to relationships with men. Kathy's first and abiding impulse was to help her.

Kenneth's fabrications aside, it was apparent to Kathy that Susan was enthralled by Mark, a situation that she accepted with the equanimity of a faculty wife toward a female student with a harmless crush on the professor. Besides, in close-knit Pikeville, where Kathy didn't know many people, it was nice to have someone to talk to.

Susan began to ask Kathy's advice on grooming and etiquette, while probing for information about Mark. She found out that he ran every night, and told him that she had started running, too. Did he read? Susan began showing up at their meetings with a paperback in hand. As they got to know each other, Mark noticed little changes in her, as if she were trying to become more like the women he knew. Even her manner of speech changed; she would correct herself crossly when she said "heered" instead of "heard," for example.

Susan began calling at all hours, sometimes several times a day. Soon after she started working as an informant, she began showing up at the courthouse nearly every day, looking for Mark in the FBI office. Since he was often out, Susan would pass the time bantering with courthouse employees, especially the officers in the probation and marshal's divisions, where she managed to establish the impression that she and Mark had a close working relationship.

Mark's take on Susan was less complicated than his wife's. He had noticed that Susan boasted about sexual relations with men at the courthouse, men who he was quite sure had never been involved with her. "She has a big mouth, Kat," he warned his wife. "Watch out."

But Susan's dependence on Kathy grew as the friendship deepened. They sometimes spoke for hours, Susan's troubles spilling out one after the other to a receptive ear. The dead-end relationships, money problems, despair, abysmal self-esteem, half-baked aspirations, and chronic ineptitude—Kathy readily recognized these afflictions because she had overcome them herself. She believed that in time she might be able to help Susan do the same.

Patiently she would say, "Listen, Susan, I have been there. Believe me, you can get yourself together."

To look at her then—poised and happy, ensconced in a solid marriage, with a spouse who loved her deeply and a bright-eyed daughter who would be a delight to any parent—it would have been difficult to imagine what similarities in their lives Kathy was alluding to.

Kathy Ponticelli and her younger sister, Christine, were daughters of an autocratic but devoted second-generation Italian American father, and a mother who offered quiet, unassuming encouragement to her girls. The household had strict rules: help out around the house, be home by curfew, make good grades, go to Mass on Sunday, and don't get in trouble with the nuns.

A smart and perceptive girl who felt that there was probably more to life than the small-town tedium of Manchester, Connecticut, Kathy coasted through St. James' parish school and then East Catholic High School, sullen and bored. Unable, she thought, to do anything right, she compensated for her lack of self-confidence with a brashness that some misconstrued as brazen effrontery. If social acceptance meant opening a purse to brandish a stash of joints, talking street-tough, copping cigarettes in the girls' bathroom, flouting the rules—then so be it. She was in, and who cared? At East Catholic High, such an attitude led right down the slippery slope to what her devout parents saw as the worst of all ignominies: public school, to which Kathy was banished in her junior year, and from which she dropped out a few months later, days after she turned eighteen.

After Kathy left high school, the similarities to Susan's life became more pronounced. She horrified her parents by moving into an apartment in a run-down, crime-ridden part of East Hartford with a jealous boyfriend who drank heavily. The young man's mother tended bar in a club that featured go-go dancers, where Kathy took a job as a waitress and bartender.

The boyfriend was thrown into jail after a fight with a man who had flirted with Kathy in a bar. After his release she resumed the relationship, driving off with him to North Carolina, where they rented a trailer near a military base. When their money ran out, he stranded her there. Ashamed, she phoned her parents for the plane fare home. In the stultifying sanctuary of their house—"If you're going to come home, you're going to live by our rules"—she tried to accommodate herself to their diminished expectations. When a man ten years her senior, who had a steady job in a gravel factory, entered her life, she married him on impulse. Her father gave her a job managing an apartment complex that he and his father had built in Manchester, and she got her high school equivalency diploma and enrolled in community college. It looked like things were working out at last.

But there was a dark side to her new husband that Kathy hadn't seen. He deeply resented the "airs" he said she was putting on by continuing in college. He was also insanely jealous. The marriage, which lasted four months, ended one night when, in a drunken rage, he smacked her around in the car and pushed her out, bruised and mortified, onto her parents' well-tended front lawn.

By the age of twenty-one, however, Kathy was on track at last. "I was no longer married, and I got my associate degree. I had a decent job managing the apartments; I was living in a nice apartment that I'd furnished beautifully from secondhand shops. I even had a new Datsun two eighty ZX. Then I saw Mark and he changed my life."

They met serendipitously on a Friday night in July of 1982, two days before his twenty-third birthday. In the apartment next door to Kathy lived an avuncular, hard-drinking elderly man who had asked her to join him for dinner at a local restaurant where a woman he was dating would be singing. At dinner, however, he drank so excessively that he was listing severely by the time the singer came on. At an adjacent table a sprightly middle-aged widow sitting with a male friend noticed Kathy's plight and caught her attention.

"Men," the older woman commiserated, rolling her eyes.

Kathy smiled back. "What are you going to do with them?"

The woman looked Kathy over appraisingly and asked a few questions about her age and marital status. "You know," she said, pulling her chair closer, "my son would be perfect for you. He's good-looking. He just graduated from the University of Tampa, and he's going to be an FBI agent. I can call him and ask him to come over."

Sure, Kathy thought. Some guy sitting at home on a Friday night while his mother hustles dates for him? And what kind of guy wants to be an FBI agent? But the woman was engagingly persistent. "Come on," she said, getting up. "*Come on!* We're going to call him."

"Listen, we need to leave," Kathy protested, noticing that her companion's elbows were sliding off the table. "I have to get him home." He got unsteadily to his feet and wobbled across the dance floor to join his friend the singer between sets, announcing that he was going home with her.

On her way to the ladies' room, Kathy passed the older woman at the pay phone. "You've got to meet this girl," the woman was saying into the phone. "She's beautiful." She grabbed Kathy by the elbow and thrust the receiver into her hand. "Talk!"

Flustered, Kathy mumbled, "Hello?"

There was embarrassed laughter on the other end, and a deep voice said, "I have to apologize to you for my mother's putting you on the spot. The woman is incorrigible."

Kathy was intrigued by the sound of his voice. They talked for a while and seemed to have things in common. She liked his sense of humor. She heard herself saying, "Well, why don't you come down here, then, if you want to talk?"

Twenty minutes later a dark-haired young man with flashing eyes and a dazzling smile walked in. He shook her hand, held her chair, made her laugh, and treated her like the most important person in his life. By the end of the night she was hopelessly in love.

"We connected right away," she recalled. "It was very clear very fast that this was the man I really wanted in my life, and he felt the same way about me. We talked and laughed, and we made love for the first time in my apartment as the sun came up."

WHEN he met Kathy, Mark was two months out of the University of Tampa, where he had been the captain of the soccer team and from which he had graduated with a degree in criminology. In September he was to start work as a clerk at the FBI office in New Haven.

Mark, his younger brother, Tim, and his sister, Cindy, had spent part of their childhood in a housing project in East Hartford. But their father worked hard to provide a better home. A burly, soft-spoken man, who always had another job or two to do after his regular workday driving a truck for Sears, Walter Putnam soon put together the down payment on a comfortable house in middle-class Coventry. He had dropped out of high school to enlist in the navy, and he and his wife, Barbara, placed great value on their children's education.

In his freshman year of high school Mark was offered an athletic scholarship to the prestigious Pomfret School in Pomfret, Connecticut, fifty miles away. Going off to prep school posed a tough decision for a boy who stayed close to home and was already a star soccer and baseball player in high school. His mother opposed it, advising him, "Stay at home. You're going to be all-American." Characteristically, his father's response was to throw the question back at him. "I know the answer, but think it out."

In time Mark knew, too. He recognized the opportunity. His father, delighted that Mark had opted for Pomfret, told him, "If you want to go, you go. I'll handle your mother."

Despite the scholarship, it would cost Mark's parents about $1000 a year to send him. They'd make do, his father said.

At Pomfret, Mark rapidly assimilated. "Friends started coming, girls started coming around. My grades were good, and I worked hard for them."

Meanwhile, his relationship with his father, who had overcome a drinking problem a few years earlier, underwent a significant change. The man who had been a distant figure through much of his childhood became a confidant. Mark sensed that his father was vicariously living out a part of life he had never been able to experience.

"We began to have talks on the phone after I went to prep school, which was odd because the man usually hated the phone. He wanted to know what people were doing, what I was studying, what the rich kids were like, what the girls were like. He had left school at sixteen, so I guess it was a world he had always wondered about."

Mark maintained a B average, played baseball, and captained Pomfret's undefeated soccer team in his senior year. He graduated in 1978 and enrolled at the University of Tampa.

The relationship between father and son grew even closer during the summer before his freshman year in college, when Mark frequently went out on the road with his father.

"On the road at night we would come into a truck stop, and my father pointed out, many times, where guys would come up and offer him twenty thousand or thirty thousand dollars for his load. The deal was, he could leave the truck, go in for a cup of coffee, and come back and report the cargo was hijacked. He told me, 'Man, there were times when we really could have used that money. But it would have been wrong. You be honest in life, Mark. That's it.' "

Mark never forgot. At the start of his sophomore year, he decided to major in criminology. In his earnest way he told his father that he wanted to become an FBI agent because he believed in what he had learned about honesty. "My old man was the one person I knew I could talk to about the FBI and not get laughed at," he remembered.

During Mark's sophomore year his father died of lung cancer. At the funeral Mark told his mother, "If I could be half the man that he was, I will be happy. I'll have made it."

WHEN his mother introduced him to Kathy Ponticelli in the summer of 1982, he fell in love with her with the same force that she did with him. From the first night they were inseparable.

"There wasn't room for anyone else in our lives," Kathy said. "By the end of the summer we moved together to a tiny apartment in Middletown, about halfway between New Haven, where he was going to start work in the FBI office, and Hartford, where I had just got a job as a paralegal at an insurance company.

"I loved hearing about his life," said Kathy many years later. "Prep school, senior proms, college pranks, graduation day—things that I had missed. Mark had done everything the right way, always.

"We were a perfect fit. For everything I learned from him, he learned something from me. I taught him how to manage money and balance a checkbook. He was so naïve about some things—like he'd never count his change. He was a sucker for garage mechanics. I showed him life: you shop around for a garage, the bills come due, the rent has to be paid. We seemed to fill in each other's blanks."

They lived together for almost two years, putting away money for marriage and a baby. When they agreed it was time to get married, Kathy decided that it was important to tell him about her past. He listened in stony silence, then walked out without a word. She didn't see him for three days. When he came back, he said only, "I don't ever want to talk about that again. Any of it." And they never did.

On Easter weekend of 1984, without alerting either of their families, they drove to New York City to get married. The only objection came not from their families but from the bureau, which frowned on elopements, even by clerks. But they had other things on their minds than the FBI. They wanted to have a baby.

Danielle was born on New Year's Day of 1985. Eighteen months later, after years of work and a long period of anxiety awaiting the results of his application interviews and tests, Mark was finally accepted into the FBI academy to begin training as a special agent. They both would later recall this period as the happiest time of their lives.

# 4

LATE in the summer of 1987 a wild man barged into the FBI office in Pikeville, filling the doorway with his bulk.

"I'm telling you, gentlemen, it's a million-dollar operation," Charlie Trotter boomed. The agents' first impulse was to reach for their guns. But Charlie held up his palms and motioned for them to relax, settling himself into an empty chair and saying expansively, "I want to give you guys the biggest case you are ever going to work."

Suspiciously Dan Brennan said, "Yeah, what's that?"

"Stolen trucks," Charlie replied, looking from Brennan to Mark to see who was looking back hardest.

Brennan tightened his lips and found something to read.

Charlie leaned forward to scrutinize Mark, a grizzled grin showing under his Fu Manchu mustache. A solid six feet and a hundred and ninety pounds, wearing a tight muscle shirt over arms festooned with prison tattoos, Charlie adjusted the little leather cap that sat jauntily on his shaved head. Mark had never seen anything quite like him.

For the next four hours, as Mark made notes, Charlie spun out his tale of betrayal and indignation. At the heart of the story was a willingness to sell information, and perhaps to testify if the price was right, about what he described as a huge multistate operation in stolen vehicles, truck parts, and construction and mining equipment—an elaborate chop shop located on a secluded mountain just over the Letcher County border twenty miles southwest of Pikeville. A member of the ring, Charlie identified the "brains" of the operation as Vernon Mullins, who had recruited a gang of thieves who stole the trucks and other pieces of equipment throughout several states and towed them back to the Letcher County site, where they were being sold.

"It's going to cost you, but it'll be worth the price," Charlie said.

Mark thanked Charlie for his time, took a number where he could be reached, and said he'd be in touch.

When Charlie left, Mark called a cop he knew in Letcher County and asked him what he'd heard about the operation. "We've been after Vernon Mullins for a long time," the cop replied, "but you can't get near him. He supposedly runs a big chop shop somewheres."

Mark checked Charlie's record. He was a hardened criminal, involved in drugs and robbery, who had also done time for second-degree murder. Such a résumé was not necessarily a bad thing in an informant, assuming you could keep him on your side.

Brennan, looking forward to his transfer, tried to discourage his young partner's obvious enthusiasm. "Mark, you don't want to mess with that," he warned. "Stolen parts, man oh man. You're overwhelmed with paperwork." He pulled out the bureau's procedural manual to illustrate the complications: Every part, every vehicle would need to be thoroughly documented and traced to its source. Fingerprints would have to be matched; owners of the stolen equipment notified. It would require tracking down original police theft reports from every jurisdiction involved, not to mention insurance reports and claims documents. If the operation was as major as Charlie was maintaining, it would be a full-time job.

Mark considered Brennan's advice. But he knew that if Charlie's information was good and if the investigation was thoroughly professional, such a case would break new ground in the territory.

"I'll give it a shot," he told Brennan, who shrugged and said, "Suit yourself."

Obviously the first question was, what was Charlie's motive? The answer appeared to be fairly simple: money, and a desire for revenge. Charlie was angry because he hadn't been paid for the last truck he'd brought in, and he figured that if Vernon Mullins and his boys weren't going to pay, the FBI was. Charlie figured he could become a rich man and settle a score at the same time.

Mark realized that Charlie was mad, but he was wily, and before he got himself killed by spoon-feeding the FBI, the anger would have passed. Mark knew he would have to work him carefully. Eager to get going, he called him and set up a meeting.

IT HELPED A LOT THAT MARK CAME to genuinely like Charlie as their alliance evolved. They met once or twice a week. Charlie would stop by the office, and they would get in the car and drive off into the hills, where they would be able to talk without being observed.

But Mark also realized that Charlie was working both sides of the fence, maintaining his activities with the chop-shop gang. While Charlie claimed that he had returned to their good graces only to facilitate the gathering of information, Mark knew that he couldn't drop his guard against a double cross.

Bit by bit, Mark built his case. Charlie liked not only the money but, it appeared, the attention. And he delivered.

In the fall Charlie had gone along for the hijacking of three trucks in Maryland. They were coming across the mountains toward Kentucky when Charlie realized he had forgotten to call Mark, as arranged, to let him know when the convoy was on its way. It wasn't time to make arrests yet, but Mark insisted on knowing what Charlie was up to. At the Putnam house, the phone rang around ten o'clock.

"Charlie, where are you?"

"Pay phone, man. We're coming in around midnight."

"Charlie, aren't they wondering who you're calling?"

"The other two trucks went on ahead. It's just me and this old boy. I coldcocked him—punched his lights out. He's out."

"Why the hell did you do that?"

"So I could call, man."

"What are you going to tell him when he wakes up?"

"I'll just say I didn't like the way he was a-looking at me."

KATHY, already accustomed to telephone intrusions, added Charlie Trotter to the growing list of people—Susan prominent among them—who called at odd hours to talk to Mark. As she had when he was a clerk, Kathy happily pitched in to help with Mark's work, fielding calls and even spending hours some nights editing and typing his handwritten interview reports, known in the bureau as 302s.

That autumn Kathy and Mark were looking forward to the birth of their second child. Kathy had become pregnant a month after they moved to Pikeville. In late October, six weeks before she was due, Kathy intended to take Danielle with her to Connecticut, where they would stay with her parents until Mark joined them for what they hoped would be a three-week Christmas vacation centered around the birth of a son.

Life in Pikeville had settled into a pleasant routine. Agent Sam Smith had been transferred, allowing Mark to finally have his own desk and the wheezing old Dodge.

His initial apprehension about being a rookie in an unsupervised environment had abated. Mark's superiors made it clear that his work was appreciated—suddenly, with his presence, the office seemed to be bustling with activity. His success in cultivating Susan and Charlie as informants was impressive; so, too, were the reports that he had significantly improved relations between the bureau and the Kentucky State Police, whose Pikeville post was one of the busiest in the department. Veteran police officers there had never before come in contact with an FBI agent who made it a part of his routine to stop by the post and shoot the breeze, trade information, and offer to help out on minor criminal investigations that the FBI often disdained. Mark showed up even for the scut work: the excruciating nightlong surveillances in mountain backwaters, the down-in-the-mud searching for physical evidence at a crime scene, the warrant-serving in places that required a hike into the woods. Putnam worked, as one of the state cops would later recall, "like a damn rented mule."

When he wasn't working, he applied the same fervor to his family life. Mark and Kathy seldom went out, preferring intimate late-night dinners at home on weekends. He always tried to get home at a reasonable hour on Friday night, which was designated "date night" with Danielle, who wore her prettiest dress to accompany her father to the Dairy Queen or the McDonald's out on Route 23.

Kathy regarded their family routine, happy as it was, as fairly mundane, and she was baffled by the allure that it seemed to hold for Susan. She knew that Mark was concerned about Susan's intense interest, which he couldn't easily defuse, because he needed her to testify at Cat Eyes' trial, now scheduled for January. Furthermore, the bureau had encouraged him to keep Susan active as an informant, since she was promising to pass on information about other criminal matters in the Tug Valley. This meant that he met with her regularly, and, unbidden, she continued calling the Putnam home almost daily. Kathy shrugged off a disquieting sense that Susan's inquisitiveness about her family might have started to become obsessive.

The initial evidence of this was innocent enough to be vaguely flattering. By the end of the summer Kathy, five months pregnant, had decided that she was tired of having shoulder-length hair. She went to a beauty salon and had it styled and layered shorter and told Susan that night how pleased she was with it.

"I guess Mark likes short hair, huh?" Susan asked.

Kathy replied, "Mark likes women who take care of themselves."

A few days later Mark mentioned that Susan had had her long hair cut short.

Not that Mark had much time to ponder an informant's hair-styling. By late October, after months of painstaking groundwork, Mark decided to move on the chop-shop case. He had brought Brennan up to date on the investigation and alerted the Covington and Lexington offices, as well as the state police in Pikeville and the sheriff's department in Letcher County. The last step necessary before a full-scale raid was to photograph the operation itself. After Charlie drew him a map, Mark persuaded a pilot from the state department of mines and minerals to fly him over the site in a small plane. Through gaps in the thinning autumn foliage they saw it—an expanse the size of two football fields, littered with trucks, bulldozers, and hundreds of other pieces of equipment.

The raid was scheduled for the last week of October, which would be right after Kathy and Danielle were to leave for Connecticut. The timing was excellent for Mark, who knew that the real work would follow the raid and the arrests. He would have to spend weeks on the scene, taking inventory of thousands of pieces of evidence. With his family out of town he could work around the clock without guilt.

After work on Friday night the Putnams drove to Lexington, where they spent the night in a motel. When Mark went to check in, there was a message to call the office.

Kathy could see that something was wrong. "The raid is going down tomorrow," Mark told her disconsolately. "There was some kind of glitch with the search warrants, and they had to move fast."

The next day, after seeing Kathy and Danielle off at the airport, Mark drove the three hours directly to the site, but he was too late. Dan Brennan was on hand, supervising the dozen or so officers who had conducted the raid. His news was not good. There had been no arrests; someone had apparently tipped off Mullins and his men, who were nowhere to be seen when the police stormed up the hollow.

As Brennan briefed him, a heavy downpour erupted from black clouds over the mountains. Most of the officers fled to their cars, and Brennan departed. Furious that the operation had been botched despite his careful preparations, Mark stood on the hillside, ankle-deep in cold mud, and took out a notebook. He crawled under a bulldozer to look for its vehicle identification number.

For three weeks afterward he spent the daylight hours on the muddy chop-shop site, accompanied by sheriff's deputies, a state cop who had helped to prepare the case, and a technician from the National Auto Theft Bureau. They photographed hundreds of vehicles and parts, recording whatever identification numbers they could find. As Charlie had promised, it was quite a haul. After the preliminary inventory Mark estimated that they had recovered $2.2 million in stolen equipment that was traceable to its owners. Newspaper accounts of the raid called it the biggest single recovery of stolen vehicles and parts in recent memory. But they also pointed out that no arrests had been made. Police were still looking for the thieves.

The trucks and other equipment were moved to a fenced-in area nearby for safekeeping. It was almost Thanksgiving when Mark was able to get back to the office to continue his statistical work, entering the serial numbers and other data into the National Crime Information Center computer. When numbers matched, the next step was to notify the owners, who had to be interviewed one by one.

Brennan was right—the detail work was staggering.

But Mark had been prepared for that. What he didn't expect, when he returned to the site one Saturday, was to be confronted by Charlie Tackett, one of the men whom Charlie Trotter had named as a ringleader in the operation. Mark had spoken with him once in the initial phase of the investigation. Tackett, aware that no evidence yet linked him to the crime, strode right up to Mark with a broad grin.

"Mark, how you doing, son?" he said.

"Hey, Charlie, where's your boss Vernon these days?"

Tackett laughed. "Let me tell you something. Vernon and I have a lot of friends in this area. We're businessmen, son. A lot of people depend on us for parts. I don't know how many people have come up to me—"

Mark lost his cool. "Charlie, is that some kind of threat? Because if it is, you can just shove it. If they want to shoot me, go ahead and let them. But I guarantee you there'll be about eight thousand agents who'll come down and bust every business you got going, and every business your partners got going."

"Oh, man, nobody's threatening nobody," Charlie said, chuckling. "This is a game with us—a *game*. They're not going to get us. You don't even have enough to make an arrest warrant."

So far, true. Mark was depending on Charlie Trotter to supply that. "Charlie, this isn't state court, where you can buy your way out of it."

"Time will tell. Time will tell. You'll come around. We got a lot of people that we know, a lot of people on the payroll."

"I know you do."

Both men glanced off to where a local detective was standing with a clipboard, looking down at some parts.

"Like I said, there are a lot of people on our payroll."

"Shove it, Charlie. It isn't going to work."

But Mark had reason to wonder as the case wore on.

Twice, the site where the parts were stored was broken into by thieves. Angry and frustrated, Mark spent several nights there in a sleeping bag. When he went back to Pikeville, he had a call.

"Bad news," said a local cop who was also on the case. "We got broken into last night. They got all the CB radios."

In all, there were four burglaries in seven nights.

Mark was at the site one morning when a battered pickup truck pulled up. "You Putnam?" the driver called.

"Yeah," he said, approaching the pickup. "Who are you?"

"Well, I ain't going to say. But they say you're a good boy, and I hate to see you wasting your time."

"What do you mean?"

"Well, you know that guy you been working with?" He named one of the cops.

"What about him?" Mark said.

"I hear he's been selling CBs," the driver said, and rumbled off.

The next morning Charlie Trotter came by the office. He looked nervous. "I had a problem last night. I was a little drunk, and some of the boys jumped me." He lifted his shirt and turned around. From shoulder to beltline a crude X had been carved in his back.

# 5

THOUGH she hated being away from Mark, Kathy was glad she had chosen to go back home to have the baby. She felt more confident delivering in a hospital in Connecticut. In December, Mark managed to get time off to fly back east. He was with Kathy on December 9, 1987, when Mark junior was born, the image of his father.

It was invigorating to leave the problems of Pikeville behind for a few weeks, but Kathy could see Mark's distress, barely masked by the glow of the new baby. The botched raid at the chop-shop site had bolstered his conviction that he needed to do everything himself. He fretted about what had happened. His key informant had obviously blown his cover—that X on Charlie's back was a bloody message not only to its victim but to his supposed protector as well. Mark brooded over the possibility that he wouldn't be able to come up with criminal indictments of the Mullins gang. There was also the problem of Cat Eyes, whose trial was coming up right after New Year's. Susan's testimony would be crucial—with no guarantees that she would go through with it and expose herself as the accuser.

With a sense of foreboding he returned to Pikeville with Kathy, Danielle, and the baby a few days after Christmas.

Susan was in the office waiting for him with a big smile. She surprised him with a kiss on the lips and said happily, "I got you a couple of things for Christmas. I'm sorry I didn't wrap them." She set a pair of expensive running shoes and a Nike T-shirt on his desk.

He was bewildered. "I can't take these, Susan!"

Her face clouded like a scolded child's. "I will be very insulted if you don't take these. You've been very good to me this year."

Not wanting to hurt her feelings, he muttered "Thanks" clumsily. But as soon as she was gone, he got on the phone to Terry Hulse, his supervisor in Covington, and asked him for advice on what to do with a gift from an informant. Hulse told him not to worry, just to write a memo about it and put the stuff in the safe. But he also wondered whether Mark was worried about more than a pair of sneakers and a shirt. "Is there anything going on with this girl?" he asked.

Mark considered his response for a moment before replying,

"Well, she has made her intentions known, if that's what y

His supervisor didn't seem concerned. "Just be careful, told him. "And do good work. See that she testifies."

Seeing that she testified was the main reason he had been going the trouble of sustaining his relationship with Susan, who he had come to believe was a loose cannon. She continued to shoot her mouth off about working for the FBI. What little information she had managed to pass on since the Cat Eyes arrest—mostly tips on small-scale criminal activities in the Tug Valley—wasn't worth the effort. Partly thanks to connections he'd developed through her, and partly thanks to his own hard work, he had a growing network of informants. Mark was grateful to Susan, but he was looking forward to putting an end to his work with her as soon as the trial was over. Because she had, indeed, made her intentions known.

It was during their last meeting, in December, before he'd gone to Connecticut. He had been driving Susan home and, as was their routine practice, pulled off on a mountain siding to talk. She seemed unusually pleased with herself. "I lost ten pounds, you know."

He hadn't noticed, but he told her, "Jeez, you look terrific."

"I started running every night, just like you. Just in case you're interested."

"Interested in what?"

"Oh, like a little fling." She gave him a coy look.

"Susan, I'm a married man. I got a new kid on the way. I can't be doing stuff like that."

She persisted. "Come on. I like you, you like me, right?"

"What about Kathy, Susan? She's your friend, for God's sake."

"Why's she have to know?"

Mark started the car and tried to make light of the situation, but he realized that his relationship with Susan—which necessarily involved elements of flirting—had become confused, in her mind if not in his.

Nevertheless, he had to work closely with Susan as the trial date for Cat Eyes Lockhart approached. She was apprehensive about testifying, but she seemed to take comfort in the implicit protection offered by her alliance with Mark. Sometimes Susan managed to talk her younger brother Billy Joe Daniels, known as Bo, into driving her the thirty-five miles from Freeburn, a task that he resented. Bo had already decided that his sister and Mark Putnam were sexually involved.

rial valiantly. The fact that a local woman
l to testify was the talk of the courthouse.
nitting it in front of everybody was some-
impressive coup for Mark.

g her positive identification of the shot-
n's case. Cat Eyes was found guilty and

A FEW weeks after the trial Dan Brennan was due to be transferred out. Mark considered the possibility that his replacement, Ron Poole—an agent coming down from the Chicago office, with a reputation as a good undercover investigator who liked to handle drug cases—might be the man to solve his problem with Susan. Most of Susan's tips lately had to do with drug cases. If his new partner was interested, he'd be able to pass Susan on to him, neatly solving a problem with a gracious gesture of welcome besides.

Brennan asked Mark to accompany him to the Landmark motel to meet Poole, who was staying there while he found a place to live.

Brennan had already met him, and he had a word of caution on their short drive across town. "This guy's a little, uh, different from what you would expect in an agent," he said tentatively.

Mark soon understood what he meant. At over three hundred pounds, with shaggy hair, perspiring heavily, Ron Poole looked like a hill-town school crossing guard on a patronage job. Maybe this guy does such great undercover work because the last thing you'd take him for is an agent, Mark thought. It was clear from the start that this was going to be an uneasy relationship.

Poole obviously cultivated his unruly image and let Mark know right away that he had no intention of "carrying" a rookie. He said that he worked alone, without interference, which suited Mark fine. Poole also let it be known immediately that he had been transferred out of the Chicago office after receiving threats on his life by drug dealers. He was, in fact, an agent who delivered, but it was apparent that his superiors preferred to keep him at arm's length, even if it meant teaming him with a rookie in a remote office without on-site supervision.

A few days after Poole arrived, Terry Hulse phoned Mark to sound him out on his new partner, whom he extolled for his investigative expertise and bravery. But Mark's impression was that there might have been a certain laxness in the paperwork.

Does he want me to cover for this character? Mark asked himself. But all he said was, "I'll do anything I can to help."

HOWEVER skeptical Poole was about being teamed with an agent who he thought looked like a magazine model, he had to concede that Mark had obviously managed to put together sources, not the least interesting of which was Susan Smith. And Putnam certainly was amiable enough. Even his wife had made a real effort to make Poole feel welcome in Pikeville.

Kathy asked Mark to invite Poole to the house for dinner. Poole eagerly accepted. He spent much of the time regaling them with war stories about his undercover work in Chicago. He also discussed his weight problem. Immediately sympathetic, Kathy described the diet-and-exercise regimen she'd used to firm up after having the baby.

A few nights later, when Mark was working late, Kathy was surprised to get a call from Poole, asking if he could borrow a diet book she had mentioned at dinner. They talked mostly about diets, but also about the long hours Mark put in. Innocently she mentioned that she was looking forward to the day they would get out of Pikeville.

Poole reiterated his experience in Chicago, when he was transferred after receiving threats. "That's all you need," he pointed out in a tone that sounded almost hopeful. "You'd be out the next day."

It occurred to her that Poole might be jealous of Mark, and she wondered whether she should warn her husband about him. When Poole phoned a few nights later to thank her for the diet book, he told her that he appreciated the help and added that he'd make it a practice to check on her when Mark was working late. In short order Ron Poole had joined Kathy's group of regular nighttime callers.

In the meantime Mark was looking forward to the time when he could pass Susan along to Ron Poole, but his supervisor cautioned him to think about her proven value to his career.

"Listen, you started out with a bang down there," Hulse told him. "You were there a few months, and you got this informant. And she actually *testified*. Keep on this woman. Look at the potential!"

Mark agreed about the potential; he just didn't want to be the one to develop it any further. He was stretched too thin already. But he felt his resistance weakening in the face of Hulse's blandishments.

Later, annoyed with himself for not standing his ground, Mark tried to assess his position. As fond as he had become of her, he was uneasy about Susan, professionally and personally. But every time he decided she had outlived her usefulness, she managed to come up with something to make him reconsider. For example, one day in the spring of 1988 she sauntered in with new information. She named two men who she said were planning to rob a bank in Phelps, on the way to Freeburn. Overwhelmed with work on the chop-shop case, worried about Charlie Trotter wavering as an informant, Mark didn't want to encourage her. He knew she was broke and desperate to get back into action, but he didn't have the time or the energy to coddle her.

"Susan, how do you know they're going to rob the bank?"

She insisted that she had heard it directly from one of the robbers himself. She identified the man as an uncle of Cat Eyes'.

This sounded preposterous to Mark. "Susan, he knows you testified against Cat Eyes. Why would he tell you that?"

"Well, he wants to get in my pants."

Everybody wants to get in her drawers, he thought. "Susan, I can't believe this, that he would tell you something like that."

She insisted it was true. She said she had driven the man to the bank herself to look it over. To prove to him that she was not working for the FBI anymore, she had even given him the gun that he planned to use in the robbery.

"No way," Mark told Poole when she left. He wrote up a standard note summarizing what she had said, and forgot about it.

A week later Mark went to Washington for a few days of work on a case involving a fugitive terrorist. He was in the office of the FBI Technical Services Division when an urgent phone call from Poole interrupted him.

"The bank in Phelps got robbed!" Poole cried. "What the hell do I do? I don't even know where this place is!"

Mark groaned and suggested, "Call Susan."

Poole was happy to do just that. In his conversations with Kathy, he'd made it clear to her that Susan interested him greatly. He'd also said that he believed Susan was in love with Mark—which came as no surprise to Kathy, since Susan herself had confided the same thing. Kathy thought it pathetic rather than threatening. Kathy warned

Poole, who was separated from his wife, not to get involved. But Poole snapped that he could take care of himself, and hung up.

For her part, Susan realized that Mark was shunting her aside, and the knowledge only made her more miserable.

"Poole wants me to work with him on these drug cases, but I need to work with Mark," Susan told Kathy through angry tears.

But the bureau money was there, of course—and Susan was desperate to put enough together to move out of the house she shared with Kenneth into an apartment in Pikeville with her two children. So she began working small drug cases with Poole.

BY THE summer, Kathy decided that it was time for a real vacation. Except for the Christmas trip back home when little Mark was born, they hadn't been away together since before Mark went into the academy. Kathy had quietly squirreled away enough money to do it right. She announced to Mark that she had already made the arrangements. Like it or not, they were going to a place they had visited once and loved: Myrtle Beach, a resort on the coast of South Carolina. At first he resisted mightily, insisting that his workload was too staggering even to think about getting away. She was adamant.

In August they packed up the car and the kids and drove across the Appalachians and the coastal plain beyond to the sandy sweep of Myrtle Beach, where they spent ten glorious days. The vacation was a sun-drenched island of peace, serenity, and intense joy in their still young marriage, but it would be their last.

# 6

THE night after they returned, Poole phoned to tell Kathy that the bureau was cutting back on spending and that "first-office agents," such as Mark, were now likely to spend four or five years in one place before being relocated to an office of their choice.

Kathy was crying when Mark came home. He didn't want to talk about it. Instead, he read Danielle her bedtime story and went out for a longer run than usual. While he was out, the phone rang.

"Is this the FBI's wife?" a gruff voice said.

"Who's calling?"

"Just this—your old man's fooling around with a girl named Susan Smith. That's all." The caller hung up.

When Mark came back, she tried to talk to him about Susan. But all he would say was, "Don't be ridiculous."

MARK, in fact, was enraged by the rumors about him and Susan, not only because they weren't true but because they confirmed that he had allowed the situation to get out of control. He felt himself sinking under the weight of his inexperience and hubris. At the same time, at home with two small children, in a place she had come to despise, besieged by an increasingly distraught Susan, annoyed by constant calls from Poole and Trotter, Kathy had fixed her hopes on getting out soon. Not having that to look forward to plunged her into a depression that deepened as the sunlight began its steady fade into fall.

Meanwhile, Susan, dejected about Mark's indifference, depending on pills to lift her spirits in the morning and to put her to sleep at night, told anyone in Freeburn who would listen that Mark Putnam was in love with her and was planning to leave his wife. In Pikeville she did everything she could to encourage the notion, now widespread in the courthouse, that she and Mark were having an affair.

Mark understood that some of this was his own fault. He did presume a degree of possession toward Susan. He wondered whether he was exploiting Susan's trust just to prove that he had, in fact, fit in.

Susan gave him no room to maneuver, and none, either, to Kathy, who had begun to take her calls not with the attitude of a concerned friend but with that of a worker for a crisis hot line.

Susan's family was furious with her because her testimony had sent a local boy to prison. As she became brazen in her insistence that she would continue her work as an informant for the FBI, the abuse from Kenneth intensified. She made no attempt to put on a brave front with Mark. "My family doesn't like this at all," she told him. "They don't talk to me anymore. Somebody gives me a hard time in a bar, they won't come to my rescue. Shelby doesn't agree with me working with a Yankee cop."

Shelby Jean Ward was Susan's older sister. Often, during her battles with Kenneth, Susan stayed at her house in Freeburn. Mark had only spoken to Shelby on the phone a few times, when he needed to reach Susan. He was aware of her animosity toward him.

As the situation deteriorated, Susan's calls to Kathy became frantic. Kathy hardly even mentioned them to her husband anymore, although she did pay attention when Susan told her how "close" she had become to Mark. There was no denying now what she meant. Kathy discounted it as drug-induced fantasy, but still warned her husband, "Don't you ever get involved with this woman."

He scoffed, "Kat—"

She was furious at him for a naïveté that she had once found charming. "She will get pregnant, and she will ruin you."

"Kathy, I'm not stupid. I love you."

WHATEVER its social risks, informing for the FBI at least paid well. Shortly after the raid on the chop-shop site, Mark had counted out $5000 in hundred-dollar bills for Charlie Trotter's work—bringing his total to $11,000—with more to come after indictments and a trial. Yet Charlie was already broke and calling regularly, clamoring for more. He had spent most of the money on prostitutes and cocaine.

Susan, however, had lost hers to Kenneth, with whom she was still trying to live. In the fall Mark had given her another $4000, which he said was payment for assisting Poole on his drug cases, as well as for the work on the Phelps bank robbery. In reality it was charity. Kathy had been pleading Susan's case—Susan was afraid of Kenneth, she needed to find a place to live—and Mark knew there would be no problem getting the bureau to approve another $4000. But Susan didn't use the money to move out. Instead, she phoned Kathy to say that Kenneth had claimed half of it for drug debts he said she owed. The other half had gone to a used car. Kenneth had taken that, too.

Kathy wondered if it was hopeless.

Mark insisted that it was. Yet he had no stomach for the scene that Susan would undoubtedly make if he tried to break the connection cleanly. Trying to foist her off on Poole wasn't going to solve the problem, either. Susan hated working with Poole and said so. On paper Susan's cooperation continued to look good, but Mark was worried about the lengths to which she would go to ensure her usefulness. The Phelps bank robbery was a case in point. Susan had helped solve the case for the FBI, but she had also helped to *plan* the robbery, entrapping Cat Eyes' uncle. What, Mark worried, would she do next?

But he was busy elsewhere, mostly over in Letcher County. There, while working the chop-shop investigation, he was trying to make inroads into political corruption that would dovetail with a secret federal investigation he'd learned about. Letcher County, where anything and anyone could be bought, was an excellent place to do that.

He wasn't aware of the fabulous new stories Susan had been circulating in the Tug Valley. Unable so far to interest him in her sexually, Susan had simply wished it true. To hear Susan tell it—her sister Shelby was hearing all of the details now, as Susan spent many nights at her house—Mark had fallen deeply in love with her. They had gone to motels, even to his house (Kathy, she said, was often in Connecticut), where they had sexual romps that lasted until dawn. Susan told people that she had already been pregnant by him but miscarried. Still, there was plenty of time for more—a lifetime, in fact, since Susan maintained that he was going to divorce Kathy to marry her.

In Freeburn people knew Susan well enough to assume that only about half of what she said was true. But there was at least a suspicion that *some* of it was true. Shelby was furious at Susan's imprudence and warned her to forget about the FBI man. Kenneth also showed his disapproval but less benignly. As Susan had already made clear to Kathy, without fully explaining why, he beat her.

Alarmed, unable to turn her back on Susan, Kathy championed her cause to Mark, urging him to do whatever he could to help her.

Late one afternoon at the end of October, Susan called Kathy to tell her she was in the hospital. Kathy was afraid she'd been beaten again, but Susan assured her she was in only "for tests" because she was "run down" and needed to "build myself up because I lost too much weight." Kathy was considering telling her what she really thought, that she needed to cut out the pills and cocaine, when Susan suddenly burst into tears. "Nobody has been out to see me since I got here," she whimpered. "I haven't even heard from my family."

Kathy bought a get-well card, signed it, had Danielle write her name on it in her big child's scrawl, and handed it to Mark when he got in that night. He didn't want to sign it. He was even less happy when Kathy suggested that he deliver it. Kathy insisted. "You owe her, Mark. Aren't you going to visit her?"

"No way. This is business, not personal."

"Well, I think you should, Mark. That girl has helped you out. I think you owe it to her to at least go see her."

He acquiesced, but he was annoyed at Kathy's interference. Yes, he felt sorry for Susan. Yes, her work had put a feather in his cap—she had delivered, no argument. But she had also been paid well. As far as he was concerned, it was time to move on.

Unhappily Mark drove out to the hospital in Williamson, where he found Susan alone in a double room, pale and thin, but animated. She giggled over the card, then put it on the nightstand. Tugging at his hand, she said, "Why don't you climb into bed with me? Ain't nobody else in this room. The door shuts."

"Susan, that would be a major mistake. You know that."

"Not if nobody ever found out," she said.

He managed to change the subject. But on the drive home he found himself reflecting on the offer. She made it sound so simple. Pure submission, he thought. In his beleaguered frame of mind it had an appealing lack of ambiguity. Quickly he put Susan out of his mind and forced himself to think about his troubles.

He had come to see that the career potential in the chop-shop case could cut both ways. The U.S. Attorney's office in Lexington, exercising particular caution in assembling the case because of its possible use as a springboard for bigger things down the road, hadn't yet come up with the indictments of the Mullins gang. In Letcher County the delay was being read differently. On the one-year anniversary of the raid, noting that no suspects had been charged, a Letcher County newspaper had printed a story suggesting that not only certain local police officers but the "federal boys" as well had been paid off for protection. Mark was infuriated by the story, and he took it very personally, since it was the first time in his life that he had ever been accused of wrongdoing.

The pilfering of material from the site was so routine that it had become a local joke that the stuff was cheaper now than it was when Vernon Mullins was selling it. Mark was convinced, though he had no evidence, that at least one of the local cops was involved. He didn't know whom he could trust, and so he trusted no one.

He left the house early one morning and saw that all four tires of the Olds had been flattened. That was the first warning that the line between work and home had been erased. Another came when he was chopping firewood in the driveway one Sunday afternoon. He was interrupted by the light tapping of a car horn. At the curb, Poole had pulled up in the Bronco, with Susan beside him in the front seat. They waved, but he turned his back and strode into the house.

He confronted Poole in the office the next morning.

"Why in hell did you bring her to my house, Ron?"

"We were out for a drive, and she wanted to see where you live, old buddy. That's all."

"Don't you *ever* bring an informant to my house. Do you hear me, Ron?" Poole muttered that he'd meant no harm.

Mark warned Kathy to be careful. He wasn't the only one. Kathy was picking up Danielle's toys in the driveway one day when a woman who lived across the street, and who hadn't been particularly friendly in the past, came over.

"I know your husband's got that case in Letcher," the neighbor said. "You should tell him to be very careful; that's probably the worst county there is. My brother was shot and killed up there."

At the end of the day Kathy was standing at the kitchen sink, pouring milk into the baby's bottle, when she happened to glance at the window. She was startled to see a man looking directly at her. He grinned, showing missing front teeth. He wore a knit cap over stringy, greasy hair. She dropped the milk carton into the sink and in a panic grabbed the loaded .357 that Mark kept on the top pantry shelf. She glanced at Mark junior in the playpen, then yelled up at Danielle, "Stay in your room, honey."

Kathy slipped out the front door, took a breath, and edged around the corner of the house. She faced the intruder, clutching the gun with both hands.

"Don't you move!" she ordered.

Shocked, the stranger raised his hands as high as he could. "Okay, lady! Okay!" he said, practically choking on the words. From the corner of her eye she saw a figure flee behind the bushes next door.

"What are you doing looking in my window?" she shrieked.

His eyes were wide. "Okay, okay, lady. We was just a-fixing the cable wire." He turned to look for his partner.

"I said don't move!" she shouted. But then she saw the spool of heavy wire on the ground beside the patio.

"I was just looking in to see was anybody home," the man said in a high-pitched voice. "Let you know we was working back here."

She lowered the gun to her side. On the man's shirt was the logo of the local cable television company. Feeling foolish, she let loose on him. "Why didn't you simply ring the doorbell and let me know you were out here? Looking into windows. How stupid can you be?"

Just then Mark's car pulled into the driveway. They watched him approach quickly. "What's going on here, Kat?"

"This idiot. I almost shot him. He was looking in the window!"

Scowling, Mark realized that his wife had threatened to shoot an innocent laborer. He thought fast. The best way to defuse the situation was with an effective offense. No point in letting the guy see himself as a victim, he decided. Let him think he's getting off easily. Mark flashed his badge at the stranger, who looked it over carefully. "What's going on here, friend?" Mark asked in an accusatory tone, while casually taking the gun from his wife.

"I'm just a-fixing the wires, mister, and she comes out wanting to shoot me. I didn't do nothing."

"Don't you think it might be a little better to go to the front door and knock instead of looking in the window?"

"Yes, sir, buddy. We should of thought of that."

"Next time you will, right?"

"Sure will."

When the cable truck pulled away, Mark marched Kathy into the house. She felt her face burning. He tried to make a joke out of it. "Hey, Kat—I know they raised the rates, but you can't be holding the cable company at gunpoint, you know."

She was not amused. "You bastard!"

He went upstairs, pointedly taking the .357 with him. She banged around in the kitchen in a rage. How could her marriage come to this? How had she become so ridiculously afraid?

He trotted back downstairs and stretched, ready for his run before dinner. She snapped on the light and fumed, unwilling to speak.

"Come on, don't you think you're overreacting a little?" he said, patting her behind and trying to hug her. But she pushed him away and said sharply, "Don't patronize me, damn it!"

His expression darkened. "You knew what we were getting into from the beginning. You took this on, Kathy."

"I didn't take *this* on," she said, flinging a gesture toward the window. "I did my best, Mark. But I didn't bargain for this."

"Pull yourself together, Kathy," he shouted.

That did it. She threw down the fork she'd been using to fix Danielle's plate, grabbed her coat and her keys, and rushed for the door in tears. As she backed out of the driveway, she screamed at the woman next door, who was peering from her window.

A few miles out of town, on Route 23, she acknowledged that she had nowhere to go. On her way back home she pulled off in the dark near the sway bridge over the Levisa and sat there smoking, waiting for her heart to stop pounding. She forced herself to think of the last really happy time she could remember, in Myrtle Beach: sunlight on the faces of her husband and children, a startling blue sky, the surf breaking in clean white curls, walks in the cool night sand.

As she calmed down, she told herself she was overreacting. She remembered the lectures they gave for agents' wives at the academy before their husbands started training: "Know what you are getting into. The pressures of a cop's life are intense. Marriages fail. Keeping them working requires constant vigilance."

A car rattling over the bridge made her look up. Feeling the chill, she turned on the engine and went home.

When she arrived, the warmth of the house seemed artificial. In her cotton Strawberry Shortcake nightgown Danielle bared tiny white teeth to show that she'd brushed them; Mark played with the baby, who tottered into a castle of plastic blocks his father had built.

"Gonna get you!" she heard Mark say with a laugh, pretending to chase the kids up the steps.

Breathing shallowly, she sat down. The phone rang.

"Hello, Susan, how are you?" Kathy said in a monotone.

Mark caught her eye, shaking his head.

"Sure, Susan, he's right here." She slammed the phone into his chest. Wordlessly she went upstairs to check on the kids.

Mark was still on the phone when she came down, speaking in the intimate tone a man uses with his wife. "I know that, Susan. I know. I *know*. Susan, don't say that. You know that's not true."

When Kathy stepped into his sight, his tone became firmer. "If you don't want to work with Ron, just tell him. It's that simple."

Mark put the phone down with a shrug. "She hung up," he said, coming into the kitchen, where Kathy was busy with the dishes.

"What's wrong with her now?" she asked in a bored voice.

"You know, I really feel sorry for her. She's a good kid. She's just so screwed up." He went on about Susan's problems and was surprised to see his wife's face show disgust.

"You are too close to her," she snapped, as if she herself hadn't been encouraging Susan. "What's she doing for you now? You're finished with her, Mark. I thought you wanted to get her off the books. She doesn't want to let go—I can see the way she's working you. Everybody knows her game. You know how naïve you can be."

Calmly he picked up the leather billfold with his badge from the counter and tossed it onto the table. "Hey, you know so much, the job's yours. Put on the badge. Why don't you show me how it's done."

He slammed the door and went out for a run.

While he was gone, the phone rang again. This time it was Ron Poole, who heard her sniffles and asked what was wrong. Grateful for the sympathy, she blurted out her misery.

Poole lectured her sternly. "How many times have I told you? You don't have to put up with this. What are you waiting for, shots through the window? You've had threats. Those boys in Letcher County play hardball. Who do you think let the air out of your tires?"

"Mark says—"

"*Listen to me!* All that husband of yours has to do is talk to Terry about the threats. Tell them you're scared. They'll get you out. I mean it. I'll back you up. You'll be gone in a heartbeat."

"Mark says there's not enough of a real threat—"

"Mark says! What does he know, a rookie worried about his boss? *You're* smart. You do not have to stay here."

When Mark came back, he found his wife taking a hot bath, deep in thought. She asked him to close the door and leave her alone.

# 7

KATHY had come to the conclusion that Poole was right. The threat she felt to the safety of her family was genuine, no matter how amplified it was by her anguish about having to remain in Pikeville as her marriage drifted away from its moorings.

Mark didn't see it that way. He thought he could handle the situation without endangering anyone, which she knew was probably true. Besides, he was adamant about not wanting to look like a quitter.

So Poole's advice to take matters into her own hands made sense to her, even though she saw that it was offered mostly to serve his own agenda. Poole disliked Mark. Mark was intensely competitive and determined to shine in the estimation of his superiors, which made Poole look bad. Furthermore, Poole's interest in Susan was obvious— but poor, misguided Susan was in love with Mark.

The situation was crazy. They'd paid their dues. It was time to intervene for the sake of her husband, their children, and her marriage. It was time to get them out. The problem was, she didn't know how to do it without driving her husband further away.

AN ODD opportunity to force the issue presented itself in the second week of November, when Kathy's sister, Chris, flew up from Florida to visit for a week and offered to baby-sit. Kathy and Mark went out to dinner. Afterward they stopped for a drink at the cocktail lounge of the Landmark motel, the most popular nightspot in Pikeville.

As they entered the crowded lounge through a haze of cigarette smoke, Mark saw a familiar face at a nearby table.

"That's the guy I pointed out on television," he whispered, trying to ignore the man's wave.

Kathy squinted to recognize a local politician from a forlorn coal town in Letcher County. Mark knew him through one of his informants. When the official had been interviewed by the local media about a minor story out of Letcher County, Mark had pointed him out to Kathy as a man involved in cocaine dealing, saying, "That's one of the guys I'd like to get talking."

There were no vacant tables in sight, and the man kept beckoning. "We'll stop for a minute and leave," Mark muttered. "What's up?" he said as the politician scraped to his feet, practically sweeping Kathy onto a stool with a broad gesture of hospitality. Kathy was wearing a low-cut sweater and a short skirt. She was uncomfortably aware that their new companion was staring at her thighs.

"Why don't you sit down and let me buy you a drink?" the man offered, flashing Mark a look that said, Wife or girlfriend?

Mark explained, "This is my wife, Kathy."

The official was planning to go home soon and suggested they take the table when he left. But first they should have a drink. A round was ordered. The two men spoke for a few minutes; then Mark spotted a local businessman he wanted to talk to at the bar and excused himself. He kept an eye on the table, though, and noticed with some amusement that the official edged closer to his wife.

Kathy, meanwhile, was trying to think. Watching her companion light his cigarette with a flourish, she reconsidered Poole's advice—"Get involved in something. I'll help get you out of here." She wondered if she was looking at opportunity leering at her across the table.

"What about you, little lady?" he asked, his voice oddly high pitched. "Do you just sit there looking pretty, or do you say something?"

"When I have something to say, I say it," she said.

He moved close enough on the stool to press his thigh against her. She flinched but covered by saying, "I saw you on television."

"And did you like what you saw?"

"Actually, yes. I remember telling my husband, 'Now, this man is a *politician.* Not like the windbags that we have back east.' "

His leg was rubbing against hers. "Why do you sleep with a cop?" he asked, deciding to be blunt.

"I married him." She had her swizzle stick between her lips and ran her tongue languidly around its tip, not believing what she was doing. He looked at it, transfixed.

At that point Kathy pressed her leg conclusively against his. Boldly he said, "Honey, your husband don't know what he's got."

She smiled beautifully and led him on, telling him that she was bored, lonely, and looking for some fun. "It's been a long time," she said. "My husband is always working, and I think he finds what he needs somewhere else, if you know what I mean." He did. Soon Kathy had deftly brought the subject around to cocaine. "It's a lot better when you do coke first," she said with a small sigh.

"Hell, you didn't never touch no coke."

"Sure I did, back east. But now I'm an agent's wife. There aren't many chances to make a connection these days."

"Hell, that ain't no problem around here."

They stopped talking and looked up innocently as Mark approached the table with another round of beers. When the politician got up to go to the men's room, Kathy had a gleam in her eye. "Mark, this guy is doing a lot of talking. I could find out anything I want."

The prospect was enticing, but Mark was cautious. "Don't say a word. If he wants to talk, let him talk." She winked.

"Believe me, Kat," Mark said sternly. "He's smarter than he looks. When he comes back, I'll walk away again. Let him talk. But watch yourself. Just listen."

Kathy shot him a sharp glare and said, "Just get out of my face, Mark!" He stiffened, but then felt their companion looming behind his shoulder. Frowning, Mark made another excuse to leave. He placed himself in a group of people, where he could keep a discerning watch on the man. After a few minutes Mark saw him get up and leave Kathy alone at the table. Then he came back. In a moment Kathy sat bolt upright, and the two shook hands. With a quick glance around the room the Letcher County politician walked out.

Mark raced back. She was putting her coat on and handed him his. "What's going on?" Mark said, hurrying out the door behind her.

"We got talking about drugs," Kathy said when they reached the car. "I told him that I like to party, but can't because of my husband being who he is. I told him everything has to be discreet."

"What did he say?"

She giggled, imitating the official's twang. " 'You can trust me, sweet thang. You sit tight for a minute, and I'll be right back.' "

"And?"

"And this." She opened her pocketbook and showed him a wrinkled plastic bag on top. "Mark, he put a gram of coke in my pocketbook. He said there was more, anytime I was interested."

"What! Are you sure? Do you know how bad we want this guy?" Then he stiffened, glancing furtively around the darkened parking lot, suddenly afraid that she had been set up. "Don't touch it!" he ordered. "Let's get out of here."

It was well after midnight. Despite the hour, they drove to the office a few blocks away, where Mark phoned Terry Hulse at home in Covington. Hulse took it in stride, if a bit groggily. He instructed Mark to phone Poole and have him come down immediately to witness Mark's securing the cocaine in the office safe. Hulse added that he would want to interview Kathy himself "to see if this leads us anywhere."

When Poole arrived, unhappy to have been called out of bed, Mark locked up the cocaine, which was, in fact, two grams, along with a cocktail napkin on which the man had written his phone number for Kathy.

It was after three by the time they got home and into bed. They talked a little about the implications of her stunt. Entrapping a local politician certainly had allure—once a man with connections started talking, there was no telling where the lines could lead. Yet Mark was irritated by his wife's impetuous intervention. He figured that Kathy could make her statement for the record. Beyond that, he wasn't prepared for any further involvement by her. He drifted off to sleep.

Kathy stayed awake, her mind churning. The encounter had shown her an opening—there was just enough danger in it. If she involved herself in an actual sting, wouldn't that be the key to a transfer? She figured she knew what she was doing. All she needed was the chance.

It appeared as if she were going to get it, too. On Monday morning Hulse and another agent drove down to Pikeville to take her statement. They came to the house without Mark, who was instructed to wait in the office.

"I can get this guy," Kathy said. "He told me he would get together whenever I want. The only thing is, I have to call my shot soon, one way or the other, so he doesn't smell a setup." They didn't chuckle condescendingly, as she had feared they would. Instead, they spoke quietly and earnestly of the wisdom of allowing an agent's wife to participate in what would be a significant drug bust.

Saying he would be in touch, Hulse left with his colleague.

Mark was furious when Hulse told him about the conversation with Kathy. "We've got two small kids," Mark said in a testy tone that he never thought he would take with his boss. "I'm not letting my wife get involved in this kind of thing. Would you let *your* wife get involved in something like this?"

Hulse shook his head understandingly. "Yeah, I see your point."

But Kathy kept at it until Mark relented and called Hulse to say that she was available to take the next step, which would be to set up a meeting by phone. Under bureau orders, Poole came to their house with a tape recorder to supervise the call.

"That coke was really good," Kathy said during the short conversation. The man was smart enough not to incriminate himself on the phone. But he did say he would be glad to meet her somewhere. She told him she'd call when she knew she could get away.

The ball was in the bureau's court. Hulse told them he would have to notify the U.S. Attorney's office in Lexington. Meanwhile, Kathy was instructed to avoid any contact with the target. The long Thanksgiving weekend was coming up, and a decision about pursuing the matter had to wait.

Kathy was feeling a lot better now that she had at least taken some initiative, no matter what came of it, and she found herself looking forward to the holiday. She always liked to cook a big dinner for Thanksgiving, which was something of a problem in Pikeville because their social circle was small. But Kathy had a thought. When Mark came home from work, she suggested, "Why don't we invite Susan and her kids for Thanksgiving dinner?"

"I don't want an informant in this house," he said. "All I want is a day off to be with my family. I don't even want the phone to ring."

As it happened, Susan called that night, but her conversation wasn't about Thanksgiving or finding a place to live. It was about Kathy's encounter with the man from Letcher County. Kathy was astonished to hear her rattling off most of the details of the possible sting operation.

"How did you find out about that?" Kathy asked with alarm.

"Oh," Susan said offhandedly. "Ron Poole told me."

Kathy was flabbergasted. Without telling Mark, she called Poole at home and demanded to know why he had given such sensitive information to Susan. Poole exploded in anger, "I didn't tell her anything. Your *husband* probably did. Don't you *ever* talk to me like that. I'll tell you something else. Your husband has been f___ing me over on two of my cases. Tell him he better smarten up."

Kathy didn't know what to say. It was obvious to her that Mark wouldn't have told Susan. But she was stunned to hear what sounded like a threat from her husband's partner.

THE week after Thanksgiving, Mark got a call asking him and Kathy to come to a meeting to discuss the sting. They argued about it all the way to Lexington, where they met with the U.S. Attorney, Louis De-Falaise, and two assistants. Terry Hulse was also there. It was apparent that the men had discussed the idea and liked it. Mark was appalled.

It was decided that Kathy would be authorized to call and arrange a buy. Details were to be worked out in the coming week.

After the meeting Hulse, who had begun to share Mark's misgivings, sent a message to FBI headquarters summarizing the plan and requesting authorization for an agent's wife to go undercover.

The Putnams were hardly back home when they got the word. A reply to Hulse's Teletype message had rocketed back from Washington with flames coming off it. No one had ever heard of such a lamebrained idea. Relieved, Hulse called off the plan immediately.

OUT of the hospital and back with Kenneth, Susan needed money. More than that, she needed attention from Mark. Sadly aware that she had exhausted—or alienated—the sources of information she had used in the Tug, she knew that she had to develop a new forte to rejuvenate her career as an informant for Mark.

Poole suggested that if nothing in Pike County was working, she might look to her drug connections up north. She'd mentioned a cop she and Kenneth had gotten to know when they lived in Cicero, Illinois—a cop heavily into drug traffic. That was worth considering, Poole said.

Susan figured it was worth a try. First she made a call to Cicero to ascertain that the cop was still active. He was. She then called Mark to tell him she had important information on a new case.

She met him at McDonald's. They sat in the car in the parking lot while she described the scenario she had in mind, which involved infiltrating a major urban cocaine-and-crack operation run by a cop and drawing its connections to the Tug Valley.

Susan told him that she had already discussed the situation with Poole. That was fine, Mark said. Poole knew the Chicago drug scene. When Mark mentioned to his partner what Susan was considering, Poole brightened at the prospect of joining them on such a case. They decided it could work—if Susan was able to deliver a crooked cop engaged in interstate drug trafficking. Poole figured he could pose as her boyfriend and help her to infiltrate the operation.

There was a problem, however. Susan still didn't want to work with Poole.

A week before Christmas, Mark drove Susan into the hills north of Pikeville to a place where they had stopped to talk in the past—a clearing just off an abandoned coal-mine road. Mark had been brooding about his difficulties, professional and personal. Nothing was working out; nothing was being resolved. Susan could sense his mood.

It was late afternoon. The sun had dropped behind the mountains, and the air was cold. He let the engine run while Susan talked, taking notes. Then he felt Susan's hand resting lightly on his shoulder.

"Is there something wrong? You seem way out in left field, honey."

She had not called him that before.

"Oh, you know, everybody's got problems, Susan."

"I know there's problems at home. Kathy tells me about them."

He was not happy to hear that. How often did they talk?

"She's feeling as bad as you are, honey, but there isn't anything you can do about that right now. You have got to have somebody, and maybe for right now I'm that person for you. Whatever I can do to help you feel better about yourself, I intend to do. You helped me a lot. A lot. Now it's your turn for attention."

As she leaned toward him, he noticed a gold chain with a tiny cross she wore. She was rubbing his neck now, and he rolled his head to feel it.

"God, are you tense. Anytime you need a release, I'm around."

"I appreciate that, Susan. But I don't think that would accomplish anything. It would just dig me in deeper, you know? I'm already in pretty deep." He didn't know exactly what he was trying to tell her.

She moved close to him, kissed him, stroked the inside of his thigh. "I think you should make love to me right now, Mark."

"I don't think that would be a good idea, Susan."

"I think it's too late for that, honey. Just relax."

Why the hell not? he thought. Why the holy hell not?

HE DIDN'T see her for a few days after that. He told himself it had been nothing. Quick, passionless, detached.

He knew what a fraud he was a few days later, when he drove her out to the place again, like a horny teenager. Afterward he said he would take her home to Freeburn.

"You seem upset," she said as they drove back onto the main road.

"I am. I'm pissed off at myself, not at you." He stroked her hair lightly. "I betrayed myself, my wife, my kids, and my job."

She laughed at his gloom. "Mark, honey, you take yourself entirely too seriously. It wasn't no—any—big deal."

YEARS later Mark would insist that they had had sex no more than five times over a two-week period, always in his car. Then, aghast at his carelessness and disgusted with himself, he broke off the relationship.

Characteristically, instead of confronting Susan, he chose to avoid her, leaving her to wonder what had happened.

Kathy never suspected that her husband was having an affair. Nevertheless, around Christmastime she detected a change in Susan's attitude. She wasn't calling as often, and when she did call, she didn't talk much. She was cordial and correct. "She seemed like she was on top of the world for once," Kathy would later recall. Kathy was heartened by the improvement. At least, she thought, *something* seemed to be getting better.

Kathy wished she could say the same about her own situation, which had deteriorated rapidly. Later she would struggle to analyze the breakdown, trying to sort out its causes. What parts were depression and paranoia, and what parts were a reasonable psychological response to real threats?

This much was sure: there were deliberate attempts to frighten her. The most terrifying came in the middle of January, with Mark out of town on a bureau training session. The phone rang around midnight. Picking it up, Kathy heard a voice growl, "We ain't sure whose side who is on no more. We think you been sleeping with cops too long. You're alone with them babies tonight, ain't you?" Frantically she grabbed the .357 from the shelf and stormed around the house snapping off lights. She spent the night on the living-room floor in the dark, with the gun aimed at the door.

On February 2 there was another late-night call, at four thirty a.m.—this one from Kenneth. Although Kathy had never spoken to the man before, he wasted no time on social niceties with her.

"Kathy, this is Kenneth. You listening?"

"Kenneth?" she said huskily. She gestured to Mark in the dim glow of the night-light.

She heard scuffling. Susan, crying hysterically, grabbed the phone. Gasping, she said, "Kathy, I'm so sorry that he did this. He doesn't understand. Kenneth, *quit it!*" There was more struggling and the sound of a sudden crash. Kenneth got on again long enough to blurt out the astonishing declaration that Susan had been pregnant—by Mark. "Is that all right with you, Kathy!" Kenneth shouted. "Is that all right with you?" His message delivered, he apparently handed the phone to Susan, who stammered through sobs, "He found out I was pregnant and lost it last month, and he says it was Mark's baby. It ain't true. I swear, Kathy. I told you how jealous he is."

Kathy said nothing, trying to clear her head. Mark was looking at her apprehensively. Kathy heard Kenneth shout something about a private detective, about pictures of Mark and Susan coming out of a motel, before Mark took the phone from his wife's hand and said sharply but with a measure of stern control, "Kenneth, you can't call people up raving like this." Mark listened quietly for a moment more and said, "Kenneth, I am just not going to listen to this." He dropped the receiver into its cradle.

Kathy and Mark were silent for a full minute while she listened to him breathe.

"Mark?" she said. "I thought she couldn't have any more kids."

He exhaled heavily. "What are you talking about?"

"She told me there were complications with the last one. That she couldn't have any more."

"So what's your point?" There was wariness in his voice.

"Well, now she says she was pregnant last month and lost it."

Mark was silent.

"Mark? Kenneth said it was your baby."

She was nursing a brief doubt, but discounted it as a reaction to being awakened in the middle of the night. She had already considered the possibility that Mark might have slept with Susan. She had asked him in the fall point-blank: "You didn't have sex with this woman, did you?" His reply had made her feel both foolish and disloyal. "Of course not, Kathy. How well do you know me?" She didn't see a need to ask him again.

Still, there was Susan's newfound air of assurance. She was less desperate in her need to glean everything she could about Mark from Kathy, as if she already knew all she wanted to. If she didn't know better, Kathy would have described her manner as *possessive* of him.

"Mark?"

"Kathy, you don't learn, do you? Leave it alone," he said. "Okay? It's not even worth discussing. They're both whapped out on drugs."

He pulled the blanket over his shoulder and went to sleep.

AND then, astonishingly, it was over. After more than a year the indictments in the chop-shop case were handed up. In February 1989 Vernon Mullins; his nephew, Charles Edward Tackett; his son, Michael; and four other Letcher County men were charged with conspiracy to violate federal law by receiving, possessing, concealing, storing, and altering the identification numbers on stolen motor vehicles and equipment that had crossed interstate boundaries. They all pleaded not guilty.

In early March a detention hearing was held in the federal courthouse in Pikeville. Tom Self, the assistant U.S. Attorney who would prosecute the case, asked that the men be held without bail and specified that Vernon Mullins and Charles Tackett presented a threat to the community.

Almost frantically Kathy began to apply fierce pressure on her husband to make his own case in court. Less reluctant now that the indictments were in place, but still uneasy because he believed he was stretching the facts, Mark testified at the detention hearing that the defendants presented a danger to his family. He alluded to information from Charlie Trotter that some of the defendants had made veiled threats against him, his wife, and his children.

The judge allowed the men to go free on bail after warning them not to have any contact with Mark or his family.

But the implied threat was enough for Hulse. After the hearing he sent a memo to his supervisor in the Lexington office to request that Mark and his family be transferred. Noting the threats, Hulse added that Trotter had been working "both sides of the fence" and had told Mark that Mullins knew "where Putnam lives and what bedroom Mark and his wife sleep in, as well as his daughter."

Within days it was over. Kathy barely had time to pack. The bureau sent the movers in and ordered her and the children to leave, with Mark to follow in a few weeks. They were going to Miami.

Kathy thought it was like hitting the lottery.

# 8

WITH Mark gone, Susan was more disposed to return the attentions of Ron Poole, which gratified the beefy FBI agent. With Susan he could have an attractive woman at his side, as well as the possibility of undercover assistance that could lead him out of Mark's shadow. As Poole had discovered, sometimes she actually delivered.

Susan had her own agenda, but it fit Poole's, too. She was lonely, afraid, and destitute. He offered friendship, protection, status of sorts—and income. She understood the game well enough to know that she needed to provide sufficient information to establish her credentials. Then she would be back in business.

But this was no easy thing to accomplish in the remote hills of southern Appalachia. Cocaine was a complicated city-based industry involving financing, manufacture, import, wholesale distribution, and retailing. Only the end of the process had any appreciable base in a sparsely populated rural area. It had been a long time since Susan ran with the city crowd; most of her friends had forgotten her. She tried to rewire her connections, but in the urban drug business Susan Smith of Freeburn, Kentucky, wasn't a high priority.

By spring her sense of rejection was nearly total. She had been measuring her days with whatever drugs she could obtain and with self-destructive visits to Kenneth. One or two nights a week she drove across the river to stay with him and be with her children. She and Kenneth fought constantly; she got the worst of it, but she always came back.

The rest of the time, Susan was living with Shelby and her husband, Ike, in Freeburn, where she watched television incessantly. Shelby was distressed that Susan's favorite program was *Miami Vice*, featuring handsome cops fighting crime in the subtropical settings of Florida.

In the ramshackle jumble of Freeburn, Susan retreated into fantasies. Her romance with Mark had been more than a couple of quick tumbles in a car with a good-looking man having troubles at home. No. They had been happy lovers for two years. It was only a matter of time until they would be together; even now he was down in Miami making the arrangements to leave his wife and marry her. As was her habit, Susan shared this fantasy with anyone who would listen.

What's more, she was pregnant with his child, she told people. Why, they even had names for the baby she carried: Mark, if it was a boy; Markella for a girl. It did not seem to matter that Mark already had a namesake. In Florida it would all work out. It might be complicated, though, given her activities as an undercover informant on major drug cases. Susan even suggested to a few people that they should not worry if she disappeared. That was how the federal Witness Protection Program worked.

Susan told some of her stories at a beauty shop in Freeburn. She did not know that the older women had begun to look at her with pity. Her girlish audacity and brassy boasts had once been a diversion, but now she seemed shrill, desperate, and somehow past her prime.

The women talked among themselves about how different she had become with her children, on whom she once doted, seven-year-old Miranda especially. They got slaps across the face for interrupting, and they had learned to wait for her silently in the beauty parlor, their eyes watchful.

EARLY in May, Susan filed charges with the police against her ex-husband. She said that in one of his rages Kenneth had tied her up and dragged her through the house in West Virginia. He called her a whore from his car outside Shelby's house, and when she got in to settle him down, he drove off, shoving her out the door a few blocks away. She said that he threatened to shoot her.

Kenneth retaliated by reporting her to the West Virginia welfare office for receiving benefits from two states. As a result she lost her West Virginia check and was left with the $249 a month from Kentucky. Desperate for cash, she turned to Pikeville.

Almost every Thursday night she took a room in a motel on the four-lane out of Pikeville. A motel night clerk later recalled that Susan was working as a prostitute. "It was obvious what she was doing," the woman said. "She was always with a different man."

Adrift, frightened, strung out on whatever cocaine and amphetamines she could scrounge, Susan was coming perilously close to the end of the line. In the middle of May, Susan was beaten up by Sherri Justice, Cat Eyes Lockhart's girlfriend, who threatened to kill her. The beating was witnessed by Kenneth, Susan's brother Tennis, and Tennis' girlfriend.

Confused and battered, Susan sought protection from the FBI man who was still in her life, Ron Poole. As she did, she focused the blame for her problems on the one who had walked out of it—Mark Putnam.

In April, in a telephone call to Mark in the Fort Lauderdale hotel where the bureau had put the Putnams up while they found a new place to live, Susan had told him that she was pregnant and asked what he intended to do about it. Stunned, Mark asked her if she was sure. She said she was. He was due to come back to Pikeville to finish up work on the chop-shop trial. They would talk then, he promised.

The call from Susan shattered any illusions he had about leaving Pikeville behind. He had convinced himself that the affair with Susan was a mistake that he had gotten away with. All he could do, he decided, was keep the trouble to himself and find a way to work it out.

Mark was actually scheduled for two trips back to Pikeville for pretrial hearings on the chop-shop case. During the first—a stay of only a few days in May 1989—he managed to avoid seeing Susan, who didn't find out he had been back in Kentucky until after he left.

Shelby had been pressing her sister to confront Mark about the pregnancy, but Susan had been afraid. After he had gone, Susan lied to Shelby, saying that she had seen him. She said they'd argued and he had tried to push her out of a car, just as Kenneth had done.

The next time Mark was scheduled to return to Pikeville, on June 5—this time for a few weeks of work—Ron Poole made sure that Susan was forewarned.

On Tuesday, May 30, Susan went to the public health center in Pikeville to have a pregnancy test and get a report confirming it. Based on what she said, the doctor who interviewed her gave her an estimated due date of November 19—indicating that the date of conception had been near the end of February. The doctor also noted that Susan had had a miscarriage and a D and C on January 2, 1989. Susan took the report to Poole, who made a photocopy of it.

That weekend, Susan visited her children at Kenneth's place. It was the last time they would see her.

On June 4 Mark Putnam, full of dread, boarded a flight in Fort Lauderdale. The chop-shop investigation that had consumed him for eighteen months, and on which he had staked his personal reputation, was nearly ready for trial. And waiting for him in Pikeville was a woman threatening to expose him as a fraud and an adulterer.

On the plane he wondered how he had blown it all so easily and with so little thought to the consequences. He shut his eyes and considered how he had disgraced himself, his family, and his badge.

A man who couldn't tolerate even small failings in himself, Mark was staggered by a big one. How could he possibly explain it when they came to him with the proof? He had compromised the bureau.

There would be a scandal. Was resigning the only way? Could he simply say, "Look, guys, I screwed up. I'm sorry. Give me my punishment. I won't mess up again"? No, he could not.

He did not consider discussing this problem with the person who knew him best and loved him unconditionally—his wife. He was in a terrible jam, but he would face it, and somehow overcome it, alone. Having never ever been in trouble before, Mark Putnam simply did not know how to ask for help.

IN HUNTINGTON, West Virginia, which has the closest commercial airport to Pikeville, a hundred miles away, he rented a Ford Tempo and told the clerk that he expected to keep it for about three weeks.

As Mark drove gloomily south, Ron Poole hurried out to Freeburn to meet Susan. He had arranged a room for her at the Landmark motel. Another person was already there on the FBI's tab. Charlie Trotter, the nervous star witness in the chop-shop case, had been salted away there for weeks, to keep him out of trouble. Mark knew he was going to see Charlie at the Landmark. Susan would be a surprise.

AFTER a restless night at the Landmark, Mark walked into the FBI office in downtown Pikeville and found Ron Poole on the phone.

"Hey, guess who's here," Poole boomed into the phone. Mark's heart sank. Winking, Poole handed over the receiver as if he were doing Mark a favor.

Susan's voice had a brittle edge. "We are going to get together, aren't we?"

Mark tried to keep his voice down. "Susan, I'll be here for at least three weeks. We'll hook up, I promise you."

"It'd better be soon, damn it. I'm sick of this. You f___d me over."

The hostility surprised him as much as the crudity. Susan had always tried to be civil and "proper" in front of Mark, even when she was in a fury about something. That pretense was gone.

"Yes," he said patiently. "We'll talk, Susan."

Poole tossed him a sly smile when he hung up and said, "Hey, buddy, hand me that piece of yellow paper on the desk?"

Mark picked up the document. It was dated May 30; on the top was Susan's childish signature, and at the bottom, that of a technician at the Pike County Health Center. It read, in part:

I fully understand that if the pregnancy test reading is NEGA-TIVE, it does not necessarily mean that I am not pregnant. I also fully understand that if the pregnancy test reading is POSITIVE, this does not necessarily mean that I am pregnant. False positive readings can occur for such reasons as misinterpretation of re-sults, undiagnosed medical problems. I have been informed that in order to lessen the chance of serious problems it is my respon-sibility to have the test results confirmed by a physician before considering myself pregnant or nonpregnant.

At the bottom was the notation "TEST RESULTS POSITIVE."

Mark felt sick. He glared at his ex-partner. Why was Poole involved in this? How many other people had he shown the report to? Clearly this was not going to be a private matter between him and Susan. She was pregnant, sure enough. And he was the father, she said. Given the proof of one premise, he accepted the other.

Mark got back to the motel in the early evening. He went down for something to eat, called Kathy and the kids, and climbed into bed to watch television. After a while the phone rang. Susan.

"Where are you?" he said. The connection from Freeburn was usually slightly fuzzy; now it sounded as if she were next door.

"I'm in the motel," she said. "I need to talk to you."

"Susan, I'm beat to hell. I have to be up at five to drive to Lexing-ton. I promise you, we'll talk when I get back tomorrow."

"We are going to talk about this. Don't think we're not!" She abruptly ended the conversation.

HE WAS up before dawn. He did not look forward to the three-hour drive to Lexington, where Tom Self, a prosecutor known for being methodical, wanted to conduct intensive reviews of the evidence be-fore the trial, which was scheduled to begin in late June.

Mark was there at nine and felt greatly put out to learn that Self had been called to court. He cooled his heels for six hours in the U.S. Attorney's office. When Self came in around three, he only had a few minutes to talk. He asked Mark to come back the next day.

No sooner was Mark back at the motel, showered, and trying to relax, when Susan stormed in. Her mood clearly hadn't improved any, and her eyes were bloodshot.

"You're avoiding me," she said.

"Hello to you, too, Susan. How are you?"

"Don't give me that. We are going to *talk*."

"Listen, Susan, I am beat to hell. I just can't do it now."

"That's just like you. You put everything before me. I should have killed them all when I had the chance."

"Killed who?"

She shrugged.

It was obvious that Susan was high. Afraid of a commotion, he asked her if she wanted to go out to McDonald's for something to eat. With that an amazing transformation occurred—the old Susan came back. They ate in the car and talked. Crying now, she poured out her misery. She described the beatings by Kenneth, by Sherri Justice. Shelby and Ike were threatening to turn her out. She had no money. Kenneth was keeping her children away from her. And he, Mark, a man she had trusted, had gotten her pregnant and abandoned her.

"Would you consider having an abortion?" he asked.

She most certainly would not. The fury came back. He could see no solution. As he took her back to the motel, he glanced at her and thought, If this is my kid, she's five months pregnant. The last time was before January. Shouldn't she be showing? But he dismissed the thought as craven and wishful. She went back to her room without replying when he said he would find more time to discuss it next week.

MARK found Charlie Trotter sitting in a lawn chair outside the room where Poole had installed him a month earlier. Living at the Landmark was an arrangement Charlie liked just fine, and not only for the security it offered. He considered it the height of luxury to be able to pick up the phone, order a sirloin and a six-pack, and, when they came, sign a piece of paper saying the U.S. government was buying.

But Charlie had gone jittery. He told Mark that he was afraid the "Letcher County boys" were watching him. A couple of them, he thought, had been driving by every night. "They know where I am, Mark," he said with grave eyes.

"Charlie, we can change motels if you want."

Charlie thought it over and said he would be okay. The FBI payment for his work was going to be substantial—$30,000, on top of the money he'd already gotten. Charlie said he would stick it out.

THE NEXT DAY, MARK AGAIN made the drive to Lexington, wasted more time waiting for a meeting that could have been handled on the phone, and made the long trip back. When he got to his room, it was nearly nine o'clock. Too tired to eat, he pulled down the bedspread and lay on the bed. His eyelids drooped and closed. He had been asleep for about a half hour when the phone went off.

"Hello!" he barked, more forcefully than he had intended.

"Heeeey! How's it going, buddy?" Poole asked.

Trying to conceal his annoyance, Mark said evenly, "We're all set to go with the trial, Ron."

"You talked the stuff over with Susan?"

"No, not really, Ron," Mark replied warily. "I've been too preoccupied with this case."

"Well, I can understand that. I'll bet you can't wait to be done with that and get out of here, huh, buddy?"

"Yeah, I'm anxious to get back to Miami."

"Talk to you later," Poole said abruptly, and hung up.

Mark was annoyed at his own cordiality. Why didn't he just tell Poole to take a hike? Mark thought back to Kathy's warnings about Poole, which he had largely written off to her desperation to get out of Pikeville. "You're naïve," she had said. "This guy has his eye on Susan, and he thinks you're in his way. This guy will do you harm."

AGAIN Mark had fallen into a deep sleep, this time dreaming of his children, when the insistent ringing of the telephone broke through. It was Susan. In a slurred voice she asked, "Sleeping? You sleeping son of a bitch."

"Susan, would you shut up and let me get some sleep?"

She banged the phone down. His anger was raw now with dislocated sleep. He hated Susan, wished he had never recruited her, used her, paid her, comforted her, depended on her, and finally, stupidly, dropped his guard enough to have sex with her. That was where she had him, pregnant with his child or not, and they both knew it.

That was his abject ruin, the mortal sin for which absolution could not be had. The fact was, as he knew very well, Susan had been there when he needed her, and cared greatly for him. She helped get him on the map. Working cases, she was as patient with Mark as he had to be with her. They had always tacitly maintained the fiction of her unsullied reputation, and in a funny way, between them it was true. She had offered herself not only in desperation and desire but out of simple trust. Their passion hadn't been devoid of love, no matter how flickering and transient. Furthermore, she had shown physical and even moral courage, beyond the lure of the $9000, to turn against people she would have to face for the rest of her life. Mark knew that his sacred career had benefitted substantially. She was an indelible part of his record.

Now she was charging hard at him—hostile, impatient, unreasonable, and dangerous. It was going to be like working the bomb squad; disarming her would be tricky, especially with Poole lurking in the background. It could blow up in his face at any time.

He thought of what she had said the other night: "I'm going to be a thorn in your ass, Mark. I'm coming down to Florida to make sure you don't forget me."

# 9

**M**ARK had pulled the motel-room curtains tight the night before, but they did not fit the window well, and the gloom seeped in with the dawn. He opened his eyes and looked at stains on the ceiling.

At least it was June. By noon the sun would be high enough in the sky that the light came over the hilltops. The trees were full and green on the mountains. Spring was a good time to sell a house in Pikeville, although now spring was almost over and still their place on Cedar Creek remained unsold. Tending to the house was another of the unwelcome chores Mark had to do before he could go home.

He turned over and pressed his face into the pillow, imagining south Florida—Danielle hopping off her bike to run to him in the front yard when he got home from work, Kathy happy again, little Mark bright and mischievous, a miniature of his old man. It had taken a lot to get there; all he wanted now was to get back.

Kicking off the thin blanket, Mark sat up on the edge of the bed, feeling sore and dizzy. He made his way to the bathroom. In the shower the spray was weak, but at least the water was hot. He closed his eyes and let the water beat on his face.

There was a pounding on the door as he was drying off. He

wrapped a towel around his waist and had barely pulled back the dime-store bolt when Susan pushed her way in, red-eyed.

"Don't you look nice," she said, smiling broadly and tugging at the towel till it came off. "Is that your new *Miami Vice* outfit?"

"Hello, Susan," Mark said wearily. "You're up early."

She brushed past him and went to the bed. He turned to face her, thinking she didn't look pregnant in her shorts and University of Kentucky T-shirt. When had Kathy started to show? He couldn't recall.

"I've got to leave for Lexington in five minutes, Susan."

"Are you avoiding me again, Mark?" Susan demanded, planting herself on the bed. "How many times do you and those guys need to meet, anyway? Why didn't you just get a room up in Lexington?"

"Because I wanted to straighten out some problems here, Susan," he said pointedly.

"Don't give me that bull, Mark."

He walked over to put a hand on her shoulder and was surprised to feel her flinch. "We'll talk this weekend, okay?" he said. "I've got to get dressed and get out of here."

When he came out of the bathroom, she was still sitting on the edge of the bed. "I've got to go, Susan."

"Wait, wait. I need to borrow a pair of shorts," she said.

"For what?"

"I didn't bring enough clothes with me. You'll get them back."

This didn't make any sense, but he wasn't in the mood to argue. He grabbed his bulging files off the top of the television and caught her injured look in the dingy mirror. "Okay. Grab your shorts, and close the door when you leave," he called back as he went out.

As he shut the door, he heard her mutter, "Bastard."

IN LEXINGTON, he was once again kept waiting until late in the afternoon. Though Mark resented having his time wasted, he regarded Tom Self as one of his few mentors in eastern Kentucky. Trying to please him during a prosecution was like trying to get an A from a particularly exacting teacher. Often he would ask Mark to go back and reinterview people he had already talked with, to fill in more detail. Self never let investigators relax until the jury adjourned.

The chop-shop case was solid and ready to go, assuming Charlie Trotter didn't bolt. Still, it was never a sure thing with a mountain

jury. Mark never forgot his first trial, when witness after witness osten-
tatiously crossed his fingers as he swore on a Bible while the judge
pretended not to notice.

He also knew that the bureau was watching this case carefully—
after all the time and trouble, after the emergency transfer out of
town, he knew that he had to bring a clean conviction to the table.

Feeling that he had wasted another day, he started back into the
hills around five o'clock. As the afternoon sun edged the ragged
mountains and cast deep shadows over the valleys, he realized that
the past two and a half years had caught up with him—everything,
even his nightly three-mile run, seemed to take extra effort. In a
month he would be thirty. He no longer felt young.

SUSAN waited all afternoon for Mark to return. Every fifteen minutes
after four o'clock she left her room and stood on the balcony of the
motel, looking for his car.

Mark saw her at the railing when he turned into the parking lot. At
the end of a frustrating day he was furious to know that the next thing
he could expect was a confrontation. He went up to his room, with
Susan hard on his heels.

She followed him inside and stood by the door. She had changed
into his gray gym shorts and T-shirt since their morning encounter.

"Are we going to talk about your baby now?" she said.

"Not tonight, Susan. Please. I have some calls to make, and I need
to spend some time with Charlie."

He was surprised when she sauntered out without a commotion.

Mark made a few calls and then walked down to talk with Charlie
Trotter, again installed in his lawn chair. "It's going to be tough
looking them boys in the eye when I'm on the stand," Charlie said.

Charlie slumped in the chair and turned slightly away, which Mark
recognized as a sign of inner conflict, signaling a potential for deceit.
"Give empathy, not sympathy," he recalled from his classes on psychological manipulation of informants and suspects.

"Charlie," he said, "I won't even try to understand what you're
going through right now. Just do the best you can, man." He stood
up and clapped Charlie on the leg. "What do you say we grab something to eat and have a few beers? Uncle Sam's buying."

"Already et," Charlie said.

A LITTLE LATER SUSAN THUMPED at Mark's door. She stood at the threshold with her arms crossed over her breasts. He knew she was high. She lunged at him the moment he shut the door behind her, slapping him hard across the cheek. She was crying.

"You're avoiding me. High-and-mighty FBI—I'll see you burn in hell!"

Spit flecked the corners of her mouth. Her hair was unkempt. Another ten years and forty pounds, he thought, and this was a woman framed in defeat in the doorway of a mobile home, yelling at the kids. "Now you are going to pay for it!" she vowed.

He wasn't sure what she meant, but he looked around quickly to make sure his gun was in the bureau drawer.

"I'm not having no abortion," she screamed.

"Susan, I understand about the abortion," he said, struggling to control the situation. "If this is my baby, I don't want you to bring up that child. Kathy and I would raise it."

He had not anticipated making such a suggestion; immediately he regretted the hurt the words caused.

Susan was sobbing. "I am a good mother. This is your baby, Mark."

"Susan, keep it down. I don't want the neighbors to know our business."

That let her regain the offensive. She stamped her foot. "The damn neighbors? You're so concerned with your reputation? Your reputation ain't nothing now, Miami Vice!"

Her pupils were dilated. Whatever was going on, he wanted to negate her ability to threaten him with a public scene. Exhaling loudly, he suggested, "Look, let's go for a ride and cool off." She surprised him by taking his hand as if he had asked for a date.

They drove deep into the mountains, talking but getting nowhere. Again and again he asked her what she expected of him. Susan's replies were threats. She insisted that the baby was his and that she would tell the FBI, his wife, and his children about it. But unless it was to renounce everything else and stay with her forever, he could not figure out what she wanted him to do.

"Ron says they'll fire you when they find out," Susan said.

He bristled at that. "What about Ron?"

But she backed off. "Nothing. He didn't say nothing. They will fire you, though, Mr. FBI."

He kept quiet, but he believed that what she said was true—that was the real threat.

He had instinctively driven out Route 23 and turned off onto the seclusion of Route 119, the only good road east into the Tug Valley. At Meta he turned right onto Route 194, a narrow two-lane that winds into the rugged hills that border the valley.

The closer they got to Freeburn, the more distraught Susan became. As they approached the crest of Peter Creek Mountain, she suddenly lunged across the seat at him, slapping him with both hands. Fighting to keep control of the car, he made a right turn onto a coal-road turnoff. Stones rattled under the car as he drove about fifty yards up the road. He shut off the engine and the lights, and silence fell with the darkness. Mark rolled the window down and felt the air cool his hot cheeks and burning eyes.

Placing his hand on Susan's shoulder, he said, "Let's try and work this out instead of acting like a couple of idiots." This was exactly the kind of setting that had led to sex on other occasions, but even the intimation of affection now caused Susan to recoil in revulsion.

"What's gotten into you, Susan?"

"What do you mean *me?* You're messing with me, Mark. I know that now. I don't know why I didn't see it before. I'll be damned if I'm going to let you prance down to Florida with your little wife and your spoiled kids to resume your wonderful life. You owe me, buddy!"

He had the sense that these were lines someone else had given her. Susan was a verbal chameleon. Buddy wasn't a word she normally used, and Mark thought he knew where she had picked it up.

"Susan, I've given you everything I could. Leave Kathy and my kids out of this."

"You sure did give me everything you got," she said, patting her belly. He watched this, thinking again that she did not look pregnant.

"And now I'm going to have a little Mark junior," Susan went on. "I'm going to bring this baby down to Florida and knock on your door and put the little bastard right into your precious daughter's arms. I can't wait to see the look in your wife's eyes. Then I'm going to your FBI *Miami Vice* office and tell your new friends there how you solved your cases by f---ing an informant and leaving her pregnant to look after herself in Kentucky. I own you, Putnam! I own you and your precious job. Ron says they'll fire you and Kathy will leave you!"

"Susan, just tell me what you want from me. From day one, all you've done is feel sorry for yourself." His heart was pounding.

Suddenly Susan was all business. "We are going to have this baby. You will be there when it's born and sign the birth certificate as its daddy. You will leave that whore Kathy and those spoiled kids and marry me. If you don't, I'll ruin your life." She smiled triumphantly.

Mark went for the immediate opening. Kathy hadn't done any injury to Susan. Kathy had been Susan's friend. "Hold it, damn it. If you ever call my wife a whore again, I'll smack the s___ out of you."

"You don't have the balls to hit me, Mark. You're no man. You're nothing—you're nothing but a spoiled rich kid!"

This floored him. He thought of his father, taking on odd jobs to scrape together the thousand dollars a year that wasn't covered by his scholarship at Pomfret. The insult infuriated him. He smacked Susan across the face. The blow barely fazed her.

"Well, the little boy hit a woman! That's the first real emotion I ever seen in you. I hope I didn't hurt your delicate little hand."

He was breathing in gulps. Sweat burned his eyes. She kept at him. "The only reason I worked with you was because I saw how pitiful you were. Seen how they sent a pretty little Yankee boy down here with real men. All the cops used to make fun of the pretty Yankee boy who wanted to work all the time." Delighted to have found a vein, she stabbed at it: "They laughed at you behind your back!"

"You're a bitch, Susan, you know that?" he said, desperate to control the quiver in his voice.

"Oh, the great one spoke out! My hero spoke!" Her breath was sour on his face. "Your life sure ain't so perfect now, is it, honey?"

He tried reasoning again. "Okay, Susan. This is what I think about our problem—"

"*Our* problem? Oh, no, Mark. *Your* problem. I've never been happier myself. I told all my friends I'm going to have an FBI baby. I can't wait to see Kathy's face when I show her our baby."

He resisted the urge to hit her again. "Since you won't have an abortion, after the baby's born, I'll come back and take a blood test to establish paternity."

She screamed. "I ain't no whore. How dare you say that!"

"Well, that isn't what I heard, Susan. I heard your sister threw you out of her house—"

"That's not true!"

Sensing advantage, he brandished the option he had not yet even considered discussing with his wife: "If the baby is mine, Kathy and I will adopt it. You've proven what kind of a mother you are by signing over custody of your kids to that drunken ex-husband of yours."

Shrieking, she slammed into him, slapping and scratching wildly. She was on top of him, pounding down with her fists. He struggled into a dominant position, working to pin her arms.

"You bastard," Susan shrieked, flailing at him. With a guttural moan, she dug a long fingernail at his eye. Stunned by the sudden pain, he swung at her with his fist. But he missed. His hand slammed into metal on the dashboard.

Blood oozed from the gash across his knuckles. She saw the bleeding hand and bit it, with her feet pressed stiffly against the windshield. The pain was astonishing. She hissed through her teeth. He needed silence. Shut up! he thought, wrenching his hand free and grabbing her neck with both hands. He held her that way, pressing for silence, until her fury and his abated. He let out his breath steadily while she struggled weakly and then submitted to his grasp. His breath fully exhaled. His grip relaxed, and his arms fell heavily to his side.

Susan was quiet. He opened his eyes and inhaled unsteadily, his face stinging from the slaps. She was a fighter, all right. But now she was leaning against him, the fight gone.

"Susan, are you going to take it easy now?" he said, nudging her gently, as if to wake her up. "Let's go. I'll drive you home."

She slumped forward when he removed his arm. As he tried to ease her gently off the console and into the passenger seat, her neck craned at a grotesque angle.

He blinked and said, "Oh, my God. Oh, my God." He shook her. He sat her back and pounded on her chest. "Susan! Susan!" He tried blowing air into her mouth, but her lips were cool and unyielding. He pounded on her chest and felt frantically for a pulse. Then he knew that she was dead and he had killed her.

He cradled her head and rocked back and forth, sobbing. I have killed this person, he thought in disbelief. A mother of two children. This woman in my arms.

Trembling uncontrollably, he got out of the car, as if to walk away from it. The door slammed, and the sound reverberated from black-faced mountain walls. He screamed; that came back, too, with the same empty echo. He fell back against the car, hearing only his breathing and the grunts of bullfrogs in the brush.

He got back into the car and replayed the scene in his mind, looking for excuses—the threats, the fury, the tears, the blows and flailing arms. He went over the story he would tell to the state police or, better yet, Bertie Hatfield, the deputy sheriff who had introduced him to Susan. He would expect no special treatment. He would take his medicine. Bertie would know what to do. He would tell him how to break it to Kathy. Kathy would tell the kids.

Another image crept into his mind—that of Danielle as an infant, three or four weeks old. It was the time of their marriage when he and Kathy were happiest. He was working a day job clerking in a liquor store, nights clerking at the FBI in Hartford. When he came home after work at one o'clock one morning, the baby lay curled in her crib. Gently he woke her, and she smiled at him sleepily. He scooped her tiny, sweet-smelling body into his arms, held her to his chest, and whispered hoarsely, "I am going to be the best father I can be. You will always be proud of me. I promise you that, Danielle."

One life was destroyed. Why destroy the rest? He was on a lonely mountain road. Not a single car had passed. Furthermore, they hadn't seen anyone else when they left the motel. Chances were, no one even knew that he and Susan had gone out together.

He got out and walked around the car several times. All of my life, he thought, I stayed out of trouble. I kept my nose clean. Now he was on a mountaintop with the body of a woman he had killed.

He ran to the passenger door, opened it, and struggled to lift her out, astonished at how heavy she was. He had eased the body almost out of the car when it abruptly toppled to the ground, the head hitting the gravel with a whack. Mark screamed in fright, as if he had injured her anew. He fell to his knees and cradled her head, rocking on his heels, praying, She is not dead. She is badly injured, in a terrible coma. It would be horrible, there would be some jail time, but she would be alive, and maybe someday she would forgive him.

A light drizzle materialized from the mist. The rain became heavier, beating hard on the rocks and leaves as it fell.

He saw the lights of a vehicle coming up the mountain road from far away, blurred through the rain. He watched, squatting beside his darkened car. A big yellow bulldozer lumbered into sight and passed by, emergency lights throbbing. It emitted an insistent beeping sound that changed pitch as it disappeared over the crest of the road.

At some point the rain stopped. Mark was cold, and his clothes were drenched; he had no idea how much time had passed. With the end of the rain the sky was full of stars.

It was time to go. Shakily, his muscles aching, he managed to lift Susan's body into the trunk of the car. Laying a hand on her small breast, he said, "Susan, Susan, how did we ever let this happen?"

## 10

MARK drove through the fog that lay in the valley, both hands locked on top of the steering wheel. He had decided to go back to his motel room and wait. He wasn't sure what he would wait for, but he needed time to consider any options beyond the single judgment that blared in his mind: You are done, pal. You are done!

There was the service revolver, of course. It lay in the motel-room drawer where he had left it. He diverted himself for a moment with the idea of putting the barrel in his mouth and pulling the trigger, but it was not a real consideration. He took inventory, standing at the mirror like a suspect in a lineup. He had wrapped a towel around his damaged hand. The index finger throbbed. Susan had fought hard; he could see scratches on his arms and some on his jaw and neck. He looked as if he had been in a fight.

It was almost three o'clock. He took a shower, dressed, walked across the road to the all-night convenience store and bought some Band-Aids and antiseptic. When he returned to the motel, he dressed the cut and got into bed. For the rest of the night he stayed awake and alert. He couldn't think of anything to do except to go on with the day and see what happened. He had no idea what he would do about the body.

In the morning he forced himself out of bed, and an hour later he was surprised to find himself in the car, dressed and shaved, his briefcase on the seat beside him, holding it steady at fifty-five on the Mountain Parkway into Lexington. The sun was shining brightly. For the first time, he noticed the long crack in the windshield on the passenger side. He thought about Susan in the trunk.

This meeting with the assistant U.S. Attorney was long and detailed. Somehow he got through it. Around lunchtime Tom Self sat back and asked what had happened to his hand, and to his amazement, Mark heard himself saying, "I was out to our old house in Pikeville, taking care of a mess in the garage, and I ripped it on a nail."

He watched Self's reaction carefully, and it didn't show anything other than friendly concern. Was it that easy to lie? As a kid, anytime he had told a lie, no matter how inconsequential, his red face had always given him away. Now that he was a killer, had it become easy?

Self kept him occupied all day with the minutiae of the chop-shop case. If he noticed the scratches on Mark's neck, he did not mention them. In fact, Self seemed completely comfortable with him. Mark realized that people, even those with sharp police instincts, can overlook a lot when their guard is down.

By the time Self turned him loose, it was after four. From the courthouse steps Mark spotted his car, alone on a side street. He approached it uneasily. Off and on during the day he had wondered about the smell, figuring that if someone noticed and called the cops, that would be it. Amazingly, there was no smell yet; the trunk was tight.

It was not yet seven o'clock when he got back to Pikeville. He found himself sitting in the car, engine off, in a parking slot in front of the state police barracks. He had no idea how he'd gotten there. Numbly he stared at the lighted windows. Lieutenant Paul Maynard, the supervisor of the post's detective squad, usually stayed late. Maynard was a friend. Maynard would hear him out, at least, and maybe he'd have some advice to offer before he put the cuffs on.

He forced himself to think through the contempt and rage that seeped into his consciousness. Okay, hotshot, here you are with a body in the trunk. Now what? Without realizing it he was mouthing the words, as if addressing himself from nearby. But nobody caught you yet. Nobody *knows* yet. Why not wait and see what happens? He argued with himself for a while, then started the car and drove off.

He took the four-lane north out of town. Just down from Marlow Tackett's country-western bar he turned right onto Harmons Branch, a side road he and Susan had taken before. About a half mile up was the first mine road, now unused. Beside it was a ravine with a small creek at the bottom, thick with weeds. The area wasn't isolated, but he knew that not many cars used the road.

When he turned in to the spot he knew and stopped the car, he could hear the brittle noise of dirt bikes—kids racing up and down one of the mine roads. He couldn't see them, but they were not far away. This was where he would put her, at the edge of a ravine thick with brush and saplings. This, he figured, was where she'd be found.

THE body was heavy. His arms trembled; it was impossible to be gentle. Using his legs for leverage, he dragged her a little way down the ravine, just out of sight from the road. His feet got tangled in roots; he stumbled and fell with a shout. He began to cry. Then, getting a better hold under her arms, he pulled her down the hill as far as he could. They were about fifteen feet below the roadbed now, and this is where she would stay—barely concealed, like his guilt. Kneeling beside the body, he cried, stroking her face, and said, "I'm sorry." Carefully he removed the clothes, tugging the T-shirt off. His shorts slid off easily. She wore no underwear. He did not think about whether she looked pregnant. She was barefoot; the sandals had come off in the trunk. He gathered the clothes under his arm and left her behind in the branches and leaves.

IT RAINED again that night. Holed up in his motel room, Mark managed to call his wife and children, though he could not remember what he said to them. Afterward he was very hungry. He drove to the Log Cabin, on Route 23, where he ate a steak and drank a beer.

It was here that he had his first real scare.

Myra Chico, a part-time reporter for the local radio station who knew all of the local cops, had a job tending bar there on weekend nights. She came by his table and asked, "Can you meet me after work? It's very important, Mark. I've got to talk to you about Susan."

Mark had known Myra for quite a while. He studied her pleasant expression and asked, "What time do you get off?"

"A half hour. Come on over to my place for some coffee."

He followed her home in his car, anxious and miserable, but strangely glad for the company.

He wanted a glass of 7-Up, not coffee, and when she had brought it, they sat on either end of her couch and talked.

"Do you know where Susan is?" she asked.

"No. Why?"

"Ron Poole told me she left the Landmark sometime yesterday and didn't go home."

"You know Susan."

"Listen, you got a problem, do you know that? She's pregnant. Ron showed me the test. He says you know."

"She told me."

"She's telling everybody you're the father."

"I never touched her."

"Ron asked me to ask you—he wants to stay out of it—where Susan went to."

"I don't know where Susan is."

Myra had no reason not to believe him, and none even to question him. They talked about other things. He seemed very tired, a little emotional. She figured it was the strain.

BACK at the motel, Mark fell into bed, exhausted. He switched off the lamp and tried to force everything that was bad out of his mind; after a while, with much effort, he succeeded.

The next thing he knew, it was after nine a.m. He hurried down to get a Lexington newspaper out of the box by the service elevator. On his way he pushed a plastic bag holding Susan's clothes into a trash receptacle. He scanned the headlines as he walked back to the room. There was nothing. Not today.

Numbly he pressed on with his work. The last subpoena in the chop-shop case had to be delivered to a man out in Magoffin County, which took a good part of the day. When he got back into town, it was late afternoon. The condition of the car was on his mind. He went to a service station on Route 23 and in the car-wash area vacuumed the interior of the Ford. He found an earring on the floor and fed it into the vacuum hose. Using a bottle of kitchen cleaner he had bought, he carefully washed his bloodstains from the dashboard and console. He bent down to look at the rubber floor mat on the passenger side and noticed what looked like dried mucus. He was afraid to throw out the mat in the gas station, where he could be clearly seen.

Kathy had told him to make sure he stopped by the house on Cedar Creek to check things over. On his way there he dropped the floor mat out of the car into a trash-strewn ditch.

The next day, having cleaned the car, he got rid of it. He drove back up to the Huntington airport and said that the windshield had been cracked by a chunk of coal falling off a speeding coal truck. They gave him another Ford Tempo without any problem.

ON MONDAY, three days after he'd left Susan's body in the ravine, Mark took another decisive step. He made a phone call to Shelby Jean Ward and asked whether she had heard from Susan.

"No, I haven't heard, and I'm worried. It ain't like her," Shelby said tentatively, thinking that Mark Putnam had monumental nerve expressing concern for Susan at this point. Ron Poole had kept Shelby well posted on Mark's evasiveness.

"Listen, I'm worried, too," Mark said. "I was thinking that if you don't hear from her, you should probably file a missing persons report."

"I know that. Somebody already told me I should do that."

Mark didn't need to ask who that might be.

After talking to Shelby, Mark called the Pikeville state police and spoke with Paul Maynard. Mark told Maynard that he was worried about Susan. He said she had left the motel on Thursday or Friday and not returned to her sister's house. He made sure to mention that Susan had told him she was planning to meet some of her drug contacts from up north on Saturday, when they came through West Virginia on their way south. He also told Maynard that he had called Shelby and advised her to make a missing persons report. "She thinks something may have happened to her sister."

"Mark," said Maynard, "this girl has a habit of taking off."

Aware that Poole had already told people about his problem with Susan, Mark anticipated Maynard's next thought. "Well, I've known her pretty well for two and a half years. If you need any help, send a couple of the boys to talk to me."

Shelby also phoned the state police that day. The initial report summarized her call succinctly:

SHELBY WARD of Freeburn, Kentucky, telephoned Post to report that her sister SUSAN SMITH of Freeburn, Kentucky, was missing.

Victim was brought to Pikeville by the FBI and left at the Land-mark motel. She arrived on June 5, 1989, and stayed until June 8,

1989, when she left the motel for unknown reasons. She left a few articles of clothing and makeup in the room. Her sister talked to her last about noon on June 8, 1989. FBI agents state that they do not know where she went.

A report of this kind is routinely filed for possible reference in case an unidentified body is found. It is not regarded as an indication of a crime. The standard police procedure is to wait seventy-two hours before initiating an investigation, by which time most missing people either return home, call, or turn up dead.

Susan Smith had done none of those things by the time that period expired. When Detective Richard Ray came to work on Friday morning, he found her missing persons report on his desk. On it was a note from his boss, Lieutenant Maynard, instructing him to get in touch with the woman's sister and see if anything had turned up.

The detective called Shelby and took down the information: Susan Daniels Smith; white female; twenty-seven years old; short brown hair; five feet five; one hundred and thirty pounds; tanned complexion; no occupation. Address, Freeburn, Kentucky; lives with sister, Shelby Ward; missing as of June 8. Sister last saw her wearing white shorts, blue University of Kentucky T-shirt, gold necklace with gold cross.

Ray was the kind of detective who notices the wayward rustle of a curtain or the dent on a car even when he is not working, and he detected in Shelby's voice an angry undertone. He asked her a few questions, listening intently to the answers. Then he told her he would be out to see her.

AT THE age of fifty-four Richard Ray was the most experienced detective in the Pikeville post, a distinction that gave him more leeway than most other detectives, who complained that they had to get permission for virtually every move they made away from their desks. Understaffed and chronically underfunded, the Kentucky State Police tended to keep its detectives on a short leash.

In Pike County, where the per capita felony statistics always came in near the top among the state's one hundred and twenty counties, a detective might handle a hundred and thirty or more cases a year. As a result case coverage tended to be, as one detective said, "forty miles wide and one inch deep."

Freeburn was a forty-five-minute drive away, but Ray was glad that he took the time to indulge himself on a hunch. It seemed that the missing woman had enemies. She had worked as an informant and put one local boy in the penitentiary. Yes, she had run off before, but she always called to check on her two small children, who were with their father. Ray was also interested to hear that the missing woman had been to the health center a couple of weeks earlier for a pregnancy test—and had named as the father FBI special agent Mark Putnam. Shelby explained that the other Pikeville FBI man, Ron Poole, had checked Susan into the Landmark motel so that she could confront Putnam. And then she had disappeared.

Ray knew Mark Putnam slightly. He thought of him mostly as a typical FBI man who had been taught never to trust the local cops. On the other hand, he had run into him on enough major investigations to regard him, if only grudgingly, as a hard worker who wasn't afraid to get his hands dirty.

On Monday, Mark was out of town serving a subpoena. The next day, Ray and another state police detective found him at the federal building for a pretrial hearing on the case. During lunch break they borrowed an empty office and spoke with him for about an hour.

Ray gave Mark a copy of the missing persons report. Mark read it quickly and saw that it had only routine information. In the space beside the words TATTOOS OR DEFORMITIES, he saw that Ray had printed "None," but added, between parentheses, "5 months pregnant."

Watching him, Ray thought Mark was nervous but cooperative—a little too cooperative. The detective had to scribble fast to get everything down:

> Agent Putnam told me . . . he knew Susan Smith and that she was a witness against Carl "Cat Eyes" Lockhart in the bank robbery trial. He said that Lockhart's girlfriend, Sherri Justice, had beaten up Susan while Susan's brother watched. Susan was paid about $9000 for being a witness and an informant.

Mark described Susan's dependency on him and Kathy. He said that the last significant work Susan had done for him was in the fall, but that they had stayed in touch after he went to Florida.

Mark also told the detectives that he had spoken about "her problems" with Susan at the motel several times during the week before she disappeared. He said they discussed the possibility of her having an abortion, and that he had offered to help her find the money for it. She did not want to have an abortion, Mark said.

He said that the last time he spoke with Susan was about ten thirty on Wednesday night, when she phoned his room and asked him to join her in the lounge for a drink. He told her he was too tired. She then told him about a "strange phone call" she had received about a meeting in West Virginia in a few days with drug contacts, some guys from Chicago—the amigos, she called them. She described one as a Spanish cop from Cicero. Mark said that she declined his offer to follow her to the meeting in case of trouble.

Why was Susan at the motel? Mark told the detectives that Poole had brought her there "to do some undercover work" for him.

Did Mark know for certain she was pregnant? He knew she was saying so, he said. Had she told him that he was the father? No, he replied. Furthermore, he wondered if Susan really was pregnant, since she didn't appear to be showing. Did she ever tell him who the father was? "No," said Mark. "She wouldn't tell me."

THE conversation with Putnam gave Detective Ray a lot to consider, not the least of which was the extent to which Susan had been dependent on the largesse of the FBI.

For his part, Mark fretted over the encounter, unable to decide what he would have done if they had asked him directly, "Did you have anything to do with this girl's disappearance?"

He thought that his answer might have been, "Yes."

What if they had then asked, "Did you kill her?" He tried to be honest with himself, but his mind was swimming with thoughts of guilt and survival. Before he fell into a feverish sleep, he decided that his answer might have been, "Yes. Yes, I did." But perhaps he was deceiving himself. At any rate, they hadn't asked.

MARK flew back to Florida a few days later. Then a coal-mine strike in the county turned violent, and Ray was barely able to keep track of the Susan Smith case. On June 23 he managed to get a few hours free to sit down with Ron Poole. Curiously, Poole claimed that he had been concerned about Susan's assertions that she felt threatened by both her ex-husband and Tug Valley outlaws vowing retribution for her work as an informant, and had thought that registering her at the Landmark would be a good way to look after her. But he said that his main reason for putting her in the motel was to give her and his ex-partner the opportunity to discuss her being pregnant. Poole said he was "tired of hearing about it" from Susan.

Poole, too, seemed to be excessively helpful. He even suggested that Mark come back to Pikeville to take a polygraph test. That struck the detective as a fine idea.

After his brief conversation with Poole, Ray studied his notes. There was the pregnancy and the bureau's proclivity for protecting itself, not to mention the ill-defined undercover operation that Susan was apparently telling everybody about. Maybe the FBI had stashed her in the Witness Protection Program, although Ray couldn't imagine that this particular source had information momentous enough to earn that kind of treatment.

Another complication was Susan's reputation. Even Shelby, worried as she plainly was, conceded that Susan had run off in the past without telling anyone where she was going.

Yet Ray couldn't put out of his mind how helpful Putnam had been in providing details of his activities. *Too many details.* He wondered if he would have the time to see which of them didn't check out.

Ray found the maid who had worked the second floor of the Landmark that week. She told him that the woman in room 224 had kept mostly to her room. She had not seen her with anyone. Her checkout bill, which Poole had paid, showed that she ordered room service and ate in her room. There were a couple of short local calls, and three long-distance calls to her sister in Freeburn. The maid had collected a few of Susan's clothes, her purse, and some makeup that she had left behind. The fat FBI man had taken them with him.

In July, Ray finally raised his concerns with his superiors. He was convinced it was time to formally question Putnam about Susan's disappearance. But he was told that there were better things he could be doing with his time. Putnam had long since left town; there would be no state police junkets authorized to Miami, not without a good reason. Besides, wasn't the bureau itself looking into it? Why waste time on a routine missing persons case?

The girl was wild, Ray was told again and again when he asked questions out on Peter Creek. Hadn't she run away before? Hadn't

Mark Putnam (right) at his graduation from the FBI academy, in 1987

Mark and Kathy Putnam with baby daughter, Danielle

Mark with Danielle and
Mark junior in Florida

Pikeville—population 4500—
situated in the coalfields of
eastern Kentucky

Left: Susan Smith in her seventh-grade yearbook.
Below: The adult Susan.

Barrenshea Hollow in Freeburn, Kentucky, where Susan grew up, the fifth of nine children

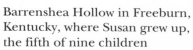

Susan's father, Sid, and her sister Shelby Ward at Susan's graveside in 1991

Mark Putnam in the courtroom of the Pike County courthouse, Pikeville, Kentucky, June 1990

she always returned? And if she was double-crossing a drug operation, she'd turn up for sure—in the morgue or Chicago.

Yes, he thought. That much was probably true.

BY AUGUST she still hadn't turned up. Ray still had only speculation and instinct to go on. If there had been any sort of unpleasant confrontation between the missing woman and either of the FBI men, he could find no one who knew about it. No one had seen Susan and Putnam together on the day she disappeared; moreover, Charlie Trotter said that Mark had made it clear he was doing everything he could to avoid her. Reasonable enough, Ray thought, since she was accusing him of getting her pregnant and running off.

The complications troubled him. He tried to separate what little he actually knew from the nagging suspicion that something was very wrong. A poor mountain girl who has been on the FBI payroll as an informant turns up missing. From the way it looks, she and this FBI man were involved; she gets knocked up, he's gone to Florida with the wife and kids. He comes back to town on government business, the FBI sets her up in the same motel. And she turns up missing.

But the FBI man isn't the only one this girl has been involved with. To hear people tell it, she gets around pretty good. She is also a wildcat who fights at the drop of a hat, and just before her disappearance she gets coldcocked by the girlfriend of the bank robber that she sent to the penitentiary. She turns up missing.

Furthermore, he thought, this is a girl messed up on drugs, whose ex-husband beats her, not to mention the other enemies she made as an informant. She ran with a bad crowd out of Chicago in the past and has supposedly been in contact with some of that crowd recently. And her sister Shelby takes a phone message for the girl, while she's in Pikeville, that she is supposed to meet some drug dealers on Saturday in West Virginia. On Friday she turns up missing.

Assuming something bad had happened to her, Ray thought, that made for a fair number of suspects. Even in normal circumstances the first suspect was always the husband or ex-husband or boyfriend. And here was an ex-husband who abused her and whom she keeps going back to. Then there were the drug dealers she was supposedly going to see. Add the bank robber's girlfriend, the bank robber's buddies, any *other* outlaws she'd informed on—and maybe even some still unidentified pillar of the Pikeville community whom she'd tried to shake down in a motel. Even without Putnam, that was a Las Vegas chorus line of star suspects—assuming she hadn't just run away.

And Ray had to assume first that she had, in fact, merely left town on her own. What he couldn't understand was why, given that—given all of the other suspects if foul play was actually the case—the earnest, well-chiseled face of Mark Putnam stayed in his mind.

# 11

THE change from Pikeville to Miami had been abrupt. Overnight they'd traded the black and gray of an Appalachian late winter for the sudden Technicolor blare of southern Florida in spring.

"Daddy, you can see the sky all over!" five-year-old Danielle had exclaimed with delight from beside the pool of the hotel where the bureau had installed them while they looked for a new house.

Kathy felt like a woman awakening from a trance. She felt young again, not haggard and ashen as she had been in the last months in Kentucky. The troubles in Pikeville swirled out of mind.

Only the phone calls intruded, and these she accepted with mild annoyance. When Susan called for Mark, as she did several times a week, Kathy exchanged a few arm's-length pleasantries, handed the phone to Mark, and walked away to do other things.

There was plenty to do. It fell largely to her to settle her family into a new home. Mark had a new job to acclimate himself to and old business in Kentucky to finish. She figured that after the chop-shop trial, Pikeville, and all that went with it, would be history.

With help from the bureau's relocation office she found a condominium in a new subdivision beside a canal. It had three bedrooms, beige walls, palmettos out front, and neighbors on either side. The town, Sunrise, lay on the fringes of the Everglades, but was only a forty-five-minute commute to the FBI office in North Miami Beach.

And then, in June, the phone calls from Susan had stopped. With so much emotional and physical distance between them, Kathy accepted the news of her disappearance impassively. She had done her best with Susan, who never had listened.

So eager was she to embrace a new life that Kathy failed to see signs that her husband was deeply troubled in the summer of 1989. He wasn't sleeping or eating normally. He was losing weight, and he had developed a nervous habit of scratching his chest, to the point where a raw patch of skin appeared on his sternum.

These symptoms she attributed partly to Mark's anxiety about establishing himself in a new job. And the echoes from Pikeville hadn't totally ceased with the end of Susan's calls. Poole still checked in, usually with word that nothing had been heard from her. Myra Chico also called from time to time to pass on Pikeville gossip.

One night, after speaking with Poole, Mark abruptly mentioned to Kathy that Susan had been saying that she was pregnant right before she disappeared. "So who's the father?" Kathy said with a trace of sarcasm. Mark shrugged his shoulders.

"When are you going to put that behind you?" she demanded. "Forget about Susan. She isn't your problem anymore."

"How can I?" he said almost plaintively.

"Look, if she's still missing, the next thing you know, Mark, you could be pulled into this. She could be lying dead somewhere."

His face darkened, and he replied quietly, without meeting her eyes, "Don't ever say that."

KATHY believed that, Mark's sluggish recovery aside, they had settled in happily. The cost of living in south Florida was higher than in Kentucky; they had to make the money stretch. To put a little aside for their next summer vacation, she took a part-time job on Saturday and Sunday mornings waiting tables at an International House of Pancakes. One of the waitresses she met there was a woman with two children, whose husband was in prison. When Kathy told Mark how sorry she felt for her, he looked away and changed the subject.

For Mark there were many such moments as he contemplated the calamity that he knew lay ahead. Yet outwardly he projected a sense of purpose. The new environment offered both the collegiality of a large group of fellow cops and the reassurance of being adequately supervised. He appreciated his circumstances with a sense of poignancy, aware that they would last only until he was exposed.

Nevertheless, he impressed his bosses. Without exception his supervisors in Miami regarded him as likable, talented, and extraordinarily hardworking. With his steady demeanor, polished manners, physical bravery, and good looks, Mark represented the FBI's image of itself. It was obvious that the young agent had a bright future.

On July 5, the day after his thirtieth birthday, not long after he got back from Pikeville, Mark was summoned to the office of the special agent in charge of the Miami bureau, William Gavin. But instead of arresting him, Gavin slid a memo across the desk from Louis De-Falaise, the U.S. Attorney for eastern Kentucky. It read in part:

> I want to formally express to you our thanks and appreciation for the work of Special Agent Mark Putnam of your Miami office. Special Agent Putnam, prior to assignment to your office, was in the Federal Bureau of Investigation office in Pikeville, Kentucky.
>
> While there only two years, his reputation for hard and diligent work left its mark. Our office had the pleasure of working closely with him and I can say confidently that he is a unique Special Agent whose career with the bureau will be long and fruitful.
>
> I want to specifically call your attention to the excellent job he just completed leading up to the successful conviction of seven defendants in the case of *U.S. v. Vernon Andrew Mullins* et al.
>
> Special Agent Putnam's departure has left a real void. You have gained a topflight agent in Miami in Mark Putnam, one who exemplifies the dedication and professionalism of a fine Special Agent. Please convey to him our devout appreciation for his service to eastern Kentucky and to our office.

Despite the new camaraderie in Mark's work life, there were no close friendships. He declined invitations to dinner, cookouts, and drinks after work. His time was running out, and he did not want to embarrass any other agent who might be close to him when the end came. As a consequence some of his new colleagues saw him as aloof—a man who could be trusted, but a hard man to get to know.

The year was full of painful irony. Once, he and Kathy invited a young agent who was having personal difficulties to dinner at their house. Warmed by the glow of affection and security he had felt in their home, the agent told everybody he saw in the office the next day what a wonderful time he'd had.

"This guy has everything—a beautiful wife, good looks, two beautiful kids, a great job," he told a group of colleagues, clapping a hand on Mark's shoulder when he came by.

If only they knew, Mark thought. He had lost fifteen pounds since the summer. Nearly every day he had diarrhea. Nights were worse. He was afraid to go to sleep. He did not know if or when he would confess. He always assumed they would find Susan and arrest him, and he was bewildered that so much time was passing without any indication that an end was in sight.

THAT winter Kathy's younger sister, Chris, came to stay with the Putnams temporarily while she was going through a divorce. Chris, as easygoing and laconic as Kathy was intense and expressive, admired Mark very much. He had helped her to find a job as an officer with the Florida Marine Patrol. She regarded him as an ideal husband and father, who had become almost a big brother to her. When she'd visited Mark and Kathy in Pikeville, she had known that their life was difficult and stressful. In Florida she didn't notice anything alarming about the way Mark was behaving.

PASSING time burnished Mark's nerve. He wondered how long he could wait. He still heard from Poole often, but Poole had his own anxieties about Susan, who had told people that she'd slept with him, too. Perhaps suspecting that Mark knew more than he let on about what had happened to Susan, Poole told Mark of Richard Ray's request, unsuccessful so far, that they be given polygraph tests.

"Ron, I don't care," Mark said boldly. "I'll take their polygraph."

Poole replied, "I'll take one, too." He added, "Well, buddy, you and I got to stick together on this thing."

What thing? Mark thought contemptuously. What did Poole feel he had to hide? It was almost amusing to think that his ex-partner was worried. For the first time, Mark felt that he had the advantage in these verbal jousts.

Still, Mark resisted the urge to probe for information on the Pikeville investigation, preferring to be seen not as disinterested but as disengaged. With Myra Chico he remained circumspect, afraid that if he gave any indication that he was worried, that anxiety would be conveyed to the state police.

Had they found the body? That was the main thing he didn't know. How could it *not* have been found, lying there just out of sight in a place where people came by on horses and dirt bikes? Maybe they had found the body and were keeping it quiet, building their case. Every time the phone rang, he jumped.

He had no respite from his obsession. Susan was the first thing he thought of every day: she flashed into his mind the moment he awoke, and she stayed there until he managed to fall asleep at night. To live with himself, he had settled on a term to describe what had happened: tragic accident.

There were frequent reminders of what he had already lost. The most painful came when his supervisor, Roy Tubergen, took him aside one afternoon to ask if he would consider a transfer to a smaller office in Florida, where he would be promoted to a supervisory rank. What would have once been fabulous news now had a bitter sting. Mark mentioned the overture to Kathy, but told her that he had turned it down because he didn't want to see his family uprooted again so soon. In his mind he knew that he was protecting the bureau from the public disgrace of having a supervisor led away in cuffs.

There had been times during the year when he had edged toward confession and pulled back. As early as September he had told Tubergen about the rumors in Kentucky that he had been sexually involved with an informant who was now listed as missing. Mark asked Tubergen if he would contact OPR, the Office of Professional Responsibility, the Justice Department's internal affairs unit, and request them to investigate the disappearance of Susan Smith to "clear up" the ambiguities associated with his relationship to her.

Literally he was told not to make a federal case out of it. A missing persons case was a state police matter. The rumors had already filtered down to Miami through the FBI grapevine, where discreet inquiries had been made to assure supervisors that Susan Smith ran with a dangerous crowd and had gone off before. Mark was seen as naïve, a young man who had been through a tough tour of duty and had acquitted himself with distinction, even if he had stupidly become involved with an informant. He was a man above suspicion.

By the winter Mark reached the point where he realized his guilt was diminishing his effectiveness as an agent.

He had been investigating an organized theft ring operating out of the port of Miami. Laboriously working informants and poring over insurance records, he made inroads until he had a suspect in a major insurance-fraud case, a man named Tito, who owned a computer-parts business. Finally Mark had enough evidence to nail the man, who tried to bluff his way through a polygraph.

"Listen," Mark said as they sat alone at a conference table in the office. "I've got documents here, with your fingerprints on the documents. You took a lie detector test and flunked it. The people who receive my report will know that you did it, and continuing to lie to me will only make it worse."

Insulted, Tito insisted that he had not lied.

Assuming a frown, Mark opened his thick folder and turned pages slowly, occasionally grunting at something he pretended to read. Out of the corner of his eye he noticed Tito was unconsciously telegraphing the classic signs of a worried man—clearing his throat, squirming, brushing imaginary dust from the table.

Mark heard the telltale sound of a sniffle and looked up expectantly. Tito met his eyes and said, "I got a wife and kid. You know how those guys down the port are. They can lean on you pretty good."

"I know what you're going through," Mark said sympathetically, thinking how nice it was to actually have a textbook example of how to usher a wavering suspect into a confession:

*You aren't the typical criminal. You seem like a man under terrible pressure. This is probably the first time you have done something like this. You seem to be basically an honest man, with a wife and kid that you obviously love. But could you put your arm around your kid right now and feel right?*

Tito started crying.

Mark looked at him with disgust that curled inward as he thought, I'm busting this guy for some lousy computers. Who the hell am I? I killed somebody. There are two kids who don't know where their mother is because of me.

"Tito, get out of here. I don't want to see you again," Mark said abruptly, standing up.

Tito was stunned. "What do you mean, man?"

"Tito, go home. Just leave me the hell alone."

Tito's feet found the floor. He backed out of the office like a court attendant and practically ran to his car in the lot.

Later that day an agent Mark passed in the hall said, by way of greeting, "How you behaving, Mark?"

"Above reproach," he said quietly.

No one looking for Susan Smith could have anticipated how many threads of her life she had left tangled. One of the first calls Richard Ray made when he began his investigation was to the man who was the source of the mysterious phone message for Susan. This man was not the drug contact from Cicero that she had been telling Mark and Poole about. He was another contact—a man from Milwaukee.

No, he told the detective, he had not met with Susan the weekend after she disappeared. In fact, she had never returned his phone call. The man said that Kenneth had called him the next week, looking for her. An FBI man also called.

Ray ventured a guess. "Poole? Ron Poole?"

"Yeah, something like that."

This should have been an indication that the FBI was investigating, but like everything else in this case, the answers were ambiguous. Although the FBI generally declines to confirm or deny whether it is investigating, Ray had determined informally that there was no "active" investigation into the case. What then was Poole doing?

Ray worked quietly and moved easily among a great range of ordinary people who felt comfortable with him because he didn't come on like a cop. Gossiping with people outside a lunch counter, he kept track of the social undercurrents of the Peter Creek communities. Usually he could get a fairly good line on current events.

Susan Smith was a tough one, though, because there were so many conflicting opinions about her. Everyone in Freeburn knew that she'd fight at the drop of a hat, that she was a heavy drug user, that she had a mouth on her. But there was another side to this woman that took a little more patience and trouble to find. She seemed also to be someone who always picked up a phone and called when she was away. Susan's mother, Tracy, said that Susan never forgot to send a birthday card, Christmas card, Mother's Day card—"no matter where she was living."

Something was not adding up.

The rumor mill also made it difficult to sort out information. Almost weekly Ray drove out to Peter Creek to check out the latest hearsay. Much of it was difficult to evaluate. He also had to consider Shelby's speculations. Perhaps, she mused once, Susan had followed Mark to Florida and was simply lying low, waiting for him. Or maybe she had gone to hide out with another sister, who lived in Texas.

On August 8, 1989, Ray had called Shelby for an update, and she told him that a man from Phelps named Johnny Stump had gotten a phone call from Susan. But when Ray drove out to see him, that turned out not to have been the case. Stump explained that Susan had bought a 1979 Ford from him and had not made the payments. He had complained about her, but he hadn't said he'd heard from her.

Bewildered, Ray decided that Shelby ought to take a polygraph test "to see if it was some kind of plot, if she knew where her sister was at." Shelby was insulted, but on August 22 she took the test and passed. The results showed that she didn't know where Susan was and that she was very worried about her. Moreover, she insisted that they ought to strap Kenneth Smith and Mark Putnam to the machine.

This proved to be no easy chore. Ray and Paul Maynard went to Captain Gary Rose, the commander of the Pikeville state police post, who in turn called Terry Hulse, Mark's former supervisor. But word came back that while the FBI would of course cooperate in any investigation to the extent it deemed necessary, it saw no reason to involve an agent. "Polygraph the ex-husband," Captain Rose said he was told. "Maybe he had something to do with it."

Meanwhile, Ray would later recall, "The FBI people just kept putting us off." What he did not know was that Mark Putnam had already approached his superiors and volunteered to take a lie detector test, and they had told him he was being silly.

In October, Kenneth Smith was sentenced to thirty days in jail for a series of motor vehicle violations. Because he was the sole guardian of seven-year-old Miranda and four-year-old Brady, the judge allowed him to serve an alternate ninety-day incarceration at his place in Freeburn. With an electronic device strapped to his leg to monitor his movements, Kenneth wasn't available to come to Pikeville to be polygraphed until January. By then Kenneth was making an effort to straighten himself out and provide a decent home for the children. He had a job as a night watchman at a strip-mining company.

On January 16 Kenneth took a lie detector test at the state police post in Pikeville. The operator believed that Kenneth was telling the truth when he said he knew nothing about what had happened to Susan, but it was difficult to get a good reading because of the drugs in Kenneth's system.

After two inconclusive tests on successive days Kenneth was kept overnight in a Pikeville motel under state police guard "to try to straighten him up." But the next day's test was not much more conclusive. Finally Ray concluded what the machine could not. Kenneth apparently didn't have a clue.

Nor long afterward Ray tracked down Charlie Trotter at his home in McRoberts, far up in the hills of Letcher County. Charlie confirmed that he had stayed at the Landmark on the FBI tab for nearly five months, including the week Susan and Mark were there in June. After testifying successfully in the chop-shop trial, the nervous star witness had checked out in August. Soon afterward he got his final payment of $30,000 from the FBI.

Charlie said that he hadn't seen anything at the motel to indicate any problem between Mark and Susan. He said that Mark was usually gone most of the day, not getting back till late at night. He didn't think Mark saw her for more than a few minutes during that week.

"Why do you think that?"

"I saw her come out on the balcony a couple of times looking for Mark. He would park in the lot under the balcony. She gave me the impression that she was coming on to Mark, and he would hide in his car and try to dodge her. I don't think Mark was fooling with her."

By January, Richard Ray figured he had run down every lead. The holidays were past, and Susan hadn't contacted a soul since the day she disappeared. He went to his boss and told him it was time to demand that the FBI have a talk with Mark Putnam, preferably with a polygraph machine strapped to his arm.

The supervisors in the FBI's main regional office in Lexington once again responded civilly but firmly to the entreaties from Pikeville. They were not prepared to produce a federal agent for questioning by Kentucky cops just because the state police were unable to find Susan Smith.

The reasoning behind their attitude was logical. First, there was no evidence that a crime had even been committed. Furthermore, there was plenty to suggest that the missing woman had simply gone off somewhere. Yes, there was speculation, but there always was speculation in places like the Tug Valley. Mark Putnam had compiled a distinguished record fighting crime in eastern Kentucky, speculation about his personal relationship with the woman notwithstanding.

But Ray was certain that Mark Putnam knew more than he said about what had happened to Susan. Convinced now that she was dead, and stymied by the FBI, he decided to go outside channels. Early in January, 1990, he stopped by the office of the county prosecutor, Commonwealth Attorney John Paul Runyon, to ask for advice.

Ray told the prosecutor that he thought the FBI's refusal to take any role in the investigation was inexcusable, Mark Putnam aside. The woman had worked for them, after all. "They don't seem to understand that they have a special responsibility to this girl," he said.

Runyon readily agreed. He himself had long been troubled by what he regarded as the cavalier way the FBI used its money to buy informants. He thought it encouraged a kind of outlaw welfare state, with little genuine long-term law-enforcement benefit.

This seemed to be a perfect example, he decided. A poor mountain girl disappears; the federal agent who has put her in danger pulls up stakes and goes off to Florida. Didn't the FBI owe her family at least the courtesy of an active investigation? Missing persons cases were not under FBI jurisdiction, but tampering with a federal witness sure as hell was. Besides, as Ray pointed out, the FBI had always managed in the past to find a way to insert itself into a local investigation when it felt like it. Where was the bureau now?

KENTUCKY's county-based commonwealth attorneys perform the function of district attorneys: prosecuting felonies. But in the state's unusual political structure, where power is concentrated within the county courthouses, a commonwealth attorney wields significant influence over a wide swath of civic life, especially in poor rural areas.

Now in his sixties, approaching the end of his fifth term in office, John Paul Runyon was the dean of Kentucky commonwealth attorneys, a man both widely admired and feared in Pike County. He also happened to be an occasional hunting buddy of Richard Ray's, and he respected the detective's levelheaded comprehension of the societal currents in isolated regions such as Peter Creek.

While Ray sat in his office, Runyon called Lou DeFalaise in Lexington. The U.S. Attorney told the prosecutor that he happened to be on his way to the Justice Department in Washington.

"Well, kick somebody there and get them working on this, will you, Louie?" Runyon said.

Runyon also got together with Captain Rose, who recounted his own frustration in dealing with the FBI. He was especially unhappy, he said, since the state police had now heard, from Poole and other sources, that Mark Putnam would agree to a polygraph test. Yet every time the state police tried to take Putnam up on the supposed offer, the bureau stalled and finally, in early February, said no.

Rose said that Putnam was now the main suspect in Susan Smith's disappearance. He strongly suggested that Runyon meet with Shelby Jean Ward, who, he warned, was threatening to call a press conference to charge that law-enforcement authorities were engaged in a cover-up of the murder of her sister, a federal informant.

On February 9 a very unhappy Shelby Ward met with Runyon and state police officials in the prosecutor's office.

Explaining that no solid information had been developed, Runyon asked Shelby to consider that if the FBI man was, in fact, involved in her sister's disappearance, premature publicity could "run Putnam to ground" and let him escape. They knew where Putnam was, and he wasn't going anywhere. Runyon asked Shelby to stay quiet for "two or three weeks to see if I can get this thing moving." Shelby agreed.

When she left, the prosecutor, now believing that a full-scale federal investigation was the only way to "shake this thing loose," called Terry Hulse and suggested strongly that the FBI should get involved in the case, if only to clear their own man's name.

Hulse made some calls. In Washington, the bureaucracy stirred. There was a request from the Justice Department for Ray's case file.

A month passed. The case was reported "under review." In April two federal officials visited Pikeville for a briefing on the case. Hulse drove down from Covington to participate in the meeting.

The federal agents conceded to Runyon that there was no current investigation into the allegations against Mark Putnam. If Poole had been investigating, he had been working on his own.

Ray would later recall, "After talking to them, I had a little hope. They read my report. They seemed pretty concerned. They assured us that once they got back to Washington, this case would take a little higher priority than what it had been before, which was apparently none."

A few weeks later Captain Rose called Runyon. He had heard back from the Justice Department. The message essentially was, "We're not interested. You handle it."

Runyon told Rose, "That's a serious mistake. To start with, you don't have the resources. You don't have the jurisdiction—the boy you need to talk to is in Florida. And you can't talk to him without permission from the Justice Department. Let me see what I can do."

This time Runyon was less delicate in his approach to the FBI. "You people are in this up to your eyeballs," he said angrily. "You threw this girl to the wolves, and if you don't get off your ass, I'm going to have Geraldo Rivera breaking down your door, sticking a camera in your face, and saying, 'Where is your missing informant?'"

# 12

WITH twenty-three years in the bureau, Supervisory Special Agent Jim Huggins had seen his share of hotshot rookie agents roar out of the academy in a blaze of energy, then burn out before they qualified for their second week's vacation.

Not so, he thought, with this Putnam. Huggins had run into him only a few times when Mark came up to Lexington for gun training, but he knew enough about his reputation to regard him as one of the best young agents he had ever encountered.

Huggins had heard the scuttlebutt that Putnam "had some problems" because of a personal relationship with a female informant who had disappeared. That would be a shame if it was true. The kid would spend a few years atoning for it. But in time, if Putnam kept his nose clean, he could get back on track.

On May 1, 1990, Huggins was called in to see Terry O'Connor, the special agent in charge of the Lexington office. O'Connor told Huggins he was being dispatched immediately to head a special squad that would get to the bottom of the allegations about the disappearance of Susan Smith. It would be a joint investigation with the state police, who had been on the case since June and had come up with nothing. The questions "needed to be resolved."

Resolving them would turn out to be the most unhappy experience of Huggins' career.

FROM THE BEGINNING HUGGINS and the other agents believed that they were looking into a situation that had been thoroughly mishandled by the state cops. Not that the bureau was totally clean. It was clear that Putnam had a lot of explaining to do. And there was the delicate underlying problem of an office out of control—a rookie agent doing the work of four people, in partnership with a veteran who'd been moved out of the mainstream and sent to Pikeville. Clearly, the bureau's vaunted public image was in peril.

Huggins met first with Captain Rose, who, he said, "made available all of the resources of the post." These consisted primarily of Detective Richard Ray, who was somewhat resentful at being assigned to escort the FBI agents as they essentially duplicated his own investigation. It was clear to him that the elite squad had been sent down to straighten out the mess the hillbilly cops had made. Their attitude, he thought, was, "Let's do a thorough job, clear our guy, and find the guy that really did it"—assuming "it" had been done at all.

The agents quickly got mired in the muddled theories, half-baked speculation, and false leads that had confounded Ray for many months. They, too, soon gathered plenty of indications that Susan was unreliable and disreputable, a drug user with outlaw friends—and enemies. If this woman had been harmed, Mark Putnam did not even make first cut on the list of likely suspects.

Just as Ray had found, the FBI discovered that the people who knew Susan Smith had a variety of theories to explain her disappearance.

According to one bureau report, Shelby's husband, Ike Ward, described Susan as "the type of person who would make stories up and make statements that she knew who was involved in a criminal act when, in fact, she would have no idea who committed the crime." He also told agents that Susan was a heavy cocaine user. Personally, he said, he thought that Susan was dead, "possibly killed by drug dealers or someone she testified against."

Ike reported that he had never observed Mark with Susan, although he had once seen Poole pick her up at the car lot. Still, Susan was "in love" with Mark, Ike said, and would have done anything for him. Although Ike seldom believed anything Susan said, he did believe she had had an affair with Mark and had been pregnant by him.

Ike also told the agents about the beating Susan had received from Sherri Justice, who, he said, had "threatened to kill her." Further clouding the picture, he confirmed that while Susan was at the Landmark, Shelby had relayed the phone message from a contact of Susan's who was believed to be a drug dealer. He added that Susan had said in the past that the man and his family "would keep her" if she needed a place to live.

The agents' report concluded: "Ward advised that he was not trying to get anyone in trouble and would not swear against Mark Putnam or Ron Poole because all the information he has is hearsay and that Susan was a cheat and a liar."

MARK was aware of what had happened in Pikeville, because both Poole and Myra Chico had called to say that Huggins and his men were in the area retracing the state police investigation. Mark received the information with an odd mixture of dread and relief. In a month Susan would be dead for a year. Mark was intensely aware that she had been out there in the woods all that time. The thought, he later said, never left him. When he looked at his own two children, he often thought of hers—a little girl and a little boy who had no idea where their mother was.

In early May, as Huggins' team was starting work in Pikeville, Mark had gone in to see Roy Tubergen again, repeating his request for an OPR investigation "into the allegations against me."

"No way," the supervisor said flatly, aware of the damage this could do to an innocent man's career. But, he asked, "if the Kentucky state cops want you to go on the box, would you do it?"

"Yes," Mark said.

A week went by without further mention of the situation. Then at the end of a workday Tubergen took Mark aside and said that Jim Huggins and a couple of state police detectives wanted to come to Miami to talk to him.

"It's strictly your call," Tubergen said.

Mark felt a coldness in his toes and fingertips. He forced himself to be steady. "I have no problem with that," he said.

He needed a little time, he thought, to draw a deep breath and brace himself. He had been overwhelmed with work lately on a major undercover theft investigation. His unit had rented an apartment in Fort Lauderdale to set up a sting. It had been a heady experience, almost like the thrill of the chop-shop case, except that this time he was part of a well-oiled unit—not a lone wolf—a professional among professionals, all prepared to go the extra mile for one another. He could see himself now, however transiently, as the agent he had always wanted to be. He had achieved that, at least.

Okay, he thought, I'm ready. But he wasn't about to simply surrender. The outcome was inevitable—he would lose it all, and soon—but he wouldn't just give it up, not after all of the decent things he had done to earn it. They were going to have to take it away. And then that's it.

ON THE afternoon of May 15 he left the office, telling the receptionist that he had an interview to do. Knowing he would be alone, he drove to the apartment they had rented for the sting. He sat on the couch, holding his bureau-issue Smith & Wesson .357. The metal was cool in his hand. He raised the barrel and pressed it hard against his right temple. How would it look? Who would find the mess? Would there be pictures? He lowered the gun and tapped the barrel thoughtfully on the palm of his left hand. If I do this, who benefits?

He put the gun down. Had he just spared his life, or was this an exercise, another step he had to take to face his fate like a man?

He was cop enough to know they didn't have much of a case. Had the flurry of FBI activity in Pikeville meant that they had found the body? If so, why hadn't they simply arrested him? Why talk now? If they had the body, then they obviously didn't have any other evidence. Did this mean that he could make his inner peace with himself and with Susan, whatever the cost for the rest of his life, and brazen his way through the rest for the sake of his family? All trouble got easier over time. Why not this?

He left the apartment unable to decide. He stopped at the office to check out before heading home. Tubergen spotted him at his desk.

"They're coming down tomorrow," Tubergen said.

MARK barely remembered driving home that night. He found himself turning into the driveway, his temples throbbing. It was almost six o'clock, the usual time. The kids tackled him at the door. Little Mark tottered off into the playroom while Danielle wrapped her arms around his legs and held on, chattering about her day. But when he only stood there silently, she stopped talking and looked into her father's eyes. He thought that she read there a deep and sudden sorrow. He knew then that he was going to prison for a long time and that when he was a part of her life again, she would be grown.

At dinner Kathy hung back, sensing that something was very wrong. She guessed it was Pikeville again. After the kids were in bed, they talked for a while in the screened-in porch outside the kitchen. Was everything okay? No problem, he said. Just work. He got up and went out for his run.

HE DREAMED of Susan again that night. He knew that he had called out her name, because the sound of his voice woke him. Kathy slept on gently. He looked at her beside him and groped for the right emotion. Was love even possible, with what he had done to her? Would remorse ever be enough?

At work, he busied himself with papers on his desk, avoiding the phone, until he saw them come in. As he had expected, the Pikeville policemen, Richard Ray and Paul Maynard, were there. Jim Huggins, from the Lexington bureau, led the way.

At eleven o'clock sharp he was called into the conference room. Mark took a place at the table. Huggins nodded at him. Maynard and Ray avoided eye contact. Each of his interrogators had files and a legal pad in front of him.

Huggins cleared his throat and advised Mark of his right as an employee of the Justice Department to answer questions voluntarily. Huggins nodded to Maynard, who looked directly at Mark and recited, "You have the right to remain silent. Anything you say can and will be used against you in court. You have the right to talk to a lawyer for advice. . . ."

Mark closed his eyes.

"You're sure about the lawyer, Mark?" Huggins asked.

Mark looked up. "Positive. I don't want a lawyer. I'm ready."

He was asked to provide a detailed day-by-day account of what he remembered about the week during which Susan Smith had disappeared. But Mark was not going to make it that easy for them. He would confess, but he had decided he would make them sweat for it. A good detective—and Putnam could claim to be that—is one who instinctively collects the minutiae, sifting it endlessly in search of a tiny nugget. It was all in the details, he thought. Let them figure it out.

Speaking slowly, Mark went over his career in Pikeville, incident by incident, as it reflected his association with the missing woman. He described how Bertie Hatfield had introduced him to Kenneth Smith and Susan in the summer of 1987. He explained that from the first time he met with Susan in a car parked in plain view of a restaurant where Kenneth, Bertie, and Tennis waited, their relationship was dogged with rumors that he was having a sexual relationship with her. Susan herself was one of those who spread the rumors, he said.

As he listened, Richard Ray perked up. Even in denying it, Putnam had already introduced the subject of his sexual relationship with the woman. Ray wondered what Mark was up to. Did he sense that Ray knew he had killed Susan? Was the agent toying with them, aware that they couldn't prove a thing unless he slipped up? Why talk on at length, then? Why not just answer each question succinctly and wait for the next? Ray took careful note of every nuance in the account. He watched and listened for false clues.

Mark did not wander from the subject, the way most guilty suspects would. He kept the focus on himself and Susan: the payments to Susan for informing on Cat Eyes and others; Susan's clamoring for more money; his and Kathy's attempts to help her find a new life away from Kenneth; the gifts Susan pressed on him; the drug operation she had resumed contact with, and Poole's interest in that.

He recounted the four thirty a.m. phone call in early February, in which Kenneth had told Kathy that Susan and Mark had had an affair. "He was extremely jealous of me because of the informant relationship with Susan," Mark said, effectively highlighting the potential motive of another suspect.

When had he first heard that Susan was pregnant? Maynard asked, narrowing the focus.

"Around the middle of April, 1989," Mark said. He had been transferred to Miami; Susan called to discuss her personal problems: she was broke, strung out, battered, afraid, and pregnant. "I asked her who the father was, and she said it was none of my business."

Later, in Miami, there were odd telephone calls from Poole, imploring him to call Susan and try to help. When he did, Mark said, "She started crying and told me I was leaving her out in the cold."

Two hours had passed since Mark started talking. Ray could sense the agent's mind racing as the chronology moved inexorably toward that final week, in June of 1989. He thought, This guy is going to slip up. He's just too cocky.

Mark described his return to Pikeville in June and recalled his surprise at finding Susan at the motel when he checked in. How had she known he was coming? "I assume Poole told her," he said. He said Susan came to his room to talk about her troubles. That was news to both Ray and Huggins. It was a detail that no one had turned up.

What did they talk about in his room? "Again, she never accused me of being the father of her child," Mark said.

Ray watched him, wondering if he had caught a whiff of panic.

"I got upset with her." Mark paused. *Upset?* He couldn't believe he had used such a stupid word! His heart pounding, he went on evenly, and made another mistake. "During this conversation, I raised my voice and grabbed her by the arm, but did not in any way hurt her."

The cops at the table, Mark included, felt this tactical blunder like an electric shock. No glances were exchanged. Mark's mind flashed urgent warnings about the "indicators of deceit" that every good cop watched for in a suspect. He took instant stock of how he was projecting his mental state. Body language: Do not shift position. Do not move! Keep your voice at the same pitch. Do not lick your dry lips. Do not sigh or yawn. *Do not swallow!*

If any one of them had stood up and pointed a finger at him at that moment, he would have admitted everything. The impulse to confess was crushing, yet the need to go on was overpowering. No one rose to denounce him for murdering Susan Smith. Grimly he drifted on.

He explained that he flew into the airport in Huntington, West Virginia. "At Huntington, I rented a car—"

Huggins interrupted him. "You rented a *car?* What kind of a car?"

Mark shot an incredulous look at his fellow agent. Was this a bluff to knock him off balance? How could they not have known about the rental car? How the hell did they think he got around that week? There were rental records, expense vouchers—easy-to-check, routine stuff. He paused for an instant, sifting possibilities. They didn't know about the car! What else didn't they know?

He had always believed that Susan would be found, that he would be confronted, and that he would confess. In the past few weeks, as they closed in on him, he had assumed that they had new evidence, that perhaps they had the body. Now, looking around at his questioners' faces, suddenly blank with the realization that they had over-looked the *car,* he knew for certain that they had not found her.

"Yes, I rented a car—a blue Ford Tempo," he said calmly.

"Go on."

In a weary voice, he touched on each of the points of the chronology that he assumed they had already established: his talks with Charlie Trotter at the motel; his trips to Lexington; his several encounters with Susan (he was careful to mention the phone message she said she had received from Shelby about meeting her drug-dealer friend); his routine on the night she was last seen.

Uninterrupted, he went on, describing his trip to Lexington the next morning. Dinner at the Log Cabin, followed by the friendly talk long into the night with Myra Chico.

So far it checked out as well as the evidence could support, Ray knew. But Mark was going too fast, layering in too much detail. He had passed over the critical time, the hours during which Ray believed he had killed Susan Smith, but there was something Mark seemed impatient to explain.

On Saturday, June 10, two days after Susan disappeared, Mark said that he left the motel at about eight thirty a.m. and drove out of town to serve a trial subpoena on a witness. "I returned to Pikeville around noon," he said. "I then went to my old house, which still had not been sold. I pulled my car in the garage, checked out the house, and went back to the garage to discard some paint cans that were stored under a workbench. Reaching under a shelf, I cut my right hand on a nail that was protruding from the shelf. The wound began bleeding very heavily; I got in the passenger side of the car and started slinging my hand up and down, causing blood to splatter on the seat and on the dash. I wrapped my hand in a towel to stop the bleeding."

Mark paused. They didn't know about the car! Why was he telling them something else that they never knew about? Besides, the blood was his, not hers. He thought about the cracked windshield and struggled to explain it: "While sitting in the front passenger seat, I was extremely angry over cutting my hand; in an act of frustration I kicked the front windshield with my right foot. It caused the windshield to slightly shatter between the mirror and the right post."

If Richard Ray had had any doubts, he now knew for certain that Mark Putnam had killed Susan. Only a guilty man in his last shrieking ride down the chute would babble on, providing new information about something like that without prompting. Ray felt a strong urge to stand up and arrest the suspect immediately. But he remained silent as Mark went on and on: how he took the car back to the rental agency, blamed the cracked windshield on a chunk of coal flying off a truck, and got a replacement car—"I lied about the damage because I didn't want to have to pay for the windshield"; how he had lent Susan his gym shorts and shirt; how Susan had told him about rebuffing Poole; how she "may have met up with the group from Illinois on a drug deal" and come to harm; or how "her ex-husband, Kenneth Smith, could have harmed her, since he had beat her up in the past."

He was exhausted, morally and physically. "I have no idea where Susan Smith is at the present time," he said. "Both Ron Poole and I cared about her very much and are concerned as to what happened to her. I certainly did not kill her intentionally or accidentally, because I could never do anything like that."

Ray stared at him with a calculated look of malice. The signs were clear. Mark had bowed his head. He was perspiring and seemed to be fighting back tears. Ray shot a glance at Maynard, who nodded almost imperceptibly in reply. The detective reached into a folder in front of him and slid out an eight-by-ten photograph of Susan Smith. When Mark looked up, Ray was prepared to fling it right across the table at him and demand, "Man, where did you put her body!"

Mark was braced for it, too.

But a chair scraped. Huggins stood up, his face pale. "That's enough for today," he said, staggered by what he had just realized.

AFTERWARD Ray was furious. It was one of those times a cop knows— He's breaking. He is going to tell me what I want to know. Sensing the detective's quiet outrage, Huggins told him he had just taken Mark aside and asked him to take a polygraph test at FBI headquarters in Washington, to "clear this thing up." Mark had requested time to think about it overnight. He would let them know the next day.

It was little consolation. The Kentucky detectives, bound to a meager expense authorization, had to fly home the next morning. Ray was convinced that the opportunity was lost, that the FBI had thwarted him again, and Mark would once more be untouchable.

# 13

Kathy was in the kitchen making dinner. Absently she glanced up and saw her husband standing mutely on the other side of the breakfast counter, his shoulders slumped and his tie undone. As he peeled off his suit coat and dropped it onto a chair, he sagged with weariness. He tugged at his holster and took out the .357 and, to her annoyance, laid it on the counter. They had an inviolate policy about that gun. It belonged on the upper shelf of the pantry. She pointedly placed the gun atop the refrigerator. When she turned, he took her in his arms and kissed her clumsily.

"You know I love you."

She did, but she hadn't been hearing it much lately and was curious about why she was hearing it now. Laughing uneasily, she moved away and studied his face. His eyes looked sunken; his skin was pale.

"What's the matter with you? You look awful."

"They came down to interview me today. I'm a little worried."

"The thing with Susan?" she asked warily. "Has she turned up?"

"No. That's what they wanted to interview me about."

"Mark, who came to interview you?"

They had gone in to sit on the couch in the living room. "A guy named Jim Huggins from the Lexington office," he said. "He came down, and so did Richard Ray and Paul Maynard."

Kathy could see he was holding back. She had met Richard Ray and knew that he would lock up his granny if he had evidence. She did not like the idea that the Kentucky State Police, who were normally so cheap, had sent detectives to Florida for what should have been a mere formality.

Kathy felt her anger rise. The bureau questioning Mark was one thing. She welcomed that as a way to finally clear the air. But the Kentucky State Police? What business was this of theirs?

She said in a tone of exasperation, "*Richard Ray* is handling this investigation?"

"Yeah." Mark got up unsteadily and trudged upstairs to change.

Later, after watching Mark talk to the kids with forced animation and pick listlessly at dinner, she put Danielle and little Mark to bed and came down feeling it was time for the nonsense to end. The more she thought about it, the more insulted Kathy was at the idea that her husband should be put in the humiliating position of being questioned by a pair of hillbillies from the Kentucky State Police who couldn't find a missing person.

"Mark, you are just too trusting," she said in the sternly reproachful tone she used when she thought his good nature overwhelmed his good sense. "Tomorrow morning I want you to call in and tell them you'll be a few hours late. I'm going down to the office first thing. They're going to hear me out before this goes on any further."

He didn't object. And he didn't ask her what she was going to say. She figured he was so beaten down that he didn't care.

He went out to run. When he returned, he found her smoking on the dark porch. He pulled up a lawn chair and sat facing her. She pressed her palms against his cheeks, which were hot.

"Is there anything you haven't told me about, Mark? No matter what, we'll work it out."

He felt tears again. He broke eye contact. "Do you remember when the windshield broke in the rental car?" he asked.

"Mark, what does that have to do with it?"

"Well, if they ask you about that, I just wanted you to know that it wasn't a piece of coal that broke that window."

"What does that have to do with anything?" she asked.

"Do you remember when I smashed my hand?"

That same trip. Cleaning the garage; a nail. When he got back, his hand was gashed across the knuckles. Of course she remembered.

"Well, I said it was a piece of coal off a truck because I was worried about what you would say," Mark continued. "The truth is, I was working in the garage, and after I snagged my hand, I got mad and kicked the windshield of the car. I didn't want to tell you that because you would think, How could he be so stupid?"

A warning bell went off in Kathy's head. She realized that she was not the first person today to hear this piece of incidental information, this *adjustment.* "Did you tell them that when they interviewed you today?" she asked sharply.

Uneasily he replied, "Yeah, I did."

"Mark! Why did you even mention the damn windshield? Don't you realize how that makes you look? How could you be so stupid?"

"They wanted to know about my activities that week," he said wanly. "I have to tell them everything that happened as it happened." He explained that after the meeting he dug the car-rental agreement out of his travel-voucher file and gave it to Huggins.

"This is totally out of hand!" Kathy shouted. "You're fueling this yourself now!" She stormed into the house, letting the screen door slam behind her.

An hour later she was awake when he climbed into bed. She lay on the far side of her half of the mattress so their bodies did not touch. They lay awake for a long time, but neither of them spoke.

Grinding her teeth, Kathy thought, I am damned if this is going to continue. We worked hard to get where we wanted to be—the nightmare was supposed to be behind us. Finally she drifted off to sleep.

EARLY the next morning Kathy gulped down a cup of coffee and drove to the FBI offices in North Miami Beach. She stated her business at the reception desk with a cool succinctness. "I'm Kathy Putnam, Special Agent Mark Putnam's wife. And I'm here to see Mr. Huggins."

As she waited, she studied the agency's seal on the wall and snorted quietly at the slogan depicted on a banner beneath the scales of justice: FIDELITY—BRAVERY—INTEGRITY. We'll see about that, she thought.

After a few minutes a door opened, and a man who looked to be in his fifties appeared with a hand extended. He introduced himself as Roy Tubergen and asked her in with a cordial flourish. It was the first time they had met. Kathy shook his hand, then got right to the point.

"I don't mean to be rude, Mr. Tubergen, but I came here to see Jim Huggins and that state trooper from Kentucky."

The FBI official had repaired to his desk. He smiled benevolently at his visitor, who sat erect in her chair.

"I know you're upset, and I know Mark's upset," he said with studied sympathy.

Her brown eyes flashed anger. "You don't seem to understand. This is not a matter of my being upset. When an agent's name— *Mark's* name—is thrown out in the way it obviously has been in Kentucky, the FBI should have been all over it before it escalated to the point where my husband's integrity is on the line. I want it straightened out. I demand to be interviewed."

"Let me get Mr. Huggins for you," Tubergen said, lifting the phone with palpable relief.

Tubergen vacated his office, and Huggins took his place behind the desk. A soft-spoken man, he had no desire to cause any further grief to a woman whose fierce loyalty he found heartbreaking. Yearning to comfort her, Huggins heard himself giving assurance to Kathy's obvious belief that the investigation was routine. He told her that the FBI was only investigating a possible kidnapping. He did not mention his own reactions to the previous day's questioning.

"I understand why you're angry," Huggins said. "Look, all I can do is explain what the FBI is doing. We are officially involved now in the investigation, and we're going to see to it that this thing is taken care of once and for all. There are questions that need to be answered—you know as well as I do the kinds of allegations that are flying around in Pikeville. Everything's going to be fine once the air is cleared."

Kathy relaxed a bit. She figured the investigation would get the questions answered—Mark would take a few lumps, of course. He had been sloppy with Susan. But Mark had plenty of credit in the bank. Besides, Kathy wasn't about to let her husband take the heat alone—she remained determined to make the bureau confront and concede its own culpability, sending a rookie agent to a hellhole like Pikeville with all of sixteen weeks' training and no daily supervision.

"Mr. Huggins," she said calmly, "it's no secret that we went through a terrible ordeal. My family was almost destroyed because of what happened in Pikeville. Nearly a year has gone by since Susan supposedly disappeared and all of this talk started. Mark is distraught over this thing. And it's his own people doing this now. Mark's former partner is taking part in the whispering campaign. That has to stop!"

"Kathy, I hear what you're saying. Why don't you tell me what's on your mind." He took out a yellow legal pad to make notes.

She obliged, launching into an indictment that she had mentally prepared for months. Right off she threw in the person she held almost as responsible for Mark's difficulties as Susan was.

"As far as Mr. Poole is concerned, I have absolutely no respect for that man. He's got no business carrying a badge. If you want to talk to somebody who's had a relationship with Susan, don't forget Poole. From what Susan told me, Poole spent an awful lot of time trying to get her to go to bed with him."

"Poole?" Huggins scribbled some notes, realizing that this could get complicated. One by one Kathy spelled out her grievances about the Pikeville office, impressing him with her command of details about FBI business. Huggins' pencil worked furiously trying to keep up. He hadn't known about the aborted drug sting; he'd never heard of an agent's wife being encouraged to risk her neck like that. That alone was very irregular. And then Kathy's allegation that Mark's partner leaked it to an *informant?* Clearly, Putnam was not the only one who needed to come up with some answers.

When she wound down, Huggins sat back and exhaled loudly. "I can't believe what went on down there," he said, then asked, "You don't think Poole killed her, do you?"

"No," Kathy replied. The fact was, she didn't even believe Susan was dead. She assumed that Susan was hiding out somewhere, lying low because she had shot off her big mouth once too often and someone was threatening to shut her up permanently.

Huggins cleared his throat and thanked her for coming. "We're going to see to it that we check all these things out and that this is resolved as quickly as possible."

That sounded vague but promising to Kathy, who drove home satisfied that she had given them enough information to investigate properly and let Mark get on with his career and them with their lives. So confident was she that she welcomed Huggins' offhand suggestion, delivered as she was leaving, that Mark might want to take a polygraph test—just for the record. "Oh," she had said with an airy wave of her hand, "he'll have no problem with that."

SHE was glad to find Mark out back watching Danielle and little Mark splashing in the inflated wading pool. She could tell he was nervous by the tentative way he asked her how it went.

"Everything's going to be fine," she said. "You've got to relax. I gave them enough information to clear this thing up."

Mark remained apprehensive. "Well, I'm going to get dressed and go to the office." He kissed the kids and turned to go into the house. "I just want you to know how much I appreciate your going to bat for me."

"We're in this together."

He didn't say so, but Mark knew that was no longer true.

WHEN MARK ENTERED THE OFFICE that Friday morning, the level of chatter fell noticeably. So they know, he thought, heading straight for the conference room. Inside, Huggins was alone.

"Mark, how about that polygraph?" he said in a measured tone.

"Let me think about it a little, okay?"

Mark had already decided he was going to take the test. It was the next step, and it would probably be the big one. A polygraph operator was not going to worry about insulting his professionalism. A polygraph operator would look at him and coldly ask, at last, "Did you kill this girl?" He wasn't sure how he would reply. But he knew the rules of the game would change at that point.

As lunchtime approached, he took Huggins aside.

"Okay, I'll go on the box. Let's get this over with."

Huggins told the agent in charge, Gavin, who quickly arranged for Mark and Huggins to fly to Washington that night. The test would be administered at FBI headquarters the next morning.

MARK went home early to pack. He was measuring his time in hours now. He felt like a man desperate to extend a vacation. Would there be one more night with the kids? He did not know.

Kathy had hoped to see a glimmer of optimism in her husband, but he looked worse than ever. With more resignation than she thought appropriate, Mark told her that he had decided to take the polygraph. To get it over with, he was flying to Washington that night. The test was the next morning.

To Kathy the important thing was to get this behind them. After thinking for a moment, she accepted his decision. "I guess it makes sense for you to take the polygraph and straighten this out. Calm down. This is going to work itself out. How could it not?"

"You're right." He seemed to brighten.

KATHY made an early dinner. Before Mark left for his flight, he went through his usual ritual of reading the kids their bedtime story. Kathy lingered in the hall and looked at the three of them on Danielle's bed, a tableau of familial trust, fatherly love, childlike devotion. Kathy unconsciously hung it like a photograph in her mind. Then she went out back to smoke and think.

Her afternoon courage faded with the daylight; with a sick feeling she considered what she should have realized a long time ago: the likelihood that her husband had had an affair with Susan. Nothing else that she knew of could explain his prolonged agitation, and what she now recognized as his abiding guilt.

If that was true, agreeing to the polygraph was a mistake. When he came out to say good-bye, she said, "Look, Mark, something's obviously wrong. Whatever it is, you've got to know by now, with everything we've been through together, that we'll work it out. If there's something you have to tell me about, about you and Susan, tell me now before you go and do this thing tomorrow. If there's something that you're hiding when you take this polygraph, it's going to make you look guilty. Whatever it is, you can tell me. There isn't anything you can't tell me—"

"What if I had—"

"*Nothing*, Mark," she repeated, fighting tears.

"I want you to understand something. I have to take the polygraph tomorrow. And then I'll tell you everything. And you'll understand."

And then he left.

ON THE plane, he and Huggins spoke uneasily, quickly exhausting bureau gossip. Each gratefully grabbed a magazine when the flight attendant came by.

It was late when they got in to Washington National Airport. Mark remembered arriving there in 1986 on his way to Quantico, a new agent in training, on top of the world. At the same airport on Thanksgiving weekend, on a three-day leave from the academy, he was met by Kathy and Danielle, almost two. They stayed at the Crystal City Marriott and visited the monuments with the happy tenacity of tourists. Would the baby remember the sense of proprietorship her old man felt when he showed her the Capitol, the Lincoln Memorial, the White House? Would she ever think of her father as a federal agent, in this city, that wonderful time, the three of them in love?

He and Huggins took a cab to the hotel. Huggins went his own way. Mark put his things in his room and went back out to wander the empty streets of the capital. In a while he managed to straighten up a bit as he walked. He was still an agent of the government he was sworn to protect. A damned fine agent—one of the best. Hardworking, focused, a guy you only had to tell once. He wasn't the smartest or the best educated or the craftiest. He was naïve. But he was honest, and he would match his dedication against anybody's.

He thought of getting rip-roaring drunk, but quickly ruled that out. He walked for hours. This is where he belonged, this dignified capital with its alabaster monuments.

He turned back to the hotel. As he walked, he spoke with her. "Well, Susan, my time is up. It's time to get this thing squared away. It's time to get you back home."

He went to bed amazingly at peace.


His wife had no peace that night. Okay, she thought. He did it. Yes, the bastard slept with Susan. She closed her eyes and thought hard. When and where did they do it? How did they keep it from her? Susan blabbed about everything else—how could she have kept her mouth shut about such a coup? For that alone, Kathy hated her, for mocking her so effortlessly.

But her imagination recoiled. No, she decided abruptly, it was not true. Mark never lied to her. It had never happened.

She kicked off the covers and lay there wide awake, her thoughts spinning. She steadied her impressions; fixed on them one at a time. Come *on,* she told herself brutally. There was something seriously wrong with Mark, and there had been all year. She could see it now. A man who was never sick, suddenly always complaining about diarrhea. That scratching at his chest.

And that rental car! The cracked windshield, his bandaged hand. Why had he lied about it? She could see his boyish face, lying as brazenly as a child. And Susan throwing her head back with that shrill laugh. Susan always looked for the easy way. Susan was a thief. She took what she wanted. Of course she took Mark.

How stupid Kathy felt. She should have seen it. But a worse fear was overwhelming her: the possibility that the rumor she'd dismissed as ridiculous—that Susan had been pregnant with Mark's child—might be true. Kathy struck her clenched fist on the mattress with each word: *"That's why this had such an impact on him."*

The only sensible thing to do was divorce him. But marriage is often not sensible. She groped through doubts: Can I live with this? We have two children. Do I throw away eight years, especially knowing what I know about Susan? She meant nothing! Then it struck her: if he had had an affair with her, and he was trying to cover it up, it was going to make him look guilty if Susan really was dead. She thought of the damaged hand. What if he *did* know something about her being missing? What *about* the lies about that windshield?

How about, okay, they're having an affair; they have a fight in the car. There's a big argument, Mark gets pissed off, punches the windshield; Susan storms out of the car and wanders away . . . and later that scummy ex-husband catches her and beats her once too often, or one of the drug dealers or bank robbers she knows kills her. So Susan is dead, and Mark is indirectly involved. This is possible.

Kathy weighed her own role. She was a child of the 1970s, a graduate of the sexual revolution. So he had a tumble with someone else. He came home to his wife, didn't he? It wasn't the end of the world; affairs happened to the best of people. But why did it hurt like this? She'd found the false base on her life, that's why. Her husband, once a part of her being, suddenly seemed alien.

SHE opened her eyes to a dull headache. The sun warmed the bed, flooded the room. Downstairs she could hear Danielle lecturing her brother on the proper way to pour cereal into a bowl.

In the kitchen, as she banged the kettle down on the stove, the phone rang. It was Mark. His voice was shaky.

"I just wanted you to know that this is not going to go well today. I'm really scared about this. I don't know if you're going to understand," he said.

"I'm glad you called. Don't do this. I want to talk to you first." She wanted to hear the truth in his own words.

"I told you I have to do this. But be prepared." His voice broke.

She thought fast and said, "Whatever happens, whatever the results of the polygraph, don't talk to them until you talk to me. Don't give them a statement or any information. You don't have to."

He was noncommittal. "I'll talk to you afterward."

THE test was in FBI headquarters. Huggins and an FBI supervisor watched it on a closed-circuit television from an adjoining room. The questions were short. The polygraph technician paused between each to read the machine and make notes. He asked about kids, college, cases. Finally, he asked about Susan.

"Did you ever have any sexual relationship with Susan Smith?"

"No," Mark said.

"Did you cause the disappearance of Susan Smith?"

"No."

"Was she wearing your clothes at the time of her disappearance?"

"No, not that I know."

AFTERWARD the technician told Mark that his voice had dropped perceptibly in pitch on the questions on which he had lied. "The real Mark Putnam told the truth about college and his family and the cases he worked. But he lied about Susan, didn't he?"

Mark knew that it was over. So did Huggins, who looked at him sadly. "Mark, we have some problems."

"Yeah, I know you got some problems," Mark said.

"Why don't you talk about it with me?"

"No. I want to go home and talk to my wife about it first. After I've done that, I'll do whatever you want to get this squared away."

Huggins said he could call.

"How did it go?" Kathy asked.

"Not very well. Things are bad." Mark said he was calling directly from the interrogation room.

She was trembling. "Are they holding you there?"

"No, but they want me to talk to you over the phone. They have a stenographer here to take down whatever I say."

"No! Mark! Mark? Don't say anything. If they'll let you come home, come home, and we'll talk about it here. Don't say anything else. You don't have to. Do you hear me? Come home."

"Okay. I'll try."

Mark sensed a flurry of activity around him as he spoke to Kathy. Someone on another phone, papers being shuffled. A different process being set in motion. It was quite clear that the rules had changed. Much of the professional courtesy was gone. They wanted to know everything, and he said they would have it, but he insisted he had to see his wife first.

There was a hurried conference out of his earshot. Obviously, there was no evidence except his confession. There was some concern about suicide. He was asked if he had brought his gun. He had not. Finally they agreed. He was allowed to fly back to Fort Lauderdale.

His FLIGHT WAS THE LAST ONE INTO Fort Lauderdale Airport that night. Kathy found Mark waiting alone at the far end of a wide, empty corridor. He started to speak, but she held up her hand and said, "Just—don't—talk—yet."

In the car, she suggested that they stop at a Holiday Inn near the airport for a drink. It was a conversation neither of them wanted to have at home, where Kathy's sister, Chris, was still living with them.

It was nearly one o'clock when they walked into the Holiday Inn lounge. At the bar Kathy ordered a double Black Russian for herself and a beer for Mark. Carrying the drinks, she led him silently to a table in the darkness.

Defiantly, Kathy lit a cigarette and blew the smoke at a point just over Mark's shoulder. She looked directly at him for the first time that night. She waited.

"This is really serious," he sputtered. "I'm sorry . . . "

Get on with it, she thought angrily.

"It's—"

"Look," she said, "did you *kill* her?" She spat out the words with a street swagger she hadn't used since she was a teenager.

"Yes."

This was not the answer she had anticipated. She blinked slowly, her mind two beats behind the words.

"So you slept with her."

"Yeah, I did."

"And this could have been your baby."

"Kat—"

"Don't talk to me! . . . How did this happen?"

Confused, he did not answer right away. He was crying. Briefly she indulged her contempt, then demanded, "Was there a car accident?"

"No."

This elicited a furious, thin stream of smoke. "Did you *shoot* her?"

"No. I choked her." Mark made a feeble choking motion.

"You choked her," she said in a flat tone. "How do you know she was dead? Are you sure, Mark? They haven't found the body. She was unconscious. Maybe she just got up and walked away."

"I thought that a million times. She was dead. I know she was. I want to explain—"

"All right," she said abruptly. "Tell me how it happened."

He said that he hadn't lied to her when she first asked him about Susan, back when Susan was shooting her mouth off about Mark. He hadn't slept with her then. That happened later. All the pieces of his story fell together. Another round of drinks was brought by a waitress. As Mark spoke, Kathy's mind careered through uncertain frames of time: Mark and Susan drive into the mountains; they park, argue; suddenly she's screaming, hitting—and he loses it. It's over in sixty seconds. He pulls her out onto the ground, desperate, but she won't breathe. Like that, she's dead.

He succumbed to wrenching tears just as the reality of what Kathy was hearing slammed finally into her consciousness. In a flash of contempt she walloped him so hard her arm resonated with pain. He tried to duck the blow, which caught him forcefully on the right side of his face. As he dodged, he lost his balance and fell to the floor, one hand grasping the little table on which the drinks had spilled. He was crying like a three-year-old when he came back up. She had never seen Mark shed more than a few sentimental tears and watched the spectacle with detached interest.

"I want to get out of here. Kathy, please let's go home and talk."

She wasn't budging. "No. I'm not moving and you're not moving. I'm simply not ready to get up yet." She had mustered a degree of haughtiness now and caught the eye of the waitress. "Another double. And he'll have a beer."

Kathy turned back to Mark. Several rounds of drinks later, she and the man she had long loved and respected, the father of her children, had explored every facet of the fact that he had killed Susan Smith.

# 14

**K**ATHY slept for less than an hour. With her mind reeling again, she bolted up in bed, sensing Mark lying beside her with his eyes open. She squinted at the glowing red numerals on the alarm clock. It was five thirty. She was due at her waitressing job at the International House of Pancakes at seven. Her first cogent thought was that she needed to phone her manager to say that she wasn't coming in, but it was still too early to call. Mark had to be in the office at ten to talk to the special agent in charge. She wanted to go with him.

Not knowing exactly what to do, she dressed quickly and walked down the hallway to Danielle's bedroom, where the sight of Chris, asleep in the spare bed, vaguely irritated her. Shaking her sister until her eyes were open, she demanded, "Wake up. I need you."

"What in the world is wrong?" Chris asked sleepily.

"Mark killed that woman!" Kathy hissed like a madwoman.

"What woman?" Chris gasped.

Kathy began to cry with frustration, sensing that this was only the start of the explaining that lay ahead of her. "The one in Kentucky."

Fully awake now, Chris's own police instincts snapped into place. "Should I get you and the kids out of here?"

"What for? No. He's fine." Kathy sobbed, afraid of awakening Danielle, who slept on, with her face turned to the wall.

THERE was no protocol for starting such a day. Kathy found herself in the kitchen, staring in bafflement at the wall phone in her hand. She put it to her ear and heard it ringing at the other end.

Her father answered huskily. Her voice quavering, she managed to say, "It's Kathy. I need you guys to come down here right away," but that was all she could get out. Sensing Mark's presence behind her, she slammed the receiver down on the breakfast counter.

"I'll handle it," Mark said, rushing back upstairs. Wordlessly she put the phone to her ear. She heard Mark pick up the extension in the bedroom and say, "Ray, it's Mark. There's something I have to talk to you about." Trembling, she placed the phone in the cradle.

By now it was after six; little Mark had wandered into Danielle's bedroom, waking her. Kathy's sister took charge of the kids and didn't ask questions.

When Chris brought the kids down for breakfast, Kathy was in the kitchen making coffee, which was reassuring in itself, although Chris did observe that her sister had spilled the grounds in a small heap on the counter and had not poured any water into the machine. Chris took over the coffee making and said nothing.

KATHY broke down again when she called her boss at the restaurant. Gently Mark took the phone and explained that a family emergency had come up and she wouldn't be in. The manager was considerate and concerned. To Mark's relief, he didn't pry for details.

Around nine Kathy and Mark drove to the office to talk with Gavin, the special agent in charge of the Miami FBI bureau. At some point before they left the house, Mark telephoned his mother. Kathy could not imagine what he said to her.

Gavin was waiting in his office, fully apprised of a situation that was unprecedented in the eighty-three-year history of the FBI: an agent—one of his people—appeared to be facing a charge of criminal homicide. While Putnam had not confessed, he had badly failed the polygraph—and he wasn't protesting his innocence. Making the situation even worse, the offender wasn't some rogue cowboy on some drug-addled flameout. Of all of the eight thousand agents in the bureau, it had to be *this* guy—this earnest, likable, gifted, indefatigable young man who seemed to project every virtue that the bureau imagined itself as representing. The guy they would have put on a recruiting poster now qualified for a wanted poster.

Gavin was accompanied in the office by his second-in-command, Larry Torrence. Gavin greeted Mark and Kathy, asked if they were comfortable, if they wanted coffee. All Kathy wanted was to smoke; seeing her desperation, Gavin went out himself to find an ashtray.

The social preliminaries were excruciating for Kathy, who was shaking with fright. She cried quietly, aware that if either Gavin or Torrence had any question at all about Mark's guilt, one look at the state of his wife would give them their answer.

She followed the conversation between Mark and the two supervisors only in phrases that pierced her staggered consciousness. She heard Mark apologize for the disgrace he had brought on the bureau. "The FBI family" was invoked several times. She heard "worst-case scenario" mentioned. She struggled to focus. On the sofa beside her, Mark was bowed, repentant, and, she saw with alarm, compliant.

She fought to resist the allure of the empathy that wafted over the desk of the supervisor, aware that so far they had talked around any specific mention of Susan's death itself. Then she heard Mark utter the words, "I would like to take care of this and clear the air," and she saw the trapdoor at his feet, triggered to spring open. Her husband was about to confess to a capital crime.

"No!" she protested, causing the three men to fix her with surprised stares. "Mark," she said, glaring, "we have to talk."

The interruption broke the momentum. There was a small bend in

Gavin's tone. Of course, if Mark wished to take care of this thing, he could make a statement now. On the other hand, perhaps Mark and Kathy wanted to discuss it privately. Gavin said that it was not his role to recommend a course of action. Nevertheless, names of good defense attorneys could be provided if Mark wished.

"Could we talk privately?" Kathy asked.

Gavin told them to go into an adjacent office and talk it over.

Jumping up, Kathy marched her husband next door. Just as she thought, Mark wanted to spill his guts. "I have to take care of this thing," he protested. "This is the *FBI.* They'll treat me right."

She shook her head violently. "Those men are *cops!* They will *do their jobs.* They can arrest you and put you in jail *today,*" she shouted. "We haven't even told the kids!"

For the first time, they talked about what would happen after he confessed. Thirty years? Life in prison? *Execution?* Neither of them knew. In all the time that he had been obsessed with his guilt, Mark had never thought through his options. It had never occurred to him that he had any, except to confess, to "put things right" and accept whatever punishment the authorities saw fit to impose.

When he and Kathy came back in, Mark apologized for not being able to give his statement immediately. He asked for the names of some lawyers. Torrence made a phone call to a Fort Lauderdale defense attorney who had previously been an assistant U.S. Attorney in Miami. Mark and Kathy retreated again to the privacy of the spare office, where he picked up the phone. "Don't say another word until you see me," the lawyer ordered.

THE appointment with the lawyer was scheduled for Tuesday. On Monday the Putnams decided to see a child psychologist. Huddled together in their bedroom, with Kathy's parents and sister in the house and Mark's mother on her way down to Florida, having no idea what anyone would say, they struggled with the need to tell Danielle that her father had killed someone and was going to prison.

"What do we tell her?" Kathy said. "How do we not destroy her?"

Mark didn't have an answer. Kathy went down a list of psychologists in the yellow pages and made an appointment with the first one who was available that day. As soon as they saw her, they realized how impossible it was to explain their situation coherently to a total stranger. But the psychologist surprised them by restating the problem succinctly: "Your husband is going to jail for killing someone, and it is a total shock. You are both loving parents. How do you explain this to your daughter, who is five years old and loves her daddy?" She suggested practical ways to begin sorting out the situation for both Danielle and little Mark. Find a previous example of how the child had handled adversity well, explain it, and hold it up as a way to approach the current situation. Offer love and as much stability as possible. Above all, hear the child out.

That night Kathy told Mark to wait upstairs until she got Danielle. Sitting on the bed, he said, "I don't know if I can handle this."

"Just get yourself together. I'm going to bring her in, and we'll do it together, just the way we discussed this afternoon."

Kathy brought Danielle in. She scampered onto the center of their bed between her parents and asked her father why he was crying. He got up and went into the bathroom, sobbing loudly.

Kathy told her to wait. She returned with Mark leaning on her. Danielle watched quietly.

"Danielle, Daddy is so very sorry," he said, unable to go on. They both looked at Kathy.

She held her daughter. "Listen, do you remember when a couple of weeks ago you were in the kitchen and Mommy was by the sink making supper, and little Mark went over to the stove and he was going to reach up and maybe get burned? And you pushed him away and he fell and bumped his head, and he cried? And Mommy only saw you push him, she didn't see him reaching up for the stove?"

"Yeah, I remember it."

"And do you remember how you felt when I yelled at you?"

"I felt bad."

Drawing a deep breath, Kathy explained that another bad thing had happened. Her father had done something wrong; he had not meant to do it. There had been a fight. A lady in Kentucky had been hurt very badly. The psychologist had stressed the need to explain that Mark was not bad, that the situation was.

"It wasn't as though Daddy had time to think," Kathy said. "He reacted quickly, just like you did. Daddy had to tell the truth about what happened. It was a terrible mistake. He's going to have to go away for a long time."

Danielle started to cry. She jumped into her father's arms and said, "If you're telling the truth, why do you have to go away?"

"Because what Daddy did was very wrong."

He told her that he would always love her, that he was proud of her, that he wanted her to be brave. "Can you do that for me?"

She said she could. "Me and Mommy can take care of things." She told her father not to cry. "You're making your nose all red." And Danielle left the room.

Mark was shaking violently. Kathy put her arms around him and rested her head on his chest.

"I can't believe I did this to you and the kids," he said.

THE commonwealth attorney's office started moving on the prosecution of Mark Putnam the day after the state police detectives got back to Pikeville. Captain Gary Rose had called John Paul Runyon at home on Saturday to tell him that Mark had just taken the FBI polygraph and failed it. Runyon supposed this meant that Putnam had a lawyer or would soon be getting one.

On Monday, Runyon held a meeting with the state police; Terry O'Connor, the FBI's representative from Lexington; and the U.S. Attorney, Lou DeFalaise, to discuss the options. They knew that all they had on Mark was that he had made false statements in an interview and during a polygraph test. There had been no admission of guilt. They believed that he had killed Susan, but there was still no way to prove it in a courtroom. There wasn't even enough to file a charge.

Runyon insisted that they evaluate the potential criminal case: In the absence of a confession, what did they have? Well, they could establish that Mark had a motive. Witnesses would testify that Susan had said she was pregnant by Mark and had threatened to hound him until he met her terms. However, no one had actually heard her say these things to him. The motive was weak but presentable.

Furthermore, Mark had had the opportunity to commit the crime. His presence in Pikeville at the time Susan disappeared could easily be established; the two had been registered at the same motel. However, no one had actually seen them together.

That was their "case," Runyon acknowledged morosely. They had no physical evidence, no witness to a threat—and no body. All they could do was wait for the killer's next move.

RUNYON WAS A FORMIDABLE opponent for any defense lawyer. Not only was he smart, he was *convincing*. He knew that if he could get Mark Putnam indicted and in the dock in a Pike County courtroom, obtaining a conviction would be no great problem. But no matter how he shuffled the cards, he knew he did not have enough evidence to indict Putnam. And he worried that Putnam and his lawyer knew the same thing.

Runyon waited impatiently to hear from that lawyer, whoever it was. Monday passed without a word. Runyon was bewildered.

Finally, late Tuesday afternoon, he received a phone call from a Fort Lauderdale attorney who introduced himself as Bruce Zimet, a former assistant U.S. Attorney now in private practice, representing Mark Putnam.

Zimet said he wanted to talk, but first he needed to invoke rule 11 of the federal rules of criminal procedure. Rule 11 is a standard procedure that enables a guilty party to discuss a plea to a lesser charge without being subject to criminal liability for anything that is divulged during those discussions. True statements "made in the course of any proceedings under this rule" are inadmissible if the plea is ultimately rejected or withdrawn. Prosecutors with a solid case do not agree to hold discussions under rule 11.

Carefully, Runyon told Mark's lawyer to go on.

Speaking hypothetically, Zimet explained that while a client might be willing to confess, he was not willing to take the maximum penalty for a charge on which the state apparently had no evidence.

Two weeks of negotiations commenced.

Down in Florida, Mark insisted that he was going to prison for thirty or forty years. "I killed somebody, Kathy. I've got to go to prison for a long, long time. You and the kids need to cut your ties to me," he told her in conversations that started at dawn and continued until they fell asleep exhausted at night.

BRUCE Zimet had been stunned by the story that Mark and Kathy told him when they came to his office on Tuesday morning, but he immediately saw the advantages in negotiating a deal. It did not make sense that Mark wasn't interested. In fact, when Kathy stepped out for a minute to have a cigarette, Zimet asked Mark whether he was actually protecting someone else, such as his wife.

A suspicion of misguided gallantry was perhaps reasonable for someone who didn't know the Putnams. Not many criminal suspects begin their case stipulating that they are guilty, even to their lawyers. Fewer still insist that they intend to admit to their crime. It took a while for Zimet to understand that Mark Putnam meant everything he said.

It also took Zimet some time to see that, stricken as she appeared to be, Kathy Putnam could be a strong force on her husband's will. For Kathy the disaster had just happened. But as she got her bearings and began to look ahead, she tried to impress on Mark the idea that assuaging his conscience was not the only consideration. There was also the fate of his family and any hope they had of putting a life together at some point, no matter how far in the future. She worked hard to persuade him that he owed it to his family, if not to himself, to begin thinking like a defendant. She realized that without Mark's confession the authorities did not have a good case. If they had one, they would have made it by now.

On Wednesday, when she and Mark returned to Zimet's office to hear his assessment after his initial conversation with Runyon, Kathy had decided the most sensible option was to deny everything. Let them make their case and prove it in court.

Zimet had come to the same conclusion. "You don't want to plead out on this," he told Mark. "You won't have to do a day. They don't even have enough to indict you."

But Mark wanted to put an end to the ordeal. His reasoning had little to do with legal strategy and much to do with guilt and pride. If he could avoid it, Mark had no intention of letting a Pike County prosecutor put him on trial. He would rather prosecute himself by pleading guilty. Furthermore, he had been tormented for a year knowing that he had abandoned Susan in a mountain ravine. She would have to be found, and he would have to confess to killing her. There was no other way he could live with himself.

Zimet suggested that Mark and Kathy go to lunch to talk it over.

At a restaurant across the street Kathy tried to breach the wall he had erected around his guilt. "What do they really have, Mark? You're going to give them everything. I understand that. But you can get some concessions in return. You don't have to spend the rest of your life in prison. *Think* about what you're doing to us, Mark."

"Kathy, I killed that girl."

"Mark, if you go to jail in Kentucky, they'll kill you. Think of Danielle and Mark and me. You have some power in this." She was imploring him as she never had before. Finally his mind managed to move past the word "deal." By the time they went back, he had agreed to let his lawyer negotiate one.

IN PIKEVILLE, the prosecutor had guessed Putnam's rationale. A more cynical man might have scoffed at the notion, but Runyon sensed that Mark was being impelled by his conscience. He didn't know how long that situation would last—consciences can fade when things get tough. He had no idea how far he could push.

In what quickly evolved into a high-stakes poker game, phone calls flew back and forth between Kentucky and Florida every day for two weeks. As Runyon told his associates at the onset of the plea negotiations, "I can never be sure when I hang up the phone today whether he's going to be talking to me tomorrow."

Under instructions from the Putnams, Zimet proceeded on plea negotiations. A prison term was inevitable. "I wanted ten years," Zimet told them at the end of the first week of talks. "If this had happened in Florida, you'd serve no more than four. But Runyon says he won't sleep with less than sixteen."

Early the following week Zimet made a formal offer: Mark would plead guilty to first-degree manslaughter in exchange for a guarantee of an eight-year sentence.

Runyon said, digging in hard with a bluff, "It's got to be eighteen." The fact was, he was prepared to take twelve.

The next day Zimet had a new gambit. If Mark pleaded guilty to whatever sentence they agreed on, he wanted to serve his time in a federal prison, not a Kentucky penitentiary.

Runyon replied that he was willing to go along with that. On June 1 the Kentucky Department of Corrections tentatively agreed not to object to Putnam's serving his sentence in a federal facility. This handed Runyon his last card to play.

"Runyon won't go for twelve," Zimet told the Putnams when they came in that day. "It's got to be sixteen." He broke it down. "Sixteen years. You won't do more than twelve; you're eligible for parole after eight, and it's in a federal facility."

Mark looked at Kathy, who nodded shakily. "Let's go," he said.

Runyon's letter spelling out the plea agreement was drafted and faxed back and forth until both sides signed off on the final language. It was dated June 1, 1990.

On Monday morning, June 4, Paul Maynard and Jim Huggins flew to Florida. A state police unit was ordered to stand by in Kentucky to recover the body of Susan Smith. They arrived at Zimet's office just after five o'clock. Mark had asked Kathy to stay home. He was ready this time when Maynard read him his Miranda rights.

Speaking softly, Mark confessed that he had killed Susan Smith and told them where to find her body.

The directions he gave were so simple that the officers standing by in Pikeville didn't believe him. "There's no way she could be there," Ray scoffed over the phone. "Somebody would have found her."

When this was repeated to him, Mark muttered that that was the point. He thought they would have, long before now.

With a scrawled map and the directions, Ray led a small and dubious group of searchers up the mine road above Harmons Branch. Accompanying him were two FBI agents and two state police officers. With the light fading, they wouldn't have much time.

Driving slowly over the deep ruts, Ray found the turnoff and stopped the car on a mud-caked siding beside a mound of fresh dirt and debris. They climbed over it and peered into the ravine, which was thick with undergrowth. After the first ten yards the ground fell off sharply. They used ropes tied to the truck to ease down one by one. About halfway down, the way was blocked by a weed-covered pile of dirt and trash, remnants of tangled wire-mesh fencing, rotted mine timbers, and moldering trash bags.

Ray heard a shout from the brush about ten feet below. "Hey, it looks like there's some bones here!"

Ray slid down to where one of the FBI agents had braced himself between two bushes and was staring at the bones, which appeared to be from a skeleton that had come apart. A flashlight glinted off metal; prodded with a stick through the dried mud and matted leaves, it proved to be a thin gold chain with a tiny cross.

Shaking his head, Ray squinted toward the top of the ravine. The remains of Susan Smith lay not fifty feet from the road.

A radio transmission was made back from the scene to the state police post in Pikeville, where the message was relayed to the small group in the lawyer's office in Fort Lauderdale. Maynard put down the phone and said, acknowledging Mark's distressed look, "They found her just where you said."

Mark took a few minutes to collect himself. Then he continued talking as a stenographer took down the rest of his confession.

ON FRIDAY, June 8, Mark Putnam's brief career with the FBI officially came to an end. He had typed out a short letter of resignation, which he planned to take to the office personally. Gavin and Torrence said they would come by his house instead.

When they arrived, the two supervisors asked Mark if he had any bureau property in the house besides his gun and credentials. He did not. Wanting to find a neutral site, they suggested a short ride. Mark and Kathy accompanied the two agents in their car. They drove in silence to a McDonald's a few blocks from their house.

It had started out proudly in a crisp ceremony at the FBI academy in Quantico. Now it was ending with three cops and a grieving woman parked outside a fast-food joint.

"I'm sorry it has to be like this. Doing it this way is in the best interest of the bureau," Gavin explained.

"I understand," said Mark.

The agents were ready to get back to the office. Numbly Kathy watched her husband pass his credentials, his gun, and his holster to Gavin. He then handed over his letter of resignation.

And that was the end of the bureau business. His resignation was official. Mark and Kathy didn't want a ride back. They got out of the car and walked home silently along the sandy shoulder of the road.

# 15

SHELBY Jean Ward knew that Susan had been found when she got a call from John Paul Runyon late Monday, asking if she could come to his office the next morning at nine o'clock. He wouldn't say why, but she could tell from the tone of his voice.

Runyon and Captain Rose from the state police were already there when she arrived, shaken and subdued. They told her that Susan's remains had been found and tentatively identified.

"Mark Putnam?" she asked.

"Mark Putnam," Runyon replied. "He confessed last night." Runyon tried to explain the necessity of a plea arrangement.

"Why? It's cold-blooded murder," she protested.

Runyon went over the prosecution's case, which came down, he said, to the fact that there was no evidence without that confession. He said a sixteen-year sentence was substantial, far in excess of the average for manslaughter.

Shelby wasn't buying it. She left his office in a tearful fury, and Runyon knew he had a problem even before he got the grand jury into session to prepare the indictment. On Tuesday, June 12, Mark Putnam would be brought to Pikeville to plead guilty. Until then Runyon hoped that the situation could be kept quiet. But by Wednesday the news that an FBI agent had been implicated in the death of a young woman was moving on the Associated Press wire out of Pikeville.

"It's cold-blooded murder," Shelby told a reporter from the Miami *Herald,* which had been alerted to the story because it involved an agent assigned to the Miami FBI bureau. "He took the body and dumped it over the hill like it was nothing," Shelby said.

"Like some dog," said her brother Billy Joe.

Other reporters soon gathered details of the sordid relationship between Susan Smith and Mark Putnam. "She was possessed by him, madly in love with him," Shelby said. "She swore that it was his baby. She was threatening to tell his wife about the baby, and he was scared to death."

On Monday, June 11, when she came to the courthouse to testify to the grand jury, Shelby was surrounded by reporters and cameras. "Because he was a big FBI, they don't want him to get justice," she said, denouncing the plea agreement, which had not yet been publicly disclosed. "It was brutal murder. Brutal, brutal murder."

GRAND juries are pliant tools of the prosecutor, but there is no law that says a grand jury can't refuse to go along, especially with the media going full tilt on Shelby's impassioned denunciation of the deal as a miscarriage of justice—a cover-up orchestrated by the feds, in collusion with the prosecutor. It was highly unlikely, but Runyon knew that if grand jury members decided they were being bamboozled, they did have the legal authority to defy the commonwealth attorney and return a murder indictment. That would present Runyon with the worst of all possible scenarios—not only would the plea agreement be null and void, but he would have to prosecute a case on which he had no evidence, on a charge he could not support.

Runyon and his staff had worked diligently all week to prepare a presentation designed to foreclose that possibility. When the grand jury opened its session Monday morning, Runyon called Richard Ray as the first witness. He had the state police detective describe his long and frustrating investigation.

Turning to the plea agreement, Runyon asked, "Up until the time that he openly was Mirandized and waived his rights on June fourth, 1990 . . . did you have any admissible evidence or evidence that you could obtain a criminal charge against Mark Putnam?"

"No, we didn't."

"You didn't have a body then?"

"Didn't have the body. . . . I was pretty sure that she was dead, but didn't have any information that we could have charged him with."

In his testimony Jim Huggins reiterated that point. The plea bargain, he stressed, was the only viable option. "We had no choice whatsoever, or Mr. Runyon didn't. If he hadn't entered into this agreement, we wouldn't be here today. We would have an unsolved homicide, or would have worse than that—an unsolved homicide where we know who did it, but we would not have a body."

Captain Rose testified that without the agreement "that fellow would have walked. He would never have pulled one day in the penitentiary." On the question of premeditation, Rose added, "I personally do not believe that he intended to kill her. He didn't know she was going to be at the motel. He came back here for court, and there she was. The evidence we obtained during the investigation was that he actually tried to avoid her."

Shelby Jean Ward was an important witness, but it was clear that she had no evidence that gave legal weight to her insistence on a murder indictment. The grand jury quickly saw that her knowledge of the relationship between Susan and Mark was strictly hearsay. Shelby conceded that all she knew about Mark was what Susan had told her.

"Did she tell you that she would come to Pikeville and see Mark Putnam?"

"Yes."

"You don't have personal knowledge, I take it, that she did, but that she told you she did—you weren't there when she met with him?"

"No, she told me she did. I've never seen the guy. I've talked to him on the phone. He called my house wanting to know if she was there."

"But you didn't have any personal knowledge of whether they met or didn't, or what their relationship was?"

"No."

Before dismissing Shelby, Runyon wanted her on the record about whether she understood and agreed with the plea arrangement.

"Incidentally," he said, "I doubt you are aware that all the officers have testified that we had no choice, that if we had not done this, he would be walking free today without any punishment. Do you understand it and accept it as being the thing that had to be done?"

"Yes," Shelby replied.

AFTER working well into the night and early the next morning, the day Mark was coming to court, the grand jury handed up the indictment in the form Runyon had wanted. It read, in part:

> It is the Grand Jury's opinion that the charge of manslaughter and the recommendation of 16 years in prison reflect the realities of this case. Obviously, Putnam would not cooperate with the investigators and reveal the location of the body without assurances that the Commonwealth would recommend less than the maximum possible sentence. The information given by Putnam and his plea of guilty have two positive results. First, the family of Susan Smith can now know her fate and can begin to adjust and reconstruct their lives with this painful knowledge. Second, a guilty man will be punished for his crime.

WHEN Mark Putnam entered the courtroom that day to plead guilty, every seat was taken, and spectators were crowded at the entrance, straining to see inside. He could hear whispers and titters. Whenever he turned his head, he saw faces hidden by cameras.

Court was called into session. Pike circuit judge Bayard Collier opened the proceedings with a soliloquy on the majesty of the law. Drifting out of time and place, Mark thought about handcuffs. At the academy they called them silver bracelets. They had explained that the bracelets had both practical and psychological functions: one, to disable a prisoner; the other, to humiliate him. Mark rubbed his wrists together, wondering how they would feel.

"It was sixteen years or nothing at all," Judge Collier was intoning from the bench, calling Mark back to attention. "If I had not accepted, or expected to deny, the motion to accept the plea, then according to the law, I would have had to tell Putnam and his attorney that in advance. At that point he simply would have withdrawn his confession and we would have been back to square one." The judge peered down at the cameras. "No evidence, no case."

The judge then looked at Mark and asked if he was in agreement with the terms of the plea arrangement.

Mark said firmly and loudly, "Yes, sir, I am."

A voice whispered in Mark's ear to put his hands behind his back. The cuffs snapped on with the resonance of a car door slamming. The cameras clucked with satisfaction. The judge imposed the sentence. The whole thing was over in less than a half hour.

MARK left the Pikeville courthouse with two state police officers and had no idea where he was going. He felt himself carried along like a stick on a current, head down through a sea of yapping faces, cameras scattering like gulls. Propelled headlong, he fell into the back seat of the police cruiser, his feet pushed in like cargo. The vehicle lurched forward. He righted himself and pressed his cheek against the cool glass, not caring about the pictures.

At a brief stop at the state police post he stared mutely at fingertips stained with fingerprint ink. Firm hands on his shoulder, averted eyes. Men stumped by uncertain protocol. Not knowing words to say, they were glad to see him leave.

To where they did not say, except that it was on an airplane. Two detectives with whom he once worked cases were assigned to accompany him. En route to Lexington, making talk from the back seat, Mark said, "You guys are coming up in the world," referring to the new car they were driving. Detective Joel Newsome, the big man at the wheel, replied silently with stricken eyes in the rearview mirror. But the cuffs were off for the ride. And in the hills they relaxed a little. Riding shotgun, Detective Claude Tackett, tall and wiry, sat back, draped his arm across the seat, and told the prisoner, as if sharing a secret, "We're going to Otisville, New York." Otisville was a medium-security federal prison in the foothills of the Catskill Mountains.

Mark said, "Claude, you remember when I first arrived in Pikeville, you were the only detective who traded business cards with me?"

Claude remembered and said that he was sorry about the way it worked out. He coughed and fell silent.

Mark asked about a robbery case he knew they had going. Neither replied. That was the moment Mark realized he was no longer a cop.

The weather was nice, a warm and fragrant afternoon, with big clouds in the sky. They listened silently to the hum of the road winding down from the mountains into the open bluegrass flatland of Kentucky, radiant in late springtime sunlight.

On the road skirting busy Lexington, the driver stiffened. He gaped at the signs and exit ramps flying by and slowed to forty.

"Do you know where the airport is?" Joel asked.

From the back seat Mark said softly, "You can take the Versailles Road, two exits ahead." He pronounced the word the local way: Ver-*sales*. Joel frowned, watching for the turn.

THERE was a two-hour layover at O'Hare before the connection to New York. They made him feel comfortable, not obviously watching while he ducked into the men's room, clearing their throats and standing back a way while he went to a pay phone and called Kathy collect. Kathy, numbly composed, told him that the television pictures from Pikeville had been on the Miami news and on CNN, but not on the network news programs, which she and Chris had monitored from the bedroom so the children wouldn't see.

ON THE second leg of the flight Mark dug out of his pocket a photograph of himself and the children. He and Danielle and little Mark all had their arms outstretched, as if beckoning to the photographer. Kathy, as usual, had taken the picture; she seldom appeared in family photos.

The twin-engine plane touched down in darkness at a quiet airport in a small city called Middletown. Near the terminal, three uniformed New York State policemen waited, arms folded with impatience, as the three men got off the plane and approached across the asphalt.

"Which one of you men is the prisoner?"

Feeling foolish, Mark raised his hand. Ignoring the Kentucky officers, two of the New York State cops grabbed him, locked his arms in theirs, and duckwalked him over to one of their cars, then pushed him onto the hood and roughly patted him down. Jerking his arms back violently for cuffing, one of the cops used the opportunity to yank Mark's elbows upward, sending a searing jolt through his shoulders that almost knocked him out. As he reeled, his eyes hot with rage, Mark thought of the occasions he had done the same thing to a particularly distasteful prisoner, a cheap cop stunt to release a little aggression and send a painful message about who was in charge.

They drove for a long time on country roads over dark, rolling farmland, the Kentucky troopers in the car behind. One of the New York cops told his partner that this prisoner wasn't the only "hotshot fed" who belonged in jail, but he would do for now.

Mark worried about how he would handle himself. Contempt and rude treatment from state cops were one thing; in prison, with the cops on the other side of the bars, it was going to be a different story. As he rode, he devised a new challenge for himself, handling that inevitable first confrontation with another prisoner eager to hassle a cop in jail—not backing down, not whining, complaining, or asking for help, not behaving in any way that would embarrass the FBI.

Ahead, against a black sky, on the crest of a hill, he saw the prison in white light. Razor wire glinted like ice atop a twenty-foot fence. The gate swung open; he was taken from the car and hustled inside.

Propelled along a gleaming hallway through gates that doubled like decompression chambers, he kept his chin up, steeling himself. He would prevail, he vowed, even if they kept him there until the very last day of his sixteen years.

# Epilogue

Susan Smith went to her grave surrounded by the people she had known all her life. A sheriff's car led a small procession of vehicles up the steep path beside the creek in Barrenshea Hollow to her mother's family plot, on the side of the hill next to the frame house where Susan had grown up.

Addressing the mourners, the preacher asked, "How could this ever happen in America, in Pike County? With as many Christian people as there are among us, how could this have ever happened? Yet it did happen. And every one of us is part of the guilt." He took as his text the Lamentations of Jeremiah:

> *She weeps bitterly in the night, tears on her cheeks; among all her lovers she has none to comfort her; all her friends have dealt treacherously with her, they have become her enemies.*

AFTER Mark pleaded guilty, the FBI conducted an internal review into the case, but did not release its findings and has declined to comment on it.

Ron Poole was transferred to the Lexington bureau, where he continued to do undercover work.

In March 1992 Kathy Putnam gave a lengthy statement to the FBI concerning Poole's conduct in the Pikeville office and his relationship with Susan. According to sources, Poole has denied any improper conduct. The FBI has forbidden Poole to comment publicly.

DETECTIVE Richard Ray was named Trooper of the Year by the Kentucky State Police in 1991. He took his plaque and resigned, disgusted by the department's general penny-pinching on investigations, in particular its foot-dragging in pressing the FBI on the Putnam case.

John Paul Runyon, the Pike County commonwealth attorney, was reelected to a sixth term in 1992. He continued to be distressed by the FBI's casual attitude toward using informants and by what he saw as its failure to heed the warnings sent up by the Putnam case.

IN MAY 1992 Susan Smith was reburied in another spot farther up Barrenshea Hollow, next to her brother Raymond Daniels, who had been killed earlier in the year in a car wreck. Only a handful of people, including her father and her sister Shelby, stood by in a cold drizzle to see her laid once more to rest.

SUSAN's ex-husband, Kenneth Smith, lives in a trailer with their two children, Miranda and Brady, in Johnson Bottom. Kenneth denies ever physically abusing Susan.

Kathy Putnam sold the condo and most of their furniture in Fort Lauderdale and moved with her children to Minnesota to be near Mark, who was transferred from Otisville to a federal prison in Rochester, Minnesota. A year later she and the children returned to Connecticut, living with the help of welfare payments.

Three years after he went to prison, she continues to proclaim her love for her husband. On sleepless nights she blames herself for not being able to prevent the tragedy.

Kathy says she is haunted by the thought of Susan. "I never sleep more than three hours at a time. Some nights I actually wake up with the phone in my hand, thinking I'm talking to her."

Meanwhile, Kathy struggles to provide as normal a life as she can for the two children and to shore up her husband in prison. She is making plans to move back to Minnesota to be near him.

"He tells me from prison, 'I think about the kids, how I screwed up their lives'—and I say, 'You can't think about that anymore, Mark. It's done. You have a responsibility not to give up and not to become a product of that place. Your responsibility is to come back to us as the man we knew. Think about what we still have. We love each other. We have beautiful, healthy children who are getting through this. Time is all that's between us. Time will pass, and we'll be okay.' "

IN PRISON Mark endlessly analyzes the circumstances that led to his downfall. "I often think about whether Susan was really pregnant. I don't think she was. If she was, I don't think now that it could have been mine. That's one of the places I get totally aggravated with myself—in the hysteria of the moment, I never looked in a cool way at the situation. Was I stupid? I don't know. Here I am for the next twelve or fourteen years, whatever. Maybe I am just stupid. If I could take back those two minutes in that car . . .

"But I had a responsibility to live up to, and I failed it. For what I did, I sentenced myself. I didn't have to give myself up—I know that better than anybody. And even then I didn't have to take sixteen years. Confessing was the only way I could see of even being able to start over with a clean slate.

"I know I could be on the beach right now with my family in Florida. I lost all of that. I lost my children's childhood, and they lost their father. But I also know that now I can sleep at night; I can look myself in the mirror. I couldn't do that for a whole year. Slowly I am becoming at peace with myself.

"One of the things that hurts me most is the effect on my relationship with my son—we never got to know each other. Danielle and I had five years together, five good years. My son knows me as a voice on the phone."

In prison he reads and rereads the letters he gets from his daughter, especially the first one, folded and creased until it is nearly in tatters:

Dear Old Pop:

I got this special paper for writing to you. I hope you like it. I have been a very good girl. I have been helping Mommy around the house sometimes without even being asked. I have been eating all my suppers. I stay up later now because I am older than my brother. And I should be able to. He is still being a pain. But I love him anyway. I can't wait until we'll be able to visit you and give you hugs and kisses. I want you to know that we are ok. We miss you but we are taking care of business. You take care of yourself for us. Eat good, sleep good, and brush your teeth. I got your letters and my heart puffed with love. Please write when you can and I will. I love you as big as the universe. Be good, and be careful.

Love,
Danielle Your #1 Girl

# Wings *of the*

# Morning

One Man's Courageous Flight to
Save His Wife and Children

## ORESTES LORENZO

Translated from the Spanish by E. K. Max

. . . We made a final effort to calm ourselves, and we walked to the door. Looking into Vicky's eyes, I whispered, "I don't know how long it will take for us to be reunited, but I'll never give you up. If they don't let you leave, I'll be back for the three of you. I don't know how—but I'll come back. This is a struggle of truth against the lie, of love against hatred. Never doubt that love will triumph."

Turning, I ran down the stairs, asking God to give me the strength to undertake that flight to a new destiny, where my children might grow up in freedom.

*—Wings of the Morning*

# *Prologue*

ALABAMA, March 20, 1991, 10:45 a.m.
Colonel Barton halted in front of the door, glancing at the panel of buttons to his left and swiftly pressing in the required code. A green light went on above the door, and the whir of an electrical motor could be heard from behind it. The fifteen-ton mass of the door began to open with a groan, revealing a familiar room lit with a pale glow that appeared to emanate from nowhere in particular.

With their eyes fixed on a twenty-foot screen looming above, a team of operators sat facing a wide panel cluttered with switches and colored lights. Moving across the screen within the contours of a map of the United States were hundreds of luminous dots, with a trail of digits and symbols. The eerie hum of high voltage was interrupted by occasional beeping sounds or brief communiqués uttered over the loudspeaker system. Although the overall effect was something out of science fiction, the leaded concrete walls enclosing an operations room several stories below ground level, and the miles of communications lines emanating from its core, framed the neurological hub of a very real United States Early Defense Warning System. This was the control room, a marvel of engineering, situated under Southern Strategic Air Command headquarters. At their posts, coordinating and directing the system, were the men and women of the morning watch.

The colonel made his way to the central panel. He stood behind one of the operators seated at the controls of the radiolocation system, glanced up at the screen and its accompanying data monitors covering the entire wall, and inquired, "How are things, Captain?"

"Everything in order, sir," Captain Lee replied.

Colonel Barton liked to keep an eye on things personally.

A few years back, learning he was to be reassigned to the command post in Alabama, the colonel had assumed that at last he would be relieved of the constant stress that pervaded his years of service in Southeast Asia and Europe. In Alabama there was no enemy with nuclear striking capability within a radius of 5000 miles, and the climate was also superb. And his married daughter, Kathy, lived less than three hours from his new post.

More recently, however, his peace of mind had been troubled. A brigadier general of the Cuban air force, Rafael del Pino, defecting to the United States in 1987, had suggested at a debriefing that Fidel Castro, in the event of any open conflict with the United States, was prepared to launch a MiG attack upon the Turkey Point nuclear reactor complex in Florida in order to produce the equivalent of a nuclear strike against our southern perimeter. Castro's MiGs were based just a few minutes away from their target.

But now Colonel Barton was smiling. Only a few more hours till the end of his shift. Then he was all set to enjoy five days' leave, when he and his wife would visit their daughter and son-in-law. He thought of his four-year-old granddaughter racing across the front lawn to greet him: "Grandpa, Grandpa! What'd you bring me, Grandpa?"

He came back to reality, letting his eyes wander from the large screen to the digital clock above it: 10:50 a.m.

## *Chapter One*

IN CUBA, at Santa Clara Air Base, less than 750 miles to the southeast, fourteen MiG-23s sat under a blazing sun awaiting the pilots who might have to board them at any given moment. The squadron of MiG-23 BN fighter-bombers was poised to carry out the day's mission.

"Permission to address the major!"

The request, barked from behind me, interrupted my thoughts as I stood examining the meteorological map for weather conditions to the north of Cuba. "Go ahead," I replied, turning around.

"Number seven twenty-two is ready to go, sir!"

"Let's try it out," I told the young engineer, inviting him to precede me onto the field as I realized I'd probably never see him again.

Gleaming in the sunlight, my MiG stood waiting for me—and for its maiden voyage following a complete overhaul, including a fresh coat of dark green and blue paint. For the past ten years I had flown only the less sophisticated MiG-21s, but now we had fourteen MiG-23 BNs, all recently arrived at the base, and this was to be my first mission in one of them—and most certainly my last in any MiG.

I was about to make the most dangerous journey of my life. There would be no points of reference on my navigational chart, nor any parameters for my heading, airspeed, altitude, or fuel consumption. For this flight the only data was in my own head: two alternate routes to my secret objective, jealously guarded in my brain. My worldly possessions consisted of a pair of photographs, cropped to fit the contours of my pockets, keepsakes of all that was dearest to me in life: my wife, Vicky, and my sons—Alejandro, four, and Reyniel, nine.

As I walked up to the plane, I found the flight technician and his mechanics standing at attention, waiting for me. I greeted each of them with a quick handshake and began to climb into the cockpit.

"How're you feeling for your first flight in a 23, Major?" my technician asked with a smile.

"Just like a beginner," I answered, hoping to deflect the real reasons for my anxiety.

"Falcon, one four six one, permission to start engine," I radioed the control tower after hearing my flight technician tell me over the headphones that I could proceed with ignition.

"Engine start, six one."

"Roger, Falcon." As I flipped the engine-start switches, my hands were trembling. "One four six one, permission to taxi."

"Cleared for taxiing, six one."

The aircraft wheeled slowly toward the runway.

You sure you want to go through with this? I asked myself, staring through the Plexiglas windshield at that landscape I loved so dearly. In the heat of the narrow cockpit I was already sweating heavily and feeling the discomfort of the oxygen mask glued to my face.

I stopped just short of the runway. A plane was coming in for a landing, and I would have to wait. Meanwhile, the heat, the oxygen mask—everything seemed meant to torture me.

How long before I see Vicky again, and the kids? Maybe never. What'll my parents say when they find out? My brothers? My friends? And what's going to happen to Vicky once they realize what I've done?

Finally the runway was clear.

"One four six one requesting permission to access runway."

"Taxi into position and hold, six one."

*Well, here goes!* "Falcon, one four six one, request takeoff."

"Six one, cleared for takeoff, zone one."

Thrust 100 percent. Revolutions, temperature, oil pressure—all normal. Voltmeter okay. Afterburner!

A sudden, overwhelming force mushroomed behind the plane, shuddering its nineteen tons of aluminum and steel straight forward. I released the brakes, and in a few seconds I was airborne.

I racked my mind, attempting to summon the data I had memorized: heading, minimum possible altitude, airspeed.

My breathing was becoming desperate. Finally I tore off the oxygen mask, leaving it dangling from my helmet.

*This is like meeting death face to face.*

NOT far from the Santa Clara base, Vicky was on her way to the market with Alejandro when they heard the deafening noise produced by an afterburner at takeoff. They glanced up to watch a MiG soaring into the air—impetuous, blue, and gleaming in the sun.

"Mommy," Alejandro asked, "is that Daddy's plane?"

"Yes, Alé, that one is Daddy's."

Vicky did her utmost not to cry, and asked God to see me safely to my destination. Help him, Lord. Help him get there safely. And please, dear God, help us to be reunited with him again, she prayed, hurrying off with Alejandro to pick up their daily ration of milk and bread.

MEANWHILE, I sat struggling with myself in the terrible confinement of that narrow cockpit, absorbed in fevered speculation: What in God's name are you doing? Have you lost your mind? What makes you think you know the truth? How can you be sure that what you saw on the Russian television or read in the Soviet papers isn't all lies? How do you know the Americans won't just turn you over to the Cuban authorities? Or send you to prison? After all, you've been their enemy practically from the day you were born.

But what about my sons? Am I going to let them have the same kind of life I had? Do I let them grow into slaves without a word of protest? Do I watch while their lives are poisoned with the hatred that infected my own?

I'd rather die first! If that world is just as bad as the one I already know, if whatever I've read and seen lately turns out to be just as false, then there's no point in living. . . . But I've got to find out!

In a cold sweat, panting for breath, struggling with my conscience and my soul, I was taking my MiG out over the blue waters of the Straits of Florida to a destination known only to Vicky and myself.

"One four six one . . . four seven here."

The pilot's voice exploded from the headphones of my helmet, severing my thoughts. I was already halfway gone, keeping just a couple hundred feet above the water, and those few minutes had been enough to lose contact with my flight controller out of Santa Clara.

"Go ahead, four seven. Six one here."

"Falcon is calling you."

"Tell Falcon I don't read him."

The pilot repeated to the tower that he had talked to me.

"Six one, Falcon is asking your position," he resumed after a pause.

"At the center of zone one," I said, "and about to go into my dive."

Four seven relayed my reply to Falcon; then after a few seconds he added, "Six one, Falcon has you cleared to proceed."

"Roger, four seven," I replied.

*Cleared to proceed—all right!*

That was my last radio contact with the Falcons of Santa Clara.

Alabama, 11:10 a.m.

Colonel Barton's vacation plans were shattered by the howling of the control room's computerized alarm system. Then came the ringing voice of one of his subordinate officers: "Enemy target approaching at sea level. Quadrant two five three two, heading three fifty, airspeed five hundred knots."

On the screen a luminous dot to the southeast of Key West was moving north at high speed. The colonel read its flight parameters and was struck with a feeling of foreboding. He was accustomed to picking up various aircraft attempting to evade radar detection, but those were without exception small craft flying at low speed, hoping to penetrate U.S. airspace covertly to deliver narcotics from Central and South America. The target he now observed on the screen was a supersonic fighter, very likely armed with bombs and missiles, and less than twenty-five knots from the coast of Key West. It would take that baby under three minutes to overfly Boca Chica Naval Air Station, and only ten minutes to hit the nuclear complex at Turkey Point!

The magnitude of the implication froze Colonel Barton's blood. Although it seemed highly improbable, no one could afford to ignore the possibility of a surprise attack by Castro against the United States. "Scramble interceptors out of Homestead and put out a yellow alert for ground-to-air for Southern Strategic and for the interceptors at MacDill," he ordered. His complement ran to their stations.

One of his officers got on the intercom, talking to a distant radar operator, hoping to obtain more precise data on the approaching target. Another was snapping out orders over his scrambled line of communication. The colonel kept checking the screen, only to confirm what he had suspected all along. He felt a chill creep up his spine.

One minute had already elapsed since the target had been picked up by radar. Now it was some nine miles farther north. It would take another minute to issue and digest the various commands needed to implement a military response from appropriate units of the armed forces. The ground-to-air missiles would need another six minutes to locate the target and destroy it. At the same time, the pilots at Homestead Air Force Base would require about five minutes to get their F-16s airborne, lock onto and knock out the target.

The squadrons at MacDill had been put on alert in view of the distinct possibility that this lone aircraft was actually part of a much larger strike force. Anything was possible.

The only thing certain was that as the seconds ticked away, the enemy aircraft would continue to make for its objective. If its intention was to hit Boca Chica Naval Air Station, only the base itself could take any preemptive measures now, because you couldn't knock that target out of the air before it reached Key West. But if its mission was actually to strike the Turkey Point reactor complex, then at least there was time to intercept and destroy it before it produced a disaster worse than Chernobyl.

The colonel suddenly thought about his granddaughter, and millions of other innocent children and adults, unconscious of the impending danger approaching the Florida coast. He picked up the phone, a direct line to the chief of staff of the Southern Strategic Air Command, and briefly explained the situation to his superior. The orders came back over the wire just as briefly.

Secret communiqués went out over the scrambled lines to military units scattered throughout south Florida. Instructions were relayed back and forth with increasing urgency. The change that came over the control room was dramatic. "We're going to take out the enemy target at the second line." The commander's voice was firm, sure.

The F-16s out of Homestead could only lock onto their target a few miles south of Turkey Point, but the ground-to-air missiles could take him out well before that—as soon as he crossed the second line of antiair defenses. Fighter pilots and missile crews were rushing to their aircraft and the silos. The military response had been set in motion.

However, by the time the alert reached Boca Chica, it was too late.

TIME to climb and cut back power, I told myself after calculating that I ought to be about fifty knots off Key West. I had no wish to alarm the United States authorities any more than I had to. I had expected to be able to climb to approximately 7000 feet and to reduce my airspeed to about 250 knots while still at a prudent distance. Radio contact was out, since I had only the twenty preset channels with coded military frequencies, impossible to adjust from inside the cockpit. I was not going to have the opportunity for direct communication with North American traffic controllers. Thus I hoped to facilitate being peaceably intercepted by some of the F-16s based at Boca Chica. Once the North American fighters reached me, I could use internationally recognized visual signals to explain my intentions. So my luck would depend on how they interpreted my presence.

It's time to climb. I'd better not cross the line at Key West, I warned myself.

As I climbed, however, the outline of Key West rolled over the horizon, and I was thrown into a panic. This was much closer than I had supposed. I was already on top of the Keys, with no alternative but to overfly the naval air base at Boca Chica.

They must have already given the order to take me out at the slightest penetration farther north, I told myself, desperate at my blunder. Just keep this side of Key West if you want to stay alive.

I cut back on power and, banking gradually, dropped altitude to make a low pass over runway number 07 at Boca Chica, waggling wings to signify my peaceful intentions.

One more pass over the runway—low, slow, and dirty—to let them know on my next pass I'll be coming in for a landing.

As I touched down, I felt my legs trembling. Could they be consulting with the Cuban government before coming to a decision? Well, whatever happens now, let it!

Suddenly I noticed someone up in the control tower observing me through binoculars.

The drag chute swinging from the MiG's tail rose and sank at intervals, whenever the exhaust from the engine's tail nozzle and an occasional gust of wind conspired to fill its canopy. It just hung there, lifting and falling in agonized convulsions, like a dying bird, imparting a feeling of captive desolation to the flat, deserted landscape of the base.

Eventually a truck with a yellow blinking light above the cab pulled up to the aircraft, signaling me to follow. Slowly, with the drag chute clawing me back, I managed to taxi behind him, crossing the length of the airfield under a bright sun—the driver and his truck, me and my MiG-23, as if we were all that was left on earth.

When we reached the far end of the field, the driver got out of his truck and raised his arms and crossed them, indicating that I should cut the engine. Seconds later, after the shrill drone of the turbine had ceased, a red automobile drove up to my plane. At the wheel was an officer, who turned out to be the base commander, accompanied by a sergeant who seemed to be Hispanic. Both stepped out of the car as soon as they saw the MiG's canopy slide open.

I took off my helmet, dropped it into the cockpit, and sprang onto the pavement, presenting myself at military attention to the senior officer. Then I proceeded to declare in Spanish with a trembling voice, *"Mi nombre es Orestes Lorenzo."*

"His name is Orestes Lorenzo."

*"Soy mayor de la Fuerza Aérea Cubana."*

"He says he's a major in the Cuban air force."

*"Y pido protección a las autoridades de este país."*

"He's asking for protection by the authorities."

*"Por razones políticas."*

"Political asylum."

The colonel nodded to the sergeant as he listened; then he fixed his eyes on me. Suddenly he broke into a smile, stepped forward, and extended a hand. "Welcome to the United States."

## Chapter Two

MY EARLIEST memories go back to my birthplace in Cabaiguán, a small town almost exactly at the center of Cuba. In those days Cabaiguán was famous for its tobacco and its women. "The most beautiful women in Cuba come from Cabaiguán," the grown-ups would say over and over again. "This black soil is the richest on the whole island. We have the best vegetables and the finest tobacco."

Cabaiguán also boasted several *escogidas*—stripping barns—where tobacco leaves were sorted and graded, their midribs manually removed, and the remainder of the leaves bundled and sent to cigar factories. There artisans called *torcedores* hand-rolled them into the distinctive *puros* from Cabaiguán.

In 1950 my parents met each other at the Zorrilla stripping barn, where they had both been driven by more or less the same destiny. My mother was the seventh of nine daughters and a son, from the marriage of María—a young peasant woman from the fields of Pedro Barba—to Casildo, a Spanish emigrant from the Canary Islands, both of whom had found each other in the midst of the direst poverty.

My paternal grandparents, María and Cristino Lorenzo, lived with their nine children on a farm, where the owner allowed them to build a shack with a dirt floor that my grandmother swept down each afternoon with the ashes left from the charcoal she used for cooking.

My father had been able to study up to the third grade in a small public school, and he began to discover what would turn out to be one of the passions of his life—reading.

Hounded by debt and despair, my paternal grandparents decided finally to move to the long-feared town, where after a few years my father found work as a reader in the Zorrilla stripping barn. My mother had also arrived there, at fourteen years of age, in search of the six pesos she could earn weekly by stemming and sorting tobacco leaves during the three months of the year the stripping barn was operative. And here was that young man of twenty, seated in the middle of a room filled with working girls, looking up at intervals from the newspaper he was reading aloud to them as they worked, fixing his eyes on the wild adolescent girl seated there before him, her head bent over the table full of tobacco leaves.

One day my father paused near my mother's workstation and remarked to the friend in his company, "That girl is going to be the mother of my children."

Hearing what he said, the young girl blushed, then turned to him with an arrogant stare that made my father burst into laughter.

It was 1955 when they decided to marry and go to live in a small, fragile wooden house, where they spent their first years together, watching every cent of their meager salaries to be able to eat and pay the rent. Around that time the government passed a law requiring the owners of stripping barns to pay higher salaries in response to workers' demands. But the owners decided to move their *escogidas* to other towns with more docile labor forces instead of paying the increased wage. My parents found themselves in the desperate situation of not having five centavos each morning with which to purchase the liter of milk needed by their first wailing little glutton—me—born in 1956.

At that time the men from the Twenty-sixth of July Movement were already in the mountains, promising to make a revolution that would give justice to the country, and my father began to collaborate with the rebels. In the last days of 1958 the troops commanded by Che Guevara entered Cabaiguán in triumph after a few skirmishes, to establish their headquarters in the Breña stripping barn, very close to our house. Three days earlier my father had left to join the combatants of the Twenty-sixth of July before the taking of the town, and now my mother was cowering in a corner of the kitchen, already eight months pregnant with their second son, her face extremely pale with the panic she felt at the sporadic gunfire she could still hear nearby. She was worrying about my absent father when she suddenly heard the desperate cries of her neighbor and went out to see what had happened. The woman was ill and had sent her adolescent nephew to the pharmacy for medicine some two hours earlier. Now they brought her the news that an army sniper, stationed on a rooftop, had killed the boy as he crossed the street attempting to reach the pharmacy. My mother felt invaded by the terror of her neighbor's tragedy and was running with me in her arms back to the house when she heard the familiar sound of an airplane swooping over the house, followed by the sound of explosions.

"Everybody into your houses! They're machine-gunning headquarters!" she heard someone yell as he ran down the street. She hurled herself under the bed with me.

The old government fled, and the guerrillas entered the capital like heroes, enveloped in the triumphal rejoicing of the adulating masses. All the *escogidas* returned to Cabaiguán, and the owners agreed now to pay the established wage, increased to some twenty pesos a week. The rent for houses was lowered significantly, and each day more and more laws were passed in favor of the poor. The rejoicing was great; the Revolution was victorious.

My father was now employed as reader in the Bouzac tobacco factory. He had a small room in the factory loft, which held a huge amplifier and an old microphone. Here my father spent the workday reading aloud from works by great authors—from Cervantes to Victor Hugo and Hemingway—as the *torcedores* rolled the cigars. Thus the cigar workers of Cabaiguán acquired a remarkable literary education.

IN THOSE days we lived with my grandparents in a small wooden house situated at the end of a narrow stone lane that ambled over a gentle hillside. I spent a lot of time with my grandparents, watching them roll their own cigars, the leaves of which they'd guard jealously in a wooden box on the dining-room table. My grandmother smoked her rough-hewn *puros* mostly in the kitchen, while my grandfather chose an old easy chair next to the living-room window. Tobacco permeated our lives back then. When I was only fourteen months old, my father had brought me to a photographer's studio, where they took my picture with a *puro* between my lips.

In the evenings when my father arrived home from work, I'd be waiting for him by the doorway. I remember how I'd try to catch sight of him as he came up the lane, always with something in hand. Then I'd take off for him like a bullet, and he'd crouch down for me to throw myself into his arms, kissing him on both cheeks. He would carry me back into the house and sit me up on the table to show me what he had brought. Sometimes a sweet; other times, fruit juice.

LATE ONE NIGHT SOMEONE WOKE me with a kiss. It was my uncle Orlando, the youngest of my father's brothers, who lived in the United States. He was holding up a large airplane he'd brought for me. We all sat up in the living room that night, excited at his arrival. And there I was with my new toy, taxiing between the legs of my parents and grandparents, taking such pleasure in the winged apparatus that transported me on a fantastic voyage around the world that no one could persuade me to go back to bed. From that night on, whenever anybody asked me what I was going to be when I grew up, I would answer, "A pilot!" That airplane, the first I ever flew—on the imaginative wings of my three years of age—would be my last toy.

It was December, and Orlando was only the first of many relatives who arrived for the Christmas holidays. My father had three other brothers and four sisters, all with children of their own, who filled our home that season with a happiness I was not to experience again during my childhood. My father's sister Miladis came from the United States as well, along with her husband and children. One afternoon they brought over a projector with slides from "up north," which they projected that night onto the white wall of the house across the street, causing a sensation in the neighborhood.

On Christmas Eve the men sat out on the patio and the women stayed in the kitchen, while we boys ran through the house in an all-out war, cap guns blazing away. The men were gathered around the rectangular fireplace, swigging occasionally from their beer bottles and laughing boisterously as the pig roasted.

Christmas dinner was held in the living room, around a long table covered with white tablecloths. There we all sat, children and grownups together, to partake of the suckling pig and to hear grandfather give thanks to God for the preservation and happiness of our family. Those were the last Christmas memories I have.

One day the leaders of the Revolution decided that Christmas traditions were imported—and harmful to the economy, since they coincided with the most important period of the sugar harvest, the best moment to cut the cane for its highest yield in sugar. Nor was there any reason for the children to be celebrating the Day of the Magi on the sixth of January. That celebration could be shifted to the twenty-sixth of July, the day of the attack on the Moncada Barracks by a group of young men led by Fidel Castro—the highest leader. Those charming figures on camels who answered our letters by leaving toys under our beds before dawn were to disappear from our dreams.

Never again would the entire family be seated around the table; never again would thanks be given to God. Never again would I receive a blessing before going to sleep.

Our life returned to its accustomed routine when the new leaders of the town offered to send my father to the School for Revolutionary Instruction, since they needed new cadres to direct the creative tasks of the Revolution. And we watched him go off, happy to seek wider horizons than those of a tobacco reader.

My father spent what seemed to me to be a long time away at school and then began working in the Ministry of Education. One afternoon I saw him emerge from my room, furious, holding a picture of the Virgin Mary that had hung over my bed. "I told you I don't want any more of this garbage in the boy's room!" he cried, and flung it onto the patio. My mother broke into sobs, and I, confused and frightened, ran for my grandmother. She pressed me to her.

At night I would often find my grandparents by the radio, listening to a faraway station with the volume turned low. In the morning, after my parents had gone off to work, my grandmother's brother Modesto usually stopped by. While he and my grandparents awaited Grandma's delicious coffee, he'd invariably bring up the previous night's broadcast. At the time, I couldn't figure out what they were talking about or why they had to listen to the radio so cautiously.

"What we need is for the Americans to come here and straighten things out," Modesto insisted.

"This guy is worse than Batista," my grandmother would add in a sad, low voice. Grandfather nodded his head.

THE following year my father went off to another province, eventually returning for us in a Russian truck with a tough young driver at the wheel. My father eagerly described his new job as "director of education." Then, piling the few things we owned onto the back of the truck, we all took off together—my father, my mother, my little brother Faure, myself, and the driver—all crammed into the front, heading for the town of Matanzas. That day I discovered that the world went much farther than Cabaiguán.

Our home in Matanzas was on the fourth floor of a modern apartment building, where my parents and my brother still live. From up on the balcony we caught our first glimpse of the sea—the sea, which was going to be the focal point of all our adventures and our mother's greatest worry. The other tenants were blond, blue-eyed foreigners. "They're German technicians," people said, and from then on, the building was called the Technicians' Quarters.

My father worked tirelessly throughout the province, often returning home dirty and exhausted. Then he would explain how he had been to Ciénaga de Zapata, inaugurating some little school for the illiterate charcoal burners who lived there. My father's work was his obsession. The word revolution was forever on his lips, and he would speak of it—to my brother and to me—as his reason for living.

As a family, we seldom traveled anywhere. The few times we went to see a movie or to eat out, my father and mother would argue because he didn't want to dress up properly. He preferred to wear his gray khakis or the simple blue militia shirt he wore each day to work.

"Orestes, please do me a favor and don't dress so shabbily. We're going out," my mother would scold him.

"A man's worth is on the inside, not on the outside," he insisted. "Dressing fancy is a bourgeois habit, not mine."

He had given himself over, body and soul, to the tasks of the Revolution, which also began to attract us youngsters.

WHEN I was seven, my father told me I was to be sent away to a new school on a government scholarship. I realized he meant I wouldn't be living at home. It was my first baptism by fire.

"I never had schooling," he explained, "but today the Revolution gives everything to children. At boarding school you'll have an education, clothing, meals—all free. Not just you, but every child. It makes no difference if you're the son of a government minister or a shoemaker. That's the justice of the Revolution."

The boarding school was located in the hills, with a distant view of Matanzas. Our week began Sunday evenings at eight, when parents dropped their children off at the front gate, and it ended only on the following Saturday at noon, when we went home for the weekend.

About sixty of us, all boys, slept in a large dormitory. We would make our beds at six in the morning, as soon as our teacher entered shouting, "On your feet!" After brushing our teeth, we formed two lines outside in the schoolyard, then marched to the dining hall in step with the teacher's commands: "Attention! Forward, march!" And as we marched, we would sing the revolutionary songs they taught us: *"Marching we go, armed with the truth, knowing we'll find the solution. United we stand, the Cuban youth, our faith in the Revolution."*

In the afternoon, after classes, we would wash up in a room near the dormitory, supervised by a woman whose job it was to make sure we were clean. She would have several five-gallon cans of cold water ready to douse us with as soon as we were naked and properly soaped up. When the cold water hit, it took our breath away.

At night there was always a man with an old rifle posted on guard duty. He told us that there was the possibility of a North American invasion and that there were counterrevolutionaries trying to turn us into slaves again, which was why he stood guard with his big gun while we slept—to defend us against imperialist aggression.

Whoever behaved badly would be punished at night. The teacher would hand the night guard a list of the guilty ones, and they'd be called in by him and made to stand at military attention for several hours. On one of those nights, I had to stand like that until early morning, and when I finally returned to the dormitory, I walked to my bed relieved and half asleep. Hardly had my head hit the pillow when two distant explosions rattled doors and windows in the dormitory. The next morning we were told that a plane coming from Miami had dropped two bombs on one of the port factories. That was the first time I began to think how bad the Americans were.

BEING separated from my parents made me very homesick, and the weekends when I could go home again were the happiest moments of my life. Together with my brother, Faure, I would go hiking in the fields of agave or wander off to catch sea snails in the bay.

One afternoon my father came with Faure to pick me up, telling me, "You have a new brother! He was born yesterday, and his name is Orlando." And so the three of us went off in the jeep to the hospital. But we were only allowed to greet Mother from the street as she waved to us from the hospital window.

My father had changed a lot since we'd moved to Matanzas. I didn't see him often, and when he talked to me, it was mainly to scold, contrasting his harsh childhood to my own. "At your age I was a man already," he would tell me. I felt ashamed of my infantile pranks; yet I felt too shy to ask him what it was I was supposed to know at my age. And I never told him about my problems, for fear of his reproach.

Then one Sunday evening, as my parents were taking me back to the school, I wanted so much to stay at home that I told my father.

"Don't be a softy," he replied. "At school you have everything."

"Please, Orestes—why don't we let him stay home this week?" my mother interceded.

"Onelia, he's a big boy now and has to stop his whining. When I was his age, I was breaking my back in the fields with my father. I couldn't even dream about school." He turned toward the back seat, where I sat, crushed by his words. "We mustn't forget that it cost a lot of lives to get where we are now and that it still takes a lot of effort to hold on to what we've won, so we're not going to coddle Orestico."

"But Orestes, try to understand. You hardly ever spend time with the boys. All you do is work day and night." My mother was trying to make him see that we hadn't talked like father and son in a long time. Whenever we did talk, it was as revolutionary to revolutionary, which at seven years of age made me rather bitter.

"Onelia, I work hard because I owe it to the Revolution, which made it possible to have schools for everybody."

"But Orestes, the family—"

My mother was interrupted by a quick slap from my father, who, livid with anger at her insistence, said in a choked voice, "Get it into your head, Onelia: first the Revolution and then the family."

I shrank in the back seat of the jeep, feeling ashamed. I wanted the earth to swallow me up because I was less than dirt. Yet when they left me at the gate of the school that evening, I ran along the fence in tears, crying out to the jeep, which was already heading down the road, "Daddy, Mommy . . . Don't leave me!" After that I never again had the courage to ask for my father's affection. I went into the dormitory, where a cold bed awaited me, and cried myself to sleep.

AFTER the third grade I was transferred to a recently opened school at Varadero Beach, a popular resort famous for its fine white sand. This time Faure would come with me. The school, which specialized in swimming, comprised a row of mansions on a street lined with palm trees. These were houses of the "old well-to-do," who had left the country for the United States because the Revolution, we were told, had not permitted them to continue exploiting the poor. The houses were filled with fine furniture, but the pupils, mostly peasants or children from modest families, didn't take long to destroy everything.

We were taken by bus to the finest hotels in Varadero for swimming lessons, but soon an Olympic-sized pool was built on the school grounds, and we would train there three times a day. Our lives became a shuffle between swimming pool, classrooms, and dining hall, always marching to the instructors' orders, intoning revolutionary songs.

Early in the morning a silver plane would fly over the school to land at the nearby airport. It was the period when those emigrating to the United States would leave from Varadero. Twenty-six years later I would learn that the Cubans who left the country on those flights had dubbed them Freedom Flights. My father would often bring up the emigrant question, saying such people preferred to exchange their love of family and country for the various articles they could obtain in the United States. Those who wanted to leave were referred to as *gusanos*—worms—meaning those who crawled, unable to hold up their heads. "Those who stay here live modestly but with dignity, and dignity is the most valuable possession one can have," said my father.

One day I heard him arguing with my mother, but I didn't understand why. "Even if it is your sister, they're not going to spend the night in this house."

My mother's sister Felicia and her husband, Raúl, owned a small store that provided them with a modest living. Once it was confiscated by the government, they decided to leave with their children for the United States, via Camarioca. As they lived quite a distance away, in Cabaiguán, they hoped to spend the night before departure with us.

"I will have nothing to do with anybody who is against the Revolution," my father declared. My mother ran off to her room in tears, thinking of the sister whom she might never see again.

SOMETIMES on Sundays my father's friends would meet at our house to discuss various political and historical subjects. I listened attentively. My father's opinions gave meaning to the doctrines we learned at school. The conversations always centered around Fidel's greatness and around the powerful but fraudulent enemy, the United States, which despised us and wanted to humiliate us. In school we were taught that for more than a century the giant to the north had coveted our island. To prove this, our teachers would cite newspaper articles of a hundred years ago in which journalists lobbied for the annexation of Cuba, referring to Cubans disdainfully as intellectually and morally inferior. Nowadays the Revolution was giving our lives a new dimension; we had dignity and would not allow ourselves to be treated as lesser beings. Death was preferable to that kind of humiliation.

My father and his friends dreamed about the bright future opening up to all Cubans. "Look at the Soviet Union," my father would remark. "A country that has made the leap from feudalism to socialism and turned out to be the first to send a man into space. What won't we accomplish in just a few years?"

In school we were taught to worship the Revolution. We were Young Pioneers, the sons of scientists, military officers, peasants, and laborers, and I felt lucky to be living where the same rights were given to everybody and where our parents' income didn't matter.

Sometimes when his friends were around, my father would quiz me on some political issue. My knowledge of politics, acquired so early, made him feel proud of me. Once when they were talking about the *gusanos,* he asked me, "What would you say if tomorrow your mother and I decided to leave for the United States?"

"I'd rather see you dead than traitors to your country," I answered gravely. My father smiled his approval.

One Saturday, when Faure and I arrived at home from school, we were told that Father had been taken to the hospital. The doctors diagnosed an ulcer and recommended that he change his job. His passion in performing his duties—often not eating or sleeping while he traveled—was the cause of his illness.

Concerned about his health, the so-called party officials from the Ministry of Education began to visit us. They were surprised to see that we had no television or refrigerator, since they took it for granted that, given my father's position, we had been allotted them. They didn't understand that my father was proud of his austerity. "The more humble a man, the greater he is," we had often heard him say. Nevertheless, a refrigerator and television were delivered to the house one day. "So he can observe his diet properly," the deliveryman explained to my mother, pointing to the refrigerator, which was not available in stores, being only assigned by the state.

AT THE END OF THE SIXTH grade I was sent to the countryside for forty-five days to do agricultural work for the Revolution. They called it School in the Fields, and every year secondary school students were assigned a period to work in the fields. Our dormitories consisted of two large barracks crammed with iron bunks. A slit-open jute bag sewn over the frame served as a mattress, and when the temperature dropped at night, you could measure it by the chill of the metal bars coming through the jute. A four-foot fence marked the boundary of the camp, and beyond it was an isolated dairy farm on whose pasture a herd of emaciated cows grazed, although we never saw them milked.

At five in the morning a teacher would burst into the dormitory shouting the dreaded "On your feet!" and we would hurry off to our breakfast, which too often consisted of bread and sugared water. Outside, a pair of tractors, each with three country carts in tow, would be waiting to haul us out to the fields.

Work began in the huge sweet-potato fields as soon as the sun broke over the horizon. Peasants on horseback would distribute hoes, and slowly we began weeding. By midmorning the sun became unbearable, and we'd start peering up at the road, expecting to see the water cart, hauled by another peasant with a team of oxen.

In those fields we developed a taste for raw sweet potatoes. We would bite off the peel and chew the inside to ward off hunger. Around noon the tractor arrived with lunch, which we ate greedily despite the constant menu of chickpeas, rice, and dried hake. Then back to pulling raw potatoes out of the ground. For dinner it was more of the same. By the time we went to bed, we had only one thing on our minds besides food—home.

Since the nourishment was so bad at the School in the Fields, parents would bring their children enough food on the weekend visits to supplement their diet for the rest of the week: condensed milk, biscuits, *gofio*—sweet roasted cornmeal—and other treats. I spent my time pining for weekend visits, when I would get to have my own picnic lunch with my parents in the trees beyond the fence. When Sunday finally came, one by one the students would go off with their parents and spread their blankets. Soon I'd be the only one left in the dormitory, pretending to read while awaiting my parents, expecting them to surprise me at any moment. But they never came.

Four lonely and sad Sundays went by like that, and finally, in despair, I wrote a note to my mother: "Mommy, please, we're all so hungry. Have someone from Matanzas bring me something, if only some brown sugar." It's true we were all very hungry, but that wasn't my real reason for writing to my mother. I just wanted to know they loved me and to have them show it, like the other parents did.

Three days later, on a rainy afternoon, my mother arrived, exhausted from the trip. She hugged me, saying, "My poor boy, you look like a ghost!" I was twelve years old, a man by my father's standards, and so I refused to let myself cry. "Your father's as stubborn as ever," she told me. "I begged him to come, but he refused, insisting you should be acting like a man. This time he got really angry with me and refused to even take me in the jeep. So I made my way as best I could, hitchhiking bit by bit along the highway."

I felt terribly ashamed to have made her go through this for me, and I grieved over what she must have suffered, embroiled in a conflict with my father because of her maternal love and my stupidity.

My mother left at dusk, and I turned back to the dormitory—remembering those faraway days with my grandparents in Cabaiguán and those lively Christmas holidays with all my relatives, wondering whether I'd really lived them or if they were simply a dream.

The last Sunday, my parents and my brothers came to visit in the shiny jeep my father had been given by the Ministry of Education. I felt so proud that I wanted all my campmates to meet them.

My mother kept asking me about conditions there, obviously to have my father hear the answers. But my father tried not to give much importance to my mother's complaints. "Nonsense," he remarked. "They're having a better time than you imagine." But you could see in his eyes he didn't believe what he was saying. When they were ready to leave, he turned to me and said, "Don't give in. You can take it. You're a man." Watching the jeep drive away, I suddenly felt able to deal with anything. I no longer felt alone.

When I returned home soon after, my father was so proud that I had passed the test. "You're becoming a revolutionary," he said, patting me on the shoulder. And then he continued, "When I say 'First the Revolution and then the family,' that doesn't mean I'm against you. On the contrary, you are part of a world I call the Revolution. It's you, the suffering people of the earth, the children everywhere—that's the Revolution. I'm tough with you because I don't want you to become selfish, callous about other people's suffering. Millions of human beings die in misery every day around the world because of the self-seeking interests of those who exploit them. These people need us. A revolutionary doesn't live to provide privileges for his own children. What makes us different is a constant readiness to sacrifice ourselves for others." As my father continued, I began thinking, Those who have nothing . . . First them, then us—yes, that's what it means! First the Revolution and then the family!

HAVING stood the test of the School of the Fields, at twelve years old I was ready to face anything. I was no longer a weakling in my father's eyes, and I in turn looked up to him as the wisest, most important man in the world. I considered myself a model revolutionary—the "new man" that the highest leader had proposed to be molded in the likeness of Che Guevara. I wanted to be like the legendary commander, strong and just, ever ready for sacrifice. So I asked my parents to let me continue my studies in the most highly acclaimed military academy in the country. If everything went well, I might eventually be chosen to become a fighter pilot.

The academy was new, with impressive five-story buildings and a program that was unique among schools in Cuba, and I arrived full of energy, out to conquer the world.

The school's main buildings centered around an asphalt polygon on which we practiced our infantry drill. We were so well trained that not even officers of the armed forces displayed such elegance and discipline in drill. Every morning at six we were awakened with, "On your feet!" We had five minutes to line up by company on the polygon, and anybody who was late, even a second, lost his weekend pass for home. We would run and drill, wash and line up again for the march to the dining room, hitting the asphalt with military vigor.

Activities at school all took place under strong military discipline. The teachers always carried with them a little notebook for "reports," as they called them, and most anything would provide occasion for a report. If you didn't respond with alacrity when called upon by a superior, you'd be marked "slothful"; if your boots weren't gleaming, "untidy." Every two weeks we had the right to a weekend pass, but first we had to appear before the terrible "court." At the court sessions we all had to line up at attention before the commanding officer–instructor of our battalion. He would call us up one by one—those with reports. Any attempt to defend oneself or to give an explanation ended in more reports—for answering back.

"You were reported for speaking during drill formation on such and such a day. Guilty or not guilty?" the sergeant would ask.

"Guilty, sir!" the student invariably replied.

I was disciplined by the court for dirty boots, speaking during drill, and especially for answering back. And each court appearance only added to the list of my reports for answering back, because keeping silent in the face of what I considered an injustice was something I never managed. Thus I spent weekend after weekend at school, waiting for night, when I might escape home secretly by creeping along the dry streambed winding past the school. Once at home, however, my father would rail at me, "You're no good for anything," and make me go back to school, which I began to hate with all my might.

I've got to get out of this place, I told myself, no longer caring about my dream to be a fighter pilot. But what about my father? How was he going to take his son's asking to be discharged? No, he could never accept that. But I'm getting out no matter how, I told myself.

So one day I locked myself in a bathroom, took a razor blade, and made two cuts in my forearm. Someone seeing blood seep out from under the door sounded the alarm, and I was taken to the military hospital. Then came the consultations with psychiatrists and psychologists, who provided me with a medical discharge from the academy, terminating the treatment as well as the illness. I had gotten my way.

I spent the remaining two months of the school year traveling with my father throughout the province, helping with volunteer work cutting sugarcane and visiting peasants. One day I noticed he looked unusually happy. He'd been nominated for possible induction into the Communist Party. Nothing could have pleased him more.

At last the good news came. He had been accepted into the ranks of the Communist Party. He turned exuberant as a child and went off to tell his friends. The Revolution finally had confidence in him.

During those months I spent with my father, we shared everything, and I was truly happy. He had changed greatly, and I felt him to be close, trusting, a friend. Years later, when I became an adult, I thought that perhaps the psychologists treating me had spoken to him. But whatever lesson he'd learned back then had brought a change.

I don't think I really wanted to leave the world of the living when I slashed my arm, but obviously I wasn't altogether well at the time. I never mentioned the deed to anyone and tried to blot it out of my life, until a certain toughness acquired by bitter experience made me see it differently. At twelve years of age I was still far from being a man.

## Chapter Three

AFTER the adventure of traveling with my father was over, I entered our local secondary school. Leaving for school in the morning and coming home each afternoon was paradise. And so I began my adolescence, thinking about girls and flashy clothes. The latter, however, was something of a problem. There were rationing coupons to control clothing purchases, but I had grown tremendously in the past year, and the clothing allotted for my age-group was too small for me. With a minor's coupon one could not purchase adult clothing. Thus with shoes that didn't fit and pants always ending above my ankles, I looked plain ridiculous and of course felt mortified.

One day a task force from the Ministry of Education came by the school to tell us that the Revolution needed teachers. "The first calling of a revolutionary is to *be* revolutionary," they told us, reminding us of our ethic of the new man, for whom sacrifice is the very meaning of life. Without thinking twice, I signed up for a year of training at Varadero Teachers' College. Once again I had a scholarship, but this time I was not deprived of my weekend passes.

Upon finishing the program at the age of sixteen, I was sent with a classmate named Victor to teach at the Communist Party's regional school, where half-illiterate workers and peasants—members of the party—were being educated to raise their "level of culture." All our students were over forty, and most had had little schooling. Yet the worldly wisdom of these simple, honest people taught me a great deal.

We cut sugarcane with them in the fields all morning, and classes took place in the afternoon, with Victor and me teaching basic subjects like math and Spanish. The older teachers, who were part of the ideological arm of the party, gave classes in political science. It was amazing to see these students straining to read Marx, Engels, and Lenin at night, struggling to make sense of their abstract theories.

During that period my parents moved to an apartment in Havana to be closer to work, and once again I was hounded by those two eternal problems: lack of transportation and scarcity of food. On weekends I would go to the bus station and try to find a space on one of the always overcrowded buses, but usually, after having spent most of Saturday there, I would have to give up and stay at my parents' empty home in Matanzas. Then the most difficult task would be to find enough food to get through the weekend. The long lines of hungry customers in front of the pizzerias generally discouraged me, and since there wasn't a single restaurant without those long lines, it was the "Frozens" that saved me. That type of ice cream, dispensed by newly installed Italian machines, was produced by mixing vanilla-, chocolate-, or strawberry-flavored powder with water to create a paste resembling real ice cream. I'd go to one of the stands with a pitcher under my arm and buy a dozen of those ice creams, which I'd then stick in the freezer to serve as my food for the weekend.

When the school year ended, I was more than ready to join my parents in the capital. Once I was in Havana, my provisional work permit stamped and sealed, I went searching for a job, and the National Board of Adult Education placed me in a school, this time the Provincial School of the Party. My boyhood pranks and adolescent rebelliousness were definitely behind me. I was seventeen, a man now, and my parents were proud to see me working and at the same time studying biology at the University of Havana.

I STARTED receiving lots of telephone calls, and my mother would ask, "When are you going to introduce us to the girl you're going with?"

"And who told you I had a girlfriend?"

"Do you think when you're not here the telephone doesn't ring?"

"It's too early, Mom," I said, kissing her on the cheek. "I'm only going to introduce you to the one I marry." But it wasn't too long before my mother got to meet that very girl. It happened when the neighbors on our block were all celebrating—with beer and music—the anniversary of the founding of the Committees for the Defense of the Revolution. I spotted a girl in an adjacent patio, playing hide-and-seek with some children, running about, unaware that she was being observed. She had the biggest eyes, full of kindness and candor.

"Who's that girl?" I asked a boy sitting next to me.

"Who—that one? Are you crazy, man? Keep your distance from her, or her father will kill you."

"All right, but what's her name?"

"Vicky."

"Vicky," I repeated softly. I didn't see her again that night, but when I went to bed, I was still thinking about her.

EACH day in the capital brought new discoveries of Havana's charm: films, theater, concerts—a life different from anything I had known. In the early morning hours on the streets of the Vedado, people coming home from nightclubs would meet those going off to work. At night the Rampa was filled with young people strolling around the Coppelia district, sporting the latest bit of clothing or jewelry from abroad. Some carried huge portable tape systems to regale the air with the booming rhythms of Led Zeppelin and Chicago. Older people felt there was something immoral about such behavior, and they swore the young were "lost"—"parading"as they were in the streets to the beat of North American hard rock. Music to us was something we didn't judge by its politics. Let whoever sings it sing it.

Every young man's dream was to own a portable tape deck, yet only those who had somebody in the family traveling abroad—the sons of diplomats and civil servants—could indulge in such a luxury. And they became the natural elite among those taking walks along the Rampa. Thus the youth of Havana was visibly divided into two categories: those who were with it, and the *guachos*—a term of ridicule applied to anyone unfortunate enough to have to wear what the Revolution made available in the shops of Cuba.

When I asked my father to use his influence to help me get more stylish clothes, he said, "There are more important things in life than dressing up, and you ought to know what they are by now."

THE Provincial School of the Party, where I gave classes in biology, was at the west end of town, so I had to get up very early in the morning to catch the bus. Among those waiting at the stop was a reserved-looking man whom I greeted each day with a good-morning and a smile. He would return the good-morning, but not the smile. His name was Gerardo, and he was Vicky's father.

One evening there was a meeting of the neighborhood Committee for the Defense of the Revolution to approve the nominations to the block committee: president; ideologist; secretaries of culture, sports, vigilance—in short, a title for nearly everyone in the neighborhood. When I arrived, I spotted Vicky, who was accompanied by her parents. She seemed naïve and extremely timid. During the meeting I gazed obliquely at this girl whose meek aspect I found so charming. Once, our eyes met, causing her to blush terribly, which didn't pass unnoticed by her father. From then on, the encounters at the bus stop turned into a forum for Gerardo's thinly veiled interrogation about my background and my prospects for the future.

Although we were neighbors, I never ran into Vicky. Our work and study schedules didn't coincide. But I finally got to meet her at one of those boring block committee meetings.

"What's your name?" I asked her during a break.

"Vicky. And yours?"

Her voice trembled, as if she were scared. I found that amusing. At the end of the meeting she approached me. "They're screening me to be a member of the Communist Youth. I'll be having my interview, and I don't know anything about politics. I'm sure they'll ask me about things like the oil crisis and— Do you think you could help me with some materials to study?"

"I'm nearly an expert on oil issues," I replied. "Look, I could come to your house and go over it with you," I insisted, looking for some way to get to see her before the next block meeting.

"I'll ask my mother. I think it should be all right."

I began to visit Vicky's house, and we'd have long talks, but always with her mother present. We hardly ever mentioned the international oil crisis. We would pass the time talking of classical music and the theater. Vicky was studying piano, and she played beautifully. I loved to sit beside her, listening while she played Mozart and Tchaikovsky.

One evening when we were sitting outside on the curb together— posted for guard duty by the Defense Committee in the company of a neighbor—I began talking about my feelings for her.

"Vicky, I've been searching for you without knowing you existed."

She moved away nervously, as if afraid of what I was about to say.

"All my life I would have searched for you, because you're the only one I could ever spend a lifetime with."

She lowered her eyes and fixed her gaze on the pavement.

"Can I talk to your parents? I love you and don't want to hide it."

"I—I don't know. It's—" she stammered.

Feeling more confident, I took her hand. "Don't say anything now. Let's talk more later. Think about it."

"Yes. I have to think about it," she said with relief.

Later, when we said our good-byes, I saw a joyful light in her eyes. I went to bed that night with a dream in my heart.

Vicky thought it over for the next two weeks. Then one day we went to the movies, chaperoned by an aunt. There in the half-light of the theater I began to press her for her answer, running my finger softly over her forearm. "Well?"

She hesitated an instant, drawing her arm away, then stammered, "All right—"

I felt so happy. I quickly put my arm around her shoulders, drawing her to me. She shrank with embarrassment. "I love you," I whispered.

Whenever I visited Vicky, her father would remain upstairs.

"Does your mother know?" I asked Vicky in a whisper one day as she was playing the piano.

"Know what?"

"That we're engaged."

"Yes," she replied without looking up from the keyboard.

"And your father?"

"No. My mother doesn't dare tell him."

"Then I'll talk to him myself right now."

"No. Please do it when I'm not here. . . . Tomorrow afternoon, while I'm at my piano lesson."

The next day I went to Vicky's house and asked her mother whether I could have a word with Senor Gerardo. As I sat downstairs waiting, I could hear their voices above.

"I'm not going down to talk to anybody!"

"But Gerardo, the boy is waiting—"

"I have nothing to say to him!" Then after a while I heard, "All right, María, I'll see him." And with rapid steps he came down and stood in front of me. "Good afternoon!" he said in a not so friendly tone, looking me straight in the eye. I got up and stared right back at him, offended by his attitude. A few seconds passed in silence. Finally Vicky's father smiled, extended his hand, and asked me to sit down.

"Senor Gerardo, I love your daughter, and I want to marry her. I know it's important to you that she finish her studies. It's important to me as well. Please let me come see her here in your home."

Gerardo listened with a certain sadness in his eyes, as if time had surprised him—as if suddenly he comprehended that his daughter was no longer a child. But when I finished speaking, he straightened up in his chair and called, "María, please bring out some food for us." Then he began asking me a thousand questions—about my parents and grandparents, about my interests and plans for the future. He ended by saying, "All right, you can come see Vicky on Wednesday and Saturday evenings from seven to nine o'clock."

From that day on, we were officially engaged, and I began my visits as Vicky's fiancé. These brief hours spent at her house were like relics of a traditional past that had begun to disappear in Cuba. We always spoke in the presence of her mother or brothers, with hardly a possibility for the amorous interchanges normally enjoyed by fiancés. I'd write little passionate notes, which she tore up immediately. Thus a month passed, and still we hadn't had our first kiss. Finally we were allowed to go to the movies again, with one of Vicky's aunts as our chaperone. It was an American film, the story of a young blind woman alone in her apartment with a murderer. Vicky was terrified by the plot, and at the moment when the entire audience let out a scream, I turned Vicky's face toward mine and kissed her lips for the first time. Now we had a real secret. Now we were truly engaged.

Little by little my visits to Vicky's house lengthened and multiplied, and as her father and I got to know each other, we shed our initial misgivings and gradually forged ties of genuine respect and affection.

Occasionally Vicky's family and mine would get together, but Gerardo and my father usually just exchanged formalities. One day when I asked my father about his behavior toward Gerardo, he replied, "I have nothing against him, but there's little for us to say to each other. His world is totally different from mine."

And that was true. For Gerardo, a humble and semiliterate plumber, life consisted of loyalty to family and friends; for my father, party leader and professor of history, it was the Revolution, the party, Fidel. With time, the simple world of Gerardo would win out over that of my father, revealing to his eldest, most indoctrinated son that whatever is opposed to the primary importance of the family ends up weakening the whole society.

My parents didn't like the capital, and at the end of the year they returned to their apartment in Matanzas. But I, in love with Vicky, insisted on staying as long as I could in the apartment the government had assigned them in Havana. I wrote to the authorities requesting permission to go on living there, saying that should the Revolution have need of the premises, I would surrender them. I never received a reply, and I interpreted their silence as acceptance.

It was September, and Vicky and I had plans to get married the following summer. Once my parents left Havana, I had gradually become a kind of adopted son, and while I still slept in my own apartment, the rest of my free time I spent at Vicky's house. There was a cement common courtyard surrounded by eight little dwellings, each inhabited by a family of five or more. Gerardo's two-story house was located at the far end of the courtyard. On the second floor, on one side of the stairway, were three rooms; on the other side was a wooden ladder that led to a skylight through which one could get to the roof. Gerardo and Victor, Vicky's younger brother, went up there frequently to feed leftovers collected from the neighborhood to the ten hens and two roosters they raised for eggs and meat to supplement the family's diet. It struck me as amazing how that family managed to raise chickens on such a tiny rooftop in the middle of the capital.

The school year came to an end, and at last the sixteenth of July, 1976, our longed-for wedding day, arrived. Vicky had successfully completed her studies, and I was enjoying a vacation. Soon we would have those first moments of intimacy we'd dreamed of for so long.

We were married at the Matrimonial Palace at six p.m. The ceremony took place among friends and family, with a photographer—sent by someone as a wedding present—who pursued us at every moment. Afterward we all went home to celebrate in the common courtyard, everybody drinking beer and teasing the newlyweds.

We had reserved ten days at the Hotel International in Varadero, where we headed at last, feeling eager to be alone, leaving the guests in the company of my in-laws. When the car was ready to leave, Gerardo came over and kissed his daughter, and looking at me with tears in his eyes, he said, "Take care of her, my son." Then the car began moving away slowly, with the string of cans somebody'd tied to the back bouncing against the asphalt.

## Chapter Four

Our marriage unfolded like our courtship, only more romantically. Each evening we'd go for walks along the Malecón, an avenue that meandered around the northern part of Havana through an area that had once belonged to the sea. We'd sit on the seawall and dream about the future—the home we would have and the children to come after Vicky finished her studies to become a dentist.

Sometimes I'd confess to her that teaching wasn't my real vocation, but merely a revolutionary duty. My real passion was to be a pilot in one of those supersonic planes pictured in magazines, but as I told her, "It's something I could never hope to do." Vicky would listen to me, a certain sadness in her eyes, and she would say reassuringly, "I like that you're a teacher."

One day in October 1976 the media were angrily denouncing a shocking crime: terrorists from Miami had placed a bomb aboard a Cubana de Aviación flight from Barbados, and the bomb exploded shortly after takeoff, killing all seventy-three passengers. Among them were members of the national fencing team. Our leader insisted that the CIA had committed the crime with the help of Cuban exiles in Miami. Suspects were apprehended, and the first mutilated bodies were recovered from the sea and sent back to Cuba. The leader called upon the people to deliver a last farewell to our martyrs, who were lying in state in Revolution Square. And the people answered his call with a massive demonstration.

Vicky and I, along with my father, who'd come from Matanzas for the event, joined the hundreds of thousands of people—human rivers—who were pouring through the streets of the Vedado, heading toward the square.

Fidel's voice, torn by grief, echoed from hundreds of loudspeakers placed on buildings surrounding the square. It went straight to the hearts of the people assembled there. He recounted the history of CIA terrorist plottings against Cuba—the ship *La Coubre* exploding in the port of Havana, the Bay of Pigs invasion—and with this litany of the innocent dead he reminded us all that we had a cowardly enemy conspiring to bring us to our knees through terrorism.

"Our athletes could not get to the Olympics," his voice echoed above the cavern of buildings, "but have been enshrined forever in that greater Olympus—of martyrs for the fatherland." Men, women, and children alike listened with clenched fists and a lump in the throat; and we all felt closer to each other, more unified as a group, sharing our grief like a great family in the midst of tragedy.

"Let it be known to North American imperialists that they will never bring us to our knees," Fidel continued, and we clamored to vent our hatred upon the enemy. An exclamation of fury broke from our throats, rumbling like a war cry. We were invincible! We were unbending—because we were in the right.

We returned home feeling as if we had been pushed around for years without reacting to the insult. "Enough is enough!" we told each other with an irresistible urge to go out and battle our enemy. "If it were up to me, we'd declare war right now," I proclaimed in my boundless grief and hatred.

Soon thereafter Vicky passed her final examinations, and we waited anxiously to find out whether she'd be accepted in her chosen course of study. Almost every day we went to the university to check the rosters of names, and every day we returned disappointed because the stomatology lists hadn't yet been posted. Finally they appeared. We scanned the names until Vicky exclaimed, "Oré, here I am!" We hugged each other jubilantly, as if it were a triumph for both of us.

ONE day Vicky's cousin Adolfo, who was training to become a fighter pilot, came to see us. I asked him about the selection process, even though I'd given up any notion of trying such a thing.

"It's not completely out of the question," he said. "I'll ask our group leader about what you might do to apply." The next day he returned with a name and telephone number. "Lieutenant Colonel de la Paz, chief of the Pilots' Recruitment Commission. Call him, and he'll tell you what to do." I went straight to the telephone.

"Why do you want to become a pilot if you're already a teacher?" the lieutenant colonel asked me.

"I'm above all a revolutionary, and that's why I became a teacher. But I love flying, and I think I'd be more useful as a fighter pilot."

He asked a few more questions about me, then said, "Report tomorrow at eight a.m. to the Marianao Military Hospital. I'll be there with a group of candidates taking their physicals. Bring your papers."

I couldn't believe it. It was turning out to be easier than I could have imagined. I went to tell Vicky my incredible news.

"But I don't want you to go away to study in the Soviet Union," she said gravely, tears brimming in her eyes.

"I know it's a sacrifice, my love, but I don't like my job, and this has been a lifelong dream. Anyway, let's not get ahead of ourselves. I probably won't even pass the tests."

The medical exams were long and intensive, not to mention the interviews with military counterintelligence, who laid great stress on the fact that I had family in the United States.

"Have you corresponded or in any way kept in touch with them?" the officer queried.

"No, never."

"And your parents? Have they ever written to any of them?"

"Never."

"What do you think of American jeans—with that piece of leather on the back showing the brand name?"

"It's like wearing the enemy flag on your pants."

The man smiled with satisfaction.

I finally passed the tests, including the investigations by counterintelligence, and in a few days I numbered among the thirty young men selected to undergo three years of training in the Soviet Union to become fighter pilots. As men chosen to travel outside the country, we were given an allowance to buy clothing at a special store. There, for the first time, I was able to buy shoes and pants that fit me. They even had us buy a suit for the trip over. Later, when all thirty of us got together at the airport, we discovered that our suits and suitcases were all alike. Evidently we were not to go unnoticed.

They gave us a farewell party in the presence of the commander in chief of the air force. A young man close to Fidel was there too—Luis Orlando Domínguez, who brought us a personal message from Castro, congratulating us and calling us an example to Cuban youth.

I was proud and happy, and I was also excited at the prospect of becoming acquainted with the Soviet Union, the most advanced country in the world. At last I was to travel abroad and get to know other languages and cultures. Yet before we were to leave, there was a meeting with the officers of military counterintelligence, who warned us about the dangers we would encounter: "There's going to be a stopover in Morocco, a capitalist country in North Africa. Remember to stay together, and no talking to foreigners. You're not to go near the newsstands or read any capitalist literature. Reading foreign material is a direct violation of orders from the supreme commander, and you will be liable for expulsion."

They went on: "In the Soviet Union you're going to meet students from other countries, some of whom you are prohibited from having any contact with, especially the Iraqis, the Libyans, the Yemenis, and all those not belonging to the socialist camp. You are authorized to pursue friendly relations only with students from Vietnam and the socialist European countries."

Vicky, her family, and my parents all came with me to the airport to see me off. Vicky had spent the night in my arms, quietly in tears, while I stroked her hair, thinking about the time we were to be separated. At the airport, we all embraced one by one, Vicky and I last of all. As I left her standing there, I read in her eyes the long solitude she would be facing—two years before I could visit Cuba again. I felt as though I were stealing something from her. But it was only when the plane was in the air that the full reality finally struck me. A deep sorrow welled up in me, and I realized how much I loved her.

Yet the vanguard of universal justice and social well-being was opening its doors to me: the Soviet Union. There could be no greater proof of the party's confidence in me.

"I'M FIRST Lieutenant Popov of the Soviet Armed Forces Tenth Command," declared a tired-looking man in perfect Spanish. He was waiting at the foot of the ramp as we disembarked from the Aeroflot jet. It hadn't been difficult for him to spot us among the other passengers on that cold fall day; we were the only ones dressed in thin suits. "We'll be spending the night in the artillery school, and tomorrow we fly on to Krasnodar, your final destination."

We left the airport in a bus at dusk, and I sat staring out the window at the landscape. Without knowing why, I felt depressed and sad.

The next day, after a two-hour flight, we arrived at Krasnodar. The officer in charge of our training was Major Argatov, a short, stout man, and after we were shown to our dormitories, he came by to give us instructions. Our group leader, Gallardo, served as his translator.

"You may not leave the school's perimeter for the first forty-five days, the time required to learn a minimum of the language. Later you'll be allowed to go on Saturdays and Sundays, but you must be back always by eleven p.m. Anybody absent will be reported immediately to general headquarters in Moscow and subject to expulsion. Tomorrow you'll receive your uniforms and have your physicals; after that, classes begin. You will take an intensive course in Russian, alternating with classes in Marxist philosophy and the history of the Soviet Communist Party, and after this you'll begin your technical training."

Thus began our three years as aviation cadets in a country that for me would only become more and more of an enigma.

Situated some 720 miles south of Moscow, Krasnodar was a city of cossack traditions, with over half a million inhabitants. Its main avenue was bisected by a spacious walkway covered with gardens. At the far end of the walkway stood a statue of Lenin, one hand in his pocket and the other hand raised in a gesture that seemed to say "Forward!" This principal boulevard and a few secondary streets were the only paved roads in the city, and in the spring and fall one's shoes were always caked with mud.

The School of Aviation was at the western end of the city. There was the school theater, fronted by a small park with a monument to pilots fallen in World War II, and in its halls we practiced "brotherhood among peoples" by commemorating the national holidays of the various foreign contingents studying there. Opposite the theater was a monument to Lenin and, behind that, an old, well-preserved edifice that housed the school's administrative headquarters.

On Monday mornings we would assemble out front between the theater and the administration building to pass muster before the school commander, Major General Paulika. With Lenin's statue behind him, he would stand before the troops, his right hand just grazing the peak of his cap in a military salute to greet his cadets; whereupon we thundered back, "Morning, Comrade Major General!" Those Monday morning formations were our only contact with the major general, yet they provided time enough to discover his peevish nature. He always found a reason to rebuke the officer on duty or to find fault with one of the students. The first time we witnessed one of the major general's outbursts, we were petrified by the despotism with which he treated his subordinates. As Cubans, we'd been accustomed to being treated with politeness and respect.

The administration building had two gigantic wings, which housed the classrooms, all excellently equipped with materials ranging from small aerodynamic tunnels to engines and planes. But the school hospital, where we had our medicals, was a series of filthy rooms outfitted with medical instruments as crude as they were antiquated.

The dormitories, on the main street of the grounds, were dubbed hotels, given the comfortable facilities they provided for their foreign "guests." At the entrance to each building was a booth in which sat an old woman we affectionately called Grandma. The grandmas proved meticulous about recording the entrance and exit times of the students for the authorities. As a result, on Saturdays after eleven p.m., one or more ropes of knotted sheets would be hung out the back windows of our "hotel" for the convenience of tardy classmates.

Our dormitory housed students from Vietnam, Afghanistan, Yemen, Iraq, Libya, and other countries. We Cuban students enjoyed cordial relations with the Vietnamese, whom we affectionately referred to as our cousins. On the other hand, culture shock was inevitable in the case of the Libyan and Iraqi students, with whom we were absolutely prohibited to have any kind of relationship. They tended to criticize everything and spoke contemptuously of the Soviets, which offended us terribly, as we considered it vile to speak ill of those who were helping us. And to top it off, the officers of those countries were used to meting out corporal punishment, beating their cadets, something incomprehensible to us.

Our day as cadets began at six a.m., with twenty minutes of exercise outdoors and breakfast in the dining hall. Our classes filled out the rest of the day until seven p.m., with an hour's recess for lunch. Vicky was writing me every day, and I would devour her letters when I was all alone, letting my imagination transport me back to her and my yearned-for Cuba. Every month we attempted to talk by telephone, and since my salary wasn't sufficient to pay for the call at my end, I'd spend the early morning hours in the booth with Grandma, waiting for Vicky's call, which was always difficult to put through. We'd talk for six minutes, meticulously timed by the operator. I'd hear Vicky faintly, sobbing while she spoke, and I'd feel my chest tightening, which made it more and more difficult for me to speak, until our conversation was reduced to repeating the same words: "I love you."

Once the call ended, I went to bed, not to sleep but to stare at the ceiling, breathing deeply to arm myself with the strength to overcome my homesickness. You have to bear with it, I told myself. The sacrifice will make for our future happiness. And I endured.

When classes ended Saturdays, at two p.m., we'd change from uniforms to civilian clothes and take off, eager to explore the world that was the Soviet Union. We'd walk the city from end to end. We received a stipend of twenty rubles a month and an additional thirteen rubles from the Cuban embassy. With this allowance in hand—a veritable fortune by our standards—we rushed out to the stores, looking for the basic articles that were scarce in Cuba and which here we were able to purchase without having to present rationing cards. Other students, such as the Libyans, received over three hundred dollars a month from their embassies, which they could exchange on the black market for eight rubles per dollar. Some of them bought beer and soda, afterward leaving their empty bottles outside the door to be picked up by the cleaning help. But we Cubans would collect the bottles and return them to the school's small store for twenty-five kopecks each. With my thirty-three rubles and what I made on the bottles, I was able to buy soap and toothpaste, as well as clothes and shoes for Vicky and our families and even a few gifts for friends.

Russian goods available in the stores were invariably inferior in quality to products of capitalist origin, but we Cubans were fascinated by the fact that they were available at all. We all wrote home about the tremendous abundance that existed in the Soviet Union.

As our Russian improved, we came to know that world, which became by turns unbelievable and intolerable. Our disillusionment with this country we had been taught to admire began when the first students were hospitalized. A Yemeni cadet had to undergo an appendectomy without anesthesia, hygiene conditions in the hospitals were dismal, and medical personnel often reeked of alcohol. And the corruption present at all levels of society left us with an impression of overwhelming ethical deterioration in the Soviet Union.

WHEN our first year of studies was behind us, we were all set to go for a vacation to Sochi, a resort on the Black Sea. The holiday was part of our study package in the Soviet Union. But it so happened that a group of students from Libya had just arrived, and they had requested to go to Sochi. Since additional accommodations were not available at the resort, the school decided to grant the Libyans our lodgings, and we had to stay on at Krasnodar for the vacation. From then on, we noticed that it was the official policy of the Soviet command to show preference toward military personnel from capitalist countries.

After the holidays we were suddenly told to pack. An unexpected number of Arab students would be arriving, and they were to be installed in the more comfortable accommodations at Krasnodar, while we were to be sent to Primoskastarskaia, a village some ninety miles away. There we would continue our technical studies of the jet we were to fly first: the L-29.

We arrived in Primoskastarskaia in autumn, and we saw mud at every turn. The villagers were simple peasants who did nothing to hide their mistrust of foreigners. We got to the school in the afternoon and, before unpacking, had to listen to our new training supervisor, who advised, "For the moment you may not visit the village. There have been cases of aggression against students by local delinquents." The school physician added, "We also advise you not to have relations with women. Our statistics indicate that more than eighty percent are infected with venereal diseases such as gonorrhea."

How is it possible? I wondered. We realized that good hygiene was rarely practiced, but what I now heard confirmed the terrible backwardness of the nation we regarded as the beacon of civilization.

Later, when Major General Paulika visited the school, we learned from the young waitresses in the dining hall that he had an apartment reserved for himself at the base and that whenever he visited, Paulika requested that his meal be brought directly to his apartment by one of the girls. Once the waitress arrived with the food, she had to accept the general's "kindness" or suffer the consequences.

It was 1978, and in our classes our professors told us that socialism had already been "constructed" in the U.S.S.R. and that they were now at the threshold of the communist society dreamed of by Marx, Engels, and Lenin. Yet in Cuba the state of medicine was incomparably superior, and we didn't live isolated from the rest of the world. We could see American films or listen to capitalist rock stars. Furthermore, we couldn't imagine that a general would force a young girl to have sex with him. What a fraud against humanity, I said to myself. And if the Eastern European countries are socialist in the Soviet fashion, then the only country where true socialism exists is Cuba!

We completed five interminable months of theoretical studies in that place, which seemed to us like hell. Then we were sent to Morozovsk, a major rail link between Rostov and Volgograd. Our group had been reduced to twenty-six cadets after four hadn't passed the final theoretical exams and were sent back to Cuba. We were all excited about our upcoming flights, and we spent long hours in the flight simulator, dreaming of our first real solo flight and the vacation in Cuba when our first two years were up.

After we cadets had passed the exercises necessary for the solo, a designated pilot would take a test flight with each cadet before giving him final authorization to fly solo. It was at this point that our group was dramatically reduced; eight of our members were disqualified.

I soloed in an L-29, and the more I flew, the more I wanted to fly—the inexplicable malady common to pilots. Each day I'd write to Vicky giving her details of my new experiences as a pilot. And dreaming, always dreaming, about the future, when we would never need to separate again. There was nothing I wanted more in the world than to hold her once again and to tell her how much I loved her.


## *Chapter Five*


THE flight to Havana was endless, and I was in a state of perpetual excitement, watching the infinite blue cloak of the Atlantic slowly pass before my window. Then, under the plane's left wing, the peninsula of Varadero appeared. I remembered the words of Columbus upon arriving at the eastern shores of Cuba: "This is the most beautiful land that mortal eyes have ever seen." Ahead was the town of my youth—Matanzas. My parents' place! Boy, what a feeling!

The spectacle of arrival at Havana airport was decidedly picturesque. It doesn't matter where you've come from or how long you've been away; when returning from abroad, you're bound to be received by a retinue of family and friends eager to hug you passionately amid exclamations of joy. We were no exception, with tears of happiness shed by my mother and Vicky.

My father was working in the Ministry of Culture at Matanzas, and in his latest car, a ramshackle Moskovich, we drove to my in-laws'.

I had returned so disillusioned with that "great" country, the Soviet Union, that I couldn't resist telling my father how cheated I felt. "What we have *here* is socialism, but what's in the Soviet Union is a lie," I told him at the first opportunity.

"What are you talking about?"

"Just what you heard. Their medicine is fifty years behind ours. Corruption is a way of life, and the level of culture is so low that many asked us whether we'd come from Cuba by train."

"You don't know what you're saying. It's just your impression of certain individuals. How can you say that the country most advanced in the world in space technology is more backward than we are?"

"I don't doubt their scientific progress. But the basic system simply doesn't work. The standard of living is incredibly low. Alcoholism and adultery are epidemic, and family values don't exist. The supposedly revered veterans of the Great Patriotic War are rotting in the streets. Old women have to shovel snow to gain barely enough to survive. Many people openly profess racism, and the general population lives in total ignorance of the outside world, believing themselves to be the first and best in everything. It's all such demagoguery."

"You know you sound just like the enemies of socialism. I have dozens of friends who've visited the Soviet Union, and they have a very different impression than you do."

"Of course. They've been there on official visits, led around by Soviet authorities to model centers especially prepared for foreigners. But we lived with everyday people, sharing daily life with them."

"I don't have to actually be there to know how it is. What I've read is enough for me."

"Okay, Dad," I said quietly, seeing that I wasn't about to change his mind. And after all, the Soviet Union was immense, and I'd only seen a few of its remote southern villages.

That evening Vicky and I went to Varadero Beach. She'd managed to get a reservation in the same hotel where we'd spent our honeymoon, and we went joyfully to relive in all its passion the beautiful time we'd shared there before.

Then we went to my parents' home, and after a week they drove us back to Havana in their car, together with my only nephew, Faure's son. We spent nearly the whole time laughing at his three-year-old's antics, and my father kidded him while driving, asking the kind of questions the boy had already learned how to answer: "Tell me, Faurito, are you a *berraco?*"

"No, Grandpa!"

"Then what are you?"

"A revolutionary!"

"And what else?"

"Militiaman, Pioneer, Communist," the boy declared, while we laughed in pride at having such a noble descendant.

For a short time Vicky and I enjoyed studying together for her upcoming exam in biochemistry. By the time I returned from my final stint in the Soviet Union, she would have only one year of schooling left to finish. "When I return, we'll order our first baby if you like," I told her, smiling, and she hugged me in agreement. The day of my departure soon arrived, but I would be back in ten months, the time it would take to learn to fly my first real jet fighter.

THIS time we were assigned to a base outside the village of Kushi-ovskaia. There, brand-new supersonic MiG-21s awaited us. Once we finished our theoretical studies, we began flying that spirited, formidable machine, so like an unbroken colt in that it allowed not the slightest error in its handling.

One evening the chief of our squadron and the base political commissar came looking for me. They were having a party in one of the apartments and wanted me to join them. It was my first invitation to a private party among Soviet officers, and as I followed them back to the apartment, I was filled with curiosity. After I was introduced, the first toast was made to me. Then, between mouthfuls of delicious food, more toasts were raised to the friendship between the people of Cuba and the Soviet Union. My hosts seemed sincere, and after a few more drinks of wine or vodka they didn't hide their admiration for Cuba and our leader.

"We need a Fidel to bring order to our country," the political commissar remarked after expressing his distaste for Brezhnev.

"The leadership is sickly, corrupt, because of this decrepit old man who hasn't finished dying," our squadron leader added. "That's why we need a Castro here."

What a revelation this was for me. How relieved I felt. I would finally be able to give a convincing explanation to my father: the system didn't work, because of the man in power, not because of the system itself. Not everyone was corrupt, just the isolated few. This restored my confidence in the U.S.S.R. They'll sweep away the evils that have been foisted upon them, I thought with optimism.

WE WERE completing our flight training when a notice arrived from the political section of the Cuban embassy. I'd been accepted as a member of the Young Communist Union. I received the following congratulations: "In recognition of the excellent results achieved in your studies, and of your exemplary revolutionary attitude."

On our last day a solemn event took place out on the apron of the Kushiovskaia airfield. With the resplendent MiG-21s behind us and the Soviet and Cuban banners flapping in the breeze, the head of the base delivered a speech congratulating us on the successful completion of our task. "You are a bastion in the defense of universal justice, confronting North American imperialism head-on," he said. "Now that we've come to know you better, we understand fully why the United States will never vanquish the Island of Liberty."

The colonel's speech brought a lump to our throats. We had longed so much for this moment; we had overcome so many trials in that strange and sometimes hostile environment. We had finally graduated, and we were proud of it.

"Long live the Communist Parties of Cuba and the U.S.S.R.!" the colonel concluded. "Long live the undying friendship between our peoples! Long live Leonid Ilyich Brezhnev! Long live—"

Our cheers resounded wildly, showing we were as ready as the jet fighters behind us to sacrifice ourselves to make a better world. We were warriors of the just cause—the pride of our people, and of our dead. I was now to begin my life as an officer in the Cuban air force.

UPON my triumphant return from the Soviet Union as a full-fledged fighter pilot I was admired by family and friends alike. Vicky was in her last year of studies and wanted to end the year with our first child. After four years our tree would finally bear fruit.

A member of the armed forces divisional staff had been at the airport to greet each pilot, advising us to report to air force headquarters in thirty days. On the appointed day in November 1980 we all presented ourselves there. Major Santos, inspector of the air force, welcomed us, adding, "Tomorrow at eight we leave for Holguín, where we'll rehearse the swearing-in ceremony to take place the day after at the Mausoleum of the Second Eastern Front." This was the site of Raúl Castro's command post when he'd led the guerrilla fighting in the mountains of Oriente Province—a fitting stage on which to receive our epaulets designating the rank of second lieutenant.

We were flown in Mi-8 helicopters to the monument, which was surrounded by the verdant ridges of the Sierra de Niquero. The landscape was majestic, with our national flag waving among those mountains where our fathers had bravely fought. I'd been selected to recite the oath in the name of our group, so after the national anthem I took my place before my comrades and began to read. "I swear eternal loyalty to the fatherland and to the legacy of our martyrs."

And my comrades responded, each raising a closed fist as emphatic proof of his assent, *"We swear!"*

"I swear to serve the cause of communism."

*"We swear!"*

"I swear to follow the orders of my superiors."

*"We swear!"*

"I swear to be faithful to the trust placed in me by the commander in chief, Fidel Castro."

*"We swear!"*

"Let the hate and scorn of my people fall upon me, at the cost of my life, should I ever break this oath!"

*"Let it fall!"*

Afterward, with the rank of second lieutenant emblazoned on our shoulders, we were flown to Santa Clara Air Base, our final destination. Colonel Cortés was waiting to escort us to the pilots' quarters—three blocks of lodgings divided by well-kept gardens filled with roses, a dining room and club. Each room had four comfortable beds and a bathroom, plus a refrigerator and an air conditioner—appliances available only to the pilots on the base.

The right of the party and of counterintelligence to meddle in our private lives was made evident from the very start, with my unmarried comrades receiving instructions from Major Felipe, chief of the squadron: "When you begin dating a girl, you must notify counterintelligence immediately, and should you plan to get married, you'll first have to wait for an investigation of her background to obtain the necessary permit." He explained that the CIA was trying to gather classified information by using pretty young girls to seduce our pilots.

Santa Clara Air Base was situated some six miles north of the town bearing the same name, and the base extended westward toward a highway. Its boundaries were delineated by a wall, and on the side flanking the highway, the wall was dug under in certain remote spots to form pathways through which soldiers and local peasants passed freely. On the other side of the highway, outside the base, was the military community—a group of identical apartment houses where some of the officers from the base lived with their families.

Headquarters was a four-story building, behind which was the parade ground, where we drilled daily. During one of our first infantry formations, our squadron chief admonished us, "You are pilots, the first to repel a massive enemy air strike. You must keep us informed of your whereabouts at all times so that you can be located in case of an attack." Thus began our initiation as rookie pilots in a combat unit.

On my first takeoff I was astounded by the beauty of the island. Like a swift bird, I veered from one end of its landscape to the other, from the tiny islands of the north and the crystalline waters of the Caribbean to the mountains of the south. I flew from coast to coast, feeling like the guardian of my marvelous island. Whoever tried to subdue her would have to reckon with me, the jealous defender of her skies.

We'd been on the base a few days when we were roused from sleep early one morning by the air-alert sirens. We dressed in seconds, and a bus rushed us to the hangars, where the planes were armed and ready. With my pulse racing, I climbed into the cockpit. My flight technician informed me, "Number six eighteen ready, with two hundred fifty rockets, two heat-seeking air-to-airs, and a pair of radars."

I flipped on the switches while installing myself in the ejection seat and adjusting the parachute straps. Then I heard a voice crackling over the radio: "All Falcons, all Falcons, report squadrons prepared for takeoff." That's Command! Damn it, this is the real thing!

Thirty minutes elapsed, and all that I heard was the voice of one impatient pilot or another calling Command, and the invariable response: "Hold position."

Evidently the U.S. fighter-bombers had yet to take off. How had our leaders learned of the impending air strike? Most likely through operatives from state security who'd infiltrated the very heart of the enemy.

From my cockpit I saw the first glimmers of sunlight cross the horizon. I'd spent three hours harnessed to a hard ejection seat, and still no enemy planes had come.

The reason for our state of alert was the U.S. decision to hold war games in the Caribbean, which included deploying an aircraft carrier near Grand Cayman, just to the south of Cuba. The Cuban high command considered such initiatives an ideal cover for a surprise attack on the island.

Ten years later I would discover that the U.S. government announces its military maneuvers with sufficient advance notice, but the Cuban command liked to keep such information from the public. Just beforehand they would announce the U.S. troop movements as a secret strategy leading to a "probable invasion," and thus mobilize the people and the armed forces in defense of the Revolution.

For a month there was no letup in preparations for an imminent U.S. invasion. Yet every night as we'd retire to an air-conditioned area reserved for pilots, we'd see captains, majors, and lieutenant colonels slip away into the darkness, crawling through gaps under the wall to spend precious hours with their wives and children. I spent that time in almost complete isolation from Vicky, who learned through the press about the danger of a U.S. invasion.

There were no telephones on the base linked to the civilian network, so at night I would sneak off to town, like the others, to spend a few minutes on the telephone with Vicky, in Havana.

Vicky thought she was pregnant and said she needed me, but duty kept me from her. I considered going to Havana, but the thought of an enemy air strike during my absence always dissuaded me.

The state of alert was finally lifted. This time the Americans had decided not to invade, but we were told that a deputation from the joint chiefs of staff was to arrive on a tour of inspection, and we would continue to be restricted to base.

One morning when I was alone in my room getting ready for my shift on standby alert, I was paid a visit by Captain Yánez, head of military counterintelligence at the base, who wanted to have a "very private" conversation with me. Although they had their office in a section of military headquarters, the men who worked for this branch of the armed forces enjoyed total autonomy. They were not subordinated to the air force command, but reported directly to the minister of the armed forces. They went about cloaked in an air of mystery, brashly entering and leaving the base on their motorcycles, dressed in civilian clothes, with their shirttails hanging outside their pants to conceal the pistol they always wore at the hip. Their regulations were in notable contrast to those for the rest of the officers, who were required to wear their uniforms at all times while on the base and were not permitted to wear side arms except during alerts.

Yánez sat opposite me, took out a pad of notes, and, staring me in the eye, asked in confidential tones, "What do you think of the security organs of the state?"

"I think they carry out one of our more difficult and delicate jobs." Why is he asking me this? I wondered.

"And about the men who do the job?"

I admired such anonymous heroes. Among the martyrs of the Revolution there were many names, guarded in secret, of heroes who'd died at the hands of the CIA without even receiving proper recognition from the people, who still considered them traitors.

"They're the most selfless of all. They can't even aspire to the respect and admiration of relatives and friends when they have to infiltrate the enemy."

Yánez smiled, making a few circles with his pen on a blank page of his pad. "We've studied your file. You're serious, intelligent . . ." And he continued with additional superlatives, concluding, "We want you to work with us."

He'd hardly finished the phrase before I was imagining myself in the United States, infiltrated into the ranks of the CIA, radioing to Cuba the latest information obtained, just like the heroes from state security did in the TV serials I'd watched.

"What? Work with you?"

"Correct."

"But I'm a pilot. . . . My whole life's been as a revolutionary. I don't think I could infiltrate anywhere."

"It's not a matter of that. We want you to collaborate with us in the protection of your comrades."

"In the protection of—"

"Pilots are a priority objective of the CIA, and the United States would give anything to have just one of you defect with a MiG. Besides, it's impossible to control a pilot once he's airborne. Can you imagine what the CIA might pay to get a fighter pilot to drop a few bombs on Central Committee headquarters?"

"Of course. . . . I see. But what do I have to do?"

"Nothing. Just keep in periodic contact with us. We'll give you instructions, and you'll look out for the security of your comrades. We'll give you a code name."

"But I don't have to hide to do it."

"Discretion is important. At times the confidence others have in you is what allows you to find out about things."

"My comrades are totally trustworthy, aren't they?"

"Yes, but no one knows what could happen tomorrow."

"Exactly. Anyone can become a traitor. But I don't have to hide to combat it. I would be the first to take action even before calling upon you people."

"So then . . . you don't accept?"

"It's not that I'm refusing. I'll always defend the Revolution, but openly. To infiltrate the CIA is one thing, and quite another to spy on my comrades. I trust them, but if one of them ever betrayed us, you can be sure I'd be the first to act."

"I think you don't realize—eighty percent of the officers in the armed forces actively collaborate with counterintelligence. Think about it; someday we'll have another talk."

Yánez left as silently as he had come, but for many days I was disturbed by the details of my conversation with him.

For a month and a half none of us could leave, and finally I went to my squadron leader to request two days' leave. The request was denied. That was when I decided I would go see Vicky no matter what, and I relied on my buddies to cover for me as best they could. I awaited darkness, ran for the wall, and slipped away as anxious and gleeful as a child committing a prank. What a surprise I'd give Vicky!

WHEN I finally reached Havana, I went directly to Vicky's parents' house, where, as always, the door was wide open. There was Vicky, seated forlornly at the table, her head lowered in thought. I tiptoed to the old piano and picked out a few notes of a piece we both loved. She raised her head and jumped up and threw herself upon me in a frantic embrace, sobbing as she cried to me, *"Papitoo!"* I held her close, stroking her hair and whispering, "Yes, yes, I'm here."

Little by little she calmed down. Then, caressing her belly with the look of an accomplice, I asked, "You really think that you're—"

She dropped her head with a shy smile. "I think so."

Whereupon I bent to kiss her belly, saying, "It's not right that I haven't yet greeted the future ruler of the household."

That evening my mother-in-law's pots were fuller than usual, and we celebrated my arrival with a delicious meal. Then Vicky and I retired to the intimacy of the apartment where we lived. How we desired each other! And caught up in our passion, we embraced each other, drowning in the tender innocence of love. I fell asleep next to Vicky, exhausted from tension and nights without sleep.

The next evening I returned on the bus, arriving at the base by dawn. I was assaulted by the possibility of my absence being discovered but was quickly put at ease by my buddies, who assured me, "Don't worry, we spent the whole day yesterday closeted like idiots, and nobody even asked for you."

## *Chapter Six*

OUR lives were spent in a constant flurry of preparations for war with the United States, and we rookie pilots gradually gained confidence in the art of aerial combat. Our daily aerial maneuvers grew more complex and the precise conditions more challenging. An atmosphere of professional pride pervaded our efforts as we developed that special competitive spirit that is usual among combat pilots. But as always, we spent most of the time restricted to base.

One day during dive-bombing runs over a white target at the side of the runway, a MiG-21 flashed the bright blue of its fuselage as it circled to come in for the target. It entered its dive from about 5000 feet, like a missile hurling itself downward, and leveled out at an altitude of 700 feet. It was one of the rookie pilots, Prado, and he was skillful at flying. The dive completed, he began to climb and banked to circle. But something inexplicable happened. The plane flipped over and, in an incredible maneuver, descended in a circular trajectory, smashing into the ground. Prado hadn't had time to even think about ejecting. I couldn't believe it. It didn't seem possible that he was dead—someone who had been so full of life just a minute before.

A commission was formed to transmit the bad news to his family, and off it went on its heavy mission. The funeral took place in Havana, where the young man was laid to rest in the Armed Forces Pantheon. Next to the tomb were two floral wreaths that stood out from the rest, sent by the country's top leaders.

I took advantage of my presence at the funeral to go see Vicky. I arrived home distressed, and I pulled Vicky close to me and stroked her belly, which had grown considerably.

"He'll be born in a month now," Vicky said, putting her hand over mine, holding it against her.

"Does he kick?" I asked, nodding toward her abdomen.

"Yes, a lot," she answered, smiling.

"Let me listen." I put my ear to her belly and listened. Suddenly there was a movement, as if something were skidding along the inside of her abdomen. I raised my head in surprise and cried out, "It's true! It moved, it moved!" We began laughing, filled with happiness.

I returned to the base, and that very first night the sirens sounded an alert. We pilots rushed to our planes and waited in our cockpits until dawn. Again it was the threat of a North American invasion. Days of extreme tension passed without my leaving the base.

Barely a week remained before Vicky was to give birth. When the alert was lifted, I requested leave to be with her. "Impossible," was the reply. "There are already too many pilots away from the base."

Then one evening I got word from air force headquarters that somebody had called in to say that my wife had been taken to the maternity hospital with labor pains. I couldn't sleep at all that night. When we assembled on the parade ground in the morning, I requested permission to address my squadron leader, and I explained, "My wife's in the hospital, about to give birth."

"So what," Major Felipe retorted coldly.

"I'd like to be with her, that's all."

"The child will be born without any problem, and you'll see it when you get a leave."

The reply stung me with its harsh, humiliating tone.

That night, the ninth of July, 1981, I got a call from command post. Vicky's sister had informed headquarters in Havana that my wife had given birth to an eight-pound boy and both mother and son were absolutely fine. My comrades hastened to congratulate me, but I went to my room and fell on the bed without undressing, and I took an imaginary journey to see them that lasted until dawn.

I was brought back by a few soft knocks at the door. "Come in!"

The door half opened, and Lieutenant Colonel Eloy—the base commander—peeked in. He was a man of profound scruples, strict but good-natured, and highly respected. I jumped up to stand at attention, but Eloy stopped me with a wave of the hand. "I hear your wife gave birth. I came to congratulate you and to tell you that you've got two weeks' vacation."

"Thank you, Comrade Lieutenant Colonel!" I exclaimed, overjoyed. And in a few minutes I was on my way to Havana.

I ARRIVED shortly after noon and searched desperately for some flowers for Vicky. But in vain, and in the last shop I looked, I was told that the flowers they had were destined solely for mortuary wreaths. Tired and sad as I walked to the hospital, I saw a single faded rose among the weeds in a poorly kept garden. Jumping over the fence, I plucked it and continued joyfully on my way to Vicky and my son.

When I entered the room, Vicky saw me and responded with an exclamation. I kissed both our mothers and approached her without saying a word. We looked at each other quietly, and after I kissed her, I offered the pale rose to her, confessing in a whisper, "I love you."

Vicky held the rose close to her breast. She reached for my hand and squeezed it. Then she looked down at the little metal cradle next to her bed. The baby was sleeping peacefully on his back, his legs outstretched and his arms resting on his chest.

"Did you register his birth yet?"

"Yesterday, after the birth."

"What name?"

"Reyniel, like we agreed."

"Can I pick him up?"

"Of course. . . . I have to feed him."

As if he understood what we were talking about, Reyniel suddenly awoke, screaming his lungs out, and nervously I took him in my arms, rocking him awkwardly to quiet him while Vicky prepared to nurse him. Our mothers were laughing, and when the boy finally seized Vicky's breast, with an appetite that seemed to me voracious, she burst out laughing and regarded me with mocking eyes.

"What's going on? Why are you all laughing?" I asked.

"At your frightened face while you were holding a crying baby."

We all laughed then, as Reyniel suckled away.

I spent the afternoon with Vicky, sitting next to her and holding Reyniel in my arms, happy at being a father and the husband of the tenderest mother I'd ever seen. The next day I accompanied them home, and the three of us spent a marvelous vacation together.

Reyniel grew vigorously, but I saw him no more than once or twice a month until some wonderful news arrived in May: I'd been assigned one of the new apartments just completed by the entrance to the base. I went quickly to Havana, and after giving up our old apartment, we loaded a van with our few belongings—clothes, an old repainted cradle, a mattress, a chafing dish—and went happily to our new home.

And so we began our lives in that small prefabricated apartment we called our nest, sleeping on the mattress on the floor, Vicky cooking with our makeshift chafing dish. At the base I obtained a coupon allowing us to buy our own bed, and our life was a happy one despite its primitiveness, for we had our first opportunity of sharing most nights together, and I could now watch my son grow.

We were so happy that we hardly missed having a television or refrigerator; nor was I troubled by the wearying trips to the well of a neighboring peasant and the walk up four flights with two gigantic buckets filled with water. Each day began and ended with the same romantic joy, seeing Vicky and Reyniel sending me off to work and welcoming me back home.

One day while I was on guard duty, the base commander came to see me. Eloy asked after Vicky, the baby, my health—and I realized he wanted to tell me something, but couldn't find the right words. Finally he explained. "The war in Angola is taking an unexpected turn. The South African air force has made several incursions into Angolan territory, and we don't have a sufficient number of pilots there. They've asked for reinforcements."

"When do I leave?"

"Tomorrow."

Vicky accompanied me the next morning to headquarters in Havana, where our group of pilots were assembling to leave for Africa. A bus waited to take us to the airport. Vicky and I hugged each other, with the baby pressed between our bodies. We finally separated, and from the bus window I saw her waving good-bye as a tear ran down her cheek. The bus pulled out slowly, and Vicky and Reyniel were becoming smaller as the war insinuated itself between us.

OUR final destination was Lubango, a town on the edge of the vast African jungle. The war turned out to be different from what we'd imagined. Instead of combat, we spent our time awaiting the enemy attacks, which, as in Cuba, never happened. But the isolated incursions by South African pilots—who were detected almost always just as they were leaving our airspace—resulted in our spending days in a state of total alert. In the meantime some of the higher brass were often out filling their suitcases with articles unobtainable in Cuba. Instead of making an effort to establish simple human contact—so vital in a war—with the men under their command, they would visit us only long enough to inspect our rooms and toss at us a list of reprimands over trivial details. Like them, we lived in the city, and thus came to witness firsthand what ordinary troops assigned to the battle-field could not: their luxurious living quarters, staffed by Angolan service personnel to satisfy their private needs; their parties, for which they squandered food that the troops were lacking, as well as the quotas of alcohol destined for the soldiers. It was a thoroughly corrupt way of life, the opposite of that of a revolutionary and a military leader. It was not uncommon to hear the pilots referring to their leaders as the bourgeoisie to express disgust at their behavior.

The same old story, I told myself.

While I was away, Vicky remained for some time at the base in Santa Clara, where she was unable to work, because there was no spot open for Reyniel in any of the local day-care centers. Finally she went to live in Matanzas with my parents, who managed to help her find a day-care center for Reyniel and a job as a dentist. We wrote almost daily, I striving to make Vicky believe that I was not in any danger, but she never stopped asking me to take care of myself.

One day we were called upon to strike positions of the UNITA (Union for Total Independence of Angola) troops, which had attacked Cuban food-supply convoys. We were to destroy their airfield, built in the heart of the jungle, through which they were receiving supplies from South Africa. The brigade commander warned that UNITA had ground-to-air missiles and sufficient antiaircraft artillery to repel our attack. We took off before dawn, following our squadron leader. A very thin cover of mist hung over the region when we reached the target, but our leader preferred to exaggerate the poor visibility and return with our full ordnance rather than attempt to seek out the objectives we were to hit.

That had been the youngest pilots' first combat mission, and we returned feeling cheated by those who appeared to seek the slightest pretext to avoid combat. And again I felt disoriented in this world of truths and lies, where what we said differed from what we did.

After my tenth month in Angola I became tormented by the idea that Reyniel could forget me, that he might not recognize me and would reject me as a stranger when I returned. Four months had passed from the date I was supposed to have had vacation leave in Cuba, but I was still awaiting my replacement. He finally arrived, and I boarded the plane to begin the journey back to Cuba.

WHEN I arrived home, the whole neighborhood was out to welcome me. Vicky ran to me first, throwing herself around my neck, crying. Then my mother-in-law walked over to us, carrying Reyniel in her arms. He wrestled free of her and ran to me, reaching out his little arms and calling, "Daddy, Daddy!"

I swept my child up into my arms and ran into the house, hiding my face in his little body, ashamed of my own tears. There I wept in the arms of my family, as I hadn't done since I was a child, and Reyniel watched me tenderly, kissing me and wiping my tears away with his small hands, saying, "There, there. . . . I love you so much, Daddy."

We went for vacation to our favorite spot. The days passed swiftly at the beach, always together, the child filling our lives with happiness. I returned to Angola at the end of the month, after witnessing Reyniel's innocent good-bye—a kiss and a smile, waving his little hand as Vicky looked at me sadly, saying only, "Come back."

In Angola, things had changed for the worse.

In August a group of pilots was summoned because a battalion of Cuban troops at Cangamba had been surrounded by thousands of enemy reinforcements from UNITA, against whom they were resisting heroically from the underground fortifications where they were pinned down. But the numerical superiority of the enemy was winning out and threatening to exterminate them all, despite the decisive role our airpower was expected to have through the constant bombardment of enemy positions.

I remained in Lubango with the bulk of the pilots, but I felt the need to be with my comrades in battle—not to sit like a parasite while others died. It kept me awake at night, filled with impatience, recalling the reports we'd received about some pilots shot down in their helicopter, their mutilated bodies found by our troops. They'd been captured alive by UNITA, then murdered, their hearts and livers cut out later and eaten. Our men poured out their heroism at Cangamba, and after the battle, which—incredibly—they won, the feats of the dead became legendary, like that of the medic who was blown to bits by a mortar shell as he crawled out of the bunker to reach the last of the wounded still lying outside.

It was October 1983 when my replacement arrived. I was given a medal denoting Internationalist Combatant First Class in recognition of the combat missions in which I had participated. I took the little plastic box with its gilded medal and tossed it into my pocket. I had completed my mission, and I felt that the horrible experience of the war had matured me. But even years later I would wake up at night seized by a nightmare: I saw myself once again back in Angola.

## *Chapter Seven*

THE final months of my stay in Angola had been especially hard on my mother, who, because she worked in the offices of the provincial government, received the names of those from the region who had fallen in combat. The most recent news referred to the bloody combatants at Cangamba and the death or disappearance of helicopter pilots, and my mother was consumed with anguish each time she found on her desk that envelope containing the lists of the dead.

I'd arrived in Matanzas thinking of the happy surprise I'd give my family, and I went to the old building where my parents worked. My father embraced me strongly in silence, then looked me in the eyes, sadly saying, "Let's go see your mother—she needs you."

We walked to her office, and there we saw her behind her desk, gazing at that envelope she feared to open. She had changed a great deal in those last months. Instead of her usual happy self I found someone forlorn and pensive, absorbed in her private worries.

"Mom," I called to her softly from the doorway.

She turned toward us and, lifting a hand to her face, broke into a series of exclamations, "*Ay*, my little boy! *Ay*, I can't believe it!" And she threw herself upon me, drowned in tears. "But why didn't you let us know? Look how you've made me suffer!" And turning to her comrades, she exclaimed, "Look, my boy's come home!"

SCARCELY had I relaxed with my family when I was called back to the base. The United States had invaded the island of Grenada. It seemed that the constant U.S. threat would again deny us the right to our happiness. While Vicky stayed at home, I once again had to remain at my post with my comrades, searching the horizon for enemy planes, awaiting the North American invasion.

Once we had moved back into our apartment on the base, another surprise awaited us. Our neighbor Captain Allende, a pilot of the 1st Squadron, had been dishonorably discharged from the armed forces and had moved away. Military counterintelligence had discovered that he was corresponding with an aunt who had abandoned the country many years ago and now lived in Miami. "For maintaining relations with the enemy . . ." read the order expelling him.

Two, three weeks went by, and the U.S. attack never came. Gradually the details of the "bloody battles" engaging our outnumbered Cuban troops in Grenada began to be known. The overwhelming majority had been taken prisoner by the enemy, and the legendary commander of the Cuban forces, Colonel Tortoló, had fled, seeking asylum in the embassy of "a friendly nation"—the Soviet Union.

All the returning prisoners were later accused of cowardice, and dishonorably discharged. I could never fathom why they were obliged to commit suicide against such overwhelming superior forces while we sat safely at home.

Soon after that, my squadron leader was sent to the Soviet Union to pursue advanced studies in military sciences, and I was his replacement. Thus began a new experience for me, that of being a military commander. Our squadron, with its roster of instructors, had the responsibility of training the youngest pilots, and we were to be flying with unusual frequency, preparing the rookie aviators to carry out real missions in case of war.

The living quarters on the base had been built some ten years before, with no plumbing or sewage system whatsoever. More than a thousand men inhabited the base, and now I began to understand how men act under extreme conditions. Many of the soldiers were young, seventeen to twenty years old, legally obliged to serve for three years, with monthly salaries that barely sufficed to buy two packs of cigarettes. Forced to live in humiliating conditions, they expressed their rebellion by being absent from their units, stealing any article possible for their private needs—and finally by deserting. And we commanders, along with counterintelligence, spent more time hunting deserters and thieves than studying the enemy.

As the problem increased, Minister of the Armed Forces Raúl Castro unleashed a war against deserters. Commanders were mobilized, with contingents from the military police, to drive through towns in search of deserters, who were gradually filling up the military prisons.

The situation reached such proportions that the minister decided to open the jails and to resort to more persuasive methods of patriotic education. And our commanders began to understand that the problem was not the existence of deserters, but acknowledging that they existed. As a result, their communiqués to headquarters began to leave out any reference to deserters. It was the lie, arrived at finally, that pleased the leaders at the top as much as those below.

Upon my return from Angola I had been processed to enter the party, and now, after the required investigations, I was admitted. I called my father to give him the news.

"Welcome to the family of Communists," he told me proudly. And he didn't hide the fact that his son—now a pilot, captain, and leader of a combat squadron—was his greatest pride.

MONTHS passed in which I worked day and night on the base in Santa Clara without even a day of rest. Vicky spent all her energy in the slow daily effort to get to work and then make her way back home. Each morning, with Reyniel in her arms, Vicky battled to obtain a space on the bus, which always pulled up crammed with people. She'd race against the clock to the nursery school where she left the child, and then to her job. On the return trip the struggle to get onto the bus was even more fierce. Finally she'd arrive home totally exhausted.

Little by little Reyniel was growing up, and we were spending less and less time together. I'd get home when he was already sleeping, and I'd leave before he even woke up. Saturdays and Sundays were the same as Mondays and Tuesdays in my exhausting schedule. Then, in the last days of 1985, the base commander summoned me.

"You've been selected to spend four years in the Soviet Union, where you'll receive advanced officer training," he told me. And then he said that after the first year, my family would be able to join me. Although I still retained the worst memories of the Soviet Union, I received the news overjoyed. We could escape from that insane, grinding pace. Vicky was pregnant with our second child, and the prospect of my simply being a student when the child was born made me doubly happy. I ran to tell her the news.

"I'll have to spend the next five months in Havana reviewing Russian and math before our departure. Will you come with me?"

Vicky went immediately to phone her parents, who were euphoric at the news and readied a room for our arrival. We left for Havana in early February, and I began my preparation at the Military Technical Institute while Vicky and Reyniel enjoyed the attention showered on them by my in-laws. Each evening the three of us would go and sit on the same seawall at Malecón where we'd gone during our courtship.

Before dawn one morning in May, Vicky felt her labor begin, and I accompanied her to the maternity hospital, among effusive comments by Reyniel, who didn't stop repeating, "Now my baby brother's coming! Now my baby brother's coming to play soccer with me!"

By early morning Vicky still hadn't delivered, so I ran in search of flowers. This time I managed to get a wonderful bouquet, which I gave to her after the birth, when they permitted me to visit.

The baby was a boy of a little over seven pounds, whom we named Alejandro. He was a beautiful, energetic baby, and Reyniel contemplated his little brother with a tenderness that moved us all.

The day of my departure for the Soviet Union arrived. A process of change had been started a few months earlier in that country, and its name, perestroika, could be heard with increasing frequency. We were promised that following our first year of studies, we'd be assigned apartments in order to allow our families to be with us for the remaining three years. So with the hope of returning soon to get them, I left at the end of August, 1986, together with eight comrades, on a voyage that would radically change our lives. I was thirty years old.

THE NINE OF US HAD BEEN selected—from among the youngest battalion commanders of the air force, the radiotechnical forces, and the antiair missile defense forces of our country—to receive advanced officer training, which would enable us to direct large military units. We'd been met at the airport and seen to the station, and now we were traveling on a train from Moscow to Leningrad.

Our stop was Kalinin. We got off the train, and a friendly man in civilian clothes addressed us. "I am Colonel Kustiukov, in charge of your studies. Outside, there's a bus waiting to take you to your hotel."

The hotel turned out to be an old but well-preserved building close to the Volga River, which flowed through the middle of the city. Our rooms were on the third floor, and we ascended a wide granite staircase accompanied by Colonel Kustiukov. He opened the door to one of the rooms. "This room should be occupied by three of you; the others hold two apiece," he informed us, dropping keys on the table. "You may distribute them among yourselves as you see fit. From now on, you are students of the Marshal Georgy Konstantinovich Zhukov War College, one of our most prestigious military institutions."

The college was made up of eight different faculties, seven for Soviet officers who studied specialties that included the secretive system of antimissile defense, the Soviet version of Star Wars. And the eighth faculty was for foreign students.

We foreign students took classes in groups separated by nationality. Technical subjects, such as electronics and armament systems, as well as military subjects, like operational procedures, were classified, with access to information on the most recent models of armaments given only to the Cubans and members of the Warsaw Pact. We had valises in which we were obliged to keep all the texts and notebooks. At the end of each day we would tie them closed with a string, covering the knot with a paste on which we pressed our individual seals, then handing them back into the room labeled CLASSIFIED LIBRARY, whose door and windows contained iron bars.

Perestroika captured all our attention, with its flood of new ideas—discussed openly now—for constructing what they called a democratic socialism based on a society of citizens' rights. New and more openly critical programs were aired daily on television. We began to discover a society plagued with corruption, which bureaucrats were attempting to cover up. And a talented new generation, unknown until then, began to appear on the cultural scene. We viewed those reforms with happiness, watching that society transformed little by little into a more open and courageous one in which corruption and vice were being publicly acknowledged in order to remedy them.

My brother Orlando was studying in the port city of Odessa, on the Black Sea, and I decided to visit him during my winter vacation. I went on the long trip by train, sharing the compartment with two economists from Odessa who conversed between sips of vodka, and for the first time, I heard someone speak of Stalin's crimes.

"But if it's true about the millions murdered, why is nothing known about it?" I asked with open mistrust of my companions.

"Truth will out sooner or later, and the day will come when they'll speak of it openly," the older of the two economists replied.

"I'm not blind," I insisted. "I just find it hard to believe that one can hide the death of millions of people for so many years."

The man continued. "Obviously it's not possible to hide such crimes. More than half the world knows about them. Except for people like you, who have only read the official versions of history—"

"Enough!" the younger one interrupted. Placing a hand on my shoulder, he said, "My dear Cuban, please excuse my friend. If anything is worthwhile, it is friendship among ordinary people."

I saw that my interlocutor in the debate was smiling. He said, "You know? You remind me of myself when I was young. I was loyal and impetuous like you . . . until life obliged me to look elsewhere for answers. It was then that I started listening to Radio Free Europe."

I spent a week with my brother in warm Odessa, and when I left, the words of the old economist kept hammering in my brain. Back in Kalinin, when I looked at the old radio on the table in my room, I felt the desire to turn the dial to the shortwave broadcasts abroad. But I gave up the idea. Listening to foreign radio stations could earn me a dishonorable discharge from the armed forces.

One night in May, watching the news on Russian television, I heard the newscaster announce that Brigadier General Rafael del Pino, of the Cuban air force, along with his family, had defected to the United States in a small plane. I simply could not believe it. I'd known General del Pino from the time I was a cadet. His son Ramsés, who had fled with him, had been my buddy at aviation school in Krasnodar. Both were good men, devoted to the Revolution. I searched for a reason to account for del Pino's desertion, and all I could think of was that he must have been working for the CIA and that the whole of his exemplary conduct had been nothing but a sham to mislead us all.

AT LAST the long-awaited month of July arrived, and they gave us the apartments we'd inhabit with our families upon our return to the Soviet Union. With keys in our pockets we went to Cuba, content to know that we wouldn't be coming back alone.

Vicky and Reyniel were waiting at the airport that evening. I was surprised to see how Reyniel had shot up in the eleven months I'd been away. With him in my arms we headed home, where Alejandro was sleeping blissfully in my in-laws' bedroom. I carried Alejandro into our room. The next morning, while Vicky and I were talking in bed, Alejandro got up and, holding on to the crib bars, stared at us.

"Look, Alé, Daddy's home now," Vicky told him, and the child smiled while jumping gently on the mattress and repeating over and over, "Daddy, Daddy, Daddy!" Alejandro had been only four and a half months old when I'd left for the Soviet Union, and his attachment to me, as well as Reyniel's, despite the time that had passed, was the result of Vicky's perseverance in talking to them daily about their daddy while showing them my photograph.

When it came time to depart for the Soviet Union, we were advised that we couldn't take more than fifty-five pounds of baggage per adult and twenty-two pounds per child, though we were moving abroad for three years. The nine families finally boarded the plane, and Alejandro and Reyniel slept deeply, without an inkling as to the great changes awaiting them—the cold, the language, the culture. I looked at them with compassion. How hard these next years were going to be for them!

## *Chapter Eight*

WE ARRIVED exhausted in Kalinin during the last days of August, 1987. There we would be living in a ten-story building that housed some two hundred tiny apartments, all identical. We had been given a sofa bed, two armoires of pressed wood, and a bed for the children. By noon the following day we had arranged what would be our home for the next three years—a small room, a bath, and a tiny kitchen.

Vicky and I didn't want our sons to feel isolated from the other children because of the language barrier, so quickly we enrolled Reyniel in the neighborhood school and Alejandro in a nearby nursery school. Much to our happiness, in just a few months the children began to speak fluent Russian with no trace of an accent.

My classes began, and I returned home every night to have supper with Vicky and the children in the confined space of the kitchen. Then we would retire to the only other room in the house, where we stretched out on the floor and played with the kids until it was their bedtime. Afterward I would sit and watch the news on television.

I became more and more a prisoner of that television, which I'd watch till past midnight, so involved was I in discovering more and better cultural talent, which until then had been underground.

The boys and I spent each day immersed in our respective schoolwork, and we wished for Vicky to become involved in the outside world as well. Since the salary the school paid me barely gave us enough to live on, Vicky decided to accept one of the jobs that the nearby soda factory offered to the wives of Cuban students.

The harsh winter had arrived, and Vicky left early each morning for work while I dressed the children and served them breakfast. Then I set off with them, starting with Reyniel's school and continuing on to Alejandro's nursery school, some five blocks away, pulling him along in his sled as we sang silly songs that we made up along the way. We sang at the top of our lungs, gladdening our day, but not that of some of the aggravated passersby who begged us to be quiet. But we were far too happy! More than enough reason to be singing each morning.

ONE day we were visited by a commission from the Cuban high command. They had the task of explaining to us the Process of Rectifying Errors and Negative Tendencies that was being carried out in our country, led by Fidel. It was a kind of Cuban perestroika, whose motto proclaimed: Now we're really going to construct socialism! And many who had devoted their lives to the Revolution began to ask themselves with stupefaction what it was that they had been constructing for so many years before.

During their visit the high command spoke to us about the "vain North American hopes for a change in Cuba led by the younger officers in the armed forces." As for Soviet perestroika, they said, "It's a giant, and we've no idea where it's going." This was the manner in which they spoke of the will of the people—which had begun imposing itself more and more each day. Without Gorbachev's intending it at the beginning of the reforms, the relaxation of censorship had provoked an unquenchable thirst in people for the truth about their history, and each day new documents appeared in print, revealing the crimes of Stalin and the reigning corruption under Brezhnev.

Around this time the controversial Boris Yeltsin had rudely criticized Gorbachev for the slow pace of reform. The media were overcome with fear of the people—and of the younger officers in the Soviet armed forces, with whom I was studying—and the appeal and indisputable popularity enjoyed until then by Gorbachev began to wane.

With secret archives being opened to public scrutiny, I was able to read some of the documents from the time of Stalin. Corruption, sexual abuse, cases of torture . . . Reading such revelations horrified me. Such was the "heroic history" of Soviet socialism!

Each month we held a party meeting to review the academic progress of each of us. Daily relations between families were also subjected to analysis at the meetings. If someone preferred to spend his free time with his own family, that could be interpreted as a symptom of conflict with others. Why don't you visit your comrades? Why aren't your families getting together in your spare time?

At those party meetings everybody had to speak; each one had to offer criticism of others. And nothing produced more panic in any of us than the idea of having the collective point its finger at us, while judging how we ought to be doing things in our own home.

THAT year's classes ended, and I had to return to Cuba for a month for my annual flight practice. Vicky and the children were not allowed to accompany me. I knew that they would feel anxious during my absence, and so I finished my flight exercises as quickly as possible and returned at once to the Soviet Union.

From the kitchen window Vicky saw the taxi pull up, and she ran down to meet me. "It's been so hard without you," she said, throwing her arms around me. Then I noticed that her right hand was bandaged.

"What happened to you?" I asked, taking her hand.

"I had an accident yesterday at the factory. I was trying to extract a bottle that had gotten jammed in the machine, and a comrade accidentally turned it on."

"It might have mangled your arm," I insisted, horrified.

"Don't worry, it was a small cut and only required two stitches, which they did right away at the hospital."

I let out a sigh of relief, and we went up to the apartment arm in arm.

The first day of classes Vicky woke up earlier than necessary. She was sitting on the edge of the bed, looking at her arms worriedly. "What's the matter?" I asked, caressing her cheek.

"I didn't sleep well last night. I think I may have been poisoned."

I noticed then a reddish blotch along her arm, then discovered the same irritation on her back and abdomen. Suddenly I remembered that the night before, we'd had some wild mushrooms we'd bought from an old woman at the market, and the idea that Vicky might have eaten a poisonous mushroom terrified me. Luckily, the children hadn't wanted any. I quickly gave them their breakfast, dropped them off at school, and got Vicky to the hospital.

"I feel like I can't stand up. My blood pressure must be way down," she told me, nearly fainting as we entered the small hospital.

Supporting her with my arm, I found the doctor on duty, a young woman who stood up quickly and hastened to check Vicky's blood pressure. A look of concern darkened her expression.

I took Vicky in my arms and laid her on a nearby bed while the doctor went for medication. She returned with a syringe and asked me to hold Vicky's arm while she looked for the vein. "Her pressure's very low, sixty over forty. I'm injecting her with a stimulant."

In scarcely a few hours Vicky had lost all her vitality. I watched her withering like a dying flower. I wouldn't—I couldn't—allow her just to die in my arms. I felt lost, demented, engulfed in a void of pain.

"She'll recover in a few minutes, but you must get her to the regional hospital as fast as possible," the doctor explained. "She needs to be looked at by one of their allergy specialists."

We set off in an antiquated ambulance, and although Vicky remained conscious under the effect of the stimulant, larger and larger reddish swellings were covering her body. And I kept shouting, begging the soldier who was driving to go faster.

The regional hospital was on the outskirts of the city, and we went into the emergency room and asked for an allergist. While we waited,

Vicky showed me the hand she'd injured a few days before, remarking that this was the hospital where they'd sutured her wound. Then she added, "I don't like the way they're taking care of their patients."

When the allergist finally appeared, she questioned Vicky and concluded she had been poisoned by the mushrooms. She gave her an antihistamine injection and recommended that she be admitted to the hospital for observation.

"I'm not staying here," Vicky told her, upset by the suggestion.

I tried to convince her to stay, but it was useless. With a look of pitiful entreaty in her eyes she said, "Please understand, I'm scared to stay here. I don't trust this place."

Thanking the doctor, we returned to the apartment. But there things got worse. The swelling continued, and by midnight the effect was almost monstrous. I felt desperate, unable to do anything except take her back to the hospital that so terrified her.

Vicky resigned herself, and when the boys were asleep, I went to the apartment of one of my buddies and asked him to come stay with them. "Go and don't worry," Jiménez reassured me.

It was close to two a.m. when we got back to the hospital, but this time we found no doctor on duty able to attend her. An old nurse filled out the forms, and we followed her down the hall to a room just opposite an office where the duty nurse sat nodding off. "The bed's the last on the left," the elderly nurse stated, and walked away.

Vicky, leaning heavily on me, made it to the last bed.

Her condition had significantly worsened in the last few hours. Now her skin looked like a sort of thick crimson mantle covering her entire body. "I think my bronchial tubes are also inflamed," Vicky commented in a low, sad voice. And she added, "I don't want to die!"

It was as if a glass world had shattered in my head. "What are you saying? You're going to be all right!" But I knew I was lying, just as I knew she would take my soul with her. *Don't leave me, Vicky.*

Vicky sobbed, "The children . . . My poor little boys."

"It's going to be all right," I repeated over and over. "Tomorrow the doctor will see you, and you'll be better in no time." And I didn't know whether I was trying to convince Vicky or myself. For the first time in my life I felt defeated.

I stayed several more hours, talking to her now and then while I wiped away the tears that rolled down her fevered cheeks. Then I said,

"I'll get the kids to school and come right back," and I left the room, leaving Vicky behind and, with her, my soul.

At home, I thanked my friend and sent him off. I covered the sleeping boys and kissed their foreheads. And seated on the edge of Reyniel's bed, I stared at the floor and recalled the day I met Vicky, our first kiss, the first dreams shared.

She had become the meaning of my life, the same as my children. What materialistic ideology, what Marxist philosophy could explain this emotion, which concerns existence itself?

I got up slowly and walked to our bed. And I fell on my knees, staring up at the sky through the window. I clasped my hands against my chest and cried, "Lord, forgive me! How could I have ignored You? How could I have denied You when You've always been inside me? Please—don't take her from me! Give her the strength to live!"

And I doubled over, crying uncontrollably—as if with each tear I might finally clear my soul of the many lies inculcated throughout my life—until the first rays of the morning sun told me that it was time to wake the children.

"Where's Mommy?" was the first question they asked.

But I was unprepared to answer. "She had to go off to work a little earlier this morning," I said. Then I got them ready, took them to school, and ran off to the hospital.

It wasn't yet eight o'clock when I arrived in Vicky's room. I apologized to the patients for the intrusion and made straight for Vicky's bed. From the window, rays of sunlight fell directly on her face, and I saw with horror how terrible she looked.

"Has the doctor seen you yet?"

"Nobody's come."

Vicky was getting worse and worse, and whenever she spoke, she had difficulty drawing her breath. I went out to the nurse on duty and said, "We need a physician. My wife is very ill."

"All the doctors are in conference. As soon as the meeting is finished, someone will come to see her."

I hurried back to Vicky's side.

"It's getting hard to breathe. I don't know if I'll be able to talk much longer." Vicky was speaking so low I could barely hear her. "What's happening has nothing to do with mushrooms. I think I'm going into anaphylactic shock—a reaction to the tetanus shot they gave me in this hospital when I injured my hand last week." She paused to get her breath, then continued. "They checked me first by inoculating me with a small dose of the serum under the skin to see if I had any reaction. But the doctor was in a hurry and didn't wait long enough. After they gave me the vaccination, I noticed that my skin had become irritated around the spot where they'd given me the test."

"Damn!"

"Forgive me. I've been so frightened I hadn't remembered."

I couldn't contain myself. I stormed out of the room like a shot. "Where are the doctors?" I demanded of the nurse.

"I told you they're having their morning meeting."

"I insist on knowing where they're holding it!"

"Next to the last door on the left," she replied, pointing down the corridor in the direction of the elevator.

"Come in!" a voice responded from the other side of the door after I knocked repeatedly. I opened the door.

There were five or six physicians seated around a table. "Please, we need a doctor urgently. My wife is very bad!"

A white-haired man with a large forehead answered curtly, "Comrade, can't you see we're busy with the morning's decisions? Tell your wife to wait." He seemed to be the chief physician.

"What do you mean *wait?*" I demanded, closing the door behind me and going up to the indifferent physician. "Don't you understand that she's dangerously ill—that she could be dying?"

I don't know what he read in my expression, but he stood up and signaled one of the other doctors to follow him. "Come on!"

Seated next to Vicky's bed, the chief physician started questioning her. "Doctor," I interrupted, "my wife can barely speak. She's a dentist, and she believes that she's suffering anaphylactic shock due to the tetanus vaccine she was given last week."

"That's the key!" the doctor declared, and he ordered his companion to bring an intravenous serum at once. Then, turning to me, he said, "I'll have them give her an electrocardiogram immediately."

I stayed with Vicky until it was time to pick up the boys that afternoon. I was amazed at how quickly she began to recover. By the time I had to leave, the welts covering her body had almost disappeared.

"She's out of danger," the doctor had told me a little after midday, "but she should remain a few days to watch her heart."

Overjoyed, I went off to pick up the children. That night I explained to them that Mommy was sick in the hospital and we'd see her soon.

Each morning I'd get up early to wash their clothes and iron whatever they were to wear that day. Then I made breakfast. I spent the days going back and forth between the house, the hospital, the school, and the nursery. Cooking, washing, ironing, cleaning.

One afternoon the chief physician called me into his office. He took out Vicky's file and explained to me the manner in which her sickness had developed. The tetanus vaccine they had given her had been made from animal plasma. "The country still lacks sufficient human plasma to prepare enough vaccines," he commented, and then added, "I'm terribly sorry. Tomorrow we'll do a final electrocardiogram. Afterward you can take her home."

The next morning Vicky and I bid the physician farewell with warm handshakes, and then we went home. And as in romantic movies, I picked her up in my arms to carry her across the threshold.

We embraced. I ran a hand through Vicky's hair and, without thinking, I said, "Thank God it's all over."

Vicky stared at me. "I've never heard you mention God before."

"And you— Do you believe in God?"

"I've always believed," she replied in a quiet voice.

"You never told me."

"You never asked me. And you?"

I didn't answer for a moment. I turned and walked to the window. The sky was particularly clear that day. Thank you, dear Lord, for giving me life, I thought, without saying a word. I felt Vicky's arms wrap around my chest as she hugged me from behind.

"Forgive him, Lord," she whispered.

## *Chapter Nine*

I REIMMERSED myself in my studies, but now I also launched an effort to learn the truth about the political questions that were beginning to haunt me. I spent long hours each evening reading the daily papers and magazines, which were reporting events in history that had been kept hidden until then. One article recounted the brutal manner in which the czar and his family, including the children, had been murdered by the Bolsheviks. What cause could justify the murder of a child? So that is the history of communism!

Lenin was a murderer. He had been my hero. Now I saw him as *the* person responsible for the crime against those children. But it wasn't only Lenin. The heroes of the great October Revolution whom I'd been taught to worship—they too approved of the crime. And wasn't it a crime to have kept hidden from me the real history of my heroes until today? I asked myself. Why had they done it? By what right?

They had hidden and distorted the facts, presenting Stalin as the most tireless defender against fascism and the supreme artist of its defeat. The same Stalin who had congratulated Hitler when the German troops entered Warsaw. The same Stalin who was being accused of the murder of more than forty million Soviets.

Now came the crimes committed by other important figures from the more recent past, under Brezhnev. Each magazine, each newspaper, each parliamentary discussion broadcast over television constituted for me a revelation of the evil of a world I had been willing to die for. I read, and with the pain came the outrage against the kind of enslavement of my consciousness that had been imposed through ignorance and lying since my childhood.

I spent the days in torment. One night when Vicky was observing my growing preoccupation, she commented, "You're going to drive yourself crazy if you continue like this. What can you do?"

"I don't know. I feel as if I haven't lived my own life."

"But you have to resign yourself to it. You can't change history."

"Right, but I refuse to live with lies! I refuse to accept the idea that in Cuba the same sort of thing is going on this very minute."

"Perhaps in Cuba things aren't that way."

Passages kept hammering in my brain from the recently published interview with Armando Valladares—that "dangerous terrorist" freed by Fidel in 1982 at the request of the French government—who now was United States ambassador to the U.N. Commission on Human Rights. Twenty-two years in prison, ten of them naked in a tiny punishment cell; eleven hunger strikes protesting ill-treatment, torture—such were the recollections of that man about Cuba. Could what Armando Valladares says be true? From now on, nothing is ever going to be the same, I thought with apprehension.

PERESTROIKA HAD GIVEN US ALL a new awareness, which made us examine more critically the stereotypes upon which we had been raised. Thus the tedious classes in Marxist-Leninist philosophy and dialectical materialism were converted into open debates between professors and their students.

One professor, Colonel Telux, a decorated veteran of World War II, was liked and respected by all, in spite of his being thought of as a man devoted to the cult of Stalin. One day when we were commenting in class on the decision to have a monument built in memory of the victims of the Stalinist purges, we asked our beloved professor his opinion on the matter.

"I know you think I'm an admirer of Stalin, " the colonel began in a barely audible voice. "I can only feel loathing over it, knowing the millions of victims of his dictatorship. But only today, under perestroika, have I been able to know it. It's like suddenly realizing that my whole life, of which I have always been proud, has been spent in a world that makes no sense." He paused for a long moment, swallowed dryly, then went on in a broken voice. "I wanted to live it over again. But as you can see, we don't have two lives, and as for this one, I wouldn't want to spend what is left of it wading through manure."

A total silence fell over the room. How terrible I felt for him!

I will never accept seeing myself in your situation, I vowed. If no one will tell me the truth of my country, then I'll find it out myself!

A NEW wave of information about the "mysterious West" swept over the media, and we watched with interest the first TV newscasts transmitted directly from the United States, West Germany, and the United Kingdom. We began thus to understand the workings of the democratic systems of such countries. This was the case with the United States Congress veto of President George Bush's choice of Senator Tower for Secretary of Defense. It was the best proof we could have had that the "all-powerful president of the United States"—as our leader called whoever happened to occupy the White House—did not remotely have the powers that Castro himself wielded.

The repercussions of perestroika in Cuba could be seen in the inauguration of the Process of Rectifying Errors announced by Fidel in 1986, and many of us interpreted it as a positive step in the fight against corruption. What fools we were!

Now our leader announced a ban on Soviet publications, which were previously sold in Cuba. "We have absolutely no use for such garbage," he declared. Fidel called Gorbachev a traitor, and leveled his most injurious attacks on figures like Yeltsin and other humanists highly respected by us, such as Andrey Sakharov.

History is the way it is, not the way we want it to be, I told myself, condemning the actions of my leaders. They're simply afraid of the truth.

ONE day we received some news that alarmed us all: Arnaldo Ochoa, the most brilliant of the Cuban generals, had been arrested on suspicion of drug trafficking with the United States. And with each day's newspapers—which we received from Cuba a week late—came new revelations implicating a group of high officials from the Ministry of the Interior who, with Ochoa, had collaborated with the Colombian cartel in the transshipment of cocaine via Cuba to the United States. The greatest corruption scandal involving the decadence of the Cuban Revolution was now being revealed.

Ochoa was one of the youngest Cuban generals, considered by those who served under him during the war in Angola to be a kindly officer, independent-minded and strong. His oft repeated praise for perestroika was no secret to anybody; nor was his sharp criticism of the deterioration that had taken hold of Cuba. His views were shared by many of the men now returning from Angola, and our highest leader swiftly realized how dangerous such men might become.

The audacity to think for himself and divulge his thoughts would cost this remarkable general his life. I watched the unfolding of the trial, predicting its outcome, and each day's session only confirmed my suspicion of political intrigue. In the midst of all this, one thing was becoming very clear to me: from now on, it would be impossible for me to follow those in whom I no longer believed, and I considered for the first time the possibility of defecting.

I decided to speak with Vicky about it, and one afternoon I asked her to take a walk with me to the Volga River, a half mile from our apartment house. The existence of some system of auditory surveillance in the building might have dire consequences, given the things I had to say. We stretched out on the sandy shore and watched Reyniel and Alejandro playing in the small park in front of us. I took

Vicky's hand and said to her, "I've been thinking about defecting."

"What?"

"Remaining in Canada when the plane stops for refueling."

Vicky first stared in astonishment; then a smile of complicity formed on her lips. "You really have gone crazy."

"Hope is called insanity nowadays?"

To my surprise, she appeared more convinced than I had hoped for. We talked about doing it the next year, after I'd finished my studies. This was a radical decision, and I realized we'd have to think hard about it. The prospect of starting a new life in a country where we didn't know anybody involved many unknowns.

WHEN August came, we left for vacation in Cuba, enveloped in happiness at the impending reunion with our loved ones. On our arrival, my father hastened to Havana with my mother and brothers, and after we all embraced each other with great emotion, he asked me to come outside to see something.

"Look, it's got yellow plates now," he said, pointing to the Soviet auto he had used for work all these years. It now displayed the yellow license plates reserved for private vehicles. It had already been his, for all practical purposes, but now they'd allowed him to buy it and thus have free use of it.

In previous years, when Vicky and I were at Santa Clara and he would visit, he was pained by the difficulties Vicky experienced going to and from her job. I realized that he would have liked to help us by lending us that official car, but unlike others, my father would in his nobility never conceive of allowing his children to use something that belonged to the state. Now, patting me on the shoulder, he said with evident pleasure, "It's yours. You can use it whenever you wish."

I knew quite well my father's dedication to the so-called work of the Revolution. He had lived his whole life as a romantic idealist, refusing opportunities for wealth and privileges that the positions he occupied might have brought him. Now I was filled with pity at the thought of how difficult it was going to be for him when the moment for facing the truth arrived. I made a few attempts to share with him the indignation I felt for what I considered a betrayal of myself, of him, of all the Cuban people. But I ran up against his preconceptions. His attitude brought back to me the memory of my professor in the U.S.S.R., dear

Colonel Telux, and I made the decision to respect my father's peace.

On the way back to Moscow, our plane stopped in Canada, and while we sat in the transit lounge waiting to board again, I noticed Vicky looking longingly through the plate-glass window, toward the street.

"Next time," I promised softly.

The last year of study began as we anxiously continued to watch developments in Cuba. The execution of General Ochoa and the jailing of the principal officials of the Interior Ministry was followed by a purge at the lowest echelons. Thousands of students being educated in the Soviet Union were recalled to Cuba, and educational exchanges were suspended.

That autumn of 1989 a wave of revolutionary changes swept Eastern Europe, taking the world by surprise. We shared unreservedly the jubilation of our German friends over the fall of the Berlin Wall, but this event created a truly ridiculous situation. The decisions we made during war games began with the well-known refrain "Because of the threat represented by the NATO bloc to the socialist countries . . ." And now it turned out that the German officers with whom we studied had become part of NATO's forces. "So *you're* the threatening enemy," we would chide them when we met between classes.

With the arrival of spring I was devoting all my energies to finishing my diploma project. General Popov, who held the chair in tactical aviation, was my director in preparing the defense of my project.

One day when we were discussing the situation in Cuba, he told me, "Fidel has betrayed all of you, son, just like Stalin did to us. Don't allow them to tarnish your life."

"You can be sure I won't," I replied. We never again spoke of Cuba or of how I was going to avoid their tarnishing my life.

Finally all that remained was to finish our final exams, go through our graduation ceremony, and take the leap into the unknown that I'd proposed to Vicky the previous year. I took a Russian-English dictionary out of the college library and memorized the words I'd have to say to the Canadian police at Gander airport: "We're Cubans, and we don't want to continue our flight. We need your protection."

I also began to instruct Vicky—on our walks to the river—but each time I brought up the subject, she'd become very serious and say with pleading eyes, "Please . . . I don't want to talk about it now."

Day after day I'd let it pass. Then one night I whispered into her ear that the moment was approaching and we should be prepared for it.

Immediately she broke into tears. "Please don't say anything more about it. It's driving me crazy!"

Vicky, I realized, had changed her mind. I took her in my arms. "Let's walk to the river. We have to talk."

Seated on a bench in a park where the children enjoyed playing, I turned Vicky's face toward me. "What made you change your mind?"

"My parents. . . . They'll be waiting for us at the airport. Can you imagine what will happen? Your comrades will walk out of the airport yelling at them, 'Scum! Vermin! Your children are traitors!' My mother would have a heart attack. It would kill her. Forgive me, I couldn't endure it. I'm not ready yet."

"It's not a matter of waiting until later. This is the only opportunity we're going to have."

I felt sorry for Vicky and sorry for myself and my sons. We were hostages to the system because of our love for our family.

"Have you thought of the children, of their future?" I asked her.

"I don't know. I don't know! And have you thought of how it could be if in Canada we find ourselves thrown out on the street without a penny to buy milk for our children?"

I realized that Vicky might be right. "All I have is faith, nothing more," I said. "I only know that going on like this, I wouldn't survive; that if I can't exercise my freedom, it would be like slowly dying—without dignity, without honor, ashamed of my existence."

"But think of your parents, of your brothers."

"All right," I began, already exhausted by the collapse of my dream, "we won't talk about it again. We'll go back!" Vicky's mood improved, and I hid as best I could an already unbearable despair.

GRADUATION day arrived, and we were splendidly dressed for the solemn proceedings in the courtyard of the war college.

After we were lined up in formation in the courtyard, standing at attention as we listened to the address given by the commander of the college, Reyniel suddenly broke out of the ranks of families attending the ceremony and raced across the parade ground, shouting at the top of his lungs, "What are you doing? Stop it, you dirty rats!"

More than a thousand faces turned to watch Reyniel running to fight off a group of boys who were trying to remove some baby pigeons from a nest that, curiously enough, had been built in the mouth of one of the old cannons enshrined there as museum pieces.

"*How embarrassing!* Do you see what your son's doing?" someone behind me muttered, lightly tapping my shoulder.

"Of course I do, and it's the proudest thing that could have happened to me here today!"

Once the ceremony was over, we marched past the podium in a final review. In a few days we'd be leaving for Cuba. As we paraded to the measured strains of a military band, I reflected that this was the first time I was marching in retreat, to where no hope remained.

## *Chapter Ten*

"ATTENTION!"

The voice of Lieutenant Colonel Teddy Rodríguez, our chief of staff, crackled over the loudspeakers and echoed across the parade ground. From my place on the podium I observed the troops assembled for that Monday morning reveille of August 1990: four fighter squadrons, the aerotechnical support battalions, communications, security—all perfectly aligned in block formation. Standing next to me was the base commander, Lieutenant Colonel Cordero, a friend of many years. He greeted the troops, then presented me to the assembled units as the new second commander of Santa Clara Air Base.

The news of my promotion to second-in-command reached me shortly after our arrival in Cuba, and I had received it without much excitement. In the four years I'd been away, changes had taken place on the base. From a single regiment of jet fighters, the base had enlarged to house a brigade. Construction had also been completed on the magnificent bunkers for housing the latest squadron of fighters, and we were now awaiting the delivery of MiG-23 BNs from Havana. Nevertheless, the same problems continued to plague the daily lives of the troops. Each day at the end of a work shift, officers and enlisted men could be seen heading toward the nearby woods with newspapers under their arms. There was still no plumbing in their living quarters. They found themselves in an even worse situation due to the termination of Soviet aid to Cuba. Meat, eggs, milk, and other products had been eliminated from their diet, and they had to work off-hours in makeshift gardens to assure themselves of a minimum to eat.

Our country, with its exceptionally fine climate for agriculture—in which it was possible to grow two or even three harvests a year—now found itself heading irremediably toward widespread hunger. The government could have alleviated the scarcity of food simply by permitting peasants to work the land and sell their crops. But this would have inevitably brought economic independence to the peasants and to others who would sell country goods in the cities. And it would have been impossible for the government to control them. Our leaders' instincts for self-preservation compelled them to blame the impending privations on the Soviet Union's betrayal and the United States's commercial embargo. Mystifying definitions—like Extraordinary Period of War in Times of Peace—began to be repeated incessantly by the machinery of government propaganda, and directives were issued establishing privations to which the populace must submit. The notion disseminated through all the militant organizations was that the United States intended to conquer our people through starvation. Once again the leaders were inciting the nation with a lie, and very few people were still capable of understanding, in the fevered hatred toward the United States, that no embargo could be blamed for the absence of food that the country itself was capable of growing.

LITTLE by little our life returned to its rhythm of five years earlier. Vicky began work in the same dental polyclinic in Santa Clara, and I started flying again and instructing the younger pilots. Standby alerts sometimes reached two or three times a week.

One night when I got home, I heard Alejandro mentioning the inevitable war with the evil Americans and the way he was going to defeat them. I looked at Vicky and burst out, "I can't stand it!"

Vicky lowered her head and walked off to our bedroom.

The year went by, and each passing day brought home the truth of the prediction I'd made to Vicky: I felt as if I were dying. I'd lost hope, drowning in the sea of lies surrounding me. Our children talked about the "war against the Yankees," and I felt guilty and ashamed for not being able to tell them that no such war existed unless our leader provoked it. I would return home each day and lose myself in thought: My honor—what's happened to my honor? Where is my pride at saying whatever I think? I'm a coward. . . . I have to explode, even if it costs me my life. Death is preferable to living a lie.

Vicky would observe me from the kitchen doorway and ask me all the time, "What's the matter?"

And each time I would answer her, "Nothing."

One night Vicky said, "I'm the one to blame for what's happening. I shouldn't have—"

I stood up and took her in my arms. I spoke softly in her ear in case there were hidden microphones in our apartment.

"You're not guilty of anything, Vicky, and I don't blame you in any way whatsoever. But I can't take any more."

"Then go— Go away!" she whispered finally.

"What do you mean, go away?"

"In a plane. I'd rather that than have you do something really crazy." The idea she'd suggested began to hammer in my brain from that day forward, with greater and greater insistence.

On the last day of the year, I was on duty, and Vicky and the boys came to spend New Year's Eve with me. Vicky had brought along a small dish wrapped in paper. "It's a flan I made today, to celebrate the new year with all four of us together," she told me, and I understood that it was all she could do. We brought in the new year of 1991 in the small waiting room at the command post, the boys asleep in our arms, and I gazed at them with pity. We had not a single toy, not even a little tree, nothing appropriate for their age to give them.

Soon after, an inspection committee arrived from general headquarters with the task of verifying compliance with the directives regarding the Extraordinary Period of War in Times of Peace. They wanted to see how well we were managing to grow vegetables on the base, to cook with firewood—in effect, to see how we were holding up in the nearly subhuman conditions in order not to capitulate to the North American embargo.

"Tonight's the welcoming dinner for the committee at the officers club. Be sure to bring Vicky," Cordero had insisted shortly after the inspectors arrived.

Vicky and I showed up that evening and took our seats at one of the tables. The waiters began to serve beer and bring in the platters of grilled pork, served with yucca and rice with black beans—the traditional Cuban dish. I thought about what our soldiers must be eating at that moment, and staring at the meal, I felt I couldn't touch it.

One of the inspectors turned to me. "Major, you'd better eat. You don't see an opportunity like this every day!"

To conceal my real feelings, I excused myself, saying I didn't feel very well. Vicky left with me, following in silence out to the tree-shaded patio of the club.

"I can put up with all the scarcities—water, food, transportation," I said. "But this life of swallowing one lie after another—I can't stand it!" I exploded, punching a tree trunk with my fist.

"You terrify me when you get like this. One day you'll commit some insanity, and we'll lose you. You have to go away."

I lowered my head, remembering the conversation we'd had. "I've been thinking about it since the last time we spoke," I confessed.

Her eyes widened, and she asked me simply, "When?"

"I don't know. It looks like it'll be impossible to do it all together. I don't know how to obtain a boat capable of making it across the Florida Strait. Besides, the surveillance that pilots are subjected to would make it impossible for us to board a boat together. I could only do it relatively easily in a MiG, but the three of you would be left behind, and that's what I can't accept."

"But it's preferable. I know you're going to explode at any moment, and that would be the worst of possibilities for us all. Do it."

"Maybe you're right . . . but let me think about it some more."

Vicky embraced me, crying. And I remarked to her gently, "If anyone comes out here, they'll think we're having a quarrel."

She smiled and hugged me tighter, saying, "I love you so!"

"I love you too," I answered, drawing her closer.


GENERAL del Pino had escaped to the United States with only part of his family in 1987. As for those he'd left behind—like his mother—they'd been forced to repudiate him to the Cuban media, calling him a traitor. That was how the repressive system functioned. The leaders would come, loyally and generously, to the assistance of the abandoned relatives, accompanied by the greatest hoopla. And the media would manage the rest, turning the defection into a triumph.

Those relatives, forced by circumstances and fear to make declarations against "the traitor," now felt too morally vulnerable to ask permission to leave the country to be reunited with their loved one.

Fidel and Raúl Castro cut a noble image in the press, repeating in their public statements that no one was held in the country against his or her will. The commander in chief, for his part, declared over national television, "We're not to blame for the ones who can't leave—it's the United States' fault for refusing to grant them visas. On the contrary, our doors are always wide open."

All that Vicky would have to do is pretend to be shocked at my departure and then, shielded by the grief at my desertion, abstain from any declaration against me to the press, and refuse to accept the privileges offered by the leaders. That would allow her to have the temerity necessary to ask to leave the country once I obtained the proper North American visas. A plan was taking shape in my mind—filled with risks, but it was the only alternative possible.

And if they refuse to permit Vicky and the children to leave, even though I manage the visas? Then I'll turn to the foreign press. The publicity would be so adverse for them that they'd have to let the family leave.

When I finished the following day's shift, I asked Vicky to go for a walk with me and the boys to a nearby stream. The next day I was going to Havana for a week to receive basic training for the MiG-23 BNs that had recently arrived at the base.

"It seems the only possible way of doing it is for me to escape first in a MiG," I told her.

"When?"

"The first opportunity after my return from Havana. But you're going to join me one way or another very soon after."

Vicky stared at me. "How will we manage it?"

And I explained my plan to her. Then I asked her, "Do you think you can manage it, bearing up under all that?"

"I think so," was her reply.

"You can't give them the slightest indication that you were aware of my intentions to leave, or all the weight of their vengeance will fall upon you. You will have to go live with your parents in Havana. Tell the boys that I've been temporarily transferred to another base—to the Soviet Union—whatever occurs to you.

"Another thing: you have to take it for granted that every word you say at home is being heard by them. Whenever you're alone, don't hesitate to do a little thinking out loud, railing against me for what I did. That'll help make them believe that you really knew nothing."

"I understand."

"If all goes well, I'll call you from there, asking you to forgive me for never having told you. Once you've heard from me, go to the U.S. Interests Office and apply for visas for you and the children. I'll be doing the same thing at the other end. Once we have those, they can no longer keep you here. It would cause an international scandal. I think they'll let you leave quietly to avoid the embarrassment."

Vicky smiled with a gleam of hope in her eyes that I hadn't seen in many months. How innocent we were then! How mistaken we were regarding the reaction of the Cuban authorities.

I left the following day, first going to see my parents in Matanzas. Afterward, having borrowed my father's car for the trip to Havana, I attended classes at the Military Technical Institute, returning to the house of my in-laws, sure I was being followed. I visited Varadero, one of my favorite places, where I'd spent so much of my childhood, but that magnificent beach resort had changed, and was now reserved almost exclusively for foreign tourists. With the growth of the international tourist trade and the conditions of poverty pervading the country, hundreds of youths had prostituted themselves, trading their bodies for an invitation to dinner, a cake of soap, some perfume, the most ordinary consumer products.

I went for a walk through the streets of my beloved seaport. A blinking sign announced EL CASTILLITO DISCOTHEQUE at the entrance to a building, and more than a dozen young girls—wearing tight short skirts to highlight their charms—were standing there, chattering loudly, waiting for some tourist to pull up and invite them inside. New restaurants had opened up everywhere, with notices posted that they were reserved exclusively for foreigners.

Even my country they take away from me, I said to myself, feeling bitterness enter my soul. The next morning I headed back to Santa Clara with the sense of being a man without a country. Only for the time being, I told myself, now convinced that my next solo flight was going to be to the United States.

VICKY and the boys ran down the stairway to meet me as soon as they saw me getting off the bus. They'd been waiting for me up on the balcony. Now Reyniel and Alejandro were noisily interrupting each other to fill me in on the latest details about their school week. The four of us spent the remainder of the afternoon playing on the living-room floor, and when it was time to turn in for the night, I whispered to Vicky, "On the first flight I make . . ."

The following morning, Sunday, I left early for the command post to go on duty for what looked to be the last time in my life. In the afternoon Vicky and the boys made a surprise visit. Vicky couldn't hide her preoccupation. "Do you know when the next flights are yet?" she asked.

"Wednesday—" I stammered, recalling the flight schedule.

The next day at the base I locked myself in my office. I unfolded the map that included the southern sector of the United States, and I made the necessary calculations with a navigational ruler for a flight to the Boca Chica Naval Air Station at Key West from the various points in the region where we were accustomed to flying. I memorized the data, leaving no trace on that map. When I got home, even though we didn't speak of the matter, Vicky couldn't hide the nervous state she was in. The next day would be our last together.

The following morning I inspected the squadron areas and visited the men, to whom I wanted to bid a silent farewell. I was tormented by the thought that soon they would think I'd betrayed them.

Then I joined the other pilots preparing for the following day's missions. A comrade from my cadet days had come from Havana to instruct us on the new MiG-23s. I would fly first with him in the training aircraft before performing my solo . . . to freedom or death.

I left for home early. Vicky started serving dinner immediately— rice, stuffed potatoes, and black beans. "It's all we have, but I prepared it with love," she told me.

"Everything you've ever done at my side has been with love," I answered.

"Mommy, how come you and Daddy aren't eating?" Reyniel asked, seeing that we hadn't touched our plates.

"We just wanted to keep you two company before you go to bed. We'll have dinner a little later," Vicky answered.

In silence we cleared the table while the children went off to sleep, and in silence we went to our room. From the family album we picked out two pictures. We checked the biggest one against the size and shape of the breast pocket of my flight uniform, and amid tears Vicky silently cut it with a pair of scissors to fit inside. The other photo went into my wallet. Together with my identification papers, the photographs were to be the only things to accompany me on my flight.

It was perhaps the last night we'd ever have together, and we wanted to give ourselves to each other with all the passion of our lives.

"I'll pray hard for you to get there safe and sound," Vicky whispered in my ear in the midst of our vigil.

"Go immediately to Havana with your parents. Don't stay here. And keep faith; love has to triumph over lies," I told her when the clock reached the hour for my departure.

Overcome with emotion, I kissed the sleeping children, dropping to the floor beside the bed they shared. Vicky gripped my shoulders hard, then ended up dropping to her knees beside me.

We made a final effort to calm ourselves, and we walked to the door. There we embraced again. Then we separated, and looking into Vicky's eyes, I whispered, "I don't know how long it will take for us to be reunited, but I'll never give you up. If they don't let you leave, I'll be back for the three of you. I don't know how—but I'll come back. This is a struggle of truth against the lie, of love against hatred. Never doubt that love will triumph."

Turning, I ran down the stairs, asking God to give me the strength to undertake that flight to a new destiny, where my children might grow up in freedom. When I'd already left the road, I turned my head and saw Vicky waving her hand in farewell. I answered with a gesture of my own while I repeated softly, "I'll never give you up!"

## Chapter Eleven

VICKY was distractedly observing Alejandro from the kitchen doorway as he sat on the living-room floor holding the small fighters I'd carved out of wood, flying across who knew what fantastic zones. *"Errrr. . ."* Alejandro continued, mimicking the sounds of flight.

Poor little thing, she was thinking. So innocent of what's happening.

It was him, she told herself, remembering the last MiG to take off that morning while she was walking to the market with Alejandro to get their ration of bread and milk. Did he make it? Why the total silence? What if they shot him down! Oh, God, how long am I to

suffer the uncertainty? A knock at the door made her turn in fright.
She walked to the door holding her breath. "Who is it?" she asked.
"It's me, Mom."

She swung open the door with a sigh of relief. She'd forgotten that
it was lunchtime and Reyniel would be home from school.

"What's the matter, Mom?"

"I wasn't expecting the knock at the door. You scared me," Vicky
told the boy, and went into the kitchen. She came back with two plates
of rice, each with a fried egg on top. "Alejandro, put the planes down
now, and come have lunch with your brother."

I have to get hold of myself. If it'd been them, they would have
noticed how nervous I am. Why do my hands keep shaking so?

FAR away, at the southeastern tip of the United States, a group of
people began to gather around the Cuban air force MiG-23.

"She's Lienne Johnson, from the Federal Bureau of Investigation,"
the sergeant said, translating what a newly arrived woman was saying.

Only a few minutes had gone by since I'd jumped to the ground
from my cockpit to ask for asylum from that affable colonel who
had then offered me his hand in welcome. His gesture of kindness
had dissipated the last remnants of fear I'd harbored about this country, and now I turned to the FBI official and smiled timidly.

"She wants to know if you're carrying any weapon or drug with
you," the sergeant continued, as interpreter.

"This is all I have with me," I replied, taking from my pockets my
billfold, cigarettes, lighter, and the photo of Vicky and the boys.

"You have a lovely family," she remarked, returning the photo and
the other articles. She looked at me again, and at that point no
translation was necessary, for I saw an infinite compassion in her eyes
for which I'll be forever grateful.

"Will you accompany us, Major?" The colonel put an arm around
my shoulder and indicated the open door of an automobile. We
drove to the control-tower building. There a lounge—equipped with
a coffee table, easy chairs, and several telephones—served as our
refuge from the heat outside. "Have a seat," the colonel said. "Would
you like a Coke, a hamburger?"

"No."

"A coffee, then?"

It was the only thing I could have taken. My stomach seemed paralyzed by the emotions taking hold of me. "Yes, please."

The colonel asked someone to bring in coffee for everybody, while the official from the FBI took a seat opposite me. "Do you have relatives in the United States?" she asked.

"Yes. Several aunts and uncles, and cousins."

"Do you know where they live? Do you have phone numbers?"

"One aunt lives in Miami. I don't know her phone number. I believe her son Charles is an officer in the air force. Charles Armenteros."

She wrote it down in a notebook and went to a phone.

"Your coffee, Major." It was the sergeant, who passed me a cup of steaming coffee, and I felt touched by the affability of those men and women whom I'd been taught to see as terrible enemies.

"Major?" It was the FBI official calling me to the telephone. "I've got your cousin Charles on the line."

I was astonished. She'd found Charles in those few minutes, with barely any information about him.

"Hello, Charles?" I talked to him for a few moments, in which he was clearly overcome by emotion. He wanted to come immediately from the air force base in Texas where he was stationed, to see me, help me. "Hold on," I tried to reassure him. "I'm in the hands of good people who will tell you what the situation is." And I handed the phone back to the FBI official, who continued talking with my cousin.

Then I glanced around the room: a number of people were busy on the telephones, others were scribbling away in their notebooks, and still others were going in and out.

Am I the cause of all this commotion? I asked myself.

"Major, permit me to introduce you to two air force intelligence officers who've just arrived." It was the sergeant again.

"Captain Sánchez," said the younger, shaking hands.

"Rodríguez," the other said. "Welcome."

"I see you both speak Spanish."

"We're Puerto Rican," the captain replied amiably, and added, "You think we might talk for a minute, Major?"

"Of course." And realizing I would have to answer quite a few questions, I took a seat with them around an adjacent table.

I noticed Captain Sánchez's watch. It was already three p.m. What's happening with Vicky and the children? I asked myself.

VICKY HAD BEEN STANDING BY THE window, watching through a crack in the venetian blinds, and she felt her heart stop as she saw a jeep pull up to the curb and Lieutenant Colonel Cordero and two other officers got out.

"They're coming!" she murmured in fright, and making a super-human effort to control her emotions, she went and opened the door. Before her stood the three men whose faces were so familiar. Cordero's was pale. Vicky decided to take the initiative. "What's the matter? Has something happened?"

They stared at her without replying.

"What's wrong? Tell me! Is my husband dead?"

"Something worse. . . . He's alive," Cordero began, a mixture of fear and anger in his expression. "He's landed in the United States."

A shock of joy seized her whole being. Thank you, Lord! He made it! she said to herself, but she exclaimed aloud, "What?"

"He landed in the United States. I only hope it was a mechanical failure and that this is not some treason," Cordero replied dryly, and Vicky understood that this man was no longer a friend. Perhaps he never was, she thought, realizing that from then on, he would be motivated by self-preservation, putting the greatest possible distance between himself and our family.

She felt alone, terribly alone. "I can't believe it!" she exclaimed, and she collapsed into a chair. Then she covered her face with her hands and gave full vent to her desperate need to cry.

They waited in silence, witnessing that sobbing, which was not feigned. Then a thought suddenly assailed her: His parents . . . I have to break the news to them. Who knows what they might tell them! And she got up to go to the phone.

"What are you doing, Vicky?" Cordero asked.

"Calling his parents. I have to tell them what's happened."

"No. You mustn't do that. We're investigating right now. We'll tell them eventually." Cordero spoke like someone giving instructions, with no emotion in his voice. "Don't do anything for the moment. We'll be in touch with you." And without another word he marched down the stairs, followed by his companions.

Vicky went back to her seat. She had prepared herself to confront that moment, but the painful uncertainty about ever seeing her husband again made her feel desperate.

"I'll stay with you in the meantime." It was Cordero's wife, Marlen, behind her, who'd come from her apartment across the hall. And Vicky felt that at last someone had come to give her succor, but Marlen simply took a seat and watched in silence as Vicky wept. Not one word of consolation from somebody who'd been her friend.

Alejandro suddenly woke up, and luckily our friend Miriam Díaz had just come from her apartment. "I'll take Alejandro with me to play, and Reyniel too when he gets home from school," Miriam said, and Vicky felt infinitely grateful for that courageous gesture.

Marlen and she were left alone together. After a while Marlen finally spoke. "You were always a slave to that man. He never loved you, and that's why he didn't hesitate to betray you."

Vicky felt like vomiting, and ran into the bathroom. We must get out of here as soon as possible! she thought. What's happening to him now? Are they treating him well? She let her imagination fly, conjuring up in her mind that country we'd been taught to consider as hell, which had become our hope of freedom.

At Boca Chica, I was being inundated by a flood of delicately posed questions from the intelligence officers. "What made you change your ideas?" was one of them.

I'd anticipated questions on the matter of Cuban troops and armaments; however, those officers seemed more interested in the psychological process that had led to such a radical turnabout in my life.

"I couldn't answer that in just a few words," I began, and I tried to describe the indignation, irritation I felt at discovering I'd been used, betrayed—at having lost my dignity, the integrity essential to go on living.

"And do you think you'll find that here?"

"I don't think the United States is a paradise; nor did I come here to switch sides, since I'll never adhere blindly to any dogma, leader, or party organization. My whole life's experience has been sufficient to make me prefer death to falling into the same traps. I only bring the hope of finding here the truth I'm searching for—my right to keep myself informed, to make my own judgments, to choose and speak what I think. I hope to God I find this . . . because if it isn't that way, I think life won't be worth living."

Captain Sánchez would stop writing on occasion, pausing to stare fixedly at me while he listened. Sometimes I got the impression that I was talking too much or that they didn't understand me. Then I'd pause and ask them if I should be more specific.

"Not at all. Say whatever comes to mind," they would reply.

So I continued, talking and talking, feeling that infinite pleasure at being able to say—for the first time!—everything I was thinking.

"And when was the actual moment you changed your ideas?"

"There was no precise moment. I acted out of convictions, and one by one I had to admit to myself that they were false—from the leaders of my country and their system of governing to the Marxist philosophy itself in which I had been educated. It was not enough to realize that communism didn't work in Europe; I had to prove to myself that it didn't work ever, in any country, and why. I had to be sure I wasn't simply acting in an egotistical manner or betraying the helpless victims of the kind of abuses prevalent in the world. I had to prove to my own satisfaction that communism would never resolve the injustices that still exist, but would only aggravate them further."

My questioners were listening attentively when someone called Sánchez, and he stepped out for a minute, returning with two men in dark suits, officials from the FBI who'd also come to talk with me.

"I'm Rubén," said the younger one, extending his hand.

"My name's José," said the other. He was in his early fifties.

"I see you men also speak Spanish."

"I'm Puerto Rican," Rubén explained, "and José's Cuban." Rubén didn't seem older than thirty-five.

I saw that another round of informal questioning was to begin. "First, middle, and last name?" "Date of birth?" "Schools where you studied?" "When did you enter the air force, the party?" "What made you come?" They were more or less the same questions I'd already answered. Then we were interrupted by the arrival of an immigration official. She was carrying a canvas bag and smiling.

"Here you'll find some clothing and whatever else you'll need for the first few days." And slipping a hand into her pocket, she explained, "And here's twenty-five dollars. You'll need it."

"Thank you very much," I replied, although the words were inadequate to describe the impact on my heart of that touching gesture.

"It's time to be going," Sánchez said. "There's a plane waiting to take us to Homestead Air Force Base."

We were heading for a place I'd known only as one of the targets I'd studied at the military academies. Just as we were about to board the plane, the sergeant who'd been my interpreter came up to us.

"I just wanted to say good-bye, Major," he said. "I've brought you this book, which I read a while back. It was written by an exceptional human being. He talks about the Cuba you don't know."

I shook his hand warmly. On the cover of the book was the face of a young-looking man with a resolute expression—it was Armando Valladares—and the title was *Contra Toda Esperanza,* meaning *Against All Hope.* Finally I'd be able to hear the voice of this man my government called a terrorist, and who was freed from a Cuban prison while I was in Angola.

The small two-engine plane flew us to Homestead. A mantle of lights blanketed the horizon when we circled the base to land. "That's Miami," Rubén remarked, upon seeing me stare out the window. And I was astonished at the immensity of that city known as the political capital of the Cuban exile community.

After landing, the pilot opened the side door of the plane, and Sánchez asked me to go out first. A red carpet extended from the foot of the ladder, and two soldiers stood in profile at the end of it, holding their rifles at attention. Beyond, the commander of the base stood waiting. They were receiving me with military honors!

I stepped forward in confusion, deeply touched and forgetting even my military protocol by not saluting smartly.

"Welcome," the commander told me when I finally reached him. "It's a pleasure to have you as a guest."

We were driven to the building where I'd be staying, and then we were led to a large room furnished with a sofa, some easy chairs, a refrigerator, and a television. I was shown the bathroom and then the bedroom, furnished with the biggest bed I'd ever seen.

"Here you have plenty of food to eat whenever you wish, Major," Rodríguez explained, opening the refrigerator.

Before they left, Sánchez said, "There will be two armed soldiers guarding the door, but that's only for your protection. You're free, and you've only to tell us if you wish to leave."

I went into the bedroom, but I knew that I wouldn't be able to sleep—I just wanted the morning to come. My mind wandered to Vicky and the boys, to my parents and my former comrades.

IT WAS ALREADY SEVEN AT NIGHT, and Vicky had not received any further communication from Cordero following his instruction that she wait at home. Since then she'd been spending most of the time on trips back and forth between the living room and the bathroom. The boys had noticed the state she was in, and she said she had a stomach-ache, which was true. Luckily, everybody had shown discretion about keeping from the children knowledge of what had happened.

One neighbor came up to the apartment, and she whispered into Vicky's ear, "They're already broadcasting news of it on American radio," referring to Radio Martí, the U.S. government station transmitted to Cuba, which many listened to in secret.

Then Vicky picked up the telephone to call my parents. "I won't have them finding out about it over the radio. It would be too terrible—"

"Hello?" It was my youngest brother, Orlando, at the other end.

"It's Vicky. Are your mother and father there?"

"Yes. . . . Something wrong?"

"Yes. Your brother landed his plane in the United States—today, sometime around noon—"

*"What?"*

"He went off to the United States. Tell your—"

She couldn't finish. Orlando had hung up and run into the kitchen. "*Ay,* Mom, what a disgrace, what a disgrace!" he cried.

"What's happened, son? Tell me what's happened!"

My father had already gotten up from his seat in front of the television, and he rushed to Orlando, a sudden pallor on his face while my mother kept yelling, "Oré, Oré! What's happened to Oré?"

"He's not killed. He's alive—" Orlando finally began.

"What happened, then?"

"He flew to the United States!"

A complete silence descended upon them. My mother stared at Orlando as if she couldn't fathom what she'd just heard.

My father finally reacted. "It isn't true."

Vicky was now on the phone to her younger sister in Havana. "Aurora, Oré's—gone," she began in a halting voice.

"He's left you? I can't believe it."

"No, Aurora. He flew off to the United States in his plane."

"Did you say *the United States? Ay!*" And Aurora broke into uncontrollable sobbing, preventing Vicky from telling her anything more.

CORDERO CALLED VICKY, TELLING her that a delegation from counterintelligence in Havana was on its way to interrogate her. Vicky felt a chill run through her. They didn't want me preparing for this, she thought, hanging up, and immediately she heard a knock at the door.

It was Lieutenant Colonel Ernesto, head of counterintelligence, followed by a group of strangers. "We need to ask you a few questions. May we talk at Cordero's while they search your house? We still don't understand how your husband could have done what he did, and we need to look for any evidence—"

"All right," Vicky said, crossing the hall to the Corderos' apartment.

They'd barely walked in when the telephone rang, and Marlen picked it up. "It's your in-laws."

Vicky answered the call, and my father couldn't believe what he was hearing. He asked to speak to Cordero, who had just arrived from the base. In a few sentences Cordero explained what had happened.

My father listened. Then he placed the receiver slowly back on the telephone, murmuring the last words he would utter for some time: "My son's broken my heart."

Then they all understood that the story was true.

Now Vicky faced the deluge of questions from the counterintelligence officers. Other officers, meanwhile, ransacked our apartment, searching for evidence that would expose my "ties to the enemy," and they hid a number of listening devices around the apartment to monitor Vicky's activities.

"Did you hear your husband make any critical remarks lately about the Revolution?" the investigating officer asked, leaning toward Vicky as if expecting the most scandalous reply.

"No," she replied. "He normally came home and played with the kids or watched TV. But he didn't talk to me about politics."

"And the commander in chief? Did you ever hear your husband criticizing him?"

"In no way. He would never do that—"

"Understand, we need to discover the reasons for which he betrayed the Revolution, betrayed the commander in chief."

"I don't understand it myself! I can't think of any reason."

"You didn't notice anything strange about your husband's behavior lately?"

"I don't know what you mean by strange."

"Did you notice him going out without telling you where?"

Do they really think that the CIA bought him off? she asked herself. "It would've been impossible. When he wasn't working on the base, he was on standby alert. We've barely had two weekends together."

"You noticed nothing strange in his intimate behavior— I mean, you haven't noted any symptom of homosexuality in him?"

Vicky realized then what they were really looking for. They knew well enough that the CIA could never recruit her husband; the opportunity had never presented itself. They knew as well that no one had induced him to fly to the United States, that he had acted as a result of his own ideas. But if the man who had now turned traitor was a loyal son of the Revolution, how then to explain his desertion to his men? Obviously, they couldn't. So they needed some fact, some evidence—even a declaration against him by his wife—with which to discredit his image before those who'd been his comrades. They'll never get such a thing from me, Vicky thought.

"Never," Vicky began by telling them. "You all know him very well and can see well enough he's not a homosexual."

The officer stood up, ending the interview. "We'll keep in touch with you. Your husband betrayed you, but the Revolution will see to it that you are well taken care of." He left, followed by his agents.

Vicky turned to Cordero, who still remained seated in the living room. "Tomorrow I'm leaving for my parents' house."

He stared at her, obviously worried. "You should stay here until the investigation's been completed."

"They can ask me whatever they want at my parents' house in Havana. If I stay here one day longer, I think I'll die of anguish." Vicky went out the door and to our apartment.

Miriam had brought the boys home, and they were asleep. Vicky thanked her and said good-bye. Then she ran to the phone and called a neighbor of her parents, from whom she learned that they'd left Havana to join her. They'd be there by morning.

Next she called my parents' house and asked my brother Faure if he'd be able to come pick her up in my father's car. "Don't worry, I'll be there before midday," Faure promised.

It was three in the morning, but Vicky knew she couldn't sleep. She glanced at the disorder of the room after the search. I'm sure they're listening to me, she thought, and she sat on the bed and, staring at the ceiling in anguish, exclaimed for the ears of those spying on her, "*Why,* my love? Why did you do it? How could you abandon us!"

THE next day Vicky got ready for the departure in the company of her parents, who had come to help her. Earlier a friend had come up to warn her that a group of children had gathered downstairs in order to yell at Reyniel and Alejandro that their father was a traitor. Now the moment had arrived to give the children a logical explanation of events. She asked them to sit down and listen carefully.

"Pay attention. Uncle Faure is on his way here. When he arrives, we're all going to go with him."

"Hooray! To see our cousins!" Alejandro exclaimed.

"Daddy had to go to another base to work for a long time, so we're going to go live with Grandma and Grandpa in Havana."

"Hooray!" exclaimed Alejandro all over again.

They were interrupted by the arrival of Faure and his wife, Isabel, from Matanzas. Faure threw his arms around Vicky, while Isabel hugged both of them from behind. Then they discussed which belongings they'd be taking and how they were all going to fit into that little car. They were just about to leave when Marlen Cordero came in to ask Vicky to come to her apartment. There, seated in the living room, was Lieutenant Valdés from base counterintelligence.

"Is it true you're leaving, Vicky?" he asked, standing up.

"Yes, right now in fact—"

"It's necessary that you remain a few more days."

"I'm sorry, but I can't stand to be here another second. Everything around me just reminds me of him."

"But we need your help! We don't know what happened, nor why he did it. We need to clarify matters, and only you can help us—"

"I don't know what else I could tell you. I know as much as you people do. I'm sorry, but I'm going."

Valdés looked very pale. He hadn't expected such obstinacy from Vicky, and he saw himself losing his only opportunity to come up with something that would free him from blame before his superiors. He had been assigned to the base to prevent such things, and he knew that his name might end up on the list of negligent and irresponsible officers who had permitted my escape. Fear was overtaking him.

"You've got to understand, Vicky! We've found nothing, not one reason to explain why he became a traitor!" And dropping the normally peremptory tone with which he addressed people, he implored her, "Please, I beg you, Vicky, stay a few more days!"

Vicky regarded him with pity—that man whom everybody on the base feared. But there was no way of keeping her there, short of arresting her. And that, she knew, they wouldn't do. "I'm sorry. I couldn't stay even if I wanted to. It's all been too much for me."

I'D SPENT the night at the Homestead Air Force Base, thinking about my family and about the impact my defection was to have on all of them. In my sleeplessness I'd started to read the book by Armando Valladares, but the description he gave of the crimes committed from the outset of the Revolution seemed an atrocious exaggeration, so I'd tossed it aside with disappointment. I was thus absorbed in thought when I heard the door of the adjacent room open. It was Sánchez, who was surprised at seeing me as I emerged from the bedroom.

"Good morning. I didn't think you'd be up so early," he said.

"I didn't sleep very well. My wife and my sons were on my mind. But I'm happy you've come this early. I couldn't bear the solitude."

Someone knocked at the door, bringing breakfast—an ample tray of fruit, toast, butter, juice, and coffee—but I still had no appetite.

Soon Rubén and Rodríguez arrived, and Rubén said, "I have a surprise for you," and took a piece of paper out of his pocket. "I'll dial your aunt's telephone number so you can talk to her. You can tell her you're with us, but I ask you not to tell her where you are."

My aunt Miladis hadn't seen me since I was three or four years old, and now she seemed so excited that I was here. She told me how the TV reporters from the local station had marched into the place where she worked to ask her countless questions, to which she'd had no answers. She also wanted me to come live with her.

"Well, I don't know. Probably."

"What do you mean, probably?" It was that same affectionate, authoritarian tone of thirty years ago.

"Try to understand. I can't be sure."

"All right, tell me where you are, and I'll come see you now."

"I can't, Aunty, I'm—"

"They've arrested you?"

"No, no, Aunty, I'm not in jail. I'm fine and with good people."

"Who're you with there?"

"The FBI."

"You're sure you don't need a lawyer? You have rights."

My aunt's words filled me with emotion. It was the first time in my life that anybody spoke to me of my rights.

"I assure you I don't need a lawyer," I told her, laughing.

When I hung up the phone, I stood there pensively a few seconds. Something in her way of talking had particularly impressed me: her independence in speaking out, her courage in questioning, especially since she was questioning the FBI. Freedom goes this far here? I asked myself, already suspecting that it might.

We spent the morning and part of that afternoon chatting about sports, the war in the Persian Gulf, life in Cuba, and I understood that through those informal discussions I was being scrutinized. Yet it didn't trouble me; rather I was enjoying their company as casual friends.

That evening Sánchez brought a supper prepared with taste and delicacy by the staff of the military club. "They've prepared it as a special welcome," he said, lifting the cover off a tray adorned with a flower set in a tall, thin vase. For the first time in days my stomach showed signs of hunger, and I ate with gusto.

THE next day I was taken on an excursion into that impressive city I'd seen from the plane. The huge highways, the modern cars of so many makes and models, all caught my attention. But more than anything it was the grass that astonished me—hundreds of miles, millions of acres carefully cultivated and cropped at the sides of the roads and in the yards of houses. Now, that was something that had never before entered my imagination! In all my years of service at the Santa Clara Air Base we'd never even managed to cut all the grass bordering the runway, though the flocks of birds that came to eat the seeds jeopardized takeoff and landing security.

Our tour included Miami's Calle Ocho, center of Little Havana, the heart of the Cuban exile community. A group of senior citizens were gathered on the patio of a curious club that excluded those under sixty. Stopping, I watched them playing dominoes and discussing the passion of their lives: Cuba.

ON OUR WAY BACK WE STOPPED at a shopping mall, and contrary to what my friends expected, I wasn't impressed by all the products I saw there. For me it had been enough to see the cut grass.

Later I tried to get some idea of my fate. "How long do you think I should be staying with you?" I asked Rubén.

"I don't know. I couldn't say for sure right now. Perhaps a week or two." Then, looking at me, he added, "But don't worry, it won't be for very long. For the moment we want to be sure that your life wouldn't be in danger off the base. Agents from the Cuban secret service might very well be looking for you to settle accounts. We wouldn't want them to succeed."

They also needed time to check whether I really was who I said I was, I thought—to see if my story was real and to protect their country's security.

I spent another two weeks with those officials, until they concluded their investigation and my MiG was returned to Cuba. They'd allowed me to talk by phone with my relatives in Miami, New Jersey, and Texas. Then they were saying good-bye to me, telling me I was free to go wherever I wished. Before me opened up a world of relatives and friends who were ready to help me with what had been an obsession even before I'd left Cuba: to be reunited with Vicky and my sons.

IN THE house of each relative I visited, I was received by welcoming relations, including cousins who I didn't even know existed but who treated me as if I'd grown up with them. Such was the Cuban family tradition. Every one of them had something to give me, including money, which they assured me I needed to make a start. Each time, I felt myself reddening with embarrassment at their generosity.

For several days I tried in vain to call Vicky at the home of some neighbors. I spent anxious hours next to the telephone, but the lines were all busy. Then one early morning—one month since I'd left Cuba—the operator managed to put the call through. "Oré?" Vicky spoke breathlessly from the distance she'd run to get to the phone.

I wanted to speak, but the words stammered out in an unintelligible groan: "My love . . ."

Vicky could barely speak either. "Oré?"

"How are you all?" I finally managed to say in a trembling voice.

"We're okay, but very sad."

"My love, forgive me for never having told you anything." It was the first thing I had to say in order to protect her.

"But what happened? Why did you go away?"

"I can't explain it to you now, but I want you to know that I still love you. . . . Forgive me. I just want to know if you still love me too."

"My life!" Vicky broke into sobs. "Of course I love you. I don't know what you've done, but I'll go on loving you forever!"

"Are you willing to come with the children to join me?"

"It doesn't matter where you are. There or in the middle of a desert or in the Antarctic—we want to be with you."

They were her final words. Our conversation had been cut off, but we both knew that we would fight to be reunited.

VICKY and the boys were now part of that family of eleven who lived huddled together in her parents' small three-room dwelling. Her sister and her brother, though married now, had continued living there with their spouses and children for lack of a place to go. Those crowded quarters didn't go unnoticed by the special group investigating our case.

After our phone conversation Vicky had told the boys the truth about where I was, and to her surprise, Reyniel had taken the news very well, saying, "At least he's not in the Soviet Union."

The month spent in Havana had been enough for him to gather why the kids of his own age, silent witnesses to the humiliating inequality between Cuban and tourist, when asked what they wanted to be when they grew up, would reply, "Foreigners."

Vicky had been trying unsuccessfully to reach the U.S. Interests Office by phone to initiate the steps necessary to obtain visas for her and the boys, following our plans to do so once I'd called her. At last she managed to talk to someone who gave her an appointment.

"You should wait until your visas are approved before undertaking the necessary steps with the Cuban authorities for your departure. We'll contact you as soon as we have a reply."

IN THE United States, meanwhile, I was discovering through my relatives and their friends the history of horrendous crimes committed by the Cuban leaders in the name of the Revolution. Only then did I pick up Valladares' book once again, realizing that the magnitude of the crimes was even greater than what was narrated by him.

I also learned of men and women who had escaped the island but whose families had been kept hostage in Cuba, prohibited from leaving despite their having visas from other countries. I realized then how naïve Vicky and I had been to think that they would let her and the children go under the weight of international public opinion. The danger hanging over their heads filled me with terror, and only the swift granting of visas would give them some protection.

In June the long-awaited news came: "We've got the visas now," she told me on the phone. "Tomorrow I'll begin the necessary steps for emigration."

We both cried for joy, still nourishing the hope that things would go more smoothly from then on. All that was left to do was to await the reaction of the Cuban authorities.

## Chapter Twelve

THE day after receiving the visas, Vicky went to the immigration office of the municipality to request permission to leave the country. The offices were located in an old colonial house. A dozen or so people sat waiting on benches, and on one wall was a gigantic color poster of the island of Cuba, across it the phrase I'M HAPPY IN THIS LAND.

"Next!" came the call from the young woman behind the counter.

"Fill out these forms and bring them back with birth certificates and four passport-size photos of each person, plus one hundred fifty pesos in postage stamps," said the woman, holding out three packets of forms after listening to Vicky without looking at her.

Vicky ran to get the children to have their pictures taken. I can't believe it, she told herself. It's all turning out to be so easy.

It took her two days to obtain the photos, birth certificates, and stamps. And two nights to fill out those forms, which reconstructed their lives. With nervous haste she returned to the immigration office.

The woman behind the counter reviewed the documents. "And your job release?" she asked without looking up.

"What release are you referring to?" Vicky inquired.

"Don't tell me you don't know. You're a dentist, and as a professional, you have to bring a document from the Ministry of Public

Health authorizing you to leave the country. Go to the office in the province where you worked to ask for your release."

Vicky felt her hopes being dashed. She would have to go to Santa Clara for the document. "Is that the only thing I'm missing?" she asked.

"No. You must also bring a clearance from the Technical Investigations Department regarding your husband."

Vicky noted the address and hurried off to obtain the clearance.

"When did you say your husband left Cuba?" the Technical Investigations woman asked from behind the information desk.

"In March."

"I'm sorry, but the data we have on emigrants only goes up to 1989. How did your husband leave?"

"In a MiG-23."

"Oh! My goodness. . . . In that case his file is never going to arrive here. They know that very well."

Vicky returned home then, wondering whether that wouldn't be an insurmountable obstacle. In any case she asked her father to accompany her on the trip to Santa Clara for the job release.

"Let's hope your job release arrives shortly," remarked the woman who typed out the request forms at the Public Health office.

"Excuse me. You mean I can't take it with me right now?"

"I'm sorry, but the forms have to be approved at the national level. Once they do that, they send it directly to immigration."

Vicky and her father returned to Havana without saying a word the whole way. It was midnight when they arrived, and they discovered Reyniel and Alejandro asleep in the living room. Vicky kissed them both on the cheek, and they woke up, asking together, "Did you do it, Mommy? When do we go to Daddy's?"

"There's still a bit more," she answered, leading them to the mattress she shared with them, suspecting bitterly that still more difficulties would arise on the path to our reunion.

The following morning she returned to immigration. "The Technical Investigations Department says that they only have files going up to 1989," she explained to the woman at the counter.

"How did your husband leave the country?" the woman asked then, for the first time looking Vicky in the face.

"He left on March twentieth, in a MiG-23."

"But . . . you realize . . . it's a very special case. Wait a moment."

And she disappeared through a door. Minutes later she returned, accompanied by a major from the Ministry of the Interior, who addressed Vicky with a penetrating stare.

"You should know that it's not up to us to decide in such a case. Only high command can make the decision."

"How will I know the decision?"

"We should receive an answer in a few weeks."

"I understand." And thanking them, Vicky walked away slowly.

Magalis, a female armed forces psychologist, had been coming to the house almost daily to talk to Vicky, always insisting that I'd betrayed my wife, that she start a new life, that she accept an offer of a comfortable house in the Vedado district and a job at the nearby dental polyclinic. Vicky would listen and then recount with some enjoyment how deeply we loved each other. But Magalis kept insisting, even though she knew Vicky wasn't about to change her mind.

The neighbors now let Vicky know that they'd noticed strange guests sitting on the steps of the house across the street, watching and taking notes on whatever people were coming and going. And Vicky would smile each morning when she took the children off to school and she saw one of these strangers get up from his seat to follow her surreptitiously, as if she didn't see what he was doing.

After two weeks Vicky returned to see the disagreeable woman at the immigration counter. "We still have no reply. Wait at home until we send you a telegram," she told Vicky without looking up.

Ignoring the request, Vicky kept visiting the office, and at last the woman told her, "Your request to emigrate has been denied."

"But why?"

"Don't you know? Because your husband is a traitor, girl!"

Vicky felt her anger clawing at her heart. "But that's him," Vicky insisted. "What can you be accusing *us* of? The commander in chief and the second secretary of the party have said repeatedly that anybody who wants to leave the country can leave."

"That's generally speaking, but don't you realize that the Ministry of the Interior has a directive prohibiting the emigration of any relatives of traitors?"

"I don't believe in such a directive. Can I see this directive?"

"No. It's verbal." And looking over Vicky's shoulder, she nearly screamed, *"Next!"*

Vicky now felt all the weight of a system that not only prevented her from exercising her rights but forced her to deal with bureaucrats who had no authority to make decisions.

No, I won't sit still for it, she told herself over and over.

Luckily, we'd been able to talk by phone two more times, and I was kept abreast of the details of her efforts.

With each passing day the boys became more aware of the reality of their situation, and they silently despaired that we would ever be reunited again. One night Vicky heard some faint sobbing through the door to the bedroom, and opening it, she found Alejandro holding a photo of me, while the tears rolled down his cheeks. He confessed to Vicky, "Mommy, my heart can't stand it anymore."

Reyniel no longer liked to play as before, and his always smiling face had now become serious. Watching his mother and seeing her pain, he would tell her, "Mommy, please, don't be sad." Then he would go to bed, suffering his first bouts of insomnia at age ten.

I wanted to bring the matter into the open now, but friends, relatives, and even Vicky asked me to wait until all possible avenues had been exhausted. Vicky wrote to the commander in chief, the minister of the armed forces, the commanders of the Revolution, and others, and she delivered the letters to the respective offices herself.

It had been a while since she'd seen my parents, so she decided to go to Matanzas with the boys, who were now on vacation, to provide them with some distraction from the anxieties assailing them.

Arriving in Matanzas, Vicky was shocked to discover how thin my parents had grown. Suffering the painful loss of their eldest son, they still nurtured the hope that he would resurface, imagining him as a probable agent from Cuban intelligence who was infiltrated into the heart of enemy territory on a confidential mission.

I'd thought a great deal about my father. To dream up stories like a child protected him from the crushing reality that would signify the negation of his entire life.

Upon their return to Havana a surprise awaited Vicky: two similar telegrams from the offices of the second and third heads of state: RECEIVED YOUR LETTER. YOUR CASE BEING ANALYZED. AWAIT REPLY.

Vicky spent another anxious month before being told to report to the offices of Raúl Castro for an interview in which she'd be given the final decision on her case. By now it was the end of September, 1991.

She spent that night without sleep. She felt weak, and she asked her mother to accompany her to the government buildings located behind the celebrated Revolution Square. Her heart was palpitating.

A sentry armed with a rifle opened the glass door, and a gigantic vestibule with shining marble floors opened before them, lit by ostentatious lamps that heightened the beauty of the plants and furnishings. Vicky and her mother felt silenced by such opulence as they proceeded to the information counter.

A woman came over to them. "Good morning. I'm Magalis Chacón, assistant to the minister of the armed forces. Will you follow me, please? You'll have to wait here," she added to Vicky's mother, and led Vicky to a tiny office.

Another woman was waiting there. "I'm Melba Chávez, assistant to the ideological chief of the party."

"Well, let's sit down," Magalis ordered, adding, "Victoria, Comrade Raúl Castro was unable to welcome you personally, occupied as he is at the moment with other tasks, and he's asked us to attend to you on his behalf."

Vicky leaned forward in her chair, focusing all her attention on what Magalis was about to tell her.

"We want you to know that your case has been examined by the directorate of the party. And the decision they've asked me to transmit is"—Magalis paused, and Vicky felt her pulse pounding—"well . . . that your husband can come back."

"What are you saying?"

"That's right. We want you to inform him that the party and the government are giving him a chance to come back."

"But what do you expect? That he'll come back to be put on trial?"

"Well . . . it will be taken into consideration that he hasn't made any declarations against the Revolution."

Vicky comprehended now that she and the boys had been taken as hostages. If the anguish caused by our indefinite separation made me come back, then they'd be able to put on a show trial for treason before the rest of the armed forces and to give an exemplary warning by executing me immediately. The precedent set by General Ochoa could hardly make her think otherwise.

"But don't you understand that we don't want him to come back? The purpose of my letters was to find out when we can join him."

"Never!"

Vicky felt terribly fragile, insignificant, impotent. "This is unjust. The boys are suffering; they need their father."

"The one guilty for their suffering is the one who didn't hesitate to betray them. What you need to do is take the house and the job we're offering you and start a new life."

A man with colonel's stripes on his shoulder had entered the office and was listening to the exchange.

"I'll never do that," Vicky began. "I'll wait whatever time is necessary, even if it's the rest of my life, but we'll be reunited."

"In that case," interrupted the colonel, who had been silent until then, "you should know that the comrade minister of the armed forces said that if your husband had the guts to leave with one of my MiGs, maybe he has the guts to come back and get his family."

Vicky turned to face his arrogant stare, thinking what she dare not say: It's your minister who should have the guts to face up to his own crimes instead of sending you people to do it.

She stood up then, satisfied for the first time at not giving in to tears. No, they'd never again see her tears! And telling them goodbye, she left in search of her mother.

Now she felt herself toughening, ready to face with dignity the powerful system that threatened to crush her. Enough of waiting in the dishonorable silence they impose upon us! she told herself. From now on, we'll go to church, even if they interpret it as an act of rebellion. And I won't hesitate to speak to diplomats and foreign journalists to ask for help.

The children, who'd been waiting at home, received the news in silence, without shedding any tears. They had also gotten tougher. "I don't know when," she promised them, "but don't you ever doubt that we'll be reunited with your father."

IN OCTOBER I talked to Vicky again by phone and learned the story. Now I received the green light from her to start the public campaign for our right to live as a family.

"It'll be hard," I'd warned her. "From now on, all the coercive machinery of the system will be turned upon you. Until now they wanted to convince you; from now on, they'll want to destroy you. Don't trust anyone who offers you the chance to participate in internal dissidence. Even less should you think about trying to leave the country illegally; don't trust anybody who offers to help you that way."

They realized that the example of Vicky fighting for her family would weaken the authority of the government by winning the sympathy of more and more people, so they had to destroy her example. They wouldn't hesitate about setting the most devious traps in her path to send her to prison, forcing her through terror to acquiesce in silence to the permanent division of her family. I knew that only the attention of the world focused upon them could protect them. For that I had to denounce their situation as loudly as possible.

When I'd finished talking with Vicky, it was one in the morning. Aunt Miladis will understand why I'm calling at this hour, I told myself, and dialed her number. "Aunt Miladis, I'm coming to live with you. I'm going to start the public battle for Vicky and the children, and Miami's the best place to do it."

Afterward I called my always helpful cousin Paul. "Paul, I want you to help me find a good journalist interested in talking with me."

"When?"

"First thing tomorrow."

"Count on it."

Dawn was breaking when I saw the sign on the highway indicating the turnoff for Hialeah. My aunt hadn't slept either, since the moment I'd called.

Paul arrived just as Aunt Miladis was chiding me for not wanting breakfast, and he took a piece of paper out of his pocket: "Tomás Regalado," it said, and below that the telephone number of one of the most well-known Cuban journalists around. We called him, and an hour later Regalado himself came to pick me up in his car and take me to a local radio station that was heard in Cuba.

That was my first interview, the first denunciation of the outrage they'd committed against my family in Cuba. Later Paul would accompany me on a whole round of interviews with reporters from the Miami *Herald,* the *Diario de las Américas,* and the principal Cuban exile leaders in Miami. The latter, dedicated for years to the struggle for human rights in Cuba, did not hesitate to offer me the support of their organizations and radio stations, which transmitted shortwave broadcasts to Cuba.

Particularly moving was my meeting with Jorge Mas Canosa, head of the National Cuban-American Foundation, an energetic, intelligent man who spoke to me of his vision of a future Cuba—democratic and open to free-market principles. I listened, delighted to discover that his views were close to my own. "Our radio station is at your disposal," he told me, and the following day we met before the microphones of the radio station, which was heard all over Cuba. Ninoska Pérez, a journalist who'd left Cuba as a child and who remained an impassioned defender of the rights of her people, would ask us questions.

We also managed to establish telephone communication with my family, and Vicky and the boys were able to denounce publicly for the first time the abuse they were suffering. They demanded their right to leave the country, Reyniel abandoning his customary silence to say that he felt like a slave, and Alejandro repeating again and again, "Some bad men won't let me go with my daddy."

Then I spoke to the Cuban people, letting them know where Vicky and my sons lived. "You're their only help or protection," I told the tens of thousands of Cubans I knew were listening. "The only thing I ask you is that you offer them spiritual solidarity in these difficult moments. No one has the right to arbitrarily divide a family."

We hoped that if the people drew close to Vicky and the children, it would be more difficult for the Cuban government to commit any treachery against them.

We were about to conclude the broadcast when I repeated to Vicky the words I had uttered to her months ago: "This is a struggle of truth against lies, of love against hate . . . and love will triumph!"

The night the program was broadcast in Cuba, Vicky's parents' house was inundated with visitors, some arriving discreetly and others openly to offer their help. They brought prayers, food, money, and, above all, their concern. A woman sent the children some toys; a group of ten mothers from Havana wrote a letter to the highest leader, which they made public through the foreign press, asking for the immediate release of Vicky and the boys. Not a day went by without some voice raised in protest somewhere in the country.

Vicky became a popular figure, constantly being stopped on the street by people who greeted her affectionately. At the same time, she had to contend with undercover agents sent to induce her to participate in activities that would serve as a pretext to arrest her. There were those who offered to arrange for her escape, to which she would answer that she would leave the country only when the authorities permitted—knowing that instead of putting her aboard some boat, they would be handing her over to state security.

One day Paul brought me the phone number of Armando Valladares, the author of *Against All Hope*, who, after having served on the United Nations Commission on Human Rights, was continuing to work for the defense of human dignity through the foundation that he'd created in his name.

"I think he might be able to help you," Paul remarked.

Armando did offer to help, agreeing that continual public denunciation was the only way to protect Vicky and the boys. "We have to take the campaign everywhere, and the place to start should be Washington," he said. He offered me his house in Virginia to stay in while we did it, and Kristina Arriaga, executive director of the Valladares Foundation, immediately went into action using their network of contacts with human rights organizations around the world.

As the year drew to a close, the first Christmas arrived that I was to experience in freedom. Christmas trees, traditional carols, and Santa Claus made appearances everywhere. In my dismay at the absence of my own children, I felt an emptiness in my soul that nothing could fill. And when twelve chimes announced the arrival of the new year at the house of a friend, and parents and children embraced one another, I went out on the balcony to talk to my own, looking up at the stars. I swore these would be my last Christmas holidays without them.

Two or three times a week I participated in the programs of the Voice of the Foundation, inspired by the support of the men and women who worked for the Valladares Foundation. Through the radio programs, we'd obtained the support of the Cuban people in Miami and on the island, but it wasn't sufficient to generate the pressure that would force the government to allow Vicky and the boys to leave. We needed the support of everyone—men, women, and children—who would be disposed to write a letter to the Cuban authorities on our behalf. I felt convinced that if we succeeded in flooding the government offices with hundreds of thousands of such letters, my family would be granted permission to leave, for fear of the publicity. But how to reach so many people? I didn't have the money for such a campaign.

Soon, from Miami's Cuban community, hundreds of hands were

extended to help us. Not a few friends made me blush with shame when they put money in my pocket to help me with my campaign.

A friend of many years, who habitually traveled abroad because of his job, called me from Mexico. "I wanted you to know about the terrible situation Vicky and your sons are in, without the slightest chance of being allowed to leave the country," he said, then added, "I know that sooner or later you'll regret what you did, and I wanted you to know that should you decide to return, I can serve as intermediary between you and the authorities in order to have you pardoned."

I knew then that this was the first direct message I'd received from the Cuban government. "Thanks," I replied, "but I prefer to die rather than betray my children." I never got another call from him.

Paul and I had finally gotten enough money together to rent a car and drive to New Jersey to coordinate the efforts of the Valladares Foundation and a group of enthusiasts from my family, together with various relatives of Vicky's, with whom I'd also made contact. We spent two days at the home of my aunt and uncle in New Jersey, sufficient time to meet dozens of people eager to shake our hands and make a contribution to help carry our effort forward.

My aunt Fela was a wonder of kindness. And how I suffered under her delicious culinary tutelage: "Eat, my boy, eat. Look how skinny you are!" she'd tell me after I gorged myself.

They had organized a group of volunteers to initiate the campaign in the Northeast, and each day Fela's husband, Uncle Raúl, would visit dozens of commercial establishments and leave pamphlets that he and my aunt had had printed up. Meanwhile, in Washington, Armando Valladares and Kristina were waiting with a tight schedule for us to complete.

Armando and his wife, Martha, invited us to their home, which was blessed by the shouts and laughter of their three precious children. And it wasn't long before I was on the floor playing with those happy little characters, who called me uncle and stole my heart.

We saw Kristina the following morning. She had a childlike face and lively brown eyes, and she talked a mile a minute, like someone forever in a hurry. She had set up various appointments with members of Congress, and we went over the schedule she'd prepared, then followed her from office to office, astonished at her mastery at dealing with people there.

Armando and Kristina had managed to get various members of Congress to agree to sign a letter directed to the Cuban government soliciting the release of Vicky and the children. And if it didn't obtain their release, at least it offered them protection against possible reprisals, because of the reaction they might produce on Capitol Hill.

At the end of the month the U.N. Commission on Human Rights was scheduled to meet in Geneva, and I was accorded the chance to speak—through the Association for Continental Peace—to plead for international help in convincing the Cuban government to release my family. If we manage to present the case before the United Nations, they'll have to let them go, I told myself.

I was met in Geneva by Mari Paz and Valle—of the National Cuban-American Foundation—whom I didn't know, but who, through the efforts of Armando and Mas Canosa, had put their organization at my disposal, arranging for my speech before the Human Rights Commission and covering all my expenses during my stay. Mari Paz was a petite Spaniard, with jet-black hair and eyes, who overflowed with energy in the struggle she waged for respect for human dignity. Valle, a seventeen-year-old from Argentina, was filled with dreams for a more just world and devoted his energy to defending the rights of others.

They, along with Luis Zúñiga, an explicitly political Cuban, were my collaborators. Together we prepared the speech I was to deliver.

The first day I attended the meeting of the commission, I was surprised and outraged by the intervention of Vilma Espín, wife of one of the Castro brothers, who talked about the rights of the child. She condemned "Yankee imperialism for the hunger and wretchedness of millions of children on the planet." She said she preferred to see such children killed by the effects of a nuclear war rather than to see them victimized by the hunger that now plagued them. I never imagined I would hear such an atrocity at the United Nations.

I began reading in a nervous voice. "I address this assembly and the international community to demand help to put an end to the plight my wife and children are now suffering, taken as hostages by the authorities in my country." In a few words I recounted the way in which they were forced to live—mine and other families like them—separated arbitrarily, under constant fear and uncertainty, their lives depending not on laws but on the will of men who despised them.

I concluded by calling out the names of other victims, but I was interrupted by the insistent banging of a fist on a table. It was the infuriated leader of the Cuban delegation. Not even in the United Nations did they manage to behave with decency!

The sessions ended, and a majority approved the naming of a special U.N. representative to investigate the situation of human rights in Cuba. But the head of the Cuban delegation declared that they would never permit a representative of that organization to set foot in the country.

I returned to Miami disappointed with the results of my trip.

SEVERAL months later a group of wealthy businessmen offered me a Bell helicopter to rescue my family, which of course thrilled me, since I trusted these men. But my dream soon went up in smoke when they asked me to pay for it by assassinating Fidel Castro during one of his public speeches in the open air—using the same helicopter.

"Thanks, but I'm not the man you're looking for," I replied.

Each passing day made me more convinced that the Cuban government would never release my family and that I would have to go get them myself. But how? Whatever I decide to do, I'll have to prepare the thing far away from here, I reflected, realizing it would be impossible to plan a rescue in Miami without raising the suspicions of the Cuban agents blighting that city. At that time, Armando and Kristina were insisting that I come live near them in order to organize a more effective campaign, so I said good-bye to my relatives and friends in Miami and moved into a tiny apartment in Alexandria, Virginia.

Both things can progress at the same time, I told myself. The public campaign and my plans to rescue them.

I SETTLED in Alexandria, and through the efforts of the Valladares Foundation my life became one of constant activity, running from Congress to the Organization of American States to religious organizations devoted to human rights. But I was also quietly searching for a way to rescue my family on my own. I was a pilot, so a plane or a helicopter would be the ideal means to do it. Yet first I'd have to obtain my American pilot's license, and to that end I was studying English, preparing myself to enroll in a course for private pilots.

One day Armando asked me to accompany him to Columbus, Georgia, to the home of Elena Díaz-Versón Amos, director of the

Valladares Foundation and also founder with her late husband of the American Family Life Insurance Company. "She can help you a great deal," Kristina informed me, observing that I wasn't very enthusiastic.

Actually I found it extremely unpleasant to think that anybody should see me as someone looking for a handout, I told Kristina with the frankness that characterized our relationship.

"Don't talk that way; you don't know Elena."

They finally overcame my obstinacy, and soon I was flying in a private plane Elena had sent for us. In Columbus we were met at the foot of the boarding ladder by an energetic woman dressed with taste and simplicity. We got into a waiting limousine with her and set off with a police motorcycle escort. Then, looking at us with the playfulness of a child caught in the act, she confessed, "This isn't my car. It's the only limousine in town. And I borrowed it from the funeral parlor!" And she broke into delightful laughter.

Elena lived in the penthouse of a seven-story building next to the offices of her company. It took only a few hours to get to know her, and already her candor had captivated me. She wept at the details of the plight in which Vicky and my sons found themselves, and from then on, she never ceased striving to obtain the intervention of people who could help us.

Among these was Brandon Scheid, a student at George Washington University and volunteer at the foundation. He wrote to the press, to politicians, to religious leaders, to artists. He seemed possessed by an obsession to attain justice in the case. Jokingly I called him the most powerful weapon the United States had against its detractors.

On my return to Virginia I was invited to lunch by a Cuban who wished to help us. Frank Calzón was the representative of Freedom House in Washington and had been one of the organizers of the campaign to free Armando. Frank had at his disposal a wide network of relationships with Congress and the American press that would permit us to give new energy to our campaign.

As in Miami, a group of Cuban families from Virginia now spontaneously adopted me, extending invitations to dine and spend time with them so I wouldn't feel alone. Armando's home by then had turned into my second home, and I used to visit often to partake of that delightful mayhem with the children, getting down on the floor with them, playing with the dog. And when sometimes Armando or

Martha noticed that I wasn't playing as usual, they'd ask me worriedly what was wrong.

"I love the horseplay with the children," I'd say, "but sometimes the silence of my own kids is louder than the noise yours are making."

It was already June 1992, fifteen months since I'd flown out of Cuba, and thousands of postcards with the photo of Vicky and the boys had been printed by the Valladares Foundation and Freedom House, to be given to people interested in sending them to the Cuban authorities. Frank Calzón had even managed to publish an article on the case, and now, with a group of volunteers, he was managing a campaign of letters and postcards to Queen Sofía of Spain, asking her to intercede with Castro during his upcoming visit for the Summit of Heads of Ibero-American States, in Madrid.

The Madrid summit was to begin at the end of July, and I decided to go there, with the intention of carrying out a hunger strike to draw the attention of the heads of state and the press gathered there. Perhaps the public embarrassment might force Castro to let them go, I thought.

Preparations for the hunger strike turned into a sort of collective suffering, as those who loved me offered myriad suggestions to avoid anything going wrong during my fast. "You have to take vitamins"; "You have to stop smoking"; "You have to eat well to build up your reserves of energy" were some of the instructions I received.

Elena was now deeply involved, together with the churches, in organizing a chain of prayers around the world for Vicky and the children. And as the day approached for my departure to Spain, Armando, Kristina, and I were invited to join Elena for dinner. They were busy watching me eat—with the kind of hearty appetite they had lost just worrying about me—when Elena exclaimed, pointing to me, "If this hunger strike business isn't over with soon, we're all going to die of hunger except him!" And we all broke into laughter.

Armando was the only one who understood, and he gave his full support. With his own experience of eleven hunger strikes while in Cuban prisons, he knew nothing untoward would happen. "The most important thing is that you be in good health when you begin the strike," he would tell me. "The hunger is the only thing that's terrible, but it lasts only two days. After that you lose interest in food, and you even feel a certain sense of well-being."

Reassured, I felt that I could hold out for the week intended.

I set off for Spain, concentrating all my hopes on this attempt. In Madrid, Mari Paz and Valle were waiting for me, more alarmed about the hunger strike than my friends in Virginia. Nevertheless, they organized meetings with the press, and I appeared on the popular radio program hosted by Encarna Sánchez—who made telephone contact with a neighbor of Vicky's and had the conversation broadcast live. Vicky appealed to all Spanish families to write letters to the Cuban government during Castro's visit, to be sent to the office of Mari Paz. But still convinced that only the hunger strike could break the wall of silence imposed on the case by the Cuban government, I showed up on the morning of Monday, July 20, 1992, with chains and padlocks to chain me to the fence around the famous Retiro Park, barely a few meters from the hotel where the visiting presidents were staying. I knew that to attain credibility for the strike, I had to carry it out in the public's eye so there'd be no room for doubt as to whether I might be eating on the sly.

"You're out of your mind," Mari Paz told me, but she went off with Valle and her sister Alicia to break the story to the media.

Around noon, as the first photographers and reporters began to arrive, Mari Paz closed the locks on the chains wrapped around my wrists and attached to the wrought-iron fence. The only things with me were an enlarged photo of Vicky and our sons, which I'd hung on the fence with a sign that said CASTRO, STOP HOLDING MY FAMILY HOSTAGE! and a copy of Armando's *Against All Hope*. Volunteers were mobilized, and soon I found my little corner surrounded by chairs, a cooler for cold water, blankets, a radio for listening to the news, and the first letters sent by Encarna's radio listeners to the offices of Mari Paz.

In a matter of hours the place was crowded with people who'd come to offer their sympathy and their help, and that first day of the hunger strike was to be the first of my battles with dozens of elderly well-meaning Madrileña women who came with tears in their eyes and food in hand to beg me to eat a bit on the sly.

I had told Valle to take the keys to the padlocks with him, and as evening approached, I drifted off to sleep. Then toward morning two policemen came up to me, demanding that I remove the chains. Thinking to put an end to the matter easily, I told them that I'd tossed the keys down the sewer. Still polite, they nevertheless were firm,

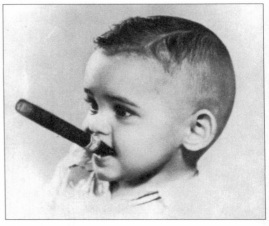

*Above: Orestes Lorenzo at fourteen months, posed by his father, a tobacco factory worker, with a Cuban cigar.*
*Left: Orestes with his younger brother, Faure, shortly after the arrival of the family in Matanzas.*

*Vicky and Orestes stroll along the Havana Malecón in 1976.*

*Orestes' (third from left) unsuccessful meeting with Mikhail Gorbachev (right) in Mexico in December 1992*

*Orestes holds up a poster of his "hostage" family before speaking to thousands of Cuban protesters in New York City, January 25, 1992.*

*Above: Marathon, Florida, December 19, 1992. Kristina Arriaga and Orestes a few minutes before the rescue flight. Right: The highway in front of El Mamey Beach, Cuba, where the rescue took place.*

*Photo taken by the author of Vicky, Alejandro, and Reyniel, minutes after the rescue, during the flight to freedom*

*Above: Vicky is the first one to land in Marathon; here, she embraces Kristina. Left: On the first day of freedom, together with Elena Díaz-Versón Amos (center) and Kristina (right) at a hotel in Miami.*

*The Lorenzos with President Bush and the First Lady a few days after the rescue. The President had called for Castro to release Orestes' wife and children.*

To Victoria and Orestes Lorenzo
with best wishes, *G. Bush*                Dec. 21, 1992
and great pride in you                     The White House
                                           and Barbara Bush

warning me that if I didn't remove the chains, they would call in a crew to cut them, and then expel me from the area.

Mari Paz and Valle arrived, and the police explained. "The use of chains is something we cannot accept. But if he removes the chains, we'll let him carry on his hunger strike as long as he wishes."

Valle was jubilant at the policemen's offer, and taking the keys out of his pocket, he began unlocking the chains.

Fidel was scheduled to arrive the next day. His photo had already appeared in the daily paper *ABC*, opposite one of me chained to the fence, and the press would be pursuing him. Perhaps now, I thought, he'd give some sort of reply about the case.

Mari Paz informed me that there was a popular demonstration in the Plaza de Colón, condemning the dictator, and that the demonstrators were planning to march, with candles lit, to where I was. As dusk was falling, I heard the police sirens and saw the crowd approaching with placards and Cuban flags. They gathered around me, and hundreds of candles glowed as we all prayed for Vicky and our sons, the smell of wax permeating all the cards and notes people were leaving as tokens of their feelings.

On my third day of the strike I still felt voraciously hungry. Just a few yards off was a kiosk selling all kinds of snacks, and how I suffered from the presence of people who innocently stopped to chat with me while they savored an ice cream or some other morsel.

The Cuban chief of state had arrived in Madrid, but he was surrounded by a cordon of security that was impossible to penetrate. He obviously feared the media, and I had a horrible premonition he might succeed in avoiding any confrontation with a reporter about Vicky and the children.

Thursday—the fourth day of the hunger strike—came, and I felt I could eat a live elephant. In the afternoon I was surprised to see Valle running toward me with a cassette recording of a press conference given by the president of Spain. Asked if he would be willing to intercede with the Cuban government on behalf of my family, he'd replied, "We are, of course, ready to intercede in the case, but we think that these matters are best resolved out of the public eye."

I listened, pained that President Felipe González was not disposed to intercede for me, but simply didn't have the courage to say so.

Early on Friday the heads of state were already leaving Madrid, and we were dismantling the material we'd put up for the hunger strike, including the more than eight thousand letters we'd received from all over Spain. The week of battle was over. I'd lost twenty-five pounds, and I wanted nothing so much as to eat, eat, eat.

As I bid good-bye to Mari Paz and Valle, I told them, "I'm fed up with the insensitivity of the powerful. I'm going to get Vicky and the kids out myself."

They stared at me for a few seconds without saying a word. "May God be with you," Mari Paz finally whispered, kissing me farewell.

## Chapter Thirteen

As A pilot, I knew the Cuban Antiair Defense System: its deployment, its radar and land-to-air missile installations, its command structure and response time, and I could put together a plan with a real possibility of success. All I needed was a plane or helicopter and somebody trustworthy who could get details of the plan into Vicky's hands.

In addition, I didn't want to violate the laws of the United States, and I first had to obtain a private pilot's license.

In September 1992 I found an aviation school in Virginia. The director, Dr. Donald O. Robb, was only too happy to help me obtain my license as soon as possible. "I need it to find a job," I'd told him in order to allay any suspicion of what I was really planning.

Then one day I found out that someone I trusted totally was going to Cuba, and I gave her a message for Vicky. "Tell her I'm coming for them myself," I confided. "Before Christmas, God willing."

I bought maps of Cuba with relief details and made the first sketch of my plan, filling in the locations of radar and missile installations and marking off the limits of their potential to locate and destroy targets. This gave me a clear picture of where I'd encounter the greatest concentration of antiair firepower and where I would be out of the reach of radar, artillery, or ground-to-air missiles.

There remained the problem of selecting the most suitable place for a landing, depending upon the terrain and the possibilities for Vicky and the boys getting there without raising suspicions.

Over and over I revised the data, and each time I came up against the same disturbing fact: the safest places for the rescue were too

distant for Vicky and the children to get to without attracting attention. I was going to have to choose a site in Havana, near her parents,
or in Matanzas, near mine, whom they regularly visited. But both
cities were surrounded by radar and antiair missile complexes.

Only one thing might give us an edge, and that was the nearly
inoperable Cuban chain of command. Convinced that the country
would never really be attacked, and fearful that their own men might
conspire to shoot them down when they traveled by air, the Cuban
leaders had concocted a chain of command in which only they themselves could authorize the firing of weapons against airborne targets.
The absence of adequate lines of communication, plus the difficulty
of locating the highest leaders, who always clouded their movements
in secrecy, afforded us precious time in which to act.

So I calculated the time, and assuming that the entire Cuban system managed to perform with precision, they'd need at least fifteen
minutes after sighting me in order to be able to fire.

How much time it would take me—from the moment of being
detected by Cuban radar on my approach, until I flew away with my
precious cargo aboard—I couldn't determine unless I knew the maximum airspeed of the plane I'd use. If this time turned out to be less
than what was needed for a Cuban response, then we could outwit the
country's antiair defenses!

I managed to get through to Vicky on the telephone. She was
terribly upset at the setbacks we'd suffered in the face of all the efforts
we'd made and at the pressure she was under. In a letter she'd managed
to smuggle out of Cuba, she had informed me that a neighborhood
youth had scribbled some graffiti on the wall of a nearby building,
demanding an end to tyranny. Somebody had reported it, and the
boy was arrested. From jail he sent Vicky a message through some
relatives: "Be careful. They're putting a lot of pressure on me to
implicate you in the graffiti incident."

Vicky then understood they'd use any pretext, even a false accusation, to put her in jail. Then they could take our sons away to be cared
for by the state. That would spell the end of our family, and I didn't
have much confidence in the reactions of a world that seemed preoccupied with too many other things to be bothered stopping the Cuban authorities from committing such a crime. I had to act swiftly.

"I'll never give you up, never. . . . Whatever it takes . . ." I repeated over and over to her on the telephone to make her realize that I'd begun preparations for their rescue.

"Don't worry, Oré. Even if they burn me alive, they'll never make me renounce you," she told me in tears.

After that, I thought I'd go mad. I was consumed by sleeplessness, desperate to finish the course for a pilot's license, to find an airplane and somebody I could trust to deliver the rescue plan to Vicky.

ONE afternoon toward the end of September, Armando called me. "Come to the office. I'm here with some Mexican women who are going to Cuba soon."

They had come to him seeking support in their struggle for the rights of the mentally ill in Mexico—Azul Landeros, with blond hair and lovely features, and la Chaparra, a young woman with lively eyes. Upon learning that they'd be attending a psychiatric conference in Cuba, Armando had explained the plight of Vicky and the children, and the two women had immediately offered their help.

"Tell me what you want us to tell them or to give them. Whatever you want, we'll do it," Azul told me, and I asked her to take Vicky and the boys some letters, photos, and tapes.

The next morning I went to the hotel where they were staying. I carried a cardboard box that Kristina had prepared, with medicines, vitamins, a little truck for the boys, and whatever else she imagined they might need, along with videos of newscasts and photos.

At the hotel I met another member of their team, who greeted me with a smile. "I'm Virginia, and I'm very moved by your family's beautiful love story." Her face seemed especially lovely beneath the thick black hair that fell softly upon her shoulders. Her eyes too were black, and shone with a kindness that completely captivated me.

I answered their questions over a cup of coffee. They wanted to know all about our lives, about our fight and our suffering, about how much I loved Vicky and my sons. When we finally said good-bye, I felt that I could trust them with our lives.

SOON thereafter the Mexican women arrived in Cuba and awaited an opportunity to visit Vicky. Several times they passed by Vicky's street in their rental car, but the constant presence of a policeman on the corner made them nervous. Virginia decided to get out of the car unobtrusively, leaving Azul to ride around the block. At the police-man's first distraction, Virginia slipped into the tenement.

Vicky was seated in front of the television, Alejandro on her knees, when that woman with black hair appeared in the doorway.

"Vicky?"

Vicky understood by the woman's intonation and dress that she wasn't Cuban, and she jumped up in anticipation. "He sent you?"

"Yes."

Virginia set down the carton and took from her bag a still camera as well as a video camera. "He sent you this, but first some photos and a video. I want to bring him back some pictures of all of you."

Reyniel had come out of the bedroom, and after greeting Virginia, he began to rummage through the carton. "Mom, photos! Dad sent lots of photos!" he said over and over.

"He loves you very much. . . . You're an amazing family," Virginia continued, taking more photos. "I've friends here with me, and we're going to help you to be reunited, to escape from here."

Azul appeared in the doorway, and they all sat down. Azul took Vicky's hands in hers: "I saw him, and he asked me to tell you that he loves you, that he's going to get you out of here somehow."

After a few minutes the house was permeated with the enchant-ment of those strange women, whom my sons were now kissing.

The next day they came back to see Vicky. "We want to buy some little things for the boys," they explained, and went off to one of those shops that sell only to foreign tourists for dollars. They filled their car with clothes, shoes, food—Vicky had never seen so much food at once or so much spontaneous generosity.

Then the moment of departure arrived. "I want you to have some-thing very dear to me," Virginia told Vicky, taking a wooden cross from around her neck. Placing it around Vicky's neck, she added, "You'll give it back to me the day you're all reunited."

And with simple tears they made their silent farewell. From then on, not a month went by when someone didn't come in their name with a load of food and a message of endearment for the family.

ONE night in October, Frank Calzón, from Freedom House, called me with some exciting news. President Bush proposed to visit Miami and would direct part of his speech to the Cuban government, asking for the release of Vicky and the children. That message would be very difficult for the Cuban leader to ignore.

I was invited to sit with the President's family during the speech, and I was touched by his clear message, calling Vicky and the boys by name and then saying, "Castro, do what's right, what's decent: Let Lorenzo's family go!"

I thanked President Bush for those words, the first to be spoken by an important world leader on behalf of my family. But days went by without any of the expected reaction in the media, without the Cuban government's responding to the plea. Disgusted by so many failures, I decided to talk to Armando about something I'd only hinted at.

"I'm going to Cuba to get Vicky and the boys," I told him as we took a short stroll in his backyard.

Armando stopped in his tracks. "Are you crazy?"

"I can't take it anymore. I think I'm going to die if I don't try it."

"You have to be strong, to put up a fight." With the example of his own experience, he felt sure that our campaign would work.

But times had changed. Then the Cuban government had felt strong; now it was intimidated by its own crimes as well as by the fall of the Eastern bloc countries. Above all, it feared the youngest officers in the armed forces and did not hesitate to send a clear message of intolerance to them.

No, my family would never be released, and now I tried to explain as much to Armando. "I fear for the safety of Vicky and the boys. Each day the net tightens around them. Imagine if something happens to them tomorrow. I couldn't go on living."

Armando was silent, and I could tell he was seeing himself in my position. Then he said, "Count on me for whatever you need. My experience in communicating by code in prison may be of help."

I hugged him, relieved that he understood. And together we worked out some ordinary phrases to utilize as codes in a phone conversation. That night I went back to my apartment much calmer. I had a friend with whom to share the greatest secret of my life. I wasn't alone anymore.

I'D ALREADY passed the theoretical examinations, and after my first few flights at the Leesburg Aerodrome I felt ready for the flight test. Dr. Robb gave me the phone number of Mr. Pears, the inspector for the Federal Aviation Administration, who would give me the test. Then, shaking my hand tightly, he said, "Good luck, son!"

Inspector Pears attended to me politely, scheduling the exam for the thirteenth of December at ten in the morning. After the thirteenth I'd be able to carry out the operation if I managed to find a plane. If God is with us, the boys will soon have their first Christmas, I told myself over and over, filled with joy.

ARMANDO and I were invited with Kristina to Columbus once more, to initiate at Elena's church the chain of prayers she'd organized around the world for Vicky and our sons, as well as to finalize the details of a meeting that the foundation's Moscow representative had been arranging with Gorbachev, who was to visit Mexico the following week. I was to serve as interpreter at the meeting, to be attended by the four of us, and we would take the opportunity to ask that prestigious statesman if he would intercede with the Cuban leader on behalf of my family. My friends still felt hopeful that a miracle would occur, making unnecessary the risks involved in my rescue plan.

Gigantic billboards reproducing the photo of Vicky and the boys loomed up before us along the highway as we approached the city, and we realized, deeply touched, that Elena was responsible for this. We attended Mass, and as I addressed the parishioners, I couldn't hold back my tears at the sight of so many people crying. Clearly, wherever we found ourselves tomorrow, their prayers and faith would accompany us.

That night the four of us met to work out the details of the trip to Mexico and to talk of my plans for the rescue attempt. I watched Elena grow sad as she listened to me. Then she took my hand and said, "Count on me. How will you find the plane?"

"I don't know. I still have to look for one."

"I have a friend who'd be delighted to help you. Just let me know when you come across that plane."

I knew that Elena was referring to herself. She'd always taken great pains not to wound my pride when she was giving me money.

I took advantage of my visit to Columbus to lunch with the pilots who worked for Elena. "I'm looking for a plane," I told them.

"I have a plane I want to sell," Ron said. "It's a 1961 Cessna 310F."

I couldn't believe what I was hearing. "Where is it? Can we see it?"

Then Gary spoke up, to Ron. "You know what he wants it for? You're going to get yourself in hot water."

I felt the blood rushing to my head. "I only want to buy your friend's plane! We're not talking about using *his* plane, but our plane, once we've bought it."

"But they'll investigate."

I wasn't looking for an accomplice to a crime, but for someone who'd sell me a plane in a completely legal fashion. "Is there any law against selling what's yours to whomever you wish?" I asked, without concealing my irritation at his meddling.

Gary remained pensive.

"I want to sell my plane," Ron repeated then.

"How much?"

"Thirty thousand."

"I don't have the money now, but I'll have it soon. Promise me you won't sell it to anybody else."

"It's a promise."

We returned to Virginia, and I had one more day to finalize my plan before leaving for Mexico. Virginia and Azul were the two people best suited to get a message to Vicky. I scribbled a brief note, which I immediately faxed to Azul: "We'll be in Monterrey. It's important we see each other there."

Azul called me back immediately. "Of course we'll go to Monterrey to meet you."

I unfolded the map on the table and began to calculate, based on the data for a Cessna 310F and the four-lane highway along the coast of Matanzas in front of El Mamey Beach—the place I'd chosen for the rescue. I'd already calculated the time needed for Cuba's antiquated chain-of-command system to launch its missiles. What I needed to ascertain now was whether the time between the moment I was spotted and the instant I was out of missile range would be less than the time they needed to be able to fire upon us.

Flying nearly at sea level, at a maximum airspeed of 212 knots, I wouldn't be spotted until I was thirty nautical miles from my landing spot. If I landed for no longer than one minute, I'd cross the perimeter of the missiles' maximum range fourteen minutes and fifty seconds after being spotted. Ten seconds less than what the chain-of-command system required to launch its missiles.

I'd need a little light to navigate and land on that highway. Dusk was therefore the best moment for the rescue. I sat in front of the computer and wrote a detailed message to Vicky, which I printed out in the smallest type possible:

> On the highway in front of El Mamey beach . . . wait there starting a half hour before sunset. Approach the plane from behind. Watch out for the propellers. Hold the boys by the hand. The codes by telephone: Mine to ask if you approve of the plan is, "How's my father?" Your affirmative reply, "He's thinner, but he's fine." To tell you that I'm coming for you the next day at dusk, "I'm sending you money for you to buy a VCR."

I finished writing at daybreak. In a few hours I had to be at the airport. In Mexico a rather interesting meeting awaited us with Gorbachev and a more important one with Azul and Virginia.

We spent the flight laughing, thanks to Elena's gift for entertaining everyone, and we readied ourselves for the meeting with Gorbachev, to be held at a small office in the convention center.

I attended the meeting with a small tape recorder in hand. I felt great admiration for Gorbachev, believing him responsible for the enormous changes that had occurred in the world, and I was grateful to him. If it hadn't been for perestroika, perhaps I'd still have been submerged in the surrealistic world in which I had grown up.

Now, after a brief exchange between Gorbachev and Armando, I addressed the statesman directly: "Mikhail Sergeyevich, my wife and small children have been held hostage for two years in Cuba—"

Gorbachev ceased smiling at that point, and taking the hand in which I'd been holding the tape recorder, he pushed it to one side, saying, "The solution to isolated family problems ought to be in the context of the solution to the Cuban problem. For that reason—"

I'd already stopped listening. I'd shut off the tape recorder, saying, "Don't trouble yourself; it's not necessary."

I left in frustration. No, a man like that didn't initiate perestroika willingly, I thought. He initiated it in order not to be destroyed!

That afternoon Virginia and Azul arrived, enveloped as always in an enchanted aura of goodwill. We met in the bar of the hotel at around six, and I explained to them all the details of my secret undertaking.

"Tell us what you want us to do to help," Virginia said.

"I need someone to take this message to Vicky," I said, taking the little folded piece of paper out of my wallet.

Virginia took it and put it in her purse, saying, "Don't you worry, Vicky will get this as soon as possible."

God willing, we'll be together for Christmas, I thought excitedly.

I'D PASSED the flight examination without a problem, and with the longed-for license in my pocket I was pacing back and forth in my room. It was Tuesday evening, the fifteenth of December. The telephone rang, and I grabbed it off the hook.

"Orestes? It's Virginia. I'm leaving tomorrow with two friends for Cuba. We'll be back on Friday afternoon."

I was trembling from head to foot. I'd waited so long. Yet what had seemed nearly impossible only months ago was progressing now with extraordinary ease. That the hand of God should have placed in our path such miraculous friends! Armando, Kristina, Elena, Mari Paz, Valle, Azul, and Virginia—I felt certain of our triumph.

I took the map with my calculations, a walkie-talkie, and the check I'd gotten from the Valladares Foundation for thirty thousand dollars, donated by Elena, and prepared to leave for Columbus to buy my plane. Armando had gone to Miami to do some work, and I called Kristina.

Together we waited for my flight in the airport lounge. She kept silent, turning to wipe away the tears she'd held back the last several days. How much I loved her! We'd fought all those long months together, each time with new illusions, then new failures. She was always present in every undertaking, continually striving to touch the sensibilities of whoever might help us.

"You won't come back to Virginia first?" she asked.

"No."

"I want to be there when you go."

It was time to board the plane. I kissed her on the cheek, and without looking back, I ran to catch my flight.

VICKY had received a phone call from Virginia, in Mexico: "I'm going to send you a Christmas present."

Now Vicky was playing with the boys in their room, and she heard her sister call her. Vicky ran into the living room just in time to see that beloved person coming in. "Here I am! I'm the Christmas present!" Virginia exclaimed, running over to Vicky to hug her.

One by one Virginia greeted everybody in the house. Then she signaled that they should go to Vicky's room. They entered quietly, and Vicky turned on the radio to its highest volume. Placing her finger over her lips as a signal for silence, Virginia opened her purse and searched for the tiny, meticulously folded piece of paper.

Silently Vicky read the note. She raised her eyes, which were radiant with happiness, and her gaze met Virginia's inquisitive look. Vicky nodded her head then and saw Virginia's fist punch the air in a gesture of rejoicing.

Vicky burned the message in the bathroom, and then they returned to the living room, where they talked loudly and happily of going the next day to the beach.

Now they were traveling, crowded into the small car, singing together and exchanging looks of complicity that went unnoticed by the children. On the way, they scrutinized the section of the highway where the rescue was to take place. Virginia insisted on stopping at a tourist shop, where she purchased three shirts and three caps of bright orange, which she handed over to Vicky, whispering, "So he can spot you more easily from the air."

On the way back to Havana they watched the sun slip below the horizon. Vicky looked at her watch: it was five thirty p.m., Thursday, the seventeenth of December.


In Columbus, I'd waited impatiently until Friday for Ron, and now we were trying out the plane before I bought it. "Can you show me its stall speed with landing gear and flaps extended?" I asked, knowing that I'd have to maneuver within the plane's aerodynamic limitations.

"Seventy-four knots," he said, cutting his airspeed and pointing with a finger to the old-fashioned indicator.

"Could we cut it down a little more until we actually stall?"

Ron looked at me questioningly, then replied, "Okay, but do you mind if we get a little more altitude first?"

I was more than pleased with the characteristics of the Cessna 310F—an extremely short run for takeoff and landing, excellent maneuverability—exactly what I needed! Like my faithful, noble friends, it had been placed in my path, and I thanked God for it.

After purchasing it, I asked Ron if he'd fly with me to Marathon, the place from which I planned to depart. I wanted him to work the radio for me, for I wanted to exclude even the remote possibility that Cuban radio interceptors might recognize my voice during radio contacts while flying to the Keys. He agreed, and we left it that afterward we'd see each other back in Columbus for dinner at Elena's.

Kristina had also arrived at Columbus, confessing to me, "I just couldn't wait in Washington."

Virginia was about to arrive back in Mexico at any moment, and now the three of us sat nervously by the phone at Elena's house.

Eight o'clock. Elena was pacing from the kitchen to the bedroom to the living room, where we sat.

Eight thirty. The phone rang.

"Hello?" Elena answered. Kristina and I listened over the intercom.

"Well, I'm back." It was the sweetest sound in the world.

"Virginia."

"It's all arranged. Our patient will be at the doctor's office at five forty-five on the day she has the appointment."

We stood frozen as we listened.

"Can you connect me to her in Havana? From here it's impossible."

"I can get her for you on the other phone. Hold on."

We waited in silence, listening to the sound of Virginia's dialing.

"Hello?"

On our line we heard, "I've gotten through!" Then Virginia said, "Hello, Vicky? I'm back home. I have your husband on the other line. He's been trying to reach you, but couldn't get through. Hold on."

I felt my pulse going through the roof.

"What shall I tell her?" Virginia spoke to us now in a whisper.

"Ask her how my father's doing."

Again we heard her distantly, on the other telephone.

"He asked how his father's doing."

Silence.

"No, not yours. He wants to know how *his* father's doing."

Once again on our line: "She says he's thinner but that he's fine."

"Tell her I'm sending money for a VCR and a TV set."

I couldn't contain myself for happiness. I hugged Elena and Kristina, who didn't know whether to laugh or cry.

When Elena had hung up, she warned, "I'm not staying here tomorrow. I want to be at Marathon when you take off." And she called Gary to tell him she'd be flying to Florida the following morning.

Ron showed up, ready to leave for Marathon, but I asked him to wait a bit. Elena had asked us to go to church, but discovering it was already closed, she called a local hospital so that we could go say a prayer in their chapel. The sister led us to the chapel and opened it up. We went in quietly, each of us kneeling in a separate pew. As we left the chapel, the sister intercepted us. She held a rosary in her hands and offered it to Kristina, saying, "The Lord be with you."

"Take it," Kristina said to me. "You'll need it on your trip."

I took the rosary, and we went back to Elena's house.

I was feeling extremely pressed to get going.

"One more thing . . ." It was Elena, extending her arms toward me. "It's a medal of Our Lady of Charity, which belonged to my mother. Take it with you, please!"

It was midnight when we took off from Columbus.

We flew the three and a half hours to Marathon in silence, interrupted only by the radio communications that Ron made. Once there, we found a motel near the airport to spend the night, and I registered under a name that came to my mind by chance: Joao Garcia. Then we went off to our rooms—Ron, to rest, and I, to go over my calculations one last time. I hadn't closed my eyes since Tuesday.

It was four thirty a.m., Saturday.

## *Chapter Fourteen*

From the moment Vicky had received her telephone call, she knew she wouldn't be able to sleep. She tried to control the excitement overwhelming her, visiting her neighbors in the tenement on some pretext or other. She'd been born and raised there, amid the clamor of those crowded dwellings. The last months had been very hard, but even though her neighbors were all from revolutionary families, they had stood by her—calling her to the phone whenever I'd telephone one of them to talk to her, and warning her of the presence of any stranger spying on her. Yes, they were part of her life. She loved them and was saying good-bye with these visits, without their knowing.

It was already late, and her mother was going to bed when Vicky told her that the next day she planned to visit my family in Matanzas. Then Vicky closed the door to her room so that they wouldn't notice the light shining. She began quietly to set her hair in front of the mirror. She realized that she hadn't bothered with it for a long time. I can't let him see me like this, she told herself. Even on the edge of life and death she wanted to look beautiful when I saw her.

Turning around, she contemplated our sons lying there fast asleep. How far they were from imagining what she was about to do. Tomorrow the outcome awaited them—their family reunited, and freedom, or perhaps death!—and she felt panic at her own thoughts.

Now it was December 19. The light of dawn was shining through her window when she finally picked up the knapsack and began to pack for the trip: the orange shirts and caps, money from Virginia, a Bible, some caramels, and a snack, which she went to the kitchen to prepare. There she found her father already quietly having his first cup of coffee.

"It's very odd, this trip you're taking to Matanzas with the boys," he remarked, staring up at her thoughtfully.

"Dad"—she squeezed his arm affectionately—"please . . ."

Gerardo lowered his gaze, and Vicky kissed him on the forehead.

As she stepped into the alley of the tenement with the children, she turned around to look at her parents standing in the doorway. She waved her hand in farewell, and they waved back, a sadness in their look. They know, she thought, regretting not having told them anything. But what for? They would've died of worry.

They walked the six blocks to the bus stop and mingled with the people waiting there. A man standing farther on kept staring at the bus stop, and Vicky felt a chill run through her. Are they following us? she thought.

"We're going to walk over to Calle Paseo," she told the boys, taking them by the hand.

"Are we going to ask one of those cars that go by to take us?" Reyniel asked her, ashamed at having to flag down one of them.

For some time, in order to alleviate people's anger at the horrible state of public transportation, the government had ordered civil servants with state vehicles at their disposal to pick up passengers along their normal routes.

At the corner, Vicky turned to check behind her, and there was the man, a block behind as before, still staring at them.

They're obviously following us around, she told herself in horror as she thought about how to lose him.

A car finally stopped for them. "I'm going to Revolution Square, no farther," the driver said, leaning out.

"Thank you, that'll be fine," Vicky answered, opening the back door. Revolution Square wasn't too far from the bus terminal. They could walk the rest of the way.

They got out of the car there, and Vicky started walking quickly, pulling the children along. She looked back, then looked up ahead on both sides of the street. The man was nowhere to be seen.

Maybe it was my imagination, but I'd better cut through those buildings just in case, she thought, and changing direction, she walked between the buildings and to the bus terminal by a less common route.

She didn't go in. On an adjacent street were parked various automobiles belonging to doctors, engineers, and other professionals who'd received them a long time ago when the Revolution had awarded them to such people. Now they were waiting there for travelers willing to pay fees amounting to several months' wages.

"We're going to Matanzas," she said to the man leaning against the fender of the Moskovich at the head of the line of cars.

"It's a hundred pesos per person."

"That's fine."

Signaling two other passengers who were waiting for him to fill his car, he opened the doors for everyone.

Vicky gave one more glance behind her and didn't notice anyone following them. She got in beside the boys and checked her watch. It was ten a.m. We'll get there in plenty of time, she told herself, rejoicing.

ELENA's plane landed at Marathon, piloted by Gary. I met her and Kristina at the bottom of the ramp. "Did you sleep at all?" Kristina asked me.

"Impossible. The time's dragging so."

"We couldn't sleep either."

"Let's go for a walk, then. I'm dying to look around Marathon," Elena added with her customary gaiety, trying to relieve the tension.

VICKY AND THE CHILDREN HAD entered the city of Matanzas and, still sitting in the Moskovich, driven past a bus that was discharging passengers. Vicky turned her head as they went by and read the sign above the windshield: ROUTE 16—CANIMAR. "We want to get out at the next bus stop," Vicky told the driver.

On the curb now, she and the boys watched the crowded bus pull over for them. There were no other cars on the road. No one seemed to be following them, and they got on the bus, pushing their way in through the back door.

They were passing the street on which my brother lived, at the edge of the city, when Reyniel commented, "We passed our stop, Mom."

"No. . . . They're at work now. Let's go to the beach for a while."

Reyniel regarded her curiously. December was not a time of year for the beach. But something in Vicky's look told him he'd better not contradict her.

When they got to Canímar, they still had to walk a good half mile to reach El Mamey Beach. They crossed the bridge, walking along the edge of the highway until they saw the sea below them.

They spotted the beach, a cove carved out by centuries of salt water, and descended to it by steps cut into the rocks. At the opposite end was a kiosk, where four men seemed to be sharing a bottle of rum.

Vicky and the children sat on a rock close to the waves, while she wondered what to do to distract the boys. There were still five hours left till the appointed moment.

"Mom, what are we supposed to do here?" Reyniel asked.

"For the moment, eat," Vicky answered, opening the knapsack. "There's no place we can go until your uncle gets back from work. The trip took less time than I thought it would."

Afterward they walked along the sand, gathering shells of various sizes, chasing tiny crabs, which would vanish back into their holes.

Vicky looked up to check the kiosk, and her heart froze. Two policemen were talking animatedly with the men. They've sent them to keep an eye on us because they suspect something! And I've no way of warning him not to land! she thought, her whole body shaking. She watched the boys running around in the sand.

After a time she looked back at the kiosk. The policemen were still there. "Go into the water—swim!" she told the boys quietly.

"But Mom, it's December. The water's still cold."

"Reyniel, please."

The boy saw something urgent in his mother's look. He turned around and ran into the water, followed by Alejandro.

Finally she saw that there was no longer anybody by the kiosk. She breathed a sigh of relief, checking her watch: five p.m.

"Reyniel, Alé. Come, change into your clothes. We're going."

WE WERE sitting in the terminal in Marathon now, leafing through magazines. I'd checked the weather reports for navigation, and the day couldn't have been better. It would take me twenty-eight minutes to reach El Mamey Beach, and according to my calculations with the wind correction, I ought to land at 5:38 exactly.

"I'm going out to the plane an hour before takeoff," I told them when I saw it was three thirty. "I've something to give you," I said to Kristina. I handed her a small bag I'd prepared. "Here are all of my personal documents. Driver's license, Social Security number, everything. I don't want this to fall into their hands if I'm captured. Who knows how they might use them. The little I have is yours."

There were tears in her eyes.

We tested once again the frequency we'd set for the walkie-talkie to communicate during my return flight.

"Connect it at six o'clock in the evening. I'll call you by the name Bicycle One. I'll be Bicycle Two."

They both smiled. We'd always referred to the plane as the bicycle whenever we talked about it on the phone.

I hugged Elena and Kristina with all my strength, and I headed out to the plane. In my hand was a bag containing audiophones, the map, a Freedom AF-35 camera, and a small ASA CX-1 flight computer.

In the cockpit, I mentally went over each step of my flight, from takeoff until my final return: Coordinates for Mamey in the loran navigation system . . . correct. I open the door this way and close like this. . . . No, no, I have to use both hands. This way.

I repeated the operation several more times, fearful of losing a second at the crucial moment.

Time to start the engines. . . . Batteries. . . . Engine start!

My hands and legs were shaking. My heart wanted to leap out of my chest. In less than an hour I'd see those I loved dearest in the world.

The airport looked deserted, no traffic. I began to taxi and then saw Elena and Kristina waving good-bye. When my watch read 5:06, I crossed onto the runway. Taking the rosary from around my neck and squeezing tightly the medal of Our Lady of Charity, I said aloud, "Thy will be done, O Lord." Then, lifting my right hand to the controls, I exclaimed, "Takeoff!"

"Is UNCLE back from work?" Alejandro asked. They were already dressed in their orange shirts and caps and now were climbing up the steps in the rocks, heading for the highway.

"No, not yet. First we're going to hunt for crabs."

"Crabs!" exclaimed Reyniel with visible astonishment.

"Yes, crabs. There's nothing else to do right now."

They reached the highway, and Vicky began to drag the boys by the arm in the opposite direction from the city. Reyniel thought his mother had really gone out of her mind. "Mom, no. . . . Why are we going farther away, with all the distance we still have to walk?"

"Reyniel!" Vicky stopped to stare at the boy angrily. "Listen to me! Do what I say without arguing. It's a matter of life and death. It has to do with your dad."

Reyniel lowered his head a second; then, looking up again, he said, "Okay, Mom, let's get going!"

Hand in hand the three of them walked along the edge of the highway. Now and then Vicky would turn around to look back. No—no one was following them. She checked her watch: 5:20 p.m.

As they walked, she searched the sky up ahead and behind, toward the northern horizon. It was 5:40 p.m.

ELENA and Kristina watched the plane turn into a dot and vanish over the horizon. They sat behind a table near the terminal and settled down to wait. Time seemed to be standing still.

"It's five thirty-eight," Kristina finally remarked.

They knew that was my expected landing time in Cuba.

Elena was rummaging in her purse without knowing what she was looking for. She said, "Whenever I'm nervous, I get a terrible urge to clean my closets. Time goes faster when you clean a closet."

They both laughed.

"It's a shame. I don't see any houses around here. We could've cleaned their closets for them!"

In Mexico City, it was one hour earlier: 4:40 p.m. Virginia had invited various friends over to her house, along with Azul and la Chaparra, and they all went into the biggest room of the house and sat on the floor, joining hands in a circle. They closed their eyes and lowered their heads.

Virginia spoke, her voice resounding, "Oh, God, they love each other. Help them make it!"

I'd climbed to 1000 feet after takeoff and flown at that altitude to ten nautical miles from the twenty-fourth parallel. Then I shut off the navigational lights and the automatic transponder, and now I was flying low above the waves.

*Have they gotten to El Mamey without a mishap? What will I find on the highway? Too much traffic? I have to land on the first try.*

Some opaque crests loomed above the horizon, drawing my attention. *Is it the slopes of Pan de Matanzas? They must have already spotted me; the radar operator must be picking up the phone by now to inform command post. . . . They're unmistakable. It's the Pan de Matanzas! The bay is just to the left. . . . They already know at divisional headquarters; they're calling Havana. . . .*

Little by little the crests of the mountains loomed larger above the horizon, slightly to the right of my route. Then I saw the contours of the coast. *The bridge! There's the Canímar Bridge!*

I checked my airspeed: 240 knots. I have to cut my airspeed!

I cut back the throttles and pulled violently at the controls in order to reduce airspeed as quickly as possible. The motors rumbled with a vibration that shook the whole airplane while I climbed to the level of the bridge.

*The motors, the motors . . . They're giving out!*

Then I was already over the bridge, turning to the left, banking steeply.

*The highway, the highway . . .*

I descended above it, searching for El Mamey Beach. Ahead, the road curved to the right. *They should be waiting about a mile beyond the turn.* Two cars were coming in my direction, and I overflew them. I followed the turn as though I were one more auto, in the air. Ahead of me appeared a trailer truck, as well as a bus attempting to pass him. They already had their headlights on.

Three bright orange dots were moving toward me a little to the left and ahead of the truck and bus.

"There they are! It's them!" I yelled in the cockpit.

Damn, another car!

A small white auto was speeding in my direction, just between them and me.

*I can't land in front of it! There's even less space than between the truck, the bus, and me!*

Overflying the car with my landing gear nearly touching its roof, I saw with horror that I still couldn't land. There was a rock in the center of the highway. I had no room to maneuver on my right—a traffic sign stood in the way. *If I hit it with my wing, we're lost here for good.*

A gentle pull on the controls, a slight banking to the right.

*Left rudder. Left rudder! You're going to miss!*

There's the truck. . . . They're braking; they're getting out of my way. Stall out! *You don't have the room! Stall it!*

The plane fell abruptly on the pavement, and I hit the brakes with all my strength. Vicky and the boys were behind me. I was a mass of emotions. The plane halted in a matter of seconds. I was nose to nose with the truck, the bus concealed behind it, and I could see every line on the truck driver's face. He was frozen at the wheel, stupefied with amazement. His eyes seemed to be popping out of his head.

Vicky had just checked behind her, peering up at the sky, when she saw me drop before her, "vertically, like a helicopter."

"It's Daddy, it's Daddy! Run!" she screamed, holding the children's hands as tightly as she could.

"It's Da-a-d!" Reyniel yelled.

"The knapsack, Reyniel. Drop the knapsack!"

He let it slide off his shoulders and ran in front now, pulling his mother by the arm.

"My shoe, Mommy. I lost my shoe!" It was Alejandro shouting now as he ran along just behind her.

"Kick off the other one!"

Can the wing make it past without hitting the truck? I wondered, watching the truck as I increased the right engine throttle and sat hard on the left brake pedal. *I've got to make the turn right now.* The plane turned swiftly and righted itself on the highway with a final jolt.

They're coming, they're coming! Vicky! My sons!

One minute! We can't wait more than one minute!

They were running toward me hand in hand. The propellers—watch out for the propellers! I turned to the left as I braked, till I was nearly perpendicular to the center of the highway. The door! Pull the seat up!

When I turned the plane, Reyniel recognized his father's face.

*"Dad!"* he screamed, tearing free from his mother. He saw the door opening and crawled onto the wing.

"Da-a-ddy!"

"Reyniel!"

I saw a thousand emotions at once in my son's face, as there must have been in mine. He was crying, shaking, frightened. He jumped into the back seat, and I felt his hand on my shoulder. "Daddy!"

Now Alejandro was by the door. Pale, shocked, happy—petrified. Vicky pushed him in, and I felt his little hands hugging my neck.

"My love!" Vicky screamed hoarsely. Her eyes were very red, wide open, and in her face were those two years of suffering. She got in and reached out with her hands to touch my own, still exclaiming, "Better to risk it all than to be slaves!"

"Don't touch me. Don't talk to me."

I grabbed the door with one hand to close it. It wouldn't close. I tried again, but it still wouldn't close. It felt as if time itself were congealing, as if everything were happening in slow motion. *Calm yourself, calm yourself!* I took hold of the door with both hands. It shut!

"We're on our way!" I cried, gunning the motors and trying to maneuver to the center of the highway.

It seems like a century, but it's all happened in seconds—it hasn't been a full minute since I touched down.

The trailer truck and bus had been left behind. The automobile I overflew was closer now, in the lane to my left. *We have to pass each other.* My wing nearly grazed the car.

"We're going to pray," Vicky told the boys.

Here comes the curve now. There's no highway left. Faster! . . . I'm not going fast enough! I have to take off!

I eased the controls softly but all the way. The plane lifted over the hillside. *We're airborne, airborne! Just don't stall out!*

The motors roared with power, and our airspeed picked up rapidly. I felt we were safe, and I banked to the right, heading north, brushing with my wing the treetops along El Mamey Beach.

Without thinking, I cried out, "We did it, you bastards! We did it!"

I could barely make out the surface of the water; it was almost dark. I heard Vicky and the boys praying behind me.

*They've already made the decision to knock us out of the air. Now they're transmitting the order to the missile installations.*

I took a quick look behind me, wanting to see my passengers, the sovereigns of my life. Alejandro was curled up, looking bewildered. Reyniel was shaking, staring at me in astonishment, unable to believe it. "Dad . . . Dad," he kept repeating.

"Cry, Reyniel, cry! Don't hold it back," Vicky told him, and the boy began crying.

*The crews are already running to their posts in the missile silos. The launching ramps and targeting antenna have already begun rotating.*

The plane was vibrating, as if it were about to disintegrate under the effects of our airspeed. I checked my watch and the loran indications. Eleven nautical miles from the missiles. Eleven and a half. . . . They've already located us. They've got our coordinates.

Twelve nautical miles. The missiles are already pointed at us. . . .

*Twelve and a half nautical miles. They can't reach us!*

We made it!

IT WAS getting impossible to fly at such a low altitude; the vault of the sky had joined the sea in a black sphere. I climbed to 200 feet, adjusting the cabin lights as dimly as possible.

*If they've scrambled any fighter to intercept us, it's already too late.*

We were arriving at the twenty-fourth parallel.

I remembered the camera then. I took it out of the bag, and holding it in my right hand above my head, I pressed the shutter four times. The drama of that instant, illuminated in the faces of Vicky and the children, was captured forever. Then I asked Vicky to do the same. Part of the instrument panel was perpetuated on film. The clock in the cockpit read 6:02.

We've passed the twenty-fourth parallel. . . . Out of danger! We continued to climb to 2000 feet. I reached back with my right arm to feel many hands seizing my own.

"We did it. We're together—together forever!" I exclaimed.

"Forever!" Vicky repeated.

I switched on the navigation lights and automatic transponder. It was time to inform Kristina and Elena. "Bicycle One, Bicycle Two here."

Silence.

"Bicycle One, Bicycle Two," I repeated.

KRISTINA was holding the walkie-talkie when she heard my voice, broken by static, too faint to make out clearly. She answered, but received no reply. The apparatus wasn't powerful enough for that distance. She ran to the phone and dialed Armando's number at home, since he was now back from Washington. Mari Paz, who'd come from Spain, was also anxiously waiting there.

"He's on his way back; we can hear his voice. But we don't know yet if he's got the family with him," Kristina said.

"If he's coming back, he's got his family with him," Armando replied. Positive of what he was saying, he hung up to call in the news to the radio stations in Miami. Mari Paz, who was sitting beside him, jumped up to hug Martha, who thanked God, bursting into tears.

Kristina ran to Elena's plane and hurried aboard. The pilots had the radio on, and she heard my voice as I radioed the Key West approach tower, reporting my position and altitude. She ran back to the cabin door to meet Elena, who was already on the ramp. "He's coming, he's coming!" Kristina was saying, when she heard another call on the walkie-talkie she was carrying with her.

"Go ahead Bicycle Two. Bicycle One here," she answered with emotion.

"Bicycle Two reporting," she heard me say in my broken voice, hoarse with excitement. "I'm bringing a plane filled with love—a plane filled with love!"

UNCLE Raúl was getting ready to take a bath. He'd gotten out of his clothes and turned on the portable radio, which he'd hung from the mirror. It was the same newscast he always heard on the Spanish station at that hour.

Aunt Fela was in the living room when she heard a cry and saw a completely naked Raúl come out of the bathroom, dripping water everywhere. "Fela, Fela!" he exclaimed, waving his arms. He reached out to grab her by the shoulders.

"What's wrong?" she replied, horrified.

"Our nephew, our nephew!"

"What's wrong with our nephew!"

"He rescued Vicky and the kids!" Raúl took a breath, then stammered on, "It's—it's on the radio."

THE lights of the Keys appeared on the horizon. "The United States!" Vicky cried.

We touched down on the runway at the aerodrome, which appeared deserted; then we taxied to the ramp where Elena, Kristina, Ron, and Gary were waiting. Vicky was the first to jump out and was swept up into their arms. Reyniel and Alejandro were hugging me around the neck in the cockpit. I felt the downy skin of their faces. Then they climbed out of the plane, and I followed behind.

ON THE ground, Vicky comes running for me and swings herself around my neck, shouting, trembling, crying.

"Together at last! How we suffered! How we suffered!" she repeats over and over as I kiss her euphorically on the forehead, on her eyes, her cheeks, her lips.

I feel Reyniel and Alejandro hugging me around the waist, and I bend over to take them too in my arms. How long since I've held them like this! I lift them up, hugging them to my chest. The whole universe is contained in my happiness.

Reyniel raises his fist and shakes it in the air, shouting, "I'm free! I'm free!"

And Alejandro imitates his brother. "We're free! We're free!"

# About the Authors

"I am a child of the fifties," says **DAVID HALBERSTAM,** the Pulitzer prizewinning journalist. "I graduated from high school in 1951, from college in 1955." After college, Halberstam, a young reporter in the South, covered the early days of the civil rights struggle, as well as the rise of the young Elvis Presley. Both events were seminal, he believes, in determining what our nation is today. "So many of the forces which exploded in the sixties," he says, "had begun to come together in the fifties." One of those forces was the U.S. entry into the Vietnam War, the subject of Halberstam's 1972 best seller, *The Best and the Brightest.* The author of eleven previous books, David Halberstam lives in New York City.

For **TERRY ANDERSON,** journalism has always been a risky occupation. During six years in the U.S. Marine Corps he was a combat correspondent in Vietnam and an anchorman and station manager for the Armed Forces Radio and Television Service in Japan. Anderson joined The Associated Press in 1974 and at the time of his capture, in 1985, was working in Beirut as the AP's chief Middle East correspondent. Since his release, in 1991, he has founded a civic organization dedicated to constitutional and political reform. He lives with his wife and daughter in a New York City suburb.

**JOE SHARKEY** is no stranger to the twisted workings of the criminal mind. In his previous book, *Deadly Greed,* he explored the notorious Stuart murder—the 1989 Boston case in which a pregnant woman was murdered, and her husband blamed the attack on a mysterious, and never located, black man. Sharkey's first book, *Death Sentence,* was a study of John List, the New Jersey accountant who murdered his mother, wife, and three children in 1971 and evaded capture for two decades. A journalist for twenty years, Sharkey is now working on an exposé of mental-health care  in the United States. He lives in Glen Ridge, New Jersey, with his wife, Nancy.

**ORESTES LORENZO** became an instant hero when he landed at Marathon, Florida, with his wife, Vicky, and their two sons. With the story featured in newspapers across America, and with his appearance on major network TV shows, Lorenzo has charmed his way into American lore. But once the spotlight began to fade, he knew he wanted to tell the story behind his escape and the reasons for his defection. The result is *Wings of the Morning.* Today he and his family live in St. Cloud, Florida, where they are settling into their new lives. *Wings of the Morning* is being published simultaneously in English and in Spanish.

## CREDITS